MOON

PORTUGAL

CARRIE-MARIE BRATLEY

Contents

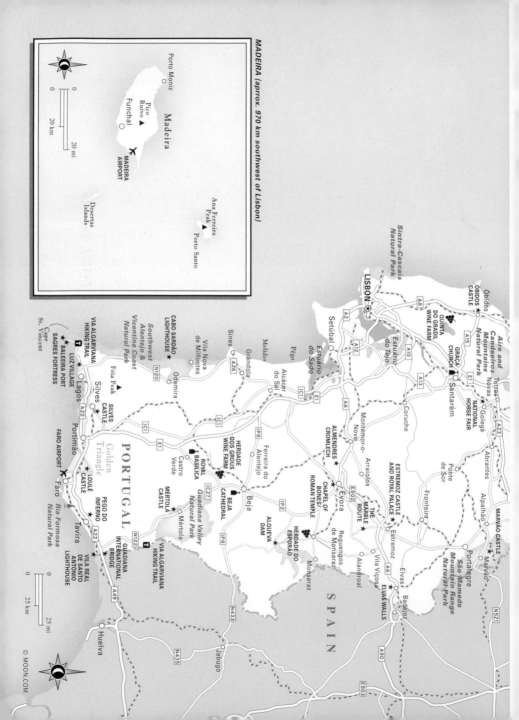

PORTUGAL

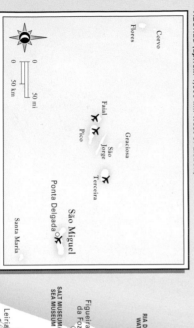

DISCOVER

Portugal

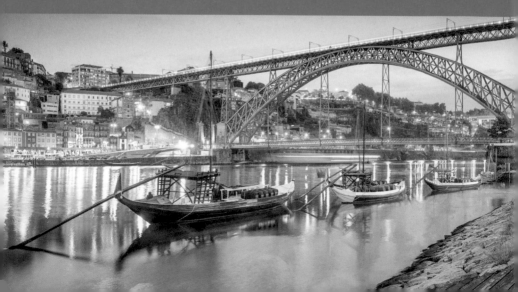

T ucked away in the far corner of the Iberian Peninsula, caressed by sunlight and ocean breezes, Portugal packs the best of Europe into one small package. The country's size belies its historic significance as the birthplace of the Age of Discoveries and center of the first global empire. As the centuries have passed, it has also been one of Europe's poorest countries, but its revitalized economy proves that the nation's industrious and resilient spirit remains intact.

Today, much of the country's allure is rooted in its old-world romanticism and laid-back ways of life, which seem untouched by the hands of time. Life stops for lunch, there's always time for a *café*, and soccer is on a par with religion. Portugal effortlessly strikes a fine balance between quaint and contemporary. Bougainvillea-framed cobblestoned streets hide chic guest houses, modern art galleries, and award-winning eateries. Lisbon's modern high-rises and high culture are not far from simple, white-washed hamlets. Porto's weathered, hardworking soul feels a world away from the lush vineyards of the Douro Valley. The

Clockwise from top left: the Alcobaça Monastery; the eggy custard tart *pastel de nata;* surfing in the Algarve; the Glória Funicular in Lisbon; azulejo tile; Porto and the Douro River.

resorts of the azure Algarve coast give way to the rustic isolation of the rolling Alentejo farmland. All hold their own importance in the intriguing patchwork quilt that is Portugal.

Here you can do as much or as little as your heart desires. Trek along majestic mountain ranges or spend a lazy day tasting port wines. Explore fairy-tale castles or relax on golden sands. A visit to Portugal is a bit like its cuisine, as characterized by the humble grilled sardine: unfussy and surprisingly packed with flavor.

Clockwise from top left: boats in Carvoeiro; *levada* trail on Madeira; Livraria Lello, the famous bookshop in Porto; grilled sardines.

10 TOP
EXPERIENCES

1 **Lisbon:** Home to soulful fado music and vivid nightlife, Portugal's capital seamlessly blends historic charm with contemporary cool (page 35).

2 **Magical Sintra:** A short trip from Lisbon, this magical town is crowned by the fairy-tale Pena Palace (page 75).

3 **Authentic Cuisine:** From grilled sardines and chicken *piripiri* to port wine, Portugal's cuisine is fresh, flavorful, and unassuming (page 26).

4 **Wine Tasting in the Douro Valley:** Up-and-coming yet down-to-earth Porto is the gateway to the breathtaking Douro Valley, which can be explored by river cruise, car, or train (pages 28 and 281).

5 **Ancient Évora:** The past is present in this Alentejo city, with Roman temple ruins and the chilling Chapel of Bones as highlights (page 168).

6 **Fado Music:** Take in a performance of Portugal's mournful folk music in the fado houses of Lisbon's Alfama and Bairro Alto neighborhoods (pages 60 and 62) and the alleyways and atmospheric venues of Coimbra (page 235).

O FADO

7 **Beaches:** Portugal has some of Europe's finest beaches, ranging from the grotto-etched Algarve coast and the Alentejo's endless stretches of sand to Lisbon's cosmopolitan Estoril coastline and beyond (page 31).

8 **Island Getaways:** Portugal's two stunning archipelagoes—sunny Madeira and the verdant volcanic Azores—are slices of paradise (page 310).

9 **Lost-in-time Villages:** Time stands still in the Algarve's fishing villages (such as Ferragudo, page 127), the Alentejo's rustic hamlets (like Monsaraz, page 177), and the schist villages near Coimbra (pictured, page 239).

10 **Experience the Landscape:** Kayak in the Algarve's bird-rich Ria Formosa Natural Park (pages 100 and 157), hike in the mountainous Peneda-Gerês National Park (pictured, page 302), or take a dip in the Azores' hot volcanic springs (page 348).

Planning Your Trip

Where to Go

Lisbon

Located at the mouth of the Tagus River, Portugal's buzzing, **cosmopolitan capital** was once the launch pad of the Age of Discoveries. Home to **fado** music and a vivid **nightlife** scene, the "City of Seven Hills" oozes charm and cool in equal measures. With tile-clad façades and red-brick roofs that tumble toward the Tagus, its **historic neighborhoods** beckon to be explored. The stunning **Setúbal Peninsula,** where the iconic statue of *Christ the King* stands with arms outstretched, is a short hop across the river. Less than an hour away are the fairy-tale town of **Sintra** and the chic coastal enclaves of **Estoril** and **Cascais.**

The Algarve

The Algarve is Portugal's number one spot for **sun-drenched holidays.** Buzzing in summer and beautiful in winter, this **year-round** destination has stunning stretches of **golden sand, crystalline coves,** and heady **nightlife.** Golfers and road trippers flock to the Algarve in winter and spring, when almond trees flourish with snowy white petals.

The Alentejo

Life in all of Portugal is **laid-back,** but nowhere more so than in the **rolling plains** of the Alentejo, where the rhythm is dictated by the slumbered sway of farm animals. Famous for its **wine** as well as its marble, this underrated area offers **rural escapes,** charming **hamlets,** and some of the **warmest weather** in the country, all under one big, blue sky. Its largest city, **Évora,** is home to its most distinctive monuments: the Gothic **Évora Cathedral,**

Lisbon

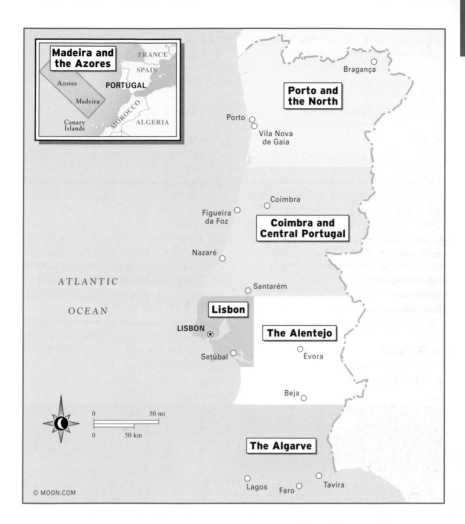

Madeira and the Azores

FRANCE
SPAIN
PORTUGAL
Azores
Madeira
Canary Islands
MOROCCO
ALGERIA

Bragança

Porto and the North

Porto
Vila Nova de Gaia

Coimbra
Figueira da Foz

Coimbra and Central Portugal

Nazaré

ATLANTIC

OCEAN

Santarém

Lisbon

LISBON

Setúbal

The Alentejo

Évora

Beja

The Algarve

0   50 mi
0   50 km

Lagos Faro Tavira

© MOON.COM

the skeleton-packed **Chapel of Bones,** and the **Roman Temple of Évora.**

Coimbra and Central Portugal

A visit to Central Portugal can feel like a journey into the past. The region captivates with its ethereal **schist villages, medieval monuments,** and the Catholic pilgrimage site at **Fátima.** Yet Central Portugal is also about the future, boasting the largest university city in the country, **Coimbra. Serra da Estrela Natural Park** is

Portugal's only **skiing** destination, while the town of **Nazaré** is one of the world's top spots for **big-wave surfing.**

Porto and the North

With a **cooler,** grayer climate, Northern Portugal also has a lusher landscape. It's famous for producing Portugal's most celebrated tipple: **port.** Cruises along the Douro River and through the **wine-making Douro Valley** are the number one pull, while cultural attractions, particularly in the up-and-coming city of **Porto,** are also popular. Farther north are **Guimarães,** the "cradle of the nation"; medieval **Bragança;** and lively fishing port **Viana do Castelo.**

Madeira and the Azores

These two **archipelagoes** are the jewels in Portugal's crown. While **Madeira** has long been a favorite for Europeans seeking an **offbeat nature destination,** the volcanic **Azores** are one of Europe's last, **best-kept secrets.** These unspoiled **slices of paradise** can be reached within two hours on domestic flights from the mainland.

Know Before You Go

When to Go

May-September offers the **best beach weather. June-August** constitutes the peak of **high season,** when Portugal (especially the **Algarve**) is at its busiest—and priciest. Most of the country's major events are held summer.

Rural inland areas such as the **Alentejo** and **Central Portugal** can be sweltering (more than 40°C) in summer, and are much more enjoyable in **spring** or **autumn.**

Spring, autumn, and winter are mild and mostly sunny, although Portugal does have rainy months, December being the wettest. Northern Portugal is generally cooler and grayer than the rest of the country and is less affected by seasonality. **Lisbon** and **Northern Portugal** are **year-round destinations.**

Getting to Portugal

Traveling to Portugal from anywhere within Europe is quick and easy—and even better, cheap, thanks to the growing number of **low-cost**

the lighthouse at Cabo da Roca, mainland Europe's westernmost point

airlines. Portugal is also served by regular direct flights from North and South America, the Middle East, Africa, and Asia.

The three main airports on the mainland are Lisbon, Porto in the north, and Faro in the south. Most flights from outside the European Union are to Lisbon. Porto also has regular direct flights from outside the EU, although far fewer than Lisbon. Faro has almost exclusively European flights.

Portugal's archipelagoes, Madeira and the Azores, are within a two-hour flight from the mainland, with direct flights from Lisbon and Porto. In addition, there are direct flights to Madeira from European destinations outside Portugal, including London, Amsterdam, and Paris. There are also direct flights to the Azores from Europe as well as the United States (Boston and Newark) and Canada (Toronto and Montreal).

Bus and train services connect Portugal with Spain, France, Belgium, the Netherlands, and the United Kingdom. Driving to Portugal from within Europe is also possible thanks to a good international road network and the EU open-borders policy.

Getting Around Portugal

Thanks to its compact size and a good road network, Portugal is easily traveled by car. Hiring a car also provides greater flexibility for exploring off the beaten track. But an efficient bus and train network also connects most major towns and cities. Train travel can often be more scenic and cheaper than bus, but train stations can sometimes be located far outside the town centers. Bus travel is almost always quicker than train.

Visas and Officialdom

All travelers entering Portugal are required to have a valid ID.

European Union nationals traveling within EU or Schengen states do not require a visa for entering Portugal for any length of stay. They do require a valid passport or official ID card. European citizens traveling between Schengen countries are not required to present an identity document or passport at border crossings, as an open-borders policy is in effect. However, it is recommended that travelers have ID documents with them, as they may be requested at any time by the authorities.

Citizens of the United Kingdom and Ireland must produce a passport to enter Portugal, valid for the duration of the proposed stay, and can stay for up to three months.

People from non-EU countries always require a passport, valid for at least six months; some may require a visa. Australian, Canadian, and U.S. travelers require a valid passport but do not need a visa for stays of up to 90 days in any six-month period. While it is not obligatory to have an onward or return ticket, it is advisable.

South African nationals need to apply for a Portugal-Schengen visa. This should be done three months before travel. Applicants must have a South African passport valid for six months beyond date of return with at least three blank pages.

Explore Portugal

The Best of Portugal

Not so long ago, Portugal was seen predominantly as a beach and golf destination, with the Algarve taking center stage for tourists. However, after carefully honing its assets, it has carved out several appealing niches that add to its appeal as a holiday destination boasting wine, nature, and adventure tourism. Both Lisbon and Porto have also achieved an enviable status as two of Europe's most up-and-coming getaway cities. Here are some ideas for building your itinerary.

Lisbon, Sintra, and Évora

DAYS 1-2: LISBON

Start your exploration of the city at the bustling riverfront **Comércio Square** (Praça do Comércio). From here, you can catch the famed yellow **tram 28,** which trundles through Lisbon's most historic neighborhoods. (The closest stop is a couple of blocks from the square on Rua da Conceição Street.) A 24-hour pass allows you to jump on and off the tram to explore at leisure; it also includes trips on the **Santa Justa Elevator** and **Glória Funicular.** Worthwhile stops along the way include the **Lisbon Cathedral** and the **Portas do Sol viewpoint,** which has a café where you can enjoy lunch with a view. In the afternoon, choose between a climb to the **São Jorge Castle,** for still more amazing views, or head to the elegant **Estrela Basilica and Gardens.** Then spend the evening in the atmospheric Alfama neighborhood for dinner and a **fado** show (make your reservation well in advance).

The next day, get an early start for sightseeing in **Belém,** a short trip west of the city center (from Comércio Square, catch Tram 15).

tram 28 in Lisbon

Sintra's Moorish Castle wall, with Pena Palace in the distance

Admire the city's most iconic monuments—the sprawling **Jerónimos Monastery,** riverside **Belém Tower,** and the **Monument to the Discoveries**. Stop for lunch and indulge in a *pastel de nata* custard tart at the famous **Pastéis de Belém** bakery for dessert. Return to Lisbon for a little rest at your accommodation before heading out again for a sunset cocktail at a rooftop bar, such as the one at **Hotel Mundial.** Then make your way to the bohemian Bairro Alto to enjoy dinner and hit some nightspots.

DAY 3: SINTRA

Head out to **Sintra** as early as possible to beat the commuter rush-hour traffic. It's a 30-minute drive via the A16 motorway, but parking is a challenge; taking the train may be the best option (40 minutes). Sintra's historic center is a pleasant stroll (1.5 km/0.9 mile) from the railway station. The 434 tourist bus runs circular loops between the station and Sintra's main sights, including out-of-town attractions like Pena Palace; investing in a day pass allows you to hop on and off.

Explore the **National Palace** in the morning, then enjoy lunch at one of Sintra's many quaint eateries. In the afternoon, make your way to the whimsical **Pena Palace.** Opposite Pena Palace, the ancient **Moorish Castle** is also worth a look before heading back to Lisbon. With more time, squeeze in a visit to the spooky Gothic **Regaleira Estate,** a five-minute walk from Sintra's center.

DAY 4: ÉVORA

Historic **Évora** lies in the heart of the rustic Alentejo, about a 1.5-hour drive east from Lisbon via the A6 motorway. Direct train and bus services run regularly from Lisbon (both also take 1.5 hours). Évora's charming walled city center is best enjoyed at a leisurely pace. Take in the grand **Évora Cathedral** with its splendid rooftop views, the regal columns of the well-preserved **Roman Temple of Évora,** and the morbidly fascinating **Chapel of Bones.**

After lunching on local delicacies like cured meats and regional cheeses, explore one of the upper Alentejo's wine farms. Located a 30-minute walk (5-minute drive) north of Évora's city center, the **Cartuxa Estate** is one of the most revered names among Alentejo wines. The century-old organic vineyard offers guided tours and tastings.

For an unforgettable overview of the vast rolling plains of the vine-meshed Alentejo, book a sunset **hot-air balloon ride.**

Despite its sleepy feel, Évora has a youthful buzz, thanks to the local university population, which means there are a good selection of **hip eateries** and **cool bars** to try out before you turn in for the night.

Southern Loop: Sun and Sand
DAY 5: TAVIRA

Head to the eastern Algarve to enjoy its long, golden beaches and warm, shallow waters.

A 2.5-hour drive from Évora via the IP2, **Tavira** oozes authenticity. Park the car and explore the quaint cobbled streets that flank the Gilão River. Admire the old **Roman Bridge,** and enjoy lunch at an alfresco café. Be sure to check out the weird and wonderful camera obscura at **Tavira Tower** observatory.

In the afternoon, jump on a ferry boat to **Tavira Island.** Set in the beautiful Ria Formosa lagoon, this barrier-island serves as Tavira's main beach. Relax on the shimmering sand bar and take a dip in the crystalline water.

In the evening, make the short trip east to **Vila Real de Santo António** (a 30-minute drive on the A22), to enjoy dinner at one of the many tavern-like seafood restaurants hidden among the backstreets. Take a moonlit amble along the waterfront, gazing over the Guadiana river toward Spain twinkling in the distance, before heading back to Tavira.

DAYS 6-7: FARO AND CARVOEIRO

Head west to **Faro,** about a 35-minute drive from Tavira via the A22. There are also frequent trains (40 minutes) between the two. Spend the morning exploring the beautiful walled **Old Town.** Wander the riverside and climb to the rooftop of the 13th-century **cathedral** for magnificent views.

Make a side trip to the fortified city of **Silves** to admire its wonderful **hilltop castle** (a 45-minute drive west from Faro via the A22). Then continue on toward Carvoeiro via Lagoa, a 20-minute drive south from Silves via the N124-1. (If traveling by public transport, skip Silves and take a 1.5-hour bus ride to Lagoa. Carvoeiro is a short bus or taxi ride from Lagoa's main bus terminal.) Settle in at

quiet street in the old town of Tavira

If you enjoy driving, have a keen sense of adventure, and want to get off the tourist track, the **legendary EN2 road** is for you. It stretches 740 kilometers (460 miles) straight down the middle of the country, from **Chaves** in the north to **Faro** in the south. Along the way, it passes through rich, unspoiled landscapes and offers access to unexplored hamlets, spa towns, and places of cultural and historic interest. It has a mystique comparable to Route 66 in the United States.

Segments of this route were **Roman roads** that crossed through what used to be Lusitania, the ancient name given to Western Iberia during Roman occupation. Successive interventions saw the main parts of the EN2 improved and connected and later used as the **Royal Road,** a network maintained by the Portuguese crown. Many of Portugal's Royal Roads were later designated National Roads, or EN roads. The EN2 is the king of them all.

Would-be road trippers should fly into Porto and rent a car to start their journeys. **Chaves** is about 1.75 hours northeast of Porto, midway along the country's northern border with Spain. Drive south, planning for stops at the northern city of **Vila Real,** as well as **Peso da Régua** and **Lamego** in the Douro Valley. Continuing south, you will pass close to **Coimbra** and **Évora** before reaching the end of the road at **Faro** in the Algarve.

It takes a good **3-4 days** to complete the full route, but allow more time to slowly savor the

stone marker indicating the beginning and end of the EN2 road

lesser-known flavors of Portugal's diverse landscape, stopping overnight in one of the many rural idylls along the way.

Plans are in place to upgrade Europe's third longest road and transform it into an official tourist route. Until then, this epic road trip remains one of Portugal's best-kept secrets.

the charming fishing village of **Carvoeiro** for the night. Choose from the colorful selection of bars and restaurants for dinner and a cocktail (or two) before turning in.

The next morning, take a grotto trip from **Carvoeiro Beach** to see the amazing **sea caves** along the coast. After lunch, hit the sand at **Marinha Beach,** one of the most famous and beautiful in the country. Once you've fulfilled your beach quota, clean up for dinner, where you'll toast to your last night in the Algarve.

DAY 8: MONCHIQUE AND NORTH TO LISBON

If you're driving, pass through the Monchique mountain range before heading back to Lisbon. Spend the morning enjoying the winding climb through eucalyptus-laden hills. From Carvoeiro, follow the M1272 toward Lagoa, then join the A22 in Lagoa, heading west to the Portimão/Monchique turnoff. From there, follow the N124 and N266 up to Monchique town. It's about a 40-minute drive (37 km/23 mi).

Explore Portuguese Cuisine

Portugal is known for fine wines and liqueurs, the freshest seafood, and a gastronomy that comes from the heart and the land. Here are some of the country's iconic dishes and where to try them.

- *Pastel de nata:* Also known as *pastel de Belém*, after the Lisbon neighborhood in which it originated, this eggy custard tart still follows the original recipe. It's Portugal's most famous sweet.

- **Chicken *piripiri:*** The Algarve town of Guia is the capital of this spicy, charcoal-grilled chicken dish, made with *piripiri* hot sauce.

- **Grilled sardines:** Any waterfront restaurant serves grilled sardines. They're simple finger food, served with a slice of rustic bread. Portimão has a trademark row of riverside sardine restaurants and hosts a festival in August dedicated to the treasured fish.

- *Cozido á Portuguesa:* Every region has its own interpretation of this meat-and-vegetable stew. The Azores' version is slow-cooked underground in the natural volcanic heat of São Miguel Island.

- **Port wine:** This traditional fortified wine is produced solely in the Douro Valley. Traditionally sweet and red in color, it's generally served as a dessert wine. Across the Douro River from Porto, Vila Nova de Gaia's legendary port wine cellars date back centuries.

- *Ginja de Óbidos:* This strong cherry liqueur (also known as *ginjinha*) is served in shops in

pastel de nata

the medieval village of Óbidos, usually in a chocolate cup.

- **Madeira wine:** This robust fortified wine is produced exclusively on the Madeira Islands, with a history dating back to the Age of Discoveries at the end of the 15th century. Ranging from dry to sweet, Madeira wine is consumed as an aperitif or dessert accompaniment.

Just before Monchique town, stop off at the fairy-tale **Caldas de Monchique** springs and spa village for an invigorating walk. Continue up to **Monchique** town and stop for a bite to eat. Sample local delicacies like cured ham and cheese platters and smoked sausage, and buy a bottle of firewater and save it for later. Then continue your climb up to **Fóia Peak,** the highest point in the Algarve, for breathtaking views of the scenic coastline. The drive from Monchique town to Fóia takes around 10 minutes (4.5 km/2.8 mi), climbing the N266-3.

Make your way back to Lisbon, a 2.75-hour drive north via the A2. If you're using public transit, head straight from Carvoeiro to Lisbon via Lagoa, a 3-hour bus ride.

Heading North: History and Wine
DAY 9: ÓBIDOS, TOMAR, AND FÁTIMA
Get up early and head to enchanting **Óbidos,** a short drive (1 hour via the A8) north of Lisbon. Allow a couple of hours to stroll the castle walls and soak up the medieval feel.

Head northeast to the Templar city of **Tomar** (1-hour drive via the A15). Allow yourself a few hours in Tomar to explore the magnificent **Convent of Christ** complex as well as visit the **Tomar Synagogue** and wander the tree-lined riverside.

From Tomar, head to **Fátima** (35-minute drive west via the IC9 road), where you'll spend the night. The ethereal holy site is particularly pretty in the evening, when the candles dance in the dusk. While the main plaza central to the **Sanctuary of Our Lady of Fátima** is open to the public 24/7, the churches close at around 6:30pm. If you arrive in the late evening and want to see inside the shrine's buildings, make the most of the next morning to explore them.

If you're on public transport, skip Óbidos and head to Tomar (2-hour bus or train from Lisbon) and Fátima (40-minute bus from Tomar).

DAY 10: COIMBRA

Head north to **Coimbra** (1-hour drive via the A1). CP regional trains (1.25 hours) run almost hourly between Fátima and Coimbra, and there are at least three daily buses (1 hour).

Take the unusual **Elevador do Mercado** funicular to uptown. Tour the famed university campus, including the opulent 18th century **Joanina Library.** Then make your way through the cobbled streets down to the riverside, stopping at the striking **Old Cathedral.** Have lunch at atmospheric **Café Santa Cruz.** Walk across the bridge over the Mondego River and visit one of the city's quirkiest attractions, the miniature village of **Little Portugal.** Then head south of Coimbra to the Roman ruins at **Conímbriga** (a 20-minute drive or a 40-minute bus ride) to see its elaborate floor mosaics. Head back to Coimbra for dinner at one of the city's trendy eateries. Round your day off at a fado bar.

DAY 11: PORTO

Head north to **Porto** by car (1.5-hour drive via the A1), train (1-2 hours), or bus (1.5 hours).

The azulejo tile-clad **São Bento railway station,** the spindly **Clérigos Tower,** the amazing **Livraria Lello** bookshop, and the opulent **Stock Exchange Palace** are must-sees, all within walking distance of one another, as is the glorious **riverfront,** lined with rainbow-colored buildings. Stop at a riverside restaurant for lunch.

the riverfront promenade in Porto

After lunch, stroll across the **Dom Luís I bridge** to **Vila Nova de Gaia** and visit one of the famous **port wine cellars** for a tour and a tasting. Round the day off with a **cable car** ride up the hill. At the top, walk to the **Monastery of Serra do Pilar** and its viewpoint before heading to the peaceful **Morro Gardens,** which has more lovely views of Porto.

Walk back across the bridge to Porto for dinner and stop for a drink at one of the local nightspots.

DAY 12: DOURO VALLEY

Take a daylong **river cruise** to see the enchanting **Douro Valley.** (One leg of the trip, either upriver or downriver, is often by train.) Choose a trip that incorporates a visit to a wine farm or at least allows time to explore one of the riverside towns such as lovely **Peso da Régua,** where the **Douro Museum** offers an introduction to the valley's history and traditions.

Alternatively, jump on a **CP train** from Porto to Régua. This journey takes around two hours one-way, but it lets you explore the town at leisure. And while not quite as glamorous as a cruise, independent train travel is much cheaper. Often the trains skirt right alongside the Douro River, so the scenery is just as good.

DAY 13: DEPARTING FROM PORTO

Return to Porto and make your way back home. The city's international airport offers connections throughout Europe as well as direct flights to the United States, Canada, South America, and Africa.

Wine Country Getaway

The captivating **Douro Valley** is one of the most beautiful and ancient wine-producing regions on the planet. The breathtaking scenery, with lacy vine terraces carved into steep riverbanks, changes with every bend of the river. In spring (April-May), it is a kaleidoscope of vivid floral hues, while in autumn (Sept-Oct), the valley is ablaze with russet tones of red and gold.

You can explore the valley by car, by train, or by boat. **All-inclusive cruises,** departing from Porto or Vila Nova de Gaia, range 2-8 days (for more information, see page 282). If you'd like to enjoy a ride on the **Douro Historic Steam Train,** time your trip so that you're here on a weekend between June and October.

Day 1
PORTO AND VILA NOVA DE GAIA

Your getaway begins in up-and-coming Porto; for suggestions on how to spend your time in the city, see pages 27 and 260. Just across the **Dom Luís I bridge** from Porto, **Vila Nova de Gaia,** serves as the gateway to wine country. Its **port wine cellars** offer regular organized tours throughout the day. The cellars right on the riverfront might be busiest, but all provide excellent opportunities to delve into the history of portmaking and sample the product, and are similarly priced.

After your tour, take a stroll along the riverfront, where traditional *rabelo* boats bob on the water. Enjoy lunch at a riverside restaurant. After lunch, jump on the **cable car** that runs from the riverside up the hill. The panoramic views of Porto from this flying gondola are amazing. At the top of the hill, walk to the grand **Monastery of Serra do Pilar,** before heading to the **Morro Gardens,** a green oasis with lovely views, particularly magical at sunset.

If you're not traveling on a budget, spend the night at the landmark **Yeatman Hotel** in Vila Nova de Gaia. Otherwise, head back down in the cable car and across the bridge to one of Porto's myriad hotels.

Day 2
AMARANTE AND PESO DA RÉGUA

Today's destination is Peso da Régua (commonly

terraced hills covered in vines in the Douro Valley

called Régua), the Douro's largest riverside town, which makes a great base for exploring the valley. It's roughly a 1.5-hour drive east from Porto. Trains run regularly between Porto and Régua (2 hours), and most Douro cruises stop here.

If you're driving, stop off first in **Amarante,** a town on the Tâmega River (a 45-minute drive east from Porto via the A4). Storybook buildings line the river, their wrought-iron balconies overhanging the tree-fringed waters below. Spend an hour walking around the town and enjoy lunch before heading on to Régua.

From Amarante, **Peso da Régua** is a 40-minute drive southeast via the A24 and A4. Ensconced by frilly vine terraces, Régua was a shipping crossroads, pivotal to the development of Portugal's port industry. Spend an hour at the **Douro Museum** to learn about the region's winemaking history and culture. Then take a five-minute taxi to **Quinta do Vallado,** a 300-year-old wine farm, for a tour and tasting. Quinta do Vallado has a restaurant and hotel, so you can have dinner here and spend the night. Otherwise, head back to Régua.

Day 3
WINE FARM AND STEAM TRAIN EXCURSION

In the morning, head to the stunning 400-year-old **Quinta do Crasto** estate, a 50-minute drive east from Régua, for a tour and tasting on the ledge of a vine terrace. There are five trains a day that make the 15-minute journey between Régua and the Ferrão station, the closest to Quinta do Crasto (it's a 45-minute walk, or you can arrange a ride with the Quinta). Have lunch at the wine farm and head back to Régua.

In the afternoon, enjoy a ride on the **Douro Historic Steam Train,** which runs between Régua and the village of Tua on weekend afternoons June-October (3 hours round-trip). Folk dancers and singers provide on-board entertainment as the train chugs through the valley. The open windows give passengers privileged views of the incredible landscape.

Spend the night in Régua.

Day 4
LAMEGO

Across the Douro River from Peso da Régua is

petite and polished **Lamego** (a 20-minute drive on the A24, or a 20-minute bus that runs twice daily).

Spend the morning sightseeing, visiting medieval sights in the compact city center, such as the 12th-century **Lamego Cathedral** in the town's historic center and the handsome hilltop **Lamego Castle.** Pick up local delicacies for a picnic in the gardens surrounding the monumental 18th-century **Our Lady of Remedies Sanctuary**—if you don't fancy climbing the epic 686-step stone staircase to the church, you can drive up.

In the afternoon, head to the beautiful 300-year-old wine farm **Quinta da Pacheca,** a 20-minute drive south of Lamego. Enjoy a tour and tasting before dinner at the excellent on-site restaurant. Spend the night in one of Quinta da Pacheca's **wine barrel-shaped cabins** or head back to Régua for the night.

Day 5
PENAFIEL AND BACK TO PORTO
Take your time heading back to Porto via the A4. Just before reaching the town of Penafiel (50 minutes west of Régua), make a detour to the striking 19th-century **Sameiro Sanctuary,** perched on a high hilltop, for amazing panoramic views.

Carry on to charming **Penafiel.** After exploring the compact town center, make your way to **Quinta da Aveleda,** producer of fizzy and fruity green wine, for a tour and tasting (book in advance). The beautiful ivy-clad manor house is surrounded by romantic gardens, where peacocks roam freely. Enjoy lunch and head back to Porto (a 40-minute drive west, via the A4).

If you have more time...
If you want to spend an extra day or two in the Douro Valley, head to **Vila Real,** located just north of Lamego and Peso da Régua. It's famous for the 18th-century **Mateus Palace,** one of the most splendid manor houses in Europe. It is also the valley's largest city and hence has good public transport connections.

From Vila Real, you can make a day trip to the town of **Vila Nova de Foz Côa** for a guided tour of the **Côa Valley Archaeological Park,** one of the biggest collections of Ice Age rock-art engravings in the world. Another day-trip option is the quaint spa town of **Chaves,** which dates back to the Roman era.

The Algarve: East to West

Many travelers enter Portugal from neighboring Spain and experience the Algarve from east to west. The eastern Algarve, called the **Sotavento,** is quiet and unspoiled, largely untouched by mass tourism. The western Algarve, called the **Barlavento,** offers all the comforts tourism offers, including beachside resorts, while retaining plenty of character. Between them is the central Algarve, home to the region's largest city, Faro.

Two major roads traverse the Algarve, running parallel to one another: the **A22 motorway** and the **N125 national road.** Deciding which to use boils down to season and distance. In summer, the N125 becomes heavily congested with holiday traffic. Traffic always flows freely on the A22 motorway, but tolls apply on all stretches, making the N125 more cost-effective for shorter distances.

Train and bus service in the Algarve is regular throughout the day. The **CP Algarve train line** connects most towns and cities, but not coastal villages. Train stations are often on the outskirts of town, a considerable taxi ride from the town center. Bigger cities have local bus service.

Eastern Algarve
DAY 1: VILA REAL DE SANTO ANTÓNIO AND TAVIRA
Take the scenic ferry across the Guadiana River from Spain to **Vila Real de Santo António.** It's

Top Beaches

Portugal is renowned for its dramatic sea cliffs, snug coves, and of course, sweeping stretches of golden sand.

- **Guincho Beach** (Cascais, near Lisbon): Head to this windswept beach, popular among surfers and windsurfers, to enjoy sweeping views of the ocean and plains.

- **Marinha Beach** (Carvoeiro, Algarve): Encased by sheer ocher cliffs, this beach has craggy rock formations that stretch out over the soft, golden sand to a calm, translucent sea. It's one of the most beautiful beaches in the country.

- **Dona Ana Beach** (Lagos, Algarve): Surrounded by golden cliffs and fronting cool crystalline water, this romantic beach is postcard-perfect.

- **Franquia Beach** (Vila Nova de Milfontes, Alentejo): With shallow waters that are warmer than others along the coast, this crescentshaped swath of sand is a magnet for families.

- **Nazaré Beach** (Nazaré, Central Portugal): Fringed by a long seafront avenue, this huge half-moon of glimmering sand is one of the most famous places in the world for big-wave surfing.

Dona Ana Beach

worth spending an hour exploring its pretty town center. After a 1755 earthquake, the town was rebuilt in a distinct Pombaline (Neoclassical) style. See the local lighthouse and walk the palm-tree-fringed riverside, where you can enjoy a coffee while gazing back at Spain. **River cruises** depart from the marina, ranging from nature-watching trips to party boats.

Soak up the sun on one of Vila Real's long golden beaches, or at the popular seaside resort of **Monte Gordo.** Then continue on to the tiny seafront hamlet of **Cacela Velha** (about a 15-minute drive along the N125), to snack on its famous oysters. End your day at **Tavira** (a 15-minute drive west on the N125) to enjoy the freshest seafood for dinner before bedding down for the night.

DAY 2: TAVIRA

After breakfast, set out on foot to explore the streets of **Tavira.** The city straddles the Gilão River, its two sides connected by the ancient **Roman Bridge;** the main sights are mostly on the western bank. Wander the old town and garden-flanked riverside. Check out the UFO-like camera obscura at **Tavira Tower** observatory, converted from an old water tower, and the remains of the medieval **Tavira Castle.** Stop for lunch; many of the local restaurants promote an array of unusual tuna dishes to honor Tavira's past as a major tuna fishing port.

After lunch, swap land for sea and jump on a ferry boat to **Tavira Island.** This sandy barrier-island set in the beautiful **Ria Formosa lagoon** is home to Tavira's main beach. When you've had enough lazing in the sun, head back to Tavira for dinner and slumber.

Central Algarve
DAY 3: OLHÃO AND FARO

In the morning, head west from Tavira toward Olhão and Faro. Public transport connects the three cities; trains are probably the best way of getting to Faro from the eastern Algarve.

If you're driving, stop en route at the **Pego do Inferno** (a 12-minute drive northwest of Tavira via the N270 road), which includes a gorgeous waterfall and lagoon. Fearless visitors jump off the cliffside into the seemingly bottomless turquoise pool.

After you dry off, drive 25 minutes west via the A22 and N398 to **Olhão.** This fishing town has a distinct North African influence, with cubic, flat-roofed houses. Admire the fresh seafood and local produce at the waterfront market; then head to a nearby café for lunch.

Continue west to genteel **Faro** (a 20-minute drive west via the N125 road). Spend the afternoon exploring the walled **Old Town,** climb to the top of the grand **Faro Cathedral,** and stroll along the riverfront. Take a **boat trip** to explore the bird-rich **Ria Formosa lagoon.** Make the most of the city's varied restaurants and nightlife before turning in for the night.

Western Algarve
DAY 4: CARVOEIRO AND FERRAGUDO

From Faro, head west toward the charming coastal villages of Carvoeiro and Ferragudo. If traveling by public transport, take the bus from Faro to Lagoa (about 1.5 hours) and then a local bus or taxi from Lagoa bus terminal to Carvoeiro.

If you're driving, stop en route at the famed pottery shops at **Porches** on the N125 road (a 40-minute drive from Faro), just before the city of Lagoa. The drive from Porches to Carvoeiro is another 15 minutes via the N125.

In touristy **Carvoeiro,** stroll the cobbled streets and browse the boutiques before heading to the main square on the beachfront. From Carvoeiro's main square, walk up the hill to the east to the **Algar Seco** rock formation and the lovely cliff-top walkway. Or take a **grotto trip**

Pego do Inferno near Tavira

wooden boat on the beach in Carvoeiro

boats exploring the Ponta da Piedade in Lagos

(around 1 hour) in a traditional wooden fishing boat from Carvoeiro Beach to the astounding **Benagil sea cave.**

Carvoeiro's **tourist train** and the **Cliffs Route hop-on, hop-off bus** offer options for getting to neighboring **Ferragudo,** a quintessential Algarve fishing village. Start in the main square by the Arade River and walk up to the **Our Lady of the Conception Church.** Back along the riverside, take a walk along Ferragudo's main beach, **Praia Grande.**

Head back to Carvoeiro to enjoy its colorful bars and restaurants and spend the night.

DAY 5: PORTIMÃO AND PRAIA DA ROCHA

Get up early to head to **Portimão,** the sardine capital of the Algarve (a 20-minute drive west via N125 or 35-minute bus ride). An array of **boat trips** depart from Portimão's riverside—there's even one on a pirate ship. Boat tours usually depart early morning and vary from half-day to full-day excursions. After your cruise, check out the acclaimed **Portimão Museum** for insight into the city's canning industry and enjoy lunch and an ice cream on the riverside square.

Head just south of Portimão (a short taxi or shuttle bus ride) to **Praia da Rocha,** which offers beachside hotels for all budgets and a cliff-top strip of bars and restaurants. **Dolphin-watching trips** run from the marina and a **water taxi** crosses the river. Stroll on the wooden walkway along the long, golden beach. Get dressed up for a night on the town.

DAY 6: LAGOS

Head west to **Lagos** by car (a 25-minute drive along the N125), or take a train (20 minutes) or bus (35 minutes) from Portimão city center.

Laid-back Lagos is a history buff's delight. Explore the city's Old Town Center on foot in the morning, including the elaborate **St. Anthony Church,** the well-preserved **Ponta da Bandeira Fort,** and the sobering **Slave Market Museum.**

Enjoy lunch in one of Lagos's many backstreet eateries. In the afternoon, walk along postcard-perfect **Dona Ana Beach;** then continue south to the **Ponta da Piedade** headland. **Boat trips** run from the base of the promontory into arches, caves, and grottoes.

In the evening, choose between upscale nightlife at the marina and the bohemian scene in the city center.

DAY 7: SAGRES

Head west to **Sagres** by car (a 30-minute drive via the N125) or bus (1 hour).

The most southwesterly tip of mainland Europe, barren Sagres is an area of raw beauty, its soaring cliffs buffeted by huge waves and strong Atlantic winds—which also makes it a top spot for **surfing.** Retrace the steps of some of Portugal's most famous explorers as you walk along the dramatic cliffs of **Cape St. Vincent** and explore the vast **Sagres Fortress.** Enjoy the sedate but cool vibe of Sagres town, stopping for a bite at one of its inexpensive seafood restaurants.

When you're ready, head home, whether that means continuing onward to explore the rest of Portugal or returning to Spain. Traveling the entire width of the Algarve without stops takes around two hours on the A22 motorway.

If you have more time...

If you cover Sagres in a morning and have a free afternoon (or an extra day or two), head north up the Algarve's west coast to **Aljezur.** From Sagres, the charming market town is a winding 40-minute drive through the unspoiled scenery of the **Southwest Alentejo and Vicentine Coast Natural Park.** Aljezur's wild beaches appeal to surfers, motorhomers, and anyone interested in getting off the tourist track.

Lisbon

Portugal's magnificent capital is currently one of Europe's most up-and-coming cities—vibrant and culturally rich, where the historic blends seamlessly with the cool and contemporary. At the mouth of the Tagus River (Rio Tejo), the "City of Seven Hills" is buzzing and cosmopolitan, home to melodic fado music and a vivid nightlife scene. Traditional tile-clad facades and redbrick roofs conceal a tangle of charming cobbled streets and elegant avenues that beckon to be explored.

Lisbon's impressive monuments, historic neighborhoods, and edgy vibe welcome visitors to drink in stunning bird's-eye views from many panoramic *miradouro* viewpoints or hip hotel rooftop bars. Stroll the chic boulevards with their many boutiques, admire striking riverfront

Highlights

Look for ★ to find recommended sights, activities, dining, and lodging.

© MOON.COM

★ **São Jorge Castle:** On a hilltop in the heart of Lisbon, this imposing Moorish monument commands spectacular views of the historic city center and the Tagus River (page 44).

★ **Belém Tower:** At the mouth of the Tagus River, this fortified tower was the last and first sight the country's intrepid sailors had of their homeland when setting off on their voyages (page 50).

★ **Jerónimos Monastery:** Home to the national archaeological and naval museums, Belém's stunning centerpiece is a marvel of ornate Manueline architecture, which took the entire 16th century to construct (page 52).

★ **Bairro Alto Nightlife:** Historic Bairro Alto has reinvented itself as the city's liveliest and coolest nocturnal hangout, with chic wine bars, historic fado houses, and renowned jazz clubs (page 61).

★ **Avenida da Liberdade:** An appealing mix of historic and contemporary buildings, high-end boutiques, and tree-shaded cafés lines the country's most famous avenue (page 65).

★ **Pena Palace:** High above the Sintra plains, this brightly colored palace is unique and magical (page 76).

★ **Boca do Inferno:** Literally "Hell's Mouth," this dramatic coastal rock formation comes to life in winter, when the rough seas show Mother Nature in full force (page 79).

★ **Mafra National Palace:** Developed over centuries from a simple convent into a sumptuous palace, this splendid baroque monument has been restored to its former glory (page 85).

★ *Christ the King:* Arms outstretched high above the Tagus River, this iconic statue affords dazzling views over the city (page 87).

★ **Dolphin-Watching in Sado Estuary:** Take a boat trip in this tranquil, marshy nature reserve to watch its resident dolphins (page 89).

monuments, explore the many museums, or for the classic Lisbon experience, take the famous tram 28 around the city's historic nooks and crannies before enjoying mesmerizing fado in one of the many original haunts in Alfama or Bairro Alto.

Less than an hour from the heart of the city are the upscale towns of Estoril and Cascais as well as magical Sintra, which famously has a microclimate all its own. Cross the Tagus River and explore the delights of the Setúbal Peninsula, where the iconic statue of Christ stretches its arms over the capital.

ORIENTATION

Hilly Lisbon is divided into many neighborhoods and parishes, or *bairros*. Most of the city's main attractions, such as its monuments, museums, fado houses, restaurants, and hotels, are located in the historic central area. The heart of Lisbon's historic area is the **Baixa Pombalina-Chiado,** often simply referred to as the Baixa, or Baixa-Chiado; it's the main downtown commercial and banking area along the river.

The downtown Baixa is immediately fringed by several of the city's other most famous neighborhoods: labyrinth-like **Alfama** (east of Baixa), famous for fado; time-honored **Castelo** (just above Alfama); melting pot **Mouraria** (which shares a hill with Alfama and Castelo); hip nighttime hangout **Bairro Alto** (northwest of Baixa); cool and cultural **Cais do Sodré** (west of the Baixa riverfront); chic **Estrela** (northwest of Cais do Sodré) and upscale **Príncipe Real** (northwest of Baixa, behind Bairro Alto).

Farther afield are other popular neighborhoods such as hilltop **São Vicente,** with boundless views from every corner, and charming, historic **Graça,** both east of the Baixa, behind Alfama, Castelo, and Mouraria. On the western extremity of the heart of Lisbon is the culturally rich area of **Belém,** while at the opposite side, on the northeast, is the modern area of **Park of Nations (Parque das Nações),** dramatically developed for the 1998 World Exhibition.

SAFETY

As with many tourist destinations, Lisbon is afflicted by petty and opportunistic crime. Take basic precautions such as not walking along dark streets alone at night, not leaving valuables in rental vehicles, and not carrying large amounts of cash. Pickpockets are an issue, so make sure backpacks are worn in front in crowded areas and on public transport. Better still, use concealed pouches and never keep cash and documents in the same pouch. Call the **PSP tourist police** (tel. 213 421 623) or visit the nearest police station. In an **emergency,** call **112.**

PLANNING YOUR TIME

Much of Lisbon's city center can be covered in a day, but it's worth spending at least two or three days. A great way to cover the must-sees is either a hop-on hop-off bus that stops at all main attractions and landmarks, or tram 28, which circumnavigates Lisbon's main neighborhoods. Other good options to explore include a neatly organized subway, nifty *tuk-tuk* carts, and a hop-on hop-off ferryboat. Set aside another day to explore Lisbon's outskirts, such as the gorgeous villages of Cascais, Estoril, and Sintra, and another day to see anything you missed. While in Lisbon, an absolute must is dinner at a fado restaurant in Bairro Alto. Make reservations well in advance, as these are popular attractions.

In mid-June, the traditional Santo António festivities, dedicated to the city's patron saint, explode into party mode. In December, Christmas trimmings and roasted chestnuts bring warmth to the city. July and August can get very hot, and even though many of the city's residents head south for summer vacation, it is still packed with tourists. Summer and New Year are tourism high seasons, when hotel prices soar and the city is packed with visitors. Good times to visit are March-May and September-October, when the weather is pleasant and the hotels cheaper.

Previous: Lisbon's Eduardo VII Park; souvenirs from the Santo António festival; abstract tile pavement.

Lisbon

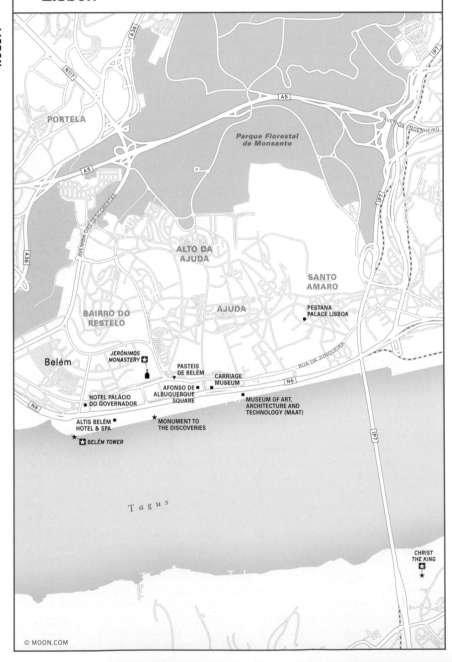

PORTELA

Parque Florestal
de Monsanto

ALTO DA
AJUDA

SANTO
AMARO

BAIRRO DO
RESTELO

AJUDA

PESTANA
PALACE LISBOA

Belém

JERÓNIMOS
MONASTERY ★

PASTEIS
DE BELÉM

AFONSO DE
ALBUQUERQUE
SQUARE

CARRIAGE
MUSEUM

HOTEL PALÁCIO
DO GOVERNADOR

MUSEUM OF ART,
ARCHITECTURE AND
TECHNOLOGY (MAAT)

ALTIS BELÉM
HOTEL & SPA

MONUMENT TO
THE DISCOVERIES

★ BELÉM TOWER

T a g u s

CHRIST
THE KING
★

RUA DA JUNQUEIRA

© MOON.COM

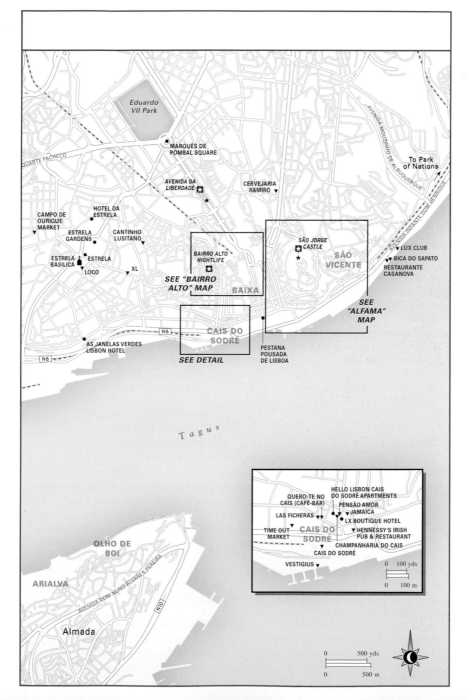

Eduardo
VII Park

MARQUÉS DE
POMBAL SQUARE

DUARTE PACHECO

AVENIDA MOUZINHO DE ALBUQUERQUE

To Park
of Nations

AVENIDA DA
LIBERDADE ✠

CERVEJARIA
RAMIRO ▼

AVENIDA INFANTE DOM HENRIQUE

CAMPO DE
OURIQUE
MARKET

HOTEL DA
ESTRELA

ESTRELA
GARDENS

CANTINHO
LUSITANO ▼

BAIRRO ALTO
NIGHTLIFE
✠

SÃO JORGE
✠ CASTLE
★

SÃO
VICENTE

▼ LUX CLUB
▼ BICA DO SAPATO

RESTAURANTE
CASANOVA

ESTRELA
BASILICA ♦ ESTRELA

LOCO

XL

SEE "BAIRRO
ALTO" MAP

BAIXA

SEE
"ALFAMA"
MAP

N6

CAIS DO
SODRÉ

AS JANELAS VERDES
LISBON HOTEL

N6

SEE DETAIL

PESTANA
POUSADA
DE LISBOA

T a g u s

HELLO LISBON CAIS
DO SODRÉ APARTMENTS

QUERO-TE NO
CAIS (CAFÉ-BAR)

PENSÃO AMOR
▼ JAMAICA

LAS FICHERAS ▼●

●◆ LX BOUTIQUE HOTEL

TIME OUT
MARKET ▼

CAIS DO
SODRÉ

▼ HENNESSY'S IRISH
PUB & RESTAURANT

CHAMPANHARIA DO CAIS

CAIS DO SODRÉ

VESTIGIUS ▼

0   100 yds

0   100 m

OLHO DE
BOI

ARIALVA

AVENIDA DOM NUNO-ÁLVARES PEREIRA

RIO

Almada

0   500 yds

0   500 m

Sights

BAIXA POMBALINA-CHIADO

Fronted by the Tagus River, the Baixa Pombalina-Chiado (BYE-shah pom-bah-LEE-nah shee-AH-doo), often referred to as just Baixa, "downtown Lisbon," or Baixa-Chiado, is the city's central shopping and banking district—and its tourist hub. The name derives from the distinctive Portuguese Pombaline architectural style employed to rebuild the city after the 1755 earthquake, under the guidance of Sebastião José de Carvalho e Melo, the 1st Marquis of Pombal. Elegant neoclassical facades and patterned cobbled streets give the neighborhood an air of graceful uniformity. Two main streets, **Rua Augusta** and **Rua da Prata,** are laden with buzzing shops and restaurants. The Chiado, situated just north of the Baixa and centered on Chiado square, is a cultural district packed with theaters, museums, and galleries. The main Metro stops in the Baixa area are Avenida, Restauradores, Rossio, Baixa-Chiado, and Terreiro do Paço, on the Green and Blue Lines.

Comércio Square
(Praça do Comércio)

This vast square, with views of the Tagus River, bustles with visitors and has the statue of King José I on his horse. The impressive colonnades that frame it on three sides house several ministries, museums, shops, and restaurants.

Two museums on the square are worth a visit. The **Beer Museum (Museu da Cerveja)** (Terreiro do Paço, Ala Nascente 62-65, tel. 210 987 656, www.museudacerveja.pt, 11am-midnight daily, €5, Metro Terreiro do Paço, Blue Line) boasts a plethora of different beers and ales from around the world. The **Lisbon Story Centre** (Praça do Comércio 78, tel. 211 941 099, www.lisboastorycentre.pt, 10am-8pm daily, €7, Metro Terreiro do Paço, Blue Line) recounts the key chapters of Lisbon's history through state-of-the-art interactive multimedia.

Comércio Square is one of the city's main transport hubs, with many trams and buses running from here; it's also directly across from the Cais do Sodré ferry terminal.

Augusta Triumphal Arch
(Arco da Rua Augusta)

The formal entrance to the Baixa neighborhood, the decorative **Augusta Triumphal Arch** (Praça do Comércio, tel. 210 999 599, www.visitlisboa.com, 9am-8pm daily, viewing terrace €2.50, Metro Terreiro do Paço, Blue Line) was built to mark the city's resilience and glorious rebirth following the 1755 earthquake. Historical Portuguese figures such as navigator Vasco da Gama and the Marquis of Pombal adorn the gateway's six columns, gazing over Comércio Square and out to the river. Inside the arch a narrow, spiral staircase made from solid stone climbs to a viewing terrace that offers sweeping views of the plaza.

Archaeological Center of Rua Correeiros
(Núcleo Arqueológico da Rua Correeiros)

Overlooked by many tourists, the **Archaeological Center of Rua Correeiros** (Rua dos Correeiros 15-23, tel. 211 131 004, 10am-6pm Mon-Sat, free, Metro Baixa-Chiado, Green/Blue Lines) showcases a wealth of Roman artifacts uncovered during the construction of the bank next door. Free guided tours of Roman ruins beneath the streets of Lisbon must be booked in advance and are available in English.

Santa Justa Elevator
(Elevador de Santa Justa)

Also called the Carmo Lift, the 19th-century neo-Gothic, wrought-iron **Santa Justa Elevator** (www.carris.pt, 7:30am-11pm

Two Days in Lisbon

Set aside at least two days to see the best of Portugal's capital. This itinerary covers all the main sights with free time to amble along the streets and soak up the city's vibe. End each day with sunset cocktails and chill-out music in the evening.

Lisbon is vast but relatively easy to navigate. Most of the main monuments and sights are downtown and along the river, easily reached on public transport. A handful of other worthy attractions are in towns and villages on the fringes, such as Cascais and Sintra; renting a car is the best option.

DAY 1

Begin by walking the main **Avenida da Liberdade,** heading south toward the Tagus River. Peruse the glamorous window displays and stop for a mid-morning coffee at one of the picturesque cafés. In the main downtown area, explore famous **Comércio Square** and its museums and landmarks—they're all within walking distance. A few streets back from the main square is the **Santa Justa Elevator,** also called the Carmo Lift. This historical contraption transports passengers from downtown up to the famous Bairro Alto neighborhood. Jump into the lift and admire how the old-fashioned machinery comes to life, taking you to the viewing platform at the top.

For lunch, hop on the Metro (from Baixa-Chiado to Cais do Sodré) or take a 20-minute walk west to the bustling **Time Out Market Lisboa,** set back from the Cais do Sodré quay. This eclectic food hall showcases the finest Portuguese products. After lunch, take a tram or bus the short distance from Cais do Sodré west to Belém. Drink in the beauty of historic **Belém Tower** and the **Jerónimos Monastery.** Then it's time to visit the famous **Pastéis de Belém** bakery to sample a *pastel de nata* custard tart.

Head back to Lisbon via tram, bus, or taxi, stopping at Chiado Square to enjoy a sunset cocktail on a panoramic terrace. The **Hotel Mundial Rooftop Bar & Lounge,** just off Chiado Square, is a good choice. From here, it's a 20-minute stroll northwest to **Bairro Alto** for dinner at the typical **fado** restaurant **O Faia.** After dinner, let loose in one of the many nearby bars.

DAY 2

Venture out of Lisbon today by renting a car and driving west along the Marginal coastal road, passing through the glitzy town of Estoril (roughly 25 km/15.5 mi west of Lisbon) to upscale **Cascais.** To enjoy some fresh sea air, park in Estoril and walk 3 kilometers (1.9 mi) west to Cascais along the seaside boardwalk. Spend a few hours strolling around the pretty village of Cascais; have a dip in the sea and lunch or a drink on the marina or in the main square. Or, if you visit on a Saturday, take in the sights and sounds of the regular Saturday-morning arts and crafts fair, a brilliant place for an unusual souvenir. A few kilometers out of Cascais center is the dramatic **Boca do Inferno** rock formation.

From there, drive on to windswept **Guincho Beach** (8 km/5 mi northwest of Cascais), popular among windsurfers, to enjoy sweeping views of the ocean and plains. Head 11 kilometers (6.8 mi) north to stop at **Cabo da Roca** and its lighthouse, the westernmost point of mainland Europe. From here, it's another roughly 18 kilometers (11.2 mi) northeast to **Sintra** and its highlight, the fairy-tale **Pena Palace.** After touring the palace, wander Sintra's charming cobbled streets and its exquisite buildings, including the Sintra National Palace and Moorish Castle, and enjoy dinner at one of its many quaint and cozy restaurants. After soaking up all of the romanticism Sintra has to offer, drive back to Lisbon, 25 kilometers (15.5 mi) east.

All this can be covered comfortably in one day if you rent a car. Alternatively, choose one destination—Cascais or Sintra—and use the train or bus to get there.

Lisbon's Best Restaurants

★ **Restaurante Cervejaria O Pinóquio:** The home-cooked steak and seafood are legendary (page 54).

★ **Café Nicola:** Frequented by poet Manuel du Bocage, this art deco landmark epitomizes European coffee culture (page 54).

★ **O Solar do Bacalhau:** This is one of the best spots to enjoy the Portuguese specialty *bacalhau* (page 54).

★ **Cervejaria Ramiro:** Expect long queues at this famed institution where a steak sandwich replaces dessert (page 55).

★ **Casa do Leão:** Dine inside the São Jorge Castle, where the dishes are culinary masterpieces and the views are remarkable (page 55).

★ **Chapitô à Mesa:** This restaurant is part of a famous circus arts school, so expect a fun and fanciful meal (page 55).

★ **Cervejaria Trindade:** This beautiful brewery and banquet hall dates from the mid-1800s, when it was the place of choice for writers, poets, and politicians (page 58).

★ **La Paparrucha:** Meat rules at this authentic Argentinean grill (page 58).

★ **Time Out Market Lisboa:** Hundreds of gastronomic goodies are under one roof (page 59).

★ **Espumantaria do Cais:** Add some fizz to your meal at this tapas and champagne bar (page 59).

★ **Pastéis de Belém:** No visit to Lisbon is complete without a stop at this birthplace of Portugal's famous *pastel de nata* tart (page 59).

daily May-Oct, 7:30am-9pm daily Nov-Apr, round-trip €5.15, Metro Baixa-Chiado, Green/Blue Lines) is the only vertical lift in Lisbon, connecting the Baixa area to the Bairro Alto neighborhood, saving a steep climb. Inaugurated in 1902, it is classified as a national monument. Standing at 45 meters (148 feet) tall, it was designed in a style similar to that of the Eiffel Tower by engineer Raoul Mesnier de Ponsard. The lift is stunning at night when lit up, and has a fabulous viewing platform at the top. Intriguingly, it can transport more people going up than coming down. It is accessed via Rua do Ouro at the bottom or Carmo Square at the top. The viewing platform (€1.50) is also accessible directly from Carmo Square, up the hill behind the lift.

Carmo Convent
(Convento do Carmo)

Once Lisbon's largest church, the **Carmo Convent** (Largo do Carmo, tel. 213 478 629, www.museuarqueologicodocarmo.pt, 10am-6pm Mon-Sat May-Sept, 10am-5pm Mon-Sat Oct-Apr, €4, Metro Baixa-Chiado or Rossio, Green/Blue Lines) is a stark reminder of the vast devastation caused by the 1755 earthquake, which razed the city and large swaths of Portugal. Originally built in 1389 by order

Lisbon's Best Accommodations

★ **Hotel Mundial:** The rooftop bar at this four-star hotel has one of the best views in Lisbon (page 68).

★ **Yes! Lisbon Hostel:** This hostel has it all: excellent location, fantastic service, and budget-friendly prices (page 68).

★ **Solar do Castelo:** Sleep in medieval-contemporary style at this eco-retreat within the walls of the São Jorge Castle (page 68).

★ **Memmo Alfama Design Hotel:** This chic urban retreat blends in with the historic Alfama neighborhood (page 68).

★ **Bairro Alto Hotel:** This grand 18th-century hotel enjoys a dominant position on the main square, within walking distance of shops and restaurants (page 68).

★ **Hello Lisbon Cais do Sodré Apartments:** These self-catering apartments reflect the youth and energy of frenetic Pink Street (page 69).

★ **Hotel Palácio do Governador:** Located in the 16th-century Governor's Palace is an oasis of tranquility in one of Lisbon's prettiest neighborhoods (page 69).

★ **VIP Executive Arts:** This streamlined four-star hotel is close to convenient transportation, shopping, and nightlife (page 69).

of Nuno Álvares Pereira, an influential knight who led the Portuguese army, the church and convent sit on a hill directly opposite the São Jorge Castle. Today only its naked Gothic ruins still stand. The site is also home to the Museu Arqueológico do Carmo, a museum with a collection of relics from dissolved monasteries, including sarcophagi and grisly but well-preserved Peruvian sacrificial mummies.

Rossio Square
(Praça Dom Pedro IV)

The beating heart of Lisbon, located downtown, Rossio Square (Metro Rossio, Green Line) has long been one of the city's main meeting places, a lively, genteel square of Pombaline architecture lined with cafés, trees, and two grand baroque fountains at either end. Housed in the impressive buildings framing the square are the stately **Dona Maria II National Theater (Teatro Nacional de Dona Maria II)** and the historic **Café Nicola,** which dates to the 18th century and was one of the first cafés to emerge in Lisbon. Also nearby is the ornate **Rossio train station,** which is typically Manueline in its architecture. One of the square's distinguishing features is the wavy black-and-white cobblestone paving.

Glória Funicular
(Elevador da Glória)

The quirky **Glória Funicular** (www.carris. pt, 7:15am-11:55pm Mon-Thurs, 7:15am-12:25am Fri, 8:45am-12:25pm Sat, 9:15am-11:55pm Sun and holidays, round-trip €3.60) puts the "fun" in funicular. It has become an emblem of Lisbon, its graffiti scrawl only adding to its charm, mirroring its urban surroundings. Inaugurated in 1885, it connects the Baixa (Restauradores Square) to the São Pedro de Alcântara viewpoint in Bairro Alto via a steep track that cuts straight through a dense residential area packed with

19th-century buildings. Practical for locals, it's a treat for visitors.

CASTELO

Stately and traditional, the Moorish Castelo (kash-TEH-loo) neighborhood, home to the São Jorge Castle, is known as Lisbon's birthplace. One of the city's finest neighborhoods, on a hill just east of the Baixa, it has fabulous views from almost every street corner. A wave of young international residents lives alongside older inhabitants, bringing a trendy vibe; Castelo is the perfect blend of historic and hip.

★ São Jorge Castle
(Castelo de São Jorge)
The **São Jorge Castle** (Rua de Santa Cruz do Castelo, tel. 218 800 620, www. castelodesaojorge.pt, 9am-9pm daily Mar-Oct, 9am-6pm daily Nov-Feb, €8.50) sits on a summit high above historic Baixa. The original fortress was built by the Visigoths in the 5th century and expanded by the Moors in the mid-11th century due to its prime defensive location. It contains the medieval castle, ruins of the former royal palace, stunning gardens, and part of an 11th-century citadel.

A permanent exhibition of relics uncovered here includes objects from the 7th century BC to the 18th century. The Black Chamber, a camera obscura, provides 360-degree views of the city through an optical system of mirrors and lenses, while an open-air viewpoint looks over the city center and the Tagus River. Renowned restaurant Casa do Leão and a casual café are also within the castle walls. To get there from downtown Lisbon, take tram 28 or the Castelo Bus, line 737.

ALFAMA

Alfama (al-FAH-mah) is Lisbon's oldest and most soulful neighborhood and claims to be the birthplace of fado, although Bairro Alto and Mouraria also make this claim. Inhabited from the 5th century by the Visigoths, this unpolished neighborhood southeast of the Baixa blankets the hillside between the Tagus River and São Jorge Castle. Its narrow cobbled streets create a stepped labyrinth of historic houses and quirky shops. It was once rough and home to dockworkers and seafarers. As the city's port prospered, so did Alfama, although its rugged charisma remains. Alfama boasts monuments, traditional fado houses, and many fabulous viewpoints along its slopes.

Portas do Sol Viewpoint
(Miradouro Portas do Sol)
Midway between São Jorge Castle and the Sé cathedral, this is one of Lisbon's most iconic viewpoints, a vast terrace looking over rooftops down to the Tagus River. It's also an obligatory stop for weary walkers. At the viewpoint is the cool, contemporary **Portas do Sol** (tel. 218 851 299, 10am-midnight daily), a café, restaurant, and cocktail bar all rolled into one—it's a great place to drink in the views, enhanced by a lively soundtrack of street entertainers mixed with the bustle of the city. Tram 28 stops at the Miradouro.

Lisbon Cathedral
(Sé de Lisboa)
Between the Alfama neighborhood and Castelo, **Lisbon Cathedral** (Largo da Sé, tel. 218 866 752, www.patriarcado-lisboa.pt, 9am-7pm daily, main cathedral free, tram 28 or 12) is the oldest and most famous church in the city. Its official name is the Church of Santa Maria Maior, but it is often simply called the Sé. Construction began in 1147, and successive modifications and renovations span the centuries. Its exterior is austere, with two robust towers. Inside, a wealth of decorative features reflect different eras. The neoclassical and rococo main chapel contains the tombs of King Afonso IV and his family. You'll also see lofty Gothic vaults, sculptured Romanesque motifs, stained-glass rose windows, and a baroque sacristy. The **Cloister** (10am-5pm Mon-Sat, 2pm-5pm Sun, extended hours until 7pm May-Sept, €2.50) houses Roman, Arab, and medieval relics excavated during archaeological digs. The **Treasury** (10am-5pm Mon-Sat, €2.50) on the second floor contains jewels

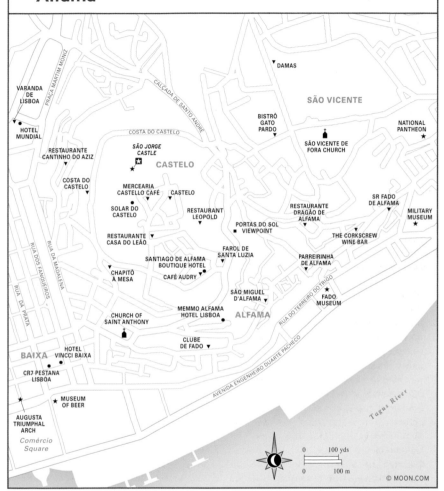

Alfama

VARANDA
DE
LISBOA

PRAÇA MARTIM MONIZ

CALÇADA DE SANTO ANDRÉ

▼ DAMAS

SÃO VICENTE

HOTEL
MUNDIAL

COSTA DO CASTELO

BISTRÔ
GATO
PARDO ▼

NATIONAL
PANTHEON
★

RESTAURANTE
CANTINHO DO AZIZ

SÃO JORGE
CASTLE

SÃO VICENTE DE
FORA CHURCH

✪
★ CASTELO

COSTA DO
CASTELO ▼

MERCEARIA
CASTELLO CAFÉ

CASTELO

SR FADO
DE ALFAMA

SOLAR DO
CASTELO ▼

RESTAURANT
LEOPOLD ▼

RESTAURANTE
DRAGÃO DE
ALFAMA ▼

MILITARY
MUSEUM
★

PORTAS DO SOL
■ VIEWPOINT

THE CORKSCREW
WINE BAR

RESTAURANTE ▼
CASA DO LEÃO

RUA DA MADALENA

RUA DOS FANQUEIROS

RUA DA PRATA

FAROL DE
SANTA LUZIA

PARREIRINHA
DE ALFAMA

SANTIAGO DE ALFAMA
BOUTIQUE HOTEL ▼

CHAPITÔ
À MESA ▼

CAFÉ AUDRY ▼

SÃO MIGUEL
D'ALFAMA ▼

RUA DO TERREIRO DO TRIGO

★
FADO
MUSEUM

MEMMO ALFAMA
HOTEL LISBOA ▼

ALFAMA

CHURCH OF
SAINT ANTHONY

CLUBE
DE FADO ▼

BAIXA

HOTEL
VINCCI BAIXA

AVENIDA ENGENHEIRO DUARTE PACHECO

Tagus River

CR7 PESTANA
LISBOA

★
MUSEUM
OF BEER

★

AUGUSTA
TRIUMPHAL
ARCH

Comércio
Square

0   100 yds

0   100 m

© MOON.COM

from various periods. Tram 28 stops right
outside the cathedral's door.

Fado Museum
(Museu do Fado)

The **Fado Museum** (Largo Chafariz de
Dentro 1, tel. 218 823 470, www.museudofado.
pt, 10am-6pm Tues-Sun, €5, Metro Santa
Apolónia, Blue Line) showcases traditional
fado, a soulful and often mournful musical
genre that is to Portugal what the blues are to

Memphis. Fado's origins are debated, but the
consensus is that it was born in Alfama in the
1820s. This interactive museum hosts a permanent exhibition with photographs, records,
and instruments. There are also sometimes
live performances.

National Military Museum
(Museu Militar)

Across the square from the Santa Apolónia
train station, the **National Military**

Best Views

Because Lisbon is laid out over seven hills, gorgeous views can be found throughout the city. Public viewing points (*miradouros*) offer views of the cityscape. Some are enhanced with cafés and restaurants, landscaped gardens, and even chic lounges. Best of all, they're free. Visit at sunset for a truly special experience.

- The famous **Miradouro São Pedro de Alcântara** (Rua São Pedro de Alcântara) provides panoramic views over São Jorge Castle and Alfama, as well as Lisbon Cathedral and the Tagus.

- The romantic **Miradouro da Nossa Senhora do Monte** (Largo Monte) is the highest viewpoint, offering bird's-eye views over the old quarters and castle all the way to the Tagus River.

- The **Miradouro Portas do Sol** (Largo Portas do Sol) overlooks the charismatic Alfama neighborhood.

- The **Miradouro da Graça** (Calçada da Graça) peers over São Jorge Castle.

Along with the *miradouros*, the **São Jorge Castle** has possibly the best views in the city. Panoramas can also be enjoyed from hotel rooftop bars, such as the **Hotel Mundial** (Praça Martim Moniz 2), where the Sunset Parties have a cult following.

Museum (Largo Museu da Artilharia, tel. 218 842 300, www.exercito.pt, 10am-5pm Tues-Fri, 10am-12:30pm and 1:30pm-5pm Sat-Sun and holidays, €3, Metro Santa Apolónia, Blue Line) is Portugal's largest and oldest military museum. Beautiful, lofty, tile-clad rooms contain 26,000 pieces of military paraphernalia spanning centuries, including the former Royal Arsenal. The building is a striking monument, built on the site of a 16th-century foundry.

National Tile Museum
(Museu Nacional do Azulejo)

Located in a 16th-century convent, the **National Tile Museum** (Rua da Madre de Deus 4, tel. 218 100 340, www.museudoazulejo.gov.pt, 10am-6pm Tues-Sun, €5, Metro Santa Apolónia, Blue Line) contains a collection of traditional hand-painted azulejo ceramic tile plaques, some dating from the 15th century. It explores the history and tradition behind the art and craft of tilework, and the building is a splendid example of the magnificence of Portuguese baroque, with carved and gilded wood features, old paintings, and historical azulejo panels.

SÃO VICENTE

Two major monuments, the National Pantheon and the São Vicente de Fora Church, are in São Vicente (sown vee-SENT), among a cascade of historic homes on the hillside toward the Tagus. Peaceful and poised most of the week, São Vicente comes alive every Saturday morning for the famous Feira da Ladra flea market, next to the National Pantheon.

National Pantheon
(Panteão Nacional)

The **National Pantheon** (Campo de Santa Clara, tel. 218 854 820, 10am-6pm Tues-Sat Apr-Sept, 10am-5pm Tues-Sat Oct-Mar, €4, Metro Santa Apolónia, Blue Line)—otherwise known as the Church of Santa Engrácia—has baroque architecture and a distinctive domed roof that can be seen from most of central Lisbon. It is on the site of the original Santa Engrácia church, which began renovations in 1681 and took more than 300 years to complete. Construction dragged on for so long that the Portuguese call any lengthy project "work of Santa Engrácia." In 1916, the church

1: the Glória Funicular; **2:** tile from the National Tile Museum; **3:** the Fado Museum; **4:** São Jorge Castle

was converted into a pantheon, a process that took another 50 years. Today, the building boasts a majestic nave with a polychrome marble decoration typical of Portuguese baroque architecture. It is home to tombs of historic personalities such as writer Almeida Garrett, fado singer Amália Rodrigues, legendary soccer star Eusébio, and Portuguese presidents. The views from the front steps and the terrace around the dome are breathtaking.

São Vicente de Fora Church
(Igreja de São Vicente de Fora)

In its present guise, the **São Vicente de Fora Church** (Largo de São Vicente, tel. 218 824 400, www.patriarcado-lisboa.pt, 10am-6pm Tues-Sun, €5, Metro Santa Apolónia, Blue Line), or Monastery of São Vicente de Fora, is considered one of the finest examples of mannerist architecture in the country. Rebuilt from a 12th-century church, it dates to the 16th century and houses one of the biggest collections of baroque glazed tiles in the world, used to clad the cloisters, stairways, and aisles. There are also two mausoleums, one belonging to the Royal House of Braganza and the other to the city's archbishops, known as the Patriarchs of Lisbon. The must-see Patriarchate's Museum showcases beautiful historic works of religious art. Enjoy fabulous views from the roof terrace.

BAIRRO ALTO

Bairro Alto (BYE-rroo AL-too) has long been Lisbon's bohemian hangout, a favorite haunt for artists and writers. In the evenings, its grid of steep streets echoes with melancholic fado. Visit after 11pm, when the innumerable small bars and colorful nightspots really start to hit their stride. The neighborhood's historical significance dates to its expansion in the 16th century to accommodate the city's booming economic and social transformation.

São Pedro de Alcântara Viewpoint
(Miradouro São Pedro de Alcântara)

A pretty, two-tiered garden embellishes this sprawling viewpoint. Located next to the Glória Lift between Bairro Alto and the Baixa, the São Pedro de Alcântara viewpoint is one of the most popular. Visitors can often be heard gasping in awe at the sweeping vistas, and telescopes are on hand.

NORTH LISBON
Marquês de Pombal Square
(Praça Marquês de Pombal)

The massive statue of the Marquis of Pombal towering in the middle of this busy roundabout is one of Lisbon's most recognizable landmarks. Sebastião José de Carvalho e Melo, the 1st Marquis of Pombal, was prime minister in the 18th century. His soaring statue faces the Tagus River, strategically between the Eduardo VII Park and the cosmopolitan Avenida da Liberdade, the start of several main thoroughfares. Get here by taking the Metro to Marquês de Pombal station (Blue/Yellow Lines).

Eduardo VII Park
(Parque Eduardo VII)

Just behind the Marquês de Pombal Square is a sprawling, manicured garden of lush lawns and box hedges that give it a regal feel, consistent with the historic buildings surrounding it. Stand at the top of the park and enjoy magnificent views down to the Baixa and the Tagus River. Covering 26 hectares (64 acres), the park was renamed in 1902 for Britain's Edward VII, who visited Portugal that year.

Calouste Gulbenkian Museum
(Museu Calouste Gulbenkian)

A major hub of the arts, the **Calouste Gulbenkian Museum** (Av. de Berna 45A, tel. 217 823 461, https://gulbenkian.pt/museu, 10am-6pm Wed-Mon, €14, Metro São Sebastião, Blue/Red Lines) is one of Lisbon's less celebrated treasures. Its collection ranges from Greco-Roman antiquity to contemporary pieces, with 18th-century French art well represented. The stunning works of French glass and jewelry designer René Lalique

Bairro Alto

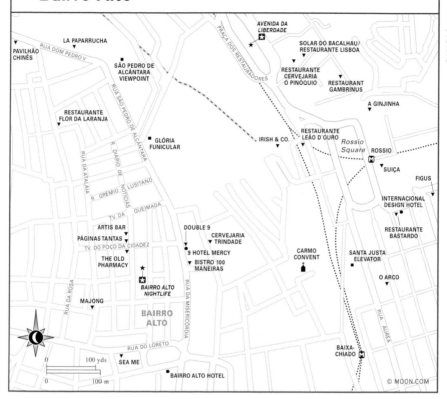

AVENIDA DA LIBERDADE

LA PAPARRUCHA

PAVILHÃO CHINÊS

RUA DOM PEDRO V

SÃO PEDRO DE ALCÂNTARA VIEWPOINT

PRAÇA DOS RESTAURADORES

SOLAR DO BACALHAU/ RESTAURANTE LISBOA

RESTAURANTE CERVEJARIA O PINÓQUIO

RESTAURANT GAMBRINUS

RESTAURANTE FLOR DA LARANJA

RUA SÃO PEDRO DE ALCÂNTARA

GLÓRIA FUNICULAR

IRISH & CO.

RESTAURANTE LEÃO D'OURO

A GINJINHA

Rossio Square

ROSSIO

RUA DIÁRIO DE NOTÍCIAS

RUA DA ATALAIA

SUIÇA

R. GRÉMIO LUSITANO

FIGUS

R. GRÉMIO

TV. DA QUEIMADA

INTERNACIONAL DESIGN HOTEL

ARTIS BAR

PÁGINAS TANTAS

TV. DO POÇO DA CIDADEZ

THE OLD PHARMACY

DOUBLE 9

CERVEJARIA TRINDADE

9 HOTEL MERCY

BISTRO 100 MANEIRAS

CARMO CONVENT

RESTAURANTE BASTARDO

SANTA JUSTA ELEVATOR

O ARCO

RUA DA ROSA

BAIRRO ALTO NIGHTLIFE

MAJONG

RUA DA MISERICÓRDIA

BAIRRO ALTO

RUA AUREA

RUA DO LORETO

SEA ME

BAIXA-CHIADO

0   100 yds

0   100 m

BAIRRO ALTO HOTEL

© MOON.COM

(1860-1945) are a highlight. The museum is housed in two separate buildings, connected by a lovely garden.

Águas Livres Aqueduct
(Aqueduto das Águas Livres)

Climb above the city to explore the formidable **Águas Livres Aqueduct** (main entrance at the EPAL Municipal Water Museum ticket office, Calçada da Quintinha 6, Campolide neighborhood, tel. 218 100 215, www.epal.pt, 10am-5:30pm Tues-Sun, €3), whose name translates as "Aqueduct of the Free Waters." Built between 1731 and 1799 to supply the city with water from Sintra, it is considered a remarkable example of 18th-century engineering, snaking over 58 kilometers (36 mi) along the trajectory of an old Roman aqueduct.

Despite its size, it blends into its surroundings. Visitors can walk the main portion of the platform, crossing the 1-kilometer (0.6-mi) stretch over the Alcântara Valley, the aqueduct's highest point at 68 meters (223 feet), with views of Lisbon. Guided tours (11am first Sat every month) require advance booking.

Take the Portas da Benfica bus 758 (every 15 minutes, €2) from the Glória Funicular to Campolide, then walk west for five minutes to the aqueduct. A taxi from central Lisbon to the aqueduct costs around €8.

ESTRELA AND LAPA

With grand properties and elegant streets, peaceful Estrela (eesh-TREH-lah) was settled by the well-heeled during the city's expansion in the 1700s and remains one of Lisbon's most affluent areas. The adjoining Lapa (LAH-pah) neighborhood is home to many foreign embassies.

Estrela Basilica

The neoclassical **Estrela Basilica** (Praça da Estrela, tel. 213 960 915, www. patrimoniocultural.gov.pt, 7:30am-8pm daily, free) was built in the 18th century by order of Queen Maria I, whose tomb it houses. The interior walls and flooring are clad in swaths of yellow, pink, and gray marble in stunning geometric patterns. Twin bell towers stand atop the striking facade, while the dome provides views over the city. The Estrela Basilica was the first church in the world dedicated to the Sacred Heart of Jesus. Take tram 25 or 28 from Comércio Square.

Estrela Gardens
(Jardim da Estrela)

The exquisitely landscaped **Estrela Gardens** is colloquially referred to as the Central Park of Lisbon, a tranquil, lush oasis in the heart of this affluent neighborhood, bordered by the main Rua da Estrela and Avenida Ávares Cabral, with the Estrela Basilica at the bottom and a statue of explorer Pedro Álvares Cabral at the top. Stroll past duck ponds, browse the library, and enjoy open-air concerts hosted in the wrought-iron bandstand on summer evenings.

National Museum of Ancient Art
(Museu Nacional de Arte Antiga)

A 20-minute stroll south of the Estrela Gardens is the **National Museum of Ancient Art** (Rua das Janelas Verdes, tel. 213 912 800, www.museudearteantiga.pt, 10am-6pm Tues-Sun, €6). Housed in a former 17th-century palace on one of the city's toniest streets, the opulent museum is laden with artifacts that span the 12th to the 19th centuries. The collection includes paintings, sculptures, textiles, and furniture. Among the most celebrated pieces are the *Panels of St. Vincent*, which depict a cross-section of

15th-century Portuguese society gathered to venerate a saint. Take the train or bus from Cais do Sodré to Santos.

BELÉM

Just west of downtown in bright Belém (beh-LAYN), iconic landmarks pay tribute to key chapters in Portugal's history, sharing a riverside location with modern museums, cafés, and gardens. During the Age of Discoveries, this is where ships set off to explore the globe. Belém can be uncomfortably busy, particularly in the heat of summer; expect long queues.

To get to Belém from downtown Lisbon, take tram 15 or 127 from the main Comércio Square, or the train from Cais do Sodré to Cascais. Jump off when you see the Jerónimos Monastery, and walk to the sights. A taxi from downtown Lisbon costs around €14 one-way.

★ Belém Tower
(Torre de Belém)

Jutting into the Tagus River, **Belém Tower** (Av. Brasília, tel. 213 620 034, www. torrebelem.gov.pt, 10am-5:30pm Tues-Sun Oct-Apr, 10am-6:30pm Tues-Sun May-Sept, €6) is Portugal's most famous monument and a UNESCO World Heritage Site due to its significance as a launch pad during the Age of Discoveries. Built in the early 16th century at the river mouth, the fortified tower was both functional and ornamental, defending Lisbon from sea raiders and also providing a ceremonial entrance to the city. The ornate white Manueline tower was the last and first sight sailors had of their homeland. The elaborate detail of the exterior belies the starkness of the interior.

Entering the tower over an ancient drawbridge, visitors access a bulwark housing artillery, in the middle of which is a small courtyard flanked by Gothic arches. Inside the tower are the Governor's Room, the King's

1: Belém Tower; 2: the famous tram 28;
3: Monument to the Discoveries; 4: Jerónimos Monastery

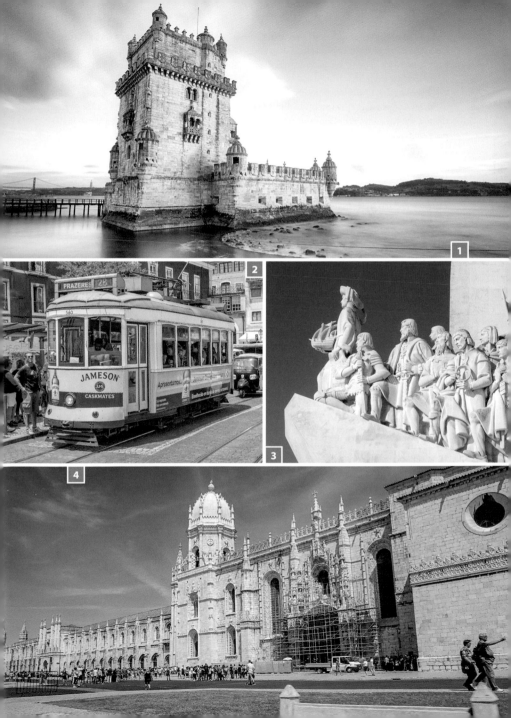

Room, the Audience Room, and a chapel, all devoid of furnishings, showcasing only the bare stonework. The tower is built over five floors, connected by a narrow spiral staircase, each floor having lovely balconies, and topped by a viewing terrace. It's worth the climb to the top for views over the Tagus estuary and the Belém neighborhood's monuments.

National Coach Museum
(Museu Nacional dos Coches)

Before cars, there were horses and carriages, and Portugal has some fine examples of horse-drawn vehicles on permanent display at the **National Coach Museum** (Av. da Índia 136, tel. 210 732 319, www.museudoscoches. pt, 10am-6pm Tues-Sun, €6). From elaborately decorated Berlins that transported royalty to children's carriages and mail buses, the various collections of 16th- to 19th-century coaches are fascinating. Located on the fringe of the Afonso de Albuquerque Square (Praça Afonso de Albuquerque), the museum also hosts a number of collections of other stately items, such as ceremonial clothing, instruments, tapestries, and horse tack.

★ Jerónimos Monastery
(Mosteiro dos Jerónimos)

Parallel to the Tagus River, with the stately Imperial Square Gardens sprawling in front of it, the exuberant **Jerónimos Monastery** (Praça do Império, tel. 213 620 034, www. mosteirojeronimos.gov.pt, 10am-5pm Tues-Sun Oct-Apr, 10am-6pm Tues-Sun May-Sept, €10, ticket including the Naval Museum and the Archaeology Museum €12) is Belém's breathtaking centerpiece. A prime example of ornate Manueline architecture, it is also a UNESCO World Heritage Site. Construction on the impressive landmark began in 1501 on the order of King Manuel I, who wanted to honor the memory of explorer Henry the Navigator, as well as to demonstrate his own devotion to Saint Jerome. The vast building took 100 years to complete. Its several architectural styles include Renaissance and the lavishly ornate Spanish plateresque style. The

magnificent riverside facade has a figure of Our Lady of Belém, while inside is the Latin-cross-shaped Church of Santa Maria, the final resting place of explorer Vasco da Gama and one of Portugal's greatest poets, Luís Vaz de Camões. Today the Monastery's long, regal wings also house the national archaeological and naval museums. To get to the Jerónimos Monastery from Cais do Sodré, take city bus lines 727, 28, 729, 714, or 751; tram 15; or the suburban train to Belém.

The **Naval Museum (Museu de Marinha)** (€6.50, ticket including the Jerónimos Monastery and the Archaeology Museum €12) occupies the western wing of the Jerónimos Monastery as well as a modern annex to the north. It grew from a collection started by King Luís I (1838-1889), who had a keen interest in oceanographic studies and was an accomplished navigator. Exhibits include historical paintings, archaeological items, and various scale models of ships, along with instruments and maps, royal barges, the Fairey III *Santa Cruz* that crossed the Atlantic in 1923, and the Portuguese Navy's first-ever aircraft, a flying boat.

Also located in the expansive wings of the Jerónimos Monastery is the **National Archaeology Museum (Museu Nacional de Arqueologia)** (€4, ticket including Jerónimos Monastery and the Naval Museum €12), devoted to ancient Iberian art. Among its collections are ancient jewelry, busts, mosaics, and epigraphs, as well as metal artifacts, medals, and coins.

Monument to the Discoveries
(Padrão dos Descobrimentos)

A short stroll from Belém Tower along the Tagus riverside is the **Monument to the Discoveries** (Av. Brasília, tel. 213 031 950, www.padraodosdescobrimentos.pt, 10am-7pm daily Mar-Sept, 10am-6pm Tues-Sun Oct-Feb, €3). First erected in 1940 and made permanent in 1960 to mark 500 years since Henry the Navigator's death, the monument celebrates the Age of Discoveries in the 15th and 16th centuries with statues of Henry the

Navigator, Pedro Álvares Cabral, and Vasco da Gama. Shaped like a caravel—a small Portuguese sailing ship—it also houses an auditorium and a museum with changing exhibitions, and has a viewing platform on top. In the square out front is the stunning **Compass Rose,** an elaborate decorative work of paving art shaped like a compass, 50 meters (164 feet) across, in black and red *lioz* limestone, in the center of which is a map of the world during the Age of Discoveries surrounded by decorative figures like mermaids, stars, and leaves.

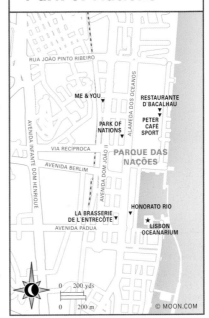

Park of Nations

RUA JOÃO PINTO RIBEIRO

ME & YOU

AVENIDA INFANTE DOM HENRIQUE

AVENIDA DOS OCEANOS

ALAMEDA DOS OCEANOS

RESTAURANTE
D'BACALHAU

PARK OF
NATIONS

PETER
CAFÉ
SPORT

VIA RECÍPROCA

AVENIDA BERLIM

AVENIDA DOM JOÃO II

**PARQUE DAS
NAÇÕES**

LA BRASSERIE
DE L'ENTRECÔTE

HONORATO RIO

AVENIDA PÁDUA

★ LISBON
OCEANARIUM

0 200 yds
0 200 m

© MOON.COM

MAAT—Museum of Art, Architecture and Technology
(Museu de Arte, Arquitetura e Tecnologia)

Inaugurated in 2016 in a contemporary building in stark contrast with its classical peers, **MAAT** (Av. Brasília, tel. 210 028 130, www. maat.pt, noon-8pm Wed-Mon, €5) is one of Lisbon's newest cultural additions. The building, by British architect Amanda Levete, has a curved design and white-tiled façade that juts out over the river like a low, gleaming spaceship. It hosts national and international exhibitions and collections of contemporary art, architecture, and technology, and is connected to the city by a footbridge. It is free to climb to the roof from outside for views over the Tagus at what has become an iconic location.

PARK OF NATIONS
(Parque das Nações)

Northeast of Lisbon, Park of Nations, or Parque das Nações (park dazh nah-SSOYNS), is an über-modern neighborhood developed for the 1998 World Exhibition, with mirrored high-rise apartment blocks and twin sail-shaped skyscrapers. It is linked to the south side of the Tagus River by the sinewy, 17-kilometer-long (10.6-mi-long) Vasco da Gama Bridge, Europe's longest. Family attractions such as the Meo concert arena and the Lisbon Oceanarium are here, along with cosmopolitan restaurants and bars.

Cable cars (11am-6pm daily, until 8pm in summer, closed in bad weather, €3.95 one-way, €5.90 round-trip) run between the Oceanarium and the modern, 145-meter (476-foot) Vasco da Gama tower, gliding over the waterfront. To get to Park of Nations from downtown Lisbon, take the Metro from Baixa-Chiado (Green/Blue Lines) to Oriente on the Red Line.

Lisbon Oceanarium
(Oceanário de Lisboa)

Inaugurated in 1998 for the World Exhibition, the **Lisbon Oceanarium** (Esplanada Dom Carlos I s/n, tel. 218 917 002, www.oceanario. pt, 10am-8pm daily late Mar-Oct, 10am-7pm daily Nov-mid-Mar, adults €16.20, children 4-12 €10.80), Europe's largest indoor aquarium, is home to a huge assortment of marine species, from seagulls to sea lions, sea dragons, and surgeonfish. The star attraction is a huge tank that houses exotic sealife, including rays, sharks, moray eels, barracudas, and sunfish.

Food

Lisbon's food scene is a crossroads of traditional and contemporary, offering everything from street food and vegan restaurants to gourmet market stalls. One thing that sets Lisbon apart from other European capitals is value for money.

BAIXA

Bustling Baixa is a hub of restaurants, cafés, and bars, plenty of them arranged around the main Comércio Square, promising people-watching and alfresco dining.

Portuguese

The home cooking at ★ **Restaurante Cervejaria O Pinóquio** (Praça dos Restauradores 79, tel. 213 465 106, www. restaurantepinoquio.pt, noon-midnight daily, €25) is a legendary variety of quality tapas and entrées, specializing in excellent steak and seafood. The decor is sparse but the outdoor terrace is charming. Although it's always busy, service is fast.

Located in the Praça do Comércio, fashionable **Museu da Cerveja (Beer Museum & Restaurant)** (Terreiro do Paço, East Wing 62-65, tel. 210 987 656, www.museudacerveja. pt, 11am-midnight daily, €20) showcases the finest beers produced in Portugal and Portuguese-speaking countries. A range of snacks and meals includes famous codfish cakes that complement the brews.

Established in 1936, acclaimed **Restaurante Gambrinus** (Rua das Portas de Santo Antão 23, tel. 213 421 466, www. restaurante-gambrinus.business.site, noon-1:30am daily, €20-40) has a dedicated following for its tapas and seafood, served in a classic setting with polished dark wood and crisp white tablecloths.

Overlooking gorgeous Rossio Square, bohemian **Restaurante Bastardo** (Rua da Betesga 3, tel. 213 240 993, www. restaurantebastardo.com, noon-11pm daily,

€15) serves up classic Portuguese cuisine with an international twist, like codfish with kombu seaweed, along with fabulous cocktails. Have there ever been so many different types of chairs under one roof?

The name of **Varanda de Lisboa Restaurant** (Praça Martim Moniz 2, tel. 218 842 000, www.hotel-mundial.pt, 6:30am-3pm and 7:30pm-10:30pm daily, €25) translates as "the veranda of Lisbon," referring to the views from its location at the top of the Mundial Hotel. It prepares accomplished dishes to match, like flambéed meats and *cataplanas* (seafood stews). There are weekly themed menus and three-course set menus.

Café

With a prime position on posh Rossio Square, the landmark ★ **Café Nicola** (Praça Dom Pedro IV 24-25, tel. 213 460 579, 8am-midnight daily, €8) epitomizes European coffee culture with its art deco interior, excellent coffees, and top-notch breakfasts. It was a favorite of poet Manuel du Bocage, who is memorialized in a statue out front. The celebrated café is excellent for people-watching, but prices are high.

Seafood

Cod is king at charming ★ **O Solar do Bacalhau** (Rua do Jardim do Regedor 30, tel. 213 460 069, www.solardobacalhau.com, 10am-midnight daily, €20), one of the best spots to enjoy the Portuguese specialty *bacalhau*. It also serves other meat and fish dishes in a setting with natural stone walls and elegantly laid tables.

At **O Leao d'Ouro** (Rua 1º de Dezembro 105, tel. 213 426 195, www. restauranteleaodouro.com.pt, noon-11pm daily, €20), dark wood and traditional tiled walls provide an almost medieval complement to rich fish and shellfish dishes such as oven-baked cod.

Established in 1956, authentic beer house ★ **Cervejaria Ramiro** (Av. Almirante Reis 1-H, tel. 218 851 024, www.cervejariaramiro. pt, noon-12:30am Wed-Mon, €20) is a famed institution featured on many travel programs. Expect long queues outside the restaurant. The rainbow of seafood includes prawns *al guilho*. The *prego no pão* is a steak sandwich with a cult following, which many eat at the end of meals in lieu of dessert. Wash it down with a chilled beer.

With simple and quaint decor that blends into its local neighborhood, **Solar 31 da Calçada** (Calçada Garcia 31, tel. 218 863 374, www.solar31.com, 5pm-midnight Mon, 11:30am-11pm Tues-Sat, €14) serves traditional Portuguese food with a focus on fresh fish and shellfish. Choose from a fantastic selection of starters and wines.

Mediterranean

Hidden on a backstreet, bright, eclectically decorated **O Arco** (Rua dos Sapateiros 161, tel. 213 463 280, noon-3pm and 7pm-11pm Thurs-Tues, €14) serves up a selection of tasty Mediterranean favorites, from spicy chicken curry to flavorful prawn dishes.

International

Elegant and sophisticated **Restaurante Figus** (Praça da Figueira 16, tel. 218 872 194, www.restaurantefigus.com, 11am-midnight daily, €20) is in the Beautique Hotel Figueira in Praça da Figueira downtown. It has a varied national and international à la carte menu and a refined selection of wines. Favorites include a *chourciço* and *morcela* sausage platter, steak in Portuguese sauce, gourmet burgers, fish, and pasta dishes. Don't miss the fig cheesecake for dessert.

Mozambican

At popular, family-run **Restaurante Cantinho do Aziz** (Rua de São Lourenço 5, tel. 218 876 472, www.cantinhodoaziz.com, noon-11pm daily, €15), savor exotic flavors from Mozambique in fare such as samosas, crab curry, and traditional Yuca Malaku and Yuca Miamba curries. The atmosphere is relaxed. Sit inside or on the long outdoor street terrace.

CASTELO

Portuguese

Located inside the São Jorge Castle, ★ **Casa do Leão** (Castelo de São Jorge, tel. 218 880 154, www.pousadas.pt, 12:30pm-3pm and 8pm-10:30pm daily, €28) takes advantage of its architectural features, including a vaulted brick ceiling, to create an elegant atmosphere. Its culinary masterpieces are concocted from fresh seasonal ingredients. Seafood *cataplana* and Portuguese-style steak are highlights. Even more remarkable are the views from the terrace outside, overlooking the city.

Set in a charming former bakery, **Leopold** (Pátio de Dom Fradique 12, tel. 218 861 697, 7:30pm-11pm Wed-Sun, tasting menu €40) puts an innovative twist on classics in intimate surroundings, with just four tables and an open kitchen. The tasting menu includes fresh, inventive daily dishes like cornbread with lime-infused goat cheese and Azores beef with algae and mizuna. As there is no stove, everything is cooked sous vide.

Part of a famous circus arts school, ★ **Chapitô à Mesa** (Costa do Castelo 7, tel. 218 875 077, www.chapito.org, noon-6pm and 7pm-1:30am Mon-Sat, 7pm-1:30am Sun, €25) offers fun, flamboyant cuisine alongside gorgeous views of Lisbon. Choose the snack bar, an alfresco grill terrace, or the elegant restaurant. Menu favorites include grilled shrimp with tropical fruit and pork cheeks with clams and sautéed potatoes.

The traditional tiled facade enhances the cozy chic-vintage interior of **Gosta do Castelo** (Costa do Castelo 138, tel. 218 870 743, noon-3:30pm and 7pm-11:30pm Wed-Mon, €25), which serves a lovely array of unusual takes on national staples, with a nice selection of wines. Try the Portuguese cheese platter with mango chutney. Entrées include duck magret with apple in port wine. Gosta do Castelo also has a brunch menu and a snack menu.

Café

Adjacent to the main entry to the São Jorge castle, **Café Audrey** (Rua Santiago 14, tel. 213 941 616, 7:30am-11pm daily, €12) is an eccentric little place with an eclectic menu, serving breakfast, lunch, and dinner dishes ranging from eggs Benedict to Goan curry.

Gourmet

Tradition meets cool at **Mercearia Castello Café** (Rua das Flores de Santa Cruz, 2, tel. 218 876 111, 10am-8pm daily, €8), a funky little eatery and grocery store. Its wood-clad interior harks back to the old days, and its location at the top of the hill near the castle is second to none. The fresh homemade fare includes quiches, crepes, and sandwiches made from quality regional products—it hits the spot after climbing to the castle.

ALFAMA

Portuguese Tapas

CorkScrew Restaurant & Wine Bar (Rua dos Remédios 95, tel. 215 951 774, www.thecorkscrew.pt, noon-2am Thurs-Sat, 1pm-midnight Sun-Wed, €10) serves great Portuguese tapas of cheeses, cured meats, and fish preserves, accompanied by fantastic Portuguese wines.

Seafood

Rustic **Farol Santa Luzia** (Largo de Santa Luzia 5, tel. 218 863 884, 5:30pm-11pm Mon-Sat, €18) is set in an 18th-century building directly opposite the Santa Luzia viewpoint, near São Jorge castle. Menu favorites include octopus salad, shellfish *açorda* (a soupy bread dish), and pork *cataplana* with shrimp, clams, and *chouriça* sausage.

Italian

Canteen-style **Restaurante Casanova** (Av. Infante Dom Henrique Loja 7, tel. 218 877 532, www.pizzeriacasanova.pt, 12:30pm-1:30am daily, €10) has a privileged riverside location with long tables conducive to sharing the authentic Italian food. Try the wood-oven-baked pizza.

Sushi

Located in an old port building on the Santa Apolónia docks, **Bica do Sapato** (Av. Infante Dom Henrique Armazém B, Cais da Pedra, Santa Apolónia, tel. 218 810 320, www.bicadosapato.com, 5pm-midnight Mon, noon-midnight Tues-Sat, 12:30pm-4pm Sun, €28) is a cool sushi bar that also specializes in contemporary and traditional Portuguese cuisine.

SÃO VICENTE

One of the city's oldest and more traditional areas, São Vicente has a more grown-up attitude that is reflected in its restaurants, which offer classic Portuguese and Mediterranean fare and cozy bistro-type eateries.

Bistro

With its exposed stone wall and brick floor, hidden hole-in-the-wall **Bistro Gato Pardo** (Rua de São Vicente 10, tel. 934 696 871, noon-10pm Fri-Tues, €15) is inviting for a snack, coffee, or a cozy meal. Tasty lamb, risotto with fish, and shrimp dishes are favorites.

Mediterranean

At no-frills hipster hangout **Damas** (Rua da Voz do Operário, no. 60, tel. 964 964 416, 6pm-2pm Tues-Thurs, 5pm-4am Fri, 7pm-4am Sat, 5pm-midnight Sun, closed Mon, €10), craft beers and excellent food accompany live music. The menu is scribbled on the tile-clad wall and changes daily. Dishes from across the Mediterranean include smoked lamb, almond tagine with falafel, and seitan meatballs. On weekends, DJ sets and live concerts are held in a small back room.

BAIRRO ALTO

Bohemian Bairro Alto might be better known for its nightlife, but it doesn't disappoint when it comes to restaurants, with a rainbow of international flavors.

1: flaming *chouriço* sausages; 2: *ginjinha* cherry liqueur; 3: outdoor café in the Alfama neighborhood

Local Specialties

Ask anyone what Lisbon's most typical dishes are, and you will hear **salted codfish** (*bacalhau*), for which the Portuguese claim to have a different recipe for each day of the year, and the ubiquitous *pastel de nata* **custard tart,** the national pastry whose home is the famous Pastéis de Belém bakery.

    Seafood features heavily on menus throughout the city, with other popular dishes including *caldeirada* (fish stew), shellfish, and octopus creations. **Bite-size snacks** like codfish pasty (*pastéis de bacalhau),* green bean fritters (*peixinhos da horta),* and codfish fritters (*pataniscas de bacalhau)* are also popular, available at most restaurants and snack bars to be washed down with a cold beer.

    Try a *ginjinha* **cherry liqueur** at its home, the historic A Ginjinha bar in the Baixa's São Domingos Square.

Portuguese Tapas

Located on the doorstep of Bairro Alto in the upscale Prince Real area, small and simple **Cantinho Lusitano** (Rua dos Prazeres 52, tel. 218 065 185, www.cantinholusitano.com, 7pm-11pm Tues-Sat, €7) is a family-run joint serving up a rainbow of Portuguese tapas. The restaurant also serves as a café and wine bar.

Brewery

One of Portugal's oldest and most beautiful breweries, bright and bold ★ **Cervejaria Trindade** (Rua Nova da Trindade 20C, tel. 213 423 506, www.cervejariatrindade.pt, noon-midnight Sun-Thurs, noon-1am Fri-Sat, €28) dates from the mid-1800s, when it was the choice for writers, poets, and politicians. Its huge medieval banquet rooms can accommodate groups of up to 200. National and international beers are accompanied by a different dish of the day, as well as typical Portuguese fish and meat dishes like steak in beer sauce.

Bistro

Owned by Bosnian celebrity chef Ljubomir Stanisic, refined and peaceful little **100 Maneiras** (Rua do Teixeira, tel. 910 918 181, www.100maneiras.com, 7:30pm-2am Mon-Sat, 7:30pm-midnight Sun, €60) serves a creative set nine-course tasting menu

based on fresh seasonal produce and typical Portuguese flavors, heavily inspired by the sea. Reservations are recommended.

Seafood

Modern, informal **Sea Me** (Rua do Loreto 21, tel. 213 461 564, www.peixariamoderna. com. 12:30pm-3:30pm and 7:30pm-midnight Mon-Thurs, 12:30pm-3pm and 7:30pm-1am Fri, 12:30pm-1am Sat, 12:30pm-midnight Sun, €28) pays homage to Lisbon's fishmongers with seafood purchased from the counter to be cooked in the kitchen, in a fusion of Japanese and Portuguese cuisines.

Moroccan

At welcoming and intimate **Flor de Laranja** (Rua da Rosa 206, tel. 213 422 996, 7pm-11pm daily, €14), authentic Moroccan food is handmade by the Morocco-born chef, who is also the owner and the waiter. Reservations are required.

Argentinean

Modern meets rustic and meat rules at ★ **La Paparrucha** (Rua Dom Pedro V 18/20, tel. 213 425 333, www.lapaparrucha.com, noon-11:30pm Mon-Fri, 12:30pm-11:30pm Sat-Sun, €25), a firm favorite among locals. Almost everything is cooked on an authentic Argentinean grill.

CAIS DO SODRÉ

This waterfront wharf has shed its former seedy image and is now a hip place to eat, drink, and be merry. It's also the location of hip Pink Street, which makes it a convenient spot to spend an evening.

Gastro Market

To try the best Portuguese cuisine, freshest local produce, and genuine regional delicacies, head to ★ **Time Out Market Lisboa** (Av. 24 de Julho 49, tel. 213 951 274, www.timeoutmarket.com, 10am-2am Thurs-Sat, 10am-midnight Sun-Wed, €10-20), which has hundreds of gastronomic goodies under one roof. This trendy food hall includes dozens of restaurants and bars run by vendors; live music adds to the ambience.

Tapas

Located on Cais do Sodré's famous Pink Street, swanky and minimalistic ★ **Espumantaria do Cais** (Rua Nova do Carvalho 39, tel. 213 470 466, 7pm-4am daily, €15) is a marble-clad quayside tapas and champagne bar. Pop open a bottle of bubbly, order a sharing platter like the popular cheeseboard or salmon tacos, and have a wonderful evening with some fizz.

Set in a lofty quayside warehouse, shabby-chic **Vestigius Wine & Gin Bar** (Cais do Sodré 8, tel. 218 203 320, www.vestigius.pt, noon-7pm Sun-Thurs, noon-1am Fri-Sat, €22) has huge windows and a terrace overlooking the water. A team of young chefs shape innovative flavors into bite-size tapas with Portuguese and Angolan influences. Dishes include calamari with aioli sauce, beef carpaccio, and beef osso buco.

Mexican

Hip and happening **Las Ficheras** (Rua dos Remolares 34, tel. 213 470 553, www.lasficheras.com, 11am-1am Sun-Thurs, 11am-2am Fri-Sat, €18) provides five-star Mexican food with great cocktails in a warm, welcoming setting.

ESTRELA

Estrela's culinary scene follows the same feel as the neighborhood: refined and upscale with a pinch of cool.

Market

Lisboetas love to meet at trendy **Mercado de Campo de Ourique** (Rua Coelho da Rocha 104, tel. 211 323 701, 10am-11pm Sun-Thurs, 10am-1am Fri-Sat, €10-20), a neighborhood gastro market with a buzzing food court that feels both traditional and contemporary. Explore the many different stalls and choose what takes your fancy.

Fine Dining

Each meal at ultra-swanky **Loco** (Rua Navegantes 53, tel. 213 951 861, www.loco.pt, 7pm-11pm Tues-Sat, €85) is a masterpiece. With two different tasting menus, this culinary experience is twice as nice.

International

Facing parliament, chic **XL** (Calçada da Estrela 57, tel. 213 956 118, 8pm-late Tues-Sun, €25) attracts a well-heeled crowd with a fusion of international haute cuisine and old-fashioned Portuguese home cooking. Specialties include soufflés, steaks, and "the best cheeseburger on the planet."

BELÉM
Bakery

No visit to Lisbon is complete without a taste of the humble, iconic *pastel de nata* custard tart. It can be found throughout Portugal, but Belém is its birthplace. ★ **Pastéis de Belém** (Rua Belém 84-92, tel. 213 637 423, www.pasteisdebelem.pt, 8am-midnight daily, €5) started making the delectable tarts in 1837, following a secret recipe from the Jerónimos Monastery. The buttery pastry contains a creamy eggy filling, slightly caramelized top, and a sprinkling of cinnamon. Other fresh-baked sweet and savory treats can be enjoyed in the large seating area, which is always packed full.

PARK OF NATIONS

The modern Park of Nations is home to eateries offering a kaleidoscope of cuisines, most located along the riverfront.

Seafood

As its name indicates, bright **Restaurante D'Bacalhau** (Rua da Pimenta 45, tel. 218 941 296 or 967 353 663, www. restaurantebacalhau.com, noon-4pm and 7pm-11pm daily, €20) specializes in codfish dishes from across the country, including a platter of four of the most traditional *bacalhau* concoctions; you can also enjoy a classic fish pasty.

French

Next to Lisbon Casino, on the main Park of Nations Avenue, classy, contemporary **Brasserie de L'Entrecote** (Alameda dos Oceanos 21101ª, tel. 218 962 220, www. brasserieentrecote.pt, noon-3:30pm and 7pm-midnight daily, €24) specializes in delicious ribs.

Gourmet Fast Food

Chic fast-food joint **Honorato Rio** (Alameda dos Oceanos, Lote 2, Unit F/G, tel. 932 561 524 or 218 967 207, www.honorato.pt, noon-midnight Sun-Thurs, noon-2am Fri-Sat, €10) boasts the best handmade gourmet burgers in Lisbon.

Nightlife and Entertainment

NIGHTLIFE

Bohemian and cosmopolitan in equal measures, Lisbon's nightlife has a different vibe in each different part of the city, from giddy Bairro Alto and atmospheric Alfama to the quirky Pink Street in Cais do Sodré and the trendy Park of Nations.

Baixa

In comparison to other parts of Lisbon, and with the exception of peak seasons like summer and Christmas, nightlife in the Baixa is rather tame. It's more about having a quiet drink at the end of the day than a big night out.

BARS

Home to Portugal's award-winning *ginjinha* cherry liqueur, **A Ginjinha** (Largo São Domingos 8, tel. 218 145 374, 9am-10pm daily) is a historic hole-in-the-wall serving tiny glasses of the sweet drink over its sticky slab of marble bar-top. *Ginjinha* is served as a shot, with a cherry in the glass if you ask. Soft drinks and beer are also available. This place is standing room only and crowded.

The swanky terrace of **Hotel Mundial Rooftop Bar & Lounge** (Praça Martim Moniz 2, tel. 218 842 000, www.hotel-mundial.pt, 6:30pm-12:30am daily) has stunning views. During the warmer months, it is a fashionable in-crowd hangout, popular for sunset parties. The views over Lisbon's downtown are worth a visit, but drinks are pricey, and the terrace can get crowded.

Alfama

Enjoy dinner and a show with spellbinding fado. Restaurants are intimate and offer traditional Portuguese dining. Many fado houses have a minimum fee that covers dinner and the show. It is customary for spectators to be silent while melodic fado is being sung, out of respect for the *fadista* (singer) and the accompanying musicians. With livelier songs, however, guests and even the staff join in. Reservations are strongly recommended.

TOP EXPERIENCE

FADO

Family-run **Sr. Fado de Alfama** (Rua dos Remédios 176, tel. 218 874 298, www.sr-fado. com, 7:30pm-midnight Wed-Sun, €25) belongs to *fadista* Ana Marina and is a cultural mainstay, with good traditional Portuguese food and a healthy dose of fado. Intimate, arabesque-styled **São Miguel d'Alfama** (Largo de São Miguel, tel. 968 554 422, www. saomigueldalfama.com, 7pm-midnight daily, €25) is famous for its fado and traditional Portuguese food.

Typical Portuguese food is served in a cozy and informal setting with great fado at **Restaurante Dragão de Alfama** (Rua de Guilherme Braga 8, tel. 218 867 737, 7pm-2am daily, €20), near the Santo Estêvão viewpoint. **Parreirinha de Alfama** (Bico Espírito Santo 1, tel. 218 868 209, www.parreirinhadealfama. com, 8pm-1am Tues-Sun, €25), a former charcoal warehouse, is a mecca for live fado and good food. Try the *arroz de tamboril* (monkfish rice), a house specialty.

In the heart of Alfama, behind an unremarkable exterior, famous **Clube de Fado** (Rua de São João Praça 86-94, tel. 218 852 704, www.clube-de-fado.com, 8pm-2am daily, €30) serves excellent Portuguese cuisine to the sound of the Portuguese guitar accompanying the *fadista*. It has a warm, romantic, and almost mystic atmosphere.

An authentic, classic fado dinner haunt, tiny tavern **A Baiuca** (Rua São Miguel 20, tel. 218 867 284, 7:30pm-11:30pm Thurs-Mon, €25 minimum pp includes dinner, drinks, and dessert) serves tasty home-cooked Portuguese fare on long tables where patrons sit snugly together. The convivial atmosphere is conducive to a great evening enjoying the magic of fado and new friends.

★ Bairro Alto

A quaint and traditional part of Lisbon that is sleepy during the day, bohemian Bairro Alto comes to life at night. The cobbled streets are packed with people and cool nightspots ranging from chic wine bars to historic fado houses and renowned jazz clubs.

BARS

One of Bairro Alto's best-known bars, **Majong** (Rua da Atalaia 3, tel. 915 214 803, 6pm-2am Mon-Fri, 6pm-3am Sat-Sun) is a favorite among the younger arty crowd, with a cool boho-chic interior where smoking is allowed. Classy cocktail bar **Double 9** (Rua da Misericórdia 78, tel. 212 481 480, afternoonlate daily), in a funky boutique hotel, is sophisticated yet laid-back.

Take a trip back in time at **Pavilhão Chinês** (Rua Dom Pedro V 89, tel. 213 424 729, 6pm-2am daily), a sumptuously upholstered tearoom with a web of nooks and crannies spread over five rooms. The walls and cabinets of this popular hangout, converted from a grocery store, are filled with a vast private collection of shiny treasures and relics: mugs, plates, books, and ancient maps. Besides more than 40 different types of tea, the Pavilhão Chinês (which translates as Chinese Pavilion) also serves wine, beers, cocktails, and liquors.

WINE BARS

The Old Pharmacy (Rua do Diário de Notícias 73, tel. 920 230 989, 5:30pm-midnight daily) is a quirky bar that offers a wide selection of wines by the glass or bottle. Wine bottles now fill the cabinets that were once stocked with medicines. Dim lighting and wine-barrel tables add to the allure. Iberian-rustic **Artis** (Rua do Diário de Notícias 95, tel. 213 424 795, 5:30pm-2am Sun and Tues-Thurs, 5:30pm-3am Fri-Sat) is the ideal place for long conversations over wine, cheese, and tapas.

Directly opposite the romantic São Pedro de Alcântara viewpoint and housed in an 18th-century palace, **Solar do Vinho do Porto** (Rua São Pedro de Alcântara 45, tel. 213 475 707, 11am-midnight Mon-Fri, 3pm-midnight Sat, glasses from €2) is run by the Port Wine Institute. It showcases more than 300 different types of port, many of which can be sampled by the glass, including rarer vintages that date as far back as 1937.

JAZZ CLUBS

Partake in some foot-tapping at **Páginas Tantas** (Rua do Diário de Notícias 85, tel. 966 249 005, 8:30am-2am Mon-Thurs, 8:30am-3am Fri-Sat, 8:30am-midnight Sun), a popular jazz bar with live music. The instrument-themed decor and portraits of jazz greats give the club a colorful, contemporary vibe. Rising and established musicians jam live nightly on a little stage in the corner.

TOP EXPERIENCE

FADO

Founded in 1947, **O Faia** (Rua da Barroca 54-56, tel. 213 426 742, www.ofaia.com, 8pm-2am Mon-Sat, minimum €50) is a famed fado house with a cult following; it hosts nightly shows and has a restaurant that serves traditional Portuguese cuisine with a contemporary twist.

Unlike other fado venues, **Tasca do Chico** (Rua do Diario de Noticias 39, tel. 965 059 670 or 961 339 696, 7pm-3am daily) is more of a fado bar than a restaurant. Dim lighting in this tiny tavern enhances the atmospheric experience. Drinks and typical Portuguese tapas, such as plates of cured meats, are served. There is no minimum consumption fee, but it's cash only.

Cais do Sodré

Created through a clever urban renewal project, the Pink Street project has taken a part of town that once was a red-light district and turned it into one of the hippest hangouts in Lisbon, with varying ambience along a short, colorful stretch.

BARS AND PUBS

The traditional Irish pub **Hennessy's** (Cais do Sodré 32-38, tel. 213 462 467, 11am-2am Sun-Thurs, 11am-4am Fri-Sat) offers live music and sports coverage in a warm and welcoming atmosphere. **Quero-te no Cais** (Rua dos Remolares 41, tel. 213 425 309, 8am-4am Mon-Fri, 10pm-4am Sat) is small and friendly, with a big alfresco drinking area to enjoy.

A former inn that once rented rooms to sailors and ladies of the night, **Pensão Amor** (Rua do Alecrim 19, tel. 213 143 399, www.pensaoamor.pt, 2pm-3am Sun-Wed, 2pm-4am Thurs-Sat) is now a lively and bohemian

hangout. **Jamaica** (Rua Nova do Carvalho 6, tel. 213 421 859, www.jamaica.com.pt, midnight-6am Tues-Sat, women free, men minimum about €8), one of Lisbon's best-known bars, is the place to go to drink and dance. It's not huge, so the dance floor can get crowded, but the DJs play a mix of '70s, '80s, rock, and current hits.

Park of Nations

Enjoy dinner and a drink in style in this funky new part of town.

BARS AND PUBS

For authentic Irish warmth and good *craic*, head to the traditional pub **Irish & Co.** (Rua Pimenta 57, tel. 218 940 558, www.grupodocadesanto.com.pt, noon-2am daily), where you'll find a friendly ambience with live music. With its vast open front on the riverside and a pub menu, it's a great place to spend a convivial few hours.

Relaxed, informal café-bar **Me & You** (Av. Dom João II, Lote 1.17.03, tel. 218 947 020, 8am-2am Mon-Sat, happy hour 6pm-8pm) is a quiet place for a light snack or to catch up on conversation over coffee. **Shisha Tea Food** (Alameda dos Oceanos 44301M, tel. 215 940 508, www.shishateafood.pt, noon-2am daily) is a funky Middle Eastern-inspired hookah bar and lounge with a warm Moroccan vibe and exotic *shisha* (water pipes) and great drinks, including teas and cocktails, and an alfresco esplanade.

CLUBS

Co-owned by actor John Malkovich, **Lux Discotheque** (Av. Infante Don Henrique, Warehouse A, tel. 218 820 890, www.luxfragil.com, 11pm-6am Thurs-Sat, cover €10-20) is one of Lisbon's most exuberant nightspots, renowned throughout Europe as the place to go to see and be seen. On two different levels, it regularly puts on live acts and DJs. Upstairs the music is mainstream, while the groove on the bottom floor is left to the resident or guest DJ. Outside is a huge terrace where you can watch the sun come up over the Tagus River.

ENTERTAINMENT

Opera

The handsome facade of the historic **São Carlos National Theater (Teatro Nacional de São Carlos)** (Rua Serpa Pinto 9, tel. 213 253 000, www.tnsc.pt), built in 1793, pales in comparison to its lavishly opulent interior. In the heart of Lisbon in the cultured Chiado district, this neoclassical National Monument hosts shows and events geared toward musical performances, such as operas and choral symphonies.

Concert and Dance Venues

Inaugurated in 1890, the famed **Coliseu dos Recreios** (Rua Portas de Santo Antão 96, tel. 213 240 580, www.coliseulisboa.com) regularly welcomes international productions, traditionally from the realm of ballet, theater, and opera, as well as pop stars, circus troupes, and comedians. Architecturally, the Coliseu was ahead of its time with cutting-edge ironwork, seen in its spectacular German-made iron dome and iron roof.

One of Lisbon's newer cultural venues, the **Calouste Gulbenkian Foundation (Fundação Calouste Gulbenkian)** (Av. de Berna 45A, tel. 217 823 461, www.gulbenkian.pt) has offerings beyond the world of art and exhibitions, with jazz, choral, and orchestral concerts, sometimes held in the lovely gardens.

Huge **Altice Arena** (Rossio dos Olivais, tel. 218 918 409, http://arena.altice.pt), formerly known as the Meo Arena, is a futuristic-looking multipurpose venue on the Park of Nations riverside, hosting the biggest concerts and events, including in recent years U2, Beyoncé, Ariana Grande, Justin Bieber, Cirque du Soleil, and the 2018 Eurovision Song Contest.

Theater

Prestigious **Dona Maria II National Theater (Teatro Nacional Dona Maria II)** (Praça Dom Pedro IV, tel. 213 250 800, www.tndm.pt) is a national jewel and cultural heavyweight on noble Rossio Square. Built between 1842 and 1846 in neoclassical style, it celebrates the performing arts with a full agenda of plays, shows, and concerts.

Soccer (Football)

The 64,642-seat **Luz Stadium (Estádio da Luz)** (Av. Eusébio da Silva Ferreira, tel. 217 219 500, www.slbenfica.pt, Metro Colégio-Militar/Luz or Alto-dos-Moinhos, Blue Line), the Stadium of Light, is the home of soccer team Benfica, one of the country's Big Three (along with cross-city rivals Sporting and northern team Porto). Architecturally impressive, its wavy roof of steel arches is designed to feel light and transparent. At the stadium there is a store, a museum, and 20-minute guided tours (10am-6pm daily, €12.50, with museum €17.50). Game tickets start around €30.

A short distance from Luz Stadium is **José Alvalade Stadium (Estádio José Alvalade)** (Rua Professor Fernando da Fonseca, tel. 217 516 164, www.sporting.pt, Metro Campo Grande), or Lions' Stadium, home to the soccer team Sporting, "the lions." Predominantly green to echo its home team's colors, the stadium was designed by architect Tomás Taveira in a mall complex with a 12-screen movie theater, a health club, and a soccer museum. There are four guided tours daily of the stadium and museum (from €14). Game tickets start at €30.

FESTIVALS AND EVENTS

Lisbon loves to party, and these annual events draw crowds. The annual Santo António festival is without doubt Lisbon's main event, the biggest traditional religious celebration in the country. Lisbon hosts an array of summer music festivals and fairs, and concerts by international artists throughout the year, mostly at Altice Arena in the Park of Nations.

Carnival

(Carnaval)

Portugal goes into party mode for Carnival, and Lisbon has a succession of colorful floats and costumed dancers shimmying through the city's main avenues in a cloud of colorful confetti and streamers to the energetic rhythms of hot South American and popular Portuguese folk music, regardless of the weather. Carnival typically falls around mid-February or early March and lasts a number of days, during which concerts, masquerade balls, and street events are also held.

Lisbon Fish and Flavors
(Peixe em Lisboa)

Discover the amazing flavors of the sea with gastronomic **Lisbon Fish and Flavors** (www.peixemlisboa.com, early Apr, €6-15), showcasing the best fish and seafood by innovative and well-known chefs and restaurants. Held in the Carlos Lopes Pavilion (Av. Sidónio Pais 16, tel. 916 442 541), the event takes place over 10 days and involves food and market stalls, cooking demonstrations, and debates.

Santo António and June Festivities

Dedicated to Saint Anthony, the city's patron, Santo António is Portugal's biggest traditional religious festival. Celebrations are staged throughout the capital for the whole month of June, reaching their peak on June 12, with jubilant parades and processions into the night. On June 13, the time-honored Casamentos de Santo António (Santo António weddings) are held. Established in 1958, these are a mass wedding of a dozen of the city's most impoverished couples, selected from hundreds of applicants. The entire ceremony, from the bridal outfits to the honeymoon, is funded by city hall and other sponsors. Over these two days, the city

parties to pay homage to "matchmaker" Saint Anthony, from the afternoon through the early morning.

During Santo António, Lisbon is at its prettiest. Every garden and square is decked out with colorful trimmings and lights. Food and drink stalls, tables, and chairs are set up with small stages for local artists to perform traditional folk songs. Grilled sardines, sangria, and traditional *caldo verde* (potato and kale) soup are served from stalls to fuel the merriment. The neighborhoods of Alfama, Graça, and Bica are the most popular for Santo António. Each neighborhood also designs a float and takes part in a grand procession along the city's main avenues in the pinnacle of the celebrations to decide which neighborhood wins. Santo António shouldn't be missed if you're in Portugal in June.

Underground Roman Galleries
(Galerias Romanas)

You'd probably walk past this house without giving it a second glance—except for once or twice a year when, for a limited time, queues form as the city opens the passageway to a mesmerizing underground world. The passageway is on the ground, a sort of utility hole, right in front of Rua da Conceição 77. Unearthed following the 1755 earthquake as the city was being rebuilt, this subterranean warren of corridors built by the Romans is remarkable. The galleries are usually flooded but are drained once a year by the local fire brigade, usually in April or September, to allow the free 20-minute guided tours. Slots on the tours are limited; sign up at least one month in advance (http://galeriasromanas. cm-lisboa.pt or www.museudelisboa.pt).

Shopping

Lisbon has a sophisticated shopping scene, from upscale stores along stylish Avenida da Liberdade to boutiques and craft shops in the Baixa. It also has shopping centers galore and plenty of open-air markets.

AVENIDA DA LIBERDADE AND BAIXA POMBALINA

The glamorous, leafy, 10-lane Avenida da Liberdade and its myriad designer stores stretch over a kilometer (0.6 mi) between Marquis de Pombal Square and Restauradores Square, leading toward Rossio Square and downtown Baixa Pombalina and the riverside. The Baixa is the heart of commerce in Lisbon, between Rossio Square and the riverside in plazas and smaller boulevards, where mainstream chain stores adjoin traditional grocery stores, boutiques, and souvenir shops. The two main shopping streets in the Baixa are **Rua da Prata** and **Rua Augusta,** parallel to each other from the main Comércio Square up to Rossio.

★ Avenida da Liberdade

Lisbon's most famous avenue, and priciest real estate, Avenida da Liberdade has serious shopping. At 90 meters (295 feet) wide and more than 1 kilometer (0.6 mi) long, this fancy street—the busiest in Portugal—has fashion's biggest players, including **Louis Vuitton Lisbonne** (Av. da Liberdade 190, tel. 213 584 320, www.eu.louisvuitton.com, 10am-7:30pm Mon-Thurs, 10am-8pm Fri-Sat), **Prada** (Av. da Liberdade 206, tel. 213 199 490, 10am-7:30pm Mon-Sat) and **Gucci** (Av. da Liberdade 180, tel. 213 528 401, www.gucci.com, 10am-7:30pm Mon-Sat).

With exquisite patterned cobblestone walkways and magnificent period architecture lining the stately boulevard, enhanced by cool, leafy gardens, it's often compared to Paris's Champs Elysées. Most buildings along the avenue date from the 19th century, built after the devastating 1755 earthquake that razed most of Lisbon.

SPECIALTY BOUTIQUES

Just off the Avenida da Liberdade at Rua Alexandre Herculano is the stylish **DeliDelux** (Rua Alexandre Herculano 15A, tel. 213 141 474, www.delidelux.pt, 8am-11pm Mon-Fri, 9am-11pm Sat-Sun), stocked with beautifully packaged gourmet products like wine, olive oil, and canned fish, which make great gifts.

Women's shoe designer **Luís Onofre** (Av. da Liberdade 247, tel. 211 313 629, www.luisonofre.com) built his brand on generations of family shoemaking history; the shoes are manufactured at a state-of-the art workshop in northern Portugal. **David Rosas** (Av. da Liberdade 69A, tel. 213 243 870, www.davidrosas.com, 10am-7pm Mon-Sat) is a family company that blends generations of craftsmanship in its fine jewelry. The design of this gorgeous store was overseen by acclaimed Portuguese architect Siza Vieira.

BAIXA-CHIADO

A trove of authentic Portuguese arts and crafts, **Atelier 55** (Rua António Maria Cardoso, 70-74, tel. 213 474 192, www.atelier55.blogspot.com) brims with handmade ceramics, embroidery, and paintings from local artists.

ALFAMA
Azulejos

Loja dos Descobrimentos (Rua dos Bacalhoeiros 14B, tel. 218 865 563, www.lojadescobrimentos.com, 9am-7pm daily) is a shop and workshop selling brightly colored hand-painted tiles and ceramics in styles from all over Portugal. Meet the artisans in the atelier and watch as they work on tiles, or paint your own.

Another top place for authentic hand-painted tiles and ceramics with a bright

Best Souvenirs: Cork and Azulejos

Two of Portugal's most distinctive products are cork goods and beautiful azulejo tiles and ceramics. Once used only to create bottle stoppers for prestigious champagnes, today Portuguese cork has become fashionable for shoes, handbags, jewelry, and even clothing. Bairro Alto is the place to go cork-hunting, and downtown Baixa-Chiado brims with local arts and crafts.

Azulejo hand-painted tile plaques adorn walls throughout the city. Many smaller-size replicas of plaques and tiles are now produced as souvenirs. Alfama is the place to head for azulejos, with shops offering miniature versions of these ceramic squares.

modern twist, **Azulejos de Fachada** (Beco do Mexias 1, tel. 966 176 953, www.azulejosdefachada.com, 10:30am-12:30pm and 2pm-5:30pm Mon-Fri) will also take customized orders and ship overseas.

SÃO VICENTE
Shopping Centers and Markets
Dating to the 12th century, the São Vicente **Feira da Ladra Flea Market** (9am-6pm Tues and Sat), which literally translates as Thieves' Fair, is a chance to experience the sights and sounds of old-time Lisbon. An eclectic mix of antiques and secondhand family heirlooms, vendors tout everything from jewels to junk. The vast market starts by the São Vicente Archway, near a stop for tram 28, and fills the streets around the Campo de Santa Clara square. While some of the traders have properly laid-out stalls, others simply pile their wares onto blankets on the ground.

BAIRRO ALTO
Cork
Everything at **Cork & Co** (Rua das Salgadeiras 10, tel. 216 090 231, www.corkandcompany.pt, 11am-8pm Mon-Sat, 5pm-8pm Sun), from hats to shoes and all accessories, is made from natural cork. **Rutz Walk in Cork** (Rua dos Sapateiros 181, tel. 212 477 039, www.rutz.pt, noon-8pm daily) is a Portuguese brand specializing in shoes, bags, accessories, and gifts made from cork.

ESTRELA AND LAPA
Shopping Centers and Markets
On a former industrial site, the **LX Factory** (Rua Rodrigues de Faria 103, tel. 213 143 399, 6am-2am daily), converted from a big old brick warehouse, is now a hub of cultural creativity and home to an array of arty retailers, trendy start-ups, and quirky restaurants. Every Sunday the locale hosts a "hippie-chic" market, as well as other forms of entertainment and events throughout the year. Inside the factory, visitors will find a slew of shops and ateliers touting a mixed range of traditional Portuguese and contemporary wares alongside buzzing offices and work centers.

Recreation

TAGUS RIVER BOAT TOURS

A nice view of Lisbon is on approach from the opposite side of the Tagus River, and, given the nation's seafaring history, a boat trip offers a uniquely appropriate vantage point to see the city.

Lisbon by Boat (tel. 933 914 740, www.lisbonbyboat.com) offers a variety of tours, from guided sightseeing trips to romantic sunset cruises, but all promise unforgettable views of the Portuguese capital. By motorboat or by yacht, trips range one to six hours, starting from around €35 pp for an hour-long historic Lisbon sightseeing cruise.

An alternative way to explore Lisbon is on the hop-on hop-off **Yellow Boat Tour** (www.yellowbustours.com, from €18). Purchase a 24-hour ticket that allows access at points of interest on both sides of the Tagus. A nonstop circuit takes 1.5 hours, with a running commentary on sights in a number of languages, including English.

SEGWAY TOURS

Lisbon Segway Tours (www.lisbon segwaytours.pt, from €35) are a fun way to zip around the city and really get into its nooks and crannies. Tours visit different areas, including a riverside tour, a tour of Alfama, a city center tour, and a Belém tour. More unusual itineraries are a Lisbon by Night tour, a gastronomic tour to discover the city's foodie delights, and a three-hour super tour that covers most of the city's main spots.

WALKING TOURS

Personalized walking tours by locals have become popular in Lisbon, allowing you to explore the city at a leisurely pace. Guided tours are available in English, and many are free. From private tours to foodie tours, pub crawls, and even sunset tours, follow a local guide who knows the city and its secrets as only a native could. Tours take place rain or shine, and their duration can range from just over 1.5 hours to the full day. On free tours, payment is in the form of tips—a suggested tip is €5-12 pp. Specialist walking-tour companies include **Discover Walks Lisbon** (www.discoverwalks.com) and **Discover Lisbon** (tel. 932 060 800, www.discoverlisbon.org).

CYCLING

Lisbon City Hall has created an extensive shared-bicycle network and a web of cycle paths. The shared-bicycle scheme **Gira** (tel. 211 163 060, www.gira-bicicletasdelisboa.pt) comprises around 50 stations around the city, with 500 electric and standard bicycles. Download the app, buy a day pass for €2, and pedal away. Lisbon has over 60 kilometers (37 mi) of bicycle lanes to explore.

Tour companies such as **Lisbon Bike Tour and Outdoors** (Rua Presidente Arriaga 112, tel. 912 272 300, www.lisbonbiketour.com) have designed exciting tours—all downhill—that cover key historic areas. **Rent-a-Fun** (www.rent-a-fun.com) includes some uphill climbs on its tours, but its bicycles are electric. Standard bike tours take three hours and cost €32 adults, €15 children. Rent-a-Fun also rents out electric, regular, and folding bicycles (9am-9pm daily, €25), including delivery, a helmet, and a lock.

Accommodations

Lisbon is awash with cool and interesting places to stay, from historic town houses to converted palaces. The Baixa area is central and convenient. Lodging is generally pricey, but there are quality budget hostels and guesthouses.

BAIXA

The **CR7 Pestana Lisboa** (Rua do Comércio 54, tel. 210 401 710, www.pestanacr7.com, €165 d) was set up with Portuguese soccer superstar Cristiano Ronaldo. It has sporty decor and a great location in the heart of downtown. Set back from leafy Avenida da Liberdade, the stately **Boutique Hotel Heritage Avenida da Liberdade** (Av. da Liberdade 28, tel. 213 404 040, www.heritageavliberdade.com, €182) is in an elegant 18th-century town house, a pleasant stroll from the Baixa area.

Despite its plain exterior, four-star ★ **Hotel Mundial** (Praça Martim Moniz 2, tel. 218 842 000, www.hotel-mundial.pt, €130) is an institution because its rooftop has a great view. Decor is tasteful, beds are comfortable, and the location is second to none. A short walk from Comércio Square, elegant four-star **Hotel Vincci Baixa** (Rua do Comércio 32-38, tel. 218 803 190, www.vinccibaixa.com, €180) embodies class and comfort in a prime location.

★ **Yes! Lisbon Hostel** (Rua de São Julião 148, tel. 213 427 171, www.yeshostels.com, €32 dorm, €140 d with shared bath) has it all: an excellent location, good service, and budget-friendly prices. Custom-made bunks ensure a good night's sleep, and reception is happy to provide tips on how to get the most out of your stay.

CASTELO

Small, romantic ★ **Solar do Castelo** (Rua das Cozinhas 2, tel. 218 806 050, www. solardocastelo.com, from €182) is the only hotel within the walls of the São Jorge Castle. Converted from an 18th-century mansion, this eco-retreat with medieval and contemporary style even has specially commissioned furniture to enhance its uniqueness.

ALFAMA

Cool and contemporary ★ **Memmo Alfama Design Hotel** (Travessa Merceeiras 27, tel. 210 495 660, www.memmoalfama. com, €193) is a 44-room urban retreat fast earning a reputation for its chic, clean design, which blends well with the historic Alfama neighborhood.

A former 15th-century palace has been reborn as cosmopolitan **Santiago de Alfama Boutique Hotel** (Rua de Santiago 10 a 14, tel. 213 941 616, www.santiagodealfama.com, €415), which oozes authenticity from its tiled floors to its prime location in Alfama.

BAIRRO ALTO

Wedged between bohemian Bairro Alto and trendy Chiado, the five-star ★ **Bairro Alto Hotel** (Praça Luis de Camões 2, tel. 213 408 288, www.bairroaltohotel.com, from €150) enjoys a dominant position on the main square and has handsome 18th-century architecture. Within walking distance of shops, restaurants, and bars, the 55 rooms are twins, doubles, and suites.

Trendy little **9 Hotel Mercy** (Rua da Misericórdia 78, tel. 212 481 480, www.9-hotel-mercy-lisbon.pt, €191) offers contemporary class, a bohemian vibe, and panoramic views from its stylish rooftop bar. Modern and clean **Bairro Alto Hostel** (Travessa da Cara 6, tel. 213 421 079, www. bairroaltohostel.com, from €60 d with shared bath) is in a historic 19th-century building. Private rooms and shared dorms are all equipped with free Wi-Fi; there's a communal lounge and kitchen facilities.

CAIS DO SODRÉ

Overlooking the Tagus River, the decadently decorated **LX Boutique Hotel** (Rua do Alecrim 12, tel. 213 474 394, www. lxboutiquehotel.com, from €165) is an atmospheric 19th-century hotel conveniently at the nexus of Chiado, Baixa, and Cais do Sodré.

Clean and comfortable self-catering ★ **Hello Lisbon Cais do Sodré Apartments** (Rua Nova do Carvalho 43, tel. 937 770 007, www.hello-lisbon.com, €159) reflect the youth and energy of their location on frenetic Pink Street. Edgy paintings provide a pop of color to the period architecture and smart interiors.

ESTRELA

A night at the plush 18th-century **As Janelas Verdes Lisbon Hotel** (Rua das Janelas Verdes 47, tel. 213 968 143, www. asjanelasverdes.com, €160) feels like staying in someone's home, with stunning views from the rooftop terrace. Occupying an old school building, the 19th-century Paraty Palace, the small **Hotel da Estrela** (Rua Saraiva de Carvalho 35, tel. 211 900 100, www.hoteldaestrela.com, €110) blends contemporary with quirky.

BELÉM

Along the river, the contemporary **Altis Belém Hotel & Spa** (Doca do Bom Sucesso, tel. 210 400 200, www.altishotels. com, €264) has a modern design inspired by the Age of Discoveries, with nautical themes in all of its 50 rooms, which include five suites. Feel like royalty with a stay at five-star **Pestana Palace Hotel** (Rua Jau 54, tel. 213 615 600, www.pestana.com, €254), in an exquisite 19th-century palace with gorgeous gardens.

Poised and polished five-star ★ **Hotel Palácio do Governador** (Rua Bartolomeu Dias 117, tel. 212 467 800, www. palaciogovernador.com, €200) occupies the 16th-century Governor's Palace, carefully conserving its original features. With 60 rooms and two pools, it is a whitewashed and manicured oasis of tranquility in one of Lisbon's prettiest neighborhoods.

PARK OF NATIONS

The stylish and streamlined four-star ★ **VIP Executive Arts** (Av. Dom João II 47, tel. 210 020 400, www.viphotels.com, €105) is within walking distance of the Oriente transport hub, the Vasco da Gama shopping center, the Altice Arena, and riverside nightlife.

Information and Services

VISITOR INFORMATION

"Ask Me" tourist information desks can be found throughout Lisbon, at the airport and major bus and train stations and monuments. Most are open about 9am-6pm daily. Also available are the main **Lisbon Tourism Visitors and Convention Bureau** (Rua do Arsenal 21, tel. 210 312 700, www.visitlisboa. com, 9:30am-7pm Mon-Fri) or the national tourist board, **Turismo de Portugal** (Rua Ivone Silva, Lote 6, tel. 211 140 200, www. visitportugal.com, www.turismodeportugal. pt, 9am-1pm and 2:30pm-5:30pm Mon-Fri).

EMBASSIES

United States: Av. das Forças Armadas 133C, tel. 217 273 300, https://pt.usembassy. gov/pt, 8am-5pm Mon-Fri
Canada: Av. da Liberdade 196, tel. 213 164 600, www.canadainternational.gc.ca, 9am-noon Mon-Fri
United Kingdom: Rua de São Bernardo 33, tel. 213 924 000, www.gov.uk, 9:30am-2pm Mon, Wed, and Fri
Australia: Av. da Liberdade 200, tel. 213 101 500, www.portugal.embassy.gov.au, 10am-4pm Mon-Fri

MONEY

In Lisbon, most hotels, bureaux de change, banks, travel agencies, and even some shops have currency exchange facilities, or use your debit card to make a withdrawal from an ATM *(multibanco)*, which can be found throughout the city. The currency exchange company **Unicâmbio** (www.unicambio.pt) has more than 80 offices around the country, including the airports at Lisbon, Faro, and Madeira, the Rossio train station in central Lisbon, the Cais do Sodré station in Baixa, and El Corte Inglês shopping mall (Av. António Augusto de Aguiar 31).

HEALTH AND EMERGENCIES

European free emergency number: 112

GNR Police Lisbon headquarters: Largo do Carmo 27, tel. 213 217 000, www.gnr.pt
PSP Metropolitan Police Lisbon headquarters: Av. Moscavide 88, tel. 217 654 242, www.psp.pt
PSP Tourist Police Lisbon: Praça dos Restauradores, Palácio Foz, tel. 213 421 623
INEM medical emergency: Rua Almirante Barroso 36, tel. 213 508 100, www.inem.pt
Lisbon Fire Brigade: Av. Dom Carlos I, tel. 218 171 470, www.cm-lisboa.pt
CUF Private Hospital: Travessa do Castro 3, tel. 213 926 100, www.saudecuf.pt
24-Hour pharmacy: Farmácia Largo do Rato, Av. Alvares Cabral 1, tel. 213 863 044, www.farmaciasdeservico.net

Transportation

GETTING THERE

Portugal's capital can be reached by land or air from anywhere in Europe. There are direct flights between Lisbon and South America, the United States, Canada, Africa, and Asia. Many low-cost carriers now serve the city, making intra-European travel easy and affordable. Lisbon can also be reached by road or rail from neighboring Spain.

Air

Portugal's national airline, **TAP-Air Portugal** (www.flytap.com), has expanded its operations to the United States and operates several direct daily flights between Portugal and U.S. cities. A number of U.S. airlines also fly to Lisbon. Lisbon's **Humberto Delgado Airport** (LIS, Alameda das Comunidades Portuguesas, tel. 218 413 500, www.ana.pt) is Portugal's biggest and busiest international airport. European flights tend to be under four hours and inexpensive. There are also daily domestic flights linking Lisbon to Porto, the Algarve, and the islands of Madeira and the Azores.

GETTING TO AND FROM THE AIRPORT

Lisbon's airport is 7 kilometers (4.3 mi) north of the city center. The **Metro** runs direct from the airport to Lisbon; the Red Line runs from just outside the airport's main entrance and connects with the Green Line at Alameda station, which runs to the Baixa and Cais do Sodré riverfront, and ends on the Blue Line, at the São Sebastião station. A journey to downtown Lisbon (€1.25) requires one change and takes 20 minutes. The **Aerobus** (www.aerobus.pt) shuttle bus runs regularly to the city center and to the financial district from outside the arrivals terminal (7:30am-11pm daily, €3.15 one-way). Municipal bus company **Carris** (www.carris.pt, €1.85 one-way) runs five bus routes between Lisbon Airport and the city center. **Taxis** can be found outside the arrivals terminal; a trip to Lisbon city center should cost up to €15. Alternatively, call an **Uber** (www.uber.com) ride-share.

The cheapest and easiest way to get around Lisbon is to buy a **7 Colinas/Viva Viagem card,** available at the airport from the newsagent on the second floor, or from main bus or Metro stations. The cards are prepaid and can be recharged. The card itself costs €0.50, and they are accepted on all local buses and Metro subways, trams, funiculars, and ferryboats. Most single trips on any mode cost €2-3. A one-day travel option has a flat rate of €6.

Bus

Eurolines (www.eurolines.com) operates regular international bus service between Lisbon and cities such as London, Madrid, and Paris. National intercity bus company **Rede Expressos** (tel. 707 223 344, www.rede-expressos.pt) operates express bus trips to Lisbon from most of the country's regions, including the Algarve and Porto, each around three hours' journey. Algarve bus company **Eva** (tel. 289 899 760, www.eva-bus.com) also runs daily routes between main bus stations in the Algarve and Lisbon.

The two main bus terminals in Lisbon are **Sete Rios** (Rua Professor Lima Basto 133, opposite Lisbon Zoo, tel. 707 223 344, ticket office 7am-11:30pm daily, Metro Jardim Zoológico, Blue Line), a Rede Expressos' hub, and the modern **Gare do Oriente** (Av. Dom João II, Park of Nations, tel. 218 956 972, Metro Oriente, Red Line), closest to the airport.

Train

Trains run to Lisbon from most major towns across the country, and train travel can be a cheap and scenic option. The two types of trains for long-distance travel are the slower Intercidades (intercity) and the Alfa-Pendular (high-speed) train. The Alfa-Pendular links Lisbon to the Algarve or Porto in around three hours, with a few stops in between. All trains in Portugal have a first-class option and are operated by **Comboios de Portugal** (CP, tel. 707 210 220, www.cp.pt).

The four main railway stations in Lisbon are Entrecampos (Rua Dr. Eduardo Neves), Oriente (Av. Dom João II), Sete Rios (Rua Professor Lima Bastos), and Santa Apolónia

(Av. Infante Dom Henrique). The Alfa-Pendular runs from Oriente, Santa Apolónia, and Entrecampos.

Car

Two main motorways connect Lisbon to the country's extremities: the A1 to the north (Porto) and the A2 to the south (Algarve). The A6 is the main motorway from the east. From outside Portugal, you'll cross the entire country from any border point to get to Lisbon. The scenery makes up for any potholes or wrong turns you might endure.

There are two crossings to Lisbon from the south over the Tagus River: the **25 Abril Bridge,** to the western end of the city, or the newer **Vasco da Gama Bridge**—the longest in Europe—to the Park of Nations area. Both provide stunning views of the city on approach.

GETTING AROUND

Getting around Lisbon can be cheap and easy on public transport, or expensive if you opt for novelty transport like the city's mushrooming *tuk-tuks*.

Lisboa Card

The **Lisboa Card** (www.lisboacard.org), Lisbon's official tourist pass, includes unlimited travel on public buses, trams, the Metro, elevators, and funiculars as well as travel on CP train lines to Sintra and Cascais; free access to 26 museums, monuments, and UNESCO World Heritage Sites; and deals and discounts on tours, shopping, and nightlife. The cost is €19 for a 24-hour card, €32 for a 48-hour card, and €40 for a 72-hour card. Children's cards are half price. These cards can be purchased online, for which a voucher is given that can be exchanged at main tourist points such as the Lisboa Welcome Center, Foz Palace, and Lisbon Airport.

Public Transit

Single trips on buses, trams, ferryboats, and the Metro generally cost under €1.50, and the rechargeable **7 Colinas/Viva Viagem card** can be bought at most newsagents and kiosks, stations, and terminals for €0.50. A **24-hour public transport pass** can be loaded onto the card; it costs €6 and covers all forms of local public transport (buses, trams, and the metro). Add ferryboat trips to the 24-hour pass and it costs €9, or €10 to also include trains to nearby Sintra and Cascais. Some public transport timetables can vary depending on the season, with hours extended later in summer.

BUS

The capital has an efficient bus service, **Carris** (www.carris.pt), which also manages the city's tram system. It provides good coverage of the city, as well as service to neighboring towns and suburbs, and is inexpensive, with most trips under €2. Most buses run 6am-9pm daily, with the busiest lines running until midnight.

TRAM

Carris (www.carris.pt) operates a network of historic trams and funiculars, a unique way to get into the city's backstreets. Five tram routes carry 60 trams, most of which are vintage vehicles. The star of the show is the famous **tram 28,** which circumnavigates Lisbon's historic neighborhoods Bairro Alto, Graça, Mouraria, Alfama, Baixa, Chiado, and Madragoa. A downside is that it is plagued by petty thieves, so stay alert. Trams and funiculars generally operate 6am-11pm daily.

METRO

Inaugurated in 1959, Lisbon's **Metro** (www.metrolisboa.pt) has consistently grown, including a stop beneath the airport, making travel fast and easy. The Metro has four main lines—Green, Yellow, Red, and Blue—and is simple to navigate, covering the city's important points. Trains run regularly and reliably. A 24-hour pass that also covers funiculars, trams, and buses costs €6. The Metro runs 6:30am-1am daily.

FERRY

Commuter ferries chug continuously across the Tagus River between Lisbon and Setúbal, operated by **Transtejo & Soflusa** (tel. 808 203 050, www.transtejo.pt) generally 5am or 6am to 1am daily, although crossings are more frequent on weekdays. Boats get busy during rush hours (before 9am and after 4:30pm weekdays) and depart from three terminals along Lisbon's riverside: Terreiro do Paço, Cais do Sodré, and Belém. The five stops on the Setúbal side are Montijo, Barreiro, Seixal, Cacilhas, and Porto Brandão-Trafaria. The Cais do Sodré-Cacilhas crossing is the busiest.

Commuter ferries are much cheaper than tourist boats, with single trips under €3. A charged 7 Colinas/Viva Viagem public transport card can be used to pay for tickets. Crossings provide awesome views of Lisbon's iconic 25 Abril Bridge and of the city.

Taxi and Ride-Share

Taxis in Portugal are plentiful and easy to spot: beige or black with a minty green roof. Each is identified with a number, usually under the driver's side mirror. There are lots of taxi stands throughout the city at train and bus stations, central plazas, and near shopping malls. Hotel reception desks will call a taxi for you, or simply hail one on the street. The main taxi firms in Lisbon are **Taxis Lisboa** (tel. 218 119 000, www.taxislisboa.com), **Cooptaxis** (tel. 217 932 756, www.cooptaxis.pt), and **Teletaxis** (tel. 218 111 100, www.teletaxis.pt).

Uber cars are also now popular and widely available in Lisbon, giving taxi drivers a run for their money.

Tuk-Tuk

A novel way of exploring Lisbon is to jump on a *tuk-tuk*. These nifty little vehicles have taken the city by storm in recent years; it's rare to turn a street corner without hearing or seeing one of the colorful three-wheelers buzzing along. They have the advantage of fitting on streets and lanes where cars can't go, and they're cute and comfortable, but they are more expensive than public transport or taxis. *Tuk-tuk* operators include **Tuk Tuk Lisboa** (www.tuk-tuk-lisboa.pt), **City Tuk** (www.citytuk.pt), **Eco Tuk Tours** (www.ecotuktours.com), and **Tuga Tours Tuk Tuk** (www.tugatours.pt). Expect to pay €55-70 pp for an hour's tour of the sights.

Car

Getting around Lisbon without a car is easy and convenient thanks to the comprehensive public transport network. A car is only necessary to visit outlying areas. Book one online and pick it up at the airport, or ask your hotel to help. Most reception desks have contacts with reputable car rental companies. In and around Lisbon Airport, the many vendors include **Europcar** (tel. 218 401 176, www.europcar.com), **Hertz** (tel. 219 426 300, www.hertz.com), and **Budget** (tel. 808 252 627, www.budget.com.pt).

Be aware that extra fees may apply to drop the car at a different point or to take it out of Portugal, and always double-check about tolls, insurance, extra fees, and hidden costs such as the collision damage waiver (CDW), better known as insurance excess. The possibility of a scratch or a bump in Lisbon is high. Investing in a GPS unit is also worth considering.

Driving in Lisbon can be fast, furious, and overwhelming. Main arteries such as the Segunda Circular ring road, which bypasses the airport, can become gridlocked during rush hour; signage is hit-and-miss (although it's slowly improving), and there are one-way roads to contend with. Lisbon's historic areas are a web of narrow, steep streets that can be daunting to drive, and finding parking, particularly in the busy city center, can be challenging. Most public parking spaces, including car parks, entail a hefty fee.

If you do rent a car to drive in Lisbon, check whether your hotel has private parking (which will entail additional cost), or find an underground car park that offers lower-cost "holiday fees," such as the one in Marquês de Pombal Square.

Vicinity of Lisbon

A rich tapestry of towns and villages blankets the outskirts of Lisbon. Just a short drive from the city, the hamlets of Estoril, Cascais, Sintra, and Mafra are worlds away from the bustle of the capital. The stunning coastline linking Estoril, Cascais, and Sintra is called the Portuguese Riviera and the Coast of Kings. During World War II, Portugal's neutral status made it a safe haven for European monarchs, aristocrats, and spies. Today it's still a playground for the rich and famous.

QUELUZ

A commuter suburb about 15 minutes northwest of Lisbon, Queluz (keh-LOOZH) is home to a fanciful royal palace and splendid gardens, making it a historic hot spot.

Sights

QUELUZ NATIONAL PALACE AND GARDENS
(Palácio Nacional de Queluz e Jardins)
Built in the 18th century as a summer residence, **Queluz National Palace** (Largo Palácio de Queluz, tel. 219 237 300, www.parquesdesintra.pt, 9am-6pm daily late Oct-late Mar, 9am-7pm daily late Mar-late Oct, last entry 1 hour before closing time, €10, audio guide €3) soon became a royal favorite for leisure and entertaining. Portugal's royal family lived here permanently before fleeing to Brazil in 1807 to escape French invasions. The palace's extravagance is a heady blend of baroque, neoclassical, and rococo styles, and its French-inspired gardens draw comparisons with the Palace of Versailles.

Vicinity of Lisbon

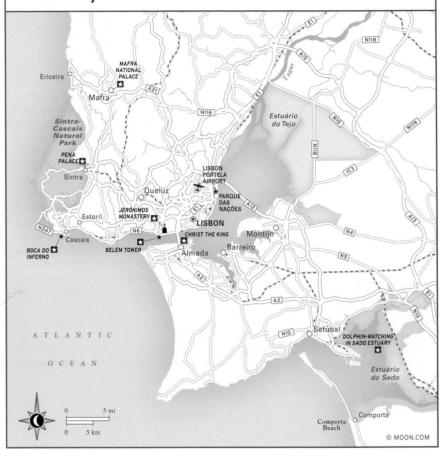

Inside are the Corridor of Azulejos (tiles); the Throne Hall, dripping with shimmery mirrors and chandeliers; the Lantern Room, which houses the palace's biggest portrait; and the opulent Ambassadors' Hall, in which every square centimeter is gilded. Outside, visitors can wander gardens decorated with fountains and statues.

Corte em Queluz, a two-hour reenactment of the 18th-century life inside the palace, is staged once a month (check dates beforehand; reservations required). The €10 fee includes entrance to the palace.

Accommodations

On a main square opposite the palace, **Pousada Palácio de Queluz** (Largo do Palácio Nacional, tel. 214 356 158, www. pousadas.pt, €130), is a luxury guesthouse that provides a taste of palace living. The building formerly housed the Royal Guards, and many of its original 18th-century features have been maintained.

Information and Services

GNR police station: Av. Doutor Francisco Sá Carneiro, tel. 214 351 121, www.gnr.pt

Main post office: Av. Luís de Camões 22, tel. 214 388 520

Getting There and Around

Queluz is a 20-minute drive, 14 kilometers (8.7 mi) north of Lisbon. Take the N117 or the A37 roads. A taxi will cost around €15 one-way.

From Lisbon's Oriente and Rossio stations, **CP trains** (tel. 707 210 220, www.cp.pt, €1.60) run on the Sintra Line every 10 minutes during the week and every half hour on the weekend. The journey to the Queluz-Belas or Monte Abraão Stations takes 20-25 minutes; both are about a 1-kilometer (0.6-mile) walk to the palace.

TOP EXPERIENCE

SINTRA

If Sintra had to be summed up in just one word, it would be "magical." Its hilltop Pena Palace is from a fairy tale, and its colorful town center is swaddled in lush hills dotted with multihued historic mansions. Sintra also has its own microclimate, with an Atlantic breeze that often makes it much cooler and mistier than its neighbors. Be prepared to bundle up. In town, a convenient tourist bus links the train station and town center to the hillside sights, which are a steep one-hour climb.

Sights and Recreation

SINTRA NATIONAL PALACE
(Palácio Nacional de Sintra)

In the town center, the **Sintra National Palace** (Largo Rainha Dona Amélia, tel. 219 237 300, www.parquesdesintra.pt, 9:30am-7pm daily late Mar-late Oct, 9:30am-6pm daily late Oct-late Mar, €10) was the residence of Portugal's royal families in the 15th-19th centuries and today is the first stop for many visitors. Its white Gothic exterior, with some Manueline features, is minimalist, a counterpoint to the extravagance of the fanciful Pena Palace on the hilltop. The wow factor of the detailed interior makes up for the exterior. A bird motif is evident in the Magpie Room and the Swan Room, with its octagonal paneled ceiling. The rudimentary Moorish kitchen is topped with huge conical chimneys. Most splendid is the 16th-century Coats of Arms room, where the paneled ceiling contains the coat of arms of 72 aristocratic families. **Guided tours** (2:30pm daily, 90 minutes, €5) are available in Portuguese, English, and Spanish. Reservations and online discounts are available via the website.

Pena Palace

Day Trips from Lisbon

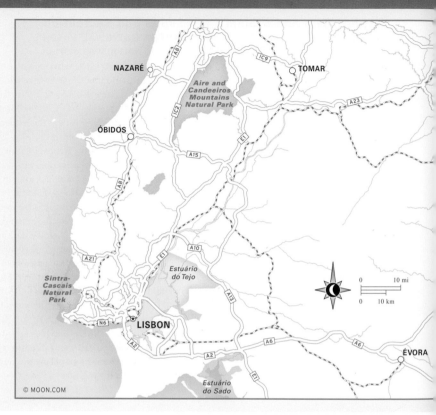

NAZARÉ

Aire and
Candeeiros
Mountains
Natural Park

TOMAR

ÓBIDOS

Sintra-
Cascais
Natural
Park

Estuário
do Tejo

LISBON

ÉVORA

Estuário
do Sado

0   10 mi

0   10 km

© MOON.COM

★ PENA PALACE
(Palácio Nacional da Pena)

Portugal's finest example of 19th-century romantic architecture, perched on a rocky peak
often shrouded in clouds, the colorful, whimsical **Pena Palace** (Estrada da Pena, tel. 219
237 300, www.parquesdesintra.pt, 9:30am-
8pm daily, €14) wouldn't look out of place in
a Disney movie. Commissioned in 1838 by the
young German-born King Ferdinand II for his
wife, Portuguese Maria II, and built on the
site of an abandoned 16th-century monastery,
the project was entrusted to amateur architect
Wilhelm Ludwig von Eschwege. The imita-
tion medieval fortress that resulted includes
a jumble of watchtowers, turrets, terraces, a
tunnel, and even a drawbridge.

The bold pink, gray, and ocher can be
seen for miles. The interior is just as eccentric, with stuccos, trompe-l'oeil murals, and
azulejo plaques. Note the exquisite carved
chairs and vaulted ceiling in the Royal Dining
Room, the rich upholstery in the Noble Room,
and the orchestra of brass pots and pans in
the kitchen. The Queen's Terrace and a clock
tower offer the best views. **Guided tours**
(2:30pm daily, 90 minutes, €5) are available
in Portuguese, English, and Spanish, and require prior booking. Reservations and online
discounts are available via the website.

Driving an hour or two from Lisbon's city center in any direction reveals a different side of Portugal.

ÓBIDOS

(page 204)

About 80 kilometers (50 mi) north of Lisbon is medieval Óbidos, popular with tour buses from Lisbon. Encircled by sturdy castle walls, the small town is a jigsaw of cobbled streets and traditional whitewashed houses. Stop to tour the castle, now a hotel, and enjoy a carriage tour or sample its famous *ginja de Óbidos* cherry liqueur. Its various festivals include a Medieval Fair (July-Aug) and the Chocolate Festival (Feb, Mar, or Apr).

NAZARÉ

(page 208)

Around 130 kilometers (81 mi) north of Lisbon, Nazaré is a small fishing town with a huge reputation. Its long sandy beaches, vertiginous hillside funicular, and fresh seafood restaurants make it a popular seaside getaway. Usually in November, monster waves roll in from the Atlantic, drawing surfers and photographers from all over the world.

TOMAR

(page 222)

The city of Tomar, 140 kilometers (87 mi) northeast of Lisbon, is heaven for history buffs. During the 13th century it was home to the Knights Templar, who governed from the sprawling Convent of Christ, an enigmatic complex that is now one of Portugal's foremost monuments. Some who visit say they feel a special spiritual energy here. Spread along the banks of the Nabão River, Tomar has a quaint town square and a picturesque riverside setting.

ÉVORA

(page 168)

Around 134 kilometers (83 mi) east of Lisbon, Évora is steeped in history and rife with relics. The most mesmerizing are the Roman Temple of Évora and the chilling Chapel of Bones, whose walls are made from tightly packed bones and skeletons. The whitewashed town emanates charm and has an energetic university student population.

MOORISH CASTLE
(Castelo de Mouros)

Surrounded by lush forest, the crumbling old **Moorish Castle** (Estrada da Pena, Parque de Monserrate, tel. 219 237 300, www.parquesdesintra.pt, daily 9:30am-8pm late Mar-late Oct, 9:30am-7pm late Oct-late Mar, €8) provides excellent views from its towering stone walls and extensive ramparts. Built in the 9th century during Moorish occupation, the castle fell into disrepair after the Christian reconquests but was later restored in the 19th century by Ferdinand II, who incorporated it into the vast gardens surrounding the Pena Palace.

REGALEIRA ESTATE
(Quinta da Regaleira)

If the Pena Palace is a fairy tale, the sprawling **Regaleira Estate** (Rua Barbosa do Bocage 5, tel. 219 106 650, www.regaleira.pt, 9:30am-5pm daily, €6), near the town center, is out of a scary movie, a spooky Gothic palace awash with gargoyles and spiky pinnacles and topped with a striking octagonal tower. Inside, a warren of hallways and stairways lead to rooms spread over five floors. The lush surroundings have hidden passages and secret spots with lakes, grottoes, wells, and fountains. The estate once belonged to the Viscountess of Regaleira, who was from a wealthy merchant family in Porto. The current building was completed in 1910.

MONSERRATE HISTORIC PARK AND PALACE
(Parque e Palácio de Monserrate)

The award-winning gardens are the main attraction at the 19th-century **Monserrate Historic Park and Palace** (Rua Visconde de Monserrate, tel. 219 237 300, www. parquesdesintra.pt, park 9:30am-8pm daily late Mar-late Oct, 9:30am-7pm daily late Oct-late Mar, palace 9:30am-7pm daily late Mar-late Oct, 9:30am-6pm daily late Oct-late Mar, €8), 4 kilometers (2.5 mi) west of Sintra town. The flora ranges from romantic to wild to exotic, with species from around the world. The estate was bought in 1856 by wealthy English textile magnate Francis Cook, who commissioned architect James Knowles to design the small palace with Gothic, Indian, and Moorish influences.

Monserrate is part of the **Sintra-Cascais Natural Park** (tel. 219 247 200, www.cm-cascais.pt), which covers a third of the Cascais region, from Sintra to Cabo da Roca. It's a popular place for hiking, biking, horseback riding, and even zip-lining.

Food

Strong meaty flavors and delicious sweets are staples in this part of Portugal. A typical dish is *vitela à Sintrense,* a slow-roasted veal dish served with roast potatoes. The traditional *queijadas de Sintra* is a decadent sweet treat, with a creamy filling of fresh cheese and cinnamon wrapped in delicate, crisp pastry.

Nau Palatina (Calçada de S. Pedro 18, tel. 219 240 962, 6pm-midnight Tues-Sat, €10) is a cute little place with scrumptious Mediterranean and Portuguese haute-rustic tapas, including regional specialties like pork cheeks, traditional Alentejo delicacies, and many vegetarian-friendly options.

The Portuguese word **Saudade** (Av. Doutor Miguel Bombarda 6, tel. 212 428 804, 8am-8pm daily, €10) roughly means

"longing." This pretty eatery across from the train station fulfills longings for tasty meals and treats with an extensive menu that includes sandwiches, fresh soups and salads, coffee, and freshly baked pastries and snacks.

Small, traditional Portuguese restaurant **O Lavrador** (Rua 25 de Abril 36, tel. 219 241 488, http://restaurantelavrador.business.site, noon-3pm and 7:30pm-10pm Tues-Sat, noon-3pm Sun €20), on the main 25 Abril road out of Sintra, has specialties that include *naco de carne na pedra* (chunks of beef on hot stone) and prawn and bacon skewers. Don't miss the Portuguese pottery hanging overhead.

Accommodations

Built from a quirky mid-19th-century building overlooking the Moors' castle, **Hotel Sintra Jardim** (Travessa dos Avelares 12, tel. 219 230 738, www.hotelsintrajardim. com, €95) is a convenient short walk from the train station and Sintra's historic center. Its 15 classically decorated rooms overlook lush gardens and a pool, a welcome oasis after a day of exploring.

In the heart of the historic center, family-run ★ **Aguamel Sintra Boutique Guest House** (Escadinhas da Fonte da Pipa 3, tel. 219 243 628, www.aguamelsintra.com, €120) offers a deluxe home-away-from-home experience. Contemporary on the inside, this cozy 19th-century property is a slice of history with a superb location in the town center.

Information and Services

GNR police station: Rua João de Deus 6, tel. 213 252 620, www.gnr.pt

"Ask Me Sintra" tourism office: Praça República 23, tel. 219 231 157, 9:30am-6pm daily

Main post office: Praça Dom Afonso Henriques 7, tel. 219 241 623

Getting There

Sintra is 25 kilometers (15.5 mi) west of Lisbon on the main A16 motorway, a 30-minute drive. Parking in Sintra is difficult, particularly in the busy summer months.

CP trains (tel. 707 210 220, www.cp.pt) to Sintra run from Lisbon's Rossio station many times daily, roughly every half hour. A one-way ticket costs €2.25 and takes about 40 minutes. Sintra train station is approximately 1.5 kilometers (0.9 mi) from town, but the **434 Sintra tourist bus** connects the station, the town center, and Pena Palace.

There is regular public transport between Sintra and Cascais on urban **Scotturb buses** (tel. 214 699 125, www.scotturb.com) about once per hour during the day, but check the schedule in advance. A bus ride from Cascais to Sintra takes 30-60 minutes and costs €5-12. Buses depart from various points in Cascais, including the Cascais Shopping Center and the main terminal on Avenida Costa Pinto and drop off near Sintra's train station on Avenida Dr. Miguel Bombarda.

Getting Around

Sintra's compact town center can be covered on foot, but most sights are farther afield. The hop-on hop-off **Scotturb tourist buses** (tel. 214 699 125, www.scotturb.com) connect all the main sights. The **434 route** (€5.50) includes stops at Sintra train station, the historic town center, Pena Palace, and Moorish Castle. The **435 route** (€2.50) goes to the Regaleira and Monserrate palaces. A full-day pass for all lines costs €12. Other fun ways to explore Sintra include a tourist train and *tuk-tuks,* both found in the main town center.

CABO DA ROCA

For invigorating sea air, stand on mainland Europe's most westerly point at **Cabo da Roca** (www.cm-sintra.pt), flanked by gigantic granite boulders and dramatic vertical cliffs that drop 100 meters (328 feet) to the Atlantic. A solitary rock monument marks the spot with a crucifix and an engraved quote from Portugal's greatest poet, Luís de Camões, who declared in his epic *Os Lusíadas* that this is where "land ends and sea begins." A short walk away, Portugal's first purpose-built lighthouse has a gift shop that offers certificates confirming

that visitors set foot on the western edge of Europe. Pack a jacket; this promontory is blustery and cold.

Getting There

Cabo da Roca is 40 kilometers (25 mi) west of Lisbon, 15 kilometers (9.3 mi) north of Cascais, and 18 kilometers (11.2 mi) west of Sintra. From Sintra it is a half-hour drive along the N247 road. The **Scotturb bus** (tel. 214 699 125, www.scotturb.com, €4) line 403, which runs from Cascais to Sintra, also stops here once an hour during the day, but services are irregular; check the schedule in advance.

CASCAIS

Perched on the western tip of the coastline, cosmopolitan little Cascais (kash-KAIZH), with its picturesque bay and elegant marina, is one of Lisbon's wealthiest suburbs. King Luís I of Portugal made the seaside hamlet his summer home in the 1870s, and it has been a magnet for the rich and famous ever since. Despite hosting some of the most exclusive resorts in the country, Cascais maintains the charm of a fishing village.

On weekends, city dwellers drive the scenic Marginal coast road from Lisbon to Cascais to enjoy people-watching in its cafés and bars. Just north of town is windswept Guincho Beach, popular among surfers. A beachside promenade connects to nearby Estoril, perfect for an after-lunch or evening stroll.

Sights and Recreation

★ **BOCA DO INFERNO**

Dramatic **Boca do Inferno** (Hell's Mouth) is a collapsed cave carved by relentless tides. Dramatic coastal views can be enjoyed from the paths up and down the cliff. In summer, when the seas are calmer, the translucent turquoise water laps gently around the formation's base. In winter, huge waves lash the rock and cliffs. It's about 1.5 kilometers (0.9 mi) west of Cascais town, a half-hour stroll along the coast. A scattering of cafés and gift shops can be found here.

GUINCHO BEACH
(Praia do Guincho)

Seven kilometers (4.3 mi) northwest of Cascais, windswept **Guincho Beach** is rugged and unbridled, with vast coastal dunes that make the landscape almost desolate. The waves rolling in from the Atlantic make it popular for surfing, windsurfing, and kite-surfing rather than for relaxation. **Guincho Surf Shop** (Praia do Guincho Estalagem Muchaxo, tel. 214 850 286, www. guinchosurfshop.com, 9am-6pm daily), right on the beach, provides everything from lessons to equipment rentals.

The urban **Scotturb bus** (tel. 214 699 125, www.scotturb.com) lines 405 and 415 run between Cascais and Guincho at least once an hour. Tickets cost about €2. Alternatively, hire a bicycle in Cascais from a shop such as the **Portugal Rent Bike** (Rua da Palmeira 39A, tel. 934 432 304, www.portugalrentbike. com, 9am-9pm daily) to ride the scenic 5-kilometer (3.1-mi) cycle track from Cascais to Guincho.

SAILING

With a capacity for several hundred vessels, **Cascais Marina** (Casa de São Bernardo, tel. 214 824 857, www.mymarinacascais.com) regularly hosts sailing competitions and international events. It's also home to elegant restaurants and boutiques.

GOLF

The **Penha Longa resort** (Estrada da Lagoa Azul Sintra Linhó, tel. 219 249 031, www. penhalonga.com) is home to one of Europe's top-30 golf courses, the 18-hole Atlantic Championship course (€74 per round) with rolling greens, world-class facilities, and the Sintra Mountains as a backdrop.

Quinta da Marinha (Rua do Clube, tel. 214 860 100, www.quintadamarinha.com, greens fees from €95) is the site of an 18-hole, par 71 course designed by Robert Trent Jones,

---

1: Cascais's beachfront; 2: Cabo da Roca;
3: Cascais's main square; 4: Boca do Inferno

with a different challenge on every hole and amazing views over the mountains and the Atlantic.

Food

Traditional Portuguese cuisine is given a modern overhaul at **Conceito Food Store** (Rua Pequena, tel. 218 085 281, www. conceitofoodstore.pt, noon-3:30pm and 7:45pm-11pm Tues-Sat, noon-3:30pm Sun, €30), an in-demand restaurant with minimalist decor. Products from local suppliers are transformed into contemporary masterpieces. Taster menus add to the gastronomic experience.

Don't miss the ★ **Marisco na Praça** (Rua Padre Moisés da Silva 34, tel. 214 822 130, noon-midnight daily, €20) for old-fashioned seafood. In the town center, this no-frills *marisqueira* is both market stall and eatery, offering fresh catch. Have the seafood cooked here and served at the table.

Time-honored Indian restaurant **Masala** (Rua Frederico Arouca 288, tel. 214 865 334, www.restaurantemasala.pt, 10am-11pm daily, €13) is a little jewel with vibrant decor to match the food. Trendy sushi restaurant **LOVit** (Av. Nossa Senhora do Cabo 101, Guincho, tel. 214 862 230, www.restaurantelovit.com, 12:30pm-11pm daily, €25) has visually stunning delicacies served overlooking the sea from the Casa da Guia cliffs, a short stroll west of Cascais center.

Romantic **Hemingway Cascais** (Marina de Cascais 58, tel. 916 224 452, www. hemingwaycascais.com, 7pm-late Thurs-Tues, €20), on Cascais Marina, is run by Pedro and Telma Vaz Moura, and its contemporary menu has cool twists on staples like fresh fish, steak, and risotto, complemented by extensive cocktail service until the wee hours. Take in a gorgeous sunset on the roof terrace.

Shopping

Every Saturday and Sunday, **antiques and handicrafts fairs** are held in the **Visconde da Luz garden** (Rua Visconde da Luz) in the heart of the town center and at nearby **Casa**

da Guia (Av. Nossa Senhora do Cabo 101, tel. 214 843 215), in a 19th-century mansion on the road from Cascais to Guincho Beach, a 2-kilometer (1.2-mi) walk west of town that takes about 30 minutes.

For local produce like cured meats and cheeses, head to the **Saloio farmers market** (7am-1pm Wed and Sat) at the **municipal market place** (Rua Padre Moisés da Silva 29, tel. 214 825 000). The lovely pedestrian street **Rua da Raita** is lined with little boutiques, designer stores, and arts and crafts shops.

The two shopping malls are **Cascais Villa** (Av. Dom Pedro, tel. 214 828 250, www. cascaisvilla.pt, 10am-10pm daily), on the road out of town to Estoril, and the larger **CascaiShopping** (Estrada Nacional 7, tel. 210 121 628, www.cascaishopping.pt, 10am-11pm daily), 9 kilometers (5.6 mi) northeast in the town of Alcabideche, on the way to Sintra.

Accommodations

In the heart of Cascais, on the beachfront, the large three-star ★ **Hotel Baía Cascais** (Av. Marginal, tel. 214 831 033, www.hotelbaia.com, €130) offers a first-rate location at accessible rates. Ideal for families or groups, it has 113 rooms, 66 of which have sea-view verandas.

Luxury hotel **Pestana Cidadela Cascais** (Av. Dom Carlos I, tel. 214 814 300, www. pestana.com, €291), converted from a 16th-century fortress, is perched on an elevated citadel wall overlooking Cascais Marina. Its exterior is centuries old, but inside, the petite five-star hotel is chic and contemporary. A short walk into Cascais town center, it offers complimentary breakfast and round-the-clock room service.

Information and Services

PSP police station: Rua Afonso Sanches 26, tel. 214 814 060, www.psp.pt
Cascais Visitors Center: Praça 5 de Outubro, tel. 912 034 214, 9am-8pm daily
Main post office: Av. Ultramar 2, tel. 214 827 281

Getting There and Around

Cascais is 35 kilometers (22 mi) west of Lisbon's city center. The two main routes are the A5 motorway, which has tolls, or the more scenic but often much busier Marginal coastal road, which runs parallel to the A5, passing pine-tree countryside, luxury villas, and old forts. On a good day, both routes take 30 minutes. With traffic, the Marginal can crawl, but the scenery is lovely. It's busiest at rush hour on weekdays and on weekends in good weather.

During the day, **CP trains** (tel. 707 210 220, www.cp.pt) run approximately every 30 minutes from the Cais do Sodré station in Lisbon along the coast to Cascais (€2.25 one-way). The journey takes approximately 40 minutes. Trains are less frequent after dark but still run until around 1:30am. The train station in Cascais is on Largo da Estação, a 10-minute stroll east of the town center.

The CP train on the Lisbon-Cascais line runs frequently and is the quickest way to travel between Cascais and Estoril's seafront station. The journey takes just three minutes, and a one-way ticket (€1.30) can be bought at the station from machines or the ticket office. Cascais is also a pleasant 3-kilometer (1.9-mi) walk west from Estoril along a lovely flat seafront promenade with lots to see—tide pools, cafés and bars, and quirky old houses.

The local urban **Scotturb bus** (tel. 214 699 100, www.scotturb.com) runs between Estoril, Cascais, and Sintra. The main bus terminal in Cascais is beneath the Cascais Villa shopping mall (level 0), just north of the Cascais railway station and town center. From here, buses depart at least once an hour for the main destinations of Guincho Beach, Cabo da Roca, and Sintra. Lines 406, 407, 411, 412, and 416 run frequently between Cascais and Estoril, while line 418 runs between Cascais and Sintra. Line 403 passes Cabo da Roca, and lines 405 and 415 run to Guincho Beach.

Once you arrive, compact Cascais itself is easily covered on foot.

ESTORIL

Glitzy São João do Estoril, better known as just Estoril (EEZH-too-reel), is a stylish seaside resort and home to the largest casino in Europe. Beaches are long and spacious, with a series of rocky outcrops and piers; calm, clean water; and a laid-back, romantic ambience. It is a popular escape for families and couples on weekends. Estoril is spread over a lengthy stretch of coastline fronted by a glorious promenade and a string of cosmopolitan restaurants and bars, and dotted with intriguing historic properties and lush green spaces.

Estoril's heyday was in the mid-1900s, when it was a playground for the Portuguese aristocracy and European high society. During World War II, the resort's reputation as a hangout for spies gave it a sense of intrigue. This is where Ian Fleming wrote the first part of *Casino Royale,* which launched the James Bond series. Mainstream tourism has stripped Estoril of a little of its elitism, but it is still one of the most glamorous beach destinations in Portugal.

A 3-kilometer (1.9-mi) **promenade** connects Estoril and Cascais, and the views along the way are fantastic, with a long stretch of golden sand along a string of historic properties, restaurants, bars, and cafés. The promenade offers a safe alternative to the short drive and is well illuminated at night.

Sights

ESTORIL CASINO

The largest in Europe, **Estoril Casino** (Av. Dr. Stanley Ho, tel. 214 667 700, www.casino-estoril.pt, 3pm-3am daily) is in the heart of Estoril, separated from the coast by sprawling, manicured gardens that slope gently upward toward the glitzy casino building. During World War II, the casino was a convergence point for spies and dispossessed royals. Its colorful history also provided inspiration for Ian Fleming's James Bond 007 novel *Casino Royale.* With nightly shows and myriad slot machines, Estoril Casino is the ultimate place

for dinner and a show. As well as the main games area, it has restaurants, bars, nightclubs, and a theater.

Food

With a prime position on the boardwalk, long-established **Bolina Restaurant** (Rua Olivenca 151, tel. 214 687 821, www.bolina. fish, 10am-7pm daily, €20) specializes in simple grilled fish, seafood, and meats—and sunset views. In the heart of Estoril with views over the bay, cozy **Gordinni Estoril** (Av. Marginal 7191, tel. 214 672 205, www. gordinniestoril.com, noon-3:30pm and 7pm-11:30pm Thurs-Tues, €15) has a huge menu of freshly baked pizzas and pastas and is famous for its sangria and *caipirinha* cocktails.

Open since 1934, celebrated bakery and cake shop ★ **Pastelaria Garrett** (Av. Nice 54, tel. 214 680 365, 8am-7pm Wed-Mon, €5) was once frequented by royalty and remains a popular haunt for Portuguese celebrities. Its displays are crammed with colorful sweet treats. It's busiest at lunchtime, and in December, queues for traditional Christmas cakes spill into the street.

Nightlife and Entertainment

Fashionable **Tamariz Beach Club** (Av. Marginal 7669, tel. 919 573 899, 11:30pm-4:30am Wed-Sun) is a popular place to be seen with a cocktail in hand. It has great views over the coast and gets lively after the sun goes down. Atmospheric **Piano Bar** (Rua Olivença 6, tel. 939 103 654, 10pm-4am Tues-Sun) is a bluesy hangout with live music every night.

Shopping

A nightly summer handicraft fair called **Feira de Artesanato do Estoril** (FIARTIL, Av. Amaral, tel. 214 677 019 or 912 590 249, 6pm-midnight weekdays, 5pm-midnight weekends, June-early Sept) is held behind the Estoril Casino, featuring about 300 artisans working on their wares, and food stands. The traditional Portuguese entertainment starts at around 9pm nightly.

Recreation

A medieval castle overlooks family-friendly **Tamariz Beach (Praia do Tamariz)**, long, wide, calm, and clean but crowded in summer. Facilities include sun beds and umbrellas, lifeguards, public restrooms, and reasonably priced restaurants and bars. Adjacent to the beach is a saltwater pool, great for swimming when the waves get rough.

Acclaimed 18-hole, par 69 **Estoril Golf Course** (Av. República, tel. 214 648 000, www. clubegolfestoril.com, greens fees from €50) is nestled in the woods above the beach. It was designed by Jean Gassiat and Mackenzie Ross and opened in 1929.

The **Estoril Wellness Centre & Spa** (Termas do Estoril, Rua Particular Hotel Palácio, tel. 214 658 600, www. estorilwellnesscenter.pt, 8am-9:30pm daily) harnesses the natural properties of the local springs for soothing treatments, including whirlpools and massages.

Accommodations

A 200-meter (656-foot) walk from the beach, four-star **Hotel Estoril Eden** (Av. de Saboia 209, Monte Estoril, tel. 214 667 600, www. hotelestorileden.com, €188) once hosted grand parties but is now a firm family favorite with 162 rooms. Most of its verandas offer nice views. Smart, unfussy **Hotel Londres** (Av. Fausto de Figueiredo 279, tel. 214 648 300, www.hotellondres.com, €158) has clean, quality rooms at sensible rates. It's a 450-meter (0.3-mi) walk to Tamariz Beach and 500 meters (0.3 mi) to Estoril Casino.

The imposing modern, glass-fronted **Intercontinental Estoril** (Av. Marginal 8023, tel. 218 291 100, www. estorilintercontinental.com, €345) stands out from the coastal landscape. All rooms have floor-to-ceiling sliding doors and private balconies, making the most of the views from its prime position midway between Estoril and Cascais.

Built in 1930, the storied ★ **Palácio Estoril Hotel** (Rua Particular and Av. Biarritz, tel. 214 648 000, www. palacioestorilhotel.com, €270) was the refuge of choice for royalty fleeing World War II. Frequented by artists, writers, and spies, it later served as a set for the James Bond movie *On Her Majesty's Secret Service.* The hotel still retains many of its original features, decor, and beautiful gardens.

Information and Services

PSP police station: just behind Estoril Casino, tel. 214 646 700, www.psp.pt

Main post office: Rua 9 de Abril 371, tel. 214 649 977

Getting There and Around

Estoril is a 25-kilometer (15.5-mi), 20-minute drive west of Lisbon. The easiest and fastest route is the A5 motorway, which has tolls. The scenic Marginal coastal road is toll-free but gets busy at commuter rush hours and on weekends.

CP trains (tel. 707 210 220, www.cp.pt) run about every half hour from Lisbon's Cais do Sodré train station 36 minutes along the coast to the São João do Estoril Station (€2.25 one-way), and continue to Cascais. Trains are less frequent after dark. There are four stations in Estoril: São Pedro do Estoril, São João do Estoril, Estoril (for the town, the casino, and Tamariz Beach), and Monte Estoril (halfway between Estoril and Cascais).

The local urban **Scotturb bus** (tel. 214 699 100, www.scotturb.com) runs between Estoril, Cascais, and Sintra, departing from outside Estoril train station. Lines 406, 407, 411, 412, and 416 run frequently between Cascais and Estoril (€3.35), while line 418 runs between Estoril and Sintra. To Sintra there is roughly one bus every hour, and the journey takes a half hour. One-way tickets from Estoril to Sintra cost €4.10. An all-day pass is €12.

A lovely and safe 3-kilometer (1.9-mi) seafront promenade connects Estoril to Cascais, providing an enjoyable walk between the two. The town of Estoril is easily covered on foot.

MAFRA

Just under 40 kilometers (25 mi) northwest of Lisbon, Mafra is famous as the home of a large, extravagant palace, which makes it a popular stop between the capital and coastal surfing mecca Ericeira. The small rural town boomed in popularity as a commuter suburb after the completion of the A8 motorway in the 1990s.

Sights

★ MAFRA NATIONAL PALACE
(Palácio Nacional de Mafra)

On a hilltop above the town center, the monumental **Mafra National Palace** (Terreiro Dom João V, tel. 261 817 550, www.palaciomafra.gov.pt, 9am-6pm Wed-Mon, €6) is the finest 18th-century baroque architecture in Portugal, built during the reign of John V (Dom João V) to fulfill a promise he made that if his wife bore him children, he would build a convent. The first stone was laid in 1717, and it took 13 years and 52,000 workers to complete it. The original plan was a monastery for 13 monks, but the project grew to immense proportions, eventually housing 300 monks and including a basilica and a royal palace. The sprawling monument's limestone facade measures 220 meters (722 feet). Painted in sunny yellow, its beautiful exterior features twin bell towers that frame the central basilica. The lavish interior comprises 1,200 rooms and 5,000 windows and doors. The Old Library is a trove of 36,000 ancient books, and the basilica has no fewer than six organs. Outside, a lovely courtyard is frequented by wild birds, and the vast decorative patio creates a border between this national monument and the town.

MAFRA NATIONAL HUNTING PARK
(Tapada Nacional de Mafra)

A 10-minute drive northeast of Mafra town on the N9-2 road, the 8-square-kilometer (3.1-square-mi) **Mafra National Hunting Park** (Portão do Codeçal, tel. 261 817 050, www.tapadademafra.pt, 9:30am-6pm daily) is a sprawling royal game reserve created for

the Mafra National Palace. Today it is still verdant and varied habitat for deer, wild boars, wolves, foxes, and birds of prey. Activities include hiking, mountain biking, horseback riding, archery, and falconry. There is no fixed entry fee, as prices are by activity: Hikes are €4 weekdays, €6.50 weekends. The Enchanted Circuit train (1 hour, adults €12, children €9) runs around the park.

JOSÉ FRANCO VILLAGE MUSEUM
(Aldeia Tipica de José Franco)

Just 3.2 kilometers (2 mi) north of Mafra town, in the village of Sobreiro, the **José Franco Village Museum** (N116, tel. 281 815 420, www.cm-mafra.pt, 9am-1pm and 2pm-5pm Mon-Sat, donation) is a detailed miniature replica of a typical Portuguese village from the turn of the 20th century. This tribute to the local people and their customs is the vision of renowned potter José Franco, who began building it in the 1960s. Among the miniature buildings are a windmill, cottages, and a schoolroom. The wood oven-baked *chouriça* sausage bread made on-site is worth the visit.

Food

Superb, unpretentious **Churrasqueira Povoense** (Rua 10 de Maio 2, Povoa da Galega, tel. 219 856 080, noon-3pm Mon-Wed, noon-3pm and 7:30pm-10pm Thurs-Sat, €8) specializes in grilled meats like the famous *tirinhas de porco,* delicious thin strips of pork, grilled on charcoal and served with fries and salad.

Getting There

Mafra is 40 kilometers (25 mi) northwest of Lisbon, about a 40-minute drive. Follow the A8 motorway from Lisbon, taking junction 5 and then heading west on the A21.

Mafrense buses (tel. 707 201 371, www.mafrense.pt) run hourly from Lisbon's Campo Grande main bus station, stopping in front of Mafra National Palace. The trip takes one hour each way and costs €4.30. Buses are less frequent on weekends.

ERICEIRA

On the coast, around 35 kilometers (22 mi) north of Lisbon, the fishing village of Ericeira attracts surfers and big-name surfing competitions. The Save the Waves Coalition has even declared it a World Surfing Reserve, only the second in the world and the only one in Europe. Laid-back Ericeira is not picturesque, but you can walk around barefoot and carefree. What it lacks in charm it makes up for with vibrant nightlife and excellent seafood. The cobbled main square, Praça da República, is lined with quaint cafés and cake shops, while Rua Dr. Eduardo Burnay, a buzzing street that runs from the square to the south beach, is packed with bars and restaurants.

Sights and Recreation

BEACHES

Praia do Sul is a crescent-shaped swath of sand on the south side of the village, backed by high cliffs and sheltered, with mild waves, making it appropriate for sunbathing and swimming. One of the top surfing spots in the region is **Ribeira d'Ilhas,** a regular fixture on the World Surf League Championship Tour, 3.3 kilometers (2 mi) north of Ericeira town, a short eight-minute drive on the N247 road.

SURFING

Ericeira has good surfing conditions year-round, with spots for beginners to experts. Dozens of different surf spots can be found on a relatively short stretch of coastline; if one doesn't suit you, you can find another. The

Ericeira Surf Center (Estrada Nacional 247, tel. 261 864 547, www.boardculturesurfcenter. com) and **eXtra eXtra Surf** (Av. São Sebastião 14I, tel. 261 867 771, www.extraextrasurf.com) are two well-established local companies that have boards, wetsuits, and other gear for rent. They also provide lessons and a wealth of information. Surfboard rentals start from €15 for a half-day; group lessons are €30-35 pp.

Information and Services

GNR police station: Largo Domingos Fernandes 7, tel. 261 860 710, www.gnr.pt
Tourist office: Rua Dr. Eduardo Burnay 46, tel. 261 863 122, 10am-6pm daily
Main post office: Rua do Paço 2, tel. 261 860 501

Getting There

Ericeira is 50 kilometers (31 mi) northwest of Lisbon, 9.5 kilometers (5.9 mi) west of Mafra. The quickest and easiest way to Ericeira from Lisbon is by car along the A8 motorway, then the A21 road west to the coast. It's about a 45-minute drive, and 15 minutes from Mafra, also on the A21.

Regular bus services operated by **Mafrense** (tel. 707 201 371, www.mafrense. com) run throughout the day between Lisbon's Campo Grande terminal and Ericeira (€6.25 one-way). Buses leave Campo Grande hourly and the journey takes an hour; the bus drops off at the Mafrense terminal, 240 meters (787 feet) north of Ericeira town center. Buses are less frequent on weekends.

Setúbal Peninsula

The Setúbal Peninsula is across the Tagus River from Lisbon, connected to the city by the historic 25 de Abril Bridge and the Vasco da Gama Bridge, Europe's longest. This fertile region is famous for its beaches, wines, seafood, and the Sado Estuary, home to a pod of bottlenose dolphins. Setúbal makes a great base for exploring Lisbon while also enjoying the lesser-known South Bank.

CACILHAS

On the northern tip of the Setúbal Peninsula, Cacilhas (kah-SEEL-yazh) is a quaint fishing town within the larger metropolis of Almada. Facing Lisbon's Belém district, it is a key transport hub and a main gateway to the "other side" of the Tagus. Cacilhas Ferries cross the river from Cais do Sodré dock, and local buses converge here.

Sights
★ **CHRIST THE KING**
(Cristo Rei)
Dominating the skyline of the Tagus's south bank is the **Christ the King statue** (Alto do Pragal, Av. Cristo Rei, tel. 212 751 000 or 212 721 270, www.cristorei.pt, 9:30am-6:30pm daily, €4), standing with arms outstretched and epitomizing Portugal's Catholic faith. The idea to build the monument came after the Cardinal Patriarch of Lisbon visited Rio de Janeiro in 1934 and was impressed by its imposing *Christ the Redeemer* statue. Built on an isolated cliff top, the statue stands 192 meters (630 feet) above the Tagus River. An express lift whizzes visitors to a viewing platform at 82 meters (269 feet), which affords dazzling views over the city. At the statue's base is a chapel. The statue's interior contains a library, a large café, two halls, and another chapel.

Information and Services
Tourist office: Largo Bombeiros Voluntários 123, tel. 212 739 340, 9:30am-1pm and 2pm-5pm daily

Getting There and Around
Cacilhas is 5 kilometers (3.1 mi) south of Lisbon, across the Tagus River. **Transtejo & Soflusa ferries** (tel. 808 203 050, www.transtejo.pt, €1.25 one-way) run approximately every 25 minutes between Cais do Sodré and Cacilhas. The journey takes 10 minutes and affords nice views. Crossing under the 25 de Abril Bridge, as the traffic whizzes overhead, is an experience in itself.

From the ferry terminal in Cacilhas, **Transportes Sul do Tejo** (tel. 707 508 509, www.tsuldotejo.pt) bus line 101 runs 2-3 times per hour to the *Christ the King* statue (about 15 minutes, €1.45). Buy tickets from the driver.

COSTA DA CAPARICA

The longest continuous stretch of sand in Europe, this 30-kilometer (19-mi) strip of coastline extends along the entire western fringe of the Setúbal Peninsula. Popular with seaside loving *Lisboetas,* Costa da Caparica is still relatively undiscovered by foreign tourists. In summer, the resort area comes alive with cool sunset parties at busy beach bars.

Sights and Recreation
BEACHES
In peak season the little *trans-praia* train connects 21 different stops along the coast. The busy north end is more developed for tourism. Farther south, you'll find vast, spacious stretches of sand. At the far southern end, the beaches are unspoiled, fringed by rugged reedy dunes. **Fonte da Telha** is famous for its mud; it's not uncommon to see people caked head to toe in the restorative sludge. There are also two nudist beaches: **Praia da Bela Vista** (Beach of Good View) and **Meco,** at the Costa's southern tip.

Setúbal Peninsula

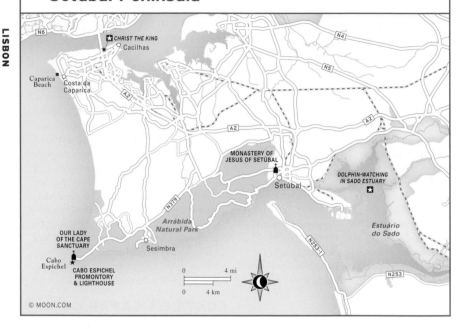

N6
CHRIST THE KING
Cacilhas
N4
N5
Caparica Beach
Costa da Caparica
A2
A2
A2
MONASTERY OF JESUS OF SETÚBAL
DOLPHIN-WATCHING IN SADO ESTUARY
Setúbal
N379
Arrábida Natural Park
Estuário do Sado
OUR LADY OF THE CAPE SANCTUARY
Sesimbra
N253-1
Cabo Espichel
CABO ESPICHEL PROMONTORY & LIGHTHOUSE
0   4 mi
0   4 km
N253

© MOON.COM

SURFING

Waves along this stretch are consistent but not in the same category as Guincho or Ericeira, which makes Costa da Caparica perfect for less experienced surfers. Top spots for surfing are **CDS beach** (Caparica town, off the main avenue) and **Praia da Riviera** (2 km/1.2 mi south of CDS beach). Local surf schools, shops, and guesthouses have flourished in the vicinity, including the **Caparica Evolution Surf School** (Estrada da Muralha, Marcelino Beach-K bar, tel. 939 124 758, www.kevolutionsurf.com). Board plus wetsuit rental is around €15 for a half-day; lessons are around €15.

Food

Costa da Caparica excels in seafood. *Canja de carapau* (mackerel soup) is a local specialty. For seafood, funky modern **Sentido do Mar** (Rua Muralha da Praia, Apoio 7, Praia do Norte 278, tel. 212 900 473, noon-11pm Mon-Sat, €10) has menus covering sushi to grilled fresh fish, complemented with fantastic sunset views. Typical *tasca* (simple, small Portuguese eatery) **Tasca do Nana** (Rua Eugénio Salvador 23, tel. 933 240 178, www.nanapetiscos.pt, 5pm-midnight Tues-Sun, €8) serves a rainbow of *petiscos,* fish and meat snacks perfect for sharing.

The name of **Borda d'Agua** (Praia da Morena s/n, tel. 212 975 213, www.bordadagua.com.pt, 10am-midnight daily, €15) translates as "waterside," and it makes the most of its beachside location, with a large deck for alfresco dining as well as enclosed indoor seating for breezier days. It's a must-visit for delicious fresh fish with a sea breeze.

Accommodations

Hotels in Costa da Caparica are varied and cheaper than most in central Lisbon. The ultimate beachfront hotel, four-star ★ **Hotel Costa da Caparica** (Av. Gen. Humberto Delgado 47, tel. 212 918 900, www.tryplisboacaparica.com, from €138) is family-friendly, with a nice swimming pool. Some of the 352 rooms over seven floors have views over the Atlantic.

Set a few streets back from the beach, small, simple **Hotel Maia** (Av. Dr. Aresta Branco 22, tel. 212 904 948, www.hotelmaia.com, €100) is unfussy and clean, with a good breakfast included in the rates.

Surfers will love **Lost Caparica Surf House** (Rua Dr. Barros de Castro 17, tel. 917 552 202, www.lostcaparica.com, €35 pp shared, €65 d), whose accommodation ranges from a shared six-bed room to a private family studio with a small bath. An added bonus is the on-site surf school.

Information and Services

GNR police station: Rua Pedro Álvares Cabral 29, tel. 265 242 590, www.gnr.pt
Tourist office: Av. da República 18, tel. 212 900 071, 9:30am-1pm and 2pm-5:30pm Mon-Sat
Main post office: Praça de 9 de Julho

Getting There and Around

Costa da Caparica is 11 kilometers (6.8 mi) southwest from Cacilhas. From the ferry terminal in Cacilhas, local **Transportes Sul do Tejo buses** (tel. 707 508 509, www.tsuldotejo. pt) run frequently to Costa da Caparica. Line 124 runs from Cacilhas (45 minutes) 6am-midnight, at least three times per hour 7am-8pm, and less frequently at other times. Express bus line 135 runs once or twice an hour 7am-8pm during the week, and always at half past the hour on weekends. This is a good option, as a single ticket costs €2.50 (bought from the driver) and the journey is quicker at 20 minutes. The bus terminal is in the heart of Caparica, at Praça Padre Manuel Bernardes.

The **Transpraia mini tourist train** (Rua Parque Infantil, tel. 212 900 706, 9am-8pm daily June-Sept) carries beach-goers from one end of Costa da Caparica to the other. It's a bumpy but scenic way to discover Costa's best beach spots. It runs 9 kilometers (5.6 mi) from Caparica town to Fonte da Telha, which takes around 25 minutes, with four little stations

and 15 stops en route. The track is divided into zone 1 (€5 round-trip) and zone 2 (€8 round-trip). The train operates only in high season. There are two departures per hour from each end, one on the hour and the other at half past. In Caparica, the Transpraia train leaves from in front of the children's beachside play park in the main town center.

SETÚBAL

The unpolished port town of Setúbal is divisive. Many are charmed by its lovely old town square, busy waterfront, and unrepentant lack of pretension; others are unable to see past its gritty industrial facade. Colorful fishing boats and commuter ferries run beside leisure vessels, a sure sign that tourism is buoying the city. With good hotels and restaurants, Setúbal is well placed as a base for exploring the wildlife-heavy Sado Estuary.

Sights and Recreation

MONASTERY OF JESUS OF SETÚBAL
(Convento e Igreja de Jesus)

Designed in 1494 by architect Diogo de Boitaca, best known for his work on Lisbon's emblematic Jerónimos Monastery, the austere gray **Monastery of Jesus of Setúbal** (Rua Acácio Barradas 2, tel. 265 537 890, www. mun-setubal.pt, 10am-6pm Tues-Sat, 2pm-6pm Sun, free) is one of the earliest examples of Manueline architecture in Portugal. Among its distinguishing features are soaring spiral granite pillars and typical azulejo murals. Outside, gargoyles and twisted pinnacles perforate an otherwise plain facade. Inside, an intricate ribbed vaulted ceiling in the main chapel and twisted-rope columns of pink and beige Arrábida stone are highlights.

★ DOLPHIN-WATCHING IN SADO ESTUARY
(Estuário do Sado)

Originating in the deep Alentejo, the Sado River flows into the sea south of Setúbal. The humid and fertile Sado Estuary is a protected natural reserve where mirror-like wetlands and surrounding banks and thickets host more than 200 bird species, including white storks and pink flamingos. A pod of bottlenose dolphins has long resided in the estuary's calm waters, a phenomenon unique in Portugal and rare in the world. **Dolphin-watching cruises** (3 hours, from €30) are available from companies including **Vertigem Azul** (tel. 265 238 000, www.vertigemazul.com), **Portugal Sport and Adventure** (tel. 910 668 600, www.portugalsport-and-adventure.com), and **Sado Arrábida Nature Tourism** (tel. 265 490 406 or 915 560 342, www.sadoarrabida.pt).

GALLEON *SAL* SADO TRIPS

A different way to explore the Sado is aboard a historic *sal* (salt) galleon. These wooden ships were converted from small fishing vessels, first used to transport salt and later used for fishing and cargo. The restored boats are now used for coastal and estuary cruises. **Sal Cruises** (tel. 265 227 685, www.sal.pt, 3 hours, €25) runs cruises on the Sado, Tagus, and Zêzere Rivers.

Food

You'll often see locals sitting alfresco, sharing a plate of local specialty *choco frito* (fried squid) with a cold beer. Small, simple dockside **Batareo** (Rua das Fontainhas 64, tel. 265 234 548, noon-3:30pm Tues-Sun, €15) only does fish and shellfish. Fish move straight off the boat and into the glass display case.

With the best sea and river produce, down-to-earth **Pérola da Mourisca** (Rua da Baía do Sado 9, tel. 265 793 689, 7:30pm-10:30pm Wed-Sun, €10) is best known for its shellfish tapas but also cooks seafood-based rice and pasta dishes. Head for the simple café-snack bar ★ **Leo do Petisco** (Rua da Cordoaria 33, tel. 265 228 340, noon-3pm and 7pm-10pm Mon-Sat, €8) in Setúbal's town center to try local delicacy *choco frito* served on a plate or—interestingly—in a sandwich.

Accommodations

Hotels in Setúbal are located in and around the town center and the port. In the heart of Setúbal, the **Rio Art Hotel** (Av. Luísa Todi 117, tel. 965 801 988, www.rioarthotel.pt, €95) retains some original features of its historic exterior. The renovated interior is gleaming and contemporary, with 23 colorful, spacious rooms and vintage-chic touches.

Just off Setúbal's main drag, Avenida Luísa Todi, in the heart of the historic part of town, two-star **Hotel Bocage** (Rua de São Cristóvão 14, tel. 265 543 080, www.hoteisbocage.com, €87) provides an unfussy, comfortable stay. It sister, Bocage Guest House, is on a side street just around the corner.

Information and Services

GNR police station: Av. Jaime Cortesão, tel. 265 242 500, www.gnr.pt
Tourist office: Travessa Frei Gaspar 10, tel. 265 539 120, open 10am-7pm daily
Main post office: Av. Mariano Carvalho s/n, tel. 265 528 621

Getting There and Around

Located 50 kilometers (31 mi) southeast of Lisbon Airport, Setúbal is a 45-minute drive from Lisbon. By car the main route is over the 25 de Abril Bridge, following the A2 motorway.

There is direct public transport between Lisbon and Setúbal. **CP trains** (tel. 707 210 220, www.cp.pt) run every hour from Lisbon's Santa Apolónia and Cais do Sodré stations and take around two hours. Single-trip tickets cost €11.20. The train station is 900 meters (0.6 mi) east of the main town center in Praça do Quebrado (Quebrado Square), near the main bus stops on Avenida 5 de Outubro.

Alternately, take the **Transtejo & Soflusa ferry** (tel. 808 203 050, www.transtejo.pt) from Lisbon's Terreiro do Paço terminal to Barreiro (€2.40), with up to seven crossings per hour; then catch a CP train from the station next to the ferry terminal to Praça do Quebrado in Setúbal (twice per hour, 30 minutes, €2.25).

Transportes Sul do Tejo express buses (tel. 707 508 509, www.tsuldotejo.pt) also run directly from Lisbon's Praça da Espanha (lines 561 and 563) and Gare do Oriente (lines 562 and 563) stations, departing once an hour; the trip takes 50 minutes and costs €4.45 one-way. National express-bus company **Rede Expressos** (tel. 707 223 344, www. rede-expressos.pt) operates a dozen buses per day between Lisbon's Sete Rios terminal and Setúbal (45 minutes, €6).

Ferries (25 minutes, €4.15) and catamarans (15 minutes, €6.85) to the Tróia Peninsula, operated by **Atlantic Ferries** (tel. 265 235 101, www.atlanticferries.pt), run hourly from the local docks in Setúbal.

Setúbal's main downtown area, with the main sights, attractions and restaurants, can easily be explored on foot.

ARRÁBIDA NATURAL PARK
(Parque Natural da Arrábida)
Blanketing a chunk of coastline between the city of Setúbal and the village of Sesimbra, the **Arrábida Natural Park** (www.natural. pt) covers 16,500 hectares (64 square mi). A rugged belt of deep green, the Serra da Arrábida mountain range is separated from the Atlantic by thin, white-gold beaches. Its tallest peak stands 499 meters (1,637 ft), and the chalky Arrábida massif is covered by a thick rug of plantlife, including rare species like rockroses and purple star thistle as well as typical Mediterranean maquis and garigue scrubland. To protect the vegetation, some areas can only be accessed with an authorized guide. Opt for a leisurely activity such as biking or hiking, or join certified guides who lead mountain climbing, caving, and diving excursions. For information, contact the **park office** (Praça da República, Setúbal, tel. 265 541 140).

An oceanographic museum occupies the historic cliff-foot **Our Lady of Arrábida Fort (Forte de Santa Maria da Arrábida)** (Portinho da Arrábida, tel. 212 189 791, 10am-4pm Tues-Fri, 3pm-6pm Sat, €3.50), next to Portinho Beach. The park is also home

to the enigmatic 16th-century **Arrábida Monastery (Convento da Arrábida)** (tel. 212 180 520, www.foriente.pt), amid dense shrubbery; it can be toured (Wed and Sat-Sun, €5) if you reserve in advance.

Getting There
Arrábida Natural Park is 2.5 kilometers (1.6 mi) west of Setúbal, a five-minute drive along the Avenida General Daniel de Sousa and the N10 road. A taxi from Setúbal should cost around €13. From Sesimbra, the 10-kilometer (6.2-mi) drive east takes about 20 minutes on the N378 road and Avenida 25 de Abril. A taxi should cost €18. Public transport is infrequent; the best way to reach the Arrábida Natural Park is by car or by asking at your hotel or the local tourist office what excursions are available.

SESIMBRA
At the foot of the Arrábida Mountain Range (Serra da Arrábida) in a protected bay, the authentic fishing town of Sesimbra (seh-ZEEM-brah) has marvelous beaches but remains largely undiscovered, allowing its genuine seaside charm to shine. It's also located at the western edge of the Arrábida Natural Park, making it a gateway to unspoiled natural beauty.

Sights and Recreation
BEACHES
With fine sand and crystalline waters, Sesimbra's beaches are glorious. **Praia do Ouro** (just west of the town center) is a generous strand of golden sand sloping gently toward calm clear water, along Sesimbra's main seaside avenue. Find comforts like sun beds, beach bars, and a children's play area. Smaller **Praia do Ribeiro do Cavalo** is on a cove with rocky beds teeming with sealife, making it perfect for diving or snorkeling. There are no diving outfitters on the beach, so bring your own gear. It's a 3-kilometer (1.9-mi) drive west of town, but you can reach it by boat from Sesimbra's port.

FISHING

Fishing trips are the main excursions in Sesimbra, and deep-sea fishing is the most popular. Tours vary but generally last around five hours and are suitable for the whole family. **Bolhas Tours—Follow Sensations** (tel. 910 658 555 or 916 205 429, www.bolhastours. com) operates from Sesimbra Marina with sightseeing boat trips, fishing trips, and dolphin watching as well as boat rentals and diving. Prices start around €35.

Food

Sesimbra's gastronomy is all about the sea. Local specialties include *arroz de marisco* (a rich, well-sauced rice stew packed with gently boiled seafood and spices) and *peixe-espada preto* (black scabbard fish).

With its charming worn tile facade and simple wooden tables, acclaimed **Bijou Casa Mateus** (Largo Anselmo Braamcamp 4, tel. 963 650 939, www.casamateus.pt, noon-3:30pm and 7pm-11pm, Tues-Sun, €15) puts all the focus on the seafood. Offerings include *caldeirada* (fish stew) and *arroz de marisco,* along with seafood delicacies such as razor clams, Sesimbra lobster, and cockles.

Unpretentious ★ **Café and Marisqueira O Rodinhas** (Rua Marques de Pombal 25, tel. 212 231 557, www.marisqueiraorodinhas.pt, noon-10:30pm Thurs-Tues, €12) serves seafood delights in a cozy and casual interior. Simple seaside ★ **Lobo do Mar** (Av. dos Náufragos, Porto de Abrigo, tel. 212 235 233, www.lobodomar.com, noon-4pm and 7pm-10pm, Tues-Sun, €15) is famous for its grilled fish.

Accommodations

Sesimbra has only a handful of hotels, including newish middle-size units and charming guesthouses. Built on a cliff overlooking Califórnia Beach and the Atlantic, modern ★ **Sesimbra Hotel & Spa** (Rua Navegador Rodrigues Soromenho, tel. 212 289 800, www.sesimbrahotelspa.com, €243) has panoramic views from all rooms as well as from its infinity pool. Its plush interior and stylish seaside decor are relaxing and refreshing.

On the beach in the heart of Sesimbra village, upscale hotel **Sana Sesimbra** (Av. 25 de Abril, tel. 212 289 000, www.sesimbra. sanahotels.com, €167) brings the luxury of an acclaimed chain to a small town. Its central location and fabulous views enhance the hotel's cool retro look.

Information and Services

GNR police station: Rua 4 de Maio, tel. 217 657 700, www.gnr.pt
Tourist office: Rua da Fortaleza, tel. 212 288 500, 9am-9pm daily
Main post office: Av. Padre António Pereira de Almeida 8

Getting There

Sesimbra is 40 kilometers (25 mi) south of Lisbon, a 50-minute drive. By car, take the A2 motorway over the 25 de Abril Bridge and head southwest toward Setúbal. At the junction of the N378 road, head directly south to Sesimbra. From Setúbal, Sesimbra is 30 kilometers (19 mi) west, a 45-minute drive along the N10 road and Avenida 25 de Abril.

Transportes Sul do Tejo (tel. 707 508 509, www.tsuldotejo.pt) runs an inexpensive express bus service (line 207 or 260) between Lisbon's Praça da Espanha and Sesimbra (1 hour, €4.35); tickets can be purchased from the driver.

Public transport between Setúbal and Sesimbra is frustratingly sparse, with around a dozen departures a day on weekdays and just four or five on weekends, making a day trip difficult. The service, line 230, is operated by Transportes Sul do Tejo and costs €3.30. In Sesimbra, the bus stops on the main Avenida da Liberdade, 350 meters (0.2 mi) from the beach.

CABO ESPICHEL

Wind-battered and rugged, Cabo Espichel is the Setúbal Peninsula's most southwesterly headland, a barren cape with massive cliffs and an eerie, desolate feel. Everything about

Cabo Espichel is wild; the waves roar, the scenery is untamed, and there are few modern comforts.

Sights

CABO ESPICHEL PROMONTORY AND LIGHTHOUSE
(Promontório e Farol do Cabo Espichel)

Perched on the promontory, this hexagonal lighthouse guards the entire Setúbal Peninsula. The structure stands 32 meters (105 feet) tall but is still dwarfed by the sheer size of the cliffs. On a clear night, sailors can see the powerful beam from the lighthouse 40 kilometers (25 mi) out to sea. It's open to the public 2pm-5pm Wednesday only. Entry is free, and visitors can climb to the top to see the lamp.

DINOSAUR FOOTPRINTS
(Pegadas dos Dinossauros)

Within walking distance of the lighthouse is a unique sight: dinosaur footprints. Likely made by sauropods, theropods, and ornithopods that inhabited the area millions of years ago, two sets of prints can be clearly seen in the cliffs. Directly above the prehistoric prints, the isolated 15th-century **Chapel of Ermida de Memória** (24 hours daily, free) perches perilously close to the cliff's edge. The chapel's interior is clad in traditional tile depicting "The Lady of the Cape"—the Virgin Mary is said to have appeared to an elderly couple in that spot in 1410.

OUR LADY OF THE CAPE SANCTUARY
(Santuário da Nossa Senhora do Cabo)

Built in 1701, the baroque **Our Lady of the Cape Sanctuary** (tel. 212 231 031, 9:30am-1:30pm and 2:30pm-5pm weekdays, 9:30am-1:30pm and 2:30pm-6pm weekends, free) was designed first as a place of defense, then to provide shelter. Two long arms stretching out from either side of the church include rooms that housed pilgrims. The church itself has a simple marble interior.

Food and Accommodations

Most visitors to Cabo Espichel plan on meals and lodging in nearby Sesimbra or Setúbal. There are a few eateries around Cabo Espichel, including **A Fátima** (Estrada do Cabo Espichel, tel. 212 685 164, www. restauranteafatima.com, noon-3:30pm and 7pm-10pm Tues-Sun, €10) restaurant and a nearby snack bar, on the road into the cape, serving traditional homemade Portuguese fish and meat dishes at good prices.

Incongruous with the wild landscape, the sleek 38-room **Hotel dos Zimbros** (Facho de Azóia, tel. 210 405 470, www.hotelzimbros. com, €150) is on the main road into Cabo Espichel.

Getting There

Taking public transport to Cabo Espichel is difficult, so most visitors drive. Cabo Espichel is 14 kilometers (8.7 mi) west from Sesimbra and 40 kilometers (25 mi) west from Setúbal. By car, take the N379 road from Sesimbra (20 minutes). From Setúbal, follow the main Avenida 25 de Abril (50 minutes).

A public bus, line 201, operated by **Transportes Sul do Tejo** (tel. 707 508 509, www.tsuldotejo.pt), runs between Sesimbra's main bus station and Cabo Espichel about eight times on weekdays, less frequently on weekends.

The Algarve

Portugal's southernmost region, the sun-drenched Algarve (al-GARV) is famous for its year-round good weather, heady summer events, golden beaches, and dramatic coastal rock formations in a sparkling sea.

With over 300 days of sunshine per year, the region is a premier destination for tourism and Northern European expats. Over 150 kilometers (93 mi) of coastline are framed by jagged ocher cliffs with golden stretches of sand and sheltered rocky coves. Large tourist towns mix with quaint whitewashed fishing villages, orange groves, and golf courses, and the entire region is peppered with Moorish and Roman ruins.

The Algarve is generally divided into the unspoiled, quiet Sotavento, eastern Algarve, which borders Spain, where the sea is warmer than

Highlights

Look for ★ to find recommended sights, activities, dining, and lodging.

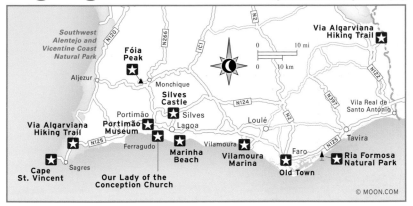

© MOON.COM

★ **Faro's Old Town:** Encircled by ancient Moorish stone walls in the heart of the city, Faro's Old Town is a warren of quaint cobbled streets and historic buildings, including the medieval Faro Cathedral (page 98).

★ **Ria Formosa Natural Park:** A wonder of nature, this offshore park comprises turquoise lagoons, sandy barrier islets, deserted beaches, and a wealth of flora and fauna (pages 100 and 157).

★ **Vilamoura Marina:** A place to see and be seen, this cosmopolitan waterfront is Vilamoura's main feature and sets the tone for the rest of the town—chic, polished, and full of well-heeled life (page 115).

★ **Marinha Beach:** Emblematic of the Algarve coast, the award-winning Marinha Beach near Lagoa regularly features on lists of Europe's top beaches but is still a hidden gem (page 124).

★ **Our Lady of the Conception Church:** Set on a hilltop overlooking the picturesque fishing village of Ferragudo, this pretty 16th-century structure enjoys a scenic setting and stupendous views (page 127).

★ **Silves Castle:** Perched imposingly above the city of Silves, this impressive medieval fortress is a legacy of the battles the Algarve once endured. Today it is the centerpiece of the city's famous Medieval Festival (page 130).

★ **Portimão Museum:** This unique award-winning museum is an interactive journey through the fascinating history and heritage of Portimão city as a major fishing and canning empire (page 132).

★ **Fóia Peak:** In the Monchique Mountains, stand on the region's highest point for panoramic views of the Algarve and the Atlantic. The journey up is pretty thrilling too (page 140).

★ **Cape St. Vincent:** No visit to the Algarve is complete without a trip to the most southwesterly point, once believed to be the world's end, a windswept, desolate area with dramatic cliffs that drop sharply into the tumultuous Atlantic (page 149).

★ **Via Algarviana Hiking Trail:** With over 200 kilometers (124 mi) of rural hiking path, this trans-region trail takes walking enthusiasts through unspoiled nature and rural hamlets (page 151).

The Algarve

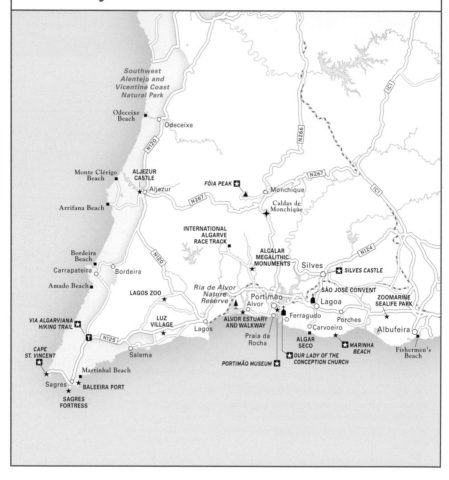

Southwest Alentejo and Vicentine Coast Natural Park

Odeceixe Beach
Odeceixe
Monte Clérigo Beach
ALJEZUR CASTLE
Aljezur
FÓIA PEAK
Monchique
Caldas de Monchique
Arrifana Beach
INTERNATIONAL ALGARVE RACE TRACK
ALCALAR MEGALITHIC MONUMENTS
Bordeira Beach
Carrapateira
Bordeira
Silves
SILVES CASTLE
Amado Beach
LAGOS ZOO
Ria de Alvor Nature Reserve
Portimão
Alvor
SÃO JOSÉ CONVENT
Lagoa
ZOOMARINE SEALIFE PARK
VIA ALGARVIANA HIKING TRAIL
LUZ VILLAGE
Lagos
ALVOR ESTUARY AND WALKWAY
Ferragudo
Carvoeiro
Porches
Albufeira
CAPE ST. VINCENT
Salema
Praia da Rocha
ALGAR SECO
MARINHA BEACH
Fishermen's Beach
Martinhal Beach
PORTIMÃO MUSEUM
OUR LADY OF THE CONCEPTION CHURCH
Sagres
BALEEIRA PORT
SAGRES FORTRESS

along the rest of the coast, and the Barlavento, western Algarve, a blend of tourist and traditional. Between the two is glitzy and glamorous central Algarve, home to the affluent Golden Triangle and the region's most exclusive hotels, restaurants, and bars. It's also home to Faro, the Algarve's largest city and the main gateway to the region.

Portugal's tourism authorities are working to shift the Algarve's image as a mere summer beach destination by adding a packed year-round events calendar and niche tourism to attract visitors in all seasons for nature and health tourism. In cooler months, the Algarve is a golfing and adventure sports destination for skydiving, scuba diving, kayaking, and surfing. Beyond tourism, the region is steeped in history.

Previous: the town of Carvoeiro; a restaurant sign in Silves; breaking waves on an Algarve beach.

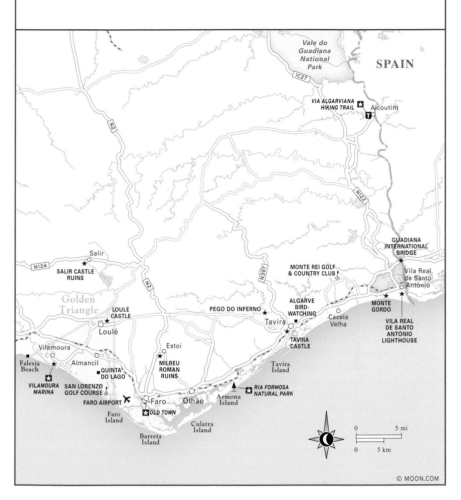

© MOON.COM

PLANNING YOUR TIME

Portugal's southern coastline spans 155 kilometers (96 mi) and takes two hours to drive from one end to the other, with Faro International Airport in the middle.

Allow at least a week in the Algarve to explore the windy, rugged west coast, the lush Monchique Mountains, the glitzy Golden Triangle, and the more traditional, unspoiled eastern end, not to mention the amazing Ria Formosa Natural Park. If you only have a few days, spend a night in each

area for a quick overview, or choose one region to soak up the local essence.

For a quiet holiday with authentic Algarve flavor and possibly a day trip to Spain, head to the Sotavento, the eastern end, home to Tavira and Vila Real de Santo António. If you appreciate luxury, central Algarve's Golden Triangle area won't disappoint. For fun in the sun and fantastic beaches with the option of interesting scenery and history, go to the Barlavento, or western end, from Albufeira to Vila do Bispo. For a break from the beach, head to the Monchique Mountains, the backbone of the Algarve, separating it from the Alentejo region to the north, or to the unspoiled west coast north of Sagres.

Beaches in the central and eastern end of the region are more popular and generally longer, with shallower, warmer water. In the western end, from Alvor onward, beaches are windier and popular for surfing and kite-surfing. Most of the Algarve's beaches are accessible, pristine, and well equipped with bars, restaurants, and other facilities, and most fly the Blue Flag award of quality and environmental standards.

June to September is a good time to visit the beaches, although prices and temperatures peak in August, and roads, amenities, attractions, and beaches get hot and busy.

Renting a car is the best way to explore the Algarve. The N125 road and the A22 motorway run parallel to the coast through the entire region. The A22 has tolls but is faster. The N125 is often subject to construction, which can cause long backups.

Faro and Vicinity

Faro is the largest city in the Algarve and home to the region's only international airport. The city itself is underrated, often passed through on the way to beach resorts but with a lot to offer.

With the exception of some tourist trappings such as the ubiquitous tourist train, Faro has remained largely untouched by tourism and is packed with historic monuments, cultural events, and genuine local life. With a busy harbor and a large university population, the city is active year-round.

In the heart of Faro is the picturesque, well-preserved Old Town, adjacent to the city's bustling main shopping street, the genteel Rua de Santo António, with cafés and restaurants. The Old Town, shopping street, and harbor are within walking distance of Faro's most popular hotels.

Fringing Faro's shoreline is the Ria Formosa Natural Park, a protected coastal lagoon that can be explored by regular boat trips that depart from various points. Head to Faro Island or Armona Island (off nearby Olhão) for a day at the beach or take a day trip to one of the nearby quaint rural villages, such as Estoi or São Brás de Alportel.

SIGHTS
★ Old Town
(Cidade Velha)

Just off the harbor front is Faro's **Historic Area (Zona Histórica),** more commonly called the **Old Town (Cidade Velha).** Encircled by Moorish stone walls, Faro's Old Town is a maze of cobbled streets with historic buildings, mostly dating from the 16th-17th centuries. It's accessed through the 1812 **Arco da Vila** gateway, an ornate monumental archway in the center of downtown.

At the heart of the historic center is the spacious **Sé Square (Largo da Sé),** an open, orange tree-dotted square that is an oasis of calm in a bustling city. This part of town is best explored on foot.

FARO CATHEDRAL
(Sé de Faro)

The centerpiece in this quarter is the Roman Catholic **Faro Cathedral** (Largo da Sé 11, tel. 289 823 018, 10am-5:30pm Mon-Sat, mass Sun, €3), a hodgepodge of architectural styles thanks to successive renovations and extensions over the centuries. The modest cathedral was erected in 1251 on the ruins of

Faro

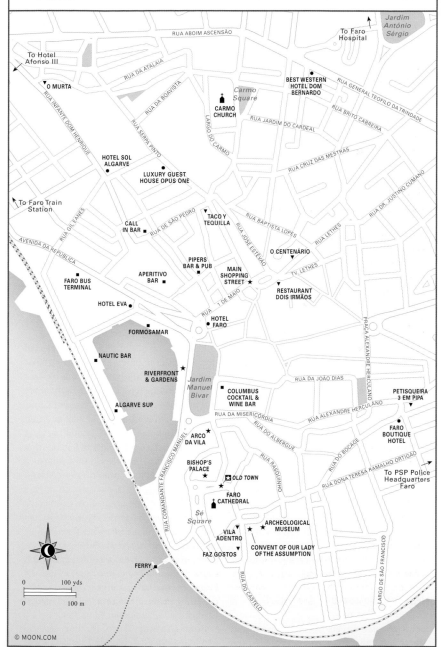

RUA ABOIM ASCENSÃO

To Faro
Hospital

Jardim
António
Sérgio

To Hotel
Afonso III

O MURTA

RUA DA ATALAIA

RUA DA BOAVISTA

Carmo
Square

BEST WESTERN
HOTEL DOM
BERNARDO

RUA GENERAL TEOFILO DA TRINDADE

CARMO
CHURCH

RUA JARDIM DO CARDEAL

RUA BRITO CABREIRA

LARGO DO CARMO

RUA SERPA PINTO

RUA INFANTE DOM HENRIQUE

HOTEL SOL
ALGARVE

RUA CRUZ DAS MESTRAS

LUXURY GUEST
HOUSE OPUS ONE

To Faro Train
Station

RUA GIL EANES

TACO Y
TEQUILLA

RUA DE SÃO PEDRO

RUA BAPTISTA LOPES

RUA DR. JUSTINO CUMANO

CALL
IN BAR

RUA JOSÉ ESTEVÃO

RUA LETHES

AVENIDA DA REPUBLICA

O CENTENÁRIO

RUA LETHES

PIPERS
BAR & PUB

TV. LETHES

APERITIVO
BAR

MAIN
SHOPPING
STREET ★

FARO BUS
TERMINAL

RESTAURANT
DOIS IRMÃOS

HOTEL EVA

RUA 1 DE MAIO

HOTEL
FARO

FORMOSAMAR

PRAÇA ALEXANDRE HERCULANO

NAUTIC BAR

RIVERFRONT
& GARDENS ★

Jardim
Manuel
Bivar

RUA DA JOÃO DIAS

ALGARVE SUP

COLUMBUS
COCKTAIL &
WINE BAR

PETISQUEIRA
3 EM PIPA

RUA ALEXANDRE HERCULANO

RUA DA MISERICORDIA

RUA DO ALBERGUE

FARO
BOUTIQUE
HOTEL

RUA COMANDANTE FRANCISCO MANUEL

ARCO
DA VILA ★

BISHOP'S
PALACE ★

RUA DO BOCAGE

RUA RASQUINHO

RUA DONA TERESA RAMALHO ORTIGÃO

OLD TOWN

To PSP Police
Headquarters
Faro

FARO
CATHEDRAL

Sé
Square

ARCHEOLOGICAL
MUSEUM

VILA
ADENTRO

CONVENT OF OUR LADY
OF THE ASSUMPTION

FAZ GOSTOS

LARGO DE SÃO FRANCISCO

FERRY

RUA DO CASTELO

0   100 yds

0   100 m

© MOON.COM

a 13th-century mosque from the Arab occupation of Portugal. The cathedral's exterior has predominantly Romanesque, Gothic, and Renaissance features. Inside are a four-nave church, a Gothic chapel, a presbytery, a museum of sacred art, a remarkable red organ decorated with Chinese motifs, and a narrow staircase that climbs to the top of a medieval tower that has stunning views over the Old Town and the Ria Formosa.

BISHOP'S PALACE
(Paço Episcopal)

The long, low, whitewashed **Bishop's Palace** (Largo da Sé 15, tel. 289 894 040 or 289 823 018) dates to the 16th century. Like many buildings throughout Portugal, it was rebuilt after the 1755 earthquake. The simple building comprises rooms clad in fabulous late-18th century azulejo plaques; of note is the azulejo-clad staircase. The building is still the official residence of the Bishop of Faro; it's open to visitors sporadically for art exhibitions (or if a request is made in advance).

CONVENT OF OUR LADY OF THE ASSUMPTION
(Convento da Nossa Senhora da Assunção)

The **Convent of Our Lady of the Assumption** (Praça Dom Afonso III, tel. 289 870 829) is an elegant national monument that was commissioned in 1519 by Queen Leonor. Its distinguishing features include a two-story Renaissance cloister and a Manueline church with a baroque dome. Since 1973 it has housed the **Faro Municipal Museum (Museu Municipal de Faro)** (Praça Dom Afonso III 14, tel. 289 870 827, 10am-7pm Tues-Fri, 11:30am-6pm Sat-Sun summer, 10am-6pm Tues-Fri, 10:30am-5pm Sat-Sun winter, €2), which includes tombstones, mosaics, and 17th- and 18th-century sacred art.

Carmo Square
(Largo do Carmo)

Set back a few streets from the harbor and north of downtown is **Carmo Square** (Largo do Carmo), opposite Faro's central post office and home to the striking **Carmo Church** (Largo do Carmo, tel. 289 824 490, 9am-5pm Mon-Fri, 9am-1pm Sat Oct-Mar, 9am-6pm Mon-Fri, 9am-1pm Sat Apr-Sept, mass on Sun and holy days 9am, €1), a fine example of baroque architecture that has a simple, quadrangular facade, two distinctive bell towers with resident storks, and elaborate gilded woodwork. Though the church is lovely, most people visit this part of town to see a different attraction: a chilling **Chapel of Bones (Capela dos Ossos)** (tel. 289 824 490, 10am-1pm and 3pm-5pm Mon-Fri, 10am-1pm Sat, €1), of which there are only a handful in Portugal. The bones and skulls in the small chapel are said to be those of Carmelite monks exhumed from a nearby cemetery, displayed to exemplify the brevity of life. It's morbid but fascinating. The chapel is set in a garden area just behind the church.

TOP EXPERIENCE

★ Ria Formosa Natural Park
(Parque Natural da Ria Formosa)

The Ria Formosa Natural Park is a protected stretch of sandy barrier islands, swirly lagoon-like canals, and reedy marshlands that stretch 60 kilometers (37 mi) along the shore of the eastern Algarve, off the coast of Loulé, Faro, Olhão, Tavira, and Vila Real de Santo António. In total it spans 18,000 hectares (44,480 acres) in a patchwork of habitats that include marshes, tidal flats, dunes, salt pans, freshwater lagoons, agricultural areas, and woodlands. The Ria Formosa is an important wetland for migrating birds, making it a popular bird-watching spot. Nearly 80 percent of Portuguese clam exports are farmed at its shellfish nurseries. The Ria Formosa's diverse ecosystems are home to a wealth of flora and fauna, including endangered species like the European chameleon, a large seahorse population, the rare purple swamp hen, and turtles. Farther out, dolphins can be spotted.

Formosamar (Faro Harbor, Av. da República, Stand 1, tel. 918 720 002, www.

formosamar.com) specializes in exploring the Ria Formosa with ecofriendly guided boating, kayaking, biking, hiking, bird-watching, dolphin-spotting, and fishing trips. Guides speak English and Formosamar operates year-round, although certain activities are weather-dependent. Some activities, such as kayaking (from €30 for 2.5 hours) and cycling (from €6 for 1 hour), can be done independently. Marine wildlife-watching tours (2 hours, Mar-Oct, €45) depart regularly from Faro and Olhão.

Faro Island
(Ilha de Faro)

Stretching 5 kilometers (3 mi), Faro Island, formally known as the Ancão Peninsula, is the westernmost tip of the Ria Formosa in Faro, just behind Faro airport, where you'll find Faro's main beach, the family-friendly **Praia de Faro,** with long and uninterrupted soft golden sand. The water is clean but cold, and the waves can be strong.

The western end is home to a traditional fishing community with typical huts and boats, and the central and eastern end is a holiday-home hot spot among Portuguese. Praia de Faro spans the island, and one long road runs its length, with more deserted beaches at either end.

The island is livelier in summer thanks to its bars, restaurants, and holiday homes, but this means it gets crowded, and parking is limited.

Clube de Surf de Faro (Av. Nascente 107, tel. 963 417 671) provides lessons and rents out boards. Kayaks and stand-up paddleboards can also be hired from the **Faro Beach Nautical Center** (Av. Nascente 25, tel. 289 870 898).

Faro Island is attached to the mainland by a narrow single-lane bridge. In high season there is significant traffic congestion and long queues. Bus 16 (€2.20), operated by Faro's **Próximo** (www.proximo.pt) service, runs every 30-40 minutes between the main bus terminal on Faro city center's harbor-side, the airport, and Faro Island. The bus doesn't cross the bridge to Faro Island; passengers must walk. This is fine to access the central part of the island and its beach, but it's a bit of a walk to the extremities. A taxi between Faro and Faro Island costs around €15.

FOOD

Faro has a multitude of restaurants and cafés that are first-rate without being flashy or overpriced. Thanks to its student population, Faro is also home to more international fare, as well as affordable fast food and trendy wine and cocktail bars.

Portuguese

For real character and typical Algarve fare, visit ★ **Restaurant Dois Irmãos** (Praça Ferreira de Almeida 15, tel. 289 823 337, www.restaurantedoisirmaos.com, 10am-11pm daily, €20), where local cuisine meshes with traditional gastronomy. Founded in 1925, it is the oldest restaurant in Faro and one of the oldest in the country. With rustic wooden-beam ceilings and brick arches inside and a leaf-covered courtyard in back, it has an extensive menu of fresh seafood and a good selection of meat and vegetarian dishes. Specialties include codfish *cataplana* (stew) and baby goat.

At beautiful, elegant **Vila Adentro** (Praça do Afonso III 17, tel. 289 052 173, 9am-midnight daily, €15), regional delicacies and traditional flavors are served with panache. In a historic building in the Old Town, the restaurant is a former art gallery clad with hand-painted tile plaques, but brightly-laid tables and clean lines give it a contemporary touch. When the weather is warm, enjoy a romantic street-side table.

Seafood

Exposed brick arches and dark wood tables and chairs give **O Centenário** (Largo do Terreiro do Bispo 4-6, tel. 289 823 343, www.restaurantecentenario.business.site, noon-3:30pm and 6pm-11pm daily, €12) seafood restaurant a warm and cozy feel, and the grub is simply divine—an ocean's worth of fresh seafood, including local and Algarvian specialties.

O Murta (Rua Infante Dom Henrique 136, tel. 289 823 480 or 933 923 606, noon-3:30pm and 7:30pm-10:30pm Mon-Sat, €15) has a vast range of unusual seafood dishes, such as *piripiri* codfish, seafood *açorda* (a soupy bread dish), and gray triggerfish pasta. This small, simple restaurant also has a decent selection of meat dishes.

Tapas

A stone's throw from the Faro Boutique Hotel, **Petisqueira 3 em Pipa** (Rua Brites de Almeida 24, tel. 914 841 090, noon-3pm and 7pm-midnight Mon-Fri, 7pm-midnight Sat, €8) is a charming, laid-back little restaurant with a tiled facade and floor. *Petiscar* loosely means "to snack" or "to nibble," here meaning delicious tapas like sweet-potato fries, miniburgers made from *farinheira* (a Portuguese sausage), and excellent homemade desserts.

Fine Dining

Located in Faro's Old Town, **Faz Gostos** (Rua do Castelo, 13, tel. 289 878 422, www.fazgostos.com, noon-3pm and 7:30pm-11pm Mon-Fri, 7:30pm-11pm Sat-Sun, €20) is classy, polished, and Michelin-listed, with rich flavors of Portuguese gastronomy cleverly complemented by international cuisine. Intriguing mains include partridge and mushroom duxelles pies served with tropical salad.

Mexican

Warm and colorful little **Taco y Tequilla** (Rua Filipe Alistão 75, tel. 289 821 844, www.tacoytequilla.pt, 7:30pm-midnight daily, €10) in Faro city center serves authentic Mexican food and is as lively as the art on the walls. Offerings include tacos, fajitas, and burritos, plus tequila shots. There are great vegetarian options, and dining here is a true fiesta.

Snacks

On Faro Island, right on the beach, **Cais 73** (Av. Nascente 25, tel. 289 037 273, 9:30am-midnight daily, €8), near the campground, is a sand-floored café with surfboards on the walls; its giant toasted sandwiches are legendary. Be warned—they are huge, enough for two people. Recently renovated, reborn from the famous O Forte café, it is a great place for a light bite on Faro Island.

ENTERTAINMENT AND EVENTS

Nightlife

Given its size, Faro has a relatively compact nightlife scene, but it's energetic and varied thanks to the city's thriving student population. Most bars are along the streets adjacent to the harbor.

A popular hangout is elegant cocktail lounge **Columbus Wine & Cocktail Bar** (Praça Dom Francisco Gomes, tel. 917 776 222, www.barcolumbus.pt, noon-4am daily), just off the riverside Manuel Bívar garden. Intriguingly set within the arcade of a 16th-century hospital, it has an impressive vaulted brick ceiling and stunning chandeliers. They say there's an Irish pub in every city, and Faro has a good one in **Pipers Irish Pub** (Rua do Prior 28, tel. 917 696 643, 5pm-4am daily). Expect a great warm welcome, live music, sports on TV, and the obligatory Guinness.

At contemporary **Aperitivo Bar** (Rua Conselheiro Bivar 51, tel. 965 410 620, www.aperitivobar.pt, 6pm-2am daily), fashionable drinks are accompanied by tapas. A popular, modern after-work meeting place, it has fabulous cocktails, an extensive wine list, and even a chic cigar room. Classy **Nautic Bar** (Doca de Faro, tel. 289 090 818, 10am-2am daily) on Faro harbor is a relaxing place to enjoy a drink and people-watching. It's perfect for a coffee or a cocktail and has a chill-out lounge vibe.

Festivals and Events

FARO BIKE MEET

The annual **Faro Bike Meet** (www.motoclubefaro.pt, mid-July) is one of Europe's largest gatherings of motorcycle enthusiasts and one of the biggest events of the Algarve

---

1: Faro Marina; **2:** *cataplana*, a seafood stew; **3:** Faro Cathedral; **4:** boating in the Ria Formosa Natural Park

summer, drawing thousands of leather-clad bikers from all over. Held on the outskirts of the city near the airport, over four days in mid-July, it is open to all, welcoming as many curious nonbikers as bikers. The large plot of pine-studded land becomes a makeshift town with campsites, a crafts market, food stalls, and a stage for nightly concerts and colorful entertainment. On the last day, always Sunday, participants mount their motorcycles and rumble through Faro in procession. The locals come out to wave their annual visitors off on their journeys home.

RECREATION

Catamaran Tours

Catamaran tours depart from the Faro quayside to explore the Ria Formosa, starting from €10, including the popular Four Islands Ria Formosa tour (4 hours, twice daily, from €30) by **Estrela da Ria Formosa** (Faro Marina, in front of McDonald's, tel. 961 129 977, www.estreladariaformosa.com), a best-seller. Relax in a comfortable modern catamaran to sail the natural beauty of Armona, Culatra, Deserta, and Farol islands. Tours are given in several languages, including English.

Stand-Up Paddleboarding (SUP)

Glide along the peaceful waters of the Ria Formosa Natural Park or discover the dramatic cliffs, caves, and grottoes of the Algarve coast from a unique vantage point. **Zen SUP** (tel. 936 735 778, www.zen-sup.com) organizes daily tours (2 hours, 3 times daily, €40) accompanied by a trained English-speaking SUP guide. Ria Formosa tours leave from Faro Marina, and coastal tours are subject to weather conditions.

ACCOMMODATIONS

Although not one of the Algarve's busiest resorts, Faro has lodgings to suit various budgets, most within walking distance of the main bus and train terminals. The city has some of the Algarve's better hostels and budget hotels, as well as strong mid-range hotels.

Excellently located in the heart of Faro, right on the marina, the 134-room, four-star **Hotel Eva** (Av. da República 1, tel. 289 001 000, www.ap-hotelsresorts.com, €142) offers reasonably-priced rooms walking distance to most attractions. One of Faro's largest and most popular hotels for business and tourism, it has magnificent waterfront views and is adjacent to the bus terminal.

Overlooking Old Town and the Ria Formosa, modern ★ **Hotel Faro** (Praça Dom Francisco Gomes 2, tel. 289 830 830, www.hotelfaro.pt, 4-night minimum, €171) boasts a prime location on the doorstep of the main shopping street, Rua do Santo António. Wi-Fi is included in the rates, and a rooftop pool and restaurant afford panoramic views.

Decent, affordable two-star **Hotel Afonso III** (Rua Miguel Bombarda 64, tel. 289 803 542, www.hotelafonso.pt, €80), 10 minutes from the airport, is near Faro's main train and bus terminals. Around half of the 41 rooms have been refurbished as part of a gradual overhaul. Rooms are basic but clean.

Standard chain hotel **Best Western Hotel Dom Bernardo** (Rua General Teofilo da Trindade 20, tel. 289 889 800, www.bestwestern.pt, €109) is in the heart of Faro overlooking Carmo Square and the church. Modern amenities include free Wi-Fi, and it is good value for money.

In downtown Faro, just a stroll from the harbor and Arco da Vila, **Faro Boutique Hotel** (Rua do Bocage 66, tel. 289 037 300, www.faroboutiquehotel.pt, €123) is bright, modern, and comfortable. Rooms are sound-proofed but small; some have balconies. Prices are reasonable for the location. The rooftop terrace is a great place for a sunset drink.

Family-run, two-star budget **Hotel Sol Algarve** (Rua Infante Dom Henrique 52, tel. 289 895 700, www.hotelsolalgarve.com, €100) is in a central older part of town near the train station. Clean and tidy, it has 38 well-equipped rooms with air-conditioning, en suite baths, TVs, phones, and free Wi-Fi.

As the name indicates, **Luxury Guest House Opus One** (Rua Serpa Pinto 37, tel.

919 503 239, www.guesthouseluxury.com, €155) is a little oasis of luxury in the heart of the Algarve's busiest city. This converted town house in Old Town has a pool and lavish touches like plush rugs and velvety throws.

INFORMATION AND SERVICES

Faro PSP police station: Rua da Polícia de Segurança Pública 32, tel. 289 899 899, www.psp.pt

Main tourist office: Av. 5 de Outubro 18-20, tel. 289 800 400, www.visitalgarve.pt, 9am-12:30pm and 2pm-5:30pm Mon-Fri

Main post office: Largo do Carmo, tel. 289 892 590

Faro State Hospital (Hospital de Faro): Rua Leao Penedo, tel. 289 891 100

Faro Private Hospital (Hospital Particular do Algarve-Gambelas): Urbanização Casal de Gambelas, Lote 2, Gambelas, tel. 707 282 828, www.grupohpa.com

GETTING THERE
Air

Fly to **Faro International Airport** (FAO; tel. 289 800 800, www.aeroportofaro.pt) on daily domestic routes from Lisbon or Porto with TAP or low-cost Ryanair. Flights from Lisbon take 45 minutes; from Porto, an hour. European carriers from France, Belgium, Germany, the Netherlands, and the United Kingdom operate daily routes to Faro. The airport is 7 kilometers (4.3 mi) southwest of the center.

Regular bus line 16 (20 minutes, every 30 minutes, €2.25), between Faro's main bus terminal and the airport, is operated by **Próximo** (www.proximo.pt), leaving the airport from outside the arrivals area. Bright yellow signs indicate where to catch it. Buy tickets from the driver.

A taxi ride from the airport into the city costs €10-12.

Bus

Buses run to Faro from most Portuguese cities, including **Rede Expressos** (tel. 213 581 460, www.rede-expressos.pt) buses from Lisbon (3 hours, under €40 round-trip). There are services to Faro from Porto (7-8 hours, from €30 one-way) with Rede Expressos, but most will require a change at Lisbon's Sete Rios station.

The main bus company in the Algarve is **Eva** (tel. 289 899 760, www.eva-bus.com), for travel around the Algarve and to other regions. An express Eva bus, the **Transrápido** (tel. 289 899 760, www.eva-bus.com), runs every few hours on weekdays, twice a day on weekends, between Lagos (western Algarve) and Faro bus terminal (2 hours, under €10 one-way), with stops at Portimão and Albufeira.

Faro has a large **bus terminal** (Av. da República 5, tel. 289 899 760 or 289 899 740, 6am-11pm Mon-Fri, 7am-11pm Sat-Sun) in the heart of the city.

Train

Faro is linked to other Algarve towns by the Algarve Line, but be aware that the train station can be quite a way from the town center in some towns.

CP (tel. 707 210 220, www.cp.pt) operates slower Intercity and high-speed Alfa-Pendular trains. The Alfa Pendular train (3 hours, 2nd class €22.60, 1st class €30.30 one-way) runs twice a day between Faro and Lisbon (Oriente, Santa Apolónia, and Entrecampos stations); the Intercity train (3.5 hours, 2nd class €21.60, 1st class €28.30 one-way) runs three times a day. Between Faro and Porto-Campanhã, there are five daily Alfa-Pendular trains (6 hours, 2nd class €52.30, 1st class €71.80) and Intercity trains (6.5 hours, 2nd class €42.40, 1st class €58.60).

Faro train station (Largo da Estação dos Caminhos de Ferro, tel. 289 830 150, 6:20am-10pm daily) is 300 meters (0.2 mi) west of the city's main bus terminal.

Car

Driving to Faro from outside the Algarve is easy on the A2 motorway from Lisbon. Faro is 280 kilometers (175 mi) southeast of

Lisbon, a 2.75-hour drive. From Spain, cross the Guadiana International Bridge and take the east-west A22-Via do Infante motorway.

Be warned: The roads in and around Faro get busy, especially at rush hour—early morning and late afternoon-early evening.

GETTING AROUND

Most attractions in Faro are in the city center and can be explored on foot. Neighboring places of interest, such as the villages of Estoi and São Brás, are a short drive or bus ride away.

Bus

An easy, reliable, no-frills way of getting around Faro is **Próximo** (tel. 289 899 760, www.proximo.pt) line 16, which continuously zips around the city's busiest spots. Tickets (€0.80-2.30) can be bought on board. Daily tickets are also available.

Taxi

Taxis ranks are at the airport, train station, main bus terminal, along the harbor-side, and in the city center. **Táxis Antral de Faro** (tel. 289 827 203) is one of the city's main companies.

Tourist Train

For a novel way to see Faro in a short time, jump on the **Delgaturis tourist train** (tel. 289 389 067, www.delgaturis.com, 10am-6pm daily Oct-May, 10am-9pm daily June-Sept, €3), which starts and finishes at the city's main harbor-front gardens, the Jardim Manuel Bívar. This ride lasts 45 minutes, departing hourly.

Car

Faro airport is a hub for car rental companies, or ask at your hotel. Rental companies with desks at the airport include **Goldcar** (tel. 707 504 070, www.goldcar.es), **Europcar** (tel. 289 818 316, www.europcar.com), and **Avis** (tel. 289 810 120, www.avis.com.pt).

Driving in Faro is straightforward, but roads can be very busy during rush hours, and the old cobblestone streets in the city center are narrow in places.

Expect to pay for parking in the downtown and city center. There are free car parks on the outskirts of town—one of the best is São Francisco Square, on the eastern side of the Old Town, a short stroll from the main downtown area.

ESTOI

Nestled in the foothills of the Caldeirão mountain range, 10 kilometers (6.2 mi) north of Faro, the pretty little town of Estoi (ESH-toy) makes a pleasant day trip. Main attractions include the stunning Estoi Palace and its decorative gardens, and the Milreu Roman Ruins, physically close but set apart by two millennia.

Sights

ESTOI PALACE
(Palácio de Estoi)

A 19th-century palace once home to the wealthy Viscount of Estói, José Francisco da Silva, and his family, **Estoi Palace** (Rua de São Jose) is today a luxury boutique hotel, the **Pousada Palácio de Estoi** (tel. 210 407 620, www.pousadas.pt, €297 d). Painted a bold pink, it boasts neoclassical architecture with neo-baroque and neo-rococo features and exquisite French-inspired gardens that roll out grandly in front of the statuesque main building. These fabulous gardens are dotted with statues, busts, and fountains, as well as two ornamental tea pavilions that have been carefully restored to their original 19th-century splendor. The Versailles-style gardens are open to the public and are worth a visit. Enjoy a refined afternoon tea.

MILREU ROMAN RUINS

On the outskirts of the village, 2 kilometers (1.2 mi) west of Estoi Palace, the **Milreu Roman Ruins** (tel. 289 997 823, 10:30am-1pm and 2pm-6:30pm Tues-Sun May-Sept, 9:30am-1pm and 2pm-5pm Tues-Sun Oct-Apr, €2) are remnants of one of the first settlements in the Algarve. Uncovered in 1877, the site dates to the 1st-2nd centuries AD. The ruins of a luxurious villa, Roman baths with columns and wall mosaics depicting fish, and a temple are highlights. It has a small museum (included in entry cost) at the entrance to the site that offers information on the ruins as well as a small-scale model of the temple. Last admission is 30 minutes before closing time.

Getting There

Estoi is a 10-minute drive inland from the coast, 10 kilometers (6.2 mi) north of Faro. By car from Faro, take the N2 road and turn onto the N2-6.

Eva (tel. 289 899 760, www.eva-bus.com) buses run regularly from Faro's main terminal to Estoi. Line 65 departs hourly on weekdays, increasing in frequency between noon and 7pm, and take around 25 minutes to Estoi. Buses leave every few hours on weekends. A one-way ticket costs €3.35.

SÃO BRÁS DE ALPORTEL

Like much of the Algarve, São Brás de Alportel (sown BRAZH dee al-por-TEL) was originally a Roman settlement; more recently it was a thriving cork producer. Today it is a bustling suburb a short drive north of Faro,

with an interesting mix of whitewashed cottages and grand old merchants' houses from the 19th-century cork era.

Sights

Tour the **NovoCortiça Cork Factory** (Parque Industrial da Barracha, tel. 289 840 150, www.novacortica.pt, 9am-5pm Mon-Fri, tours €12.50), in São Brás's industrial park, to see how cork is transformed from the bark of a tree into useful and fashionable products, and learn more about the importance of the cork industry. This is an excellent option for a rainy day. Tours of this working cork factory take around 1.5 hours and can be conducted in English. Tours must be booked in advance.

Picturesque **Fonte Férrea** (24 hours daily) spring and picnic area is shaded by trees and has a lovely café selling drinks and snacks. Take a refreshing dip in the iron-rich spring waters in summer. Fonte Férrea is 30 minutes' drive north of Faro by car on the N2 road to São Brás de Alportel, through São Brás and north another five minutes. Free parking is available at the site. **Eva** (tel. 289 899 760, www.eva-bus.com) bus lines 65 or 66 depart regularly from Faro's main terminal to São Brás de Alportel. From São Brás, take a taxi (10 minutes, €8).

Estoi Palace

Getting There

São Brás de Alportel is 18 kilometers (11.2 mi) north of Faro, a 25-minute drive, and 10 kilometers (6.2 mi) north of Estoi, a 12-minute drive. By car from Faro, follow the N2 road. São Brás is a 40-minute bus ride from Faro. **Eva** (www.eva-bus.com) bus lines 65 and 66 run every 1-2 hours on weekdays and every few hours on weekends and holidays between Faro and São Brás de Alportel, line 65 via Estoi and line 66 via the little village of Santa Bárbara de Nexe. A one-way ticket costs €4.25.

OLHÃO

East of Faro, Olhão (ohl-YOWN) is a down-to-earth fishing town, home to the Algarve's largest fishing port and known for its August seafood festival. Bursting with Moorish character, Olhão has a unique architecture of North African-inspired cubic whitewashed houses and narrow streets, influences that seeped in through the city's fishing and trading activities with Africa. It also has a thriving market and cool, leafy public riverside gardens, not to mention the highlight, Armona Island.

Armona Island
(Ilha da Armona)

Just off Olhão's coast is **Armona Island,** one of the barrier islands that make up the Ria Formosa protected wetlands. This vast pile of sand in the calm, shallow *ria* is considered Olhão's main beach and is hugely popular. Nine kilometers (5.6 mi) long and up to 1 kilometer (0.6 mi) wide, the island has a tiny year-round residential community of fisherfolk. A visit to Armona can offer a deserted-island experience—if you overlook the colorful fishing boats that dot the shoreline and the tons of other visitors in summer. The island is for pedestrians only, and all forms of motor transport are prohibited.

In the busier summer months, the island buzzes with water sports and has all necessary facilities for a relaxing day at the beach, including bars and restaurants, a kid's playground, toilets, sun beds, a mini-market, and even holiday chalets.

Ferries (under €4 round-trip) depart hourly from Olhão harbor and take 15 minutes to reach Armona Island. From arrival it is another 15-minute walk to the main beach area.

Entertainment and Events
OLHÃO SEAFOOD FESTIVAL
(Festival do Marisco)

The annual **Olhão Seafood Festival** (www.festivaldomarisco.com, Aug) is a celebration of seafood, with many delicacies, freshly caught and prepared to traditional and innovative recipes, sold from busy food stands at the festival's waterfront location. Now one of the main summer attractions in the Algarve and the biggest of its kind in Europe, the festival is held around the second week in August for several days. It usually takes place in the **Jardim Pescador Olhanense** (Av. 5 de Outubro) gardens on the waterfront from around 7:30pm until 1:30am, with live concerts by popular artists every night.

Recreation

There is relatively little to do in this part of the Algarve except to enjoy the coast, including trips to the Ria Formosa Natural Park. **Formosamar** (tel. 918 720 002, www.formosamar.com), which also operates in Faro and Tavira, runs Ria Formosa wildlife-watching boat tours that depart from Olhão Marina and popular bird-watching boat tours (2.5 hours, adults €35, children €17). Local **Passeios Ria Formosa** (tel. 962 156 922, www.passeios-ria-formosa.com) also offers regular boat tours to the Ria Formosa, ranging from simple sightseeing cruises of the islands with a stop at a deserted beach (1 hour, €12.50) to dolphin-watching (2-5 hours, €30) and bird-watching trips (2 hours, €25). Passeios Ria Formosa has a land-based guided tour in English of Olhão Market and town center (2 hours, €25) and runs aqua taxis among the Ria's islands and rents out boats, kayaks, and fishing equipment.

Getting There

Olhão is 10 kilometers (6.2 mi) east of Faro, a 20-minute drive via the N125 road. Buses and trains run regularly from Faro. **Eva** (tel. 289 899 760, www.eva-bus.com) buses run every 20 minutes or so from Faro's main bus terminal

to Olhão's bus terminal (20 minutes, €3.25), located in the city center a short stroll to the waterfront.

A cheaper and quicker way to get to Olhão from Faro is by train. **CP** (tel. 707 210 220, www.cp.pt) trains run hourly between Faro and Olhão (10 minutes, €1.45). Olhão's train station is within the city center, walking distance to the waterfront.

109

Loulé and the Golden Triangle

THE ALGARVE
LOULÉ AND THE GOLDEN TRIANGLE

A bustling traditional market town and a large inland residential area, Loulé (LOO-lay) is an attractive city rich in Moorish heritage, with cobblestone streets and petite squares. Known for its markets—Loulé was a major trade center in medieval times—the city is also famous as home to one of the biggest and oldest Carnival parades in Portugal.

South of Loulé is the Golden Triangle, the Algarve's most affluent and prestigious area, with luxury hotels, Michelin-starred restaurants, and pricey real estate. The exclusive coastal resorts of **Quinta do Lago** and **Vale do Lobo** attract the rich and famous. Farther west is the self-contained, privately owned upscale resort of **Vilamoura.**

Halfway between Loulé and the coastline, bisected by the busy N125 regional road, **Almancil** is a bustling, untouristy town with a choice of good restaurants.

SIGHTS
Loulé Castle
(Castelo de Loulé)

Loulé Castle (Rua Dom Paio Peres Correia 17, tel. 289 400 642, www.cm-loule.pt, 10am-1:30pm and 2pm-6pm Tues-Fri, 10am-1:30pm and 2pm-4:30pm Sat, €1.62) is today an important national monument and one of the city's main attractions. Loulé Castle is unusual in that it has become a part of the city's core: The castle's walls and towers have been incorporated into local buildings.

Built on the site of Roman fortifications, the Moorish castle was expanded in the 13th century under King Afonso III. The remains of the castle comprise four towers and the walls that link them. The views over Loulé's old town from the top of the towers are well worth the small entry fee.

The **Loulé Municipal Museum (Museu Municipal Loulé)** (tel. 289 400 885, www.museudeloule.pt, included with castle entry) is also within the castle, among its towers and patios. The museum includes areas dedicated to traditional local gastronomy and fruit drying.

It is free to visit the castle's courtyard, where visitors can see impressive medieval siege artillery.

Shrine of Our Lady of Piety
(Santuário de Nossa Senhora da Piedade)

From afar, the unusually shaped **Shrine of Our Lady of Piety** (9:30am-12:30pm and 2pm-6pm Mon-Fri summer, 9:30am-12:30pm and 2pm-5pm Mon-Fri winter, free), 2 kilometers (1.2 mi) west of Loulé center along the N270 road, looks like a futuristic spaceship. The sanctuary is an important Marian shrine and hosts "the largest religious celebrations south of Fátima." The interior is mostly made of wood and has an eerie candle room. There is also a small chapel at the site, believed to be around 300 years old, with a baroque altar and lovely frescoes.

Loulé and the Golden Triangle

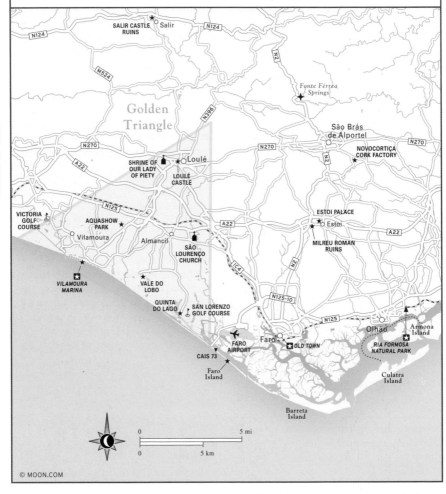

The views from the hilltop shrine are superb. The walk from Loulé takes 25 minutes, although it is strenuous, with a climb up a steep cobbled hill. A taxi from Loulé costs around €5; taxis can be found parked in the city center.

Salir Castle Ruins
(Ruinas do Castelo de Salir)

On a rural hilltop in the quaint hamlet of Salir, 16 kilometers (9.9 mi) north of Loulé, with the Caldeirão mountain range as a backdrop, the 12th-century Moorish **Salir Castle Ruins** (tel. 289 489 119, www.salir.pt, 9am-5pm Mon-Fri, free) were part of coastal defenses in the southern Algarve during the Christian reconquests.

A legend claims that the village of Salir and the castle are named for the daughter of Moorish governor Aben-Fabilla. The governor is said to have vanished when the Christians invaded, leaving behind a stash of gold and his daughter, who had insisted on staying in the castle. The young woman was turned into a stone statue by the mystical hand of her father to save her from the invaders.

There's not much left of the castle today, except some walls and scattered ruins. A small on-site museum has a glass floor so you can see the archaeological dig beneath it. A contemporary viewing platform provides 360-degree views of the countryside. This sight is well off the beaten track but worth a visit.

By car, Salir is a 20-minute drive north of Loulé along the M525 road. **Eva** (tel. 289 899 760, www.eva-bus.com) buses run every couple of hours from Loulé bus station to Freixo Verde, via Salir. Tickets for the 30-minute journey cost €2.55 one-way.

FOOD

From the outside, **O Beco (The Alley)** (Av. 25 de Abril, tel. 289 462 980, noon-3pm and 7pm-9pm Mon-Sat, €8) looks like a hole-in-the-wall with a café awning. Inside, the no-frills theme continues with basic paper tablecloths and a simple room with a high, dark-wood ceiling. Platters are piled with unfussy, tasty Portuguese food like fresh grilled fish and pork with clams. Located just off the main street, O Beco is also one of the oldest restaurants in town, a testament to its popularity among locals.

In the city center, **Bocage** (Rua Bocage 14, tel. 289 412 416 or 914 011 482, www.restaurantebocage.com, noon-3pm and 6:30pm-10pm daily, €10) is a little corner cottage popular for its traditional Algarvian cuisine, using fresh local products. Specialties include stewed rabbit, Portuguese-style pork, and tuna steak in onions.

ENTERTAINMENT AND EVENTS
Loulé Med Festival

Every year, Loulé hosts one of the country's biggest world music festivals, the **Med Festival** (www.festivalmed.pt, end of June), a four-day event with concerts around the city. Loulé transforms into a buzzing hive of Mediterranean food and culture with music from around the globe.

Carnival

Loulé's **Carnival** celebration (www.cm-loule.pt, Feb or early Mar) is the oldest and one of the most famous in the country, attracting huge crowds for samba-fueled festivities. Not quite as racy as Carnival in Brazil, Portugal's version satirizes political affairs. The allegorical floats usually feature huge papier-mâché puppets and heads parodying government leaders and sports stars. It is nonetheless a vibrant, energetic, exciting affair that goes on for three days, with parades and dancing in the streets. Loulé's main parades take place along the city's central José da Costa Mealha Avenue, which is closed off to the public; spectators must buy a ticket (€2) to enter the main parade area.

SHOPPING

Along with its famous markets, Loulé has quirky galleries and an array of arts and crafts shops. To buy local produce, head to the municipal market. For traditional handicrafts, venture off the main street and into the backstreets around the castle and city center.

Loulé Municipal Market
(Mercado Municipal de Loulé)

With striking red domes and Moorish architecture, **Loulé Municipal Market** (Rua José Fernandes Guerreiro 34, tel. 289 400 600, www.lcglobal.pt, 6am-3pm Mon-Sat) looks more Arab than Portuguese. Inaugurated in 1908, the atmospheric building is busy with vendors selling fresh local produce, jams, preserves, and oils. Stock up on artisanal specialties like cured meats, smoked sausages and cheeses, fresh bread, Algarve liqueurs, and local sweets made from figs and almonds. There are also stalls selling lovely handmade Loulé tablecloths, crocheted items, and cork products. A traditional outdoor farmer's market takes place every Saturday morning, adjacent to the municipal market.

Loulé Weekly Market
(Mercado Semanal de Loulé)

Haggle for a bargain at one of the most famous weekly markets in the Algarve. Held every Saturday morning in front of the Santo António Convent, on the road out of Loulé toward Boliqueime-Albufeira, the **Loulé Weekly Market** (Rua da Nossa Senhora da Piedade, 8am-1pm Sat) is packed with clothes, handbags, shoes, and sunglasses as well as regional merchandise by local artisans such as cork items and pottery.

ACCOMMODATIONS

Converted from an early-20th-century residence, the stately **Hotel Loulé Jardim** (Praça Manuel de Arriaga 25, tel. 289 413 094, www. loulejardimhotel.com, €119) is in the older part of Loulé, facing a leafy garden. It has a rooftop pool and is a short walk from the heart of the city.

Basic but clean and modern one-star **Hotel Star Loulé** (Rua Doutor Francisco Sá Carneiro, tel. 933 094 579, www.hotelstarloule. pt, €65) is within walking distance of the city center. It has free Wi-Fi in all rooms, modern baths, and an excellent central location.

INFORMATION AND SERVICES

GNR police station: Travessa Charles Bonnet, tel. 289 410 490, www.gnr.pt
Tourist office: Av. 25 Abril 9, tel. 289 463 900
Main post office: Rua 1 Dezembro, tel. 289 400 500

GETTING THERE

Loulé is 20 kilometers (12.4 mi) northwest of Faro airport along the IC4 and then either the N125-4 road or A22 motorway, about a 20-minute drive. The inland city is north of the A22 and the N125, which both run the length of the Algarve region.

Eva (tel. 289 899 760, www.eva-bus.com) buses run every half hour between Loulé's main bus terminal in the city center and Faro (40 minutes, €3.35), on the Loulé-Faro line. **CP** (tel. 707 210 220, www.cp.pt) runs trains

from Faro to Loulé (10-16 minutes, €3) at least once every hour 7am-8:40pm. Loulé train station is 5 kilometers (3.1 mi) out of the town center. There are taxis outside the station, or ask the desk staff to call one.

GETTING AROUND

Loulé is compact enough to walk around. A municipal shuttle bus (tel. 289 416 655, www. lcglobal.pt, €1, 48-hour tourist pass €3) runs frequently around the city as well as to the coastal resort of Vilamoura, the nearby town of Quarteira, and Loulé's train station. There are plenty of taxis in Loulé center.

ALMANCIL

Almancil is the beating heart of the Golden Triangle and the gateway to the upscale resorts of Quinta do Lago and Vale do Lobo. Catering to wealthy local holiday homeowners rather than tourists, it is a pleasant, bustling town that has an excellent selection of international restaurants. Almancil is halfway between Loulé and the coast, 13 kilometers (8.1 mi) northwest of Faro and 6 kilometers (3.7 mi) south of Loulé.

Sights
SÃO LOURENÇO CHURCH
(Igreja de São Lourenço)

A main attraction but still a hidden gem, **São Lourenço Church** (Rua da Igreja, tel. 289 395 451, 2:15pm-5pm Mon, 10am-1pm and 3pm-5pm Tues-Sat, open until 6pm Mon-Sat in summer, free), a short walk east of the town center, was built during the first half of the 18th century. The exterior of the modest whitewashed church belies its spectacular interior, with an iridescent gilded altar and traditional blue-and-white azulejo tiles from 1730.

Food

On the road heading out of Loulé toward the A22 motorway is polished **A Quinta**

1: Vilamoura Marina; **2:** Loulé's main shopping street; **3:** Loulé Castle; **4:** Loulé Municipal Market

Restaurant (Rua Vale Formoso, tel. 289 393 357, www.aquintarestaurant.com, 7pm-10:30pm Mon-Sat, €25), with a sophisticated menu in a refined setting. A firm favorite, A Quinta bases its menu on fresh seasonal produce with a gourmet twist. Fine wines and warm hospitality complement the cuisine, and the restaurant has a beautiful terrace with coastal views.

French-inspired **Restaurant Henrique Leis** (Estrada Vale Formoso 234, tel. 289 393 438, www.henriqueleis.com, lunch and dinner Tues-Sat Sept-June, dinner Mon-Sat July-Aug, €40) has a rich and refined interior, an acclaimed menu, and a wine list showcasing the best Portuguese *vinhos*. It has held a Michelin star since 2000 and is regarded as a benchmark for fine food in the Algarve. Dishes include egg *à la coque* (soft-boiled) with smoked caviar and lobster from the Algarve Coast with risotto gel.

Atmospheric **Figueiral** (Rua Cristovao Pires Norte, tel. 289 395 558, www.figueiral.pt, 7pm-10pm Mon-Sat, €25) specializes in grilled meats, and the famous onion soup and Brazilian *picanha* (a prized cut of beef) keep patrons coming back. Elegantly laid tables and fresh colors make this restaurant feel classy and airy.

Recreation

AQUASHOW WATER PARK
Aquashow Water Park (Semino N396, tel. 289 315 129, www.aquashowparkhotel.com, 10am-5:30pm daily May-Sept, adults €29, children 5-10 €19) boasts one of the highest free-fall waterslides in Europe, a watercoaster, and a speed-race slide. Cool off while having fun with the family.

Getting There

Almancil is 13 kilometers (8.1 mi) northwest of Faro, a 15-minute drive via the IC4 road, and 6 kilometers (3.7 mi) south of Loulé, a 10-minute drive via the M521 road. The main N125 road runs through the middle of Almancil.

Eva (tel. 289 899 760, www.eva-bus.com) buses run half-hourly from Faro to Almancil (20 minutes, €3.35), passing through on their way to Loulé. The bus stop is located close to the main town center. Alternatively, take the **CP** (tel. 707 210 220, www.cp.pt) train from Faro to Almancil (10 minutes, €2). Trains run several times a day between Faro and Almancil. The train station is not in the town center but is within walking distance.

From Almancil, buses or taxis, such as **Rádio Táxis de Almancil** (tel. 289 399 998), run to the coastal resorts of Vale do Lobo and Quinta do Lago.

VALE DO LOBO
Sprawling in fragrant, pine-laden countryside, **Vale do Lobo** (tel. 289 353 000, www.valedolobo.com) is a large luxury resort founded in 1962, among the first in the Algarve, on 450 hectares (1,112 acres) of beachfront. It is home to 1,500 residential and holiday properties with swimming pools; restaurants and bars; two championship golf courses; wellness and medical centers; and a tennis academy. All are open to nonguests. The resort offers exceptional service and is a destination for the rich and famous who prefer to stay low-key.

Getting There
Vale do Lobo is 6 kilometers (3.7 mi) south of Almancil. **Eva** (tel. 289 899 760, www.eva-bus.com) buses run hourly between Almancil and Vale do Lobo (10 minutes, €2). Alternatively, call **Rádio Táxis de Almancil** (tel. 289 399 998, €7).

QUINTA DO LAGO
The exclusive **Quinta do Lago** (tel. 289 390 700, www.quintadolago.com) is an upscale resort featuring golden-sand beaches and golf courses. A prestigious five-star sea-view hotel is nestled among dunes and pines, surrounded by the Ria Formosa Natural Park.

Portugal's Best Golf Courses

More than 40 acclaimed courses and good winter weather lure thousands of golfers to the Algarve to enjoy the challenging and expertly designed greens, concentrated in the Golden Triangle. The Algarve has smashed records, with more than a million rounds played annually. Europe's premier golf destination, the Algarve offers variety, from Arnold Palmer's acclaimed Victoria championship golf course in Vilamoura to the beautiful classic Penina Course in Portimão, designed by Sir Henry Cotton.

Recreation
GOLF
Award-winning **San Lorenzo Golf Course** (Quinta do Lago, tel. 289 396 522, www. sanlorenzogolfcourse.com, greens fees from €145 for 18 holes) showcases Quinta do Lago's unique landscape, with beautiful Bermudagrass greens, saltwater lagoons, and pine woodland. Shaped as a figure eight, the course was designed by Joseph Lee and inaugurated in 1988.

Accommodations
Conrad Algarve Hotel (Estrada da Quinta do Lago, tel. 289 350 700, www. conradhotels3.hilton.com, €629) is the embodiment of luxury and refinement and one of the Algarve's newest five-star hotels. In the heart of the Golden Triangle, it is cool and contemporary, with a spa; five restaurants and bars that include the acclaimed Gusto Restaurant, run by Michelin-star chef Heinz Beck; and guests who are well-known international stars.

Getting There
Quinta do Lago is 4 kilometers (2.5 mi) south of Almancil. **Eva** (tel. 289 899 760, www. eva-bus.com) buses run hourly between Almancil and Quinta do Lago (10 minutes, €2). Alternatively, take **Rádio Táxis de Almancil** (tel. 289 399 998, €5).

VILAMOURA
Vilamoura, a privately-managed resort town, is pleasing to the eye, made up of lowrise resorts, manicured golf resorts, and vast artificial lakes. At the heart of the town is its famous marina.

Sights
★ **VILAMOURA MARINA**
(Marina de Vilamoura)
Portugal's Monaco or Marbella, the award-winning **Vilamoura Marina** (www. marinadevilamoura.com) is a favorite hangout for the rich and glamorous. The largest marina in Portugal, it has capacity for over 1,000 vessels. Surrounded by elegant restaurants and trendy bars, luxury properties, and smart hotels, the marina is a place to people-watch and be seen, and a great place for a pleasant stroll. It is also home to one of the Algarve's three casinos.

Food
An institution among the well-heeled locals, **Willie's** (Rua do Brazil 2, tel. 289 380 849, www.willies-restaurante.com, 7pm-10:30pm Thurs-Tues, €35) has a solid reputation. Willie Wurger is the chef who dreams up the superlative seasonal menus for his elegant eponymous Michelin-star restaurant. Dishes include Willie's homemade seafood ravioli in a vermouth cream sauce, sautéed sea scallops on truffle risotto, and calf's liver on potato mousse.

Recreation
WATER SPORTS
Boats for big-game fishing can be chartered directly from the marina, where visitors will also find facilities for Jet Skis, parasailing, and boat tours.

GOLF

The 18-hole **Victoria Golf Course** (Urbanização Colinas do Golfe 4, tel. 289 320 100, www.dompedrogolf.com, greens fees from €90) is Arnold Palmer's only signature course in Portugal. With 90 hectares (222 acres) of manicured greens, it is also home to the Portuguese Masters and features extensive gently rolling fairways, smartly placed bunkers, and challenging water hazards that will test even the most accomplished.

CYCLING

For all its pizzazz, Vilamoura is an environmentally conscious and down-to-earth town, and cycling is a popular way to get around, with dozens of pathways for strolling and cycling. Bikes are widely available to rent, including from **MegaSport Travel** (tel. 289 393 044, www.megasport.pt, €30 per day, €126 per week) as well as through a bikeshare program, **Vilamoura Public Bikes** (www.inframoura.pt), although these are only rented for up to 45 minutes. There are many pickup and drop-off points around Vilamoura.

Accommodations

On the water at the mouth of Vilamoura Marina, overlooking the gleaming yachts and bustling bars on one side and the beautiful beach on the other, the **Tivoli Marina Vilamoura** (Marina de Vilamoura, tel. 289 303 303, www.minorhotels.com, €285) is glamorous, sophisticated, and contemporary. It comprises several pools and restaurants, a spa, and a summer beach club, and is next door to the casino. Just behind the Tivoli Marina Vilamoura is the **Dom Pedro Marina Boutique Hotel & Golf** (Av. Tivoli Lote H4, tel. 289 300 780, www.dompedro. com, €333), a swanky little hotel a stone's throw from the marina and the beach.

On the main road into Vilamoura, **Browns Sports & Leisure Club** (Caminho dos Golfes, tel. 289 322 740, www.brownsclub. com, €143), a first-rate sports facility used by top international teams for off-season training, also has a four-star hotel on-site. Facilities include a high-performance gym, a heated indoor pool, tennis courts, and an on-site sports bar and restaurant.

Information and Services

Tourist office: Praça Parlatorio Romano, Edifício Loja 9, Marina Arcadas, tel. 926 066 277

Getting There

Vilamoura is 15 kilometers (9.3 mi) southwest of Loulé on the N396 road, a 25-minute drive. Vilamoura is 25 kilometers (15.5 mi) west of Faro on the IC4 road, a 30-minute drive.

Eva (tel. 289 899 760, www.eva-bus.com) buses run from Faro's main bus terminal to Vilamoura (45 minutes, €4.10), via Almancil, almost hourly. From Loulé, catch the municipal **shuttle bus** (tel. 289 416 655, www. lcglobal.pt) that runs frequently between Loulé, Vilamoura, and Loulé train station (45 minutes, €1, 48-hour tourist pass €3).

Albufeira

Albufeira is the Algarve's best-known tourist destination and is geared toward foreign visitors, with everything from fantastic beaches and a quaint Old Town to modern neon-lit bars, a classy marina, and lots of hotels and restaurants for all budgets. As far as tourist hot spots go, it's a solid magnet for families and young travelers on holiday. It can get busy and rowdy in the height of summer.

SIGHTS

Albufeira is a town of two halves: the Old Town and the neon-lit Oura area, 2 kilometers (1.2 mi) east of Old Town. Oura is the

Algarve's ultimate party destination and home to the Strip.

Old Town

The charming historic part of Albufeira is worlds away from the loud neon lights of the Strip. With its large central square fringed with restaurants, quaint cobbled streets with little shops and cafés, and street entertainment in summer, the Old Town offers a more relaxed atmosphere, although in summer bars stay open until the early hours.

Zoomarine Sealife Park

Dive into a world of all things marine at **Zoomarine Sealife Park** (N125, Km 65, Guia, tel. 289 560 300, www.zoomarine. pt, 10am-7:30pm daily late June-early Sept, 10am-5pm daily Mar-late June and early Sept-Nov, adults €29, children under 11 €20, discounts online), one of the Algarve's most exciting theme parks, promoting ocean conservation and environmental awareness. In the town of Guia, 15 kilometers (9.3 mi) west of Albufeira, the park has attractions including dolphin and seal shows, an artificial beach and wave pool, a Ferris wheel, and water rides. You can swim with the dolphins (booked in advance, from €126). Don't forget your swimsuit and a towel. The park closes sporadically in quieter months (Mar and Nov), so check ahead for open hours.

By car from Albufeira, follow the N125 road west to Guia. Zoomarine is just past the town on the N125. A taxi from Albufeira (Rádio Táxis de Albufeira, tel. 289 583 230, www.taxis-albufeira.pt) to Zoomarine costs €12 one-way or €15 on weekends. Organize the return trip with the driver. There is no convenient way to get to Zoomarine by public bus or train.

BEACHES

Boasting 25 beaches, Albufeira's coastline has something for everyone, from secret secluded coves to long, shimmering stretches of golden sand that are among the most popular in the Algarve. Many beaches are sought out by Portugal's wealthy and famous for a break from prying eyes.

Albufeira's three main beaches that front the city are **Fishermen's Beach (Praia dos Pescadores)** along with the adjacent **Tunel** and **Inatel** beaches. The spacious bay-like **Oura** beach is to the east, and **São Rafael**, a small cove-like beach, to the west. Farther east of Albufeira is **Falésia** beach, backed by vibrant ginger-hued cliffs.

Fishermen's Beach
(Praia dos Pescadores)

Albufeira's main and most central beach, Fishermen's Beach fronts the Old Town area. Although the beach was once a hub for fishing, today the colorful little wooden boats have given way to parasols and banana boats. In summer a range of water sports occupy this beach, while in winter it hosts a big New Year's party. Escalators take beachgoers from the Pau da Bandeira bluff to the sands of the Blue Flag-awarded beach at one end. Pau da Bandeira bluff is easy to get to; it is a short walk east of Fishermen's Beach and can be seen from the sand. At the west end of the beach, the modern **Peneco Elevator** (Esplanada Dr. Frutuoso da Silva 5, 8am-9pm daily, free) sticks out from its charming surroundings like a sore thumb but is a great way to avoid the many steps down to the beach.

Falésia Beach
(Praia da Falésia)

Ten kilometers (6.2 mi) east of Albufeira, Falésia Beach is a 5-kilometer-long (3.1-mi-long) stretch of golden sand backed by ocher-red cliffs dotted with pine trees. Peppered with bars and restaurants and loved for its family-friendly shallow water, it is one of the Algarve's most popular beaches and one of the best in the country.

An **Eva** (tel. 289 899 760, www.eva-bus. com) bus runs between Albufeira's main bus station (Urbanização Alto dos Caliços, tel. 289 589 055), 1.6 kilometers (1 mi) from the city center, and Falésia Beach (every 30 minutes, €3.35).

Local Specialty: Chicken *Piripiri*

Even though grilled chicken is a staple throughout Portugal, **Guia** village, a 15-minute drive west of Albufeira, is reputedly the home of the famous dish, although this is hotly contested. Quintessential *frango assado* (grilled chicken) is juicy, crispy, and has a distinctive garlicky marinade. The ubiquitous *piripiri* dressing (a hot sauce made from olive oil, crushed chilies, pepper, garlic, salt, lemon juice, bay leaves, and paprika, among other ingredients) is optional, but if you like your food hot, make sure you ask for your chicken *"com piripiri."* The marinated chicken is grilled over charcoal and served with fries and salad. Don't be surprised at the diminutive size of the chicken pieces, though, because—according to those in the know—the smaller the chicken, the tastier it is.

For the ultimate chicken *piripiri* experience, try the legendary restaurant ★ **Ramires** (Rua 25 de Abril 14, Guia, tel. 289 561 232, www.restauranteramires.com, 11am-11pm daily, no reservations in summer, €10), which has been serving Guia grilled chicken since 1964 and claims to have invented the original recipe. The restaurant might look simple from the outside, but inside the service is fast and the food delicious.

FOOD

Cozy and casual **Stews & More** (Forte de São João, Rua Almeida Garrett 40, tel. 924 088 166, 5pm-10pm Tues-Sun, €15) serves "new-style grandmothers' cooking," old-fashioned home cooking with a contemporary twist, with typical Portuguese one-pot dishes in traditional earthenware. The space is modern-rustic, with wooden finishes and elegant tables. Stew menus are divided into seasonal items and specials.

In Albufeira's Old Town, overlooking Peneco Beach, the **Beach Basket** (Praça Miguel Bombarda 7, tel. 289 512 137, noon-midnight daily, €15) is a highly recommended beachside restaurant for long, lazy lunches or romantic dinners. Fabulous views are complemented by fresh seafood like stuffed crab, fresh sea bass, and *cataplana*.

Spacious, modern **Market Restaurant & Wine Bar** (Av. Sá Carneiro 1, tel. 289 501 441, 5:30pm-11pm daily, €20) is toward the bottom of Albufeira's main strip heading toward Oura, overlooking the sea. Market has unusual Mediterranean-inspired dishes such as tuna ceviche with coconut, suckling pig croquettes, and a shrimp and chili burger, as well as staples such as New Zealand lamb chops; it also has interesting cocktails.

One of Albufeira's most popular restaurants, **Jaipur** (Rua 1 de Dezembro 28-30, tel. 289 585 707, www.curryclubs.com, lunch and dinner daily, €10) is a spice box of fresh Indian flavors with a garish interior. It's a short walk north of the Old Town center, near the Sineira church and bell tower.

ENTERTAINMENT AND EVENTS

Albufeira is a popular nightlife destination year-round, with live music and shows throughout the town. With a big party scene, Albufeira can get rowdy. The main beach, Fishermen's Beach, hosts one of the biggest New Year's parties in the Algarve.

Nightlife

Packed with side-by-side sports bars, Irish bars, tattoo parlors, and restaurants, Albufeira's famous **Strip** is one very long and flashy road with souvenir shops by day and by night a kaleidoscope of every shade of neon. Stretching 2 kilometers (1.2 mi) from the Montechoro neighborhood almost to Oura Beach, it is the Algarve's busiest nightlife destination. The Strip can get pretty raucous most nights, especially in summer when

1: Albufeira's Old Town; **2:** Fishermen's Beach

it never seems to sleep. Many tourist-oriented international restaurants are also along the Strip.

Not as rowdy as the Strip, Albufeira's **Old Town** hangouts tend to be livelier in summer, although live entertainment is generally put on at least once or twice a week even in low season. The atmosphere at **Albufeira Marina** is more composed, with reasonably priced, classy restaurants, plenty of shops and entertainment for the kids, and lovely bars. The marina is a 30-minute cliff-top walk west of central Albufeira, or a short taxi ride.

Upstairs at **Wild & Co. Bar & Steakhouse** (Av. Sá Carneiro 29, tel. 289 583 545 or 911 700 999, www.wildandcompany.com, 11am-4am Mon-Sat, 11am-midnight Sun) is a steakhouse; downstairs it's one of the wildest bars in Albufeira, with neon flashing, music thumping, dancing on the bar top, and regular live music. Think Irish pub meets American saloon.

Open since 1981, **Kiss Disco Club** (Rua Vasco da Gama, Edifício Kiss, tel. 289 515 693, 1am-7am Wed-Mon, 9am-5pm Tues May-Oct, 11:45pm-7am Fri-Sat Nov-Apr) has DJs and live bands with the latest hits to keep the crowd dancing till the early morning. It's a place to go after other bars have closed, but drinks can be pricy. An entry fee may be applied.

Just a stone's throw from the marina, gorgeously exotic cocktail bar and chill-out lounge **Casa do Cerro** (Cerro da Piedade, near Dolphin Roundabout on the road to the marina, tel. 919 596 665, 8pm-3am Tues-Sun) is adorned with Moroccan-style loungers, scatter cushions, and *shisha* pipes, while a warm and spicy color palette and the odd statue of Buddha lend an Indian twist. A hidden gem frequented by the in crowd, it is a relaxing place to see and be seen. Casa do Cerro also serves tapas and has a full restaurant menu.

RECREATION

Water sports galore are available on all of Albufeira's main beaches in summer. Oura

Beach, 2 kilometers (1.2 mi) east of downtown and a few beaches down from Fishermen's Beach, is known for having the biggest variety of fun sea activities. Beach outfitters tout everything from pedal boats, banana boats, and kayaks to paragliding.

Horseback Riding

See the Algarve from a different perspective in the saddle of a well-trained horse at **Quinta da Saudade Riding School** (M526, Km 26, Pêra, tel. 968 054 013 or 964 942 929, www.cavalosquintadasaudade. com, 90-minute tour €35), with horseback-riding tours through the sandy dunes of Praia Grande and along the Salgados Lagoon for riders of all levels. Nonriders can tour in a horse and carriage. Quinta da Saudade is in the village of Pêra, 18 kilometers (11.2 mi) west of central Albufeira, a 20-minute drive.

Biking

Cycle from Albufeira through gorgeous central Algarve landscapes on a small-group, four-hour guided bike tour (from €30 pp) with **Algarve Bike Holidays** (Av. da Liberdade 144, tel. 913 226 954, www. algarvebikeholidays.com, head office 9am-8pm daily). Tours are conducted in English and can be customized.

Boating

Dream Wave Algarve (Marina de Albufeira, Passeio dos Oceanos, Lote 5, Loja 31, Fracção A, tel. 962 003 885 or 962 003 801, www. dreamwavealgarve.com, from €22) has sailing trips on a wooden caravel and the fastest speedboat in the region. Operating from Albufeira Marina, the boating company also offers cave tours and dolphin-watching cruises.

ACCOMMODATIONS

Albufeira offers scores of lodging for all budgets: family-friendly all-inclusive resorts, cheap self-catering apartments, charming B&Bs, and high-end hotels.

In the middle of Albufeira's Old Town, right on Fishermen's Beach, the four-star **Hotel Sol e Mar** (Rua José Bernardino de Sousa, tel. 289 580 080, www.grupofbarata.com, €221) is massively popular for its location and has 74 rooms on six floors. It dates to 1965 and was refurbished in 2002. Built into the cliff, this distinctive Spanish-looking hotel boasts first-line sea views.

Environmentally conscious low-rise five-star resort ★ **Epic Sana Algarve** (Aldeia da Falésia, tel. 289 104 300, www.algarve.epic.sanahotels.com, €432) is nestled among Albufeira's characteristic pine trees on the coast overlooking Falésia Beach. Along with 162 rooms, 24 suites, and 43 spacious apartments, it houses a large conference center. This modern and contemporary resort strikes a balance between nature and comfort.

Boutique hotel **Vila Joya** (Estrada da Galé, tel. 289 591 795, www.vilajoya.com, from €555) is pricey, but it is the epitome of exclusivity. A Moorish-inspired gem overlooking the Atlantic, Vila Joya boasts 12 rooms, 8 palatial suites, and a Michelin two-star restaurant.

On Albufeira's main Avenida dos Descobrimentos, four-star **Hotel Brisa Sol** (Rua do Município 27, tel. 289 580 420, www.hotelbrisasol.com, €159 d, €179 studio, €249 one-bedroom apartment) is a modern building with a traditional Portuguese interior of polished stone floors and tile-clad walls. This casual apartment-hotel is a 15-minute walk from Fishermen's Beach and a short stroll to the Strip.

INFORMATION AND SERVICES

GNR police station: Estrada de Vale de Pedras, tel. 289 590 790, www.gnr.pt
Tourist office: Rua 5 de Outubro 4, tel. 289 585 279
Main post office: Rua Alexandre Herculano, tel. 289 580 860

GETTING THERE

Albufeira is 45 kilometers (28 mi) and a 40-minute drive west of Faro airport along the A22 motorway. Following the N125 road takes 45 minutes.

Eva (tel. 289 899 760, www.eva-bus.com) buses run regularly between Faro and Albufeira, generally via Loulé or via Vilamoura and Quarteira. The regional bus (1.5 hours, €4.85) runs every 30-50 minutes; the Transrápido express coach (1 hour, €6) runs every couple of hours. Albufeira's main bus station (Urbanização Alto dos Caliços, tel. 289 589 055) is 1.6 kilometers (1 mi) from the city center but is easy to get to on Albufeira's **Próximo** (www.proximo.pt) bus, which stops at the terminal.

Taking the train to Albufeira is not recommended, as the train station is 7 kilometers (4.3 mi) outside the city center and requires taking a taxi.

If you arrive at Faro airport at night and want to go straight to Albufeira, arrange a private transfer. A reputable company is **Yellow Fish Transfers** (tel. 289 046 243, www.yellowfishtransfers.com).

GETTING AROUND

It is possible to walk from one end of Albufeira to the other, from the marina or Old Town to the Strip, but it is far, especially at night or in the heat. **Rádio Táxis de Albufeira** (tel. 289 583 230, www.taxis-albufeira.pt) and other taxis are readily available around town and inexpensive.

The local bus system **Próximo** (www.proximo.pt, €1.10, unlimited 24-hour ticket €5.30) stops at all the city's major attractions, including the main bus terminal. Buy tickets on board; most drivers speak good English.

Giro Bus (www.cm-albufeira.pt, day ticket €4) also runs five circular nonstop lines serving key places such as the main bus terminal; Old Town; the Montechoro, Oura, and Santa Eulália neighborhoods; the marina; and the Strip.

Lagoa and Vicinity

Flanked by flat marshland from which it took its name, the city of Lagoa (LAH-go-ah) is the heart of a traditionally agricultural area that was once an important wine-making region, and it is home to the last functioning cooperative winery in the Algarve. The small city's simplicity pales in comparison with elegant coastal villages such as Carvoeiro and Ferragudo. To the east of Lagoa is Porches and its famous pottery shops.

SIGHTS

LiR Art Gallery

Housed in the **Única—Adega Cooperativa e Lagoa** (the Algarve's last functioning cooperative winery), **LiR Art Gallery** (N125, tel. 282 356 131, www.galeria-de-arte.net, 10am-6pm Mon-Sat, free) showcases the works of 30 local and foreign artists in the unique ambience of a historic wine cellar. From the gallery, visitors can glimpse wine production, and local wines can be bought from the gift shop. There's also a café/bar as well as ample parking. The gallery is directly opposite the bus terminal, across the main N125 road, south of the city center.

São José Convent
(Convento de São José)

Converted into a cultural center that hosts exhibitions by local artists and artisans throughout the year, **São José Convent** (Rua Joaquim Eugénio Júdice, tel. 282 380 434, 9am-12:30am Tues-Fri, free) and chapel, founded in the early 1700s, originally housed Carmelite nuns before it was an orphanage and later a girls' school. A rather morose feature that has been conserved is a now disused foundling wheel, where mothers could anonymously give up their unwanted newborns.

FOOD

Perhaps due to Lagoa's essence as a rural working town, its restaurants are unfussy, down-to-earth eateries with simple grilled and hearty meat. Head toward the coast to find more upscale restaurants with seafood and international cuisine.

Fine dining in the heart of Lagoa, **Chrissy's** (Praça da República 17, tel. 282 341 062, 6:30pm-midnight Mon-Sat, €20) is a bistro-style restaurant with sophisticated food at reasonable prices. In a historic building next to the municipal market, this renowned restaurant offers blended international and French classics and the chef's daily suggestions.

Blink and you'll miss **O Casarão** (Beco 5 de Outubro 7, tel. 282 352 091, lunch and dinner Sun-Fri, €8), next to the gas station on the main N125 road through Lagoa. At this small and understated place, the specialty is grilled chicken and homemade desserts. It has a lovely outdoor patio for alfresco dining.

Homey, bistro-like ★ **Ele & Ela** (Rua do Barranco 28, tel. 282 357 509, 6pm-11pm Tues-Sun, €15) has a colorful menu of popular fare, from steak to ribs to the catch of the day. Dishes are based on fresh local produce, international favorites, and a little Asian twist. Specials include Thai fish cakes, salmon soup, lamb shank, and braised pork.

ENTERTAINMENT AND EVENTS

Candlelight Cultural Market

The **Candlelight Cultural Market** (around São José Convent, Thurs-Sun usually 1st weekend of July) runs for four nights, with the streets of Lagoa lit by thousands of candles in glass jars. Each year the traditional arts and crafts of a different culture are showcased at the convent and various locations around the city. Past themes have included Celtic, Sephardic Jewish, and African. A plethora of stalls line the streets around the São José Convent, offering a variety of local handicrafts and foods. The market is a magical experience that is at its prettiest after dark. The event starts at 7pm each night, with the lighting of the candles at around 8:30pm.

Fatacil Fair

Held every year for 10 days in mid-August, **Fatacil** (N125, Parque Municipal de Feiras e Exposições de Lagoa, tel. 282 380 465, www. fatacil.pt, from 6pm, €3.50) offers a true flavor of Portugal with agriculture, arts and crafts, tourism, and industry; hundreds of stalls offer everything from cork souvenirs to horse tack, from all over the country. It also features food and drink, farm animals, and horse shows, and culminates every night in a concert by some of Portugal's top artists. It's a great opportunity to see, sample, smell, and shop for a vast selection of typical Portuguese products.

RECREATION
Slide & Splash Water Park

From afar it looks like a tangle of blue tubes, but up close it's a refreshing opportunity to get wet. Five kilometers (3.1 mi) west of Lagoa, the **Slide & Splash Water Park** (N125 Vale de Deus, Estômbar, tel. 282 340 800, www. slidesplash.com, Easter-early Nov, adults €27, children under 11 €19, discounts online) is a popular summer attraction that gets very busy in peak season, but the fun is worth the queues.

Aqualand Water Park

Aqualand Water Park (N125, Sítio das Areias, tel. 282 320 230, www.aqualand. pt, 10am-5pm daily mid-late June, 10am-6pm daily July-late Sept, adults €27, children €19, discounts online) is the smallest of the Algarve's major water parks but is also the cheapest and has an area with water attractions for young children. It also boasts the stomach-churning Banzai skim-board slide, white-water rapids, and the aptly named Kamikaze ride, a 36-meter (118-foot) drop in four seconds. Aqualand is 9 kilometers (5.6 mi) east of Lagoa on the N125, a 10-minute drive.

ACCOMMODATIONS

On the main road through Lagoa, **Hotel Lagoa** (N125, Rua Visconde de Lagoa, tel. 282 380 130, www.lagoahotel.pt, €161) is a 10-minute drive from the village of Carvoeiro and walking distance to the local bus terminal, town center, and supermarkets. Formerly a run-down roadside motel, it was overhauled to a high standard and now boasts four stars, an outdoor pool, and a reputable restaurant and bar with an extensive cocktail list.

INFORMATION AND SERVICES

GNR police: Rua Joaquim Eugénio Júdice, tel. 282 380 190, www.gnr.pt
Post office: Rua Coronel Figueiredo 46, tel. 282 340 220

GETTING THERE

Lagoa is 60 kilometers (37 mi) west of Faro airport, a 50-minute drive on the A22 motorway. It's also a straight drive on the N125 regional road, although this is a secondary road with traffic signals, roundabouts, and intersections, and with summer traffic can take twice as long as the A22. Lagoa is 30 kilometers (19 mi) west of Albufeira, a 25-minute drive on the A22.

Lagoa's bus terminal (tel. 282 341 301) is on Rua Jacinto Correia. **Eva** (tel. 289 899 760, www.eva-bus.com) buses run every couple of hours between Albufeira and Lagoa (1 hour, €4), on the Albufeira-Portimão line.

There is no train station in Lagoa. The nearest is in Estômbar, 4 kilometers (2.5 mi) west of Lagoa.

GETTING AROUND

Lagoa's main sights, such as the São José Convent, are within walking distance of Lagoa's bus terminal. The Slide & Splash Water Park (€4-5) and the villages of Carvoeiro (€7) and Ferragudo (€15-20) are a short taxi ride.

CARVOEIRO

Having grown from a small fishing village into a tourist hot spot, Carvoeiro (CAR-voo-AY-roo) offers big fun in a petite package. The heart of the town is its main beach, nestled between two steep hills blanketed in white-washed apartments and town houses. It is a popular settlement for expats and has a lively café culture. Carvoeiro also offers a bustling choice of restaurants and bars that are busy year-round.

Sights and Recreation

ALGAR SECO ROCK FORMATION

A 10-minute walk up a steep hill east of Carvoeiro village center, Algar Seco is a remarkable cliffside rock formation, carved out by the tide. A long wooden walkway runs along the cliff tops with views of the ocean. Accessed via a flight of stairs from the top, the unusual rock formation contains a network of sinkholes, pools, and spouts. In a large pinnacle is a grotto named **A Boneca** (The Doll), with two windows to the Atlantic (the doll's eyes). Nestled in the groove of the rock formation is a popular café-restaurant, **Restaurant Boneca Bar** (tel. 282 358 391, 10am-midnight Sun-Sat). For a breathtaking treat, visit at sunset.

★ MARINHA BEACH
(Praia da Marinha)

This award-winning beach is one of the most famous and beautiful in the country. Emblematic of the Algarve and its natural splendor, Marinha Beach has been used in many advertising campaigns and frequently appears on must-see lists. Encased by sheer ocher cliffs, the beach has craggy rock formations that stretch out over the soft golden sand to a calm, translucent sea. Accessible by car or bus, this popular beach can be very busy in summer. It is accessed from the cliff-top car park by a long staircase down to the sand, which can be a challenge for the less agile. The view from the car park and a photo of Portugal's most famous beach are worth the trip.

Marinha Beach is in the hamlet of Caramujeira, 10 kilometers (6.2 mi) and 15 minutes' drive east of Carvoeiro. One bus runs in the morning and one in the afternoon weekdays between the Lagoa bus terminal (Rua Jacinto Correia, tel. 282 341 301, ticket office 7:30am-noon and 1:20pm-7pm Mon-Fri, 8am-noon and 3pm-6pm Sat) and Marinha Beach (under €3).

GOLF

Built on flat terrain, 10 minutes' drive northwest of Carvoeiro, the **Pestana Carvoeiro Golf Resort** (tel. 282 340 900, www.pestanagolf.com, greens fees from €73 June-Aug and Dec-Jan, €110 Feb, Apr-May, Sept, and Nov, €120 Mar and Oct) offers the playable 18-hole Gramacho course and the challenging and stunning 18-hole Vale da Pinta course. Inaugurated in 1991, Gramacho was designed by Ronald Fream and former world champion Nick Price. Fream also designed Pinta, inaugurated in 1992. Both courses highlight the region's natural countryside, combining olive and carob trees with ornamental sculpted lakes and bunkers.

GROTTO TRIPS

This part of the Algarve's coast is studded with caves and dramatic rock formations, and no visit to Carvoeiro is complete without a boat trip to the region's coastal grottoes on a local fishing boat. **Carvoeiro Caves** (left side of Carvoeiro Beach square, near changing rooms, tel. 965 041 785, www.carvoeirocaves.com, 9am-7pm daily) specializes in tours (1-1.5 hours, from €25) guided by experienced sailors to the stunning caves, including the popular **Benagil sea cave.**

Food

In 2015 Carvoeiro welcomed its first Michelin-star restaurant, the gracefully understated **Bon Bon** (Rua do Cabeço de Pias, tel. 282 341 496, www.bonbon.pt, 6:30pm-9:30pm Mon

1: Algar Seco in Carvoeiro; **2:** Marinha Beach near Carvoeiro

and Thurs-Fri, noon-2:30pm and 6:30pm-9:30pm Sat-Sun, 4-course tasting menu from €98), about 4 kilometers (2.5 mi) northwest of Carvoeiro village, near the Pestana Golf Resort. Seasonal specialties are gastronomic masterpieces, with a focus on Portuguese ingredients and locally sourced seafood, meat, and vegetables.

One of Carvoeiro's best-known and most colorful restaurants, **Chef António** (Estrada do Farol, tel. 282 358 937, 6pm-midnight daily, €20) serves hearty traditional Portuguese food by the charismatic opera-singing chef-owner António. This large villa-like restaurant has an elegant indoor dining area and a large alfresco terrace, and is hugely popular among locals.

No fishing village would be complete without an awesome fish restaurant. **Mar d'Fora** (Rua do Paraíso 522, tel. 282 180 735, noon-10:30pm Tues-Sun, €25), halfway down the western hill of the two hills that encase Carvoeiro village square, has ocean views as a backdrop. The beach shack-chic restaurant overlooks the beach, so you can expect wonderful sunsets to complement tasty fish dishes.

Entertainment and Events
Mid-June, don't miss Carvoeiro's famous **Black & White Night,** when the village is flooded with visitors to enjoy the bands on various stages set up throughout town, and to dance on the beach until dawn.

Accommodations
Perfectly appointed boutique B&B ★ O **Castelo Guest House** (Rua do Casino 59-63, tel. 282 083 518, www.ocastelo.net, €113) overlooks Carvoeiro Beach from high up on one of its hills. Its 12 rooms are bright and spacious, and it offers privileged sea views from all rooms.

Toward the top eastern end of Carvoeiro village is the **Tivoli Carvoeiro** (Vale do Covo, Praia do Carvoeiro, tel. 282 351 100, www.minorhotels.com, €225), thoroughly refurbished and reopened as a deluxe, modern five-star hotel in 2017. It boasts 248 tastefully decorated rooms, most with stunning sea views, and Sky Bar, one of the hippest bars in the village.

Information and Services
GNR police: Rampa Sra. da Encarnação 15, tel. 282 356 460, www.gnr.pt
Main tourist office: Carvoeiro main beachfront square, tel. 282 357 728

Getting There
Carvoeiro is 5 kilometers (3.1 mi) south of Lagoa, a 10-minute drive via the M1272 road, or bus or taxi ride from Lagoa's main bus terminal. **Eva** (tel. 282 341 301, www.eva-bus.com) buses run almost hourly between Lagoa and Carvoeiro (€2.35), less frequently on weekends and holidays, and stop in the heart of Carvoeiro village.

Neither Lagoa nor Carvoeiro has a train station. The nearest train station is in the nearby town of Estômbar, 4 kilometers (2.5 mi) west of Lagoa.

There is a permanent taxi rank at Lagoa bus terminal and one just off Carvoeiro's main village square. Taxis are readily available and travel between Carvoeiro and Lagoa (€7-10).

Getting Around
Carvoeiro can be covered easily on foot, but be warned that it involves some steep hills. A more pleasant way to get around and see the village's charms, even on the outskirts, is on the tourist train.

TOURIST TRAIN
The **Carvoeiro Tourist Train** (tel. 914 906 599), operated by **Turistrem** (tel. 965 135 466, www.turistrem.com), departs regularly daily from the main village square and does 40-minute round-trips of the village (€3-5). The train also does round-trips to Ferragudo (Tues and Fri, €10 round-trip), where it stops for a few hours for passengers to wander around before coming back. More information is at Carvoeiro's tourist office (tel. 282 357 728) on the main beachfront square. Tickets can be bought from the driver.

CLIFFS ROUTE HOP-ON HOP-OFF BUS
(Rota das Falésias)

The **Cliffs Route** (24-hour ticket adults €10, children €8, 48-hour ticket adults €15, children €12) is a new hop-on hop-off round-trip service operated by **Turistrem** (tel. 965 135 466, www.turistrem.com) in an air-conditioned minibus that departs Carvoeiro and drops passengers at some of the region's most popular beaches, coastal beauty spots, and points of interest around Lagoa, including the village of Ferragudo, Marinha Beach, and the Algar Seco rock formation and boardwalk. Buy tickets on board.

TOP EXPERIENCE

FERRAGUDO

At the mouth of the Arade River, 6 kilometers (3.7 mi) west of Carvoeiro and across from the city of Portimão, Ferragudo is a stunning 14th-century hamlet and the quintessential Algarve fishing village. Less touristy than Carvoeiro, it is a maze of bougainvillea-framed cobblestone streets lined with traditional whitewashed cottages cascading down the hillside, with the main church at the top.

An opportunity to see traditional fishing work, the village's pretty harbor is also the setting for breathtaking sunsets and postcard-perfect pictures, with small wooden fishing vessels bobbing on silken water. The harbor is particularly striking at night, as the village lights twinkle in the background.

Ferragudo's main **Queen Leonor Square (Praça Rainha Leonor)** is the core of village life, fringed by restaurants, cafés, bakeries, and ice cream parlors; in summer there is nightly live entertainment. Just beyond the square, near the Our Lady of the Conception Church, is the striking, privately owned **São João do Arade Fort**, opposite the Santa Catarina Fort, across the river in Praia da Rocha (Portimão).

It may be small and quaint, but Ferragudo has a lot to offer, from the Praia Grande main beach to art and antiques shops, artisans' workshops, and laid-back café life.

Sights
★ OUR LADY OF THE CONCEPTION CHURCH
(Igreja Nossa Senhora da Conceição)

The 16th-century **Our Lady of the Conception Church** (Rua da Igreja 10, tel. 282 461 962, 10am-noon and 3pm-5pm daily, free) sits high above the harbor of Ferragudo. Those who make it up the steep streets and flights of stairs to the pretty church are rewarded with stunning panoramic views over the Arade River to the city of Portimão. The church's exterior is bright and simple, with large whitewashed walls and sunny yellow trim. Inside, the church has a richly gilded rococo altarpiece and a number of religious works of art.

Food

On Ferragudo's picturesque quayside, **A Ria** (Rua Infante Santo, tel. 282 461 790, 6:30pm-10pm Tues-Wed, 12:30pm-2:30pm and 6:30pm-10pm Thurs-Sun, €20) specializes in traditional Algarvian seafood. Specials at the quaint and cozy family-run restaurant include razor clam rice and *caldeirada* (fish stew).

Entertainment and Recreation

In summer, the village square comes to life with nightly entertainment, including live music. Ferragudo has a popular monthly **flea and antiques market** (along the main central canal, 2nd Sun Sept-July) and a sweet **Christmas market** (1st weekend of Dec).

Ferragudo's **Praia Grande** beach is a hub of activity. The long stretch of sand has lovely water and is great for a brisk walk. In summer, beach outfitters provide plenty of activities, from pedal boats to kayaks. On the beach is the fabulous **Clube Nau** (Praia Grande, tel. 282 484 414, www.club-nau.com, 10am-midnight daily), a shack-like wooden bar and restaurant that is one of the coolest hangouts in the Algarve. Sundays are legendary, with a live band, drinks, dinner,

Best Souvenirs: Porches Pottery

A piece of Porches pottery makes a unique souvenir of the Algarve. While Porches is well-known as a wine-making region, elaborately decorated red-clay ceramics earned it acclaim. Local inhabitants still make pottery to keep the traditional art alive. Once a flourishing trade, the art in Porches had started to wane until Irish artist Patrick Swift and renowned Portuguese ceramicist Lima de Freitas collaborated to establish the famous Porches Pottery workshop in 1968. With increased tourism in the Algarve, Porches's pottery gained renewed interest and can now be found in first-class restaurants and hotels and homes around the world.

and dancing. With an eclectic menu heavily focused on fish and cocktails, it is so popular that reservations are recommended if you want a table for dinner.

Accommodations

Amid the maze of Ferragudo's streets, the swanky **One2Seven Boutique** (Rua Mouzinho de Albuquerque 12, tel. 916 542 351, www.one2seven.pt, minimum 7 nights, €623 d weekly, 3-bedroom house €1,113 weekly) wouldn't look out of place in Miami, with its petite pool and deck area and sleek architecture. It overlooks the picturesque village harbor and offers rooms, apartments, and holiday houses.

Getting There

Ferragudo is 9 kilometers (5.6 mi) west of Lagoa, a 10-minute drive along the M1272 road, and 6 kilometers (3.7 mi) west of Carvoeiro village, a 12-minute drive via the Urbanização das Sesmarias country road. It's 5 kilometers (3.1 mi) east of Portimão, across the Arade River; it's a 10-minute drive along the M530 road, over the old bridge.

Eva (tel. 282 341 301, www.eva-bus.com) buses run hourly between Portimão and Ferragudo (10 minutes, €3). There are no direct buses between Lagoa or Carvoeiro and Ferragudo.

1: São João do Arade Fort in Ferragudo;
2: Our Lady of the Conception Church in Ferragudo; 3: a bougainvillea-covered street in Ferragudo; 4: fishing boats in Ferragudo's harbor

The **Carvoeiro Tourist Train** (tel. 914 906 599), operated by **Turistrem** (tel. 965 135 466, www.turistrem.com), runs twice a week from Carvoeiro to Ferragudo (30 minutes, Tues and Fri, €10 round-trip), where it stops in the village center. Tickets can be bought from the driver.

A handy **water taxi** (tel. 927 272 784, Mar-Nov) between Ferragudo and Portimão (5 minutes, €4 one-way, €6 round-trip) crosses the Arade River on demand. It takes passengers to the museum and marina in Portimão and also stops at Ferragudo's Praia Grande beach. The water taxi stop in Ferragudo is at the far end of the riverfront quay, by the lifeboat station. Beneath a large umbrella is a little manned desk—staff there can answer questions and sell tickets.

PORCHES

The town of Porches (POR-shezh) is synonymous with pottery. Charming yet unassuming, it is overshadowed by its bigger, touristy neighbors. A smattering of pottery shops still produce ceramics using traditional artisanal methods. If handicrafts are your thing, spend a few hours browsing the colorful ceramics, have lunch, and walk around town.

Shopping

Pottery shops line both sides of the N125 road, which delimits the northern boundary of Porches, and the shop fronts are clad with the typically colorful hand-painted designs on bright-red handmade clay pots. Traditionally, Algarvian ceramics are painted blue and white, but designs today use a variety of colors and patterns.

POTTERY AND CERAMICS

The **Porches Pottery Shop and Atelier** (N125, tel. 282 352 858, www.porchespottery. com, 9am-6pm Mon-Fri, 10am-2pm Sat) produces the famous original Porches pottery. Founded in 1968, the shop produces pieces in the traditional way, handmade and then hand-painted and glazed with the region's distinctive patterns and colors, often

Silves

blue and white. From mugs to salt shakers to plates, all are painted freehand.

Getting There

Porches is 5 kilometers (3.1 mi) east of Lagoa city, a 10-minute drive via the N125 road. **Eva** (tel. 282 341 301, www.eva-bus. com) buses run hourly between Lagoa and Porches (10 minutes, €2.35), stopping on the main road within walking distance of the village center. A taxi from Lagoa bus terminal costs around €8 one-way.

The city of Silves (SIL-vesh) is an impressive sight on approach, with its imposing castle and cathedral on the hill, a crown atop a cascade of whitewashed houses and bright-red roofs staggering down to the Arade River through the middle of town. The capital of the Algarve in Moorish times and now the self-proclaimed Orange Capital of the Algarve, due to the orange groves surrounding the town, Silves is of historic and archaeological importance. Few signs of mainstream tourism are evident, but it is host to one of the biggest events of the Algarve summer, the famous Medieval Festival. Silves is an easy day trip from Lagoa or Portimão.

SIGHTS
★ Silves Castle
(Castelo de Silves)

Besides being one of the best-preserved castles in the Algarve, **Silves Castle** (Rua da Cruz de Portugal, tel. 282 440 800, www.cm-silves. pt, 9am-8pm daily, €2.80) has extraordinary medieval military architecture inherited from the Moors, who once occupied the region. Excavations suggest the first fortress was built by the Romans or Visigoths on the remnants of a Lusitanian military camp. Circa 716, the citadel was conquered by the Moors, who bolstered the existing fortifications with

new walls, including extensive ramparts to the west. Silves was later captured by the Spaniards and again by the Moors, then taken by King Sancho I of Portugal in 1189 with the help of Crusaders, and again captured by the Moors in 1191. The fortress was finally regained by Afonso III of Portugal in the 13th century during the reconquests. After reconstruction following earthquakes, including the catastrophic earthquake of 1755, Silves Castle was restored to its current glory in the 1940s.

Today, as well as being home to an interactive visitors center, in summer the solid-red castle also hosts **Sunset Secret** (6:30pm-11pm Thurs June-Aug, €5) cocktail events, where food and wine are served within the castle walls, with live fado singers and chill-out music.

It's a 20-minute climb from the riverside to the castle on Silves's steep cobbled streets. At the top, the views of the surrounding countryside, blanketed with orange and lemon groves, are a reward. Walk around the castle walls, admire the excavations, and relax in the courtyard with a cocktail or a meal. Exhibitions located in the turrets and in below-ground cisterns showcase artifacts unearthed during on-site excavations; descriptions are available in English. You could spend a couple of hours in Silves Castle; bring the camera.

FOOD

On the river, the delicious scents of grilled chicken and fish waft from simple water's-edge restaurants. Hidden in the rolling hills surrounding the city are a number of *marisqueiras* (seafood restaurants) and typical Portuguese restaurants offering hearty home-cooked dishes and local specialties.

Ú Monchiqueiro (Av. Marginal, tel. 282 182 046, lunch and dinner Thurs-Tues, €8) is a long-established typically Portuguese restaurant along the Arade River, popular for its fresh grilled fish and meats and renowned for its tasty *cozido à Portuguesa* (Portuguese stew), a rustic dish for sharing that includes boiled pork, *choriço* sausage, cabbage, carrots, and potatoes.

In the riverside municipal market, vibrant and friendly no-frills ★ **Churrasqueira Valdemar** (Mercado Municipal 11, tel. 282 443 138, lunch and dinner Mon-Sat, €7) specializes in grilled *piripiri* chicken. Regulars don't bother with a menu and go for the staple garlicky barbecue chicken (*piripiri* optional), homemade bread, fresh salad, and crunchy fries; other meats are also available. The food is basic but fabulous.

Hidden on a Silves backstreet, **Marisqueira Rui** (Rua Comendador Vilarinho 27, tel. 282 442 682, noon-1am Wed-Mon, €15) has an ocean's worth of fresh seafood in simple surroundings, at reasonable prices. Watch in awe as platters piled with steaming shellfish come out of the kitchen and onto the tables. Grilled fish kebabs are also popular.

For fantastic international food, ★ **Café Inglês** (Rua do Castelo 11, tel. 282 442 585, www.cafeingles.com.pt, 10am-11:30pm Tues-Sun, €12) is one of the most charismatic café-restaurants in the Algarve. Popular and trendy, it has an exceptional location high above the town along the castle walls, with incredible views. The menu ranges from international classics like beef tenderloin, lamb chops, and roast duck to artisanal pizzas. Live music, from jazz to world music to pop, is also available regularly.

ENTERTAINMENT AND EVENTS

Medieval Festival

Silves's main yearly attraction is the exotic **Medieval Festival** (tel. 282 440 800, www.visitportugal.com, mid-Aug), nine days when the entire city is closed to traffic and transformed into a medieval marketplace, complete with hog roasts, jousters, hay bales, belly dancers, snake charmers, and fire jugglers. It's a remarkable experience. Costumes are also available to rent for those who want to get into the spirit of things.

GETTING THERE

Silves is 63 kilometers (39 mi) west of Faro, a 45-minute drive via the A22 motorway. It's 8 kilometers (5 mi) north of Lagoa, a 10-minute drive on the N124-1 road, and 16.5 kilometers (10.2 mi) northeast of Portimão, a 25-minute drive via N124-1. Silves is easiest visited by car and offers ample parking in large free car parks along the riverside.

There are six **CP** (tel. 707 210 220, www.cp.pt) trains between Portimão and Silves (20 minutes, 11:30am-9:30pm daily, €2). Trains depart every few hours from Faro (1 hour, €5.20). The train station is on a steep hill 2 kilometers (1.2 mi) south of Silves. There are sometimes taxis outside the station, or call a taxi from the neighboring café.

Frota Azul (tel. 282 400 610, www.frotazul-algarve.pt) buses run almost hourly between Portimão and Silves (35 minutes, 7:30am-7:10pm daily, €3.35) via Lagoa. Buses stop along the riverfront, a short stroll from the town center.

A novel way to get to Silves from Portimão is by boat up the Arade River. **Algarve Sun Boat Trips** (tel. 919 919 450, www.algarvesunboat.com) operates solar-powered boats that depart Portimão's riverside year-round for Silves (1.5 hours, €30). The boats stop in Silves for three hours for passengers to wander around before they are brought back to Portimão by road. Refreshments on the boat are included.

Portimão

In its heyday, Portimão (por-tee-MOWN) was an important fishing and trading port with a thriving sardine and mackerel canning industry. The colorful, iconic designs used on the cans are now considered retro art, seen on modern tins as well as graffiti and murals around the city, embodying Portimão's former glory. The award-wining Portimão Museum is dedicated to this era, with a glimpse into life in Portimão a century ago.

Today Portimão is a blend of residential and touristy. Delimited to the south by Praia da Rocha, a well-known holiday hot spot, and the Arade River to the east, the once-impoverished city is bouncing back as a cool place to visit. And just 15 minutes west of Portimão is Alvor, one of the trendiest little villages in the region.

SIGHTS
Portimão Riverside
The riverside is delightful when the weather gets warmer. Families come to stroll the water's edge and enjoy ice cream in the gentle breeze from the sea. The riverside's bike track is popular with cyclists and joggers.

The main **Manuel Teixeira Gomes Square** is the heart of Portimão to enjoy the sunshine and watch the world go by. It's also known as Casa Inglesa square for the century-old café **Casa Inglesa** (tel. 282 416 290, 8am-11pm daily). The ice cream parlor **Nosolo Italia** (tel. 282 427 024, www.nosoloitalia.com, 10am-2am daily, €8), renowned for its huge and varied sundaes, is a must in this part of town.

★ Portimão Museum
(Museu de Portimão)
Toward the south end of Portimão's riverside and Praia da Rocha, the **Portimão Museum** (Rua D. Carlos I, tel. 282 405 230 or 282 405 265, www.museudeportimao.pt, 2:30pm-6pm

Tues, 10am-6pm Wed-Sun Sept-July, 7:30pm-11pm Tues, 3pm-11pm Wed-Sun Aug, adults €3, children under 16 free) has breathed new life into the site of a once-thriving cannery building. Inaugurated in 2008, the museum has won awards for its insight into fishing and canning traditions. An interactive recreation of the entire process, from landing catches to production lines and canning, uses state-of-the-art effects.

Also on display are local artifacts from prehistoric, Roman, and Islamic times. Part of the museum is dedicated to Portimão's most famous son, Manuel Teixeira Gomes, an acclaimed writer, diplomat, and president of Portugal 1923-1925. English translations on exhibits are scarce, although staff will try to answer questions in English. The documentary videos in the interactive experience have English subtitles.

FOOD
In summer, when the Algarve is at its busiest and the sardines are at their fattest, people flock to Portimão's trademark row of **riverside sardine restaurants.** The smell of grilled fish wafts across the city, and cooks turning fish on large outdoor grills always make a great photograph. Sardines are caught in spring and summer to allow stocks to replenish in winter, meaning some restaurants may close during low season.

Tucked away under Portimão's bridge is ★ **Dona Barca** (Largo da Barca 22, tel. 282 484 189, noon-11pm daily, €15), a favorite among locals with a festive interior that reflects the colorful characters who frequent it. The menu is all about fresh seafood, including, of course, sardines. Another riverside seafood restaurant that is popular among locals, **Marisqueira A Fábrica** (Av. Afonso Henriques, Av. Fabrica Bldg., Loja E, tel. 282 431 091, 10am-11:45pm daily, €15)

Local Specialties

A former canning heavyweight, Portimão is still an active fishing city famed for **sardines,** small silvery, fatty, and juicy fish. Sardine stocks are decreasing in waters used by Portuguese trawlers, so sardine prices are rising. Called "the queen of summer," the sardine is a national treasure and an indisputable icon.

Portimão hosts a yearly sardine festival, and part of the city's pretty riverside is set aside for grilled-sardine restaurants. The way to eat sardines, according to locals, is on a thick slice of bread, letting the juices sink in while you remove first the backbone and then the crispy skin and juicy flesh with your fingers. The bread should be saved for last. Sardines are traditionally accompanied by boiled baby potatoes and mixed salad with grilled peppers.

Other regional specialties in Portimão include the *cataplana,* fish stew cooked in a clam-like copper pan and served directly onto the plate by a waiter. The traditional Algarvian *cataplana* is made with clams, monkfish, potato, garlic, onion, tomatoes, green pepper, and olive oil, producing a sauce that is deep red, rich, and aromatic.

serves remarkably varied fresh seafood platters and a delicious Thai green or red prawn curry.

Just up the road from Dona Barca is the traditional **Taberna da Maré** (Travessa da Barca 9, tel. 282 414 614, noon-3pm and 7pm-10pm Tues-Sun, €15), a quaint place with wooden benches and a tiled counter on the bar, adding to the authenticity. On the menu are no-frills traditional dishes like grilled meats, cuttlefish, and freshly grilled catch of the day.

For something more exotic, **Masala House** (14 Rua Carlos da Maia, tel. 282 412 020, 10am-11pm daily, €9), in the center of Portimão, has a reputation for being one of the best Indian restaurants in the region. Located opposite the striking city hall building, this small restaurant serves up fresh Indian specialties and a range of vegetarian options.

ENTERTAINMENT AND EVENTS

Portimão Sardine Festival

Portimão is home to the popular summer **Sardine Festival** (tel. 282 470 700, www.cm-portimao.pt, early Aug). Held since 1985, the festival runs for five days, accompanied by nightly concerts. Entry is free, and for around €6, visitors can enjoy a plateful of sardines and a drink.

Saint Martin (São Martinho) Fair

Every fall, Portimão welcomes the **Saint Martin Fair** (early Nov), once a celebration of the saint and now a celebration of the harvest, with roasted chestnuts and *farturas* (sugar- and cinnamon-coated doughnuts) in abundance. One of the most popular in the region, it runs for 10 days before November 11, the Day of Saint Martin (São Martinho). Held annually since 1662, the fair is open from morning till midnight near the train station at the Park for Fairs and Exhibitions, with hundreds of stalls selling food, kitchenware, clothes, shoes, trinkets, and fairground rides.

SHOPPING

Meander the city's main shopping district, the Rua das Lojas (Shopping Street), and browse shops that showcase Portuguese products like leather bags and shoes, textiles, and toys.

RECREATION

Golf

Built on a former rice field, the **Penina Hotel & Golf Resort** (N125, Penina, tel. 282 420 200, www.penina.com, greens fees from €45, 2 players plus cart €105) was the first 18-hole golf resort in the Algarve, designed by Sir Henry Cotton, who described it as his greatest achievement; it also has the Resort Course and

THE ALGARVE
PORTIMÃO

the Academy Course. Inaugurated in 1966 by Portugal's president, it is one of the few true championship golf courses in Southern Europe.

Boating

Boat trips from Portimão's riverside and marina range from scenic voyages along the Arade River (from €25), fishing trips (€30-50), coastal sightseeing cruises (€35-70), sunset cruises (€30), and dolphin-watching trips (www.seafaris.net, €40).

A large wooden "pirate ship"-style caravel, the *Santa Bernarda* (Rua Júdice Fialho 4, tel. 282 422 791 or 967 023 84, www.santabernarda.com) is the most recognizable of the Algarve's recreational boats, with half-day and full-day trips (from €35) along the coast to explore caves, with options such as a barbecue lunch on the beach.

Go-Karting

Inaugurated in 2008, the **Algarve International Circuit Racetrack (Autódromo Internacional do Algarve)** (Sítio do Escampadinho, Mexilhoeira Grande, tel. 282 405 600, www.autodromodoalgarve.com) hopes to become a serious contender on the international racing calendar. It is also home to Europe's biggest go-kart track (from €26 for 15 minutes); equipment is supplied.

ACCOMMODATIONS

Hotel Globo (Rua 5 de Outubro 26, tel. 282 490 160, www.hotel-globo.portimao.hotelsalgarve.org, €70) is one of the few in the heart of Portimão city. Its glass-clad top-floor restaurant is an illuminated landmark seen for miles, offering diners stunning views. After a full refurbishment, this modern, three-star hotel now offers a boutique feel; it is within walking distance of Portimão riverside and the main shopping street.

Halfway between Portimão city and Praia da Rocha, holiday apartment complex **Apartamentos Clube VilaRosa** (Rua da Vila Rosa, Lote 1, tel. 282 430 100, www.clubevilarosa.com, €165) is within walking distance of both. A well-kept, pretty pink resort, it has a large pool, tennis courts, and plenty of entertainment in summer.

INFORMATION AND SERVICES

PSP police: Av. Miguel Bombarda 16, tel. 282 417 717, www.psp.pt

GNR police: Av. São Lourenço da Barrosa, tel. 282 420 750, www.gnr.pt

Main tourist office: Largo 1º de Dezembro, tel. 282 430 165

Post office: Praça Manuel Teixeira Gomes, near the riverfront, tel. 282 420 150

Portimão State Hospital: Estrada do Poço Seco, tel. 282 450 300

GETTING THERE AND AROUND

Portimão is 72 kilometers (45 mi) west, a 45-minute drive, from Faro airport on the A22 motorway. (Take the Portimão turnoff, which leads into the north of the city.) It's 10 kilometers (6.2 mi) west of Lagoa, a 15-minute drive along the N125 road, and 14 kilometers (8.7 mi) west of Carvoeiro, a 20-minute drive on the N125 road via Lagoa.

Buses and trains run to Portimão from Faro and other major towns in the Algarve. **CP** (tel. 707 210 220, www.cp.pt) trains run almost hourly between Faro and Portimão (1.5 hours, €6.10-15.55). Portimão's train station is in a seedy part of town, 2 kilometers (1.2 mi) from the riverfront and Praia da Rocha, but there are usually taxis on the doorstep.

The main bus terminal is on the riverfront. An express Eva bus, the **Transrápido** (tel. 289 899 760, www.eva-bus.com), runs between Faro bus terminal and Portimão (1.75 hours, every 2 hours 8am-7:40pm Mon-Fri, 12:30pm and 5:35pm Sat-Sun, under €10), with stops at Albufeira and Lagoa.

One of the best ways to get around Portimão is on the city's nifty **Vai-e-Vem shuttle bus** (www.cm-portimao.pt, €1.50, day tickets €3.50), which runs from early morning to late night and covers a comprehensive network within the city and its fringes. The Vai-e-Vem's hub is in Portimão main square, Largo do Dique; there are 10 lines around Portimão, and 7 to and around the village of Alvor. Buy tickets from the driver.

PRAIA DA ROCHA

Praia da Rocha, 3 kilometers (1.9 mi) south of Portimão, is a premier holiday destination and one of the western Algarve's most popular tourist hot spots, with a stunning beach and vibrant nightlife year-round. Spanning 1 kilometer (0.6 mi), the long golden strip of sand is backed by cliffs, with the town's main hotels, restaurants, bars, and shops on a road running along the cliff tops parallel to the beach.

In summer, the beach is packed with families and young people on school holidays. A wooden walkway runs the length of the beach along the foot of the cliffs, punctuated with restaurants selling snacks, meals, ice cream, and cocktails.

Sights

SANTA CATARINA FORT
(Fortaleza da Santa Catarina)

At the eastern end of Praia da Rocha, overlooking Portimão Marina and the Arade River mouth, the 17th-century **Santa Catarina Fort** (tel. 282 402 487, 24 hours daily, free) is a small medieval stronghold built to defend the town from pirates and maritime invasions. It is mirrored on the opposite side of the river by the São João do Arade Fort in Ferragudo. Inside are cafés and a courtyard with panoramic views over Praia da Rocha and Ferragudo. Take a steep flight of steps down to Praia da Rocha Marina and the beach. The fortress is right off the main road, Avenida Tomás Cabreira.

PORTIMÃO MARINA
(Marina de Portimão)

With 300 berths, **Portimão Marina** accommodates some of the sleekest yachts in the Algarve, lending a sophisticated atmosphere to this part of town. The marina is fringed by buildings painted bright terra-cotta, yellow, and red, complementing the Tivoli Marina Hotel. A number of bars and restaurants can also be found along the water.

Food

For a special occasion, head to ★ **F Restaurante** (Av. Tomás Cabreira, Edifício Falésia, tel. 919 115 512 or 282 483 014, www. food-emotions.com, 3pm-10:30pm Mon-Sat, €20), with excellent service. The creative menu, inspired by seasonal local produce and traditional recipes with a contemporary twist, is outshone only by the stunning views of Praia da Rocha beach.

Nightlife

Praia da Rocha, along with Albufeira, is one of the most popular nightspots in the western Algarve, drawing crowds year-round. As well as a colorful selection of bars, in summer many of Praia da Rocha's hotels put on live music events open to nonguests. Praia da Rocha is also home to one of the Algarve's three casinos.

PRAIA DA ROCHA STRIP

Not quite as long as Albufeira's Strip but almost as flashy, Praia da Rocha's main Strip, **Avenida Tomás Cabreira,** stretches the length of the beach along the cliff tops and has most of the resort's main hotels, restaurants, Irish pubs, sports bars, discos, and karaoke bars. It's busy year-round and has a more family-oriented feel than Albufeira's Strip. In summer some of the hotels near the Strip have live music and dancing that is open to everyone.

The **Hotel Algarve Casino** (Av. Tomás Cabreira, tel. 282 402 000, www. hotelalgarvecasino.solverde.pt, 6pm-3am Mon-Fri, 4pm-4am Fri-Sat, 3pm-3am Sun), one of three casinos in the Algarve, is also on the Strip, for a show (€15), dinner with a show (€35), and a little flutter on the tables. Along with standard game machines, the casino has three American roulette tables, four Texas Hold 'em poker tables, and a blackjack table.

PORTIMÃO MARINA

The upscale marina offers popular bars and trendy alfresco hangouts. The ultra-cool **Nosolo Agua Portimão Pool and Beach Club** (Portimão Marina, tel. 282 498 180, www.nosoloagua.com, 10am-2am daily Mar-Oct) is a chic place to be seen on sun loungers during the day, and in summer it becomes a premier venue for night events such as regular live music and dance, guest DJs, and huge parties hosted by the likes of MTV.

Recreation

Water sports concessionaires dot the beach, touting pedal boats, Jet Skis, and kayaks.

SCUBA DIVING

Rich in shipwrecks and marinelife, the Portimão area is a hub for diving, with several PADI schools. **Subnauta** (Rua Engenheiro José de Bívar, Edifício Scorpius, Loja B, Praia da Rocha, tel. 935 577 000, www.subnauta.pt, 8:30am-6pm daily) is a well-established dive center with a highly qualified team that organizes dives (from €50) and courses.

With the growing interest in diving and a wealth of subaquatic attractions, the **Ocean Revival Project** (Rua Engenheiro José de Bívar, Edifício Scorpius, Praia da Rocha, tel. 935 577 000, www.oceanrevival.org) seeks to create a world-class diving destination. Four decommissioned warships were sunk to create an underwater park, the Ocean Park Revival, and act as an artificial reef. It provides an exceptional diving experience.

BOATING

Dolphin-watching excursions depart Praia da Rocha's marina, from where big-game fishing trips, sunset cruises, and private charters can also be arranged. **Seafaris** (www.seafaris.net) runs regular dolphin-watching trips (from €40).

1: Silves Castle walls; 2: an exhibit in the Portimão Museum; 3: promenade along the beach in Praia da Rocha; 4: Praia da Rocha

Accommodations

Right on the lively main strip, **Hotel Jupiter** (Av. Tomás Cabreira 92, tel. 282 470 470, www.jupiteralgarvehotel.com, €185) is a mid-range four-star, family-friendly hotel. It has a heated swimming pool that's covered in winter and nightly entertainment during summer. Overlooking the beach, it has 183 rooms and suites, an on-site restaurant, and a spa.

Imposingly on the cliff edge, overlooking the beach, the historic ★ **Hotel Belavista** (Av. Tomas Cabreira, tel. 282 460 280, www. hotelbelavista.net, €378) has been voted one of the most beautiful hotels in Europe. Converted from a 1918 mansion, this gorgeous boutique hotel was one of the first hotels opened in the Algarve. It boasts stunning gardens, direct access to Praia da Rocha beach, and a fabulous spa.

Cheapish and cheerful, **Clube Praia da Rocha** (Av. das Comunidades Lusíadas, tel. 282 400 500, www.cprocha.com, studios from €90, 1-bedroom apartments €120) is the ultimate family-friendly resort, with indoor and outdoor pools, activities for kids, and bountiful buffets at mealtimes. With 300 studio and one-bedroom apartments with kitchenettes, guests can opt for self-catering packages or include one to three meals a day. The apartments are dated and basic but spacious and clean.

Information and Services

Main tourist office: in front of Hotel Jupiter, Av. Tomás Cabreira, tel. 282 419 132

Post office: Rua Engenheiro José de Bívar, Edifício Plaza, LJ 2, tel. 282 416 532

Getting There

Praia da Rocha is on the southern fringe of Portimão, 3 kilometers (1.9 mi) south of the city center. Take a taxi to Praia da Rocha from Portimão (€5) or jump onto one of the handy **Vai-e-Vem shuttle buses** (www.cm-portimao.pt, €1.50) that dart around the city. The main lines that run between Portimão's main Largo do Dique riverfront square and Praia da Rocha are numbers 33 and 11. Buy tickets on board. It is possible to walk from Portimão to Praia da Rocha in 45-60 minutes.

ALVOR

Alvor has managed to flourish from a simple fishing village into a hugely popular seaside resort without sacrificing any of its original character. With the village's smart riverfront area dotted with trendy wooden café-bars, a main street that's busy without being brash, and plentiful fish restaurants along the harbor, it's easy to see why people flock here. It is a place to enjoy a walk, the scenery, a meal, and a cocktail or two.

Sights and Recreation

The picturesque village is fringed to the south by a pretty harbor and wetlands with uninterrupted views of Lagos to the west and rugged coast to the east. Water sports are another major draw in Alvor, with kayaking, kite-surfing, and boat trips available from the harbor.

ALVOR ESTUARY AND WALKWAY

A 6-kilometer (3.7-mi) wooden boardwalk is built on the dunes that separate Alvor's waterfront from the beach, providing a serene walk through the scenic *ria* (estuary) and its wealth of flora and fauna. Benches along the walkway allow you to enjoy the view. This walkway starts by the harbor and winds through dunes and marshes, a tapestry of green and gold with abundant birdlife. Visit in the evening for a spectacular sunset.

ALCALAR MEGALITHIC MONUMENTS
(Monumentos Megaliticos de Alcalar)

In the parish of Mexilhoeira Grande, the hilltop **Alcalar Megalithic Monuments** (www.monumentosdoalgarve.pt, 10am-1pm and 2pm-6pm Tues-Sat Aug, 10am-1pm and 2pm-4:30pm Tues-Sat Sept-July, €2, €4 with museum) are a set of ancient granite burial tombs that date back to the third millennium BC. Classified a national monument, the necropolis has seen archaeological digs since the 19th century. It also has an on-site museum.

Alcalar is 10 kilometers (6.2 mi) north of Alvor and 11 kilometers (6.8 mi) northwest of Portimão; each is about a 12-minute drive. Follow the N125 road from Alvor and Portimão toward Lagos. Turn opposite the Penina Hotel and petrol station. The route is signposted. The site is easy to find and has limited parking. A taxi costs around €8 from Alvor and €12 from Portimão.

Alvor estuary and walkway

BOATING

Alvor Boat Trips (Alvor harbor-front, tel. 962 091 551, www.alvorboattrips.com, from €15) operates tours and charters along the coastline as well as down the Arade River to Silves, in a number of different vessels, among them a solar-powered boat.

SKYDIVING

The Algarve is a top winter skydiving destination thanks to excellent weather conditions. A number of companies organize packages that cover everything from airport transport to lodging. One of these is **Sky Dive Algarve** (Aeródromo Municipal de Portimão, Alvor, tel. 282 496 581, www.skydivealgarve.com, from €235), certified and experienced, operating 365 days a year. Be wowed by the stunning Algarve from a unique vantage point.

Food

Alvor's main Rua Dr. Frederico Ramos Mendes, a steep cobblestone street that runs from the top of the village to Alvor Bay, has the right mix of bars, restaurants, and shops. At the top is a municipal market, selling produce and fish and at night transforming into a popular restaurant, ★ **Churrasqueira Mercado** (Largo Castelo, Loja 2, tel. 282 458 248, lunch and dinner Tues-Sun Feb-Nov, €8). Basic pine tables and benches enhance the simplicity of the menu, which features grilled fish and chicken, so delicious, fresh, and cheap that the restaurant attracts queues from the moment it opens. Phone ahead to reserve a table.

There are many other good restaurants along the main road; at the bottom of the street along the riverfront are excellent fish restaurants.

Nightlife

Alvor's nightlife buzzes without being raucous, from smart cocktail bars to animated Irish bars that often have live music.

Popular among trendsetters is the **Caniço Restaurant and Beach Bar** (tel. 282 458 503, www.canicorestaurante.com, noon-5pm and 6pm-midnight daily), famous for its summer parties. Unusually, it is sandwiched between two cliffs and perched over Caniço beach. Enjoy a sundowner followed by a great meal of Portuguese Mediterranean fare, and then join the after-dinner party as it spills onto the beach, where a DJ plays until dawn. It can only be accessed via an elevator within the **Prainha Resort** (Praia dos Três Irmãos, www.prainha.net), 4 kilometers (2.5 mi) east of Alvor village.

Accommodations

Contemporary four-star beachside **Pestana Alvor South Beach** (Praceta do Barinel 1, tel. 282 243 000, www.pestana.com, €226) has a Miami vibe with a sleek contemporary design, art deco-inspired rooms, and palm tree-fringed infinity pools. Set on the gorgeous Três Irmãos Beach, it is a 20-minute, 2.5-kilometer (1.6-mi) walk southeast of Alvor village center.

Information and Services

HPA Private Hospital: Estrada de Alvor, tel. 707 282 828, www.grupohpa.com

Main tourist office: Rua Dr. Afonso Costa 51, tel. 282 457 540

Getting There

Alvor is 6 kilometers (3.7 mi) east of Portimão and Praia da Rocha. It can be reached in 10 minutes by taxi from Portimão or Praia da Rocha (about €10). Or jump on one of the many **Vai-e-Vem shuttle buses** (www.cm-portimao.pt, €1.50) that run among the three. Line 14 is one of the main routes between Portimão's main Largo do Dique riverside square and Alvor waterfront. Tickets can be bought on board. By car, take the main M531-1 road between Portimão and Alvor.

Monchique

The mountainside farming town of Monchique (MON-sheek) is part of the Serra de Monchique mountain range, which parallels the coast as the backbone of the western Algarve. Swaddled in eucalyptus, pine, and cork-oak trees, this part of the Algarve is a fragrant escape from the bustle of the coast. Lush and cool, Monchique's landscape changes with the seasons, emerald green in winter, a kaleidoscope of color in spring, golden in summer, and red in autumn. Monchique is a day trip from Portimão but also warrants staying a night or two.

Monchique is famous for its ultra-strong liquor *(aguardente)*, a potent alcoholic drink made from the strawberry-like *medronho* fruit. It is also famous for its spring water and traditionally made smoked meats and sausages, the centerpiece of an annual festival. Monchique is a town still steeped in tradition, where shops along winding cobbled streets display local handicrafts and artisans open their doors to anyone passing by. Notable regional arts and crafts include leather and wood.

SIGHTS AND RECREATION

Caldas de Monchique

The Caldas de Monchique natural springs and spa village are a magical place to spend a few hours, or stay a night at the **Villa Termal Caldas de Monchique Spa Resort** (Rua de Caldas de Monchique, tel. 282 910 910, www. monchiquetermas.com), which has a hot-spring spa where you can enjoy the famous warm spring water massages or soak in the pool, said to have therapeutic benefits (single entry for pool is €15 for hotel guests, €20 for nonguests).

Made up of a handful of mini palace-like properties, the hamlet is a lovely mountainside place for an invigorating walk in the

mountain air, with tall trees framing the running spring. Amid the trees are ancient stone tables and benches for picnics. On balmy summer nights, open-air movies and other events are held, while colorful lights are hung in the trees to add extra wonder to this unique spot.

The Caldas are just off the main road up to Monchique, 8 kilometers (5 mi) south of the town center.

★ Fóia Peak

At 908 meters (2,979 feet), Fóia Peak is the highest point in the Algarve. The drive up is gentle and winding and can be hair-raising at points, although the roads and safety barriers are in good condition. Visitors who don't have a car can make the journey from the town center by bus, taxi, or an 8-kilometer (5-mi) hike (which is much easier coming down than going up). Near the peak is a viewpoint with a spring-water fountain. At the peak, it's like standing on top of the world: On a clear day the view stretches to Cape St. Vincent in the west and Faro in the east—a breathtaking experience.

Fóia Peak is 8 kilometers (5 mi) west of Monchique on the N266-3 road. The drive up takes 15 minutes. Hikers generally follow the main road. There is no public transport to Fóia, but a taxi from Monchique town costs around €8. Try local company **Táxis Ginjeira Martins Unipessoal** (tel. 282 913 157).

FOOD

Monchique's gastronomy is literally from plot to plate. Meat, especially pork, is popular in Monchique, renowned for its traditional cured hams and smoked sausages. Monchique's rural essence comes to the fore in its gastronomy, with restaurants offering hearty meals at reasonable prices. Local specialties include stews incorporating cabbage,

Local Specialty: Monchique's Firewater

Besides its spring water, Monchique is famous for firewater *(aguardente)*, a clear distilled high-alcohol beverage made from the fruit of the Arbutus strawberry tree *(medronho)* that grows throughout the Algarve's interior. The drink is generally taken as a shot after meals; locals say it aids digestion. Be warned: it is very potent. A softer version, *melosa*, is *aguardente* mixed with honey, lemon, and cinnamon. *Aguardente de medronho* is homemade and not widely commercialized, so don't be surprised if it is served from an unmarked bottle from under the counter. Top tip: Start with a small sip.

pork, and beans. Platters of cured or smoked meats and cheeses, warm rustic bread, and big jugs of wine are staples. An added bonus is that many restaurants are on the mountainside and offer gorgeous views to the coast.

Established in 1958, **Cinzas** (Pocilgais, tel. 282 912 221, lunch and dinner daily, €10) restaurant is a well-known family-run eatery on the winding road up to the town, just before the Caldas. As well as serving hearty home-cooked local specialties like eel stew, Cinzas also serves platters of traditional Monchique products, like wafer-thin slices of dry-cured ham *(presunto)* and regional cheeses. Much of the food comes from the family's own farm. This place is a must to sample the real flavors of Monchique.

ENTERTAINMENT AND EVENTS

In March, Monchique throws its popular **Feira dos Enchidos** (stuffed meats fair, early Mar), showcasing the region's tasty cured and smoked *choriça* sausage and *presunto* ham as well as cheeses, honey, and *aguardente*. It takes place over two days, usually the first weekend in March. Other local specialties, such as roast kid with plums,

black pig cheeks, cabbage Monchique-style, and honey cake, are also available.

ACCOMMODATIONS

The historic **Villa Termal Caldas de Monchique Spa Resort** (Rua de Caldas de Monchique, tel. 282 910 910, www.monchiquetermas.com, €107) is in five small, charming hotel buildings. The resort also has a wine bar, a restaurant, a convenience store, and a hot-spring spa that nonguests can also enjoy.

GETTING THERE

Monchique is 32 kilometers (20 mi) and a 30-minute drive north of Portimão. From the A22 motorway, take the Monchique turnoff near Portimão and follow the signs. From anywhere in the Algarve, you can also take the main N125 road to Portimão, then head north toward the A22, following the N266 road. It's a short drive from Portimão to the base of the mountain.

Buses operated by **Frota Azul** (tel. 282 400 610, www.frotazul-algarve.pt) run almost hourly between Portimão and Monchique (45 minutes, 7:50am-8:30pm daily, €4). Buses depart Portimão from Avenida Guarané, on the riverfront, at Stop 5, and drop passengers in Monchique town center.

Lagos

At the mouth of the Bensafrim River, Lagos (LAH-goosh) has long been a favorite for backpackers and surfers thanks to its beaches, tourist-friendly attitude, laid-back vibes, and genuine Portuguese character. Add an Old Town, cool nightlife, and a variety of places to eat and drink, and Lagos pulls visitors in droves.

Lagos played an important role in the Age of Discoveries, as Prince Henry the Navigator lived and built his ships here, having founded a navigation school in nearby Sagres. Other Portuguese explorers set sail from Lagos and helped establish the city as a prosperous trading point.

Lagos's economy is tightly linked to the sea and to tourism. As one of the Algarve's most popular destinations, it is a good base for exploring the western Algarve, with proximity to Sagres, Aljezur, and Luz for day trips.

SIGHTS

Lagos begs to be explored on foot, but it is expansive, so wear comfortable shoes. Start with a stroll along the riverside promenade before crossing the main Avenida dos Descobrimentos (Discoveries Avenue), parallel to the waterfront, to wander around the Old Town. Follow the castle walls through the city along the charming cobbled streets. Then head to the southern tip of Lagos, Ponta da Piedade, with its famous tide-battered rock formations and lighthouse. Back toward Lagos, pass Praia Dona Ana beach and the Ponta da Bandeira fortress. This is a lovely walk that will occupy a few hours, or a full day if you stop for drinks and lunch, and it takes in most of Lagos's major sights.

Lagos Marina
(Marina de Lagos)
On the Bensafrim River, across from Lagos's riverfront promenade, **Lagos Marina** (www.

marlagos.pt) separates the city of Lagos from Meia Praia and the local train station. Opened in 1994, it hosts hundreds of vessels and charter boat trips. Connected to Lagos city center with a bridge, the petite marina houses a number of good bars and restaurants.

Old Town Center
(Centro Histórico)
Lagos's Old Town Center is a place to appreciate the city's history and lounge at one of the many pretty cafés. Sixteenth-century stone walls from Lagos's castle encircle the Old Town, explored by passing through the impressive **São Gonçalo Gate,** flanked to either side by watchtowers. The Old Town Center is a tangle of cobbled streets, picturesque squares, shops, simple white-washed cottages, and tile-clad town houses. Also within the Old Town is the **Gil Eanes Square (Praça Gil Eanes),** named after another Portuguese navigator, where locals meet for a *café*. It's at its most vibrant after dusk.

ST. ANTHONY CHURCH
(Igreja de Santo António)
A highlight of the Old Town is the tiny 18th-century national monument **St. Anthony Church** (Rua General Alberto da Silveira, tel. 282 762 301, 10am-12:30pm and 2pm-5:30pm Tues-Sun, church and museum €3), whose plain limestone exterior belies its lavish baroque interior, a single aisle with no side chapels, clad with ornate gilded wooden carvings and azulejo plaques. The centerpiece is an opulent golden altar. No photography is allowed inside, and explanatory notes are in English. Adjacent to the church is the **Dr. José Formosinho Museum,** packed with a random, bordering on bizarre, collection of local artifacts, from coins to model ships, dolls houses, and Roman relics.

Lagos

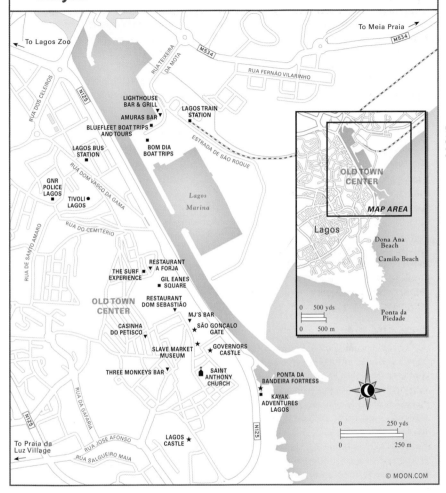

© MOON.COM

SLAVE MARKET MUSEUM
(Mercado de Escravos)

Lagos was home to the first market for enslaved Africans in Europe. The historic building, today housing the **Slave Market Museum** (Praca Infante Dom Henrique, tel. 282 762 301, 10:30am-12:30pm and 2pm-5:30pm Tues-Sun, €3), was built in the 17th century, first to house the Royal Overseer's office and later the local customs house. The museum is on two floors, the upper floor accessed via a staircase on a side street. The museum offers a sobering look at the history of slavery in Lagos and throughout the Algarve, from the arrival of the first boatload of enslaved Africans in 1444. Artifacts include weapons, manacles, and maps used during the slave trading era.

GOVERNORS CASTLE
(Castelo dos Governadores)

Lagos's most prominent feature is the impressive 17th-century **Governors Castle** (Jardim da Constituição, 24 hours daily, free). In its heyday, it housed kings and explorers and was the seat of the region's governors. The entrance to the stout stone fort is guarded by chunky towers, and many parts of the pentagonal medieval city walls are well preserved. There's not much to see inside, but the castle is an excellent photo opportunity. Follow the castle walls around the city for excellent views. The pretty gardens to the front and side of the castle are also worth a visit.

PONTA DA BANDEIRA FORT (Fortaleza da Ponta da Bandeira)

The squat quadrangular **Ponta da Bandeira Fort** (Cais da Solaria, tel. 282 761 410, 9:30am-12:30pm and 2pm-5pm Tues-Sun, €2) dates from the late 17th century, completing Lagos's defense system and one of the last strongholds built here. It is also the city's best-preserved monument. Cross a little drawbridge to find a small 18th-century chapel, barracks converted into art exhibitions, a restaurant, and views over the sea and the city.

Ponta da Piedade

At the southernmost tip of Lagos, 3.5 kilometers (2.2 mi) south of the center, is **Ponta da Piedade** (Piety Point), a vast headland that juts into the Atlantic with a lighthouse. Centuries of tides and gales have weathered the cliffs into extraordinary formations: tunnels, arcs, caves, and pillars. Ponta da Piedade's 1913 lighthouse is dwarfed by the 50-meter (164-foot) promontory. Just over an hour's walk from Lagos, it is now decommissioned and closed, but the views from the headland are phenomenal. A web of pathways spans the area. Lovely beaches, including the popular Praia do Camilo, flank the headland. Praia do Camilo is accessed down a flight of 200 steps from Ponta da Piedade, so it is not wheelchair accessible.

Boat trips to explore this awesome feat of nature run year-round from Lagos Marina as well as from the base of the promontory, weather and sea conditions permitting. Little boats can be found at the foot of the outcrop, accessed down a flight of 200 steps. The smaller the boat, the more grottoes and narrow passages it can squeeze into. A 15-minute boat trip into the caves costs around €20 pp.

Lagos Zoo

A 20-minute drive 17 kilometers (10.5 mi) northwest of Lagos is **Lagos Zoo** (Medronhal-Quinta Figueiras, tel. 282 680 100, www.zoolagos.com, 10am-5pm daily, adults €15, children 4-11 €12, discounts online), in the hamlet of Barão de São João. The modest-size zoo has habitats for birds, mammals, and reptiles, plus a Portuguese restaurant. A taxi from Lagos costs around €15.

BEACHES

Lagos boasts a healthy selection of beaches, from long stretches of sand to small cove-like hideaways.

Dona Ana Beach (Praia Dona Ana)

A 2-kilometer (1.2-mi), 25-minute walk south of the city center, postcard-perfect **Dona Ana Beach** has recently been praised as one of the most beautiful beaches in the world. Bigger than the average cove-type beach, it doesn't feel crowded but offers a romantic feel. Golden cliffs surround the soft golden sand fronting cool crystalline water. Be warned that it gets busy on weekends and throughout summer, so parking around the area might be harder to find at those times.

Meia Beach (Meia Praia)

Meia Beach is 4 kilometers (2.5 mi) of soft golden sand from Lagos to Alvor, on the east side of Lagos Marina, offering ample space even in the height of summer. Development is low-rise and sparse in places, so it can feel quiet and secluded. The western end, a 40-minute walk (7 km/4.3 mi) from Lagos

---

1: Ponta da Piedade in Lagos; **2:** Fóia Peak near Monchique; **3:** Caldas de Monchique; **4:** Dona Ana Beach in Lagos

city center, over the bridge to the marina and past the train station, tends to be the busiest section, but a bit farther along is all the space and peace you could want. The sea tends to be shallow and calm, albeit cooler than in the eastern Algarve. Beach beds and parasols are provided by outfitters (from €10 per day), along with equipment for windsurfing, kite-surfing, and Jet Skiing.

Camilo Beach
(Praia do Camilo)

Camilo Beach is a sensational little sheltered cove-beach between Dona Ana Beach and Ponta da Piedade, on the outcrop's western face. Its 200 wooden steps lead down from the cliffs. Just around the corner, west of the Piedade headland, is **Porto de Mós Beach,** the second longest in Lagos after Meia Beach. Camilo Beach is 2.2 kilometers (1.4 mi) south of Lagos center, a 30-minute walk.

FOOD

Lagos has an eclectic mix of dining options, from warehouse-like cantinas to food trucks and international restaurants.

A few streets back from the river is **Restaurant A Forja** (Rua dos Ferreiros 17, tel. 282 768 588, noon-3pm and 6:30pm-10pm Sun-Fri, €14), from the outside little more than an unremarkable doorway. But inside, this typical *adega* (wine cellar) has a strong local feel, serving generous portions of home-cooked, unfussy Portuguese food, including grilled fish and steaks.

Close to A Forja, just back from the river, **Restaurant Dom Sebastião** (Rua 25 de Abril 20-22, tel. 282 780 480, www. restaurantedonsebastiao.com, noon-10:30pm daily, €12) is a classically rustic Portuguese restaurant with polished cobblestone floors and dark wood tables and chairs, making it feel cozy and intimate. With a dedicated following since opening in 1979 and a vast underground wine cellar, it provides fine dining with accomplished dishes from local ingredients.

Casinha do Petisco (Rua da Oliveira 51,

tel. 282 084 285, noon-2:30pm Mon, noon-2:30pm and 6pm-10:30pm Tues-Sat, €12), "Little House of Snacks," offers tapas-size dishes of local and regional specialties, made for sharing with beer or wine and good company. On Lagos Marina, British pub-style **The Lighthouse Bar & Grill** (Marina de Lagos, tel. 282 762 115, 9am-2am daily, €8) is a top spot for a comfortable beer and a bite. With a laid-back atmosphere, it serves pub grub like fish-and-chips, chili, and a Sunday roast. There's live music and karaoke during the week.

ENTERTAINMENT AND EVENTS

Lagos has vibrant, easygoing nightlife for surfers, backpackers, and the more discerning. The city center has an eclectic assortment of bars and nightclubs, many in historic buildings on the city's cobbled backstreets. The marina boasts classy upmarket bars, while Meia Beach is for a chilled cocktail and a beach party that goes until daybreak.

One of Lagos' top nighttime haunts, just off the waterfront, colorful **MJ's Bar** (Travessa de Sra. de Graça 2, tel. 969 923 639, 7:30pm-2am daily) is a cool little place serving great cocktails and playing old school music (requests taken).

One place where the party always gets started, **Three Monkeys Bar** (Rua Lancarote de Freitas 26, tel. 282 762 995, www.3monkeys. me.uk, 1pm-2am daily) is close to hostels and draws a young and energetic crowd fueled by shots, happy hours, dancing, and a great variety of music.

Comfortable, laid-back **Amuras Bar** (Marina de Lagos, Shop 4, tel. 282 792 112, 9am-2am daily) on Lagos Marina has a friendly, lively atmosphere, televised sports, and live music most evenings. A popular meeting place for locals, it attracts a more demure clientele and serves pub grub.

RECREATION
Boating

A variety of boat trips and charters are run

from Lagos Marina, including dolphin-watching trips and grotto exploring. Stroll around the shops and stalls to see what takes your fancy. **Bom Dia Boat Trips** (Lagos Marina, Shop 10, tel. 282 087 587, www.bomdiaboattrips.com) offers coastal sightseeing tours, dolphin-watching, and grotto trips on sailing ships (€20-55). **BlueFleet Boat Trips and Tours** (Lagos Marina, tel. 911 963 309, www.bluefleet.pt) has grotto trips, dolphin-watching, kayaking, and the Blue Cruise (3.5 hours, 11:30am Mon-Sat, adults €50, children €25) along the Lagos coastline past Ponta da Piedade, including appetizers, lunch on board, and a swim.

Kayaking

Explore iconic Lagos coastal spots from the water with **Kayak Adventure Lagos** (Av. dos Descobrimentos, Cais da Solaria, Lugar 2, tel. 913 262 200, www.kayakadventureslagos.com, from €29 pp) and its English-speaking guides. Paddle through caves and grottoes and find deserted beaches at sunrise, sunset, or try a kayak and snorkel trip.

Surfing

The most popular pastime in Lagos is surfing, and a number of surf schools and camps have popped up in recent years. Many instructors are foreigners, and all speak good English.

Established in Lagos since 1992, **Surf Experience Lagos** (Rua dos Ferreiros 21, tel. 282 086 012, 919 830 591, or 916 137 082, www.surfexperience.com) is run by a mix of experienced surfers of various nationalities who know the area well. Boot camps, surf safaris, longboard weeks, surf school, and yoga are among the wave-based programs. Accommodations and airport transfers are available. Weeklong surf camps include breakfast and lunch, beach transfers, lessons, and equipment (from €428).

Filsurf (tel. 917 127 517, www.filsurf.com) provides surf lessons (from €50), surf camps, day trips, and surfboards and wetsuits (from €25 per day) for beginners to boasters.

Hiking

Don your comfiest walking shoes for trekking with **West Coast Adventure Company** (tel. 918 903 899, www.westcoastlagos.com). Led by an experienced English-speaking guide, tailor-made group adventure hikes (from €69 pp) show off the west coast's secret beauty spots, with sunset picnics.

ACCOMMODATIONS

Relaxed, whitewashed **Tivoli Lagos** (Rua António Crisógono dos Santos, tel. 282 790 079, www.minorhotels.com, €134) hotel has three restaurants and three pools and is at the entrance to Lagos, within walking distance of the town center and a short walk to the train station and marina.

INFORMATION AND SERVICES

GNR police: Largo d'Armas 28, tel. 282 770 010, www.gnr.pt

Main tourist office: Praça Gil Eanes 17, tel. 282 764 111

Post office: Rua da Porta de Portugal 25, tel. 282 770 251

GETTING THERE

Lagos is 90 kilometers (56 mi) west of Faro, an hour's drive on the A22 motorway from Faro airport, or follow the N125 road west to Lagos. It's 23 kilometers (14.3 mi) west of Portimão, a 25-minute drive along the N125 road.

An express Eva bus, the **Transrápido** (tel. 289 899 760, www.eva-bus.com), runs between Faro bus terminal and Lagos (2 hours, every 2 hours 8am-7:40pm Mon-Fri, 12:30pm and 5:35pm Sat-Sun, under €10), with stops at Albufeira and Portimão. Eva also operates a half-dozen buses on Interurbanos (Intercity) and Litoral (Coastal) lines between Portimão and Lagos (35 minutes, €4). The **Lagos Bus Terminal** (Largo do Rossio de São João, tel. 282 762 944) is in the city center.

CP (tel. 707 210 220, www.cp.pt) trains run between Faro's main station and Lagos Station (1.75 hours, every 2 hours, €7.50-16.05). Trains run almost hourly between Portimão and Lagos (20 minutes, 8:30am-10pm, €2.05). **Lagos Station** (Estrada de São Roque) is on the opposite side of the waterway, behind the Lagos Marina, a 15-minute walk from the city center.

GETTING AROUND

The best way to explore Lagos is on foot, but to go beyond the center, the **Onda** (www.aonda. pt, €1.20-1.60, day pass €3.60) bus network runs nine color-coded lines from the center to all attractions as well as popular villages in the suburbs. The red and turquoise lines circulate in the city center, while the yellow, pink, and green lines run to Luz village and Barão de São João, where the zoo is. Tickets can be bought from the driver or at the main bus station.

Taxis (tel. 282 763 587) are readily available in Lagos and can be found along the waterfront.

LUZ VILLAGE

Family-friendly and welcoming, the delightful seaside village of Luz (LOOZH), or Praia da Luz, is a 15-minute drive west of Lagos. It has soared in popularity but has been sensibly developed to retain its classic charm. Luz centers on a bay-shaped beach flanked by an unusual volcanic black-rock cliff, in remarkable contrast with the red sandstone of the rest of the coastline. The challenging hike to the top of this cliff is rewarded with views over the Atlantic.

Compact but comprehensive, Luz has banks, supermarkets, cafés, and arts and crafts stalls well presented and in close proximity. A pretty cobbled promenade along the waterfront west of the beach is an excellent spot to enjoy an ice cream or sunset. In the heart of the village is the medieval Our Lady of Light Church, a short stroll from the ruins of what were once Roman baths, tucked behind the promenade wall.

Luz is 12 kilometers (7.4 mi) west of Lagos, on the yellow, pink and green lines (30 minutes) of Lagos's **Onda** (www.aonda.pt, €1.20-1.60, day pass €3.60) buses. Buy tickets from the driver or at the main Lagos bus station. A **taxi** (tel. 282 763 587) from Lagos to Luz costs around €10.

SALEMA

At the western end of the Algarve, the tiny coastal town of Salema is a little jewel for its beach, a sandy bay with calm water backed by sloping cliffs. Inaccessible by train and largely overlooked by tourists, Salema is an unspoiled fishing hamlet for escaping the crowds. Large hotels and resorts are encroaching on Salema, but so far it retains its unspoiled seaside hideaway feel.

Salema is 20 kilometers (12.4 mi) west of Lagos and 10 kilometers (6.2 mi) west of Luz. **Eva** (tel. 282 762 944, www.eva-bus.com) buses run from Lagos bus terminal to Sagres, passing through Salema (30 minutes, almost hourly 7:15am-8:30pm Mon-Fri, less frequently Sat-Sun, €3).

Sagres

Windswept and rugged, Sagres (SAH-grezh) is a surfer's paradise at the western tip of the Algarve, 33 kilometers (20 mi) west of Lagos, on a remote headland. The dune-like terrain, combined with dramatic cliffs, tumultuous sea, and sweeping beaches, incites adventure. Intrepid Portuguese explorer Prince Henry the Navigator founded his famous navigation school here, and Sagres remains adventurous. With long beaches, a sweet fishing port, Cape St. Vincent, and Sagres Fortress, Sagres is a great day trip from Lagos or a weekend stay.

Sagres town is small and sleepy, but the region is expansive, with much to see and do, so pack sturdy hiking boots.

SIGHTS
★ Cape St. Vincent
(Cabo de São Vicente)

Wind-battered Cape St. Vincent headland is Europe's most southwesterly point, jutting into the Atlantic some 60 meters (197 feet) above the sea, with dramatic cliffs topped by the commanding **Cape St. Vincent Lighthouse (Farol do Cabo de São Vicente)** (N268, tel. 282 624 234, 10am-6pm Tues-Sun, €3), the second brightest in Europe, built around the turn of the 20th century and perched close to the cliff edge. The lighthouse itself is closed to the public, but it's part of a larger complex that includes a cafeteria, a gift shop, and a little museum with information on the lighthouse.

Standing on these blustery cliffs at the tip of Europe feels like teetering on the edge of the world. Europeans believed that Cape St. Vincent was literally the edge of the world prior to the 15th century. On Cape St. Vincent, where the lighthouse stands today, Prince Henry the Navigator had his private residence, and he set up a school for explorers in nearby Sagres town, making it a launching point for exploration in the Age of Discoveries.

Cape St. Vincent is located on the

Vicentine Coast, a belt of wild protected natural park that stretches from the western tip of the Algarve north to the Alentejo. The winding road from Cape St. Vincent, 7 kilometers (4.3 mi) west of sleepy Sagres, snakes through rugged, remote, boulder-littered landscape, with captivating and eerie desolation.

Sagres Fortress
(Fortaleza de Sagres)

Sprawling, imposing **Sagres Fortress** (tel. 282 620 140, www.monumentosdoalgarve.pt, 9:30am-8pm daily May-Sept, 9:30am-5:30pm daily Oct-Apr, last admission 30 minutes before closing, €3) was built in the 1400s where the prosperous Mediterranean and Atlantic maritime routes crossed. It played a key role in Portugal's strategic defenses, protecting the coast from North African invaders. Just south of Sagres town, this vast, squat fort has an impressive arched entrance, a restored 15th-century church, a 16th-century monastery, and the remnants of a 43-meter-wide (141-foot-wide) cobbled compass, the Compass Rose, one of the first of its kind in the country. It was here in the fortress that Henry the Navigator spent much of his time planning voyages. He died in the fortress in 1460.

Spend a few hours strolling the perimeter of the fortress, punctuated by cannons, and taking in the ocean views. It can be windy, so go prepared with warm clothes or at least a windbreaker, even in summer. There are restrooms inside, and free parking in front of the fortress.

Sagres Fortress is 1.4 kilometers (0.9 mi) south of Sagres town, a five-minute drive. The regular Lagos-Sagres buses (tel. 282 762 944, www.eva-bus.com, €3) also stop here.

Baleeira Port
(Porto da Baleeira)

The charming traditional little fishing port of

Baleeira, 2 kilometers (1.2 mi) east of Sagres town center, harbors scores of typical fishing boats that supply the local market. A fish auction is held every morning in the building just above the docks, where there is also a small café-snack bar from where visitors can watch proceedings. Diverse boat trips also operate from Baleeira Port.

BEACHES

Given the unique weather on the southwestern tip of the Algarve, the beaches are more frequented by surfers and kite-surfers. Despite usually being a few degrees cooler and breezier than the rest of the region, on a good day, Sagres's beaches offer a chance to escape the crowds and enjoy tranquil, unspoiled sand without a banana boat in sight.

Martinhal Beach
(Praia do Martinhal)
Fringed by reedy dunes, **Martinhal Beach** is a bay-like stretch of sand that sweeps around to Baleeira Port and the Sagres promontory and its fortress. In summer, outfitters operate for surfing, body-boarding, kite-surfing, and windsurfing, with rental equipment and English-speaking instructors. Off-season, the hardy can take a bracing walk on the beach.

Conveniently, a large free car park borders the beach.

FOOD
Fresh seafood is the dish in Sagres, and local delicacies hard to find elsewhere are gooseneck barnacles, sea urchins, and cuttlefish. Local fisherfolk sometimes risk their lives to collect these animals, often in rough conditions. An eclectic cross-section of restaurants varies from typical Portuguese to vegetarian and international.

For the freshest seafood, head to **Telheiro do Infante Restaurant** (Praia da Mareta, tel. 282 624 179, www.telheirodoinfante.com, 10am-10pm Wed-Mon, €15), overlooking Mareta Beach. What started as a small factory around 1910 has evolved into Sagres's finest eatery, where specialties include monkfish *cataplana* and a lobster rice pot.

Near Tonel Beach, the cozy and casual **A Sagres Restaurant** (Ecovia do Litoral, tel. 282 624 171, www.a-sagres.com, 1pm-11pm Thurs-Tues, €12) is warm and rustic, reflected in its menu, showcasing interesting seafood creations such as seafood pasta stew and octopus rice.

Intriguingly named ★ **Mum's Restaurant** (Rua Comandante Matoso, tel.

Sagres Fortress

968 210 411, www.mums-sagres.com, 7pm-2am Wed-Mon, €15) promotes a slow-cooking approach based on organic produce, with a wide variety of vegan and vegetarian options. The highly creative menu includes dishes such as purple rain soup, made with red cabbage, and a codfish cappuccino.

RECREATION

The town of Sagres is on a headland bordered by one of Portugal's natural parks, **Southwest Alentejo and Vicentine Coast Natural Park (Parque Natural do Sudoeste Alentejano e Costa Vicentina).** One of the finest preserved stretches of coast in Europe, the park covers 100 kilometers (62 mi) from Porto Covo in the Alentejo to the village of Burgau, 23 kilometers (14.3 mi) east of Sagres. The dramatic cliffs and beaches are home to hundreds of unique plant and animal species. Coupled with Sagres's water-sports beaches, it is the perfect place for active tourists, with unlimited hiking, trekking, and surfing.

★ Via Algarviana Hiking Trail

The **Via Algarviana Hiking Trail** (www.viaalgarviana.org) is an old pilgrims' path that runs 300 kilometers (185 mi) from Cape St. Vincent to the Spanish border. It is the backbone of the region's popular hiking routes, launched in 1995 to promote walking, ecotourism, sustainable development, and the Algarve's inland areas. The Via Algarviana offers a landscape starkly different from along the coast, and it changes with the seasons, passing through rural hamlets, lush countryside, historic sites, and natural beauty spots.

Those who have hiked the trail from one end to the other take a couple of weeks to do so. The Via Algarviana website offers information on specific stretches, with advice on accommodations, viewpoints, and where to stop for drinks and food.

Shorter **themed routes** have been drawn up for a few hours' or a day's hiking. These include the intriguing Contraband Route, the Water Route, the Monumental Trees Route, and the Geology Route. See the trail's website. The **main office** (Association Almargem, Project Via Algarviana, Rua de S. Domingos 65, Loulé, tel. 289 412 959) is in Loulé.

Surfing

With rough Atlantic waves, Sagres is a top spot for surfing and has decent conditions most of the year. The west coast's beaches, including the western tip of the southern coast, are generally windier and the water much cooler than east along the southern coast—which means they're also less crowded, even in the height of summer.

Companies that specialize in surfing lessons, equipment rentals, and camps and lodging include **Casa Azul Sagres** (tel. 282 624 856, www.casaazulsagres.com), which runs a surf school, organizes four- to seven-night surf camp packages, and runs a B&B guesthouse.

Boating

Dolphin-, whale-, and seabird-watching excursions (from adults €35, children under 12 €25) sail from Baleeira Port with **Cape Cruiser** (Porto da Baleeira, tel. 919 751 175, www.capecruiser.org), which also does fishing trips and coastal exploration, narrated in English. Trips depart three times a day October-March, and four times a day April-September. If you're lucky, you might even spot a shark.

ACCOMMODATIONS

Homey, spotless **Casa Azul Sagres, Rooms & Apartments** (Rua Dom Sebastião, tel. 282 624 856, www.casaazulsagres.com, €175 d, €240 2-bedroom apartment) is a pretty little bed-and-breakfast finished to high levels of comfort. Anywhere in Sagres is a 10-minute walk, and Casa Azul runs its own surf school. Weekend barbecues are the main attraction. Double or twin rooms have en suite baths, and there are self-contained studio and one- and two-bedroom apartments.

Eco-conscious ★ **Martinhal Sagres Beach Family Resort Hotel** (Quinta do

Martinhal, tel. 282 240 200, www.martinhal.com, €362) is among Europe's finest luxury family resorts. Overlooking the bay-like Martinhal Beach, which sweeps to the pretty Baleeira Port, the hotel has lodging in rooms, apartments, houses, and luxury villas. The restaurant uses fresh local ingredients, and the design complements the surrounding landscape. Among its facilities are a sumptuous spa, a kids' club, heated swimming pools, sports facilities, and a village square where guests can meet and socialize.

INFORMATION AND SERVICES

GNR police: Rua de Santa Fé, tel. 282 630 010, www.gnr.pt
Main tourist office: Rua Comandante Matoso 75, tel. 282 624 873
Post office: Rua Comandante Matoso s/n, tel. 282 624 890

GETTING THERE

Sagres is 33 kilometers (20 mi) west of Lagos, 30 minutes' drive on the N125 road. Head west after Sagres for Cape St. Vincent. **Eva** (tel. 282 762 944, www.eva-bus.com) buses run from Lagos bus terminal to Sagres (1 hour, almost hourly 7:15am-8:30pm daily, €4), stopping at the fortress in Sagres as well as in the town center.

CARRAPATEIRA

Carrapateira is the ultimate unspoiled west coast community, a hamlet of whitewashed cottages amid sandy dunes with a plain church and ruins of an old fort, along with two massively popular surfing beaches that book-end the village: the main Bordeira Beach to the north, and Amado Beach to the south.

Beaches

BORDEIRA BEACH
(Praia da Bordeira)

Flanked by rugged untamed countryside, **Bordeira Beach** is a long creamy swath of sand that offers large waves year-round, a 20-minute walk north of town. At low tide the beach increases in size, making it one of the largest in the Algarve. A stream also flows into the sea, sometimes forming a shallow lagoon that children love to play in.

AMADO BEACH
(Praia do Amado)

A 30-minute walk south of town, **Amado Beach** is one of the best surfing spots in the region. It is a long sandy strip of beach with great year-round waves and a wooden hiking trail around it. The spot is usually occupied by a good-looking surf crowd and is also popular among campers. **Amado Beach Rentals** (tel. 913 810 449, www.amadobeachrentals.com) has a large range of surf equipment for hire, right on the beach.

Getting There

Carrapateira is 22 kilometers (13.6 mi) north of Sagres and 21 kilometers (13 mi) south of Aljezur, a 20-minute drive via the N268 road in either direction. A taxi from either Sagres or Aljezur costs around €25 one-way.

Aljezur

Sleepy Aljezur (al-zheh-ZOOR), the main town on the Algarve's west coast, has stunning countryside beaches. Untamed and unpretentious, the Algarve's west coast is one of the region's best-kept secrets.

Aljezur is a small town built on a valley plain about 30 kilometers (19 mi) north of Lagos. The drive from Lagos is relaxing and scenic, following a winding road through shaded countryside dotted with farmhouses and cottages. The easygoing town straddles a pretty river, its older and newer halves connected by an old Moorish bridge. Local folklore has it that the new part of Aljezur emerged when an outbreak of malaria struck the older part in the 18th century, and the Algarve bishop moved inhabitants away from the disease to the other side of the river.

The nearest beaches are 10 kilometers 6.2 mi) away on the rugged western Vicentine coastline and are among the best in the Algarve for surfing, which adds to the town's laid-back feel.

SIGHTS

Aljezur Castle
(Castelo de Aljezur)

Aljezur's skyline is dominated by the ruins of the once-imposing medieval **Aljezur Castle** (Rua do Castelo, tel. 282 990 010, 24 hours daily, free), on a hill above the town. Excavations indicate the site could date to the Bronze Age. The castle was likely built by the Moors in the 10th century. Its distinctive circular stone tower can be seen from afar, and the steep 10-minute walk up to the castle is a challenging 300 meters (984 feet); it's also possible to drive up. There are views of the countryside from the top, and interesting relics inside the ruins have explanatory boards in English.

BEACHES

Popular beaches for surfing include Arrifana and Monte Clérigo, both within Southwest Alentejo and Vicentine Coast Natural Park. The west coast beaches are best accessed by car or taxi, as public transport is unreliable.

Arrifana Beach
(Praia da Arrifana)

The views from the cliffs above medium-size **Arrifana Beach** are mesmerizing. The secluded beach is protected by the cliffs and is off the tourist track but is very popular among locals. Constant unintimidating waves are great for beginner surfers. Parking at the top of the cliffs is scarce in summer, and the walk down to the beach is steep. Off-season it is a tranquil hideaway for strolls and sunsets. Arrifana fishing village is along the top of the cliffs above the beach and has a cluster of cafés, snack bars, and restaurants. Arrifana is 10 kilometers (6.2 mi) west of Aljezur town; a taxi from Aljezur (tel. 282 991 176 or 917 574 630, www.taxiluis.com) is around €13 one-way.

Monte Clérigo Beach
(Praia de Monte Clérigo)

Monte Clérigo Beach is low and open, flanked by hills on either side, scattered with cottages and topped with sandy dunes. This beach is great for families, with rock pools and restaurants, plenty of parking, and easy access, although it is a 10-minute walk from the car park to the beach below. A 10-minute, 8-kilometer (5-mi) drive northwest of Aljezur, this is one of the west coast's quieter beaches, even in summer.

FOOD

Aljezur's gastronomy is a mix of land and sea, with abundant fresh fish, game, and produce.

Local specialties include sweet potato cake and sweet potato pasties.

In a quaint, rustic, whitewashed cottage with blue-framed windows, the **Pont' a Pé Restaurant and Bar** (Largo da Liberdade 12, tel. 282 998 104, www.pontape.pt, 9am-midnight Mon-Sat, €10) is one of the oldest in town, specializing in the genuine flavors of Aljezur like beans, cabbage, sweet potato, and whelk stew.

Warm and welcoming **Restaurant-Bar A Lareira** ("The Fireplace") (Rua 13 de Janeiro, tel. 282 998 440, 9am-11pm daily, €10) showcases authentic Portuguese cuisine, with a focus on local specialties and products. The unfussy dishes include fish *cataplana*, pork loin, and specials like duck rice. There's also a guesthouse with rooms above the restaurant.

RECREATION

Surfing

Near the Algarve's best surfing beaches and with great conditions almost year-round, Aljezur has numerous surf trips and schools. Established in 2005, the **Arrifana Surf School & Camp** (Urbanização Vale da Telha 31, tel. 927 310 441 or 961 690 249, www.arrifanasurfschool.com) has group surf lessons and equipment rentals and full surf packages with lodging. Its Surf House overlooks Arrifana Beach, with lessons (from €35) and surfboard and wetsuit rentals (from €20 per hour).

Horseback Riding

With often deserted beaches and luxuriant terrain, Aljezur is prime riding country. **Algarve Horse Riding** (tel. 967 607 840, www.algarvehorseriding.com) has safe trails (from €25 for a beginner's walk) throughout the Southwest Alentejo and Vicentine Coast Natural Park on beaches and rugged terrain; all levels of riders can be accommodated.

Jeep Safaris

Explore the remote terrain of the western Algarve on a customized, family-friendly 4WD jeep safari (6 hours, from €70) with **Sandy Toes Algarve** (tel. 282 998 063, www.sandytoes-algarve.com), taking in hidden hamlets and unspoiled secret spots. Safaris are mindful of the environment and include a picnic of local produce. Local sights such as Aljezur Castle can be incorporated, along with lake swims, sand-boarding, and off-roading.

ACCOMMODATIONS

Lodging in Aljezur tends to be cozy guesthouses or private rental cottages and villas. The surf companies also have their own lodging.

In town, the small but well-equipped **Vicentina** (Av General Humberto Delgado, tel. 282 990 030, www.vicentinahotel.com, from €120) is a great base for exploring the Vicentine Coast. A short stroll to the river and town center, it comprises 26 rooms and apartments, and has a pool and an on-site restaurant and bar.

Also in a prime location in the heart of Aljezur is the **Amazigh Design Hostel** (Rua da Ladeira 5, tel. 282 997 502, www.amazighostel.com, €29 dorm, €109 d), nestled amid historic walls and picturesque alleys. Clean and unfussy shared dorms and private doubles are complemented by well-equipped social areas and a decorative courtyard.

Camping

The **Serrão campground** (Herdade do Serrão, tel. 282 990 220, www.campingserrao.com, adults €5.50, children €2.75, plus €5-9 per tent, €7-9 per RV, cottages from €75) is on the edge of the stunning west coast, swaddled by the protected Southwest Alentejo and Vicentine Coast Natural Park, just a few minutes' drive from the town of Aljezur and within walking distance to the Monte Clérigo and Arrifana Beaches. It is superbly equipped with clean communal shower and toilet facilities, a swimming pool, a sports field and tennis courts, summer entertainment, an on-site minimarket, a bar and restaurant, and even a crepe and waffle shop.

Shared bungalow dorms with bunk beds and one-bedroom cottages with a kitchen and bath are available.

INFORMATION AND SERVICES

GNR police: Rua da Escola 3, tel. 282 998 130, www.gnr.pt
Post office: Rua 25 de Abril 75, tel. 282 997 275

GETTING THERE

Aljezur is 30 kilometers (19 mi) north of Lagos, a 40-minute drive north on the twisty N120 road. Heading west on the A22 motorway, take the last exit north on the N120 road for 20 minutes.

Alternatively, take a train from Faro or elsewhere to Lagos, then catch a **Rede Expressos** (www.rede-expressos.pt) bus to Aljezur (30 minutes, twice daily, 3 daily summer, €6-8). **Eva** (tel. 282 762 944, www.eva-bus.com) buses run more frequently but take longer from Lagos to Aljezur (50 minutes, every few hours Mon-Fri, 1 bus Sat, €4). Aljezur doesn't have a train station.

ODECEIXE

The coastal village of Odeceixe (oh-deh-SAYZH), 17 kilometers (10.5 mi) and 20 minutes' drive north of Aljezur, spills down a steep hillside in the Seixe valley with a river at its foot, a jumble of tightly packed whitewashed houses and red roofs to explore. Odeceixe is on the border between the Algarve and the Alentejo, within the Southwest Alentejo and Vicentine Coast Natural Park. Surrounded by lush pastures and orderly fields, this sleepy village, with a cute windmill at the top, is very popular with RVers, surfers, anglers, and families.

Life in the hamlet centers on the main 1 de Maio Square, flanked by colorful buildings housing a handful of restaurants, bars, cafés, and reasonably priced guesthouses. It has enough charm to merit spending a night or two here. In the village center, **Residencia do Parque** (Rua da Estrada Nacional 15, tel. 282 947 117, www.residenciadoparque.com, €50, €60 with balcony) is a simple and clean little B&B.

Odeceixe Beach (Praia de Odeceixe) is 3 kilometers (1.9 mi) west of the village, a wide patch of sand sandwiched between the Seixe River and the Atlantic. Sheltered by cliffs, it is adjacent to a clothing-optional beach, one of Portugal's few officially recognized naturist beaches.

Odeceixe is 48 kilometers (30 mi) north of Lagos and 16.5 kilometers (10.2 mi) north of Aljezur. **Eva** (tel. 282 762 944, www.eva-bus.com) buses leave Lagos for Odeceixe (1.25 hours, every few hours Mon-Fri, 1 bus Sat, €4.55), passing through Aljezur.

Tavira

The handsome traditional fishing town of Tavira dates to the Bronze Age and may be one of the first Phoenician settlements in western Iberia. Once an aristocratic town, today a small city, Tavira straddles the Girão River, connected by a photogenic seven-arch bridge known as the **Roman Bridge,** although it is more likely Moorish in origin.

Amid the closely-packed whitewashed houses and red roofs are quaint cobblestone streets, monuments, and sleepy squares. Discover traditional architecture, grand buildings, historic ruins, and over 30 churches; Tavira is nicknamed "the Town of Churches." Unique four-sided hipped roofs, striking red, have a strong Moorish look and are emblematic of the town. The design is thought to allow air to circulate in summer and retain warmth in winter.

Tavira's pretty riverside is lined with cafés and seafood restaurants. Its shoreline is illuminated by white salt pans, from where the

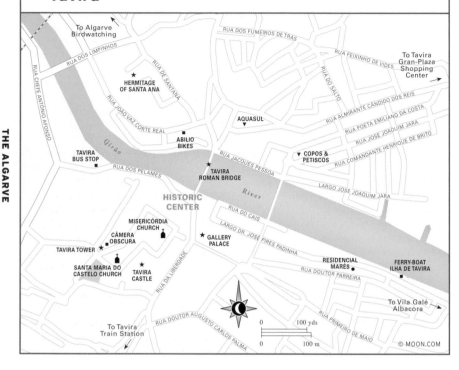

Tavira

Algarve's famous *flor de sal* rock salt is harvested. Neat rows of pristine white salt merge with the turquoise water and golden dunes of the Ria Formosa protected wetlands fronting Tavira. Despite being a coastal town, Tavira does not have a beach, but a number of beach-islands in the Ria Formosa lagoon are easily reached by ferry or water taxi from the town center.

SIGHTS
Historic Center

Tavira's main monuments are clustered in the town center, on the western bank of the Girão River. Here you will find the medieval Tavira Castle, the local town hall, and many churches.

TAVIRA CASTLE
(Castelo de Tavira)

The medieval **Tavira Castle** (Urbanização

Tavira Garden, 10am-7pm daily, free), in the southwest part of Tavira near the water tower, overlooks the town and its jumble of bright red roofs and ornate chimneys. On the highest point of the city, the castle is thought to have been built during Moorish rule in the 11th century, although its origins could be older. Castle walls were added in the late 13th century. Despite being partially ruined, two towers and the walls and their battlements are well preserved. Inside are pleasant, well-kept gardens. Walk around the battlements for views over Tavira and the coast.

MISERICÓRDIA CHURCH
(Igreja da Misericórdia)

Misericórdia Church (Rua da Galeria, tel. 289 247 120, 9am-5pm Mon, 9am-6pm Tues-Sat, €2, plus €1 for the bell tower), built 1541-1551, is a fine example of Renaissance architecture. It's in the heart of the Old Town near the castle, on the way to the main square; the striking white and gray facade, with its austere carved archway, covered by a canopy with a statue of Our Lady of Mercy, is particularly impressive. The sober exterior belies the church's unique interior, clad in decorative traditional blue-and-white azulejo murals; there's also a gilded altar. Visitors can climb to the bell tower for views of Tavira.

TAVIRA TOWER
(Torre de Tavira)
Converted from a 1931 water tower, **Tavira Tower** (Calçada da Galeria 12, tel. 281 321 754, www.cdepa.pt, 10am-5pm Mon-Fri, 10am-1pm Sat-Sun, €4) houses the Algarve's first and only **camera obscura.** On an odd-shaped observation platform, from the camera obscura, visitors can observe the city in real time through a series of lenses, mirrors, and magnifying glasses that project images onto a 2-meter-wide (6.6-foot-wide) screen inside the tower. This gives the extraordinary experience of seeing the city in 360 degrees, almost like hovering above it. A lift and stairs provide access to the tower.

GALLERY PALACE
(Palácio da Galeria)
Emblematic of Tavira, the elegant 16th-century **Gallery Palace** (Calçada da Galeria, tel. 281 320 540, www.museumunicipaldetavira. tavira.pt, 9am-4:30pm Tues-Sat, €2) is a historic baroque building that hosts a variety of exhibitions throughout the year on themes such as olive oil production and the Mediterranean diet. High on Santa Maria peak, site of an ancient Phoenician settlement, this Tavira municipal museum was once the home of illustrious magistrate João Leal da Gama e Ataíde.

Hermitage of Santa Ana
(Ermida de Santa Ana)
The **Hermitage of Santa Ana** (Largo de Santa Ana, tel. 281 320 540, 9am-12:30pm and 2pm-5pm Tues-Sat, free) is one of the oldest religious buildings in the city. Set in its own little square, it dates from the early 14th century and was completely rebuilt in the 18th century following the devastating 1755 earthquake. From then on, it functioned as a private chapel in the palace of the governor of the Algarve. After a period of abandonment, the building was again renovated and made a museum in 2006. Today it hosts a variety of exhibitions.

Pego do Inferno
A short drive from town is the breathtaking **Pego do Inferno** (M514-2, Santo Estêvão, 24 hours daily, free), literally "Hell's Pit," a gorgeous waterfall and a little lake that until recently were a local secret. Now the site is overgrown but captivating in its raw beauty. Folklore has it that a horse-drawn carriage fell into the lake and was never found, and that anyone who falls into it goes straight to hell. As the spot grew in popularity, supporting infrastructure was improved, and today it is a main attraction. Pego do Inferno can only be accessed by car; there is no public transport. From Tavira, take the N270 road and then the M514-2. Pego do Inferno is about 10 kilometers (6.2 mi), a 12-minute drive, northwest of Tavira.

TOP EXPERIENCE

★ Ria Formosa Natural Park
(Parque Natural da Ria Formosa)
Ria Formosa is a protected coastal lagoon made up of a chain of barrier islands and peninsulas that stretch from Faro east to Tavira. A swirl of gold and turquoise when viewed from above, the shifting landscape adapts to the seasons, shaped by the tides. Many of the sandy islets, such as Tavira Island, the city's main beach, are popular beach destinations accessed by regular boat trips from the mainland. Ria Formosa is also home to varied indigenous flora and fauna, particularly birds and marine wildlife, that attract nature enthusiasts.

Formosamar (tel. 918 720 002, www.

formosamar.com) runs ecotourism activities on the Ria Formosa, including nature sightseeing boat trips (2 hours, €25), seabird-, turtle-, and dolphin-watching boat trips (2 hours, €40), and kayak tours (2 hours, €35).

Tavira Island
(Ilha de Tavira)

Tavira Island, one of the bigger barrier islands at 11 kilometers (6.8 mi) long and up to 1 kilometer (0.6 mi) wide, is part of the Ria Formosa reserve. In summer this sandbar is a popular beach day trip for families and camping. Flamingos, among other bird species, are often spotted here, making the island a favorite for bird-watchers. Tavira Island has a campground, bars and restaurants, and a handful of houses. It also has spots for nude sunbathing. Parasols and sun beds are available on the beach.

The island is only reachable by ferry or water taxi from Tavira city center's riverside or the Quatro Águas docks, where the river meets the ocean, a half-hour walk south of Tavira center. Ferries (€1.50 round-trip) run daily year-round, except in poor weather, generally 9am-5pm, although working hours are extended in busy holiday periods. Water taxis operate 24 hours daily in July-August; hours are limited outside this peak season. The taxi is more expensive than the ferry as it runs on demand and is faster.

FOOD

Tuna, octopus, shellfish, and grilled fish are on the menus of most Tavira restaurants; roast kid is also among local specialties. Sweets are one of Tavira's fortes and widely available at the many coffee shops and *pastelarias* around town.

Tavira's finest seafood restaurant is classy **Copos & Petiscos** (Rua Poeta Emiliano da Costa 6, tel. 916 562 645, 6:30pm-10:30pm Mon-Sat, €20), with abundant fresh seafood and excellent wines. This inconspicuous restaurant looks unremarkable from outside, but the inside looks smart, with the bottom half of the walls clad in deep green tiles.

Arty **Aquasul** (Rua Dr. Augusto da Silva Carvalho 11, tel. 281 325 166, 6:30pm-10pm Tues-Sat, €20) is a colorfully decorated eatery with an experimental menu that spans the Mediterranean with a heavy Italian accent. Dutch-owned, this atmospheric restaurant is on a flower-draped backstreet near the riverside in the heart of Tavira.

RECREATION
Bird-Watching

There are a series of prime year-round bird-watching spots along the Algarve coast, but few rival Tavira's dazzling salt pans on the Ria Formosa. These unique salty marshes and brackish lagoons are home to flamingos, spoonbills, black-winged stilts, Kentish plovers, scores of wader species, waterfowl, and gulls. Portugal's most beautiful and important wetland, the Ria Formosa shelters 30,000 migrating birds every year and is a must for birders.

Many types of bird-watching trips are organized from Tavira. **Algarve Birdwatching** (Urb. Pezinhos, Lote 9 EH, tel. 960 170 789, www.algarve-birdwatching. com, from €50 half-day) has years of experience with the best spots for indigenous, migrating, and rare birds. It organizes private and group tours as well as wildlife photo excursions.

Cycling Tours

Abilio Bikes (Rua João Vaz Corte Real 23A, tel. 281 323 467, www.abiliobikes.com, from €30) has cycling routes for guided tours of Tavira, including the eco-friendly Ria Formosa tour, a Forts and Castles tour, and more.

Ria Formosa Boat Trips

To sunbathe on a beach-island or cruise the Ria Formosa, hire one of the taxi-boats

---

1: the Pego do Inferno waterfall; **2:** a Kentish plover; **3:** café overlooking the Girão River in Tavira; **4:** flamingos on the Ria Formosa

(from €8 per boat, up to six people, 1-hour tour from €12 pp). **SequaTours** (tel. 960 170 789, www.sequatours.com) runs water taxis from Tavira, Quatro Águas (a little dock at the mouth of the Gilão River, halfway between Tavira town and Tavira Island, a 30-minute walk from Tavira town center), and Tavira Island.

ACCOMMODATIONS

Tavira lodging ranges from quaint, spotless guesthouses to sprawling, manicured resorts. Absent are high-rise concrete eyesores; all construction conforms with and enhances the town's character.

★ **Vila Galé Albacora** (Quatro Águas, tel. 281 380 800, www.vilagale.com, €190) is a charming beach resort full of character and Portuguese features, sited where the Girão River meets the ocean, 4 kilometers (2.5 mi), a 40-minute walk or a 7-minute drive, south of Tavira center. This 162-room eco-hotel, part of the Vila Galé group, is converted from former fishing houses, workshops, warehouses, and an old chapel—buildings that reflect what was once the local way of life on the Ria Formosa.

Residencial Marés (Largo Dr. José Pires Padinha 134, tel. 281 325 815, www.residencialmares.com, from €86 d, €346 3-bedroom villa) is in the heart of Tavira on the riverside, a historic town house transformed into a 24-room lodging with a private villa, within walking distance of anywhere in the city. It has panoramic views over the river and local decor, with polished terracotta floor tiles and beachy colors.

INFORMATION AND SERVICES

GNR police: Rua de Santa Margarida 2, tel. 281 329 030, www.gnr.pt
Main tourist office: Praça da República 5, tel. 281 322 511
Post office: Rua da Liberdade, tel. 707 262 626

GETTING THERE

Tavira is 38 kilometers (24 mi) east of Faro, a 35-minute drive on the A22 motorway. It's 22 kilometers (13.6 mi) west of Vila Real de Santo António, a 30-minute drive on the A22.

A dozen **Eva** (tel. 289 899 760, www.evabus.com) buses run from Faro's main bus terminal to Tavira (1 hour, 7:15am-7:30pm daily, €4.45) on weekdays, and about seven buses run on weekends and holidays. Tickets for buses departing from the terminal must be bought at the ticket office, inside the terminal. Eva runs buses slightly more frequently between Tavira and Vila Real de Santo António (1 hour, €4.15). The **Tavira Bus Terminal** (Rua dos Pelames, tel. 281 322 546) is on the northern edge of town, on the west side of the Gilão River, a short walk to the town center.

Trains to Tavira are slightly faster and cheaper than the bus. **CP** (tel. 707 210 220, www.cp.pt) trains run from Faro to Tavira (40 minutes, €3.20), and there are around a dozen departures a day. CP also runs about a dozen trains daily between Faro and Vila Real de Santo António (1.25 hours, €5.25). The small train station in Tavira is on the southwest side of town, a 10-minute downhill walk to the center.

Vila Real de Santo António

Vila Real de Santo António is Portugal's southeasternmost city, separated from Spain by the Guadiana River. On a clear day—most days—you can see Spain from the river's edge. Vila Real is easy to explore as it is built following a neatly organized grid, unlike most Algarve towns. A long, elegant riverside walkway enhances the relaxed, peaceful pace of life.

Like Portimão for sardines, in the late 19th century Vila Real prospered as a canning center for tuna. Toward the end of the 20th century, as tuna stocks were depleted, the prosperity dried up. The tuna fish's heritage is still celebrated, and most local restaurants feature it on their menus.

The novelty of being able to cross to Spain never seems to wear off, and with crowd-free beaches, excellent restaurants, and boat trips along the glorious Guadiana, Vila Real may be the last port on the Algarve's coast, but certainly not the least significant.

SIGHTS

Running along the eastern side of Vila Real parallel to the Guadiana River, attractive **Avenida da República** is a long cobblestone walkway dotted with palm trees that stretches between the town's port and marina south to manicured gardens and beachfront. The town's **port** (Av. da República, tel. 281 513 769, www.anguadiana.com) is where the Guadiana boat trips and ferry crossings operate from.

A few streets back from the river is the main town square, the **Praça Marquês do Pombal,** fringed with orange trees. The town center is said to be inspired by central Lisbon, and it certainly has a similar feeling of splendor and stateliness.

Vila Real de Santo António Lighthouse
(Farol de Vila Real de Santo António)
South of the city, just before the beach, **Vila Real de Santo António Lighthouse** (Av.

Min Duarte Pacheco, tel. 281 544 402, 2pm-5pm Wed, free), one of the Algarve's largest, is an impressive structure dating to 1923. It has 224 steps or an elevator up to the 40-meter-high (131-foot-high) circular viewing platform, with views of the city, the coast, local salt pans, and Spain. A little museum at the base offers snippets of the lighthouse's history.

BEACHES

As at most beaches in the eastern end of the Algarve, the sands of Vila Real de Santo António are sweeping and golden, and the water shallower and warmer than farther west.

Santo António Beach
(Praia de Santo António)
Fronting Vila Real is the vast **Santo António Beach,** where finding a spot away from other beachgoers is never difficult. Santo António Beach starts at the mouth of the Guadiana River, and its flat creamy sand and tranquil water stretch 12 kilometers (7.4 mi) to the Ria Formosa estuary.

Monte Gordo
A five-minute, 4-kilometer (2.5-mi) drive west from Vila Real de Santo António along the main N125 road is the smaller and lesser-known summer resort town of **Monte Gordo,** with one of the longest and finest beaches in the Algarve, popular with Portuguese families. Monte Gordo's formerly dated beachfront area now has a gorgeous 3-kilometer-long (1.9-mi-long) wooden walkway that will be extended to Vila Real de Santo António. Monte Gordo town consists of a long beachfront avenue lined with bars and restaurants

FOOD

Vila Real's gastronomy is rich and diverse, with strong Roman and Arab influences. Tuna takes center stage, a legacy of the town's canning industry. A local delicacy is *espinheta de atum*, tuna and potato stew.

It might not look like much from the outside, but quaint and traditional **Caves do Guadiana** (Av. da República 89, tel. 281 544 498, noon-4pm and 7pm-10:30pm Fri-Wed, €15), on the riverside, is renowned for fresh fish, particularly tuna. It serves excellently prepared regional and Portuguese classics.

Guadiana riverside **Sem Espinhas Guadiana** ("No Bones") (Av. da República 51, tel. 281 544 605, www.semespinhas.net, noon-midnight daily, €16) revives age-old traditional cuisine from the eastern Algarve for younger crowds. This trendy, glamorous restaurant, one of four Sem Espinhas restaurants in the area, serves gastronomic history with contemporary cool.

Tucked away on one of Vila Real's backstreets is the rustic ★ **Pisa II** (Rua Jornal do Algarve 44, tel. 281 543 157, 8am-midnight Thurs-Tues, €8), a husband-and-wife-run restaurant that has been attracting patrons for decades. Nondescript on the outside and snug on the inside, this former tavern is so popular for its seafood that queues form long into the night. Its reputation hinges on its star dish, fried squid with french fries.

RECREATION
Hiking
The **Via Algarviana Hiking Trail** (www.viaalgarviana.org) runs the 240-kilometer (149-mi) length of the Algarve from Alcoutim west to Vila do Bispo, crossing 11 of the Algarve's 16 municipalities and countryside. The website has suggestions for restaurants and lodging in villages along the way. No fees are charged, but donations help maintain the route.

River Cruises
TransGuadiana River Cruises (Av. Infante D. Henrique, tel. 966 089 341, www.transguadiana.com) offers sightseeing cruises, a river and mountain cruise, bird-watching cruises, and a sunset party cruise to explore the Guadiana River (from €47). Stop at a local village for a sumptuous lunch. This is a must-do if you're spending any time in the region.

Golf
The **Monte Rei Golf & Country Club** (tel. 281 950 950, www.monte-rei.com, greens fees from €165) is an exclusive golf development and boasts a stunning Jack Nicklaus signature course. Monte Rei North opened in 2007 and is ranked among the best in Europe by golf publications. This par-72 course is a unique design in the undulating hills north of the A22 motorway; water comes into play on 11 of the 18 holes.

ACCOMMODATIONS
Lodging in Vila Real is limited but clean and affordable. In the center of town, a couple of streets west of the main square, large and brightly colored three-star **Hotel Apolo** (Av. Dos Bombeiros Portugueses, tel. 281 512 448, www.apolo-hotel.com, €144) has 56 rooms, ranging from singles to family size, as well as a pool and a restaurant. Sleek-looking **Arenilha Guest House** (Rua Dom Pedro V 55, tel. 964 722 018, €100) offers 30 modern rooms and a great central location just off the main square, just a three-minute walk from the river that overlooks Spain.

INFORMATION AND SERVICES
GNR police: Rua Dr. Manuel de Arriaga 19, tel. 281 530 150, www.gnr.pt

Tourist information: Rua 5 de Outubro, António Aleixo Cultural Centre, tel. 281 542 100

Post office: Rua Teófilo de Braga 50, tel. 281 510 450

GETTING THERE
Vila Real de Santo António is 63 kilometers (39 mi) east of Faro airport, one hour's drive on the A22 motorway, or longer on the N125 road, which gets congested in summer. The Guadiana International Bridge connects Vila Real with Ayamonte in Spain and connects to the A22 motorway.

CP (tel. 707 210 220, www.cp.pt) trains and **Eva** (tel. 289 899 760, www.eva-bus.com) buses both run frequently between Faro and Vila Real de Santo António, on the same lines that pass through Olhão and Tavira. There are a dozen departures per day of both trains and buses. The train takes 1.25 hours and costs around €5.25; the bus takes under 2 hours and costs €5.60. Buses run slightly more frequently between Tavira and Vila Real de Santo António; the 22-kilometer (13.6-mi) journey takes 1 hour and costs €4.15. The Vila Real de Santo António **train station** (tel. 281 543 242) is a 15-minute walk north of the town center. Buses stop in the town center on the riverside, next to where the ferries leave for Ayamonte.

Ferry crossings (15 minutes, adults €1.90, bicycles €1.20, cars €5.50) from Vila Real to Ayamonte in Spain run every half hour throughout the day from Vila Real's port.

CACELA VELHA

High on a hill overlooking the Ria Formosa's easternmost lagoon, 12 kilometers (7.4 mi) west of Vila Real de Santo António along the N125 road, Cacela Velha is a charming walled hamlet that oozes character. One of the quaintest in the eastern Algarve, the village is a tiny cluster of whitewashed fishing cottages with bright blue trim, the remnants of an ancient 16th- and 17th-century fort, a 16th-century church, and a couple of eateries. The church and fort cannot be visited.

Fronting the hamlet is a huge, pristine beach where colorful fishing boats can still be seen. Famous for its oysters, Cacela Velha strikes an interesting balance of being highly popular among tourists yet almost completely untouched by tourist infrastructure.

The modest **Casa da Igreja tavern** (Rua de Cacela Velha 2, tel. 289 952 126, 4:30pm-10pm daily, €10) specializes in fresh oysters from the Ria Formosa.

The Alentejo

Making up one-third of Portugal, the vast

Alentejo (ah-len-TAY-zhoo) is underrated. One of Western Europe's poorest and most sparsely populated regions, it makes no apologies for its rustic, unkempt beauty. Situated south of the Tagus River and north of the Algarve, bordering Spain to the east and the Atlantic to the west, the rusty Alentejo—whose name derives from the Portuguese *além Tejo* (beyond the Tagus)—is deeply traditional and predominantly agricultural.

Life moves more slowly in Portugal's hottest and driest region, and the searing summer heat, which can peak above 45°C (113°F), means it is impossible to spend much time outdoors. The golden wheat fields—which give Baixo (lower) Alentejo its nickname "the Breadbasket of

Highlights

Look for ★ to find recommended sights, activities, dining, and lodging.

★ **Chapel of Bones:** This eerie-sounding monument in Évora is the most famous of a handful of Portugal's unique bone chapels. Its walls, arches, and pillars are clad entirely with tightly packed human bones and skulls, making for a chilling but fascinating experience (page 168).

★ **Roman Temple of Évora:** Often referred to as the Temple of Diana, this ancient site is one of Évora's most distinctive monuments and an important landmark of Roman civilization in Portugal (page 168).

★ **Monsaraz:** Perched on a hilltop overlooking the vast Alentejo plains, this whimsical walled village has a true medieval feel (page 177).

★ **Elvas:** One of Portugal's few remaining undiscovered treasures, this well-preserved fortified town oozes charm and character (page 182).

★ **Franquia Beach:** With shallow waters that are warmer than others along the coast, this beautiful swath of sand, a river beach, is a magnet for families (page 191).

★ **Southwest Alentejo and Vicentine Coast Natural Park:** Stretching from Porto Côvo in the Alentejo to Burgau in the Algarve, this belt of protected coastline is home to a wealth of unique flora and fauna as well as superb landscapes (page 194).

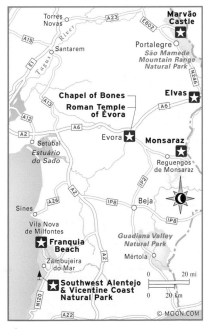

★ **Marvão Castle:** On a rocky granite peak in the São Mamede mountain range, this preserved medieval castle offers sweeping vistas and historic village ambience (page 198).

The Alentejo

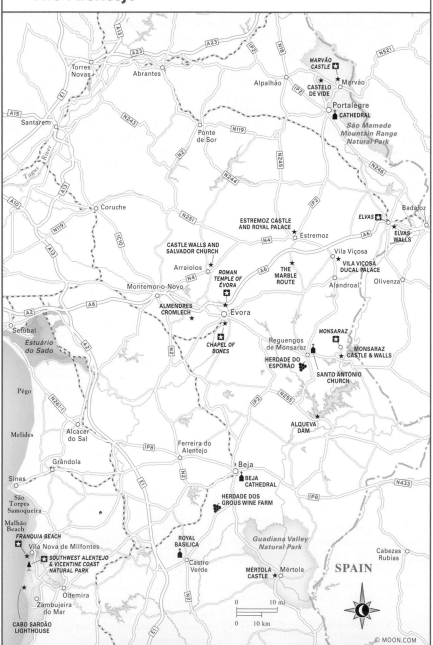

MARVÃO CASTLE

N521

Torres Novas

Abrantes

Alpalhão

CASTELO DE VIDE

Marvão

Portalegre

CATHEDRAL

São Mamede Mountain Range Natural Park

Santarem

Ponte de Sor

N119

N245

Tagus River

Coruche

N251

ESTREMOZ CASTLE AND ROYAL PALACE

ELVAS

Badajoz

Estremoz

ELVAS WALLS

CASTLE WALLS AND SALVADOR CHURCH

Vila Viçosa

Arraiolos

ROMAN TEMPLE OF ÉVORA

THE MARBLE ROUTE

VILA VIÇOSA DUCAL PALACE

Montemor-o-Novo

Alandroal

Olivenza

ALMENDRES CROMLECH

Évora

Setúbal

Estuário do Sado

CHAPEL OF BONES

Reguengos de Monsaraz

MONSARAZ

MONSARAZ CASTLE & WALLS

HERDADE DO ESPORÃO

SANTO ANTÓNIO CHURCH

Pêgo

Melides

Alcácer do Sal

Ferreira do Alentejo

ALQUEVA DAM

Grândola

Beja

Sines

BEJA CATHEDRAL

São Torpes Samoqueira

HERDADE DOS GROUS WINE FARM

IP8

N433

Malhão Beach

FRANQUIA BEACH

Vila Nova de Milfontes

ROYAL BASILICA

Guadiana Valley Natural Park

Cabezas Rubias

SOUTHWEST ALENTEJO & VICENTINE COAST NATURAL PARK

Castro Verde

MÉRTOLA CASTLE

Mértola

SPAIN

Odemira

Zambujeira do Mar

CABO SARDÃO LIGHTHOUSE

0   10 mi

0   10 km

© MOON.COM

Portugal"—are devoid of movement as cows and sheep seek refuge from the relentless sun under the cork oak trees that dot the landscape. In the heat of summer days, 1pm-4pm, shops close and locals hide in their homes.

In cooler months, wheat fields are green, stretching as far as the eye can see. The coast is a string of quaint whitewashed villages and beaches backed by sandy cliffs. Coastal Alentejo is rugged and breezy, with a majestic rawness that appeals to surfers and outdoors enthusiasts. In Alto (upper) Alentejo, the landscape darkens to gray as the rolling plains give way to jagged granite hills that border Spain. Alto Alentejo is a trove of medieval walled towns and hilltop fortresses off the beaten track.

The Alentejo is an important wine-producing region and the world's largest producer of cork; regional cheeses, cured meats, and olive oil also boost local incomes. Tourism is growing, but the region is not as traveled as the Algarve, Porto, or Lisbon. Several large dams in the region have created reservoirs popular for boating and other sports. Burgeoning wine tourism supports excellent boutique lodgings and wine-pairing menus. Many vineyards welcome visitors to take part in the traditional *vindimas* (grape picking) during grape harvest season.

Many people speed through the Alentejo as they travel between the north and the south, making it a relatively untapped, unexplored region. Its historic hamlets remain unspoiled, hiding fascinating relics of bygone eras. Come here to slow down, enjoy great food and drink, and discover a charmingly genuine part of Portugal.

PLANNING YOUR TIME

Vast, sleepy Alentejo varies by region and season. Pleasant times to visit are spring and fall, warm but without the severe summer heat. In spring the rolling plains bloom with wildflowers. In autumn the meadows blaze with color and vines are laden with fruit.

Head east from Lisbon to Évora and make your way south toward the Algarve through Beja and the coastal towns of Vila Nova de Milfontes and Odemira (allow four days). For a northbound route, head east from Lisbon to Évora and visit the enchanting historic walled towns of Elvas, Marvão, and Castelo de Vide (allow three days; Marvão and Castelo de Vide can be seen in one day).

The Alentejo is famous for wine, and a self-guided wine tour (www.vinhosdoalentejo.pt) is a popular option. Pick the wineries and villages that grab your attention, hit the road, and follow the signs.

More than a few days can be spent in the sprawling Alentejo among the historic whitewashed hamlets. A good road network connects major towns, but roads in rural areas can be narrow, winding, poorly maintained, and sparsely signed.

Previous: cork oak trees on rolling Alentejo plains; wall detail from the Church of Saint Francis in Évora; an iron gate in Estremoz.

Évora

In the heart of the Alentejo, Évora (EH-voh-rah) is the region's biggest city, built on a small hill amid the surrounding plains 133 kilometers (82 mi), or a 1.5-hour drive, from Lisbon. It is home to unusual monuments and leading wine producers, and is a university city that blends the old with the demands of modern youth.

Often called the megalithic capital of Iberia, Évora, a UNESCO World Heritage Site, has sites that date from prehistory. The most famous is Almendres Cromlech, on the city's outskirts, with menhirs (stone sculptures) that predate England's Stonehenge. Évora's city center is well preserved. First inhabited by Celts, the city was conquered by the Romans in the 1st century BC, and relics of their occupancy, such as the Roman Temple, remain along with surviving architectural influences from the subsequent Moorish occupancy. In the 15th century, Évora was home to Portugal's kings, which brought great wealth, and more prestige came in the 16th century when Évora was elevated to an ecclesiastical city.

Plan to spend at least one day in Évora exploring the monuments, maze-like cobbled streets, and the many excellent cafés and restaurants. Allow another day or two to venture outside the city center and discover a host of acclaimed vineyards and quaint villages.

SIGHTS

Évora is not that big, and its sights can be covered on foot in one day. Central **Giraldo Square (Praça do Giraldo)** is the city's main meeting point. Flanked by historic monuments and buildings and lined with elegant cafés and restaurants, it has a grand feel.

★ Chapel of Bones
(Capela dos Ossos)
The odd and chilling **Chapel of Bones** (Praça 1 de Maio 4, tel. 266 704 521, www.

igrejadesaofrancisco.pt, 9am-5pm daily winter, 9am-6:30pm daily summer, €4) is next to the entrance of the **Church of Saint Francis (Igreja de São Francisco)** in the heart of the city. The inner walls and pillars of this 16th-century chapel are clad with the tightly packed human bones and skulls of 5,000 local residents who were exhumed from the overcrowded cemeteries that once sprawled on the city's fringes. Local monks decided to put their remains on display as a warning about the superficiality of materialism and the certainty of death. This is explained in a message above the chapel door: *"Nós ossos que aqui estamos, pelos vossos esperamos,"* or "We bones that are here are awaiting yours."

★ Roman Temple of Évora
(Templo Romano de Évora)
A sacred site dating from the 1st century AD, the **Roman Temple of Évora** (Largo do Conde de Vila Flor, tel. 266 769 450, www.cultura-alentejo.pt, 24 hours daily) is one of the best-preserved Roman temples on the Iberian Peninsula. Also referred to incorrectly as the Temple of Diana, it is one of Portugal's most recognizable landmarks. The temple is believed to honor Emperor Augustus, who was worshipped as a god. Its remains are a series of Corinthian stone columns on a solid base, but the Roman architecture is still evident. In the historical center, near the cathedral, the temple is on the highest point in the city in front of the manicured public **Garden of Diana (Jardim de Diana)**, pleasant for a shady stroll and with a café with glorious views over Évora.

Évora Cathedral
(Catedral de Évora)
The grand **Évora Cathedral** (Largo do Marquês de Marialva 809, tel. 266 759 330, www.evoracathedral.com, 9am-5pm daily, cathedral €2, cloister, roof, and museum

Évora

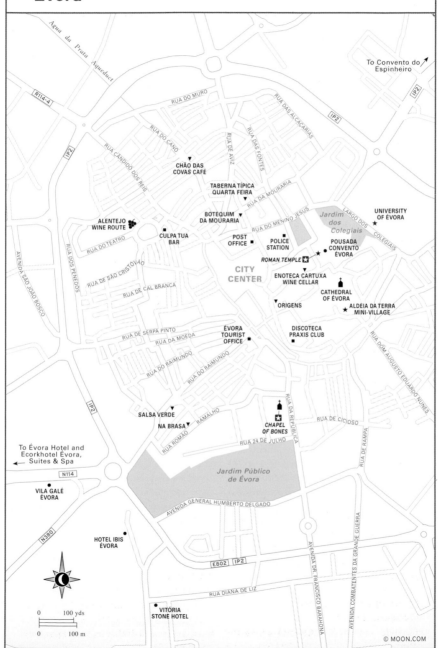

To Convento do Espinheiro

Água da Prata Aqueduct

R114-4

IP2

RUA DO MURO

RUA DAS ALCAÇARIAS

IP2

RUA DO CANO

RUA CÂNDIDO DOS REIS

RUA DE AVIZ

RUA DAS FONTES

CHÃO DAS COVAS CAFÉ

TABERNA TÍPICA QUARTA FEIRA

RUA DA MOURARIA

BOTEQUIM DA MOURARIA

RUA DO MENINO JESUS

Jardim dos Colegiais

LARGO DOS COLEGIAIS

UNIVERSITY OF ÉVORA

ALENTEJO WINE ROUTE

RUA DO TEATRO

CULPA TUA BAR

POST OFFICE

POLICE STATION

POUSADA CONVENTO ÉVORA

RUA DE SÃO CRISTOVÃO

ROMAN TEMPLE

CITY CENTER

ENOTECA CARTUXA WINE CELLAR

RUA DE CAL BRANCA

CATHEDRAL OF ÉVORA

ORIGENS

ALDEIA DA TERRA MINI-VILLAGE

RUA DOS PENEDOS

AVENIDA SÃO JOÃO BOSCO

RUA DE SERPA PINTO

RUA DA MOEDA

ÉVORA TOURIST OFFICE

DISCOTECA PRAXIS CLUB

RUA DÔM AUGUSTO EDUARDO NUNES

RUA DO RAIMUNDO

RUA DO RAIMUNDO

IP2

SALSA VERDE

NA BRASA

RAMALHO

RUA DA REPÚBLICA

CHAPEL OF BONES

RUA DE CICIOSO

RUA ROMÃO

RUA 24 DE JULHO

RUA DE RAMPA

To Évora Hotel and Ecorkhotel Évora, Suites & Spa

N114

Jardim Público de Évora

VILA GALÉ ÉVORA

N380

AVENIDA GENERAL HUMBERTO DELGADO

HOTEL IBIS ÉVORA

AVENIDA DR. FRANCISCO BARAHONA

AVENIDA COMBATENTES DA GRANDE GUERRA

E802 IP2

0   100 yds

0   100 m

RUA DIANA DE LIZ

VITÓRIA STONE HOTEL

© MOON.COM

€4.50), or Sé, is the largest medieval cathedral in Portugal. Similar to Lisbon's monumental cathedral, Évora Cathedral has two massive towers, Gothic cloisters, a Manueline chapel, and a magnificent baroque chapel. Also of note, among many other unique features, are the striking six-turret lantern-tower and the main portal, whose huge marble columns have impressive carvings of the apostles.

Built on the highest ground in the city, near the Roman Temple, the Gothic structure also bears Romanesque, Manueline, and baroque architectural touches in its add-ons over the centuries. Construction ran from 1280 to 1350 to mark the victory of the Christian Crusaders over the Moors. The cathedral has the look of a fortress, evident in features such as the battlement-encircled terrace. Its main facade is made of rose granite. Inside are ornamental cloisters and beautiful rose windows that give an ethereal feel, a contrast to the simple exterior.

Évora Cathedral also houses a **museum** packed with religious art and has the only Gothic statue of the pregnant Virgin Mary in Portugal, over a gilded altar inside the church. An added bonus is the view from the rooftop; the climb up is via a narrow 135-step spiral staircase through the bell tower, suitable only for the agile.

University of Évora
(Universidade de Évora)

The **University of Évora** is monumental but overshadowed by the city's more famous attractions. Founded in the 16th century, the university comprises several restored historical structures around the city, identified with a dove sculpted into a marble circle above the main entrance. The university's main building is the spectacular square **Espírito Santo College** (Largo dos Colegiais 2, tel. 266 740 800, www.uevora.pt, 9am-8pm Mon-Sat, adults €3, children under 12 free), a magnificent edifice with an imposing facade of successive grand arches on marble columns, encasing a courtyard and central fountain.

Construction took place 1550-1559. Visitors can explore on their own the lecture halls and hidden works of art, which include ancient tile plaques and an old bookshop with a mural.

Aldeia da Terra Mini-Village

The quirky **Aldeia da Terra Mini-Village** (Rua de São Manços 15-19, tel. 266 746 049, www.aldeiadaterra.pt, 10am-6pm daily, €3) is a tongue-in-cheek portrayal of Portuguese village life. Translating as "Village of the Land," it is a colorful collection of pint-size clay sculptures by artist Tiago Cabeça. Opened in 2010, this open-air attraction comprises 2,000 clay figurines that were relocated in 2017 from the nearby town of Arraiolos to Évora.

Água da Prata Aqueduct
(Aqueduto da Água de Prata)

Supplying drinking water over a length of 9 kilometers (5.6 mi), this 16th-century stone aqueduct, literally "Silver Water Aqueduct," was a complex and challenging construction project for its era. Massive arches, at points 25 meters (82 feet) high, rise from the ground. The main arches are located outside the city walls, north of Évora near the ring road. In the city's core it blends in seamlessly, fused to houses and shops. Originally the aqueduct ran to a marble fountain in the main Giraldo Square, with a series of public fountains along the way. It is possible to follow the route of the aqueduct by foot or bicycle through the city on the Água de Prata Route (Percurso da Água de Prata), which leads to the outskirts of the city, through farms and cork oaks. A shorter route is from Porta da Lagoa, where the aqueduct crosses the R114-4 road from Évora to Arraiolos, into the city center; follow the aqueduct and enjoy the sights along the way. Charming little shops have been built beneath some of the arches, and there is a Renaissance-style water box with a dozen Tuscan columns on Rua Nova. Other streets where you can

---

1: the ancient Roman Temple of Évora; 2: Chapel of Bones; 3: fountain in Giraldo Square; 4: cloister of Évora Cathedral

see the aqueduct are Rua do Cano, Rua do Salvador, and Travessa das Nunes.

Wine Routes and Tours

Wine lovers are spoiled for choice, and the **Alentejo Wine Route (Rota dos Vinhos do Alentejo)** (Horta das Figueiras, Rua Fernanda Seno 12, Apartado 498, tel. 266 748 870, www.vinhosdoalentejo.pt, 11am-7pm Mon-Fri, 10am-1pm Sat) takes visitors through the region's various wine-growing areas, listing dozens of wineries. It aims to promote regional wine-making as well as other aspects of regional culture. The headquarters are just outside the historic city center, between the hospital and the train station. Staff can help organize a trip and winery visits.

Alternately, head to the central **Wines of the Alentejo (Vinhos do Alentejo)** (Praça Joaquim António de Aguiar 20, tel. 266 746 498, 11am-7pm Mon-Sat) tasting and information center, which harnesses the essence of the region's wines. As well as showcasing two different wines to taste from three different producers, the beautiful center, with vaulted ceilings, stone walls, and windows on a beautiful square, also provides information on what to see in the Alentejo.

One of Évora's most iconic vineyards is the **Cartuxa Estate** (Quinta de Valbom, tel. 266 748 383, www.cartuxa.pt, 10am-7pm daily), 1.7 kilometers (1.1 mi) from the town center, a half-hour walk, a five-minute drive, or €5 by taxi. Producing iconic EA, Foral de Évora, and Pêra-Manca wines, the century-old 15-hectare (37-acre) organic vineyard offers guided tours (1 hour, in English, by appointment only), as well as wine and olive oil tasting (€10). Just next door is the Cartuxa Convent, built between 1587 and 1598, which houses monks.

FOOD

Évora's food scene spans rustic restaurants to fine dining, centered on hearty, meaty regional dishes, although international cuisine and vegetarian restaurants can be found. Many of the city's best-known restaurants are in the Moorish Quarter (centro histórico).

Unpretentious and atmospheric, the family-run ★ **Taberna Típica Quarta Feira** (Rua do Inverno 18, tel. 266 707 530, 12:30pm-3pm and 7:30pm-10pm Tues-Sat, 7:30pm-10pm Mon, €20) serves tasty local and regional specialties such as Alentejo-style pork meat and grilled black pork chops.

Don't be misled by the "café" in the name of **Chão das Covas Café** (Largo Chão das Covas Évora, tel. 266 706 294, 11am-11pm Tues-Sun, €10); this cute little eatery might be small, but its home-cooked Alentejano dishes and tapas are huge in flavor.

Cosmopolitan ★ **Enoteca Cartuxa Wine Cellar** (Rua de Vasco da Gama 15, tel. 266 748 348, www.cartuxa.pt, 10am-10pm Mon-Sat, noon-3pm Sun, €20) is a polished restaurant by the producers of the famous Cartuxa vineyard wines. The estate's wines are paired with Portuguese regional dishes such as cow tongue, pork cheek, sheep and goat cheese, smoked sausages, and cured meats.

One of Évora's most popular restaurants, **Botequim da Mouraria** (Rua da Mouraria 16A, tel. 266 746 775, 12:30pm-3pm and 6:30pm-9:45pm Mon-Fri, €15) is small, rustic, and tavern-like, run by a husband-and-wife team who prepare simple, unfussy, traditional Portuguese food. Be sure to try the presunto cured ham.

Offering contemporary Portuguese fare, **Origens** (Rua de Burgos 10, tel. 964 220 790, www.origensrestaurante.com, 12:30pm-3pm and 7:15pm-11pm Tues-Sat, €18) is modern and gleaming, with a sleek menu to match. Don't miss the chilled fresh tomato cream soup with cottage cheese, dried fruit, and honey.

Vegetarian restaurant **Salsa Verde** (Rua do Raimundo 93A, tel. 266 743 210, www.salsa-verde.org, 11am-3:30pm and 6pm-9:30pm Mon-Fri, 11am-3:30pm Sat, €10) is an airy, colorful setup in a former convent, a true haven for veggie fans in a land of meat lovers. Meat-free twists on traditional Portuguese

Local Specialties

Two local delicacies are *porco preto* (**black pig**) and the sweet treat *queijada d'Évora*. Black pig, also known as Alentejano pig, is a darker-skinned animal than its relatives. Its origins can be traced to wild boars. The black pig is traditionally free-range and feeds on acorns, so the meat is moister, more succulent, and more fragrant, with a nutty taste.

Queijada d'Évora is a small, sweet tartlet with a thin, crispy pastry crust and a creamy filling made from egg yolks and fresh sheep milk cheese. It is a form of *doçaria conventual*, traditional Portuguese sweets whose closely guarded recipes come from convents.

dishes use fresh local produce and herbs. There are no fixed menus; every day the offerings are fresh and different.

Lofty barnlike steakhouse **Na Brasa** (Rua Romão Ramalho 82, tel. 266 771 609, 11am-4pm and 6:30pm-midnight Mon-Thurs, 11am-4pm and 6:30pm-1am Fri-Sat, 6:30pm-midnight Sun, €15) serves fabulous meat straight from the grill as well as seafood dishes.

ENTERTAINMENT AND EVENTS

Évora has a vibrant alfresco social scene. In summer especially, locals socialize in the cooler temperatures after dark, giving the city a bustling café-culture feel, topped with the energetic vibe of the university students.

Many of the city center hotels have upscale wine and cocktail bars, while the other bars around the historic center buzz with students and younger people, particularly on Wednesday night. **Discoteca Praxis Club** (Rua Valdevinos 21, tel. 963 937 388, www.praxisevora.wixsite.com, 11pm-6am Tues-Sat) has four bars and two dance floors popular with the younger crowd. Its packed calendar features resident and guest DJs, live bands, and themed evenings.

The rustic **Culpa Tua Bar** (Praça Joaquim António de Aguiar 6, tel. 969 533 692, 5pm-3am Mon-Sat, 5pm-midnight Sun) is a busy little bar showcasing great local liquor, wine, and fruity cocktails. The bar is in a characterful old building with a vaulted ceiling, brick arches, and a cobbled floor.

RECREATION

Skydiving

Contact **SkyDive Portugal** (Évora Municipal Airdrome, tel. 910 999 991, www.skydiveportugal.pt, from €115) to jump out of a plane over the stunning Alentejo plains.

Hot-Air Balloons

Enjoy the beauty of the Alentejo from the serenity of a hot-air balloon. Watch the sunrise as you glide over Évora, the aqueduct, and the rolling plains and vineyards with a glass of champagne in hand. **Balonissimo** (tel. 935 646 124, www.balonissimo.com, from €140) offers free pickup from anywhere in Évora. Flights last about an hour, with the full excursion taking 3-4 hours.

ACCOMMODATIONS

Luxury boutique hotel ★ **Convento do Espinheiro** (5.2 km/3.2 mi north of Évora city center, tel. 266 788 200, www.conventodoespinheiro.com, from €180), converted from a 15th-century convent, is one of Portugal's most famous and emblematic hotels. Surrounded by gardens, it offers 92 rooms (including 5 suites), divided between sumptuous conventual rooms and a modern wing with midcentury-inspired decor.

The serene 36-room **Pousada Convento Évora** (Largo do Conde de Vila Flor, tel. 266 730 070, www.pousadas.pt, €183), with a swimming pool, is in Évora's historic center, converted from a low-rise, whitewashed monastery dating to 1487. The luxurious rooms are former monks' cells.

Sprawling, modern, upscale **Évora Hotel** (Av. Túlio Espanca, tel. 266 748 800, www. evorahotel.pt, from €100), a five-minute drive from the city center, captures the essence of the Alentejo. Surrounded by quintessential countryside and decorated with tones and textures of the region, it has two outdoor pools and an indoor pool.

Sleek, modern, four-star **Vila Galé Évora** (Av. Túlio Espanca, tel. 266 758 100, www. vilagale.com, €109) is a short walk from the city center, just outside the city walls. It has high-quality rooms, indoor and outdoor pools, a spa, and an on-site restaurant. Built using natural materials, refined countryside ★ **Ecorkhotel Évora, Suites & Spa** (Quinta da Deserta e Malina, tel. 266 738 500, www.ecorkhotel.com, from €128) has an eco-friendly ethos with 56 private suites a 10-minute drive from the city center in the rolling Alentejo plains.

You'll find bright, clean rooms at no-frills, contemporary **Hotel Ibis Évora** (Rua de Viana 18, Quinta da Tapada Urbanizacao da Muralha, tel. 266 760 700, www.accorhotels. com, €59), a 10-minute walk west of the center, just outside the city walls. Trendy, stylish **Vitória Stone Hotel** (Rua Diana de Lis 5, tel. 266 707 174, www.vitoriastonehotel.com, €103) offers a hip rooftop pool and a cool bar. It is just outside the city walls, 10 minutes' walk west of the center.

INFORMATION AND SERVICES

PSP police station: Rua Francisco Soares Lusitano, tel. 266 760 450, www.psp.pt
Main post office: Rua Olivença, tel. 266 745 480
Évora Hospital: Largo Senhor da Pobreza, tel. 266 740 100
Évora Tourist Office: Praça do Giraldo 73, tel. 266 777 071, 9am-6pm Mon-Fri, 10am-2pm and 3pm-6pm Sat-Sun Nov-Mar, 9am-7pm daily Apr-Oct

GETTING THERE
Car

Évora is 1.5 hours' drive east of Lisbon, about 140 kilometers (87 mi), following the A6 motorway, and 2.5 hours from the Algarve, 230 kilometers (143 mi) north of Faro following the A2 motorway and the IP2 road.

Bus

Rede Expressos (tel. 707 223 344, www. rede-expressos.pt) runs air-conditioned buses almost every half hour from Lisbon's Sete Rios bus station (1.5 hours, from €10.60). Tickets can be bought at the ticket office at the station or booked online.

From the Algarve, Rede Expressos operates four buses daily between Faro and Évora (4.5 hours, €15). The bus stops in Quarteira, Vilamoura, and Albufeira in the Algarve, as well as Castro Verde and Beja in the Alentejo. Évora's main bus station (Av. Tulio Espanca, tel. 266 738 120) is a 10-minute walk west of the walled city center.

Train

CP (tel. 707 210 220, www.cp.pt) trains run four times daily from Lisbon's Oriente, Sete Rios, and Entrecampos stations (1.5 hours, 2nd class €12.40, 1st class €16.50). Train travel between Faro and Évora (4.5 hours, 2nd class €25.90, 1st class €35.10) is not practical as there are just two services daily, one in the early morning and one in the early afternoon, with several stops en route, and the journey requires a change at Pinhal Novo station in Setúbal.

The train station in Évora, Largo da Estação, is outside the city walls, 1 kilometer (0.6 mi) south, a 15-minute walk. The station is simple, but look for the old azulejo tile murals depicting local life.

GETTING AROUND

Most of Évora's sights can be covered on foot, but the old cobbled streets can be slippery and uneven. **Horse-drawn carriages** (around €30) can be found outside the cathedral for sightseeing trips.

Car

Hire a car to explore the surrounding wine farms, villages, and Almendres Cromlech. Hotels work with local car hire companies; ask at reception. South of the walled city, between the IP2 road and the Circular de Évora ring road, are a number of car rental offices, including **Europcar Évora** (Estrada de Viana, Lote 10, tel. 266 742 627, www.europcar.pt), **Hertz** (Rua da Revendedora, Lote 7, Bairro da Torregela, Horta das Figueiras, tel. 219 426 300, www.hertz.pt), and **Sadorent** (Rua Manuel Correia Lopes 118, tel. 266 734 526, www.sadorent.pt), all open 9am-6pm weekdays.

Finding **parking** within the city walls can be difficult, and must be paid for 8:30am-7:30pm weekdays, 9am-2pm Saturday. There are spacious car parks outside the walls, such as at Portas de Lagoa, near the aqueduct, north of the city center. It is within walking distance of the center, with no steep hills or stairs. Parking outside the city walls is usually free.

Taxi

There are plenty of **taxis** near places of interest and the train and bus stations. Local company **Associação de Rádio Táxis de Évora** (Rua dos Altos, tel. 266 735 735) provides service anytime.

Bus

Local bus service **TREVO** (www.trevo.com.pt, €1 for 24 hours) serves Évora and its immediate fringes. Lines 51 and 52 on the Blue Route cover the old city continuously 8am-8pm weekdays, 8am-2pm Saturday.

The regional public bus service **Rodalentejo** (tel. 266 738 120, www.rodalentejo.pt) runs daily between Évora and neighboring towns such as Reguengos de Monsaraz, Arraiolos, Elvas, and Vila Viçosa, but on most routes there are only two or three buses per day, meaning a stay overnight might be required. Reguengos de Monsaraz can be done as a day trip, as there are four daily buses (1 hour) during the school year, two in the morning and two in the afternoon, and three daily buses when school is out. National bus company **Rede Expressos** (tel. 707 223 344, www.rede-expressos.pt) runs buses between Évora and Reguengos de Monsaraz (35 minutes, 9am and 7:45pm daily, €6.70).

ALMENDRES CROMLECH
(Cromeleque dos Almendres)

One of several Neolithic stone arrangements around the Alentejo, mysterious **Almendres Cromlech** (www.cm-evora.pt, 24 hours daily, free), on the outskirts of Évora on the gentle

Almendres Cromlech

THE ALENTEJO ÉVORA

slope of Monte dos Almendres, is a group of 95 granite standing stones haphazardly arranged in twin rings overlooking the plains. One of the oldest stone circles in Europe, built 6000-3000 BC, possibly for ceremonial or astronomical purposes, the site was discovered in 1966. Look closer and you'll see the stones are engraved with patterns. Public transport to the site is poor, so go by car. The enclosure is located 17 kilometers (10.5 mi) west of Évora center, a half hour's drive on the N114 road.

REGUENGOS DE MONSARAZ

Small, beautiful Reguengos de Monsaraz is the main gateway to the nearby walled medieval village of Monsaraz. Perched on the banks of the expansive Alqueva reservoir, near the Spanish border, Reguengos de Monsaraz is surrounded by sweeping plains dotted with Neolithic menhirs and dolmens. With interesting architecture, excellent wines, and local arts and crafts, the city has seen its tourism flourish in recent years.

Sights

Reguengos de Monsaraz sprawls around the main square, **Praça da Liberdade,** in a jigsaw of whitewashed houses and red roofs. Little arts and crafts shops dot the town, many run by working artisans.

SANTO ANTÓNIO CHURCH
(Igreja do Santo António)
In the middle of Praça da Liberdade, **Santo António Church** is unusual, with a hexagonal tower front and fanciful Gothic-Manueline style. Its origins date to 1887 when it was commissioned to replace a hermitage on the site, and it was designed by António José Dias da Silva, the architect who created Lisbon's bullring.

ALENTEJO WOOLEN GOODS FACTORY
(Fábrica Alentejana de Lanifícios)
The **Alentejo Woolen Goods Factory** (Rua dos Mendes 79, tel. 266 502 179, www.mizzete.

pt, 10am-4:30pm Mon-Fri), a 10-minute walk south of the main square, is one of the country's last remaining traditional handloom producers of wool blankets, rugs, and carpets. You can walk around the factory and watch the artisans work.

ESPORÃO WINE ESTATE
(Herdade do Esporão)
The name Esporão is a heavyweight in wine and olive oil and has placed Reguengos de Monsaraz on the wine map. Founded in 1277, the **Esporão Wine Estate** (tel. 266 509 280, www.esporao.com, 10am-7pm daily, closed Mon Nov-Mar), overlooking the Caridade dam 4 kilometers (2.5 mi) south of Reguengos de Monsaraz, a four-minute drive, opened its doors in 1997. Spanning 1,884 hectares (4,655 acres), the estate is open to the public to explore. It also has a **wine bar and restaurant** (10am-6:30pm daily Apr-Oct, 10am-6pm daily Nov-Mar) for wine-tastings and lunch; no reservations are necessary.

Guided tours (1 hour, in English 11am and 3pm daily, €15) of the wine cellar, vineyards, and olive groves include wine-tasting. Alternatively, skip the tour and head straight to the bar for a wine-tasting (from €8) or an olive oil tasting (from €3) accompanied by local cheeses and cold meats.

Esporão Wine Estate's cluster of medieval buildings comprise the Esporão Arch, the hermitage of Our Lady of Remedies (Nossa Senhora dos Remédios), and the **Esporão Tower,** outwardly plain and square, believed to date to the mid-1400s, built as a symbol of power. Today it is the symbol of Esporão wines and houses an archaeological museum, and can only be visited as part of a tour.

Getting There
Reguengos de Monsaraz is 200 kilometers (124 mi), a two-hour drive, east of Lisbon via the A2 and A6 motorways. From Évora, Reguengos de Monsaraz is 38.5 kilometers (24 mi) southeast, a 35-minute drive on the IP2 and N256 roads.

Rede Expressos (tel. 707 223 344, www. rede-expressos.pt) runs buses almost every half hour between Lisbon's Sete Rios station and Reguengos de Monsaraz (via Évora, 2.5 hours, from €14.30). Rede Expressos runs two other buses between Évora and Reguengos de Monsaraz (35 minutes, 9am and 7:45pm daily, €6.70).

The regional public bus service Rodalentejo (tel. 266 738 120, www. rodalentejo.pt) runs four times daily between Évora and Reguengos de Monsaraz (1 hour), two buses in the morning and two in the afternoon during the school year, and three buses a day when school is out.

The bus station in Reguengos de Monsaraz is on Avenida Dr. António José de Almeida, in the town center, just north of the central public gardens.

TOP EXPERIENCE

★ MONSARAZ

Within castle walls atop a jagged hill that rises from the endless Alentejo plains, the petite medieval village of Monsaraz, 16 kilometers (9.9 mi) northeast of Reguengos de Monsaraz, sits like a crown. Between the castle tower at one end of the village and an old bell tower at the other, Monsaraz is a cluster of whitewashed houses, restaurants, and guesthouses along steep schist-stone streets, with a statuesque church right in the middle. Bunches of bougainvillea provide color along the cobbled streets, and the views from the village over the Alentejo plains to the Alqueva reservoir are stunning. Monsaraz has a whimsical feel but is a down-to-earth village, one of the oldest in Portugal.

Sights

MONSARAZ CASTLE AND WALLS
(Castelo de Monsaraz e Muralhas)

It is thought that Monsaraz was a fortified settlement as far back as prehistoric times. The limestone and schist village's high position, over the Guadiana River and the Spanish border, made it a desirable and contested location that played a pivotal role in many battles.

Centerpiece Monsaraz Castle, a national monument, was built in the 14th century by King Dinis. After its military functions ended in the 19th century, the castle's main formation square was used as a bullring. Today the arena is used for little more than annual religious celebrations.

At the heart of the hilltop village is the Largo Dom Nuno Álvares Pereira square and the striking Our Lady of the Lagoon Church (Igreja da Nossa Senhora da Lagoa), in front of which is the 18th-century village pillory, another of Monsaraz's landmarks. Leading to the square is the main street, or Rua Direita, lined with whitewashed 16th- and 17th-century houses.

A large car park just outside the walls helps preserve the village from motorized traffic, and also means visitors can amble the cobbled streets at leisure. There are cafés, restaurants, and shops in the village, but they blend in discreetly so as not to detract from Monsaraz's authenticity.

The long wall around Monsaraz has four key entrances; the main one, the Porta da Vila (Village Door), is flanked by a pair of semi-cylindrical towers, and above its Gothic arch is a memorial stone dedicated to the Immaculate Conception, laid in 1646 by King João IV. On the north side of the wall is the Porta d'Évora (Évora Door), another Gothic arch cosseted by a chunky turret. The Portas d'Alcoba and Buraco have full arches and overlook the splendid Alentejo plains.

A high point of visiting Monsaraz is the 360-degree views over the countryside, from the vast Alqueva reservoir to Spain.

Getting There

Monsaraz is 16 kilometers (9.9 mi) northeast of Reguengos de Monsaraz, a 15-minute drive on the M514 road.

Buses operated by Rodalentejo (tel. 266 738 120, www.rodalentejo.pt) run four or five times a day between Reguengos de Monsaraz and Monsaraz village (lines 8174 or 8930, 30 minutes, €2-4). The bus drops passengers off just outside the village walls.

Visitors can also take a taxi from **Táxis Antral Reguengos Monsaraz** (tel. 266 502 671) from Reguengos de Monsaraz (around €13).

ARRAIOLOS

Charmingly rustic Arraiolos is a small village north of Évora that is famed for its rugs. Laborious traditional carpet-making, a skilled artisanal craft, dates to Moorish times and produces colorful handmade woolen carpets, tapestries, and cushion covers. Just as colorful is the sloping town itself, quintessentially *Alentejano* with its whitewashed houses, red roofs, and a church within the walls of a medieval castle.

Sights

CASTLE WALLS AND SALVADOR CHURCH
(Muralhas do Castelo e Igreja do Salvador)

Dominating the town's skyline, the 14th-century **castle** (24 hours daily) has a long circular wall in a big ring atop St. Peter's Hill (Monte de São Pedro). The area within the castle walls was initially a hive of local activity, but villagers eventually started to head to the plains at the foot of the mound to escape the wind and cold. There's nothing of the actual castle left, but its walls were restored in the 1960s when the fortification was declared a National Monument. On the hill's peak, in the very center of the castle walls, the 16th-century **Salvador Church** is impressive in white with sky-blue trim. From inside the castle walls, views over Arraiolos town are worth the seven-minute climb up the hill.

ARRAIOLOS CARPET INTERPRETIVE CENTER
(Centro Interpretativo do Tapete de Arraiolos)

Most people come to Arraiolos to see the **Arraiolos Carpet Interpretive Center** (Praça do Município 19, tel. 266 490 254, www.tapetedearraiolos.pt, 10am-1pm and 2pm-6pm Tues-Sun, €1), in a former hospital that's one of the oldest buildings in the village. Get insight into the local craft, believed to have been introduced by the Moors. Carpets were once a status symbol, indicative of wealth, and Arraiolos has been producing carpets since the 16th century. The center has a permanent collection of woven tapestries and carpets on display alongside temporary exhibitions by local artists, with signage in English.

Getting There

Arraiolos is 23 kilometers (14.3 mi) north of Évora, a 30-minute drive on the R114-4 road.

Rodalentejo (tel. 266 738 120, www. rodalentejo.pt) buses run sporadically between Évora and Arraiolos (1 hour, €6-8), generally a bus in the early morning, one at lunchtime, and one in the afternoon. The bus stops just outside the pedestrianized town center, near a taxi rank and post office.

ESTREMOZ

Busy, down-to-earth Estremoz is a small walled market town with an authentic feel and dramatic history. The graceful historic center, with tree-shaded streets and picturesque squares, was a key military headquarters and home to Portugal's kings and queens. From afar the town appears piled high on a mound where the 13th-century castle and walls sit. The fortified architecture is modest, built from regional marble, with 13th-century walls and a 30-meter-high (98-foot-high) solid marble keep within. A second fortified wall runs around Estremoz, which has a newer section, the Vila Nova (New Town), as its lower band. Local blush-pink marble is used liberally for everyday paving and cladding.

Estremoz's fantastic large **Saturday morning market** (Rossio Marquês de Pombal Square, 8am-1:30pm Sat) has

---

1: medieval hilltop castle of Arraiolos; 2: tapestry in Arraiolos; 3: church in Monsaraz; 4: cobbled street in Estremoz

The Marble Route

Estremoz is at the heart of the Alentejo's Marble Route, a region pitted with marble quarries and where the rock is widely used. The route runs along the Serra d'Ossa mountain range from Alandroal north to Estremoz. The main towns bedecked in marble include Estremoz, Sousel, Borba, Vila Viçosa, Redondo, Mourão, and Alqueva, giving the regional architecture a radiant character in ethereal iridescent white-gold and pale pink.

Guided tours and **visits to quarries** are organized by the **Rota Tons de Marmore** (Rua 5 de Outubro 20, Vila Nova de Baronia, tel. 284 475 413, www.rotatonsdemarmore.com) association, set up to promote the region's natural resources. Its headquarters is in Vila Nova de Baronia, 36 kilometers (22 mi) south of Évora near Viana do Alentejo.

extensive local produce, smoked sausages, and cheeses. Enjoy a *fartura* (like a churro) rolled in sugar and cinnamon, sold fresh from snack vans. The flea market usually sets up next to the farmers market; look for local red clay pottery, especially the traditional *bonecos de Estremoz,* colorful pottery figurines, and unique twin-spout stoneware jugs.

Sights
ESTREMOZ CASTLE AND ROYAL PALACE
(Castelo de Estremoz e Paço Real)
Nestled in the heart of the historic town center, **Estremoz Castle** (tel. 268 332 075, 24 hours daily, free) was built in the 13th century by King Dom Dinis in honor of his wife, Isabel of Aragon. The narrow, winding roads from the compact town surrounding the castle climb up to it. Its centerpiece is the impressive **Tower of the Three Crowns (Torre das Três Coroas),** a keep that stands 30 meters (98 feet) tall, made of local white marble. This tower is widely regarded as one of the most beautiful keeps in Portugal, and its 70 steps can be climbed for 360-degree views over the Alentejo. On a clear day you can see as far as the Serra da Estrela mountain range in central Portugal.

The castle's courtyard, Largo Dom Dinis, offers the former **Royal Palace,** once inhabited by King Dom Dinis and Dona Isabel and today an exclusive luxury hotel, the Pousada Castelo de Estremoz. One of the rooms, where Queen Isabel died in 1336, has been converted

into a **chapel** and remains open to the public. The Tower of the Three Crowns is accessed via the hotel.

MUSEUM OF LIVING SCIENCE
(Centro Ciência Viva)
Occupying a building that was once a 16th-century convent, Estremoz's **Museum of Living Science** (Convento das Maltezas, tel. 268 334 285, www.ccvestremoz.uevora.pt, 10am-7pm Tues-Sun, adults €9, children 7-17 €5, children 4-6 €3, family €16) is an interactive setup where science and technology offer insight into the history of the planet, with a particular focus on local geology. Exhibits include a dinosaur skeleton, the Estremoz Yellow Submarine deep-sea experience, and a vast fossil collection. This museum is a great place to keep kids entertained for a few hours if the weather is dreary.

SANTO ANTÓNIO DOORWAY
(Portas de Santo António)
Built into the castle wall, the Santo António Doorway, or Saint Anthony's gate, one of the main gateways into the city of Estremoz, is the prettiest of its formal entrances, full of carvings and engravings. Made from creamy-colored, chunky stone blocks, it pops out from the whitewashed town walls. With barely enough room for a car to squeeze through, the long tunnel from the doorway is publicly accessible for pedestrians and provides a memorable introduction to the town.

Accommodations

Pousada Castelo de Estremoz (Largo Dom Dinis, tel. 268 332 075, www.pousadas. pt, €162) is a luxury hotel in the former royal residence adjacent to the Estremoz Castle. It is packed with local historic artifacts and antiques and makes a great base to discover the gems of Estremoz on foot.

Information and Services

PSP police station: Rua 31 de Janeiro, tel. 268 338 470, www.psp.pt
Main post office: Rua 5 de Outubro 30, tel. 268 339 190
Estremoz Health Center: Rua Prof. Egas Moniz, tel. 268 337 700
Estremoz Tourist Office: Rossio Marquês de Pombal, tel. 268 339 227, 9am-5:30pm daily

Getting There

Estremoz is 48 kilometers (30 mi) northeast of Évora on the A6 motorway, about a 35-minute drive.

Rodalentejo (tel. 266 738 120, www. rodalentejo.pt) buses runs from Évora to Estremoz (1.25 hours, €4.55) three or four times a day, but buses back from Estremoz to Évora are less frequent.

Rede Expressos (tel. 707 223 344, www. rede-expressos.pt) express buses run between Évora and Estremoz (40 minutes, €7.60) at least twice a day, mostly in the afternoon, and are quicker than the regular buses. Rede Expressos also operates direct buses between Lisbon's Sete Rios terminal and Estremoz (2.5 hours, €14.70), departing every two hours. Some Lisbon-Estremoz services may require a transfer in Évora, so double-check when booking.

There are no trains to Estremoz. Estremoz bus station (Av. Rainha Santa Isabel, tel. 268 324 266), a short walk east of the city, occupies the disused train station.

VILA VIÇOSA

A short drive southeast of Estremoz is Vila Viçosa (VEE-lah vee-SSOH-sah), a pretty little town with an aristocratic feel that also has its own castle and a grand royal palace. A relaxing place to wander along the wide boulevards, marble-encased Vila Viçosa is so pretty that it is referred to as the "Princess of the Alentejo" and dubbed an open-air museum. Small but charming, this lush and regal town was the birthplace of famous Portuguese author and poet Florbela Espanca (1894-1930) and is her final resting place. Packed with history and magnificent monuments, it's worth a stop on the way to Estremoz.

Sights

VILA VIÇOSA DUCAL PALACE (Paço Ducal)

The magnificent 15th-century **Vila Viçosa Ducal Palace** (Terreiro do Paço, tel. 268 980 659, www.fcbraganca.pt, 2pm-6pm Tues, 10am-1pm and 2pm-6pm Wed-Sun June-Sept, 2pm-6pm Tues, 10am-1pm and 2pm-5pm Wed-Sun Oct-May, €7) has a simple and unique beauty. For centuries it was the seat of the House of Bragança, an important noble family.

An eerie point of interest is the private quarters of Dom Carlos I, king from 1889 to 1908, and his wife, Marie-Amélia. He left the palace one morning in 1908 for Lisbon and was murdered there that day, the first Portuguese king to be assassinated. His rooms have remained as they were following his last night here, laid out with clothes and toiletries, awaiting his return and untouched since.

The palace's mannerist architecture boasts a long symmetrical facade clad in marble from local quarries. Inside, the palace comprises 50 rooms that are open to the public and house collections such as Chinese porcelain, jewelry and gold, armaments, and coaches and carriages. Some of these exhibitions require an additional fee (€2.50-3).

Guided tours (in English 11am Tues-Sun, included in admission) are conducted in various languages.

VILA VIÇOSA CASTLE (Castelo de Vila Viçosa)

Dating from the 13th century and

reconstructed in the 17th century, the intriguing **Vila Viçosa Castle** (Rua Sacadura Cabral 2, tel. 268 980 128, www.fcbraganca.pt, 2pm-5pm Tues, 10am-1pm and 2pm-5pm Wed-Sun, till 6pm June-Sept, €3) houses an archaeology museum; a hunting museum showcasing the collection of Dom Carlos I, with taxidermy animals and skins on display; and an old Gothic chapel. Nearby is the cemetery where renowned Portuguese author Florbela Espanca (1894-1930) is buried. The walled fortress was home to the Bragança dynasty prior to the ducal palace being built. Wander the castle and its walls and museums, exploring its hidden tunnels and vaulted ceilings, as well as absorbing the views from the castle walls over pretty Vila Viçosa.

Getting There

Vila Viçosa is 70 kilometers (43 mi) northeast of Évora and 27 kilometers (17 mi) southeast of Estremoz. As with many of the little towns and villages skirting Évora, the easiest way to reach Vila Viçosa is by rental car. From Évora, follow the N245 road for 50 minutes, or take the N4 and N255 from Estremoz, around 35 minutes.

Rodalentejo (tel. 266 738 120, www.rodalentejo.pt) buses make at least three journeys a day between Estremoz and Vila Viçosa (30 minutes, €2-4). There are at least two direct daily **Rede Expressos** (tel. 707 223 344, www.rede-expressos.pt) buses from Lisbon's Sete Rios terminal (2.5-3.75 hours, from €14.30), with some trips making more stops. The bus stops in Vila Viçosa on the western fringe of town, a 10-minute walk from the center.

★ ELVAS

The grandly titled Garrison Border Town of Elvas sits on a hilltop above the Guadiana River 15 kilometers (9.3 mi) from Badajoz, Spain, flanked by lush plains and renowned for olives and plums, brandy, and pottery as well as for the iconic star-shaped fortified bulwarks that make the area famous.

Despite being heavily fortified, Elvas has charming churches, quaint streets, a pretty café-flanked main square, and good restaurants. It's one of Portugal's few remaining undiscovered treasures, but it can get extremely hot in the height of summer. Elvas is remote but easily accessible with regular bus services from both Lisbon and Évora.

view of the old town of Elvas and its surroundings

Sights

ELVAS WALLS
(Muralhas de Elvas)

A UNESCO World Heritage Site since 2012, Elvas is a good example of *trace italienne* (star fort) military architecture and has a large bulwarked dry-ditch system. The unique star-shaped walls were heavily fortified in the 17th-19th centuries. A solid band of ramparts and moats with gates and bastions protected the historic town. Unlike the residents in other walled towns, Elvas's community remained within the walls rather than relocating outside them. This fortification complex is excellently restored.

Inside the walls, the town is a cluster of narrow, flower-lined cobbled streets with traditional whitewashed buildings, churches, and small businesses.

AMOREIRA AQUEDUCT
(Aqueduto da Amoreira)

Towering over Elvas, outside the city walls, is the massive 16th-century **Amoreira Aqueduct,** which took over 100 years to complete (1498-1622), following the design by architect Francisco Arruda. The town's water supply is still delivered by the trellis-like conduit, which in some places looks like an extension of Elvas's walls and at points reaches four stories high, one arch on top of another. Elongating like a chunky knitted ribbon between two hills, the impressive aqueduct has a total of 843 arches, stretching 8 kilometers (5 mi) southwest of the city, and is one of Portugal's five most notable water conduits.

OUR LADY OF GRACE FORT
(Forte da Nossa Senhora da Graça)

Elvas has two outlying forts on opposite sides of town—the Santa Luzia Fort (Forte de Santa Luzia), within walking distance south of town, and, slightly farther afield on a hilltop to the north, the larger **Our Lady of Grace Fort** (tel. 268 625 228, 10am-5:30pm Tues-Sun, €5, with guided tour €8). Built in 1763 and officially known as Conde de Lippe Fort, it is one of Elvas's most distinctive bulwarks, a 10-pointed site in the hamlet of Alcazaba, 1 kilometer (0.6 mi) north of Elvas.

Getting There

Elvas is 210 kilometers (130 mi) east of Lisbon on the A6 motorway, two hours' drive. From Évora, Elvas is an 84-kilometer (52-mi) drive (1 hour) northeast, also on the A6 motorway. From Estremoz, it's a 40-kilometer (25-mi) drive (40 minutes) east on the N4 road.

Rede Expressos (tel. 707 223 344, www.rede-expressos.pt) runs buses between Évora and Elvas (1.5 hours, €12) around four times daily, usually from 1:45pm. From the Sete Rios bus station in Lisbon, there are seven buses 8:30am-7:30pm daily to Elvas (3.25 hours, €17.50). Buses run between Estremoz and Elvas (45 minutes, €8.50) five times daily. **Rodoviária do Alentejo** (tel. 266 738 120, www.rodalentejo.pt) offers similar service between Estremoz and Elvas (1 hour, €3-6). The bus station is just south of the town, outside the city walls; a taxi costs around €6.

Beja

Occupying a commanding position on a 277-meter (909-foot) hill, the city of Beja (BAY-zhah) is a rural hub with roots in the fertile plains surrounding it. From its earliest days it has been a strategic, important location. Beja was named Pax Julia by Julius Caesar in 48 BC, when he made peace with the Lusitanians and raised the town to capital status. During the reign of Augustus, the prosperous town, by then an established strategic junction, was renamed Pax Augusta. The largest city in the lower Alentejo, Beja is not as famous, grand, or monument-laden as Évora, but it has countrified simplicity.

From a distance Beja is a whitewashed cluster that looms above the surrounding golden plains, its skyline dominated by a statuesque medieval castle with a large tower. It is also infamously the hottest district capital in Portugal. Great restaurants, boutiques, and pretty squares await in its labyrinth of cobbled streets.

SIGHTS
Old Town
Most of Beja's monuments are in the historic old town. A cluster of splendid buildings including the cathedral and castle surround the city's main cobbled square, the Praça da República.

BEJA CATHEDRAL
(Catedral de Beja)
Beja Cathedral (Largo do Lidador 7, tel. 284 388 196, www.diocese-beja.pt, 10am-noon and 3pm-7pm daily, free), known locally as the Sé, was built in 1590 on the site of an earlier church dedicated to Saint James the Great. Mannerist in style and currently the seat of the Diocese of Beja, the cathedral is one of the oldest churches in the area.

CONVENT OF THE CONCEPTION
(Convento da Conceição)
The **Convent of the Conception** (Largo da Conceição, tel. 284 323 351, www.

museuregionaldebeja.pt, 9:30am-12:30pm and 2pm-5:15pm Tues-Sun, €2) houses one of the lower Alentejo's most important historical artifact collections, the **Beja Regional Museum (Museu Regional de Beja)**, also known as Queen Leonor Museum (Museu Rainha D. Leonor). Inside, a rich mix of tiled plaques, baroque carvings, paintings, and statues provide history. The palatial building is in the decorative Manueline style with some late Gothic influences, such as the flamboyant portal, double-arched windows, and lacy trimmings, which mark the transition to the Manueline. Entry to the Beja Regional Museum also includes entry to the Visigothic Museum.

BEJA CASTLE
(Castelo de Beja)
Built on the orders of Dom Dinis, a 14th-century king, on the site of a Roman fortress, imposing **Beja Castle** (Rua Dom Dinis 3, tel. 284 311 913, www.cm-beja.pt, 9:30am-12:30pm and 2pm-6pm daily, free) appears tired even though it is well preserved. Sections have been repaired over the years, but its most famous feature, the 40-meter (131-foot) keep, has retained its full splendor. A regional landmark, the keep is made entirely of marble. Inside, visitors can roam freely, ambling the walls at will, or climb a flight of worn steps to the top of the keep to take in the view. This is a solid, old-fashioned castle that is fun to visit.

SANTO AMARO CHURCH AND VISIGOTHIC MUSEUM
(Igreja de Santo Amaro e Museu Visigotico)
Adjacent to Beja Castle is 4th-century **Santo Amaro Church,** one of only a handful of preserved Visigoth churches in the country and one of just four churches in Portugal that date to the Roman era. A rare example of

Beja

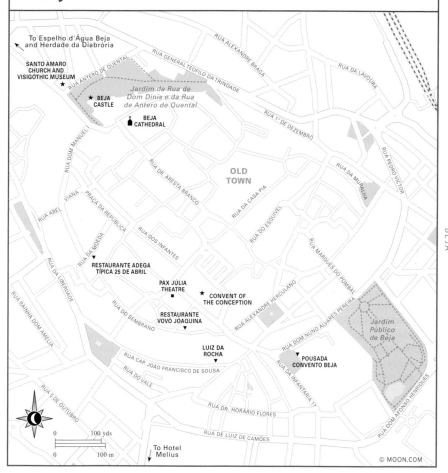

Paleo-Christian architecture, it has a simple whitewashed exterior and a trove of mosaic-tiled walls, carved columns, and motif-covered capitals on the inside. Today the building is home to the **Visigothic Museum** (Largo de Santo Amaro 26-27, tel. 284 321 465, www. museuregionaldebeja.pt, 9:45am-12:30pm and 2pm-5pm, Tues-Sun, €2), with artifacts dating from the 5th-8th centuries, among them tombstones and swords. Entry to the Visigothic Museum also includes entry to the Beja Regional Museum.

FOOD

★ **Luiz da Rocha** (Rua Capitão João F. Sousa 63, tel. 284 323 179, www.luizdarocha.com, 8am-11pm Mon-Sat, 8am-8pm Sun, €12) is a well-known, century-old restaurant and café in the heart of Beja where art and regional gastronomy go hand in hand. Traditional convent sweets fill the cabinets, while colorful tile murals depicting life in the Alentejo clad the walls. Specialties include Alentejo-style pork, *açorda* (soaked bread with garlic), and *ensopado de borrego* (lamb stew).

Wine Farms of the Alentejo

The Alentejo is a primary wine-producing area, divided into eight wine-making subregions: Portalegre, Borba, Redondo, Évora, Reguengos, Granja-Amareleja, Vidigueira, and Moura. Wine tourism is a growing trend, and many traditional vineyards have built elegant restaurants and accommodations on-site.

The **grape harvest** is in mid-August to early September, when visitors can help out with the harvest for a day. Vineyards that participate are listed on the **Alentejo Wine Route** website (www.vinhosdoalentejo.pt). Besides having a hand in making wine, you can meet local residents. Given the soaring temperatures in late summer, wear a hat and sturdy shoes and drink plenty of water. And be warned—harvest requires an early start. Some wineries, including Herdade dos Grous, on the outskirts of Beja, host mystical-sounding moonlight harvests.

Tavern-style **Restaurante Adega Típica 25 de Abril** (Rua da Moeda 23, tel. 284 325 960, 12:30pm-3pm and 7:30pm-10pm Tues-Sat, 12:30pm-3pm Sun, €10) offers traditional local and Portuguese specialties in a cozy, rustic environment. The grilled black pork is delicious.

Inside the luxury Pousada Convento hotel, once a refectory for the Franciscan friars, elegant, airy restaurant **Pousada Convento Beja** (Largo D. Nuno Alveres Pereira, tel. 284 313 580, www.pousadas.pt, 1pm-3pm and 7:30pm-10pm daily, €25) has high walls and vaulted ceilings. It offers a classic fine-dining experience based on fresh seasonal local produce and regional specialties.

At quaint ★ **Restaurante Vovó Joaquina** (Rua do Sembrano 57, tel. 961 302 815, www.vovojoaquina.pt, 12:30pm-2:30pm and 7pm-10:30pm Tues-Thurs, 12:30pm-2:30pm and 7pm-11pm Fri and Sat, €15), walls are adorned with old photos, there's a piano in the corner, and meals are delicious and home-cooked traditional Alentejano food with a quirky twist.

Hidden away in a corner of Beja's public city park, contemporary Portuguese cuisine restaurant **Espelho d'Água Beja** (Rua de Lisboa, City Park, tel. 284 325 103, www.espelhodagua.com.sapo.pt, noon-3pm and 7pm-10:30pm Tues-Sun, €15) overlooks a waterfall and a lake. Modern and light menu items include fresh fish, tapas for sharing, and typical Alentejo specialties.

ENTERTAINMENT AND EVENTS

Hidden on the streets of Beja are assorted cool bars and cafés, or head to the local **Pax Júlia Theater** (Largo de São João, tel. 284 315 090, http://paxjuliateatromunicipal.blogspot.pt) for cultural recreation. The biggest and most entertaining agricultural fair in the country is Beja's annual **OviBeja Fair** (www.ovibeja.pt, end of Apr), a five-day event that attracts tens of thousands to see the latest in farm animals, machinery, and products as well as to enjoy nightly entertainment, regional food, and drink.

ACCOMMODATIONS

Converted from a historic 13th-century convent, the upscale **Pousada Convento Beja** (Largo D. Nuno Álvares Pereira, tel. 284 313 580, www.pousadas.pt, from €155) is set amid extensive manicured grounds in the heart of Beja, a 10-minute walk to the castle. The large, clean, and comfortable four-star **Hotel Melius** (Av. Fialho de Almeida, tel. 284 313 080, www.hotelmelius.pt, €64), on the edge of the city, has a fitness center and a snack bar.

On the outskirts of Beja, 6 kilometers (3.7 mi) northwest of the center, near the brand-new and largely unused international airport, **Herdade da Diabrória** (N121, tel. 284 998 177, www.diabroria.com, €70) is a tranquil, rural Alentejano refuge amid wheat and sunflower fields. This agro-tourism hotel was converted from a 300-hectare (741-acre) hacienda with an enormous lake at its heart.

INFORMATION AND SERVICES

PSP police station: Rua Dom Nuno Álvares Pereira, tel. 284 313 150, www.psp.pt

Main post office: Rua Diogo Gouveia, tel. 284 311 270

Beja Hospital: Rua Dr. António Fernando Covas Lima, tel. 284 310 200

Beja Tourist Office: Largo Dr. Lima Faleiro 1, in the castle square, tel. 284 311 913, 9:30am–12:30pm and 2pm–6pm daily

GETTING THERE

By car, Beja is 178 kilometers (110 mi) southeast of Lisbon, under two hours on the A2 motorway and the IP8 road. From anywhere in the Algarve, take the A22 motorway to the A2 and the IP2, a 1.5-hour trip. From Évora, Beja is 82 kilometers (51 mi) south, under two hours on the IP2 road.

There is frequent bus and train transport between Beja and Lisbon. Buses are easier because the train trip requires a transfer.

Rede Expressos (tel. 707 223 344, www. rede-expressos.pt) runs a dozen daily buses between Lisbon's Sete Rios station and Beja (3 hours, €13.30). From Évora, there are nine daily Rede Expressos express buses (1.25 hours, €7.60). The bus station in Beja (Rua General Humberto Delgado 44, tel. 284 313 620) is a short 600-meter (0.4-mi) walk south of the historic center.

By train, **CP** (tel. 707 210 220, www. cp.pt) operates four Intercity trains (2 hours, 7:10am, 9:10am, 5:10pm, and 7:10pm daily, 2nd class €14, 1st class €17) between Lisbon's Entrecampos station and the train station in Beja (Largo da Estação, a 10-minute walk east of the city center). There are four daily trains from Évora to Beja (2.25 hours, €7.40 one-way), two early in the morning and two in the afternoon).

ALQUEVA DAM
(Barragem de Alqueva)

This vast reservoir, also known as "the Great Lake of Alqueva" (al-KEH-vah), spreads between Beja and Évora, covering 250 square kilometers (97 square mi). From Beja, the Alqueva Dam is around a 45-minute drive north, 63 kilometers (39 mi) on the IP2 road. Completed in 2002, the Alqueva project was controversial, completely submerging the local village Aldeia da Luz.

One of the largest artificial lakes in

Alqueva Dam

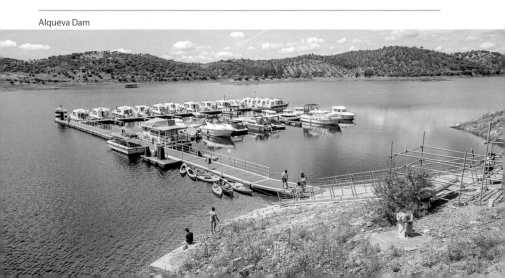

Europe, the Alqueva Dam's waters irrigate five Alentejo municipalities and provide for water sports and family-friendly leisure. Canoeing, kayaking, boating, water-skiing, wakeboarding, fishing, or lounging on a sun bed on the beaches are enabled by outfitters such as **Amieira Marina** (tel. 266 611 173, www.amieiramarina.com, 9am-8pm daily), the largest infrastructure on the Alqueva, located in the village of Amieira, a 63-kilometer (39-mi) drive north of Beja on the IP2 road that takes 45 minutes. No public transport serves the marina.

Rent a houseboat to explore the historic villages around the reservoir's banks, such as the rebuilt Aldeia da Luz and Reguengos de Monsaraz. Rentals from Amieira Marina start from around €200 per night, and piloting a houseboat doesn't require a driver's license.

There are at least four beaches around the Alqueva, in the towns of Monsaraz, Mourão, Cheles, and Tapada Grande.

CASTRO VERDE

Larger-than-life Castro Verde is a vibrant farming town said to have been the backdrop for the famous Battle of Ourique on the plains between Castro Verde and nearby Ourique on July 25, 1139. Portuguese Prince Afonso Henriques defeated the Moors, led by Ali ibn Yusuf, after which Afonso declared himself the first king of Portugal. The only action on the plains today is the grazing of sheep and other livestock. The town is packed with interesting churches and has an emblematic windmill in the town center. Every year on the third weekend in October, Castro Verde hosts the Feira de Castro, the biggest fair in the lower Alentejo, celebrating the region's culture, traditions, and produce.

Sights
ROYAL BASILICA
(Basílica Real)
The legendary Battle of Ourique is depicted in eye-catching ancient tile murals that clad the nave of Castro Verde's main church, the sizable 17th-century **Church of Our Lady of the Conception (Igreja da Nossa Senhora da Conceição)** (Largo Doutor João Guerreiro Mestre, tel. 286 322 176, 10am-12:30pm and 2pm-6pm Wed-Sat Apr-Oct, 9:30am-12:30pm and 2pm-5:30pm Wed-Sat Nov-Mar, mass noon-1pm Sun, basilica free, museum €2), more commonly known as the **Royal Basilica.** This little gem, nestled in the heart of the quaint town, also has a gilded hand-carved altar, an unusual large weight-driven machine clock dating to 1875, and a remarkable painted wooden ceiling. The Royal Basilica is also home to a museum brimming with sacred art, known as the Treasure.

Accommodations
Family-friendly wine estate and farm **Herdade da Malhadinha Nova Country House & Spa** (Herdade da Malhadinha Nova, tel. 284 965 432, www.malhadinhanova.pt, from €300)), 22 kilometers (13.6 mi) north of Castro Verde, offers rustic charm and modern amenities. Sprawled around a vast lake, 28 kilometers (17 mi) north of Castro Verde, ★ **Herdade dos Grous** (Albernôa, tel. 284 960 000, www.herdade-dos-grous.com, €145) is a beautiful wine estate and farm with a luxury rustic-chic feel, where rest and relaxation blend seamlessly with food and wine. Horseback riding, wine-tasting, cycling, and canoeing are available on-site.

Getting There
Castro Verde is a 40-minute, 47-kilometer (29-mi) drive south of Beja on the IP2 road. Local **Rodalentejo** (tel. 284 313 620, www.rodalentejo.pt) buses run between Beja and Castro Verde (€4.20) five times every afternoon during the week; there's no bus service on weekends.

MÉRTOLA
Built on a jagged knoll where the Guadiana River converges with the Oeiras stream, Mértola is situated in the heart of the Guadiana Valley Natural Park (Parque Natural do Vale do Guadiana) in the southeastern Alentejo on the border with Spain.

The town is a postcard-perfect vision of hodgepodge quaint whitewashed cottages on the rocky mound, with Mértola Castle at its peak. Like many Alentejo border towns, Mértola is ringed by the long arms of its castle. The town's main church was originally a mosque.

Sights

MÉRTOLA CASTLE
(Castelo de Mértola)

The 13th-century medieval **Mértola Castle** (Largo da Igreja, tel. 286 610 100, www. museus.cm-mertola.pt, 9:15am-12:30pm and 2pm-5:30pm Tues-Sun, castle free, museum €2) towers over Castro Verde at the highest point, a 600-meter (0.4-mi) walk south from the center. The centerpiece is a 30-meter-high (98-foot-high) keep that houses two exhibitions, one on the castle's history and the other on Moorish relics. From the top of the keep are sweeping views over the Guadiana River.

CHURCH OF OUR LADY OF THE ANNUNCIATION
(Igreja da Nossa Senhora da Anunciação)

Mértola's main church, the **Church of Our Lady of the Annunciation** (Rua da Igreja, tel. 286 610 100, 9:30am-12:30pm and 2pm-5:30pm Tues-Sun Oct-June, 9:30am-12:30pm and 2pm-6pm Tues-Sun July-Sept, free), was formerly a mosque, converted to Christianity in the 13th century by the Knights of Saint James. It is believed to be the only church in Portugal that retained its Moorish appearance after conversion. Just 100 meters (328 feet) west of the castle, the dazzling white building is a mix of architectural styles that give it a bit of a frilly wedding cake look. On an isolated spot on a hill below the castle, the church reveals its strong Moorish architectural roots in the keyhole-shaped doors and the mihrab in the wall behind the altar. It has a tiny museum in the basement, and the long, low interior is divided into five naves with a bright and airy feel. There is parking at the foot of the hill, but the short cobblestone road up can be challenging.

Getting There

Mértola is 53 kilometers (33 mi) southeast of Beja, 50 minutes' drive on the IC27 road. Mértola is not accessible by train.

From Beja there are three local **Rodalentejo** (tel. 284 313 620, www. rodalentejo.pt) buses (1 hour; morning, lunchtime, and afternoon daily; €6.10) to Mértola. National bus company **Rede Expressos** (tel. 707 223 344, www.rede-expressos.pt) has at least one direct daily bus from Lisbon's Sete Rios station (3.5 hours, 5:15pm daily, €16.60). Rede Expressos has a direct service between the border town of Vila Real de Santo António, in the Algarve, and Mértola (1.25 hours, €10.50).

Coastal Alentejo

Along Portugal's west coast between the Setúbal Peninsula's Sado River and the Algarve, the Alentejo's coastal region has natural beauty that's mostly safeguarded in the Southwest Alentejo and Vicentine Coast Natural Park, which crosses into the Algarve, and in the Alentejo stretches between Odeceixe in the south and São Torpes in the north. In summer the Alentejo coast can get busy as Portuguese holidaymakers flock here in search of a calmer alternative to the frenzied Algarve. Its beauty rivals the Algarve's but is less manicured and less built-up. Outside summer, the pristine beaches backed by golden cliffs and the rugged landscape, dotted with pretty whitewashed villages and the odd wind turbine, offer rare peaceful isolation.

Coastal Alentejo

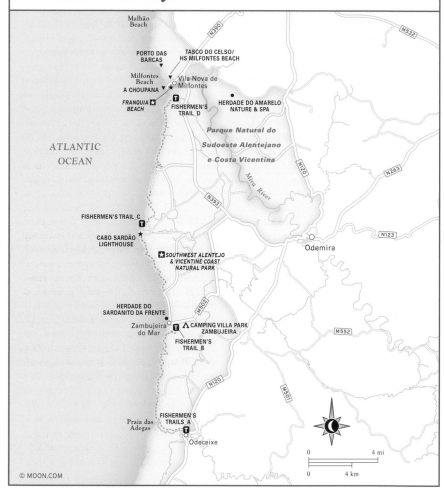

Malhão
Beach

PORTO DAS
BARCAS

TASCO DO CELSO/
HS MILFONTES BEACH

Milfontes
Beach

Vila Nova de
Milfontes

A CHOUPANA

FRANQUIA
BEACH

FISHERMEN'S
TRAIL_D

HERDADE DO AMARELO
NATURE & SPA

Parque Natural do
Sudoeste Alentejano
e Costa Vicentina

ATLANTIC
OCEAN

Mira River

Odemira

FISHERMEN'S TRAIL_C

CABO SARDÃO
LIGHTHOUSE

SOUTHWEST ALENTEJO
& VICENTINE COAST
NATURAL PARK

HERDADE DO
SARDANITO DA FRENTE

Zambujeira
do Mar

CAMPING VILLA PARK
ZAMBUJEIRA

FISHERMEN'S
TRAIL_B

Praia das
Adegas

FISHERMEN'S
TRAILS_A

Odeceixe

N390
M532
N120
N263
N123
N393
M502
M552
N120
M501

0   4 mi
0   4 km

© MOON.COM

ODEMIRA

Odemira is a sweet little hilltop town over-looking the Mira River on the edge of the Southwest Alentejo and Vicentine Coast Natural Park, providing a gateway to the Vicentine Route and some of the most popular Alentejo seaside villages within the park, including Zambujeira do Mar and Vila Nova de Milfontes. Odemira has a remarkably large foreign community of Dutch, Germans, and Asians, many of whom work in the vast greenhouses that cover the surrounding landscape and supply fresh produce. This eclectic hamlet has few historically important relics but takes pride in preserving its local arts and crafts, such as basketmaking and furniture, pottery, and hand-woven fabrics.

Recreation

Odemira is a playground for outdoors

enthusiasts, with prime terrain for hiking and cycling in the Southwest Alentejo and Vicentine Coast Natural Park. The Mira River, which starts in the Caldeirão mountain range and snakes through Odemira, has a 30-kilometer (19-mi) stretch from Odemira to Vila Nova de Milfontes that has been made navigable for paddleboarding and canoeing.

ECO-TRAILS

Local outdoors activity company **Eco-Trails** (tel. 967 155 383, www.ecotrails.info) offers guided hiking (from €27) and canoe trips (from €20 pp) on the Mira River to explore nature in the gentlest way. A variety of canoe tours are available to suit all ages and energy levels. Horseback treks (€25 per hour), cycling, camping, and fishing trips (€20 pp for 2-3 hours) can also be arranged.

Getting There

By car, Odemira is 76 kilometers (47 mi) straight north of Lagos in the Algarve, a 1.25-hour drive on the winding N120 road. The fastest route from Lisbon is the A2 motorway, turning off at Beja, a 204-kilometer (126-mi), 2.25-hour drive.

CP (tel. 707 210 220, www.cp.pt) trains run from Lisbon's Oriente, Entrecampos, and Sete Rios stations. There are three Intercity services on line 570, which passes through all three Lisbon stations consecutively, departing first from Oriente at 10am, 2pm, and 5:30pm daily, to Santa Clara-Saboia station (2.25 hours, 2nd class €17.50, 1st class €23.50), the nearest to Odemira. From Santa Clara-Saboia, take a taxi to Odemira (30 minutes, 34 km/21 mi, €26). There are taxis outside the station, or call **Taxis Antral de Odemira** (tel. 283 322 404).

There are three **Rede Expressos** (tel. 707 223 344, www.rede-expressos.pt) buses between Lisbon's Sete Rios station and Odemira (up to 4 hours, 7:30am, 3pm, and 5:30pm daily, €16.10) The trip takes longer depending on how many stops the bus makes. Rede Expressos has two buses from Lagos in the Algarve to Odemira (1.5 hours, 8:30am and 3:20pm daily, €10.50), which make three stops en route.

VILA NOVA DE MILFONTES

Halfway between the Algarve and Lisbon, whitewashed Vila Nova de Milfontes (VEE-lah NOH-vah d' mil-FON-tezh) is a gem of a seaside hamlet and one of the prettiest towns along the Alentejo coast, hence its nickname, the "Princess of the Alentejo." Vila Nova de Milfontes is surrounded by the distinctive rugged terrain of the Southwest Alentejo and Vicentine Coast Natural Park. Regulations governing the park mean that any development in the area has been kept subtle and in harmony with the landscape. For a place of such striking beauty, Vila Nova is overlooked by foreign visitors, but it is popular among Portuguese holidaymakers and comes to life during the peak July-August vacation season, when the local population soars. In other months it falls back into the region's characteristically unhurried pace.

Beaches

Vila Nova de Milfontes has excellent beaches, from small cove-like havens to vast expanses of sand that seem to go on forever.

★ FRANQUIA BEACH (Praia da Franquia)

Just a five-minute walk from the town's center is wide, crescent-shaped **Franquia Beach,** just inland from the mouth of the Mira River. One of the most photographed beaches in the Alentejo, it is Vila Nova de Milfontes's busiest thanks to its proximity and child-friendly shallow water, tucked away from the rough Atlantic behind a headland. Franquia Beach is well equipped with cafés, bars, restrooms, a lifeguard, and a canoe-rental outfitter.

Just around the other side of the headland, heading west, toward the coast, is popular **Farol Beach (Praia da Farol),** at the mouth of the Mira River. Less sheltered and more rugged than Franquia, it is not as well

Portugal's Best Hidden Beaches

The Alentejo coast might not be as famous as the Algarve's, but its beaches are just as beautiful. Less crowded even in peak season, the generous Alentejo coast is home to some glorious and still relatively undiscovered stretches of sand.

In the north, **Comporta Beach,** south of the Tróia Peninsula, is a vast swath of golden sand with excellent parking and beach restaurants. Surfers say the **São Torpes Beach** near Sines is the best in the region, while the stunning **Samoqueira Beach** in Porto Côvo, a wild alcove, is more like an oversize rock pool, studded with jagged crags, where visitors can swim or float in calm, crystalline waters. **Melides Beach,** near Grândola, is the biggest beach in Portugal, a long stretch that divides the ocean from an expansive lagoon. The 4-kilometer (2.5-mi) road from sleepy, whitewashed Melides village is a scenic route flanked by rice fields and pine groves. Nearby **Pêgo Beach** is famous for its wild beauty and has a beach bar, **Sal** (tel. 265 490 129, www.restaurantesal.pt), that has been rated one of the best in the world. Less known is **Praia das Adegas,** near Odeceixe, one of the country's few nudist beaches.

equipped, although the waves are gentle and the water shallow and calm.

MALHÃO BEACH
(Praia do Malhão)
Malhão Beach, 10 kilometers (6.2 mi) north of Vila Nova de Milfontes, a 15-minute drive on the N390 and CM1072 roads, is a long, wide expanse of dune-fringed sand open to the elements, making it popular with surfers. It is also a windsurfing and kite-surfing hot spot, although there are no outfitters on the beach to rent equipment. It's unblemished, with zero development—no beachside restaurants or bars—but parking and access have been greatly improved in recent years, though access to the beach is limited to a beaten track with viewing decks and platforms.

Food
On the outskirts of Vila Nova de Milfontes, bright and open, tastefully decorated **Porto das Barcas** (Estrada Canal, tel. 283 997 160, noon-11pm daily, €15) is the place to enjoy creative fresh seafood dishes in classy surroundings with stunning views. It is a six-minute drive (3 km/1.9 mi) north of town and an excellent spot to enjoy sunset with dinner.

Popular for its *cataplana* (a seafood stew) and other local and regional specialties, the centrally located, warm, and welcoming tavern ★ **Tasco do Celso** (Rua dos Aviadores

34, tel. 283 996 753, www.tascadocelso.com, 11:30am-3pm and 7:30pm-11:30pm Tues-Sun, €20) oozes local flavor. The dining area has solid slabs of tree for tables, a bar propped up on wine barrels, and a cozy area with deep armchairs set out around an open fire for a drink.

A Choupana (Praia do Farol, tel. 283 996 643, 10am-midnight Tues-Sun, €18), a little wooden beach shack on Farol Beach, offers fantastic grilled fresh fish and meats combined with ultimate beach views.

Recreation
In addition to water sports, the Alentejo coast offers trekking along the **Vicentine Route (Rota Vicentina)** (www.rotavicentina.com), a web of designated coastal and countryside walking routes, such as the Fishermen's Trail and the Historical Way, that span the Southwest Alentejo and Vicentine Coast Natural Park. The Vicentine Route is marked along all its routes and divided into 15- to 25-kilometer (9.3- to 15.5-mi) sections. Spring and autumn are the best times to do these walking trails, as summer is excessively hot and winter can be rainy and blustery.

THE FISHERMEN'S TRAIL
(Rota dos Pescadores)
Sturdy shoes are needed for the demanding Fishermen's Trail, along the paths etched into

the cliff tops by centuries of local fisherfolk. Portuguese fishermen are famed for their fearlessness, and on this route you will understand why. Local anglers perch on jagged cliffs with the Atlantic crashing relentlessly below. The Fishermen's Trail is a single track that runs parallel to the coastline, comprising four sections in the Alentejo plus a number of complementary circuits, totaling 120 kilometers (74 mi) of walkable trail through popular and hidden fishing spots. The trail passes through Vila Nova de Milfontes on a 15-kilometer (9.3-mi) trail between Vila Nova and pretty Almograve below it. See the website (www.rotavicentina.com) for an exact map of the route.

Accommodations

Surrounded by the lush vegetation of the Southwest Alentejo and Vicentine Coast Natural Park, the magical ★ **Herdade do Amarelo Nature & Spa** (EN 532, Km 7, tel. 930 520 706, www.herdadedoamarelo.pt, minimum 2 nights, from €195) farmhouse and estate is both rural and refined, with a large outdoor pool and 10 elegant rooms.

Four-star **HS Milfontes Beach** (Av. Marginal, tel. 283 990 070, http://hsmilfontesbeach.com, €149), with simple, unfussy rooms, is in the center of the village overlooking the river mouth. It has three on-site restaurants and an outdoor pool and deck area, and is a short walk to anywhere in town.

Information and Services

GNR police station: Rua António Mantas 28, tel. 283 990 020, www.gnr.pt
Main post office: Rua Custódio Brás Pacheco 9, tel. 283 990 000
Vila Nova de Milfontes Tourist Office: Rua António Mantas, tel. 283 996 599, 9am-1pm and 3pm-6pm daily

Getting There

By car, Vila Nova de Milfontes is 28 kilometers (17 mi) northwest from Odemira, a 30-minute drive on the N393 road. A **Rede Expressos** (tel. 707 223 344, www.rede-expressos.pt) bus runs twice daily between Odemira and Vila Nova de Milfontes (20 minutes, €6), once in the morning and once in the afternoon. The bus stop in Vila Nova de Milfontes is just north of the town, close to the campsites, a 15-minute walk to the center.

ZAMBUJEIRA DO MAR

Spread out over steep, dark cliffs, Zambujeira do Mar (zam-boo-ZHAY-ray doo MAHR) is the Alentejo's most southwestern seaside village, a tiny hamlet popular in summer among young Portuguese. The village's whitewashed cluster of cottages stretches along one main road toward a bay-like beach. Sleepy Zambujeira bursts into life in summer, particularly during the Sudoeste music festival when the petite locale is inundated by revelers who party at night and bask on the beach by day. Outside peak season, this tranquil fishing village offers invigorating cliff-top walks and dramatic, isolated scenery.

Sights
CABO SARDÃO LIGHTHOUSE
(Farol do Cabo Sardão)
An 8-kilometer (5-mi) detour north of Zambujeira do Mar village is the **Cabo Sardão Lighthouse** (Cavaleiro, tel. 283 958 218), dating to 1915, with breathtaking views from its base over the coast and surrounding landscape. The lighthouse is at the heart of a network of walking trails that explore the area's raw beauty. A number of viewing decks have been built around the lighthouse, but sadly their positioning is too far back to afford the spectacular coastal views in full. Cabo Sardão Lighthouse is a 15-minute drive on the CM1158 and CM1124 roads from Zambujeira, or an 80-minute walk on a designated pathway along the cliff tops. The lighthouse building is open to the public only 2pm-5pm Wednesday.

Entertainment and Events
MEO SUDOESTE MUSIC FESTIVAL
The massive annual five-day **Meo Sudoeste Music Festival** (www.sudoeste.meo.pt, 1st

week in Aug) takes place on the Herdade da Casa Branca estate, a huge field on the fringes of Zambujeira do Mar village. The site provides camping facilities with modern comforts, but many revelers stay in the nearby towns, filling local accommodations, bars, and restaurants to the rafters. By night, music from international superstars keeps the crowds partying, while by day they reenergize on the beaches. Three stages play different genres of popular music simultaneously. Past performers include the Chainsmokers, Lil Wayne, Jamiroquai, Dua Lipa, Steve Aoki, Sia, Wiz Khalifa, and James Morrison.

Accommodations

Rural tourism at its finest, 140-hectare (346-acre) ★ **Herdade do Sardanito da Frente** (Sardanito, tel. 283 961 353, www. herdadedosardanitodafrente.com, €165 d, €210 4-person bungalow) has cozy rooms and bungalows around a glorious lake, an indoor and outdoor pool, a jetted tub, and a petting farm. It's a 10-minute, 6-kilometer (3.7-mi) drive south of Zambujeira do Mar center.

At the entrance to the village, a short stroll from the center, **Camping Villa Park Zambujeira** (main road into Zambujeira do Mar, tel. 968 292 236, www. campingzambujeira.com, tenting €6.10 plus €6.55 pp, RV €6.95, RV over 6 meters/20 feet €7.95, €109 1-bedroom, 4-person bungalow) is a clean, well-equipped, and popular campsite with a pool, a tennis court, and other amenities. It accommodates tents and motor homes and has 24 cute little Alentejo-style cottages.

Getting There

Zambujeira do Mar is a 17-kilometer (10.5-mi), 25-minute drive east from Odemira on the CM1159 road. **Rede Expressos** (tel. 707 223 344, www.rede-expressos.pt) operates at least two daily direct buses year-round between Lisbon's Sete Rios station and Zambujeira do Mar (3-4 hours, 4pm and 5pm daily, €17). Buses run more frequently in summer.

Buses from the Algarve include service from Lagos (1.5 hours, 9am Mon-Thurs, 9am and 3:20pm Fri-Sun, €10.90), with stops in Aljezur and Odeceixe on the way. The small bus station in Zambujeira is west of town on Avenida do Mar, a few hundred meters from the main seafront square.

★ SOUTHWEST ALENTEJO AND VICENTINE COAST NATURAL PARK
(Parque Natural do Sudoeste Alentejano e Costa Vicentina)

The **Southwest Alentejo and Vicentine Coast Natural Park** is one of the finest preserved coastlines in Europe. Rugged and wild, it spans 100 kilometers (62 mi) from Burgau in the Algarve to Porto Côvo in the Alentejo and is a magnet for scientists drawn to its unique indigenous flora and fauna, including 700 species of flowers, a dozen of which exist only in the park. Also here are various orchids and unusual plant species such as *Biscutella vicentina, Cistus palhinhae,* and *Plantago almogravensis,* adapted to the limestone terrain and salty breeze. This diverse plantlife attracts butterflies and 200 species of birds, including fishing eagles, choughs, and white storks, which nest in the cliffs.

The landscape is sheer, multicolored cliffs carpeted in plantlife and bordered by beaches. A network of walking trails and scenic routes, all well mapped and marked, traverses the park, but be warned that winter weather can be severe. Low-key traditional eateries and lodgings are in sleepy hamlets, and the park's office (Rua Serpa Pinto 32, tel. 283 322 735) is in Odemira.

Getting There

The main points of entry to Southwest Alentejo and Vicentine Coast Natural Park are the towns of Odeceixe, São Teotónio, Odemira, and São Luís.

Portalegre

In the São Mamede Mountain Range Natural Park in northeastern Alentejo, on the border with Spain, charming whitewashed Portalegre is the biggest city in the upper Alentejo region and a base to explore a cluster of fortified hilltop villages and rural hamlets. A textile powerhouse in the 15th century and renowned for tapestries, silk cloth, and religious tableaux, faded and humble Portalegre provides glimpses of more affluent times in the once-grand baroque facades of worn mansions and elegant main streets. Much of the old town is still embraced by city walls, but the newer part of Portalegre and its pretty Rossio Square are amid a modern hub of transport terminals and apartment blocks.

SIGHTS

Portalegre Cathedral
(Catedral de Portalegre)

The majestic little **Portalegre Cathedral** (Praça do Município, tel. 245 309 480, www. portalegre-castelobranco.pt, 8:15am-noon and 2:30pm-6pm Wed-Sun, 8:15-noon Tues, free) is on the main square. Construction started in the mid-1500s and took two centuries to complete. Two pointy bell towers, vaulted arches, and exposed brick give the cathedral an austere, almost military look. Inside, it is packed with more than 90 mannerist paintings. As with many religious sites, it is built on the highest point of the city and can be seen from afar.

Tapestry Museum
(Museu de Tapeçarias)

Tapestry was once a flourishing industry in Portalegre and remains a traditional artisanal craft. The **Tapestry Museum** (Rua da Figueira 9, tel. 245 307 530, 9am-1pm and 2pm-6pm Tues-Sun, €2) is a hidden gem with a marvelous collection of labor-intensive tapestries, explaining the history of the craft and the work. The building is a modern wood and glass structure with exhibits marked in English throughout. A video is available, as is a guided tour in English (on request, extra fee).

Santa Clara Convent
(Convento Santa Clara)

Santa Clara Convent (Rua de Elvas 54, tel. 245 307 520, www.biblioteca.cm-portalegre. pt, 10am-1pm and 2pm-6pm Mon-Fri, 3pm-6pm Sat, free) was built on the orders of Queen Leonor Teles in the 14th century, and then added on to over successive centuries. Only the cloister preserves the original features, the centerpiece of which is a solid-marble baroque fountain. The convent currently houses the city's library.

FOOD

Cozy and casual **Solar do Forcado** (Rua Cândido dos Reis 14, tel. 245 330 866, 12:30pm-3:30pm and 7pm-10:30pm Mon-Fri, 7pm-10:30pm Sat, €10) serves traditional regional dishes that showcase the best of the Alentejo's meats and wines. Dark woods and exposed brick arches add to the rural feel.

Tucked away on a backstreet in the center of Portalegre, unassuming, cozy little **O Escondidinho** (Travessa das Cruzes 13, tel. 967 419 084, lunch and dinner, €10) offers hearty helpings of home-cooked Portuguese fare with local cheeses and desserts, served on traditional earthenware crockery.

In the heart of Portalegre's historic center, friendly, upscale tavern ★ **O Poeiras** (Praça da República 9-15, tel. 245 201 862, 11:30am-9:30pm Tues-Sat, 11:15am-4pm Sun, €10) serves tasty local and regional specialties, such as the famous meaty *pedra* (stone) soup, as well as a range of vegan options.

ENTERTAINMENT AND EVENTS

The city's **Center for Performing Arts** (**Centro de Artes e Espetáculo de Portalegre**) (Praça da República 39, tel. 245 307 498, http://caeportalegre.blogspot.pt) showcases performances of all types, from fado to rock and jazz. The annual **Conventual Sweets Fair** (1st or 2nd weekend in Apr) showcases traditional sweets that originated in the country's convents.

RECREATION

São Mamede Mountain Range Natural Park
(Parque Natural da Serra de São Mamede)

Seven kilometers (4.3 mi) northeast of Portalegre and sprawling over 29,694 hectares (115 square mi) of the northeastern Alentejo, the **São Mamede Mountain Range Natural Park** is a stark contrast to the gentle plains of the region. The park is a mix of bizarrely shaped quartzite peaks scattered with chestnut trees and Pyrenean oaks, cork oaks, Holm oaks, and olive groves, a unique landscape conducive to exploration. The highest peak south of the Tagus River is here, at 1,025 meters (3,363 feet), and the range has its own microclimate. The park is home to rarely spotted birds of prey such as the vulture, kite, and Bonelli's eagle, symbol of the park, as well as wild boars and deer.

Open year-round, the main hiking trails are Marvão (PR de Marvão, moderate, 8 km/5 mi round-trip), Galegos (PR de Galegos, moderate, 11.5-km/7.1-mi loop), Alegrete (PR3, moderate, 11 km/6.8 mi round-trip), and Esperança (PR de Esperança, moderate, 16-km/9.9-mi loop). Alegrete and Esperança can also be done on a mountain bike. The trails are signed. A section of the park is set up for experienced rock climbers; check with the park office (Rua Augusto Cesar Oliveira Tavares 23, Portalegre, tel. 245 309 189, www.icnf.pt).

1: Zambujeira do Mar; 2: Portalegre Cathedral; 3: Southwest Alentejo and Vicentine Coast Natural Park; 4: Marvão Castle

ACCOMMODATIONS

With one of the best locations in Portalegre, a short walk from all of the city's main sights and overlooking a lovely fountain and gardens, modern-looking **Hotel José Régio** (Largo António José Lourinho 1-5, tel. 245 009 190, www.hoteljoseregio.com, €70) is practical and plush in equal measures. It is inspired by one of Portalegre's most famous sons, writer José Régio.

Nestled in the heart of the São Mamede Natural Park a few kilometers out of Portalegre, **Quinta da Dourada** (hamlet of Ribeira de Nisa, tel. 937 218 654, www.quintadadourada.pt, €65) is a delightfully rustic farmhouse-style hotel with a warm and welcoming interior and a refreshing outdoor pool.

GETTING THERE

By car from Lisbon, Portalegre is a 230-kilometer (143-mi), 2.5-hour journey northeast on the A1 and A23 motorways. From Estremoz, Portalegre is a 57-kilometer (35-mi), 45-minute drive north on the IP2 road.

At least three **CP** (tel. 707 210 220, www.cp.pt) trains run daily from Lisbon's Oriente station to Portalegre (3.5-4.25 hours, €13.85-27.40), ranging from the slower regional train to the faster Intercity train. The train station in Portalegre is 12 kilometers (7.4 mi) south of the center, requiring a taxi or bus ride; both are just outside the station.

There are six **Rede Expressos** (tel. 707 223 344, www.rede-expressos.pt) buses daily between Lisbon's Sete Rios station and Portalegre (3.5-4 hours, €14.70), with stops in other main cities in the region such as Elvas, Évora, and Estremoz. The bus terminal in Portalegre is near the Rossio Square in the new town.

MARVÃO

Marvão (mar-VOWN) is a magical little hilltop village on the highest crest of the São Mamede mountain range. Fortified by encircling walls, some of which date to the 13th century, the village is the prettiest in the

Alentejo, with tangled narrow streets and typical Alentejano houses with Gothic arches, Manueline windows, and wrought-iron balconies. In summer the village's intrinsic cragginess is cheered up with bright flowers and stunning sunrises and sunsets. Visit Marvão for its chestnut festival (Nov), when the roasting nuts, smoking chimneys, and winter mist enshroud the village in a mythical aura.

Sights
★ MARVÃO CASTLE
(Castelo de Marvão)

The 13th-century **Marvão Castle** (tel. 245 909 138, www.cm-marvao.pt, 10am-5pm daily, €1.50) sits atop the 900-meter (2,953-foot) granite peak, with views of the Alentejo plains toward Spain. As Portuguese Nobel laureate writer José Saramago said, "From Marvão one can see the entire land." An austere medieval structure, Marvão Castle has thick granite walls that encircle most of the village, except in the east, where the village extends outside. Inside the castle walls are two cisterns and a tall central keep, from which the views are even more astounding. The castle also conceals a cistern chamber that has become a popular wishing well. To the side of the castle are peaceful manicured gardens that add vibrant green and seasonal color to the rocky landscape.

MARVÃO MUNICIPAL MUSEUM
(Museu Municipal de Marvão)

Housed inside the whitewashed 14th-century church is the **Marvão Municipal Museum** (Travessa de Santa Maria, tel. 245 909 132, www.cm-marvao.pt, 10am-12:30pm and 1:30pm-5pm daily, €1.90). Most of the artifacts on display, from armor to religious art, were donated by locals, giving the exhibition a homegrown feel. In spring the gardens surrounding the church and the castle add color to the mountainous scenery.

AMMAIA ROMAN VILLA
(Cidade Romana de Ammaia)

In the heart of the São Mamede mountain range is the **Ammaia Roman Villa** (São Salvador de Aramenha, tel. 245 919 089, 9am-1pm and 2pm-5pm Mon-Fri, 10am-1pm and 2pm-5pm Sat-Sun, €2), the outstanding ruins of a 1st-century town. Among the ruins are a residence, a forum, a temple, parts of a public bath, and the remains of arch doorways and towers. The most interesting artifacts are jewelry, coins, and glassware, displayed in the on-site museum. Ammaia is between Marvão and Castelo de Vide, in São Salvador de Aramenha.

Getting There
Marvão is 21 kilometers (13 mi) northeast of Portalegre, most easily visited by car via the N359 road, a 30-minute drive.

Public transport to Marvão is unreliable, but there are one or two buses daily from Portalegre (1 hour, €6) with **Rodalentejo** (tel. 245 330 096, www.rodalentejo.pt). **Rede Expressos** (tel. 707 223 344, www.rede-expressos.pt) runs one bus between Portalegre and Marvão (35 minutes, 11:15am daily, €6).

CASTELO DE VIDE
Twenty minutes northwest of Marvão is the enchanting fortified town of Castelo de Vide, unspoiled and charismatic yet not heavily visited. It is famous for the sparkling spring water in the decorative village fountain. Life in Castelo de Vide has changed little over the years. The town covers a sloped foothill in the São Mamede mountain range, a huddle of whitewashed town houses and red roofs with the main church in the middle and more than two dozen other churches among the village's cobbled streets. At the top is a 14th-century castle that overlooks the village and its surroundings. Given the town's overall natural beauty and numinous ambience, it is dubbed the "Sintra of the Alentejo."

Sights
The imposing castle and the Jewish Quarter are reason enough to spend a few hours in town, comfortably explored on foot.

CASTELO DE VIDE CASTLE
(Castelo de Castelo de Vide)

Clinging to the mountainside, what's left of the once-handsome quadrangular 14th-century medieval fortress **Castelo de Vide Castle** (free) almost blends in with its surroundings. The strategically important castle was built in 1310 by order of Dom Dinis. To get to the castle from the town, you have to climb many steep steps, along quaint streets lined with historic houses and little shops. Today the castle is in need of repair but is open for exploration of its ruins and battlements. Inside there is also a little exhibit on the Portuguese Inquisition. Panoramic views from the castle extend to the Spanish border.

JEWISH QUARTER
(Judiaria de Castelo de Vide)

Wedged between the local market square and the 16th-century marble and granite Renaissance **village fountain (Fonte de Villa)**, surrounded by columns and statues, is Castelo de Vide's beautiful **Jewish Quarter,** home to the oldest synagogue in Portugal, with sculpted Jewish symbols on doorposts and Jewish street names. In the heart of the Jewish Quarter is the former **synagogue** (Rua da Fonte, tel. 245 908 220, 9:30am-1pm and 2:30pm-6pm daily), a 12th-century home converted in the 14th century to a temple, which also served as a school and a social meeting point. It reverted to a private residence in the 16th century when the Jews were expelled from Portugal. At the corner of Rua da Judiaria and the fountain street, the synagogue is now an evocative museum of Castelo de Vide's Jewish history and the persecution of Jews by the Inquisition.

VILLAGE PILLORY
(Pelourinho)

Contrasting with Castelo de Vide's gentle beauty is the somber 16th-century **village pillory,** a stone column atop four octagonal steps in the middle of a picturesque plaza, in front of the local prison and clock tower, where offenders were publicly shamed or punished.

Getting There

Castelo de Vide is 12.5 kilometers (7.8 mi) northwest of Marvão, a 15-minute drive on the N246-1 and N359 roads. **Rede Expressos** (tel. 707 223 344, www.rede-expressos.pt) buses run at least once daily between Marvão and Castelo de Vide (15 minutes, mid-afternoon daily, €5-7).

Coimbra and Central Portugal

In the heart of Portugal, between Lisbon, the Alentejo to the south, and Porto to the north, Central Portugal is a vast region of historic towns and extraordinary landscapes. Medieval Óbidos, the holy site Fátima, and the Templar city Tomar are infused with tradition and legend.

The **Silver Coast (Costa da Prata)**, one of the Iberian Peninsula's lesser-known *costas*, stretches the length of the Central Region's coast between Lisbon and Porto, offering long, pristine beaches that aren't crowded, even in high season. Construction is sparse, which means the increasingly elusive feeling of an unspoiled beach can still be found. Move inland and explore the region's remarkably intact historic cities, like Coimbra and Santarém, which played a key role in

Highlights

Look for ★ to find recommended sights, activities, dining, and lodging.

★ **Óbidos Village:** One of Portugal's most historic and well-preserved medieval villages, beautiful Óbidos is famous for its castle walls and *ginja* cherry liqueur, served in a chocolate cup (page 204).

★ **Surfing in Nazaré:** The monster waves that roll into Nazaré have catapulted the formerly sleepy fishing town to global fame as one of the top big-wave surf spots on the planet (page 210).

★ **Alcobaça Monastery:** Be amazed by this staggering monastery, an astounding feat of Gothic architecture and home to a large medieval Cistercian cloister (page 214).

★ **Almourol Castle:** Rising from the Tagus River on a solitary islet, this remote 12th-century castle is a symbolic monument of the Christian reconquest and a significant medieval military monument (page 221).

★ **Convent of Christ:** Looming over the historic town of Tomar, this 12th-century complex is one of Portugal's greatest works of Renaissance architecture, famous as the local headquarters of the Knights Templar (page 222).

★ **Sanctuary of Our Lady of Fátima:** Spellbinding Fátima is an important pilgrimage site and a hub of mysteries, miracles, and monuments (page 226).

★ **Coimbra University:** The beautiful old buildings of Coimbra's university complex crown its historic hill, encapsulating the elegance and prestige of learning in times gone by and buzzing with the energy of today's youth (page 230).

★ **Schist Villages:** Hidden away in deepest

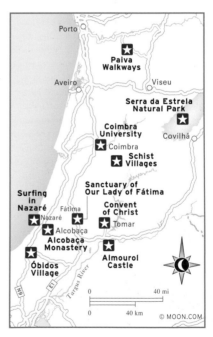

Central Portugal is a string of unique fairy-tale villages built entirely from schist stone (page 239).

★ **Paiva Walkways:** Explore the unspoiled landscape of rural Central Portugal along this award-winning 8.7-kilometer (5.4-mi) raised wooden walkway (page 246).

★ **Serra da Estrela Natural Park:** This park is home to majestic mountains, rocky glacial valleys, and dramatic lakes—and Portugal's only ski resort (page 249).

shaping Portugal, as well as hidden caves and schist villages. In the majestic Serra da Estrela mountain range, you'll find the only skiing in Portugal.

Discover welcoming hospitality, hearty meals, awesome sights, and enthralling tales around every bend.

PLANNING YOUR TIME

The expansive Centro comprises four key areas: the **Oeste,** the lower portion of the Silver Coast, just north of Lisbon and home to the medieval village of Óbidos and the surfing town of Nazaré; **Santarém,** home to momentous cities such as Tomar and Fátima; the famed ancient university city **Coimbra,** along with Figueira da Foz and Aveiro at the upper end of the Silver Coast; and the emblematic **Serra da Estrela** mountain range and its gateway town, Covilhã.

Most people visit the Oeste region while traveling between Lisbon and Porto, stopping in its lovely towns and villages for lunch or a sunny stroll before jumping back on the main A1 motorway to the north. Nazaré, Óbidos, and Tomar are also popular day trips from Lisbon.

Set aside a few more days to explore the region and discover some of its myriad natural charms. Some suggested routes:

- **North from Lisbon:** Start with the Oeste, passing through Óbidos and Nazaré, before traveling inland to Santarém to explore Fátima and Tomar. From here, go to Coimbra and then head to the snowcapped Serra da Estrela. Head toward coastal Aveiro before completing the route in Porto.

- **South from Porto:** Do the north-from-Lisbon trip in reverse.

- **Lisbon loop:** Starting from Lisbon, pass through the Oeste (Óbidos and Nazaré) and travel up through Leiria to Coimbra. Move on to Covilhã and explore the Serra da Estrela before heading back south to Santarém (Fátima and Tomar), ending in Lisbon.

- **Porto loop:** Starting from Porto, pass through Covilhã and the Serra da Estrela, Santarém (Fátima and Tomar) and the Oeste (Óbidos and Nazaré) before heading back north to Leiria, Coimbra, and Aveiro, ending in Porto.

The easiest way to do these tours is by car over at least four days and up to a week.

Getting around Central Portugal by road is easy, as all the main towns are connected by good roads and motorways. Public transport among big towns is also relatively frequent, but getting to smaller places can be difficult. The main routes through Central Portugal are the A1 motorway between Porto and Lisbon, the A8 between Lisbon and Leiria, the A13 from Setúbal to Santarém, the A14 from Coimbra to Figueira da Foz, and the A15 between Santarém and Peniche.

Previous: the city of Coimbra; detail of an azulejo tile; interior at the University of Coimbra.

Coimbra and Central Portugal

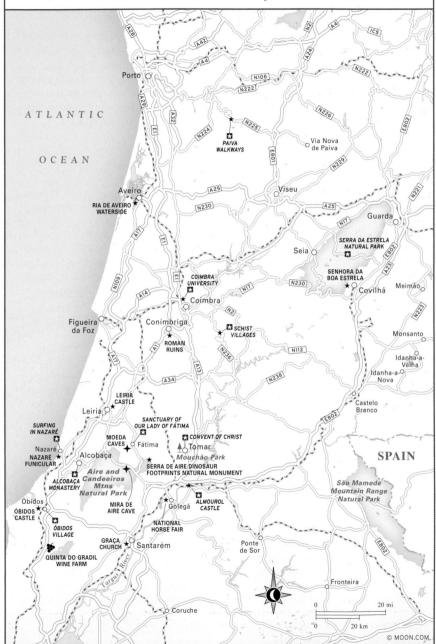

© MOON.COM

Oeste

Formerly in what was known as **Estremadura Province,** the Oeste (West) subregion of Central Portugal loosely refers to the lower Silver Coast, which runs north from Lisbon. This region's 12 municipalities are some of the Silver Coast's most spectacular seaside towns, like the surfing mecca Nazaré, the renowned medieval village Óbidos, and history-drenched Alcobaça with its colossal monastery.

Often referred to as "the land of vineyards and sea," the Oeste is a popular destination for a balance between rural and coastal. Castles and aqueducts sit alongside beaches, spas, and golf courses, all with the area's lovely weather.

ÓBIDOS

Not to be missed, enchanting Óbidos (AW-bee-doosh) is a pretty example of a fortified town and a quintessential Portuguese village, with whitewashed houses that exude undiluted charm huddled within the walls of the castle. The local car park is usually packed with tour buses from dawn till dark. Over the centuries Óbidos's natural beauty and perfection made it a favorite among royals. In the 13th century, King Dom Dinis gifted the village to his wife, Queen Isabel, starting a tradition, and centuries later, in 1441, King Afonso V famously wed his cousin, Princess Isabella of Coimbra, here when they were ages 9 and 10, respectively. The regal favoritism gave the village its nickname "Village of Queens," a legacy that makes the town treasured and well looked after by its residents.

Home to some of the country's biggest and best-known festivals, which take over the entire town, Óbidos is always buzzing. Walk through the main archway, the ancient tile-clad Porta da Vila, to a maze of cobblestone streets lined with gorgeous whitewashed houses adorned with flowers, and cute crafts shops touting souvenirs, including *ginja*, the famous Óbidos cherry liqueur. For a special

view of the town (if you can handle heights), circumnavigate the historic center on the elevated battlements.

Allow at least a few hours to really explore the town's attractions, or spend a night here to enjoy the less busy hours before 9am and after 8pm, when the tour buses leave.

Sights
★ ÓBIDOS VILLAGE
(Vila de Óbidos)

Authentic and magical, Óbidos is the archetypal fortified Portuguese town, referred to locally as the "wedding gift town." Its classic beauty and layers of history make it a top destination for day trips from Lisbon, competing with Sintra and Cascais. Due to the high number of visitors, especially during popular annual events, its narrow streets can often be crowded.

The main entrance to Óbidos, the **Porta da Vila** (village gateway), is a sight in itself, cased in traditional blue-and-white azulejo tiles depicting the Passion of Christ. Absorb the historic ambience of the atmospheric town as you stroll the main shopping street, **Rua Direita,** from the Porta da Vila to the castle, with its plethora of traditional shops and delightful little houses with colorful flowers hanging from roofs and doorways. No trip is complete without trying a *ginja de Óbidos,* strong cherry liqueur served in shops throughout the town, usually in a chocolate cup. Plenty of shops along Rua Direita offer tastings. To flee the crowds, wander off the main street and explore Óbidos's cobbled labyrinth of side streets.

In the middle of town, in a little square, the Praça de Santa Maria, along the main Rua Direita, is the pretty 12th-century **Santa Maria Church (Igreja de Santa Maria)**

1: Óbidos village; **2:** the Porta da Vila gateway in Óbidos; **3:** Bar Ibn Errik Rex in Óbidos

(Praça de Santa Maria, tel. 262 959 633, 9:30am-12:30pm and 2:30pm-5pm daily Oct-Mar, 9:30am-12:30pm and 2:30pm-7pm daily Apr-Sept, free), with its striking white bell tower and fancy Renaissance portal. Inside, the walls are clad from the floor to the painted wooden ceiling in 18th-century azulejo tiles, and the church also houses the tomb of Dom João de Noronha, a 16th-century commander of Óbidos. In front of the church is the 15th-century **town pillory,** decorated with fishing net in homage to the fishermen who recovered the body of Afonso, the son of Queen Leonor and King João II, who died in a riding accident by the Tagus River.

ÓBIDOS CASTLE
(Castelo de Óbidos)

Originating from the 12th century, Óbidos's excellently-preserved medieval castle dominates the village. The main part, including the keep, is today an outstanding luxury *pousada* (hotel). The castle was gifted as a wedding present by King Dom Dinis to his new wife, Queen Santa Isabel, in 1282 when they were married here. From then until 1834, the village was owned by each queen of Portugal, earning its nicknames "Vila de Rainhas" (Village of Queens) and "wedding gift town." Over the centuries, the queens spent much time in Óbidos, and each left her influence on the village, including the local aqueduct.

The castle remains one of Óbidos's most impressive and romantic features, invoking a real sense of a bygone era, protectively guarding the village. The castle was extensively reinforced during the 14th century, so most of what can be seen today is from that era, with little surviving evidence of its earlier incarnation. A visually interesting structure, it blends four main architectural styles that characterize the centuries of its origins and expansion: Romanesque, Manueline, baroque, and Gothic.

The hub of the town's main events is the grounds adjacent to the castle, the Old Arms Square. The sturdy **castle walls** (24 hours daily, free), accessible via stony flights of stairs dotted around the village, were built in the 14th century when the castle's keep and battlements were reinforced; the walls encircle Óbidos and make for a unique stroll around the town. The circuit takes an hour and offers bird's-eye views over the village center. Note that walking the walls is not for everyone—the height, lack of railings, and unevenness underfoot require balance, agility, and a tolerance for heights.

ÓBIDOS AQUEDUCT
(Aqueduto de Óbidos)

On the outskirts of town, across from the main car park and Porta da Vila entrance, is the long, spindly Óbidos Aqueduct, also known as the Aqueduct of Usseira. Remarkable in its slenderness and intactness, it was built at the order of Queen Dona Catarina of Austria, wife of Dom João III, in 1573 to bring water from the nearby Usseira spring to the village's fountains.

QUINTA DO GRADIL WINE FARM

South of Óbidos in the parish of Cadaval is the **Quinta do Gradil Wine Farm** (Estrada Nacional 115, tel. 262 770 000, www.quintadogradil.wine), a unique 120-hectare (297-acre) estate between sea and hills that once belonged to the family of the Marquis of Pombal, an important 18th-century Portuguese statesman. It sits on the western foothills of the Montejunto mountain range in a region of varied geology, climate, and vegetation that create a distinctive terroir that produces fine wines. These include Mula Velha, the eponymous Quinta do Gradil, and Castelo do Sulco. The farm's endless rows of vines make an excellent stop to learn more about wine-making.

The elegant Quinta opens its doors to the public every harvest (Sept-Oct) for visitors to take part in the grape-picking process, and year-round wine-tastings (11:30am and 3:30pm Mon-Sat, 11:30am Sun, from €9) are offered that can be combined with degustation menus (from €70). Dinner is also an option at the excellent on-site **Restaurant Quinta do Gradil** (tel. 917 791 974, lunch

10am-6pm Wed-Mon, dinner 7pm-10pm Fri-Sat, €25), converted from a former cereal storehouse. Large groups should reserve in advance.

From Óbidos, Quinta do Gradil is a 20-minute, 25-kilometer (15.5-mi) drive south on the A8 motorway. The easiest way to get here by public transport is by taxi, which costs around €25 one-way. Taxis are available just outside the Porta da Vila.

Entertainment and Events

NIGHTLIFE

Don't miss **Bar Ibn Errik Rex** (Rua Direita 100, tel. 262 959 193, 11am-1am daily), one of the oldest and best *ginja* bars in town, open since 1956. A medieval-style, family-run bar on the main street, it has over 1,800 dusty miniature bottles hanging from the ceiling.

MEDIEVAL FAIR
(Feira Medieval)

Every year from a Thursday in mid-July to the Sunday in the first week of August, Óbidos's quaint streets are transformed into a medieval village for the **Medieval Fair,** complete with colorful bunting, fire-eaters, wizards, court jesters, jousting knights on horseback, falconry, and medieval gastronomy. The hub of activity is in the Old Arms Square, adjacent to the castle, where little shacks form a medieval marketplace (www.mercadomedievalobidos. pt, €7) selling food and handicrafts typical of the era. A costume shop rents outfits for just €5 if you want to get into the theatrical spirit of the fair. This is one of Portugal's most famous events and well worth a visit.

INTERNATIONAL
CHOCOLATE FESTIVAL
(Festival Internacional de Chocolate)

A 12-day event over a series of weekends in February, March, or April, the **International Chocolate Festival** (www.festivalchocolate. cm-obidos.pt, Fri-Sun, €4) is staged in the Old Arms Square, next to the castle, where small shacks emit the glorious sweet scent of warm chocolate. The festival showcases cocoa-based goodies from traditional Portuguese sweets to contemporary concoctions, and the obligatory hot chocolate or *ginja* liqueur served in a chocolate cup. Guests can also take cocoa-making classes for all ages.

CHRISTMAS VILLAGE
(Óbidos Vila Natal)

Every year during December, Óbidos becomes a real-life snow globe, full of festive spirit and sparkly trimmings, when it hosts its famous annual **Christmas Village** (www.obidosvilanatal.pt). Hundreds of stalls sell gifts and hot chocolate, and fairground rides, shows, and entertainment fill the quaint streets. Dress warmly; this open-air event has an authentic winter chill.

Accommodations

Spend a night in the heart of Óbidos town in the imposing 700-year-old ★ **Pousada Castelo Óbidos** (Paço Real, tel. 210 407 630, www.pousadas.pt, €280) castle, which is today a luxury *pousada* hotel. Each of the 11 rooms, 3 of which are in the castle keep, is individually decorated, while the adjacent 8-room Casa do Castelo cottage offers authentic yet comfortable medieval lodging.

Inside the town walls on the main street, the charming and casual three-star **Albergaria Rainha Santa Isabel** (Rua Direita 63, tel. 262 959 323, www.vivehotels. com, €68) is in a historic whitewashed building, with 20 simple old-fashioned rooms and a cozy guest lounge. Breakfast is included.

The sprawling ★ **Praia D'El Rey Marriott Golf and Beach Resort** (Av. D. Inês de Castro 1, Vale de Janelas, tel. 262 905 100, www.marriott.com, €225) is on the coast, 23 kilometers (14 mi) west of Óbidos and 57 kilometers (35 mi) south of Nazaré. This upscale place has 177 airy rooms and suites, a spa, and an 18-hole golf course.

Information and Services

National emergency number: tel. 112
GNR police: Rua Direita, tel. 262 955 000, www.gnr.pt

Tourist office: Rua da Porta da Vila, ground Fl., tel. 262 959 231, www.obidos.pt, 9:30am-6pm Mon-Fri, 9:30am-12:30pm and 1:30pm-5:30pm Sat-Sun
Post office: Praça Santa Maria, tel. 262 955 041, www.ctt.pt, 9am-12:30pm and 2:30pm-6pm Mon-Fri

Getting There

CAR

Óbidos is 80 kilometers (50 mi) north of Lisbon, a fast and easy drive on the A8 motorway (tolls apply) that takes just over one hour. Cars can be parked in a large car park (€2 for 1.5 hours) just outside the Porta da Vila gate, opposite the tourist information center. When it gets full, especially common in summer, there is a large overflow car park just across the road, by the aqueduct.

BUS

An express bus service named the Rápida Verde (1 hour, hourly Mon-Fri, less frequently Sat-Sun and holidays, €7.70), operated by bus company **Rodoviária do Tejo** (tel. 249 787 878, www.rodotejo.pt), runs between Lisbon's Campo Grande station, near Alvalade stadium, and Óbidos's car park, just outside the city walls near the Porta da Vila gate. The same service also runs to Alcobaça and Nazaré. National bus service **Rede Expressos** (tel. 707 223 344, www.rede-expressos.pt) operates a similar service from its main Lisbon hub, Sete Rios.

Getting Around

Óbidos is easily seen in one day and can be explored comfortably on foot. Cars are not allowed within the historic center and must park in the car park just outside the city walls, a two-minute walk south of the Porta da Vila gate.

CARRIAGE RIDES

Take a step back in time and rumble along the cobbled streets in an old-fashioned horse and carriage (30 minutes, 4 adults from €30 outside the walls, €65 inside the walls).

Charretes do Oeste (tel. 262 835 562, www.charretesdooeste.com) and **Mundo dos Cavalos** (tel. 968 881 805 or 918 509 521, www.mundodoscavalos.pt) operate year-round, awaiting passengers in the main car park, but rides are subject to weather conditions.

NAZARÉ

Before becoming a monster-wave surfing hot spot, Nazaré was a fishing town and popular traditional seaside resort. Today the town's charming main seafront avenue is flanked by dense construction. Famed for its excellent fresh seafood as much as for incredible surfing conditions, Nazaré can feel overrun, especially in peak season, and modern development has taken the shine off its fishing-town charm. Nonetheless, authentic traits and traditions persevere.

Watch the laden dragnets brought in to the shouts of local fisherwomen, who still wear the traditional seven skirts and headscarves. Along the beachfront, you'll see boards of butterflied fish left to cure in the open air, sold by the fisherwomen as a local delicacy. You can also enjoy the fresh catch at one of the many local beachfront seafood restaurants.

Sights and Recreation

NAZARÉ FUNICULAR
(Ascensor da Nazaré)

The dizzying **Nazaré Funicular** (Rua de São Lázaro, tel. 262 550 010, www.cm-nazare.pt, 7:30am-8:30pm daily Oct-May, 7:30am-midnight daily June-mid-July and late Sept, 7:30am-2am daily mid-July-mid-Sept, €1.20) takes passengers from the urban beachfront up to **Sítio,** an older extension of the town on a headland atop cliffs to the north. From Sítio's main piazza, it is a short walk down to the lighthouse, where you can view the underwater canyon made famous by the photos of the huge monster waves.

The modern funicular cabs climb a historic track, ascending 318 meters (1,043 feet) in 15 minutes, between residential buildings at the bottom, through a tunnel, offering

Nazaré

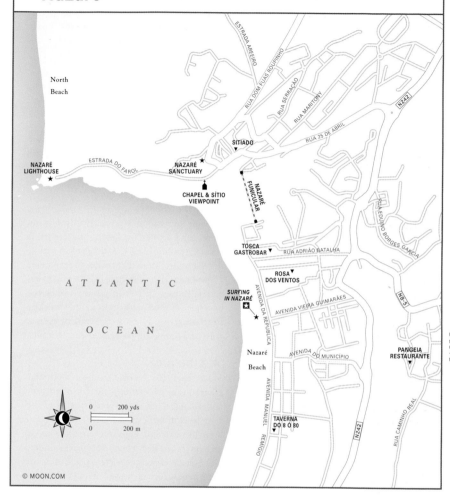

astounding views of Nazaré as they ascend to the top. This fun, easy, and cheap experience is a short trip and a good way to get to Sítio without a car—parking at the top can be hard to find, especially on weekends. The funicular runs every 15 minutes or so.

SÍTIO

Soar up the vertiginous rock face on Nazaré's famed funicular to the elevated part of town, on cliffs to the north of Nazaré main beach, known as Sítio, comprising a lovely large square flanked by stunning views, quaint shops and restaurants, a large sanctuary, and a chapel. In summer, Sítio can offer some respite from the throngs in the main part of town.

The best place to observe the fearsome spectacle of the monster waves is at the **Nazaré Lighthouse** (Estrada do Farol, tel. 265 561 967, http://wlol.arlhs.com, 10am-6pm daily, €1), within the stone walls of the São

Local Specialty: Octopus with Olive Oil

Given the town's seafront location, Nazaré's local gastronomy is based on fresh seafood. A typical dish is *polvo á lagareiro* (octopus cooked in a pressure cooker and served with lashings of hot olive oil). The octopus should be soft, not chewy, and is usually served with small baked potatoes and lots of garlic. Two top places to try this local delicacy are **Pangeia Restaurante** (Rua Abel da Silva 50, Nazaré, tel. 917 934 726, www.pangeiarestaurante.com, noon-3pm and 7pm-10pm Thurs-Tues, noon-3pm Wed, €20) and tapas eatery **Cantinho dos Petiscos** (Rua Alexandre Herculano, Nazaré, tel. 915 064 325, 10:30am-2am Wed-Mon, €20).

Miguel Fortress on a promontory near North Beach (Praia do Norte), a short walk from the Sítio headland's main square. This outcrop was made famous in 2011 after photos of Garrett McNamara's big-wave victory traveled the globe, showing the tiny lighthouse dwarfed by the huge swells in the background. As well as spectacular views, the lighthouse also hosts an exhibition of paraphernalia relating to the local surfing scene.

Once upon a time, the Sítio promontory teemed with deer, and a bizarre contemporary **statue of a surfer** with a deer's head, which stands halfway down the road to the São Miguel Fortress, pays tribute to the locale's blended history. According to local legend, in 1182 nobleman Dom Fuas Roupinho was hunting in dense fog and stopped just short of the edge of the cliff where his deer vanished. Just as he was about to fall to his death, he cried out to Our Lady of Nazaré, who appeared before him and stopped his horse. The rider ordered a chapel, the **Memorial Hermitage (Ermida da Memória)** (Rua 25 de Abril, 24 hours daily, free), built in honor of this miracle; it can be visited just off Sítio's main square. This enthralling piece of folklore is depicted in the traditional 17th-century azulejos that completely clad the interior of the small, square chapel, with its pyramid-like roof. A supposed hoofprint of the nobleman's horse is engraved in a stone found in a crypt beneath the chapel. Other folktales claim explorer Vasco da Gama prayed here before setting off on his voyages. The chapel was built above a cave in the cliffs where,

during Moorish occupation, there stood a small statue of a black Madonna nursing the baby Jesus.

NAZARÉ BEACH (Praia da Nazaré)

A huge half-moon stretch of glimmering blond sand favored for fishing and surfing is Nazaré's calling card. Due to the offshore underwater formation that creates the famously huge waves, the water here can be rough and cool, although calmer in summer, when the beach is packed with holidaymakers. The beach is fringed by a long seafront avenue with end-to-end shops, bars, and restaurants.

★ SURFING

Since the 1960s, Nazaré has been a popular place among experienced surfers looking for a challenge—but recently it gained a whole new level of fame as one of the planet's top spots for extreme big-wave surfing. Once a year, typically in November, Nazaré's underwater canyon creates perfect conditions for enormous waves. In November 2011, U.S. professional big-wave surfer Garrett McNamara conquered a monstrous 24-meter (79-foot) wave in Nazaré, setting a world record for the largest wave ever surfed. His name is now synonymous with Nazaré's surf scene, having almost single-handedly catapulted the once-sleepy coastal resort onto the must-surf map. (McNamara's record has since been smashed

1: half-man, half-deer statue paying tribute to Nazaré's surfers; **2:** a Nazaré fisherwoman selling dried fish; **3:** fishing boats on the beach in Nazaré

Leiria Castle

Grand **Leiria Castle (Castelo de Leiria)** (Largo de São Pedro, tel. 244 813 982, www. visiteleiria.pt, 9am-6:30pm Mon-Fri, 10am-6:30pm Sat-Sun Apr-Sept, 9am-5:30pm Mon-Fri, 10am-5:30pm Sat-Sun Oct-Mar, €2.10) is worth a trip if you are visiting the Oeste region or on the way to Coimbra, Serra da Estrela, or Porto. This magnificent hilltop monument is symbolic of the region's history, central to the Christian reconquests.

On a green hill above the cobbled city, this beautiful 12th-century bastion is a fine example of medieval architecture, believed to be built on the remains of a Roman settlement. Originally defending the fledgling kingdom's southern border from being recaptured by the Moors after the Christian conquest of Leiria (LAY-ree-yah) circa 1135, the castle was lost twice and regained twice by King Afonso Henriques I and his soldiers. It was from this castle that Dom Afonso Henriques drove forward his strategy to reconquer Lisbon, Sintra, and Santarém, still under Moorish rule. The castle also hosted an important formative moment in Portugal's early history when, in 1254, Dom Afonso III summoned the first Royal Parliament (Cortes).

Later, in the early 14th century, King Dinis and his wife, Queen Santa Isabel, who wed in Óbidos, used the castle as their main residence, restoring it after a period of abandonment. During the late 14th and early 15th centuries, John I (João I) converted the castle into a royal palace, with arched galleries that framed sweeping vistas over the town and the Lis River beyond. Much later, in the 20th century, the palace was restored after again falling into disrepair, but thanks to the thoughtful preservation of the castle keep through the centuries, visitors can still climb to the roof for the view.

Within the castle walls are various well-preserved points of interest, including the ruins of the 12th-century Santa Maria da Pena church, the 14th-century Royal Palace and Keep, gardens, and, of course, the views. Leiria's majestic walled centerpiece is a great spot to soak up local history; guided tours (10am and 2pm Tues-Sat) are available. There is also a museum inside the keep.

by Brazilian surfer Rodrigo Koxa, who surfed a 24.4-meter/80-foot wave in November 2017.)

The monster waves are formed by a unique underwater canyon off Nazaré, a finger-shaped crevice pointing toward the town; the colossal waves create a year-round attraction, as visitors hope to witness Mother Nature's full fury unleashed. Outside November, the waves can still be big, but nowhere near as spectacularly fearsome. There are plenty of surf schools and shops throughout Nazaré and along the beachfront, where boards can be rented.

Food

It might not be a beachfront place, but the seafood at **Rosa dos Ventos** (Rua Gil Vicente 88, tel. 918 267 127, noon-3:15pm and 7pm-9:30pm Fri-Wed, €18) is second to none. Set back from the beach on the main road through the top end of town, near the funicular, Rosa dos Ventos serves fresh fish and shellfish, simply boiled or grilled. Tasty fish stews and homemade desserts round out the offerings.

Local products meet international favorites at **Tosca Gastrobar** (Rua Mouzinho de Albuquerque 4, tel. 262 562 261, noon-3pm and 7pm-10pm Thurs-Tues, €15), a small, trendy gastropub where creative snack-size dishes take center stage. Baked camembert with walnuts and red fruit coulis, shrimp pasta, and spinach, apple, and cheese strudel are on the innovative menu. Reservations are recommended.

The quirky vintage decor at **Sitiado** (Rua Amadeu Guadêncio, tel. 262 087 512, 11:30am-3pm and 7pm-10pm Wed-Mon, €15), a colorful, petite restaurant (note the bicycle hanging on the wall), does little to convey the traditionally Portuguese essence of its menu. Simple salads, juicy grilled tuna steaks, beef steaks, and a range of tasty tapas (try the *casquinhas*, potato skins) make up the menu.

GETTING THERE AND AROUND

Leiria is connected to the rest of Portugal by the A1, A8, A17 and A19 motorways. It's 145 kilometers (90 mi) north of Lisbon, a two-hour drive by car on the A1, and 187 kilometers (116 mi) south of Porto (two hours) on the A1. From Batalha, Leiria is a 14-kilometer (8.7-mi), 15-minute drive north on the A19. Tolls apply on all motorways in Portugal.

CP (tel. 707 210 220, www.cp.pt) runs trains directly to Leiria from major towns. From Lisbon, trains leave frequently from the main stations (Santa Apolónia, Entrecampos, Sete Rios, Rossio, and Oriente), a journey of under four hours. A change might be required on some lines, and prices start from €11.50 one-way. There are six daily trains from Porto's Campanhã station to Leiria (3.5 hours, €17-20). The regional Western Line (Linha do Oeste), operated by CP, links Cacém to Figueira da Foz and serves the central stretch of the western coast through Leiria. The railway station is 2 kilometers (1.2 mi) from the city center, accessible via the local urban bus service, Mobilis (tel. 244 735 735, www.mobilis.pt, €1.30, day ticket €3.05); buy tickets from the driver.

Rede Expressos (tel. 707 223 344, www.rede-expressos.pt) operates buses to Leiria from Lisbon's Sete Rios station (2 hours, hourly 7am-9pm daily, last bus at midnight, €12.20) and from Porto's Campo 24 Agosto station (2.5 hours, hourly 6am-9:30pm daily, €15.20), which often involves a transfer in Coimbra. Rodoviária do Lis (tel. 244 735 735, www.rodoviariadolis.pt) and Batalha's urban bus system, the Gira (www.girabatalha.pt), operate a dozen daily buses between Batalha and Leiria (30 minutes, €3-7). Leiria's main bus terminal is a four-minute walk southeast of the main town center.

From Leiria's center, the easiest way to get to the castle is either a 10-minute uphill walk or by taxi (€2-3).

Busy, sociable tavern-turned-wine bar Taverna do 8 ó 80 (Av. Manuel Remígio, tel. 262 560 490, www.tavernado8o80.pt, noon-midnight Wed-Mon, €20) is a beachfront restaurant that specializes in traditional favorites with a modern twist. The food is pricey because of the restaurant's location and reputation; specialties include sea bream ceviche, fried goat cheese, and mushrooms with *alheira* sausage.

Getting There

By car, Nazaré is 122 kilometers (76 mi) north of Lisbon, an hour's drive, following the A8 motorway (tolls apply). From Óbidos, Nazaré is a 40-kilometer (25-mi), 30-minute drive north along the A8.

Rodoviária do Tejo (tel. 249 787 878, www.rodotejo.pt) operates the Rápida Verde express bus service between Lisbon's Campo Grande station and Nazaré (1.75 hours, hourly Mon-Fri, less frequently Sat-Sun and holidays, €9.85). Rede Expressos (tel. 707 223 344, www.rede-expressos.pt) operates similar bus service from its main Lisbon hub, Sete Rios (1.75 hours, €10.90).

Rodoviária do Oeste (tel. 262 767 676, www.rodoviariadooeste.pt) operates buses three times a day between Óbidos and Nazaré (1.25 hours, €4), and there is an evening Rápida Verde bus between the towns. The main bus station in Nazaré is a few streets back from the beachfront, about a 10-minute walk.

ALCOBAÇA

Understated Alcobaça (al-koh-BAH-ssah) is on the tourist map for its staggering focal monument, the Alcobaça Monastery. A 15-minute drive inland from coastal Nazaré, it's worth passing through, even just to gaze at this feat of Gothic architecture.

Alcobaça grew from the valleys along the Alcoa and Baça Rivers, which merge into one in Alcobaça and give the town its name. Another story holds that the town's Arabic name was split into two to name the rivers. Either way, the town became noteworthy in the 12th century when Portugal's first king, Afonso Henriques, built the country's biggest church here to commemorate reclaiming Santarém from the Moors in 1147. That church evolved into the Alcobaça Monastery, one of Portugal's most important monuments.

Perhaps due to the masses of tourists visiting the monastery, Alcobaça has taken a turn toward the touristy, but it still has plenty of genuine features, such as its pretty town center with the picturesque Alcobaça River running through it, and a traditional town market every Monday near the local Continente supermarket. Alcobaça is also famed for its quality crystal, earthenware, and porcelain.

Sights

★ ALCOBAÇA MONASTERY
(Mosteiro de Alcobaça)

Founded by the Order of Cistercians in 1153, **Alcobaça Monastery** (Praça 25 de Abril, tel. 262 505 120, www.mosteiroalcobaca.pt, 9am-6pm daily Oct-Mar, 9am-7pm daily Apr-Sept, €6), also known as the Royal Abbey of Santa Maria, is one of Portugal's foremost monuments, a masterpiece of Gothic architecture whose purity and finesse earned its classification by UNESCO as a World Heritage Site. It was Portugal's first truly Gothic building, constructed by Afonso Henrique I after victory over the Moors at Santarém in 1147. Construction began in 1178, with the main central church—the largest church in Portugal at the time—completed in the mid-13th century. Additions were made in the centuries that followed.

Hidden behind the monastery's lavish baroque facade is the phenomenal Gothic **church** (free), whose narrow length and soaring ribbed ceiling in the nave let light flood in, illuminating the interior. It is the final resting place of 14th-century Pedro I and Inês de Castro, famous for their tragic love story. Their intricately carved tombs face each other.

Added to the monastery in the late 13th century, the **Cloister of Silence (Claustro do Silencio)** is one of the largest medieval Cistercian cloisters in Europe. Its sheer size and exquisitely carved Gothic architecture are remarkable, its name evocative of the silently moving monks who inhabited its walls. The cloister centers on a peaceful garden with a lovely Renaissance fountain in the middle.

More features worth seeing inside the monastery include the **Kings Room (Sala dos Reis),** where sculptures of Portuguese kings peer down on visitors and old azulejos clad the walls; the **Chapter House (Sala do Capítulo),** where monks gathered to discuss the daily running of the complex; a huge upstairs **dormitory;** a **refectory** (dining hall) with a pulpit embedded in the wall; and the impressive **kitchen,** with its gigantic tile-clad chimney.

A combined ticket to the Alcobaça Monastery, Batalha Monastery, and Tomar Convent of Christ (€15) is valid for seven days.

Getting There

Alcobaça is 122 kilometers (76 km) north of Lisbon, a 1.5-hour drive via the A8 motorway; 41 kilometers (25 km) north of Óbidos, a 30-minute drive on the A8; and 16 kilometers (9.9 mi) east from coastal Nazaré, a 15-minute drive via the IC9 road.

The best way to get to Alcobaça by public transport is the direct bus service from Lisbon. **Rodoviária do Tejo** (tel. 249 787 878, www.rodotejo.pt) runs several express buses (2 hours, €9.85), leaving Lisbon's Campo Grande almost hourly on weekdays, less frequently on weekends and holidays. **Rede Expressos** (tel. 707 223 344, www.rede-expressos.pt) operates similar bus service from its main Lisbon hub, Sete Rios (2 hours, €10.90).

Rodoviária do Tejo (tel. 249 787 878, www.rodotejo.pt) also operates over a dozen daily services between Nazaré and

Pedro I and Inês de Castro: Star-Crossed Lovers

An enthralling aspect of the Alcobaça Monastery is an epic ill-fated love story. The monastery's church is the final resting place of 14th-century King Pedro I and his doomed lover, Inês de Castro. The third but only surviving son of Afonso IV, Pedro was forced into royal duty from an early age. He was also set up in marriage by his father to Infanta Constanza of Castile, whose lady-in-waiting was Inês de Castro. Pedro fell in love with Inês, and following Constanza's death shortly after their marriage, the pair eloped to live in Coimbra. The affair ended when Inês was murdered in 1355 on the orders of Afonso IV, as she and her family were perceived as a threat. A ghastly twist is that shortly after the death of his father, Pedro announced that he had secretly married Inês prior to her assassination, and in a morbid ploy to exact revenge on her killers, he had her body exhumed and embalmed, had a crown placed on her head, and had all the courtiers kneel and pay homage to her decomposed hand.

Alcobaça (20 minutes, €2.30). The bus station in Alcobaça is on Avenida Manuel da Silva Carolino, a 10-minute walk east of the monastery.

BATALHA

A few kilometers north of Alcobaça is the lovely old town of Batalha (bah-TAL-yah), home to another extraordinary monastery, a masterpiece of intricate ornamental late Gothic-Manueline architecture. In the middle of town, the Batalha Monastery is one of a trio of must-sees in the region, along with the Tomar Convent and the Alcobaça Monastery.

Sights

BATALHA MONASTERY
(Mosteiro da Batalha)

The **Batalha Monastery** (Largo Infante Dom Henrique, tel. 244 765 497, www. mosteirobatalha.gov.pt, 9am-5:30pm daily mid-Oct-Mar, 9am-6:30pm daily Apr-mid-Oct, €6, includes audio guide), a Dominican convent, was constructed to celebrate victory after the 1385 Battle of Aljubarrota, when John I (Dom João I) defeated the Castilians, ensuring two centuries of independence from Castilian invaders.

Built between the late 14th and early 15th century, the Batalha Monastery is awash with pinnacles and ornamental masonry, giving its exterior an extravagantly frilly look. The combination of strikingly Gothic and intricate Manueline architecture is impressive and beautiful. Some would argue that in comparison to the Alcobaça Monastery, the Batalha Monastery is the more stunning. The soaring vaulted interior and original stained-glass window in the nave of the main church are classically Gothic, flooding the building with light, but more streamlined than its ornamental facade.

The **main church** is free to visit, but to truly appreciate the full magnificence of the monastery, see the paid sections, which include the **Founders Chapel (Capela do Fundador),** Portugal's first royal pantheon, whose unique octagonal chamber contains the combined tomb of John I and his wife, Queen Philippa, while the tombs of their children, including Henry the Navigator, line the walls; two contrasting cloisters, the fancy Gothic-Manueline **Royal Cloister (Claustro Real)** and the austerely medieval **King Afonso V Cloister (Claustro de Dom Afonso V);** and the **Unfinished Chapels (Capelas Imperfeitas),** final resting place of Duarte I, eldest son of John and Philippa, and which takes its name from the fact it has no roof.

A combined ticket to the Alcobaça Monastery, Batalha Monastery, and Tomar Convent of Christ (€15) is valid for seven days.

Getting There

Batalha is 22 kilometers (13.6 mi) north of Alcobaça, a 25-minute drive along the IC9 and IC2 roads. From Lisbon, Batalha is 122 kilometers (76 mi) north, a 1.5-hour drive along the A1 and N1 roads.

By public transport, from Lisbon, **Rede Expressos** (tel. 707 223 344, www.redeexpressos.pt) operates buses six times daily from its main Lisbon hub, Sete Rios (under 2 hours, €10.90). **Rodoviária do Tejo** (tel. 249 787 878, www.rodotejo.pt) and **Rodoviária do Oeste** (tel. 262 767 676, www.rodoviariadooeste.pt) operate 10 daily connections between Alcobaça and Batalha (25 minutes, €3.30). The main interurban bus stop in Batalha is in Largo 14 de Agosto, next to the parish church.

Santarém

Santarém (San-tah-RAYN) is a sprawling district of flat, fertile, cattle-rich farmland along the north bank of the Tagus River in the heart of Central Portugal. The region is famed for wine, bullfighting, and the legendary *sopa da pedra* soup. Encompassing much of the former **Ribatejo Province,** it is also home to a number of Portugal's most important religious and historic landmarks, among them the Holy Shrine of Fátima; Tomar, seat of the Knights Templar; and the fabled Almourol Castle.

SANTARÉM CITY

Despite its formidable history as one of the most strategically important strongholds in Portugal, Santarém city, an hour's drive northeast of Lisbon, is a lesser-known and untouristed city. Built atop a large plateau on the northern bank of the Tagus River, it offers views over the marshy wetlands that surround it. This advantageous position made it a desirable location during the 11th- and 12th-century *reconquistas,* with Afonso Henrique I ultimately reclaiming the country from the Moors.

Wedged between the Aire and Candeeiros Natural Park to the top and the Tagus River to the bottom, and skirted by traditional towns and villages, Santarém had been home to the Lusitanian people, then the Greeks, Romans, Visigoths, and the Moors, before being claimed by the Portuguese Christians. Local legend claims the city is named after the Visigoth saint Irene, Santa Irene in

Portuguese; the city later became Santarém. Afonso Henriques's reconquest of Santarém on March 15, 1147—along with regaining Lisbon later that year—gave way to the *reconquista* of Portugal as a whole and its foundation as an independent nation. Today the tranquil whitewashed city is a hub of tradition, its monuments, including a large, varied collection of Gothic churches, paying testament to its role in history.

Sights
GRAÇA CHURCH
(Igreja da Graça)

One of the fanciest churches in the land, flamboyant little jewel of Gothic architecture **Graça Church** (Largo Pedro Álvares Cabral, tel. 243 304 441, 9:30am-12:30pm and 2pm-5:30pm Tues-Wed and Sat-Sun, 10am-12:30pm and 2pm-5:30pm Thurs-Fri, free), built in 1380, features a magnificent portal embedded with a rosette-style window, carved entirely from a single block of stone, looming above a very elegant ribbed doorway. Inside rivals the lovely front, with light from the rosette window creating an ethereal feel. The church is packed with the tombs of nobles, including explorer Pedro Álvares Cabral, the first European in Brazil in 1500. An 18th-century decorative tile plaque depicting Saint John the Baptist between Saint Rita and Saint Francis, in the chapel's right-hand nave, adds another layer of interest to the interior. This former

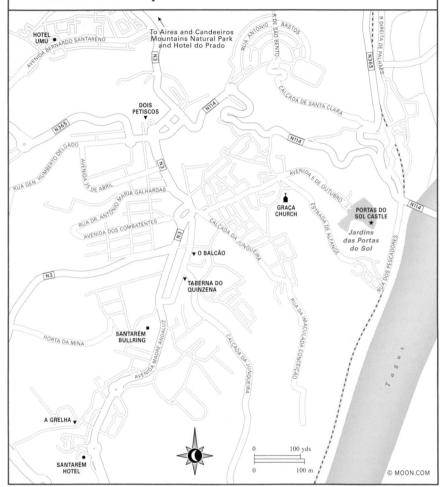

Santarém City

COIMBRA AND CENTRAL PORTUGAL

SANTARÉM

---

monks' convent is also an important example of Gothic architecture.

PORTAS DO SOL CASTLE AND GARDENS
(Portas do Sol Castelo e Jardins)

Within the citadel of the old castle, the **Portas do Sol Castle and Gardens** (Largo das Alcaçovas, tel. 243 304 437, 8:30am-9pm daily June-Sept, 9am-8pm daily Oct-May, free) have sun-dappled lawns, huge trees,

and a picturesque bridge crossing a blue lake. Within these grounds, Dom Afonso Henriques, first king of Portugal, and his soldiers ambushed the occupying Moors at night, and consequently conquered the land in 1147. The Portas do Sol (Doors of the Sun) are two imposing old gateways built into the toothy citadel walls. With views over the Tagus River and the region's distinctive *lezírias* (low-lying, lush meadows), this small park is a lovely place to wander and enjoy a

Local Specialty: Stone Soup

sopa da pedra (stone soup)

In the small village of **Almeirim,** a 20-minute drive from Santarém city, is one of the most famous restaurants in the whole district, O Forno, famous for its *sopa da pedra* (stone soup), a Portuguese peasant soup with a fascinating fable. The traditional version includes beans, potato, pig ears, pork ribs, *chouriço* sausage, *morçela* (black blood) sausage, *farinheira* (flour) sausage, bay leaves, coriander, and mint.

The legend, said to originate from Almeirim, is that a poor friar on a pilgrimage stopped in the village. Famished, he asked around for donations to buy food, but no one had alms to spare, so the friar announced he was going to make a marvelous soup from just a stone and water. Enthralled, the villagers gathered round. Having borrowed an old pan, he got water boiling and threw in a stone. The villagers were fascinated. Tasting the water, he commented that it might need seasoning, which the villagers happily provided. Then he said it might benefit from some spicy *chouriço* sausage or pork belly to add more flavor; the curious villagers obligingly supplied them. Then the friar asked for some vegetables like beans or potato to add substance, and these were also promptly provided. By the time the soup was finished, the villagers had to agree the scent from it was indeed mouthwatering. After his meal, the friar took the stone from the bottom of the pan, washed it off, and put it back in his pocket, ready for the next time. Perhaps the most poignant part of this story, which is arguably about helping and sharing, is that traditionally the soup is served in large metal terrines with a ladle, placed in the center of the table for all to enjoy.

★ **O Forno** (Largo Praça Touros 23, Almeirim, tel. 243 241 163, www.restauranteoforno.pt, 11:30am-3:30pm and 6:30pm-10:30pm Wed-Mon, €12) is a famed restaurant in the heart of Almeirim town, widely seen as the ultimate place to enjoy real *sopa da pedra*. Most days, queues form around the door as busloads of tourists come to eat at this unassuming traditional restaurant. There are many other restaurants in the area that serve *sopa da pedra,* but O Forno boasts a cult following. Located near Almeirim's bullring, it also serves up other meaty regional specialties. Reserve a table well in advance to avoid a long wait.

Almeirim is a 20-minute, 13.7-kilometer (8.5-mi) drive south of Santarém city along the N3 and N114 roads. **Ribatejana** (tel. 707 201 371, www.ribatejana.pt) runs a half-dozen buses daily between Santarém's main bus station (Av. do Brasil) and Almeirim (€2.10), more frequently in the afternoon than in the morning. **Rodoviária do Tejo** (tel. 249 787 878, www.rodotejo.pt) operates almost hourly buses between the towns (15 minutes, €2.10).

coffee at the little on-site cafeteria. Within the gardens are children's play areas and the **Urbi Scallabis Interpretation Center and Museum** (Largo das Alcaçovas, tel. 243 357 288, 9:15am-12:30pm and 2pm-5:30pm Wed-Sun, free), offering insight to the city's history and locally found relics.

Food

A swanky little place with contrasting dark and bleached woods on the outskirts of town, **A Grelha** (Rua do Ateneu Comercial de Santarém, ground Fl. left, tel. 243 333 348, www.grelhasantarem.blogspot.pt, 11am-11pm Tues-Sun, €15) serves typical Portuguese food—lots of it grilled, as the name (The Grill) suggests—in generous portions. Smoked hams and cheeses, octopus salad, seafood rice, meat kebabs, and grilled veal ribs are favorites.

Popular, rustic **Taberna do Quinzena** (Rua Pedro de Santarém 93-95, tel. 243 322 804, www.quinzena.com, 10am-midnight Mon-Sat, €20) has changing daily specials of meaty regional staples like roast *chouriço* sausage and oven-roasted kid served in large helpings.

Not much about the minimalistic, brilliant-white and bleached-wood interior can distract from the food at **Dois Petiscos** (Cerca da Mecheira 20, tel. 243 095 552, noon-3pm and 7pm-11pm daily, €15). The food is as fresh and clean as the decor, with a creative menu based on the concept of taking regional *petiscos* (snacks) to a new level. Modern twists on local classics include melted cheese with dry fruits, oxtail sandwich, and elegant desserts like lemon cake and mango sorbet.

One of Santarém's most popular taverns, **O Balcão** (Rua Pedro de Santarém 223, tel. 243 055 883, noon-11pm Mon-Sat, €18) has a warm ambience and serves authentic country food like fishcakes, meat croquettes, and tuna or Angus steak sandwiches with a modern twist.

Entertainment and Events

Every year for 11 days in late October, Santarém hosts the **National Gastronomy Festival (Festival Nacional de Gastronomia)** (www.festivalnacionaldegastronomia.pt, €2), celebrating Portugal's gastronomic heritage through regional foods and drink (think amazing cheese, meat, and wine). Since 1981 it has attracted the region's top restaurants, chefs, and producers, usually in the city's exhibition and trade center, **Casa do Campino** (Campo Emílio Infante da Câmara, tel. 918 638 507). It is a unique opportunity to indulge in regional cuisine with the locals.

Accommodations

One of the lodgings closest to Santarém city center, **Hotel Vitória** (Rua Segundo Visconde Santarém 21, tel. 243 309 130, www.hotelvitoria.com.pt, €55) is cheap, cheerful, and highly rated, with all the amenities. It's in a nondescript residential building, and all rooms have air-conditioning and cable TV. Decor is slightly dated, but it's a clean and comfortable place to stay, a 15-minute stroll to the riverside Portas do Sol Gardens.

Equipped with pools, terraces, and a fitness center, the smart, bright, airy, and clean four-star **Santarém Hotel** (Av. Madre Andaluz, tel. 243 330 800, www.santaremhotel.net, €65) is on the outskirts of Santarém center, a six-minute drive to the city's main attractions. In a tranquil residential area south of the center, perched on a plateau, the hotel has some rooms with views over the Tagus, and rates include breakfast and parking.

Amid typical whitewashed buildings on a leafy street on the outskirts of Santarém, **Hotel UMU** (Av. Bernardo Santareno 38, tel. 243 377 240, www.umu.pt, €59-65 d) is a basic three-star hotel. Some of the rooms have been refurbished; others are dated but cheaper. The hotel is 2 kilometers (1.2 mi) from the Portas do Sol Gardens.

Near a petrol station off the motorway, 15 kilometers (9.3 mi) north of Santarém, **Hotel do Prado** (Auto-Estrada A1, Km 84, Área Serviço B.P., tel. 243 440 302, €50) is a cheap and cheerful place with 30 well-equipped rooms and a pool, as well as lots of peace and quiet, thanks to the vast gardens surrounding it.

Bullfighting in Portugal

The staunchly traditional region of Santarém is one of few in Portugal where bullfighting, an activity not to everyone's taste, remains widely appreciated. Visitors might note the presence of bullfighting paraphernalia on the walls of restaurants and hotels, as well as depictions on azulejo plaques that dress the streets. The most central of Portugal's traditional provinces, Santarém is at the heart of bullfighting, and is regarded by many as the unofficial bullfighting capital. It is one of the few places where the activity still takes place, but unlike in neighboring Spain, in Portugal the bull is not killed in the ring but behind the scenes (with the exception of the Alentejo town of Barrancos, on the border with Spain). Bullfighting is an age-old tradition in Portugal, generally scheduled before sundown from Easter until late summer. The noble Portuguese Lusitano horse is the star of the show, along with traditionally attired riders, or *cavaleiros*, and *forcados*, a group of eight men who challenge the bull directly without protection or defense. Portugal also has a number of female bullfighters, who for many people are like pop stars.

Information and Services

National emergency number: tel. 112
PSP police: Av. do Brasil 1, tel. 243 322 022, www.psp.pt
Tourist office: Rua Capelo e Ivens, tel. 243 304 437, www.cm-santarem.pt
Post office: Rua Dr. Teixeira Guedes 2, tel. 243 309 730, www.ctt.pt, 9am-6pm Mon-Fri
Santarém District Hospital: Av. Bernardo Santareno 3737B, tel. 243 300 200, www.hds.min-saude.pt

Getting There

CAR

Santarém is 84 kilometers (52 mi) northeast of Lisbon on the A1 motorway (tolls apply), an hour's drive. It is 135 kilometers (84 mi) south of Coimbra, a 1.25-hour drive along the A1, and 51 kilometers (32 mi) east of Óbidos, 35 minutes on the A15.

BUS

Two bus companies run regular services between Lisbon and Santarém city center: **Rede Expressos** (from the Sete Rios station in Lisbon, tel. 707 223 344, www.rede-expressos.pt, 1 hour, €7.60) and **Rodoviária do Tejo**'s Rápida Laranja line (Campo Grande station, tel. 249 787 878, www.rodotejo.pt, 1 hour, €7.65). Both operate about six buses daily, every few hours. From Coimbra to Santarém, Rede Expressos runs three daily buses (2-4 hours, €14), which take longer if there is a transfer in Lisbon. From Santarém's main bus station (Av. do Brasil), it is a 15-minute walk west to the town center.

TRAIN

From Coimbra, **CP** (tel. 707 210 220, www.cp.pt) trains run almost hourly to Santarém (high-speed train 1.5 hours, 2nd class €19, 1st class €26.70; regional train 2.5 hours, €10.75). CP also runs trains between Lisbon and Santarém (1 hour, €7.50-18.30). Santarém train station is 2 kilometers (1.2 mi) north of the city, a 45-minute uphill walk into town. Taxis are available outside the station, or call **Taxis Santarém** (tel. 243 102 500, www.taxis-santarem.net); the trip into the town center should cost under €5.

GOLEGÃ

Known as the horse capital of Portugal, Golegã (GOH-leh-gah) is home to the annual National Horse Fair, which showcases the country's beautiful Lusitano horse, prominent breeders, and showmanship as well as regional food and drink. The petite village is a quintessential farming community that offers romantic gardens and striking churches. Visiting Golegã during the Horse Fair is a thrill, but its charm and character are evident any time of year.

National Horse Fair
(Feira Nacional do Cavalo)

Every year at the start of November, peaceful Golegã is inundated with visitors, and every hotel room and campsite in the area is booked up well in advance for the time-honored **National Horse Fair** (www.cmgolega.pt). Purebred horses, particularly the magnificent Lusitano, take pride of place at the 10-day event, which reaches its pinnacle on November 11, the Feast of Saint Martin, when people eat roast chestnuts and drink new wine to celebrate the occasion, and dress in traditional Portuguese equestrian attire. Competitions such as show jumping, dressage, and carriage driving are a staple, as are local gastronomy and wines, which liven up the crowds after hours.

Historically, Golegã has been a place for farmers and cattle breeders to display their products. The Horse Fair emerged in the 18th century, when special celebrations in honor of Saint Martin were staged, and horse breeders seized the opportunity to put their best horses on show. The fair is Portugal's biggest equestrian event and one of its most traditional celebrations, drawing over 150,000 people to little Golegã.

Getting There

From Lisbon, Golegã is a 1.5-hour, 122-kilometer (76-mi) drive north on the A1 and A23 motorways. Halfway between the cities of Santarém and Tomar, Golegã is a 25-minute drive south of Tomar on the A13 and IC3 roads, and a 35-minute, 30-kilometer (19-mi) drive north from Santarém on the N365 road.

CP (tel. 707 210 220, www.cp.pt) runs trains between Lisbon's Entrecampos, Oriente, and Sete Rios stations and the town of Entroncamento (1-2 hours, €10-17), from where it is a short taxi ride to Golegã (about €10). There are also CP trains to Entroncamento from Santarém (20-30 minutes, twice hourly, €3.30-11.90) and Tomar (1 hour, hourly, €5.20).

★ ALMOUROL CASTLE
(Castelo de Almourol)

Set on a solitary islet that juts out into the Tagus River, in a parish known as Praia do Ribatejo (Ribatejo Beach), the **Almourol Castle** (Ilhota do Rio Tejo, Praia do Ribatejo, Vila Nova da Barquinha, tel. 249 720 358, www.igespar.pt, 10am-1pm and 2:30pm-5pm daily Nov-Feb, 10am-1pm and 2:30pm-7pm daily Mar-Oct, €2.50 includes boat trip) rises from a rocky outcrop. The castle dates to the 12th century, and its origins are shrouded in mystery. It is believed to have been built on the site of an ancient Lusitanian *castro* (a pre-Roman fortification) that was conquered by the Romans in the 1st century BC and later held by invading Visigoths and Moors. It remains unclear when the structure was founded, although an inscription on the main entrance suggests it was circa 1171.

Enigmatic and powerful, Almourol is symbolic of the Christian reconquest, distinguished from other monuments by its riverside location on land that once fell under the protection of the Knights Templar. Almourol Castle forms part of a protective belt that was a frontline of defense along the Tagus River in the Middle Ages, along with the castles of Tomar, Zêzere, and Cardiga. It was abandoned with the extinction of the Knights Templar in Portugal, but from the 19th century it was rediscovered, and in the 20th century the castle was used by the government to host many important meetings.

Reach the castle from the nearby Tancos boat pier, in the parish of Vila Nova da Barquinha, sailing across the Tagus on a little boat to the islet. Boats depart hourly and allow visitors 40 minutes to wander the castle before the return trip. The castle is a magnificent fairy-tale sight as the boat approaches. The views from the castle are phenomenal.

Getting There

Vila Nova da Barquinha and Almourol Castle are a 40-minute, 56-kilometer (35-mi) drive northeast from Santarém city on the A1 and

A23 motorways. From Tomar it's a 25-minute, 22-kilometer (13.6-mi) drive south on the N110 and A13 roads.

CP (tel. 707 210 220, www.cp.pt) trains run six times daily from Tomar to Tancos train station (1-2 hours, €3.15); the journey may require a transfer at Entroncamento. CP trains run more frequently from Santarém to Tancos; take the Regional (R) train (30 minutes, €3.90), which is more direct and sometimes requires no change at Entroncamento. Tancos train station is a 10-minute walk east of the boat pier.

TOMAR

A sense of history pervades the town of Tomar, which straddles the pretty Nabão River. Shrouded in mystery and packed with fascinating sights and ruins, the town was a key pillar in the formation of Portugal. During the 13th century, Tomar was a powerful town as the seat of the Knights Templar, a Catholic military order founded in 1119. For at least 130 years Tomar's Convent of Christ was the hub of the Templars in Portugal as they fought to free the country from Moorish control. In 1190 a Moorish invasion crossed the Tagus River and attacked Tomar, capturing nearby castles, but the Templars withstood a six-day siege and eventually claimed victory. With this and similar conquests in the region, the Templars gradually started the reconquest of Portugal from the Moors.

The Knights Templar order came to an abrupt end in the early 14th century when Philip IV of France, allegedly jealous of their prowess and conquests, convinced the pope to extinguish the order. While most Templars had their wealth and land repossessed, in Portugal they were spared that fate by King Dinis. He protected the Templars by persuading the pope to agree to a new order, renaming them the Order of Christ and moving their hub to Castro Marim. A century later, Tomar was restored to its full glory as the headquarters of the Order of Christ by Prince Henry the Navigator, an exceptional figure who played a pivotal role in the Age of Discoveries.

In addition to ruins with intriguing history, Tomar offers leisurely, picturesque walks along the Nabão River or a stroll through lovely Mouchão Park. Browse the many traditional shops and cafés in the sleepy town center and indulge in one of Tomar's typical cakes, such as the almond and squash *queijadas* (sticky cakes) or the *fatias de Tomar* (Tomar slices) made with egg yolks, sugar, and water slowly cooked in a bain-marie in a special pan invented by a local tinsmith in the mid-20th century. As the locals say, the secret is in the pan.

Sights

★ CONVENT OF CHRIST (Convento de Cristo)

The 12th-century **Convent of Christ** (Igreja do Castelo Templário, tel. 249 315 089 or 249 313 434, www.conventocristo.gov.pt, 9am-5:30pm daily Oct-May, 9am-6:30pm daily June-Sept, €6) is a great work of Renaissance architecture, blending Romanesque, Gothic, and Manueline features in its remodeling over the centuries. The compound is on a hill overlooking Tomar, its lofty location dominating the skyline and enhancing the feeling of power and secrecy that cloaked the Order of the Knights Templar.

The Templars settled in Portugal in the early 12th century and built what is today the Convent of Christ in 1160 under the leadership of Gualdim Pais, provincial master of the order in Portugal. In the early days the convent was a symbol of the Templars' privacy and their desire to recapture the kingdom, but later, having been occupied by Henry the Navigator in the 15th century, it became an emblem for Portugal opening to the world.

The sumptuous interior outweighs the striking exterior and should be seen. The Convent of Christ refers to a complex of buildings rather than just the convent used by the Templars (who later became the Order of Christ) for at least 130 years as their seat in Portugal. The complex is a mix of a classic 12th-century castle and eight cloisters added in the 15th and 16th centuries, plus vast gardens. The centerpiece is the castle's unusual **Charola,** the oratory of the Templars, an exuberantly decorated, light-filled church built by the first great master of the Templars and inspired by the architecture of the Holy Land. Outside, the church has a 16-sided polygonal structure, while inside it has a central octagonal structure, its lavish decor with floor-to-ceiling paintings indicative of the order's wealth and power.

It's possible to spend a few hours wandering this incredibly beautiful complex. Construction began in the 12th century on land donated by King Afonso Henriques to thank the Templars for their role in the *reconquistas.* It evolved into an impressive military complex. Henry the Navigator added a palace in the 15th century, when he was grand master of the order. He extended the monastic premises by adding two new cloisters and transformed the military house into a convent to be used by the clergy. The complex was completely remodeled in the 16th century by Manuel I, who also became master of the order, and was embellished throughout with elaborate sacred art, mural paintings, and decorative plasterwork. Classified a UNESCO World Heritage Site in 1983, it has intricate details and surprises around every corner,

such as the many masons' inscriptions that linger from its days as the seat of the Templars.

Audio guides are available. A combined ticket to the Convent of Christ, Alcobaça Monastery, and Batalha Monastery (€15) is valid for seven days. Note that there are narrow, uneven passages, cobbled floors, and lots of worn stairs; accessibility could be problematic for people with limited mobility.

TOMAR SYNAGOGUE
(Sinagoga de Tomar)

Built in the 15th century in Tomar's historic center, the **Tomar Synagogue** (Rua Dr. Joaquim Jacinto 73, tel. 249 329 823, www.cm-tomar.pt, 10am-1pm and 2pm-6pm Tues-Sun Oct-Apr, 10am-1pm and 3pm-7pm Tues-Sun May-Sept, free) is a rare example of a medieval Jewish temple in Portugal, and is the best preserved. Tomar's Jewish community thrived until 1496-1497, when the Jews were forced to convert to Roman Catholicism or be expelled by Manuel I. Subsequently, the synagogue served as a prison, a Christian chapel, a hay storehouse, and a grocery warehouse. From the outside, it blends in with the simple whitewashed houses on the street, distinguished by the blue Star of David above the door. Inside, Gothic vaulted ceilings connecting to the

Convent of Christ

floor with spindly stone columns are an impressive sight. The synagogue's present-day north-facing entrance is not an original feature; the pointy Gothic east-facing arch was the main entrance in the Middle Ages. In 1921 the building was classified a National Monument, and it also houses a small Jewish museum, which hosts several medieval tomb slabs from across Portugal.

PEGÕES AQUEDUCT
(Aqueduto de Pegões)
Looming above the Ribeira dos Pegões valley, on the northwestern outskirts of Tomar, the 16th-century **Pegões Aqueduct** was originally built to supply the Convent of Christ with water. Like a caterpillar on long legs, the colossal water channel with its succession of lofty double-tiered arches winds around the hills for over 6 kilometers (3.7 mi). Its highest point is 30 meters (98 feet). Construction started in 1593 by Italian architect and engineer Filipe Terzi and was completed in 1641 by Portuguese architect Pedro Fernandes Torres.

MATCHBOX MUSEUM
(Museu dos Fosforos)
The quirky, colorful **Matchbox Museum** (Av. Gen. Bernardo Faria, tel. 249 329 814, 10am-1pm and 3pm-6pm Tues-Sun, free), located in the São Francisco convent, houses an extraordinary collection of 43,000 matchboxes, collected over 27 years from 127 countries and dating back to 1827, filling cabinets and creating a striking visual effect. The collection was started by local man Aquiles da Mota Lima and donated to the municipality in 1980. His fascination with matchboxes started when he traveled to the United Kingdom to attend the coronation of Queen Elizabeth II in 1953, and his first box features the British monarch.

Entertainment and Events
TRAY FESTIVAL
(Festa dos Tabuleiros)
One of Tomar's most ancient local traditions, the **Tray Festival** is a spectacle like no other religious celebration. Staged every four years in June or July (there was one in 2015, with another scheduled for 2019), it takes its name from the festival's high point: a procession of local girls wearing headdresses made from bread piled staggeringly high, parading through the streets with male partners as attendants. The headdresses, called *tabuleiros,* are decorated with colorful flowers and topped off with a white dove, symbolizing Christianity's Holy Spirit. The festival also features other traditional ceremonies and celebrations. The day after the procession, the *pêza* takes place, when bread and meat are shared among the local people. The festival is believed to have originated in rituals dating to the 13th century. Almost the entire local population—thousands of men, women, and children—takes part in this event.

KNIGHTS TEMPLAR FESTIVAL
(Festival dos Templários)
The annual **Knights Templar Festival** (tel. 249 310 040, www.templarknights.eu) is a series of celebrations dedicated to the Templars, held over four days at the beginning of July. These include a torchlit Knights Parade, medieval banquets, and a reenactment of the 1190 Moorish siege of Tomar. The festival dates to 2013, when Tomar was chosen to be world headquarters of the International Order of the Knights Templar (OSMTH)—the oldest Knights Templar organization in the world. The entire town dresses in its best medieval finery to recreate the mysticism and magic of the bygone era, with costumes, arts and crafts, and food and drink galore.

Recreation
MOUCHÃO PARK
(Parque do Mouchão)
Straddling the heart of Tomar town and a sliver of land called Mouchão Island in the Nabão River, **Mouchão Park** (Rua do Parque, tel. 249 313 326, 24 hours daily, free) is a public park with many trees for shady tranquility on hot days. Stroll the lovely gardens and hear the river running nearby. An

old wooden waterwheel stands guard near one of the park's entrances, and a campsite is located nearby. The park is divided into two areas, with a playground, a sports field, and pavilion on one side and the verdant island on the other, connected by a bridge.

Accommodations

Overlooking the Nabão River, at the foot of the Convent of Christ hill, the central, four-star ★ **Hotel dos Templários** (Largo Candido dos Reis 1, tel. 249 310 100, www. hoteldostemplarios.com, €92) has spacious rooms and sizable indoor and outdoor pools. Its great location makes a good base for exploring the region.

In the heart of historic Tomar, modern little **Thomar Story Guest House** (Rua João Carlos Everard 53, tel. 925 936 273, www. thomarstory.pt, €60) occupies a late-19th-century building that oozes character and charm. Each of the 12 tastefully decorated rooms is designed to reflect the town's history.

In a good location on the eastern side of the Nabão River, within walking distance of Tomar's attractions and an 11-minute walk to the train station, **Hotel Kamanga** (Rua Major Ferreira do Amaral 16, tel. 249 311 555, www.hotelkamanga.com, €55) is budget lodging at its best. Rooms are clean, with simple wood furnishings and colorful, crafty quilts; some offer views of the convent.

Information and Services

National emergency number: tel. 112
PSP police: Rua Dom Lopo Dias de Sousa 8D, tel. 249 328 040, www.psp.pt
Tourist office: Av. Dr. Cândido Madureira 531, tel. 249 329 800, www.cm-tomar.pt, 8am-6pm daily
Tomar Health Center: Rua Nabância 14, tel. 249 329 710, 9am-12:30pm and 2pm-5:30pm Mon-Fri

Getting There
CAR
Tomar is a 1.5-hour, 140-kilometer (87-mi) drive north from Lisbon on the A1 motorway;

a 45-minute, 70-kilometer (43-mi) drive north of Santarém city on the A1; and a 35-minute, 39-kilometer (24-mi) drive east from Fátima on the IC9 road.

BUS
Rede Expressos (tel. 707 223 344, www. rede-expressos.pt) runs four daily buses between Lisbon's Sete Rios hub and Tomar (1.75 hours, €9.50). **Rodoviária do Tejo** (tel. 249 810 700, www.rodotejo.pt) has seasonal buses (May-Sept) that connect Santarém's main destinations (Tomar, Fátima, and Nazaré, stopping at the monasteries of Batalha and Alcobaça) along the IC9 road, including Fátima to Tomar (€4 one-way). Tomar's bus station is located on the west side of the Nabão river, a 10-minute walk south of the Convent of Christ.

TRAIN
CP (tel. 707 210 220, www.cp.pt) trains run from Lisbon's Santa Apolónia and Oriente stations to Tomar (2 hours, €10.10) roughly every couple of hours. Tomar's railway station is a short walk from the historic city center.

FÁTIMA

This once sleepy rural backwater is today one of Europe's top Marian shrines and pilgrimage spots. It's hard not to be gripped by the sheer scale of the town's main sanctuary or by the devotion of the pilgrims, crawling on their knees along the sanctuary's stone strip to the Chapel of Apparitions.

Nearly every street, hotel, and restaurant has a religious reference in its name. Formerly inhabited by sheep farmers, Fátima had a change of fate in 1917, when three children claimed to have witnessed an apparition of the Virgin Mary, who gave them important messages to convey over several months. The Roman Catholic Church's belief in these apparitions brought the faithful flocking to the hamlet, hence the Fátima of today, where sheep-dotted pastures gave way to the paved place of worship.

The millions of visitors have fed the

In 2017 Portugal celebrated the 100th anniversary of the apparitions of the Virgin Mary, Our Lady of Fátima, culminating with a visit by Pope Francis to the sanctuary to meet pilgrims; he also made two of the three shepherd children into saints. The pinnacle of the Centenary of the Visions was marked by a canonization mass, attended by 500,000 people in the sanctuary's central plaza.

According to the tale, the Virgin Mary first appeared to the three shepherd children—Lúcia dos Santos, age 10, and her cousins, siblings Francisco and Jacinta Marto, ages 9 and 7—on May 13, 1917, as they watched their flock of sheep pasture at the spot where the Chapel of Apparitions now sits. Emerging from flashes of white light like lightning, above a holm oak tree that still exists, the Virgin asked the young shepherds to return on the 13th of every month until October to receive and relay her messages of salvation for those who embrace her Immaculate Heart, with the promise of a miracle on the last apparition. During the apparitions, Mary is said to have given the children three secrets, a series of apocalyptic visions and prophecies.

On October 13, 1917, Mary's last apparition was known as the Miracle of the Sun. As on the previous occasions, she emerged from a strong light in the sky above the holm oak and asked that a chapel be built at the spot in her honor. By then a large crowd had gathered in response to the children's prophecy that she would appear and perform a miracle. Numerous newspapers published reports from eyewitnesses that the sun danced and zigzagged across the sky, catapulted toward earth, and radiated vibrant multihued light. This was the final event in the cycle and lasted around 10 minutes. Many theories have been put forward to explain the phenomenon, but little detracts from the mystic magnetism of Fátima.

As the young shepherds said the Virgin had predicted, Francisco and Jacinta died just a few years later. Lúcia went on to become a Carmelite nun in Coimbra until her death at age 97 in 2005. She was buried alongside her cousins at the Basilica of Our Lady of the Rosary in 2006.

emergence of tourist shops around the sanctuary laden with religious souvenirs, including not only candles to be lit at the sanctuary but also glow-in-the-dark Virgins and fridge magnets.

Sights

★ SANCTUARY OF OUR LADY OF FÁTIMA
(Santuário de Fátima)

In the urban heart of Fátima, the **Sanctuary of Our Lady of Fátima** (tel. 249 539 600, www.fatima.pt/en, 24 hours daily, free) is an expansive site comprising a cluster of religious buildings constructed after the 1917 apparition. It is one of the most famous Marian shrines in the world, and five million people pass through the site annually. May 13 and October 13 are the main dates for international pilgrimages, mass vigils, and special services.

Central to the sanctuary is the main plaza, a large paved esplanade flanked by the neo-baroque **Basilica of Our Lady of the Rosary (Basílica de Nossa Senhora de Fátima)** (7:30am-6:30pm daily, free) at one end, built 1928-1953, and the contrasting contemporary **Basilica of the Most Holy Trinity (Basílica da Santíssima Trindade)** (7:30am-6:30pm daily, free) at the other. The three shepherd children, siblings Francisco and Jacinta and their cousin Lúcia, are buried in tombs inside the Basilica of Our Lady of the Rosary, where mass is still held. The Holy Trinity Basilica, inaugurated in 2007 to accommodate growing visitor numbers, is a minimalistic sleek round structure of ghostly pale stone that borders on the sterile. It is one of the largest churches in Europe and an award-winning feat of structural engineering that also hosts mass.

At the heart of the sanctuary is the **Chapel of Apparitions (Capelinha das Aparições),** which marks the spot of the apparition. Enclosed by a modern structure of glass panels, it was built to fulfill one of the last instructions from the Virgin Mary to the children. The modern outer building is a simple structure, while inside a statue of the Virgin and the original tiny white chapel are flanked by rows of benches, where many sit in silent prayer. From the top of the central esplanade to the little chapel is a long strip of polished stone, named the Penitential Path, which the devout shuffle along painfully slowly on their knees.

In the middle of the main central esplanade is a fountain with holy water, where visitors can fill containers. Tiny empty flasks are sold at the many souvenir stalls around the site.

Daily masses in Portuguese are held at the two basilicas (various times 7:30am-6:30pm daily). English mass is held at the little Chapel of Apparitions (3:30pm Mon-Fri, free). Visitors can freely explore the sanctuary, although group selfies and loudness are discouraged.

WAX MUSEUM
(Museu da Cera)

There's an interesting **Wax Museum (Museu da Cera)** (Rua Jacinta Marto, tel. 249 539 300, www.mucefa.pt, 9am-6pm daily, adults €7.50s, children 7-12 €4.50) in the middle of town that tells the story of Fátima, the shepherd children and the apparitions, and other town history through 30 well-made sequential wax scenes. It is an enjoyable way to see the town's fascinating past and interesting on a poor-weather day.

Accommodations

In a key location a two-minute walk from the sanctuary, polished and tranquil four-star **Hotel Santa Maria** (Rua de Santo António 79, tel. 249 530 110, www.hotelstmaria.com, €79) provides comfort and contemporary design. Simple and pretty three-star **Hotel Genesis** (Rua de Santo António 41, tel. 249 532 550, www.genesis.fatima-hotels.com, €100) is an eight-minute walk from the sanctuary, with an on-site bar and restaurant.

Modern and minimalistic, the four-star **Hotel Anjo de Portugal** (Angel of Portugal)

(Rua Anjo de Portugal 24, tel. 249 530 240, www.hotelanjodeportugal.pt, €62) has a slick look and a swanky Mediterranean restaurant. It's about a 10-minute walk to the main shrine. On the main road through Fátima, the refined four-star **Hotel Avenida de Fátima** (Av. de Dom José Alves Correia da Silva 116, tel. 249 534 171, www.hotelavenidadefatima.com, €60) is just 100 meters (328 feet) from the main sanctuary.

On the outskirts of Fátima center, the large four-star ★ **Hotel Dom Gonçalo & Spa** (Rua Jacinta Marto 100, tel. 249 539 330, www.hoteldg.com, €85) is comfortable, with a well-equipped spa, a modern renovated wing, and an older wing. It's about a 25-minute walk to the sanctuary.

The **Hotel Casa das Irmãs Dominicanas** (House of the Dominican Sisters) (Rua Francisco Marto 50, tel. 249 533 317, www.hoteldominicanas.pt, €55) is a large convent-like building fronted by well-kept lawns and palm trees. This simple whitewashed hotel with wood accents is a 10-minute walk from the sanctuary.

Getting There

A popular day-trip destination halfway between Lisbon and Porto, Fátima benefits from easy motorway access and regular public transport.

CAR

By car, Fátima is 125 kilometers (78 mi) north of Lisbon, a 1.5-hour drive on the A1 motorway (tolls apply). Fátima is 195 kilometers (121 mi) south of Porto, a 1.75-hour drive via the A1 motorway. From Tomar, Fátima is 40 kilometers (25 mi) west, a 35-minute drive on the IC9 road.

There is plenty of parking in Fátima, including a number of large car parks, but it can be busy and crowded on major religious holidays.

BUS

Rede Expressos (tel. 707 223 344, www.rede-expressos.pt) operates up to two dozen

buses daily to Fátima from Lisbon's Sete Rios station (1.5 hours, €11.90). Rede Expressos also has regular daytime buses from Porto's Campo 24 Agosto station (2 hours, 2 buses hourly 5:30am-5:30pm daily, €17.10), plus a few at night. Tickets can be booked online in advance. From Tomar, Rede Expressos has one round-trip bus daily (40 minutes, €6.80 one-way, €13.60 round-trip), leaving at 7am and returning at 4:55pm. **Rodoviária do Tejo** (tel. 249 810 700, www.rodotejo.pt) has seasonal buses (May-Sept) that connect Santarém's main destinations (Tomar, Fátima, and Nazaré, stopping at the monasteries of Batalha and Alcobaça) along the IC9 road, including Fátima to Tomar (€4 one-way). There are a few daily connections on Rodoviária do Tejo's regular service between Tomar and Fátima (40 minutes, €4)—one early morning, one at noon, and one in the afternoon.

Fátima's bus station is a 10-minute walk west of the sanctuary.

AIRE AND CANDEEIROS MOUNTAINS NATURAL PARK
(Parque Natural das Serras de Aire e Candeeiros)

Comprising the mountain ranges of Aires and Candeeiros, the sprawling **Aire and Candeeiros Natural Park** (head office Rua Dr. Augusto César Silva Ferreira, Apartado 190, Rio Maior, tel. 243 999 480, www2.icnf.pt), a barren passageway to the heart of Central Portugal, covers 40,000 hectares (154 square mi) of hilly terrain between Santarém and Leiria, a natural limestone barrier between the coast and the interior.

The park's most famous features are an eerie web of cool caves and grottoes, fissures, and rock formations. The caves shelter 18 species of bats, the symbol of the park. Several of the larger caves have steps, elevators, and arty lighting so visitors can explore their innards.

About 15 kilometers (9.3 mi) south of Fátima, the **Mira de Aire Cave** (Av. Dr. Luciano Justo Ramos 470, Mira de Aire village, tel. 244 440 322, www.grutasmiradaire. com, 9:30am-5:30pm daily Oct-Mar, 9:30am-6pm daily Apr-May, 9:30am-7pm daily June and Sept, 9:30am-8pm daily July-Aug, adults €6.80, children €4) is the biggest, stretching 11 kilometers (6.8 mi), although only the first few hundred meters are accessible. Visits are in groups accompanied by a guide and descend 110 meters (361 feet) on stairs to the deepest part of the cave, where natural water features, rock formations, and lighting transform the gaping cavern into a magical kaleidoscopic Middle-earth. An elevator takes visitors back to the surface. Tours depart every 20 minutes. The cave's complex comprises a water park, windmills, and a restaurant.

Another extraordinary subterranean attraction in the park is the **Santo António and Alvados Caves** (tel. 249 841 876, www.grutassantoantonio.com, 10am-6:30pm daily July-Aug, 10am-5pm Tues-Sun Sept-June, €6 for 1 cave, or €9 both caves) in the parish of Alvados, 17 kilometers (10.5 mi) south of Fátima. Gaze in wonder at the spiky stalagmites and stalactites that cover Santo António cave, the larger of the two, as you follow a guide along a path that snakes around its warmly lit interior. Just down the road from Santo António, Alvados is smaller but no less impressive. Its hollowed-out insides form a labyrinth of low room-like sections, and its rock formations, while visibly different from Santo António's due to the higher moisture content, are equally fascinating. Tours (25-30 minutes) depart regularly at each cave.

Just a few kilometers west of Fátima in the parish of São Mamede are the dramatic underground **Moeda Caves (Grutas da Moeda)** (Rua das Grutas da Moeda, São Mamede, tel. 244 703 838, www.grutasmoeda. com, 9am-5pm daily mid-Oct-mid-Mar, 9am-6pm daily mid-Mar-mid-July and mid-Sept-mid-Oct, 9am-7pm daily mid-July-mid-Sept,

1: the Sanctuary of Our Lady of Fátima; **2:** a stall at the sanctuary; **3:** candles lit in pledge or prayer; **4:** two sainted shepherd children immortalized as statues

€7), spectacular caverns of immense natural beauty, with areas packed with stunning limestone formations, lighted lagoons, and moisture that drips off stalactites like sparkly diamonds. Legend has it the caves were discovered in 1971 by two hunters chasing a fox. At 45 meters (148 feet) below the entrance level, the caves' various sections have been given romantic titles like Lake of Happiness, Flawed Chapel, and Spring of Tears. Visits are in group tours (30-40 minutes, every 20 minutes) accompanied by guides, who provide information in various languages.

The park is also home to the **Serra de Aire Dinosaur Footprints Natural Monument (Monumento Natural das Pegadas dos Dinossáurios da Serra de Aire)** (Bairro village, tel. 249 530 160, www.pegadasdedinossaurios.org, 10am-12:30pm and 2pm-6pm Tues-Sun, €3), the world's largest and most important collection of sauropod dinosaur footprints from the mid-Jurassic period, making them over 175 million years old.

They are in the eastern flank of the park in the village of Bairro, about 10 kilometers (6.2 mi) south of Fátima. This unassuming patch of Portugal offers the unique chance to walk among dinosaur footprints. Wander solo at this low-key, unspoiled site or take a guided tour (1 hour, minimum 10 people, booked at least 8 days in advance).

Among other features in the park are Portugal's only inland **rock salt pans,** in the village of Rio Maior, on the southern tip of the Aires and Candeeiros Mountains Natural Park, a 50 minute, 76-kilometer (47-mi) drive south of Fátima, and a web of 16 well-mapped **hiking trails** spanning 2-15 kilometers (1.2-9.3 mi).

The park is best explored by car. While there is public transport between the various hamlets and villages, it can be inconsistent. Taking a taxi from Fátima to the Serra de Aire Dinosaur Footprints Natural Monument or to the Moeda Caves should cost under €15 one-way.

Coimbra

Piled on a large hill halfway between Lisbon and Porto is the charming city of Coimbra (koo-WEEM-brah), a trove of historic treasures and home to the country's oldest university. Dubbed "the City of Students," Coimbra exudes whitewashed splendor and was Portugal's capital in the 12th and 13th centuries. Divided into the older uptown and the newer downtown, Coimbra, the country's third most-populous city, covers the hillside and the banks of the Mondego River. In the late medieval period, when Coimbra's importance dwindled, the city became a hub of culture and learning, propelled by sprawling Coimbra University. Coimbra's well-preserved medieval center pumps with a youthful vivacity and a blend of ancient and modern. Surrounded by mountains, the densely constructed urban sprawl is famous for nightlife and its own type of fado.

SIGHTS
★ Coimbra University
(Universidade de Coimbra)

Coimbra University (Pátio das Escolas, tel. 239 859 900, www.uc.pt, 9am-7pm daily) is the oldest in the Portuguese-speaking world, founded by King Dinis in Lisbon in 1290 and moved to Coimbra in 1537. For 300 years it was the only university in Portugal and produced the country's great intellectuals. Currently spread over several campuses throughout the city, it has an ancient core that was mostly the **Royal Palace,** which has housed the university since 1537, and the **College of Jesus,** the oldest Jesuit college in the world, which dates from the 16th century. Classified as a World Heritage Site by UNESCO in 2013, Coimbra University is today a cosmopolitan place to study, with a large contingent of international students.

Coimbra

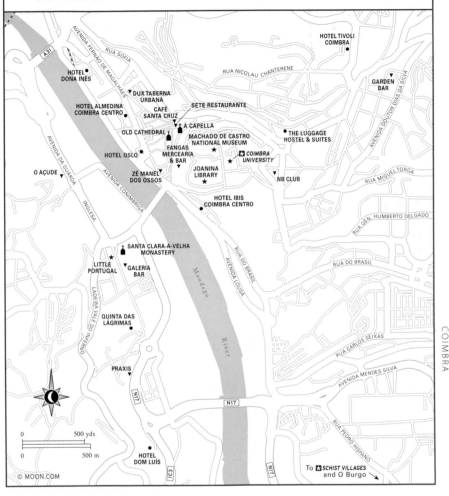

HOTEL TIVOLI COIMBRA

RUA NICOLAU CHANTERENE

A31

RUA SOFIA

AVENIDA FERNÃO DE MAGALHÃES

HOTEL DONA INÊS

GARDEN BAR

AVENIDA DOUTOR DIAS DA SILVA

DUX TABERNA URBANA

HOTEL ALMEDINA COIMBRA CENTRO

SETE RESTAURANTE

CAFÉ SANTA CRUZ

À CAPELA

OLD CATHEDRAL

THE LUGGAGE HOSTEL & SUITES

MACHADO DE CASTRO NATIONAL MUSEUM

AVENIDA DA GUARDA

FANGAS MERCEARIA & BAR

HOTEL OSLO

COIMBRA UNIVERSITY

RUA MIGUEL TORGA

O AÇUDE

AVENIDA CONIMBRIGA

ZÉ MANEL DOS OSSOS

JOANINA LIBRARY

NB CLUB

RUA GEN. HUMBERTO DELGADO

HOTEL IBIS COIMBRA CENTRO

INGLESA

Mondego

RUA DO BRASIL

AVENIDA LOUSA

RUA DO BRASIL

SANTA CLARA-A-VELHA MONASTERY

LITTLE PORTUGAL

GALERIA BAR

LADEIRA VALE DO INFERNO

RUA DO BRASIL

River

RUA CARLOS SEIXAS

QUINTA DAS LÁGRIMAS

AVENIDA MENDES SILVA

PRAXIS

N17

N17

RUA PEDRO HISPANO

0   500 yds

0   500 m

HOTEL DOM LUÍS

IC3

N17

To **SCHIST VILLAGES** and O Burgo

© MOON.COM

The historic core of the vast university complex has a hilltop location and astounding architectural treasures, such as the 12th-century Manueline **São Miguel Chapel (Capela de São Miguel),** with its 18th-century baroque organ centerpiece, and the gorgeous 18th-century baroque **Joanina Library,** also known as the Book House. Many of the campus's main attractions, such as the Joanina Library, the **Great Hall of Acts (Sala dos Capelos)** that hosted academic ceremonies,

and the **Arms Room (Sala das Armas)** with its unique collection of the Royal Academic Guard halberds, are inside the Royal Palace. There's also an **academic prison** beneath the Joanina Library, believed to be the only existing medieval prison in Portugal. The university had its own court, and the prison held unruly students.

Coimbra's fado emerged from the city's academic residents, who maintain their closely guarded academic traditions today. The

Burning of the Ribbons (Queima das Fitas) is one of Coimbra's best-known student rituals, today replicated across the country. Starting every year on the first Friday in May and running for a week, it celebrates graduation with the symbolic burning of ribbons that represent each faculty.

To visit the university, take a short taxi ride up to it from the city center, as it's at the top of a steep hill, and walk back down through the labyrinth of quiet cobbled streets away from the noisy throngs. Don't miss a trip up to the **University Tower** (10:30am-7pm daily, €2), which affords the best views in the city.

Guided tours of the campus (tel. 239 242 744, 1.5-2 hours, €20 pp) are available from the university and cover the highlights. Tours run twice daily (depending on guide availability) at 11am and 2:30pm. Book at least three days in advance, indicating preference of language and morning or afternoon tour.

Audio guides and leaflets are also available on-site, at the ticket office in the university's main library. Four **self-guided tours** include a simple trip up University Tower (program 4, €4 pp) and an all-encompassing journey (program 1, includes São Miguel Chapel, Great Hall of Acts, Arms Room, Joanina Library, and College of Jesus, €12 pp). A visit to the tower can be added to any program for an additional €1.

JOANINA LIBRARY
(Biblioteca Joanina)

In the midst of Coimbra's university complex is the lavishly decorated **Joanina Library** (Largo da Porta Férrea, tel. 239 859 841, 9am-5:30pm Mon-Fri, 10am-4pm Sat-Sun Nov-mid-Mar, 8:30am-7pm daily mid-Mar-Oct, €12), which radiates a warm glow from the rich woodwork. Amazing baroque architecture with elaborate carpentry and ancient books make this arguably one of the world's grandest libraries, named for João V, who in 1717 sponsored its construction to promote artistic, cultural, and scientific endeavors. The ornamental bookshelves, made from exotic materials from all over the world, are gilded, painted, and engraved, and covered by an elaborate trompe l'oeil ceiling to lend the room extra height. The shelves house 250,000 books on subjects such as medicine, science, philosophy, and theology, spanning the 15th to the 19th centuries; some are written by hand. Urban legend has it that bats are released at night to protect the books by eating bugs that might damage them. This is a must-see at Coimbra University.

Tickets to the Joanina Library can be bought from the ticket office at the university's main library; they are timed, specifying the time of the visit. Groups of up to 60 people are allowed in every 20 minutes, and visits are limited to 20 minutes.

Machado de Castro National Museum
(Museu Nacional Machado de Castro)

Named after the renowned Portuguese sculptor Joaquim Machado de Castro (1731-1822), most famous for the statue of Dom José I on horseback in the center of Lisbon's Praça do Comércio square, the **Machado de Castro National Museum** (Largo Dr. José Rodrigues, tel. 239 853 070, www.museumachadocastro.gov.pt, 2pm-6pm Tues, 10am-6pm Wed-Sun, €6, cryptoporticus only €3) houses a fine collection of Roman relics and classical Portuguese art. The building, near Coimbra University and within walking distance of the Sé Velha cathedral, was converted from a 12th-century Bishop's Palace and stands on the site of a Roman forum founded by the Emperor Augustus.

The building includes a remarkable 1st-century cryptoporticus (subterranean vaulted galleries that provided a level foundation for the forum) that can be explored in the museum's basement. The museum also incorporates a 16th-century church that stood on the original site and was restored. A 16th-century veranda teeters on a series of columns so spindly they are practically transparent. Besides a vast compilation of Roman relics, the museum houses a large collection of sculptures as well as traditional azulejo tiles, carpets, ceramics, furniture, gold and silver objects, medieval tapestries, and 16th- to 18th-century religious paintings.

Old Cathedral
(Sé Velha)
Coimbra's handsome 12th-century **Old Cathedral** (Largo da Sé Velha, tel. 239 825 273, www.sevelha-coimbra.org, 10am-5:30pm Mon-Fri, 10am-6:30pm Sat, 11am-5pm Sun, no entry during religious ceremonies, €2.50) is a grand example of Romanesque architecture, one of the few to survive the turbulent Christian reconquests unscathed. Its history and architecture are why many call it the most Portuguese cathedral. While its solid, blocky facade and crenellated walls give it the austere air of a fortress, the cathedral's hundreds of interior columns with sculpted capitals are true to its Romanesque roots. Inside, an early 13th-century cloister marks the transition from Romanesque to Gothic, and in the main chapel a beautiful gilded altarpiece in elaborate late-Gothic style steals the show. A number of 13th- and 14th-century tombs also pay homage to the Gothic era.

Santa Clara-a-Velha Monastery
(Mosteiro de Santa Clara-a-Velha)
On the left bank of the Mondego River across from central Coimbra are the well-preserved Gothic ruins of the **Santa Clara-a-Velha Monastery** (Rua das Parreiras, tel. 239 801 160, www.santaclaraavelha.drcc.pt, 10am-7pm daily May-Sept, 10am-5pm daily Oct-Apr, €4). Built in the 13th century, the monastery was abandoned by the resident nuns in the 17th century due to persistent flooding. After three centuries of neglect, it was excavated and gradually restored over 12 years, reopening in 2009. The building's design is believed to have been influenced by the Alcobaça Monastery. During the excavations, so many archaeological vestiges were unearthed that a modern interpretive center was built, housing a museum and a run-through of the daily lives of the Poor Clare nuns.

Little Portugal
(Portugal dos Pequenitos)
Imagine an entire nation's cultural heritage shrunk to miniature size. **Little Portugal** (Largo Rossio de Santa Clara, tel. 239 801 170, www.portugaldospequenitos.pt, 10am-5pm daily Jan-Feb and mid-Oct-Dec, 10am-7pm daily Mar-May and mid-Sept-mid-Oct, 9am-8pm daily June-mid-Sept, adults €9.95, children 3-13 €5.95) offers miniature replicas of traditional Portuguese houses and famous monuments as well as pavilions dedicated to Portugal's former colonies. Established in 1938 on the left bank of the Mondego River across from downtown Coimbra, close to the Santa Clara-a-Velha Monastery, this small theme park is a favorite attraction among Portuguese families.

FOOD
An excellent spot to enjoy fine regional cheeses and wines on the bank of the Mondego River, **O Açude** (Av. da Guarda Inglesa 63, tel. 239 441 638, 10am-midnight Mon-Sat, €15) is a low-key little restaurant that takes authentic Portuguese cuisine up a notch, with classic dishes such as Lagareiro-style octopus and codfish skewers. An extensive wine list is available.

Hidden deep in the backstreets of central Coimbra is the local gastronomic institution ★ **Zé Manel dos Ossos** (Beco do Forno 12, tel. 239 823 790, 12:30pm-3pm and 7:30pm-10pm Mon-Sat, €12.50, cash only), opened in 1942. The walls of this eccentric, snug restaurant, which has just a half-dozen tables, are plastered thick with notes penned by patrons. People queue just to say they have eaten here and tried some of Zé's famous boiled pork knuckles, roast goat, or wild boar and bean stew. It's the kind of place where finger-licking is encouraged.

Fangas Mercearia & Bar (Rua de Fernandes Thomas 45-49, tel. 934 093 636, noon-4pm and 7pm-midnight Tues-Sun, €12) merges a traditional grocery store with a bar, meaning clients can buy and try. On the menu of this atmospheric little backstreet tavern, a

former grocery store, are regional delicacies like smoked sausages and cured meats, cheeses, tinned products, wines, and sweets.

In the heart of Coimbra, **Dux Taberna Urbana** (Urban Tavern) (Rua Dr. Manuel Rodrigues 59, tel. 239 093 723, www.duxrestaurante.com, 12:30pm-3pm and 7:30pm-11pm Sun-Thurs, 12:30pm-3pm and 7:30pm-midnight Fri-Sat, €20) is a refined, trendy restaurant. Boasting a rainbow of snack-size *petiscos* (snacks) from land and sea, it also has a more limited number of main dishes, from matured steaks to tuna steak with avocado mayonnaise.

Opened in 2017, **Sete Restaurante** (Rua Martins de Carvalho 8, tel. 239 060 065, www.seterestaurante.wixsite.com, 12:30pm-3pm and 7pm-11pm daily, €20) hasn't taken long to establish itself as a serious contender on the local gastronomic scene. In downtown Coimbra next to the famous Santa Cruz café, Sete elevates traditional regional favorites and national ingredients into refined dishes like crunchy sardines, traditional "Bairrada" suckling pig patty with pineapple chutney, and a selection of vegetarian offerings.

NIGHTLIFE AND ENTERTAINMENT
Nightlife

Coimbra has a good nightlife scene without the flashy neon, with lively bars and nightclubs and more sedate hangouts for a quiet drink.

Emblematic **Café Santa Cruz** (Praça 8 de Maio, tel. 239 833 617, www.cafesantacruz.com, 8am-midnight daily) is the place to people-watch and eavesdrop. Established in 1929, the historic café has welcomed some of Portugal's leading academics and intellectuals over the decades and still witnesses debates at its marble-top tables. The main features of this lovely converted 16th-century church include a lofty vaulted ceiling and stained-glass windows. It is as famous for its prized egg and

almond *crúzios conventual* sweets as it is for its regular free fado sessions, for a slice of history with your coffee.

If you like beer, you'll love **Praxis** (Rua António Augusto Gonçalves, Lote 28-29, tel. 239 440 207, www.beerpraxis.com, 10:30am-2am Mon-Sat, 10:30am-1am Sun), a unique brewpub and beer museum on the left-hand side of the Mondego River, just over the bridge from central Coimbra. An established gastrobrewery, it produces its own beer, the secret to which is the natural brewing process and Coimbra water. A covered, heated terrace makes for year-round enjoyment.

Popular among students and locals, busy **Galeria Bar Santa Clara** (Rua António Augusto Gonçalves 67, tel. 239 441 657, www.galeriasantaclara.blogspot.pt, 2pm-2am Sun-Thurs, 2pm-3am Fri-Sat) is a café, bar, restaurant, and art gallery. This stylish place overlooks the old Santa Clara Monastery, on the other side of the river. **Garden Bar** (Rua Sá de Miranda 70, tel. 914 091 856, www.gardenbarcoimbra.negocio.site, 5pm-2am Mon-Sat) is a classy and cool hangout designed like a spacious indoor patio. Enjoy a delicious cocktail from the extensive drinks menu.

One of the top dance spots in the city, **NB Club** (Rua Venâncio Rodrigues, tel. 916 737 611, www.noitebiba.pt, midnight-6:30am Tues and Thurs-Sat, no cover) regularly hosts themed events as well as house music, pop, and rock, featuring live DJs to keep partiers moving. Geared toward clubbers of all ages, its Friday-night revival nights draw in huge crowds.

TOP EXPERIENCE

Fado

For something more cultural, Coimbra is known as the home of the "other" fado. Lisbon fado tends to be melancholic, but the Coimbra version is a medieval serenade and slightly less forlorn. Closely associated with academic traditions, Coimbra's fado is sung exclusively by men dressed all in black in an ensemble akin

---

1: Old Cathedral cloister; **2:** Coimbra University; **3:** Little Portugal; **4:** Joanina Library

to the university cloaks. Performances take place as darkness falls, traditionally in public places such as alleys, streets, and the staircases of monuments, adding to the intensity and mystique of the custom. Tradition also has it that while in Lisbon people applaud to fado, in Coimbra one coughs as if clearing the throat. Make sure to see a fado performance while in Coimbra.

Pop into **Café Santa Cruz** (Praça 8 de Maio, tel. 239 833 617, www.cafesantacruz. com, café 8am-midnight daily) to take in one of its nightly free fado sessions (6pm and 10pm Mon-Sat, 6pm Sun) in the beautiful historic vaulted interior of the former chapel.

Live fado shows (6pm daily) take place at cultural center **Fado ao Centro** (Rua de Quebra Costas 7, tel. 239 837 060, www. fadoaocentro.com, center 10am-7pm daily, fado show €10), created to promote the fado of Coimbra, showcasing some of the city's finest musicians. Reservations are advised because of the limited space.

An atmospheric converted 14th-century chapel, **aCapella** (Rua do Corpo de Deus, Largo da Vitoria, Nossa Sra da Vitória chapel, tel. 962 205 564, www.acapella.com. pt, 7pm-2am daily, cover €10 pp, includes 1 drink) offers tapas complemented with a bar and fado sessions (from 9:30pm daily). It's a popular place where culture and gastronomy merge over dinner or drinks and a show with a difference.

RECREATION

Admire Coimbra from a different angle with a kayak tour on the Mondego River. Outdoor adventure canoe and kayak company **O Pioneiro do Mondego** (Pioneer of the Mondego) (Rua da Calçada 21, Penacova, tel. 239 478 385 or 912 903 782, www. opioneirodomondego.com) runs trips daily year-round 33 kilometers (20 mi) between Penacova and Coimbra to explore the area's stunning natural scenery and unspoiled beauty at a leisurely pace. Several different routes are available, including a night excursion. The classic route (4-5 hours, €24.50 pp)

starts in Penacova (transport is provided from Coimbra) and involves a 25-kilometer (15.5-mi) guided tour down the Mondego River to Coimbra, affording unique vistas of the city.

ACCOMMODATIONS

Large, centrally located, three-star **Hotel Almedina Coimbra Centro** (Av. Fernão de Magalhães 199, tel. 239 855 500, www. almedinacoimbra.com, €55) has good value for the money. Rooms have balconies, and there is free Wi-Fi throughout.

With views over the Mondego River, and located just 300 meters (0.2 mi) from the railway station, **Hotel Ibis Coimbra Centro** (Av. Emídio Navarro 70, Edificio Topazio, tel. 239 852 130, www.accorhotels.com, €65) is central and offers the cheap and cheerful, clean comfort for which the budget Ibis chain is known.

Providing panoramic views over Coimbra, the smart three-star **Hotel Dom Luís** (Rotunda Ponte Rainha Santa Isabel, tel. 239 802 120, www.hoteldluis.pt, €75), on the western outskirts of the city on the Mondego's left bank, across the bridge from downtown Coimbra, has spacious rooms, some with balconies, and an on-site restaurant. The hotel provides a free shuttle bus into Coimbra for guests.

The elegant **Hotel Dona Inês** (Rua Abel Dias Urbano 12, tel. 239 855 800, www. donaines.pt, €88), with its tasteful decor in shades of white and beige, is a 10-minute walk north of Coimbra center. It has an outdoor pool and an on-site bar and restaurant. Family-run **Hotel Oslo** (Av. Fernão de Magalhães 25, tel. 239 829 071, www. hoteloslo-coimbra.pt, €151) is just 50 meters (164 feet) from Coimbra's train station. Modern and stylish, it boasts fabulous views of the city from its roof terrace.

A few hundred meters from Coimbra's university, the **Luggage Hostel & Suites** (Rua Antero de Quental 125, tel. 239 820 257, www. theluggagehostel.com) offers clean and well-presented budget options, including six-bed dorms (€17.10 pp) and a superior suite with an en suite bath (€95). Modern four-star **Tivoli**

Coimbra Hotel (Rua João Machado 4-5, tel. 239 858 300, www.tivolihotels.com, €101), near the Mondego River in the heart of old-town Coimbra, has spacious rooms that are bright and airy, with large windows framing good views.

★ **Quinta das Lágrimas** (Rua António Augusto Gonçalves, tel. 239 802 380, www. quintadaslagrimas.pt, €200) is a romantic retreat in an 18th-century palace surrounded by 4 hectares (10 acres) of lush gardens. It's on the left bank of the Mondego River, close to attractions like Little Portugal.

INFORMATION AND SERVICES

National emergency number: tel. 112
PSP police: Av. Elísio de Moura 155, tel. 239 797 640, www.psp.pt
Tourist office: Av. Emídio Navarro 35, tel. 239 488 120, www.turismodocentro.pt, 9am-6pm Mon-Fri, 9:30am-5:30pm Sat-Sun
Coimbra Main Hospital: Centro Hospitalar e Universitário de Coimbra, Praceta Prof. Mota Pinto, tel. 239 400 400, www.chuc.min-saude.pt

GETTING THERE
Car

Coimbra is 200 kilometers (124 mi) north of Lisbon, a two-hour drive on the A1 motorway; take the Coimbra Sul exit. From Porto, it's a 130-kilometer (81-mi) drive south, a 1.5-hour journey along the A1 motorway; take the Coimbra Norte exit.

Train

Taking the train from Lisbon or Porto to Coimbra is the fastest public transport, but it's more expensive than the bus. **CP** (tel. 707 210 220, www.cp.pt) runs the high-speed Alfa Pendular train (AP, 1.5 hours, 2nd class €23.20, 1st class €33.30) and the slower and cheaper Intercity train (IC, 2 hours, 2nd class €19.50, 1st class €24.70) hourly to Coimbra B station, the main station on the Porto-Lisbon line, from Lisbon's Oriente Station, and most also stop at the Santa Apolónia station. Trains run hourly from Porto's main Campanhã station to Coimbra B station; the AP train (2nd class €17, 1st class €22.10) takes just under an hour, while the IC train (2nd class €13.40, 1st class €17.50) takes a little over an hour. The cheaper Regional train from Porto (€9) takes two hours.

Once in Coimbra, take a CP shuttle train from Coimbra B station to Coimbra A station near the downtown area (Intercity trains do not stop there). Urban trains (3 minutes, €1.45) run between the stations three or four times an hour. To avoid a steep uphill walk from Coimbra A station to the city center, take a short taxi trip from Coimbra B station to downtown Coimbra (€5).

Bus

Rede Expressos (tel. 707 223 344, www.rede-expressos.pt) operates buses hourly and sometimes every half hour from Lisbon (2.5 hours, €13.80) and Porto (1.5 hours, €11.90). The bus station in Coimbra is on Avenida Fernão de Magalhães. From the station, it's a 15-minute walk to the city center. There is a taxi rank outside.

GETTING AROUND
On Foot

Coimbra is easily covered on foot, and the main attractions are within comfortable walking distance of each other. Most of the bars and restaurants are in the downtown area and along the riverfront. However, Coimbra is built on a steep hill that can involve strenuous uphill treks, especially to the hilltop university and the old uptown neighborhood. A glass-fronted elevator and funicular combination, the **Elevador do Mercado** (tel. 239 801 100, 7:30am-9pm Mon-Sat, 10am-9pm Sun, €1.60) connects Rua Olímpio Nicolau Rui Fernandes near the municipal market to Rua Padre António Vieira in uptown Coimbra. Tickets can be bought from the elevator operator.

Bus

Coimbra has its own bus system, the **SMTUC**

(www.smtuc.pt). Lines 27, 28, and 29 run between the main bus station, Coimbra B train station, and the main Praça da República square every 15-30 minutes. Multiuse tickets range €2.20 for three trips to €3.50 for a day ticket that includes the elevator. A single-trip ticket, bought from the driver, costs €1.60. SMTUC tickets can also be bought from kiosks and newsagents.

The Pantufinhas electric mini-buses, or **Blue Line** (8:45am-1pm and 2:45pm-7pm Mon-Fri, 9:15am-1:15pm Sat), are another way of getting around Coimbra's historic heart and between its uptown and downtown; the same tickets are accepted as on the SMTUC buses.

Taxi

Using a taxi to get around Coimbra city center and from one side of the river to the other is an option. The main taxi company is **Politaxis** (Rua do Padrão, Kiosk A, tel. 239 499 090, www.politaxis.pt, 24 hours daily). A taxi from the Little Portugal theme park, on the left bank of the river, to the university costs about €5; from Coimbra B train station to the university costs €6. There is a fare calculator on Politaxis's website.

Car

Given its hilly disposition and maze of steep, narrow streets, Coimbra can be a challenge to navigate by car, and parking is hard to find. Leave your car on the outskirts of town, on the left bank of the river, where there is plenty of designated parking. There is also free parking in the side streets flanking the university for those lucky enough to find a spot.

There are a number of car rental offices around the city, including **Hertz** (Rua Padre Estevão Cabral, tel. 239 834 750, www.hertz.com.pt), **Europcar** (Coimbra City Stadium, Rua D. João III 35, tel. 239 723 324, www.europcar.pt), and **Avis** (Rua General Humberto Delgado 297, tel. 239 834 786, www.avis.com.pt), which offer hourly, daily, and short-term rentals.

CONÍMBRIGA

A national monument since 1910, Conímbriga (tel. 239 941 177 or 239 949 110, www.conimbriga.pt, 10am-7pm daily Mar-Oct, and 10am-6pm daily Nov-Feb, €4) is a large walled Roman settlement believed to be among the biggest on the Iberian Peninsula. Open-air ruins are exposed to the elements, and the site embodies Roman Portugal with a wealth of relics from that era. These include parts of an amphitheater, an aqueduct, water gardens, ponds and jets, thermal baths, gazebo columns, and elaborate mosaic floors that survived 2,000 years, all contained by a long curtain of stone structures. The centerpiece is the beautiful House of Fountains. The Conímbriga Monographic Museum, a gift shop, and a café-restaurant are also on-site.

Conímbriga has many layers built up by the civilizations that occupied it over the centuries. The Romans arrived circa 139 BC, seizing the settlement from its Celtic inhabitants, and under Roman rule the town quickly prospered. Given the size of the amphitheater, archaeologists believe the population at that time was more than 10,000. As it evolved, Conímbriga became an important stop for those traveling between Olisipo (Lisbon) and Bracara Augusta (Braga).

After a number of attempted incursions by invaders, the Romans built a massive defensive wall through the middle of the city, made from stones from residential houses that were taken apart, sacrificed for the city's protection. But it was to no avail—circa AD 468, the city came under attack by the Suebi people, and the Romans were defeated, fleeing to nearby Coimbra.

The Roman Ruins of Conímbriga are a large site in the parish of Condeixa-a-Velha, 16 kilometers (9.9 mi) south of Coimbra. Explanatory signs in Portuguese and English dot the site. Allow a couple of hours to absorb this spectacular attraction. The site is exposed to the elements and can get very hot in summer and wet in winter, so dress accordingly. There's free parking on-site.

Sights

CONÍMBRIGA MONOGRAPHIC MUSEUM
(Museu Monográfico de Conímbriga)

Adjacent to the ruins, the small, well-organized Conímbriga Monographic Museum (tel. 239 941 177 or 239 949 110, www. conimbriga.pt) is a great place to start a tour of the ancient city. It explains the city's history and layout as well as the inhabitants' ways of life and the dynamics of the settlement. Households have been recreated, packed with hundreds of artifacts excavated at the site, allowing visitors to see how the Romans lived. It also holds an oversize bust of Augustus Caesar that originally stood in the community. Grab a map from the museum before exploring the ruins.

ROMAN RUINS
(Ruinas Romanas)

It doesn't take much imagination to conjure the grandeur of Conímbriga, and according to experts—and the relics—it was a magnificent settlement. Archaeologists believe not even a fifth of the original site has been unearthed. Among the finest ruins is the House of Cantaber (Casa de Cantaber), the palatial villa of an important resident built during the 1st century AD. The first to be excavated here, it is one of the largest known residences of its type in the Roman world.

Another must-see is the House of Fountains (Casa dos Repuxos), a former aristocratic residence built during the latter 2nd century AD, with 500 water jets, beautiful ponds, and gardens. For an additional €0.50, visitors can see the water jets switched on. Among the most impressive features of Conímbriga are the intricate, colorful floor mosaics that cover the site like carpets, depicting scenes of hunting and mythological creatures. Some of the most impressive and complete floor mosaics are in the House of Fountains.

The reign of the Emperor Augustus in the 1st century BC saw the construction of several grand civic buildings, such as a forum, an amphitheater, hot-spring baths, and a three-nave basilica, forming the town's grand civic center, to complement the many residential houses. Remnants of these can be seen at Conímbriga, along with the extensive remains of an aqueduct.

Getting There

Conímbriga is 16 kilometers (9.9 mi) south of Coimbra, a 20-minute drive along the IC2 and IC3 roads.

A regular Transdev (tel. 255 100 100, www. transdev.pt) bus runs the scenic route from Coimbra to nearby Condeixa-a-Nova's bus terminal (40 minutes, every half hour Mon-Fri, less frequently Sat-Sun, €2.55), which is 1.6 kilometers (1 mi) from the Conímbriga ruins; from the terminal it is possible to walk to the ruins or catch a taxi. Some buses go directly to Conímbriga; these are marked with a "C" on the timetable.

TOP EXPERIENCE

★ SCHIST VILLAGES
(Aldeias do Xisto)

Hidden away in deepest Central Portugal, peppering the mountains that stretch east from Coimbra, is a string of villages built entirely from schist stone, drawing droves of visitors with their one-of-a-kind architecture, heritage, traditions, and gastronomy. This unique side of Portugal is about as far off the beaten track as you can get, but thanks to eye-catching promotion it's attracting a growing number of visitors, enthralled by the rural life that goes on as it has for centuries.

The 27 ancient villages across 16 counties are in four main areas: the Lousã and Açor mountain ranges, Zêzere, and Tejo-Ocreza. Complementing the scenic setting are river beaches with sparkling water, 600 kilometers (370 mi) of hiking trails, excellent local restaurants, and cozy lodgings.

The Schist Villages Route (Rota das Aldeias do Xisto) (tel. 275 647 700, www. aldeiasdoxisto.pt) was devised by local authorities and outlines various routes to follow, what to see in each village, and where to eat and stay. The routes are available on the website.

Along the way, sample a local specialty, goat cheese, made with traditional processes passed down through the generations, accompanied by fresh bread baked in village community wood-burning ovens. Many of the villages have become havens for ecotourists, with creative environmentally conscious young entrepreneurs giving them renewed energy.

Casal de São Simão, Talasnal, and **Cerdeira,** all in the Lousã mountain range, are among the prettiest schist hamlets and are closest to Coimbra.

Casal de São Simão

A tiny hamlet formed around a single street, picturesque **Casal de São Simão** (kah-ZAL d' SOWN see-MOWN) stretches along a ridge that runs almost parallel to the Ribeira de Alge watercourse. Comprising a little chapel and a river beach, this gorgeous little stone village, with its string of rocky cottages set against a forest backdrop, offers the ultimate photo op.

Casal de São Simão is 47 kilometers (29 mi)

south of Coimbra, a 30-minute drive on the A13 motorway.

Talasnal

Characterful **Talasnal** (tah-lazh-NAL) is a unique village in verdant vegetation teeming with deer and wild boar. The pre-17th-century vine-covered stone cottages ooze medieval charm. Houses and streets have been well preserved, and local crafts can be found in abundance. In the center of the village is a natural spring offering drinking water.

Talasnal is 40 kilometers (25 mi) south of Coimbra, a 55-minute drive on the N17 road.

Cerdeira

Wedged between green slopes and often misty skies is **Cerdeira** (ser-DAY-rah), whose schist houses cling to the rocky hillside. The main bridge leads to a brook that passes through the heart of the village. Cerdeira is better known as a hub of artistic creativity, home to artisans who run lodgings, ateliers, and retreats. The annual July Art Meets Nature festival transforms the village into an open-air gallery.

Cerdeira is 36 kilometers (22 mi) southeast of Coimbra, a 50-minute drive on the N17 road. It's 13 kilometers (8.1 mi) east from

Talasnal, a schist village near Coimbra

neighboring Talasnal, about a 30-minute drive along the winding N236 road.

Hiking from Lousã

Many of the schist villages in the Lousã (loh-SSAH) hills, such as neighboring Talasnal and Cerdeira, can be visited by hiking from **Lousã Castle** (on the M580 road, in front of the Nossa Senhora da Piedade hermitage, tel. 239 990 370, www.cm-lousa.pt), on the southern outskirts of the town of Lousã. The treks are signposted from the road in front of the castle.

The hike from Lousã Castle to Talasnal (2-3 hours) follows a winding mountain road and can be challenging in places, but it's comfortably manageable and affords stupendous views. The hike from Lousã Castle to Cerdeira (3 hours) is slightly more demanding, with steeper parts en route.

FOOD

A few minutes' walk from Lousã Castle is a pretty cottage-style restaurant worth a stop. Surrounded by amazing views next to a waterfall, ★ **O Burgo** (Ermida da Nossa Senhora da Piedade, Lousã, tel. 239 991 162, 12:30pm-3pm and 7:30pm-10pm Tues-Sat, 12:30pm-3pm Sun, €10) offers superb regional dishes. Try the set mixed platter, which has rabbit, venison, wild boar, goat, and chicken.

GETTING TO LOUSÃ

Lousã is 28 kilometers (17 mi) southeast of Coimbra, a 30-minute drive along the N17 road.

Buses run regularly between Coimbra and Lousã, with frequent connections from Coimbra to the village of Serpins via the Ramal da Lousã line, which stops in Lousã. The buses are operated by Coimbra's urban **Metro Mondego** (tel. 239 488 100, www.metromondego.pt, 1 hour, hourly, €3) light rail and bus network, which is still under construction.

There are two bus stops in Lousã town: Lousã A and Lousã by the old train station, not far from the tourist office. The Metro Mondego service runs to Lousã A. From here,

it's a steep 3-kilometer (1.9-mi) uphill walk to the castle. Take a **taxi** (Central de Radio Taxis de Coimbra, tel. 239 499 090, €5) up and walk back down.

FIGUEIRA DA FOZ

Figueira da Foz (fee-GAY-rah dah FOZH), often simply Figueira, is a pretty coastal city at the mouth of the Mondego River, less than an hour's drive from Coimbra, which makes it a popular day trip. Historically a seaside resort, Figueira developed rapidly in the 18th and 19th centuries due to its port, shipbuilding, and codfish-drying industries. Today it's up-and-coming, with a massive beach, beautiful 19th-century architecture, a casino, a long seafront promenade, and a summer holiday vibe. Packed with palatial properties, it has long been a popular place among Portuguese vacationers, and nowadays attracts throngs of Spanish tourists and surfers. Thanks to its growing popularity, trendy restaurants and bars give Figueira plenty of life even off-season.

Sights

SALT MUSEUM
(Museu do Sal)

Salt has played a key role in Figueira, and the **Salt Museum** (Armazéns de Lavos, Salina Municipal do Corredor da Cobra, tel. 233 402 840, 10:30am-12:30pm and 2:30pm-6:45pm Wed-Sun May-mid-Sept, 10am-12:30pm and 2pm-4pm Wed and Sat-Sun mid-Sept-Apr, €1 pp, €2 family) opened in 2007 to explore the history, origins, uses, and production of local salt, once concentrated in the marshes along the southern arm of the Mondego River. Near those salt pans are three sites to explore: the Corredor da Cobra saltworks, the salt warehouse, and the museum. A 3-kilometer (1.9-mi) self-guided raised boardwalk runs through the ponds; see how salt is extracted and refined.

SEA MUSEUM
(Museu do Mar)

Opened in 2003, the **Sea Museum** (Rua

Figueira da Foz

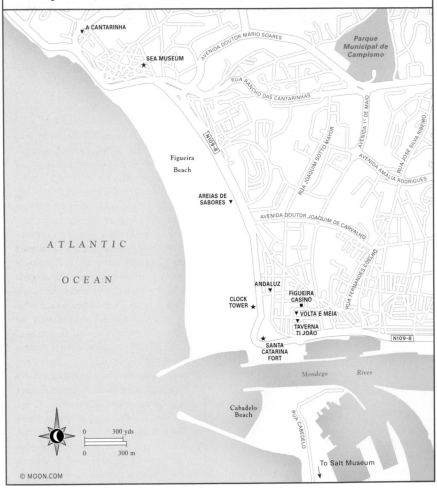

COIMBRA
COIMBRA

© MOON.COM

Governador Soares Nogueira, tel. 233 413 490, 9am-1pm and 2pm-5pm Mon-Fri mid-Sept-mid-July, 9am-1pm and 2pm-5pm Mon-Fri, 2pm-7pm Sat, mid-July-mid-Sept, free) explores the traditions, history, and paraphernalia of fishing along the Figueira da Foz coast. See mock-ups of traditional fishing boats from different eras, fishing gear, and clothing. Covering fishing communities, cod fishing, and arts and crafts, this small museum is in the traditional fishing village of Buarcos, 5.5

kilometers (3.4 mi) north of Figueira da Foz, a 10-minute drive or an hour's stroll along the seafront.

Food

Near the casino and beach, **Taverna Ti João** (Rua Poeta Acacio Antunes 7, tel. 233 094 542, 4pm-4am Mon-Sat, €18) is famed for its steaks. The small modern eatery also serves quirky dishes like codfish burgers.

Boasting original decor like a classroom

Local Specialty: Monkfish Rice

Figueira da Foz is home to the delicious local specialty *arroz de tamboril* (monkfish rice). This fishy stew, made with chunks of meaty white monkfish, is cooked in a rich tomato sauce with peppers, onions, and rice. Cooked slowly, the rice becomes soft without being mushy and soaks up the buttery taste of the stew. There are two renowned places to sample this dish:

No-frills and low-key, **Andaluz** (Rua Maestro David de Sousa 114, Figueira da Foz, tel. 233 420 454, noon-2:30pm and 7:30pm-10:30pm daily, €20) restaurant is slightly hidden toward the southern end of Figueira da Foz, but it's synonymous with monkfish. *Feijoada de búzios* (whelk stew) and sea soup are other house specials.

On the seafront in the nearby fishing village of Buarcos, long-established ★ **A Cantarinha** (Travessa da Rua das Tamargueiras 3, Buarcos, tel. 233 432 801, www.restauranteacantarinha. com, 11am-11pm Tues-Sun, €15) is famous for its barbecue sardines and *arroz de tamboril*. The restaurant has a nice esplanade area.

with mismatched chairs, **Volta e Meia** (Rua Dr. Francisco Antonio Diniz 64, tel. 233 418 381, www.voltaemeia.com, noon-3pm and 7pm-11:30pm Tues-Sat, noon-3pm Sun, €10) prides itself on fresh fare from local ingredients, such as homemade pâtés, mushrooms stuffed with regional cheese and sausage, daily soups, and cheesecakes.

Translating as "Sands of Flavors," **Areias de Sabores** (Av. Brasil, tel. 233 415 336, 10:30am-1:30am daily, €20) is on Claridade Beach on the main Avenida Brasil and has a modern seaside feel. The menu includes excellent fresh fish prepared as tuna *tataki,* ceviche, and teriyaki, as well as a selection of meat dishes including duck and steak.

Entertainment
FIGUEIRA CASINO
A few streets back from the beach behind the clock tower is the swanky midsize **Figueira Casino** (Rua Cândido dos Reis 49, tel. 233 408 400, www.casinofigueira.pt, 3pm-3am Sun-Thurs 4pm-4am Fri-Sat), run by hotel group Solverde. Looking jazzy at night when its glass facade is lit up, inside it has slot machines, live game tables, and classic table games such as blackjack and roulette as well as *banca francesa* (a popular dice game) and poker cash tables.

Beaches and Recreation
CLARIDADE BEACH
(Praia da Claridade)
Seemingly endless, Figueira da Foz's main **Claridade Beach** is a hub of activity—in summer, at least. Its proportions are staggering, so long and wide that when the tide is out, it can be a long walk to the water's edge. Facing the Atlantic, this stretch of coast can be breezier and the water cooler than in more sheltered parts of the country, but it is nonetheless a top-quality beach.

The sand is latticed by a grid of wooden walkways that stretch almost to the water, dotted with tables and benches for picnics. Praia da Claridade is hugely popular among surfers and sunseekers, offering services and amenities such as beach bars, restaurants, and surf rental shops within walking distance. The beach is nice for long, invigorating walks in low season, when it is practically empty.

Figueira da Foz's main Avenida do Brasil runs parallel to the beach, offering a pleasant hour-long walk to the nearby traditional fishing village of **Buarcos,** 5.5 kilometers (3.4 mi) north of Figueira da Foz, where the Sea Museum is located. Buarcos retains its down-to-earth authenticity even as neighboring Figueira's popularity has boomed.

CABEDELINHO BEACH
(Praia do Cabedelinho)

A five-minute walk across the bridge from Figueira da Foz, at the tip of the Mondego River mouth on the south side, **Cabadelinho Beach** is a local favorite for families in summer and a top surf spot in autumn and winter. A trendy wooden surf bar and little shops with board rentals are just off the beach. An added bonus is the fantastic view over Figueira da Foz and the Boa Viagem mountain range.

Getting There
CAR
Figueira da Foz is on the coast 60 kilometers (37 mi) west of Coimbra, a 45-minute drive on the A14 motorway. Figueira da Foz is 197 kilometers (122 mi) north of Lisbon, a two-hour drive up the A8 motorway, and 140 kilometers (87 mi) south of Porto, a 1.5-hour drive down the A1 motorway.

BUS
A **Moisés Correia de Oliveira** (tel. 239 629 114 or 239 629 238, www.moises-transportes.pt) express bus runs regularly from Coimbra's bus station to Figueira da Foz (1.5 hours, every 4 hours, €4.30). **Rede Expressos** (tel. 707 223 344, www.rede-expressos.pt) buses run four times daily from Lisbon's Sete Rios station to Figueira da Foz (3 hours, €15.20). There are no direct bus or train services between Porto and Figueira da Foz. Figueira da Foz's bus terminal is a short walk east of the waterfront marina and town center.

TRAIN
Trains run about hourly between Porto, Lisbon, and Coimbra, and from Coimbra it is possible to catch a connecting train to Figueira da Foz. **CP** (tel. 707 210 220, www.cp.pt) operates Urbano trains from Coimbra to Figueira (1 hour, €2.75) about once per hour.

CP's regional Western Line (Linha do Oeste) runs between Lisbon and Figueira da Foz, serving Portugal's central western coast. While scenic, the trip is slow and trains run infrequently, with lots of stops, and will require a change somewhere on the way to Figueira da Foz. Figueira da Foz's railway station is next to the bus terminal.

AVEIRO

At the upper end of the Silver Coast, Aveiro (ah-VAY-roo) is one of Central Portugal's most photogenic cities, positioned around a gorgeous shallow lagoon, the Ria de Aveiro. The lagoon teems with birds, *aves* in Portuguese, which could be the origin of the city's name. As well as being an important port, Aveiro also produces salt and seaweed, used as fertilizer. Crisscrossed by a series of canals that have become the city's distinguishing feature, Aveiro is referred to as the "Venice of Portugal." These canals are navigated by colorful gondola-like boats called *barcos moliceiros,* traditionally used to harvest seaweed but nowadays used to ferry tourists. Also famous for its art nouveau architecture and equipped with great transport links, quirky Aveiro is a popular day-trip destination from Coimbra and Porto.

Sights
RIA DE AVEIRO WATERSIDE
Savor the tranquility of the bird-rich *ria* (lagoon) on Aveiro's waterside, lined with pretty buildings, souvenir shops, and cafés. Enjoy a drink, cake, and people-watching as the *barcos moliceiros* sail past.

ART NOUVEAU ARCHITECTURE
Aveiro's city center is packed with distinctive art nouveau buildings, a trend that took off in Portugal at the turn of the 20th century with emigrants returning from Brazil who also incorporated typically Portuguese embellishments like azulejo tiles. While many prefer to drink in the scenic setting of the *ria* waterside, venture into the heart of the city and you'll be amazed by the architecture.

See Aveiro's foremost art nouveau buildings on a guided walking tour with **Explore Aveiro Walking Tour** (tel. 927 355 062, www.explore-aveiro.com, 2 hours, from €15).

Local guides who speak English enthusiastically point out the hidden delights and main points of interest of the city.

Aveiro's **Art Nouveau Museum (Museu Arte Nova)** (Rua Dr. Barbosa de Magalhães 10, tel. 234 406 485, 10am-12:30pm and 3:30pm-6pm Tues-Sun, €1) is worth a look, occupying Casa Major Pessoa, one of the city's fanciest art nouveau buildings with whirly wrought-iron features and whimsical azulejos of birds, animals, and flowers. The first floor of the three-story museum features a road map of a self-guided walking tour of 28 art nouveau buildings in Aveiro as well as a lovely tearoom, Casa de Chá; the second floor comprises an auditorium and an art gallery for emerging artists and architects; and the top floor hosts temporary exhibitions.

AVEIRO MUSEUM
(Museu de Aveiro)

Aveiro Museum (Parque de Santa Joana, tel. 234 423 297, www.patrimoniocultural. gov.pt, 10am-6pm Tues-Sun, €4) encapsulates the religious history and heritage of the region and explains how nuns lived over the centuries. It occupies what is today known as the Monastery of Jesus (Mosteiro de Jesus), a 15th-century former Dominican convent, one of the oldest in Aveiro, once inhabited by Saint Princess Joana, also known as Blessed Joan of Portugal. Joana was the daughter of Afonso V, and after moving into the convent circa 1472, lived a life so holy that she was beatified in 1693. The convent became famous for its association with the Saint Princess.

One of the remaining original features of the convent is the 15th-century **Church of Jesus (Igreja de Jesus)**, with a lavish gilded baroque interior, cloister, and chapels. Inside this church, in its inner choir, visitors can see one of the museum's highlights, an ornate tomb made from solid multicolored marble, which contains the ashes of Saint Princess Joana.

In the 16th and 17th centuries, the convent underwent significant renovations that added to its architectural and artistic wealth, but as you wander through, you will see its original features, such as the chapter room and refectory, the Chapel of Senhor dos Passos, and the silent Dominican rooms. The museum also houses a collection of ancient religious artifacts such as paintings, sculptures, azulejo tiles, and jewels.

AVEIRO RAILWAY STATION
(Estação Ferroviária de Aveiro)

No longer in service, beautiful **Aveiro Railway Station** still draws admirers thanks to its striking sky-blue and snowy white azulejo-clad facade, dating from the early 1900s. The tiles depict scenes from Portugal's history and regional motifs, and are fine examples of the art of storytelling on tiles. The building dates from 1864 and can't be entered, but its finest features are on the outside and visible to all. The old station is a 15-minute walk east of the city center, in Largo da Estação, next to the new train station.

Food

At **O Bairro** (Largo da Praça do Peixe 24, tel. 234 338 567, www.obairro.pt, noon-3pm and 7pm-11pm Thurs-Tues, €20), a promising young chef reinvents regional classics, including cod and duck dishes. In a lovely old-town building with original tile floors, O Bairro is small but perfectly formed, and effortlessly blends the authentic with the contemporary.

Converted from two old salt warehouses on the São Roque docks, ★ **Salpoente** (Cais de São Roque 83, tel. 915 138 619, www.salpoente. pt, 12:30pm-2pm and 7:30pm-9:30pm daily, €25) is an elegant restaurant in a lovely location. Modern furniture and colorful, plush upholstery give a fresh twist to the old warehouse. At Salpoente, known as the "cod specialists," cod is the star. Other popular dishes include seafood risotto and seafood soup. This is world-class contemporary cuisine, and all dishes have a surprising twist.

Classic little fish restaurant **A Peixaria** (Rua Mestre Francisco Jorge Gomes Pestana, tel. 234 331 165, www.restauranteapeixaria.pt, 10am-midnight Tues-Sun, €18) is bright and

COIMBRA

COIMBRA AND CENTRAL PORTUGAL

basic and serves an extensive menu of simply grilled fresh fish, unfussy seafood, and cold beer at good prices.

Recreation
MOLICEIRO BOAT TRIPS

You can't leave Aveiro without jumping on one of the city's traditional colorful little *moliceiro* boats and enjoying a cruise of Aveiro's pretty canals and natural scenery. Take a seat where seaweed was once heaped and enjoy the knowledge and insight imparted by the jolly crew. The *moliceiros* also take visitors to the nearby lagoon for bird-watching; to the *bacalhoeiros* docks, where old cod-fishing boats and colorful huts can still be seen; or to the São Jacinto Dunes Nature Reserve (Reserva Natural das Dunas de São Jacinto), with its unspoiled dunes and endless beach. The nature reserve is 14 kilometers (8.7 mi) from Aveiro at the southern tip of a string of marshy dunes that separate the city from the Atlantic Ocean.

Moliceiro boat rides are run by, among others, local organization **Viva a Ria** (along the docks, near the gardens, tel. 969 008 687, www.vivaaria.com). City canal tours (45 minutes, every 15 minutes daily, from €10) include a sampling of sparkling wine and the traditional local sweet *ovos moles* (sweet egg yolk in rice-paper casings). Other cruises, such as the *bacalhoeiros* docks (1.25 hours, €15), the São Jacinto Dunes cruise (2.5 hours, €20), and the lagoon bird-watching cruise (3 hours, €20, includes an optional picnic), require prior reservation. A romantic cruise on a *moliceiro* for two, including a bottle of champagne and sweets, costs €150.

Getting There
CAR

Aveiro is 52 kilometers (32 mi) north of Coimbra, a 50-minute drive on the A1 motorway. It's 74 kilometers (46 mi) south of Porto on the A1 motorway, a 55-minute drive, and 253 kilometers (160 mi) north of Lisbon, a 2.5-hour drive on the A1 motorway. From Figueira da Foz, Aveiro is a 73-kilometer (45-mi), 50-minute drive north on the A17 motorway.

TRAIN

CP (tel. 707 210 220, www.cp.pt) trains run regularly between Coimbra and Aveiro (every 30 minutes 5am-midnight daily). The journey takes 25 minutes on the high-speed Alfa Pendular (AP) or Intercity (IC) train, or one hour on the Regional train (R). A one-way ticket ranges from €5.20 (R) to €20 (AP, 1st class).

From Porto, trains run frequently to Aveiro (every 30 minutes 5am-1am daily). The journey takes 35 minutes on the high-speed Alfa Pendular (AP) or Intercity (IC) train, or one hour on the Urbano (U) train. A one-way ticket ranges from €3.50 (U) to €20 (AP, 1st class).

The new train station in Aveiro is next to the historic station on Rua do Dr. João de Moura, a 15-minute walk east of the city center.

BUS

There are four daily **Rede Expressos** (tel. 707 223 344, www.rede-expressos.pt) buses between Coimbra and Aveiro (45 minutes, from 1pm daily, €6 one-way), which are faster than the train but more expensive. From Porto to Aveiro (1.5 hours, 6 buses Mon-Fri, fewer Sat-Sun, €8.60), a transfer is usually required in the town of Albergaria-a-Velha. There are two daily Rede Expressos buses to Aveiro from Figueira da Foz (1 hour, 11:15am and 6:45pm daily, €8.30 one-way). The main bus terminal in Aveiro is on the riverfront, in the town center on Rua Clube dos Galitos, 1 kilometer from the train station.

★ PAIVA WALKWAYS
(Passadiços do Paiva)

Located outside the town of Arouca, a 1.5-hour drive north of Aveiro, are the award-winning

1: Aveiro Railway Station; **2:** a colorful sculpture in Aveiro; **3:** Paiva Walkways; **4:** traditional *moliceiro* boat

Local Specialties

A renowned symbol of Aveiro's local gastronomy, **eel stew with saffron** *(caldeirada de enguias com açafrão à moda de Aveiro)* is famous throughout the country, and many visit Aveiro to try this unusual delicacy. It's made from multiple layers of fresh ingredients, including eels caught in the local *ria* as well as thick slices of potato and onion. The two main ingredients in the traditional recipe, which give the dish a unique flavor and color, are "eel dust," a blend of saffron or ginger and pepper, and rancid lard. Eels cooked in rancid lard might not sound appetizing, but the end result is surprisingly good.

A popular place to try this Aveiro classic is the upscale ★ **Mercado do Peixe** (Largo da Praça do Peixe 1, Aveiro, tel. 968 073 652, www.restaurantemercadodopeixeaveiro.pt, 12:15pm-3pm and 7:30pm-11pm Tues-Sun, €25), whose name translates as "fish market." Above the João Estevão fish market on the water, the restaurant has elegant tables and a spacious, minimalist look that are a stark contrast to the bustling fish market below. It serves all things fish, from classic Portuguese dishes to local specialties, including *cataplanas* and seafood rice, as well as the typical Aveiro eel stew with saffron.

Ovos moles, literally "soft eggs," is a sweet local delicacy synonymous with Aveiro and one of the most famous sweets from the country's convents. Made of a sugary egg yolk concoction that fills rice-paper casings shaped like shells or fish in a nod to local history, these pint-size pastries can be found in practically every café and cake shop in Aveiro.

Paiva Walkways (tel. 256 940 258, www.passadicosdopaiva.pt, 7:30am-8pm, €1), a demanding but highly rewarding 8.7-kilometer (5.4-mi) raised wooden walkway through unspoiled landscape, along rivers with rapids and through the protected habitats of endangered species. The linear route runs between Espiunca and Areinho, both about 14 kilometers (8.7 mi) from Arouca town, the walkway's end points. This peaceful natural sanctuary is a trek through seldom-seen landscapes typical of the region—rugged forested mountainsides, deep gorges, sparkling waterfalls, and mirrorlike pools.

Along the left bank of the Paiva River, one of the cleanest in Europe, the walkway takes 2.5 hours walking downstream from Areinho, and twice as long coming back upstream (and uphill). If you want to do the 17.4-kilometer (10.8-mi) round-trip, start in Espiunca. The walk involves some unpaved and strenuous stretches, long flights of steps, and steep inclines, so some physical fitness is required. While Central Portugal is often cooler than other parts of the country, and the walkway is shaded in parts, it can get very hot in summer. There is a bar and a natural swimming pool about halfway along to cool down, although you should take your own water and snacks—and a good pair of walking shoes.

Getting There

The Paiva Walkways are 82 kilometers (51 mi) northeast of Aveiro and 75 kilometers (47 mi) southeast of Porto. From Aveiro, it is a 1.5-hour drive along the R326-1 road; from Porto, it is a 1.25-hour drive along the N326 road. If you visit by car and only want to walk one-way, a taxi back from either end costs around €15.

Serra da Estrela

One of Portugal's most famous mountain ranges, the snow-topped Serra da Estrela (Star Mountain Range) shines among its peers, with the country's only ski resort. The most popular parts of the Serra are near the city of Covilhã, a convenient gateway.

★ SERRA DA ESTRELA NATURAL PARK
(Parque Natural da Serra da Estrela)

Sprawling 1,000 square kilometers (386 square mi), more than half of which is above 700 meters (2,297 feet) elevation, the Serra da Estrela Natural Park has exceptional majestic mountains, boulder-littered meadows, rocky glacial valleys, and dramatic lakes. It was the first natural park in Portugal and remains the largest. Home to the highest point on mainland Portugal, the Torre summit, and the country's only ski resort, the park is also the source of the Mondego and Zêzere Rivers. It's inhabited by a wealth of wildlife, including wolves, foxes, wild boars, otters, golden eagles, falcons, and owls. It even has an indigenous breed of dog, the Estrela mountain dog used by local shepherds for centuries. In recent decades, flocks of sheep have given way to hordes of tourists who pour into Serra da Estrela, especially in winter to enjoy the snow.

The park can be explored on marked walking routes, off-road mountain bike routes, or by car, although the weather can hamper visits and should be taken into account.

Park Information

The **Serra da Estrela Natural Park Interpretation Center (Centro de Interpretação da Serra da Estrela)** (Praceta os Doze de Inglaterra 11, Seia, tel. 238 320 300, www.cise.pt, 10am-6pm Tues-Sun, €4) is a good place to learn more about the park's sights and routes, flora, and fauna. It's in Seia, on the opposite side of the mountain range from Covilhã, the main gateway to

the park. Seia is 50 kilometers (31 mi) west of Covilhã, across the mountain range, a 1.25-hour drive on the hilly N339 road.

The park also has a number of **information offices**, including **Manteigas** (Rua 1º de Maio 2, tel. 275 980 060 or 275 980 061), in the center of the park; **Seia** (Praça da República 28, tel. 238 310 440), along the northern edge of the park; **Gouveia** (Casa da Torre, Av. Bombeiros Voluntários 8, tel. 238 492 411), along the northern edge of the park, northeast of Seia; and **Guarda** (Rua D. Sancho I 3, tel. 271 225 454), northeast of the park.

The **Covilhã tourist office** (Av. Frei Heitor Pinto, tel. 275 319 560, www.turismodocentro.pt, 9am-12:30pm and 2pm-5:30pm daily) provides information on Serra da Estrela as well as useful maps.

Sights

First, visitors should see **Torre,** the highest point on mainland Portugal at 1,993 meters (6,539 feet), usually easy to reach by car. Torre is marked by a simple stone point in the middle of a roundabout, reached by following the N339 road that cuts straight across Serra da Estrela from Covilhã to Seia. The drive up is scenic and the views from the top are breathtaking. Visit the little mountaintop shops that sell local cheese, ham, and trinkets. There are also restrooms. Torre is a 23-kilometer (14.3-mi), 35-minute drive west from Covilhã, and a 28-kilometer (17-mi), 40-minute drive east from Seia.

In the heart of the Serra da Estrela range, on the way route from Covilhã to Torre on the N339 road, 21 kilometers (13 mi) or 35 minutes' drive from Covilhã, **Covão do Boi** is a remarkable section of mountain with huge eroded stone blocks affectionately referred to by locals as "cheeses." Stop here to see the 7-meter-tall (23-foot-tall) **Senhora da Boa Estrela** rock sculpture, created by

Serra da Estrela

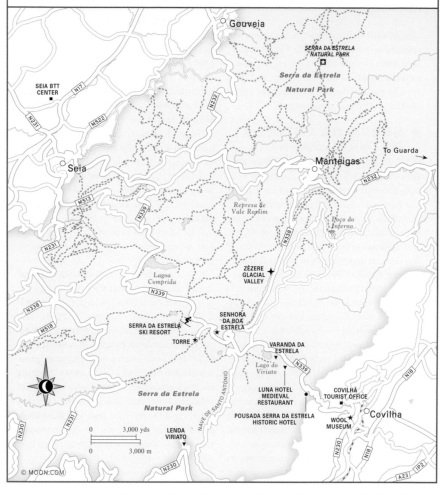

Portuguese sculptor António Duarte in 1946 when a local priest wanted to pay tribute to the Senhora da Boa Estrela, patron saint of shepherds, whose flocks are a familiar sight in the rugged terrain.

Thirty minutes' drive north from Torre, 20 kilometers (12.4 mi) along the N339 and then N338 roads toward the town of Manteigas, is the 13-kilometer-long (8-mi-long) **Zêzere Glacial Valley,** a dramatic gorge of imposing granite. The valley can also be reached

from Seia, 50 minutes on the N232 road, or Covilhã, 40 minutes on the N18 and N232 roads, before heading south, up to Torre peak. The views are best when heading down from Torre to Manteigas. The Zêzere Glacial Valley is a unique landscape in Portugal—immense, U-shaped, and ice-clad in winter, the valley is sandwiched between soaring, barren mountains of rock-strewn pastures peppered with tiny stone-built farmhouses typical of the region. The Zêzere River gushes through the valley. The valley is very popular among hikers for its easy walking.

At the foot of the Zêzere Valley is the charmingly authentic mountain town of **Manteigas,** its whitewashed houses and cobbled streets a great stop for exploring, for lunch, or to stock up on local produce. It makes a good base for spending more time in the hiking-friendly Zêzere Valley.

Also near Manteigas is one of the Serra's best-kept secrets, **Poço do Inferno** (Hell's Well), a 10-meter (33-foot) waterfall considered one of the most beautiful in the country. Despite its name, the spot is beautiful, with a clear pool at the bottom that can run dry in summer. An easy hike is a circular trek from Manteigas to Poço do Inferno, 16 kilometers (9.9 mi) on a four- to five-hour round-trip, one of the most scenic hikes in the park. By car from Manteigas, drive along the N232 road for about 8 kilometers (5 mi) to the signed turnoff, then follow a narrow, winding road through the forest for another 5 kilometers (3.1 mi) to a spacious car park and an information board.

While in the area, you can drink from Estrela's many springs, waterfalls, and rivers; it is used to produce bottled water.

Recreation

Over 100 kilometers (62 mi) long, 30 kilometers (19 mi) wide, and 300 million years old, the Serra da Estrela Natural Park is for adventure-seekers. The scenery changes with the seasons, from flower-peppered meadows in spring to snowcapped peaks in winter. Spring and summer have the best temperatures and clear skies for hiking or cycling, although the summer sun can be fierce, and many treks have little shade. Fall can bring rain, especially toward the end of the season, while December to February is prime time for snow sports.

HIKING, BIKING, AND CLIMBING

Various hiking and mountain bike trails traverse the park, although signage can be sketchy, so ask for a map at one of the park's information offices. Opportunities abound for canyoneering and mountaineering. Join a guided tour with experienced local companies such as **Trans Serrano** (tel. 235 778 938, www.transserrano.com) for riverbed hikes (4-5 hours, €17.50), canyoneering (4-5 hours, from €25), climbing, and rappelling in the Serra da Estrela's hidden nooks and crannies. Canyoneering rates include a wetsuit, helmet, harness, insurance, and supervision by accredited guides.

Six kilometers (3.7 mi) north of Seia, the **Seia BTT Center** (Rua Domingos Gonçalves Santiago, parish of Santa Comba, tel. 238 317 762, www.aldeiasdemontanha.pt, 9am-7pm daily June-Sept, 9am-4pm daily Oct-May), part of the Portuguese Cycling Federation network, can provide information on mountain bike routes and rentals.

SKIING

Serra da Estrela is the only place in Portugal for snow sports. Skiing, sledding, and snowboarding are all available at the resort. Off-season, there are artificial ski slopes. The **Serra da Estrela Ski Resort (Estância de Ski da Serra da Estrela)** (N339 road, tel. 238 031 940, www.skiserradaestrela.com, 9am-5pm daily, adults €22, children €15, rentals from €25, snowboards €15) has just four ski lifts and nine trails, best for beginners and families, but some sections are advanced. When the weather is bad, many roads are closed, meaning access is limited.

Food

In Unhais da Serra parish, 23 kilometers (14.3 mi) west of Covilhã, behind the church, rustic stone-built restaurant ★ **Lenda Viriato** (Rua Santo Aleixo 16, tel. 275 971 252, www.lendaviriato.pt, 7:30pm-10pm Tues-Fri, 12:30pm-4pm and 7:30pm-10pm Sat-Sun, €25) is renowned for traditional mountain food. Staff dress in old-fashioned costumes to enhance the authenticity, and the local meats and wines are outstanding.

Mountain-top eatery **Varanda da Estrela** (Penhas da Saúde parish, tel. 963 447 873, www.varandadaestrela.pt, 8am-2am daily, €20), 13 kilometers (8.1 mi) west of Covilhã, with a cozy atmosphere and incredible views, specializes in pure and simple Portuguese cuisine, with good-size portions and lots of flavor. Try the *arroz de zimbro* (juniper berry rice), a regional specialty.

For a real treat, head to the Luna Hotel, on the N339 road 13 kilometers (8.1 mi) west of Covilhã, for the **Luna Hotel Medieval Restaurant** (Penhas da Saúde parish, tel. 275 310 300, www.lunahoteis.com, lunch and dinner daily, €14-20), where a medieval feast awaits. With Old World decor and a tavern-style interior, the restaurant puts on a banquet-like buffet of regional food.

Accommodations

Chalets always sound cozy, and modern alpine ★ **Luna Mountain Chalets** (Penhas da Saúde parish, tel. 275 310 300, www.lunahoteis.com, €140), 13 kilometers (8.1 mi) west of Covilhã on the N339 road, are no exception. At 1,500 meters (4,921 feet) elevation within Serra da Estrela Natural Park, this warm wooden cluster of chalets is 11 kilometers (6.8 mi) east of the ski resort, with two on-site restaurants (one with a medieval theme) as well as a rustic bar, a romantic log fire-warmed lounge, and a spa.

★ **Pousada Serra da Estrela Historic Hotel** (Penhas da Saúde parish, tel. 210 407 660, www.pousadas.pt, €142) has a fascinating history. With distinct turrets and an imposing facade, it was converted from an old sanatorium, built here for the pure mountain air believed to cure chronic ailments. On a hilltop on the edge of the Serra da Estrela mountain range, it is 14 kilometers (8.7 mi) from the Serra da Estrela Ski Resort and 13 kilometers (8.1 mi) west of Covilhã on the N339 road. Most of the rooms have balconies with mountain views. The hotel has a spa and indoor and outdoor pools.

Getting There and Around

The easiest way to get to Serra da Estrela is through its main gateway, Covilhã, or from Seia. Covilhã and Seia are on either side of the mountain range, 50 kilometers (31 mi) apart, connected by the hilly N339 road, one of the main roads that traverse the Serra da Estrela. The ski resort is 24 kilometers (15 mi) west of Covilhã, a 30-minute drive along the N339 road; from Seia, it is 26 kilometers (16 mi) east, a 35-minute drive along the N339.

The best way to explore the park is by car, as public transport is limited at best. If you don't have a car, opt for an organized excursion. Ask your hotel or the local tourist office for more information on excursion companies. A taxi from Covilhã to the Serra da Estrela Ski Resort costs around €20, and from Seia €25-30.

ROAD CONDITIONS

The road network across Serra da Estrela, unlike that of some mountain ranges, is decent and well signed. Even the highest summit, Torre, is accessible by car. The park is open 24 hours daily, except when heavy snowfall closes roads. The **Roads of Portugal (Estradas de Portugal)** website (www.estradas.pt) provides current information on all road incidents and closures in the country. Road information is also on the Serra da Estrela Ski Resort's website (www.skiserradaestrela.com/ acessos). Police are posted at closed roads to inform drivers of detours.

COVILHÃ

Covilhã (KOH-veel-yah) is an impressive place thanks to its mountainous backdrop and views to Spain. On the eastern fringe of the Serra da Estrela, the city is at 450-800 meters (1,476-2,625 feet) elevation and thus cooler than most places in the country. Covilhã's setting is reflected in the rustic architecture of its handsome historic city center, whose centerpiece, the icy blue and white azulejo-clad Santa Maria Church, dates from the mid-16th century.

1: Serra da Estrela Natural Park; **2:** the Senhora da Boa Estrela in the Covão do Boi; **3:** the Poço do Inferno waterfall; **4:** the town of Manteigas

Prior to the 1980s, Covilhã was an industrious hub of wool and textile factories, a manufacturing center that was unique in its mountain location. This means that parts of Covilhã have a lackluster, factory-town feel. As the wool industry waned, the University of Beira Interior took over factory spaces. Nowadays the "Town of Wool and Snow" is a gateway to the Serra da Estrela and a hot spot of mountain culture.

Sights

WOOL MUSEUM
(Museu de Lanifícios)

In 1982, the University of Beira Interior converted two former textile factories into one large museum dedicated to the region's industrial heritage. The interactive **Wool Museum** (Rua Marquês d'Ávila e Bolama, tel. 275 319 724, www.museu.ubi.pt, 9:30am-6pm Tues-Sun, free) eventually became the hub of the Wool Route, which promotes Covilhã, Manteigas, and Seia, among others, where wool was once key in the local economy. The museum explores the region's wool industrialization from the 18th century through its demise in the 20th century and houses a collection of machinery and equipment; products such as wool, string, fabric, and garments; and even ancient documents relating to local wool production.

CHEESE MUSEUM
(Museu do Queijo)

This little gem of a museum in an unassuming old stone building is worth seeking out, especially by cheese lovers. In the village of Peraboa, 14 kilometers (8.7 mi) east of Covilhã, a 20-minute drive, the **Cheese Museum** (Rua dos Casainhos, Peraboa, tel. 275 471 172, www.roteiromuseus.ccdrc.pt, 10:30am-12:30pm and 2:30pm-5:30pm Wed and Fri-Mon, 10:30am-12:30pm Tues and Thurs, €5) explains Serra da Estrela's famous cheeses and cheese-making processes, from the type of sheep that graze on the green mountain pastures to cheese-making traditions. A tasting of three cheeses rounds off a tour of the museum, and a shop next door sells the cheeses at reasonable prices. A taxi from Covilhã to Peraboa costs €13-16 one-way.

Food

A cozy spot with wicker furniture, **Restaurante Pitadas** (Rua 30 de Junho 96A, tel. 275 333 158, www.restaurantepitadas.negocio.site, noon-3pm and 7pm-10pm Wed-Mon, noon-3pm Tues, €15) is the place to go to sample hearty Covilhã cuisine. Try the house specialty, stuffed *saloio* bread: fresh-baked bread filled with melted local cheese and ham.

In a lovely old stone town house, the gorgeously moody, sophisticated-looking little **Restaurante Bar Paço 100 Pressa** (Travessa Sao Tiago 3, tel. 925 868 877, www.paco100pressa.com, 9am-11pm Mon-Fri, 11am-11pm Sat-Sun, €20) has wrought-iron furniture, bringing a twist of trendy to the rustic mountain scene. Specialties include local wines, octopus, and codfish dishes, and bed-and-breakfast lodgings are available.

Famous for its matured local beef, the magnificent **Quinta da Amoreira** (Rua da Amoreiras 4, Canhoso, tel. 919 884 684, www.quintadaamoreira.pt, 12:30pm-4pm and 7:30pm-10:30pm daily, €15) restaurant is in a typical Serra da Estrela farmhouse, in the parish of Canhoso, a five-minute drive north of Covilhã city center. The rustic-chic interior fits with the accomplished menu of mountain specialties, many of which are cooked in a traditional wood oven.

Entertainment and Events

The **Woolfest** (tel. 916 109 764, www.facebook.com/woolfest) urban art festival couples Covilhã's illustrious past as a wool and textile producer with its aspirations to become a key hub of urban arts. The festival's featured artists take snippets of the city's history and transform them into vibrant modern street art, the main centerpieces being huge, striking murals, flooding the city with color and thought-provoking imagery. The festival features regular events such as exhibitions and concerts throughout the year.

Accommodations

In the heart of Covilhã's historic center, housed in a fancy old building in the main square opposite the city hall, affordable **Hotel Solneve** (Rua Visconde de Coriscada 126, tel. 275 323 001, www.solneve.pt, €48) is 1 kilometer (0.6 mi) northwest of the train station. Inside are modest, spacious rooms, an indoor pool, and a good restaurant.

One of Covilhã's swankier hotels, the polished, four-star **Tryp Covilhã Dona Maria Hotel** (Alameda Pêro da Covilhã, tel. 275 310 000, www.trypdonamaria.com, €110) is 2 kilometers (1.2 mi) southwest of the train station on the southern fringes of town, a 25-minute walk from the city center. A spa offers a heated indoor pool, a fitness room, a sauna, and massages.

Housed in a traditional stone building dating from the 1940s, the cozy, typical mountain inn **Residencial Panorama** (Rua dos Bombeiros Voluntários 7-9, tel. 275 323 952, www.residencialpanorama.pt, €40) is a great place to stay for authentic local atmosphere. In the city's historic center, the inn boasts wonderful views over the mountains, and all of the 25 comfortable, elegantly furnished rooms have private baths.

Getting There and Around

Behind the Serra da Estrela range in a remote part of the country, Covilhã is surprisingly easy to reach. It's 212 kilometers (131 mi) southeast of Porto, a 2.5-hour drive on the A25 motorway, and 278 kilometers (175 mi) northeast of Lisbon, a 2.75-hour drive on the A1 and A23 motorways. From Coimbra,

Covilhã is a 191-kilometer (118-mi), two-hour drive along the IC8 and A23 roads.

Rede Expressos (tel. 707 223 344, www.rede-expressos.pt) direct buses run daily between Covilhã and major neighboring cities as well as from Lisbon and Porto. From Porto, Rede Expressos buses (1.5 hours, 6am-9pm daily, €11.90) run hourly, not always on the hour. From Lisbon (2.5 hours, 6am-10:30pm daily, €13.30), buses depart almost hourly, sometimes twice an hour.

The easiest way to get from Coimbra to Covilhã by bus is **Rodonorte** (tel. 259 340 710, www.rodonorte.pt) buses from Coimbra to Viseu (1 hour, 4 buses daily, €8.30); change in Viseu for Covilhã. From Viseu there are six daily buses (2 hours, €12.20) operated by Rede Expressos and **Citi Express** (tel. 707 223 344, www.citiexpress.eu).

Traveling by train to Covilhã from Lisbon or Porto is not recommended, as the journey is extremely long, at seven hours, and requires at least two transfers.

The main bus terminal and train station in Covilhã are on a plain below the city, 1.5 kilometers (0.9 mi) east of the center, at the foot of a steep hill. The main bus station is about 450 meters (0.3 mi), a five-minute walk, south from the train station. Covilhã's local bus service, **Covibus** (tel. 275 098 097, www.covibus.com, €1.30), runs every 35 minutes between the main bus station (Central de Camionagem) and the city center. There are also **taxi** ranks outside the main bus station and the train station (Covilhã Taxis, tel. 275 323 653); a trip into the city center costs €5-7.

Porto and the North

With verdant landscapes, medieval villages, and majestic mountains, Northern Portugal is invigorating. Its defining feature is the Douro River, flowing westward through the rugged landscape to the Atlantic at its biggest city, Porto, an emerging getaway destination. Flanked by terraced vineyards, the river reflects the emerald tranquility of the Douro Valley, which yields the grapes that have made the region's port wines famous. They owe their distinctive flavor to the valley's schist terrain. Charming wine estates and guesthouses are popping up along the river.

The north is home to around one-third of the country's people, and this region is where the Portuguese trace their origins as a people and a nation. It is said that Portugal was founded here in the 12th century in

Highlights

Look for ★ to find recommended sights, activities, dining, and lodging.

★ **São Bento Railway Station:** Clad with tile plaques depicting Portugal's history, this early-20th-century transit hub is a work of art (page 260).

★ **Clérigos Tower:** Climb to the top of this spindly landmark for fantastic views of Porto (page 262).

★ **Porto's Riverfront:** Walk the Ribeira, a hive of activity with distinctive bustling cafés and haphazardly arranged houses (page 265).

★ **São João Festival:** Porto residents pay homage to the city's patron saint by being bashed over the head with leeks during one of the biggest street parties in the country (page 270).

★ **Douro River Cruises:** Drink in the breath-taking Douro Valley on a gentle cruise up the river (page 271).

★ **Port Wine Cellars:** Visit the famous Vila Nova de Gaia winemakers to learn more about the history of the tipple, and round it off with a tasting or two (page 277).

★ **Douro Historic Steam Train:** This blast from the past trundles between Peso da Régua and Tua, taking in memorable scenery (page 285).

★ **Côa Valley Archaeological Park:** This mysterious open-air gallery of Paleolithic art runs for 17 kilometers (10.5 mi) along the Portuguese-Spanish border (page 289).

★ **Peneda-Gerês National Park:** Portugal's only national park teems with wildlife as well as Roman roads and medieval castles (page 302).

★ **Guimarães's Historic Center:** The town's well-preserved center is an architectural jewelry box with gems that span centuries (page 304).

Porto and the North

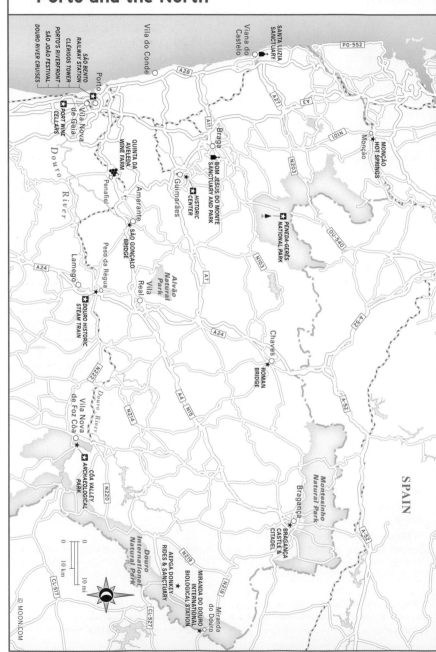

DOURO RIVER CRUISES
SÃO JOÃO FESTIVAL
PORTO'S RIVERFRONT
CLÉRIGOS TOWER
PORTO'S RAILWAY STATION
SÃO BENTO
PORT WINE CELLARS

Vila do Conde

Porto
Vila Nova de Gaia

Douro River

Penafiel

QUINTA DA AVELEDA WINE FARM

Amarante

SÃO GONÇALO BRIDGE

Lamego
Peso da Régua

DOURO HISTORIC STEAM TRAIN

A24

A24

N222

Douro River

Vila Nova de Foz Côa

CÔA VALLEY ARCHEOLOGICAL PARK

N220

0   0
10 km
10 mi

© MOON.COM

CL-517

Douro International Natural Park

CL-527

Viana do Castelo

SANTA LUZIA SANCTUARY

A28

A11

Braga

BOM JESUS DO MONTE SANCTUARY AND PARK

Guimarães

HISTORIC CENTER

Alvão Natural Park

Vila Real

A7

N103

A27

E1

A3T

N203

101N

Monção

MONÇÃO HOT SPRINGS

PO-552

PENEDA-GERÊS NATIONAL PARK

OU-540

V-52

Chaves

ROMAN BRIDGE

A4   N15

N214

N219

AFEGA DONKEY RIDES & SANCTUARY

N218

MIRANDA DO DOURO INTERNATIONAL BIOLOGICAL STATION

Miranda do Douro

Montesinho Natural Park

Bragança

BRAGANÇA CASTLE & CITADEL

A-52

A52

SPAIN

the picturesque province of Minho, home to ancient cities and the northern coastline, the Costa Verde, with authentic fishing towns and lively seaside resorts.

PLANNING YOUR TIME

Most visitors start their travels in the region at Porto or use it as a base. Porto's Sá Carneiro International Airport has direct flights from the United States, South America, and Africa as well as European routes. It receives hourly flights from Lisbon and frequent low-cost flights from Faro in the Algarve, both of which take 50 minutes. Regular train and bus services connect Porto to other main cities. It's possible to visit Porto as a two-day trip, but the city and the Douro Valley merit more time than that.

Plan on at least a week to explore Porto, the Douro Valley, and the surrounding region. Douro River cruises are a popular way to see the highlights. Cruises range from one day to weeklong all-inclusive trips with excursions and entertainment.

To explore the Douro Valley by car, stay in one of the main towns, Lamego or Peso da Régua, halfway along the Douro River. North of the valley, halfway between coastal Porto and the Spanish border, the city of Vila Real is another good base for exploring the mountainous Trás-os-Montes region. Highlights such as Vila Nova de Foz Côa and Bragança are around a 1.25-hour drive. Braga is a good base for exploring picturesque Minho, in the northwestern corner of the country, including the Peneda-Gerês National Park.

Porto

Portugal's second-largest city after Lisbon, Porto (POR-too) is flanked by vine-laden valleys and historic towns, a hard-working metropolis with newfound fame as a getaway among budget travelers. Significant investment is being made to upgrade Porto's infrastructure and image, but the city's unrefined charm is part of its allure. Shabby in parts, sophisticated in others, as a whole Porto is down-to-earth, relaxed, and endearingly genuine. Northerners are known for using expletives liberally in conversation, but despite the city's lack of airs and graces, beneath the gritty exterior is the warmth of the *tripeiros* (tripe eaters), a nickname derived from the local tradition of tripe-based dishes.

Known among Portuguese as the Cidade Invicta (Unvanquished City), Porto is one of Europe's oldest nuclei, dating to the 1st century BC, when it was known as Portus Cale. Evidence of ancient Celtic and Proto-Celtic citadels has been uncovered here, and

under Roman occupation Porto flourished as a commercial port, trading with Lisbon and nearby Braga. In the 14th and 15th centuries, Porto played an important role in shipbuilding and became a seat of power for Portuguese royalty. Porto has historic ties to Great Britain through the marriage of John I (João I) of Portugal to Philippa of Lancaster, celebrated in Porto in 1387, which cemented the oldest alliance in the world that is still in force today. Locals say the weather is more akin to Britain than the balmy Mediterranean—it is noticeably cooler than the rest of the country and one of the wettest major cities in Europe, although occasional gray drizzle does little to dampen the local vivacity.

Porto's best-known export, port wine, is reason enough to visit the city. Despite its centuries of history and culture, Porto feels young, and like port wine, it only seems to get better with age.

Previous: Porto and the Douro River; tiles at Porto's Bolhão Market; a riverside building in Porto.

One Day in Porto

Porto's major sights can be seen in a day, but spending a night or two allows you to soak up the city's energy, which picks up pace as dusk falls. While not without steep streets and climbs, Porto is an easy city to navigate on foot or by public transport.

Spend the day exploring landmark sights in the historic city center. Start off at the top, at the bustling **Bolhão Market,** followed by a walk down the main Rua de Santa Catarina shopping street to the famous belle epoque **Majestic Café** for a mid-morning coffee and a cake. Then visit the **São Bento Railway Station** with its famous tiled walls. Plan on about 20 minutes of walking time from the market to the railway station, allowing additional time for each stop. Take a 10-minute walk over to the magical **Livraria Lello** bookshop, a must for Harry Potter fans. Then head downhill toward the river, passing the baroque **Clérigos Tower,** the monumental **Porto Cathedral,** the opulent **Stock Exchange Palace,** and the **São Francisco Church,** with its museum and catacombs.

Stop for lunch at one of Porto's many eateries serving the local specialty, the *francesinha,* a monster signature sandwich comprising a stack of meats, smothered in melted cheese and a beer sauce, often topped with a fried egg. It's not for the fainthearted, but all that walking will build up an appetite. After lunch, set aside an hour for a short **river cruise** along the Douro, where you can gaze at its splendid bridges. Then walk across the iconic Dom Luís I bridge to **Vila Nova de Gaia** to see the famous port wine cellars.

Round the day off with a sunset stroll along Porto's charismatic **riverfront** area, with its mishmash of colorful houses. It's particularly lovely at night, a romantic spot for a cozy dinner. After dinner, head to **Rua Galeria de Paris** and **Rua Cândido dos Reis,** which run parallel and offer myriad bars for a Porto-style nightcap.

SIGHTS

Porto is packed with buildings and monuments that range from historically important to quirky and cool. Most can be found in the medieval downtown area, a UNESCO World Heritage Site that includes the famous Ribeira riverside area and the main Avenida dos Aliados. Public transport, such as the historic electrified trams, buses, and a modern subway system, provide easy access to the fringes.

Northwest of the city's historic hub is the stunning contemporary music hall, the Casa da Música. Farther west is the beautiful Serralves Foundation and Museum, a major player on the international modern art scene. Farther west on the coast is the cliff-top Castelo do Queijo (Castle of Cheese) fortress, which juts into the Atlantic. One long, straight avenue, Avenida da Boavista, runs between the Casa da Música and the Castelo do Queijo, connecting the heart of Porto to the coast.

Visitors looking for great photos have plenty of opportunities. For breathtaking vistas of the city's jumbled rooftops, climb the Clérigos bell tower. Take the Guindais Funicular from the foot of the Dom Luís I Bridge to Batalha Square. Or if you're brave, climb the Arrábida Bridge for the ultimate view.

Bolhão Market
(Mercado do Bolhão)

Inside an impressive neoclassical building, the loud and lively **Bolhão Market** (Rua Fernandes Tomás, tel. 223 326 024, 7am-5pm Mon-Fri, 7am-1pm Sat) is packed with stalls run by farmers, butchers, and fisherfolk, roaring with trade each morning. Browsing shoppers can indulge in a real taste of Porto in the cafés on the ground floor.

★ São Bento Railway Station
(Estação de São Bento)

More than just a railway station, **São Bento** (Praça Almeida Garrett, tel. 707 210 220, www.cp.pt) is a piece of history, built in the early 20th century with a U-shaped atrium

Porto

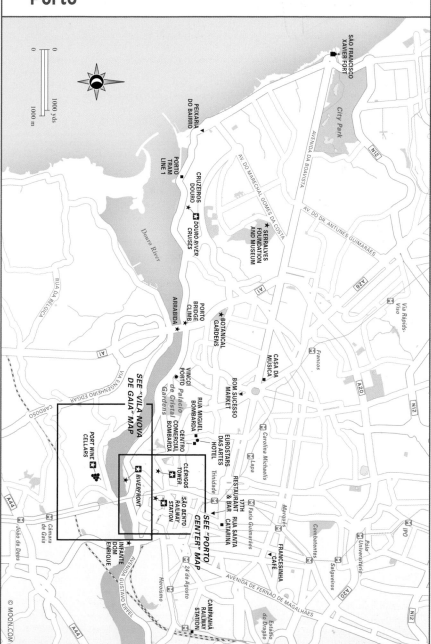

SÃO FRANCISCO XAVIER FORT

City Park

AVENIDA DA BOAVISTA

N12

AV. DO DR. ANTUNES GUIMARÃES

A28

PEIXARIA DO BAIRRO

AV. DO MARECHAL GOMES DA COSTA

PORTO TRAM LINE 1

CRUZEIROS DOURO

DOURO RIVER CRUISES

SERRALVES FOUNDATION AND MUSEUM

Douro River

A1

RUA DA BELGICA

A1

ARRABIDA

PORTO BRIDGE CLIMB

BOTANICAL GARDENS

CASA DA MÚSICA

Via Rapids- Viso

Francos

A20

N12

Carolina Michaelis

VIA EM VICENCHEIRO EDGAR

CARDOSO

SEE "VILA NOVA DE GAIA" MAP

VINCCI PORTO

de Cristal Gardens

PORTO Palacio

RUA MIGUEL BOMBARDA

CENTRO COMERCIAL BOMBARDA

BOM SUCESSO MARKET

EUROSTARS DAS ARTES HOTEL

Lapa

Trinidade

PORT WINE CELLARS

RIVERFRONT

CLÉRIGOS TOWER

SÃO BENTO RAILWAY STATION

17TH RESTAURANT & BAR

RUA SANTA CATARINA

Faria Guimarães

Marques

Combatentes

IPO

Pólo Universitário

A20

A44

João de Deus

Câmara de Gaia

INFANTE DOM ENRIQUE

AVENIDA DOM ENRIQUE

SEE "PORTO CENTER" MAP

FRANCESINHA CAFÉ

Salgueiros

Heroísmo

24 de Agosto

AVENIDA DE FERNÃO DE MAGALHÃES

N12

© MOON.COM

A44

CAMPANHÃ RAILWAY STATION

Estádio do Dragão

AVENIDA GUSTAVO EIFFEL

0   1000 yds

0   1000 m

Porto's Best Restaurants

★ **Ernesto:** Enjoy regional specialties at this warm family favorite (page 267).

★ **Petisqueira Volataria:** Share a platter of creative tapas to savor the local gastronomy (page 267).

★ **Peixaria do Bairro:** There's an ocean's worth of tasty fish on the menu (page 267).

★ **Ostras & Coisas:** Do as the restaurant's name suggests and go for the oysters (page 267).

★ **17 Restaurant & Bar:** The gastronomic experience is matched by bird's-eye views (page 268).

★ **Majestic Café:** This distinctive belle epoque tearoom is the perfect place for a refined afternoon snack or a light meal (page 268).

clad floor-to-ceiling in 20,000 hand-painted tiles that depict scenes from Portugal's history, such as the Conquest of Ceuta in 1415. The oversize blue-and-white friezes were painted by preeminent artist Jorge Colaço. Used by commuters, this open-air museum buzzes with the energy of everyday life.

★ Clérigos Tower
(Torre dos Clérigos)

The baroque landmark **Clérigos Tower** (Rua de São Filipe de Nery, tel. 220 145 489, www. torredosclerigos.pt, 9am-7pm daily, tower €5, church free) and its church were designed by Italian architect Nicolau Nasoni. Upon completion in 1763, it was the tallest structure in Portugal at 75 meters (246 feet), dominating the city's skyline. Climb the 225 steps of the inner spiral for 360-degree views of the city.

Porto Cathedral
(Sé do Porto)

Built on the highest spot in the city, **Porto Cathedral** (Terreiro da Sé, tel. 222 059 028, free) was constructed in the 12th-13th centuries in a Romanesque style, but was successively enlarged and extended, adding new styles to its mixed heritage. The fortified church has a simple whitewashed extension.

Inside are a gold-leaf altar, cloisters, and a Gothic funerary chapel. The sweeping views of Porto's jumble of rusty roofs rambling down toward the Ribeira make it worth a visit.

The church is open 9am-7pm Monday-Saturday, 9am-12:30pm and 2:30pm-7pm Sunday and holy days April-October, 9am-6pm Monday-Saturday, 9am-12:30pm and 2:30pm-7pm Sunday and holy days November-March. The cloisters are open 9am-6:30pm Monday-Saturday, 2:30pm-6:30pm Sunday and holy days April-October, 9am-5:30pm Monday-Saturday, 2:30pm-5:30pm Sunday and holy days November-March.

Stock Exchange Palace
(Palácio da Bolsa)

The magnificent **Stock Exchange Palace** (Rua de Ferreira Borges, tel. 223 399 000, www.palaciodabolsa.com, 9am-6:30pm daily Apr-Oct, 9am-12:30pm and 2pm-5:30pm daily Nov-Mar, €9) is an imposing neoclassical building that once housed Porto's stock exchange. Built between 1842 and 1910 on the ruins of an old convent, it was meant to

1: the Stock Exchange Palace; 2: Clérigos Tower; 3: Bolhão Market; 4: traditional wooden *rabelo* boats on the Douro River

Porto Center

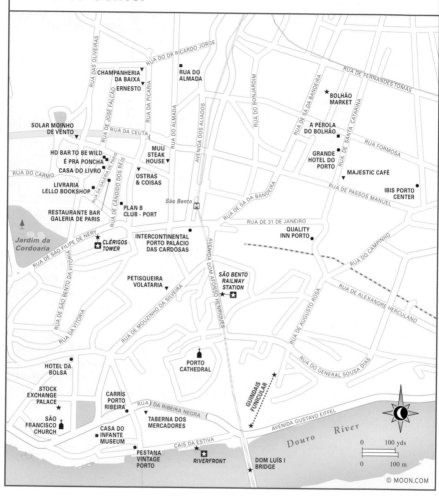

impress visiting businesspeople, dignitaries, and heads of state with the city's economic vitality. Beyond its stately facade are the even more impressive glass-domed Hall of Nations and the opulent Arabian Hall, with Moorish nuances and floor-to-ceiling gilding. Guided tours run regularly throughout the day.

São Francisco Church
(Igreja de São Francisco)

Facing the riverside, the 14th-century

São Francisco Church (Rua do Infante Dom Henrique, tel. 222 062 100, www.ordemsaofrancisco.pt, 9am-5:30pm daily Nov-Feb, 9am-7pm daily Mar-June and Oct, 9am-8pm July-Sept, €6) is a church of surprises. Its austere gray Gothic exterior hides a mind-blowing baroque interior. Construction began in 1245 but was disrupted by a huge fire that destroyed the old cloister. Over 300 kilograms (660 pounds) of gold dust clad the lavish new interior, radiating a golden glow and

Porto's Best Accommodations

★ **Vincci Porto:** In a renovated fish market, this stylish retreat has avant-garde decor and a terrace with river views (page 273).

★ **Eurostars das Artes Hotel:** Surrounded by galleries and museums, it's an art-lover's dream (page 273).

★ **Pestana Vintage Porto:** In pastel 16th-century buildings on the romantic riverfront, this five-star hotel is like a warm hug (page 273).

★ **Intercontinental Porto Palácio das Cardosas:** Feel like royalty in this opulent converted 18th-century palace (page 273).

★ **Grand Hotel do Porto:** This stately retreat is on the doorstep of the city's best monuments, theaters, and shops (page 273).

dripping with cherubs and animals, vaulted pillars and marble columns, and soaring ogival (pointed) arches. Distinguished citizens are interred in the catacombs.

★ Riverfront
(Ribeira)

You can't say you've been to Porto until you've walked the riverside, the lively Cais da Ribeira (Riverside Docks), which date to medieval times. Disorderly narrow pastel buildings of mismatched heights, sizes, and colors seem to teeter into each other. Their fronts are adorned with tiny wrought-iron balconies and freshly washed laundry as well as more modern trappings like satellite dishes. Traditional flat-bottomed *rabelo* bob up and down on the Douro, adding to the romantic ambience. Used for centuries to ferry barrels of port and other cargo on the river, the boats are today mostly decorative. At ground level, a series of busy restaurants and tourist shops run along the river. Have refreshments or a relaxed meal in one of the myriad establishments, most enjoyable during and after sunset.

Guindais Funicular

The **Guindais Funicular** (Av. Gustavo Eiffel 314, tel. 808 205 060, www.metrodoporto. pt, 8am-10pm Mon-Fri May-Oct, 8am-8pm Mon-Fri Nov-Apr, €2.50) runs between Batalha Square, near Porto Cathedral, and the riverside far below. Inaugurated in 1891, the original line has been successively upgraded for a short and swift journey, and the views over the river are phenomenal.

Six Bridges

Known as the "City of Bridges," Porto has six bridges that unite it with Vila Nova de Gaia across the Douro River. Counting inward from the *foz* (river mouth), the bridges are the Arrábida, Dom Luís I, Infante Dom Henrique, Dona Maria Pia, São João, and Freixo.

The two most famous, standing side-by-side, are named after a husband and wife, King Luís I and Maria Pia of Savoy. The **Dona Maria Pia Bridge** was designed by Gustave Eiffel, famous for the tower that bears his name in Paris. The 142-meter (466-foot) double-deck **Dom Luís I Bridge,** built between 1881 and 1886 and designed by Eiffel's disciple, Théophile Seyrig, has become emblematic of the city. While both master and disciple initially worked on the design, their relationship soured and Seyrig completed the project alone. Keen eyes will still note the resemblance in their intricate metal frameworks. Both of the Dom Luís I Bridge's decks are open to pedestrians, with the upper platform 60 meters (197 feet) above water level; the views are worth the vertigo. Cars use the lower deck, while the Metro crosses on the upper deck.

The other four Douro bridges are built from concrete with more streamlined silhouettes. Inaugurated in 2003, the modern **Dom Infante Henrique Bridge** was the last of the six to be built and boasts the longest single-platform arch in the world.

Palácio de Cristal Gardens
(Jardim do Palácio de Cristal)

Occupying 8 hectares (20 acres) in the center of Porto, the **Palácio de Cristal Gardens** (Rua de D. Manuel II, tel. 225 320 080, www. cm-porto.pt, 8am-9pm daily Apr-Sept, 8am-7pm daily Oct-Mar, free) are a jigsaw of manicured lawns, colorful flowerbeds, and beautiful water features, divided by walkways and inhabited by peacocks. The garden's terraces are called the "verandas of the Douro" for their views of the river and its bridges. Although the gardens were designed by a German landscape architect for a 19th-century exhibition, little remains of the original crystal palace, replaced in the 1950s by a modern pavilion, now slightly run-down. The gardens are about 30 minutes' walk west of the city center.

Serralves Foundation and Museum
(Fundação e Museu de Serralves)

The **Serralves Foundation and Museum** (Rua D. João de Castro 210, tel. 226 156 500, www.serralves.pt, 10am-7pm Mon-Fri, 10am-8pm Sat-Sun Apr-Sept, 10am-6pm Mon-Fri, 10am-7pm Sat-Sun Oct-Mar, €10, park only €5, free 10am-1pm 1st Sun each month) seeks to promote contemporary art, thought, architecture, and landscape. The **Serralves Museum (Museu Serralves)** features contemporary art in a building designed by distinguished architect Álvaro Siza. **Casa de Serralves,** a pink art deco villa built in the 1930s, offers insight into the architectural

and decorative details of the era; it also serves as the foundation's office. Both are surrounded by 18-hectare (45-acre) **Parque de Serralves,** with its sprawling gardens, woodland, and a farm. Serralves is 5.5 kilometers (3.4 mi) west of the city center.

São Francisco Xavier Fort
(Forte de São Francisco Xavier)

Perched on a cliff jutting out between the Douro and Matosinhos river mouths, the **São Francisco Xavier Fort** offers lovely ocean views. Built in the 17th century to protect the city from attack, it's commonly called the Castelo do Queijo, "Castle of Cheese," because it was built on a rotund granite rock that looks like a cheese round. The trapezoidal walls are built from chunky granite blocks that give the small fortress a robust look, enforced by a dry moat and drawbridge, turreted watchtowers, and cannons. Inside is an exhibition of military paraphernalia. Two of Porto's most popular beaches are on either side of the fort. It's located approximately 8 kilometers (5 mi) west of the city center at the end of Porto's main Avenida da Boavista, which links the city center to the coast.

Nearby is the idyllic **City Park (Parque da Cidade)** (Praça de Gonçalves Zarco, tel. 226 181 067, www.monumentos.gov.pt, 1pm-6pm Tues-Sun late Mar-early Oct, 1pm-5pm Tues-Sun late Oct-early Mar, €0.50), nice for a relaxing walk.

FOOD

Offal is a staple in Porto's regional cuisine, as are rice and beans. Classic dishes include chicken *cabidela* (chicken stewed with giblets, blood, and rice) and Porto-style tripe, with various meats, sausages, and beans in a rich seasoned sauce that led to the nickname *tripeiros* (tripe eaters) for the locals. No trip to Porto would be complete without trying a meaty *francesinha* sandwich—covered in thick sauce—at least once, but it's so filling you may never eat again. Rounding off a meal with a glass of port is virtually compulsory.

Regional

Cozy **Solar do Moinho de Vento** (Rua de Sá de Noronha 81, tel. 222 051 158, www. solarmoinhodevento.com, noon-3pm and 7pm-10pm Mon-Sat, noon-3pm Sun, €13) serves hearty portions of quality home-cooked local dishes, such as octopus with tomato rice, Porto-style tripe, and chicken *cabidela* rice.

★ **Ernesto** (Rua da Picaria 85, tel. 222 002 600, www.oernesto.pt, 8:30am-3pm Mon, 8:30am-3pm and 6:30pm-midnight Tues-Sat, €15) is a local family favorite. Dishes include Alheira sausage with fries and *marmota frita,* fish fried whole with its tail in its mouth. Inside, the exposed stone walls and gleaming crockery provide a fresh, warm feel.

Busy **Taberna dos Mercadores** (Rua dos Mercadores 36, tel. 222 010 510, 12:30pm-3:30pm and 7pm-11pm Tues-Sun, €20) is hidden behind heavy wooden doors on a narrow street near the riverside. The rustic and romantic interior is complemented by tasty traditional dishes and local specialties.

Francesinhas

It's generally agreed that the *francesinha* sandwich, stuffed with meats and covered in rich tomato and beer sauce, should be washed down with an ice-cold beer. However, the best *francesinha* in town remains hotly debated. A definite contender is found on the edge of downtown at the **Francesinha Café** (Rua da Alegria 946, tel. 912 653 883, 12:30pm-3pm and 7pm-11pm Mon-Sat, €8), which looks unremarkable, but the huge picture of the namesake sandwich in the window gives its secret away.

Tapas

If you can get a table at ★ **Petisqueira Volataria** (Rua Afonso Martins Alho 109, tel. 223 256 593 or 913 885 252, 11am-10pm Wed-Mon, €10), a narrow tapas place near the São Bento train station, thank your lucky stars. Sharing platters are creatively conjured with local delicacies in sample-size portions, a great way to savor the scope of local gastronomy in one sitting. Also on the menu is the ubiquitous *francesinha.*

If you like finger food and fancy drinks, you'll love sophisticated **Champanheria da Baixa** (Largo Mompilher 1-2, tel. 220 962 809, www.champanheriadabaixa.com, noon-12:30am Mon-Thurs, noon-2:30am Fri-Sat, €8) downtown. The decor is bohemian and atmospheric, and the tapas are delicious. Wash it all down with cocktails, sangria, or champagne.

Gastro Markets

Tantalize your taste buds at **Bom Sucesso Market** (Praça Bom Sucesso 74-90, tel. 226 056 610, www.mercadobomsucesso.pt, 10am-11pm daily), browsing the 40-plus stalls serving myriad gastronomic treats, from traditional savory snacks to handmade chocolates and Portuguese wines and gin.

Opened in 1917, **A Pérola do Bolhão** (Rua Formosa 279, tel. 222 004 009, 9:30am-7:30pm Mon-Fri, 9am-1pm Sat) is a gorgeous grocery and delicatessen with an eye-catching art nouveau facade. Inside, it's stuffed to the rafters with colorful traditional products, including sweets, nuts, dried fruits, cookies, local cheeses, cured meats, and, of course, port wines. It's near the busy Bolhão Market.

Seafood

Delicious fresh fish is always the dish of the day at the ★ **Peixaria do Bairro** (Rua da Senhora da Luz 142, tel. 919 400 408, noon-11pm Tues-Sat, 8am-11pm Sun, €20), whose name translates as "neighborhood fishmonger," a lively little joint a short walk from the beachfront and Castelo do Queijo. Fish from meaty tuna steaks and juicy sea bass to salmon appear on the menu.

Trendy ★ **Ostras & Coisas** (Rua da Fábrica 73, tel. 918 854 709, www.ostrasecoisas.pt, 6pm-11pm Tues-Thurs, noon-midnight Fri-Sat, noon-4pm and 7pm-11pm Sun, €25) serves fresh seafood straight from the docks. Indulge in Mozambican-style shrimp, clams Bulhão Pato-style, or, as the

Local Specialty: *Francesinhas*

the *francesinha* sandwich

It might sound elegant, but there's nothing petite about the *francesinha*, which translates literally as "little Frenchie." Porto's ubiquitous monster sandwich with a cult following is less a snack and more a gut-busting meal. This mound of a sandwich comprises cured and cold meats, such as *chouriço* sausage and bacon, piled on top of slices of roast pork or beefsteak and fresh sausage, wedged between two slices of bread, covered first in melted cheese, then in a hot beer and tomato sauce, and served with fries and a fried egg on top for good measure. Variations include hamburger patties instead of pork or beef, and a spicier sauce made with *piripiri*.

The *francesinha* is believed to derive from its daintier French cousin, the *croque monsieur* (a fried or grilled sandwich with cheese and ham). A local tale pinpoints its origins to a man named Daniel David Silva, who, after living in France and Belgium, brought the *croque monsieur* back to Porto and transformed it into today's *francesinha*. He called the sandwich "little Frenchie" because, he said, French women were the sauciest he had ever met. Silva made his name serving his creation at the A Regaleira restaurant, established in 1953 in Porto, arguably the home of the *francesinha* (it closed in 2018). Legend has it that the recipe for Silva's sauce was a fiercely guarded secret until an employee passed it on to a rival restaurant across the river in Vila Nova de Gaia.

Another theory about the *francesinha*'s origins dates to the early-19th-century Peninsular War, when Napoleonic troops would eat all sorts of meats and heaps of cheese in bread as sustenance. The sauce was Porto's contribution later on. Whatever its origins, this classic Porto dish is now served at eateries throughout the country.

restaurant's name suggests, go for the oysters. Mixed platters for two are a specialty.

Mediterranean

On the top two floors of Porto's Dom Henrique Hotel, the elegant ★ **17 Restaurant & Bar** (Hotel Dom Henrique, Rua Guedes de Azevedo 179, tel. 223 401 617, www.decimosetimo.pt, noon-2am daily, €20)

offers a fabulous gastronomic experience alongside bird's-eye city views. The menu fuses traditional Portuguese dishes with Mediterranean flavors.

Tearoom

Opened in the 1920s to cater to high society, glittering ★ **Majestic Café** (Rua de Santa Catarina 112, tel. 222 003 887, www.

cafemajestic.com, 9:30am-11:30pm Mon-Sat) has carried its splendor across the decades. Decked out with distinctive belle epoque furnishings, including elegant chandeliers and oversize mirrors, Majestic is on a busy shopping street, perfect for a refined afternoon tea, a snack, or a light meal. Fame comes at a price; be prepared to pay more (a regular coffee is around €5) and wait in a queue to get in, unless you reserve ahead online.

Steakhouse
Swanky **MUU Steakhouse** (Rua do Almada 149A, tel. 914 784 032, www.muusteakhouse.com, 7pm-midnight Wed-Mon, €30) is a mecca for meat lovers. Both the meat and the patrons are treated royally.

NIGHTLIFE AND ENTERTAINMENT
Nightlife
Porto's colorful nightlife is consistent with the city's work-hard, play-hard ethos. The city's most popular bar street is **Rua Galeria de Paris.** If one full street of bars does not suffice, try the parallel **Rua Cândido dos Reis.** Both are in the historic area, just off the Clérigos Tower. Nightlife doesn't get into full swing until after 11pm, although most bars are open earlier. Be prepared to stay up late.

Once upon a time, **Casa do Livro** (Rua Galeria de Paris 85, tel. 912 958 284, 9pm-3am Tues-Thurs, 9pm-4am Fri-Sat) was a bookshop, but now it's a nightlife classic, with diverse music from DJs and live musicians. Its walls are decorated with the bookshelves of its former life, while gleaming polished wood and low-lit lamps provide a warm glow, contributing to the intimate drawing-room atmosphere.

Housed in a former warehouse, **Galeria de Paris** (Rua Galeria de Paris 56, tel. 222 016 218, 9am-2am Mon-Wed, 9am-3am Thurs-Sat) is packed with vintage paraphernalia: old toys, musical instruments, and even bicycles hanging from the ceilings. Enjoy eclectic live acts, from jazz bands to trapeze artists and belly dancers. Candlelit tables add a touch of romance. Galeria also serves breakfast, lunch, and dinner.

Decorated with Harley Davidson memorabilia, laid-back biker bar **HD Bar to Be Wild** (Rua Galeria de Paris 113, tel. 933 347 079, www.h-dporto.com, 6pm-2am Sun-Thurs, 6pm-4am Fri-Sat) has an American jukebox and an energizing road-trip soundtrack. **É Pra Poncha Bar** (Rua Galeria de Paris, tel. 291

Majestic Café

773 571, 5pm-4am Mon-Sat), a narrow cave-like space with a wavy multicolored ceiling, is the setting for great punch-based cocktails like Madeira Poncha.

One of Porto's best dance venues, boho-chic **Plano B** (Rua de Cândido dos Reis 30, tel. 222 012 500, www.planobporto.com, 10pm-6am Thurs-Sat) offers an interesting mash-up of music and art, design and culture, and a regular lineup of DJs and live acts playing everything from R&B and techno to hip-hop.

Performing Arts

Northwest of the city's historic hub, the **Casa da Música** (Av. da Boavista 604-610, tel. 220 120 220, www.casadamusica.com, 9:30am-7pm Mon-Sat, 9:30am-6pm Sun) stages year-round concerts and events ranging from classical to contemporary. Its striking modern building, designed by Dutch architect Rem Koolhaas, has a fluid, sleek look, in stark contrast with the rugged city surrounding it. Private tours of the building (€10) are available in English twice daily.

Maus Hábitos ("Bad Habits," Rua de Passos Manuel, tel. 222 087 268, noon-2am Tues-Thurs, noon-4am Fri-Sat, noon-4pm Sun) is an art gallery, theater, concert hall, and restaurant.

Festivals and Events

★ SÃO JOÃO FESTIVAL

This 600-year-old festival, honoring Saint John, patron saint of lovers, is one of the most raucous street parties in Portugal. Every year, thousands flock to Porto for the 24-hour-long *festa* that starts on the eve of June 23.

Thousands of floating lanterns are launched, creating a dazzling picture in the night sky overhead. One of São João's quirky traditions is to bash and be bashed over the head with leeks, which in recent times have given way to squeaky plastic hammers. Even though this bashing can get quite vigorous, it's all good-natured, a wish for luck in love and fertility. Almost every home in the city is draped in cheery bunting. Stalls selling beer, sangria, grilled sardines, and kale soups spring up all over the city.

The party bubbles feverishly until a gigantic fireworks display over the Douro River at midnight, when the city's main squares and avenues become dance floors as live bands and DJs play until dawn. The day after is a much-needed local holiday.

SHOPPING

Porto's shopping scene isn't as posh as Lisbon's or as trinket-laden as the Algarve's. **Rua de Santa Catarina** is lined with a mixture of international chain stores such as Mango, Zara, and H&M along with boutiques that give it a cool cosmopolitan feel. Major brands can also be found along the **Avenida da Boavista,** while **Rua do Almada** is a hub of alternative shops. Peruse the chic window displays along **Rua Miguel Bombarda,** interspersed with arty galleries. There are two large shopping centers, **CBB Centro Comercial Bombarda** (Rua Miguel Bombarda 285, tel. 934 337 703, noon-8pm Mon-Sat) and **Via Catarina shopping center** (Rua de Santa Catarina 312-350, tel. 222 075 609, www.viacatarina. pt, 9am-10pm daily).

On the second and last Saturday of every month, Rua Cândido dos Reis hosts **Mercadinho dos Clérigos** (10am-8pm), a marketplace bursting with crafts, antiques, music, and even gastronomy. Vintage clothing, antiques, and decorative objects are found alongside the local produce market **Mercado Porto Belo** (Praça Carlos Alberto), held noon-7pm every Saturday.

A frontrunner for the title of most beautiful bookshop in the world, **Livraria Lello** (Rua das Carmelitas 144, tel. 222 002 037, www. livrarialello.pt, 10am-7:30pm Mon-Fri, 10am-7pm Sat-Sun, entry €4, deductible from any purchase) inspired author J. K. Rowling, who lived in Porto in the 1990s: The shop served as the basis for the Flourish & Blotts bookshop in her Harry Potter novels. Close to the Clérigos Tower, the bookshop dates to 1881 and is housed in a 1906 building with a magical feel, with a ghostly-white facade of neo-Gothic and

Best Souvenirs: Port Wine

Deep, rich, fortified port wine has become an ambassador not only for its namesake Porto but for Portugal as a whole. Only port wine produced in northern Portugal may be labeled port, and authentic port is produced exclusively in vineyards in the Douro Region, demarcated in 1756, with mostly native grape varieties. The exceptional terrain and climate give the port grape unique characteristics. It is transported down river and aged in barrels stored in cellars such as those in Vila Nova de Gaia.

Generally enjoyed as a dessert drink, the best-known port is typically ruby red in color. **Ruby** is the younger, lighter, fruitier variety, while **tawny** varieties are older and nuttier. Exceptional **vintage** port is produced only from the finest harvests and aged for long periods in oak casks. **Rosé** and **white** varieties have recently given the wine a trendy makeover as an ingredient of white port and tonic, a popular summer cocktail.

Some of Portugal's oldest port companies were founded by British mercantile families in the 17th and 18th centuries and are still run by their descendants. The history of port-making can be explored at the cellars in **Vila Nova de Gaia,** such as Sandeman, Graham's, Taylor's, and Croft, where guided tours in various languages, including English, end with a tasting.

The essence of the north in a bottle, port wine is the quintessential Porto souvenir. Bottles are available in sizes from miniature 50-milliliter bottles, often sold in packs containing 4-6 different types of port for around €14, to the standard 750-milliliter bottles. Port should be stored on its side to keep the cork moist.

art nouveau architecture, a sweeping crimson central staircase, and a spectacular stained-glass skylight. Outside, the front is embellished with two figurines, painted by José Bielman, symbolizing science and art, while inside, the stained-glass ceiling bears detailing of Lello's motto, *Vecus in Labore* (Dignity in Work). Besides books in several languages, the shop has a café upstairs that sells coffee, port wine, and cigars. The small shop is so popular, especially with Harry Potter fans, that long queues form at the door. It's worth braving the crowds. Tickets can be bought online or from a shop just around the corner.

RECREATION

Many of Porto's most popular activities center on its magnificent bridges and the Douro River. A top excursion is a cruise on the river, with options ranging from hour-long trips to multiday cruises that explore the Douro Valley.

Six Bridges Cruises

Each of Porto's bridges has a story to tell, and a cruise along the Douro is the best way to

hear them. Enjoy a relaxing hour sailing on modernized *rabelo* boats, learning the history of the Unvanquished City. Cruises depart regularly from the quaysides in both Porto and Vila Nova de Gaia, in all weather, and last around 50 minutes.

Douro Acima (tel. 222 006 418, www.douroacima.pt) operates cruises (every 30 minutes, 10am-6pm daily Apr-Oct, hourly 10am-4pm daily Nov-Mar, from €15) from Porto's Ribeira dock (in front of Cubo Square). **Douro Azul** (Rua de Miragaia 103, tel. 223 402 500, www.douroazul.com, from €12) operates daylong hop-on hop-off cruises that allow passengers to board either at the Gaia pier or at the Ribeira dock in Porto. Audio guides are available in 16 languages.

★ Douro River Cruises

Explore the scenery of the fertile Douro Valley with a peaceful cruise along the river, sailing past the terraced vineyards that cascade down its schist banks. **Cruzeiros Douro** (tel. 226 191 090, www.cruzeiros-douro.pt) leads daylong trips, including excursions between Porto and the whitewashed city of Peso da

Régua (10 hours, €60), an important junction for port wine transport. The cruise includes lunch on board the boat. Other charming cruise destinations include the towns of Pinhão, Pocinho, and Barca D'Alva. Weeklong all-inclusive luxury cruises packed with excursions and entertainment are also available.

Bridge Climb

Ascend to the tip of the landmark **Arrábida Bridge**'s sweeping inner arch on this unusual guided tour. The experienced guides of **Porto Bridge Climb** (Rua do Ouro 680, tel. 929 207 117, www.portobridgeclimb.com, 30 minutes, from 2:30pm daily, €13) lead you up the 262 steps to the peak of the sleek cement arch—once the longest single cement arch in the world—which in 2016 reopened for the first time since the 1960s. One of Porto's best-kept secrets, these tours run for groups of five or more people. Full-moon and sunrise climbs are also available. The minimum age is 12, and reservations are required.

ACCOMMODATIONS

Porto offers a wide range of options, from basic to high-end historic conversions, all with central locations.

In the historic center, four-star ★ **Vincci Porto** (Alameda de Basílio Teles 29, tel. 220 439 620, www.vincciporto.com, from €171 d) is a stylish retreat in a renovation of the landmark Bolsa do Pescado fish market. It has a big, bright, and airy glass-brick atrium, distinctive avant-garde decor, and a terrace with views over the Douro.

Just 100 meters (328 feet) from the Palácio da Bolsa, three-star **Hotel da Bolsa** (Rua de Ferreira Borges 101, tel. 222 026 768, www.hoteldabolsa.com, €100) offers 34 comfortable rooms, a good buffet breakfast, an on-site bar, and a great location.

A few streets back from the riverfront in the old Ribeira, 4-star **Carris Porto Ribeira** (Rua do Infante D. Henrique 1, tel. 220 965

786, www.hotelcarrisportoribeira.com-porto. info, €120) occupies a refurbished 17th-century building with chic rooms, a cozy tapas bar, and views across the Douro.

In central Porto, ★ **Eurostars das Artes Hotel** (Rua do Rosário 160-165, tel. 222 071 250, www.eurostarshotels.com.pt, €138) is an art lover's dream. In an area surrounded by galleries and museums, it features boutique accommodations, with rotating exhibitions inside the hotel, and a peaceful outdoor deck. It straddles two structures: a palatial older building with a sky-blue tiled facade and its contemporary sibling.

On the romantic riverfront, five-star ★ **Pestana Vintage Porto** (Praça da Ribeira 1, tel. 223 402 300, www.pestana. com, €227) was created from a set of 18 pastel-color historic buildings emblematic of Porto's cityscape. Some date to the 16th century. Inside it's plush and comfortable, and the on-site restaurant, Rib Beef & Wine, is excellent.

Feel like royalty at the opulent five-star ★ **Intercontinental Porto Palácio das Cardosas** (Praça da Liberdade 25, tel. 220 035 600, www.ihg.com, €256), a beautiful 18th-century palace reborn. Think grand chandeliers, polished marble floors, and Romanesque columns. It's just a short stroll from the São Bento train station and the Livraria Lello bookshop.

Just around the corner from the iconic Majestic Café on busy Rua de Santa Catarina, ★ **Grand Hotel do Porto** (Rua de Santa Catarina 197, tel. 222 076 690, www. grandehotelporto.com, €171) is a stately 94-room retreat on the doorstep of the city's best monuments theaters, and shops. Established in 1880, it embodies the grandeur of bygone eras, brought up to date with modern comforts.

Located in the city center, **Ibis Porto Center** (Rua da Alegria 29, tel. 223 400 700, www.accorhotels.com, €82) offers clean, comfortable, no-frills accommodations. Rooms are basic and small, but convenience and affordability compensate.

1: São João Festival; 2: the stairs inside the Livraria Lello bookshop; 3: bottles of port wine; 4: bridges over the Douro River

Located next to Rua de Santa Catarina, modern **Quality Inn Porto** (Praca da Batalha, 127, tel. 223 392 300, www.choicehotels.com, €111) is comfortable and clean—and just a short walk from main attractions.

INFORMATION AND SERVICES

European emergency number: tel. 112
PSP Metropolitan Police: Largo 1º de Dezembro 3, tel. 222 092 000, www.psp.pt
PSP Tourist Police: Rua Clube dos Fenianos 19, tel. 222 081 833
Santo António General State Hospital (Centro Hospitalar do Porto): Largo do Professor Abel Salazar, tel. 222 077 500, www.chporto.pt
Santa Maria Private Hospital: Rua de Camões 906, tel. 225 082 000, www.hsmporto.pt
INEM medical emergency ambulance: tel. 112
24-hour pharmacy: Farmácia Antunes, Rua do Bonjardim 485, tel. 222 007 936
Porto Tourism Office Downtown: Calçada Dom Pedro Pitões 15, tel. 300 501 920, www.visitporto.travel, 9am-7pm daily
Porto Tourism Office Center: Rua Clube dos Fenianos 25, tel. 300 501 920, www.visitporto.travel, 9am-7pm daily
Post office (main downtown branch): Allied Post Office, Praça General Humberto Delgado, www.ctt.pt, 8am-9pm Mon-Fri, 9am-6pm Sat

TRANSPORTATION
Getting There

Porto is northern Portugal's major transport hub and easily accessed from all over the country. Bus and train connections run from all major towns and cities and are cost-efficient; road routes are straightforward and in good condition; and short domestic flights link the north to Lisbon, the Algarve, and the islands. From the Algarve, it can often be cheaper to fly to Porto than to go by car or public transport.

AIR
Porto's **Sá Carneiro International Airport** (OPO, tel. 229 432 400, www.aeroportoporto.pt) has daily flights from dozens of European destinations year-round as well as regular direct flights from Canada, the United States, South America, and Africa. Daily domestic flights operate between Porto and the Algarve, Madeira, and the Azores; there's also an hourly express flight between Porto and Lisbon. Irish low-cost Ryanair is the only airline operating direct flights between Faro (Algarve) and Porto. Fares start from €30 one-way and take around an hour. From Lisbon, the hourly express flight operated by regional TAP Express takes one hour and costs around €70 one-way; in addition, Ryanair offers less frequent flights.

There are at least two daily flights between Porto and Funchal on Madeira, operated by Transavia, Easyjet, and TAP. The flight takes two hours, and return tickets often cost under €100 round-trip. To the Azores (Ponta Delgada), there are at least three daily flights, generally noon-5pm, operated by Azores Airlines, TAP, and Ryanair, which take around 2.5 hours. Round-trip flights can be found for under €100, depending on the season.

Porto's airport is in Maia, 10 kilometers (6.2 mi) north of Porto city center and served by the **Metro** (tel. 225 081 000 or 808 205 060, www.metrodoporto.pt) light rail and tram system to central Porto, every 20 minutes Monday-Friday, less frequently on weekends and holidays. It takes around 30 minutes to reach Porto by Metro, and a one-way ticket costs €2.55. Tickets can be purchased from ticket machines or the airport's tourist information office.

There is little to no public transport midnight-6am (a late-night bus service runs hourly between the airport and the downtown Aliados area), so a taxi might be necessary. Both conventional taxis and Uber operate in Porto. From the airport, the trip costs €20-30.

TRAIN

The **Celta high-speed train** (www.cp.pt) operates twice daily between Porto's Campanhã station (Rua Pinheiro de Campanhã, Largo da Estação) and Vigo, Spain. Other international trains from London, Paris, and Madrid require a change in Lisbon.

CP (tel. 707 210 220, www.cp.pt) operates high-speed Alfa-Pendular trains and the slightly slower Intercidades (Intercity) train service that connect Lisbon and the Algarve to Porto's Campanhã station (Rua Pinheiro de Campanhã, Largo da Estação) at various times daily. Campanhã station is 5 kilometers (3.1 mi) east of Porto's downtown.

From Faro in the Algarve, the Alfa-Pendular takes 6 hours to Porto and costs €52.30 one-way for second class, €71.80 for first class. The Intercity train takes around 6.5 hours and costs €42.40 one-way for second class, €58.60 for first class. There are five daily Alfa Pendular and Intercity trains between Faro and Porto-Campanhã.

From Lisbon, the Alfa-Pendular runs almost hourly from the Santa Apolónia and Oriente stations and takes three hours to reach Porto. Tickets cost €31.60 one-way for second class, €43.70 first class.

Tickets can be booked online (www.cp.pt) and can be cheaper bought in advance.

From Campanhã, local Urbano trains connect to Porto's many suburbs. There is a free train between Campanhã on the outskirts and the historic city-center São Bento station (Praça Almeida Garrett), which handles mostly urban and regional trains due to its limited capacity. There is also a Metro station at Campanhã. Metro tickets can be bought from machines or from the station's main ticket office.

BUS

Porto doesn't have a main bus terminal but instead has several hubs for long-distance buses located around the city. The main intercity bus company between Lisbon and Porto is **Rede Expressos** (tel. 707 223 344, www. rede-expressos.pt, 8am-9pm daily), whose buses are modern, comfortable, and air-conditioned. Bus travel is cheaper than rail but takes longer. From Lisbon, buses sometimes stop at Fátima. Dozens of buses depart daily between Lisbon and Porto, and the journey takes 3.5-4 hours. Rede Expressos buses depart Lisbon's Oriente station (in the Park of Nations area) every few hours, and hourly from the Sete Rios hub (near the zoo). Buses arrive at Porto's main bus hub, Campo 24 Agosto (Campo 24 de Agosto 125), about 1 kilometer (0.6 mi) east of Porto's Bolhão Market; it has a nearby Metro station with the same name. Journeys take approximately 3.5 hours, and one-way tickets cost €19.

There are services from the Algarve's main stations (Faro, Albufeira, Lagoa) to Porto with Rede Expressos, but most will require a change at Lisbon's Sete Rios station. Non-change services are longer with many stops on the way. The journey takes 7-12 hours, depending on the number of stops, and one-way tickets start from €30.

International buses from Vigo in Spain tend to stop in Porto's downtown Aliados area, although some go to the Campo 24 Agosto terminal if passengers are connecting southward. Other international bus lines, such as AVIC, Internorte, Eurolines, and Resende, stop at the Casa da Música, while many urban buses drop off and depart from the São João Hospital (Alameda Professor Hernâni Monteiro), north of the city center, and the Camelias Park (Rua de Augusto Rosa), in downtown Porto, just before Batalha Square.

Eurolines (tel. 225 189 303, www. eurolines.com) operates regular international bus services between Porto and London, Madrid, and Paris. **Internorte** (tel. 226 052 420, www.internorte.pt) is another option. Most international buses use Porto's Casa da Música or Campo 24 Agosto stops.

Northern Portugal's biggest regional bus company, **Rodonorte** (tel. 222 005 637, www. rodonorte.pt), connects Porto with all major towns and cities through the northern region, as well as Lisbon.

CAR

Porto is 300 kilometers (185 mi) north of Lisbon and 600 kilometers (370 mi) north of the Algarve. Porto is served by an excellent network of motorways, although it can be costly as tolls apply to most A-roads. The main A1 motorway links Lisbon to Porto in under three hours. From the Algarve, the main A2 motorway links the south to Lisbon and connects to the A1. From Porto, the main motorway is the A3, which connects to the Minho and Trás-os-Montes regions. Braga and Viana do Castelo are also linked to Porto by the A28 or A29 motorways.

Getting Around

Getting around Porto is easy, with several efficient forms of transport. The historic center is compact and easy to cover on foot, but the cobbled streets can be very steep. Bus, car, or Metro travel is required to see sights on the outskirts, such as the Fort of São Francisco Xavier and the Serralves Foundation.

An all-encompassing multimodal travel card called the **Andante Tour Card** (tel. 225 071 000, www.stcp.pt) covers bus, tram, Metro, and urban train lines between Espinho, Valongo, and Travagem stations. It is great for getting around stress-free and comes in two versions: Andante Tour 1 (€7) is valid for 24 hours after first validation. Andante Tour 3 (€15) is valid for 72 hours. Andante tickets can be purchased from all bus and Metro ticket machines and booths, or from tourism offices. The rechargeable card costs €0.60.

If passengers are caught traveling without a valid ticket on any form of Porto's public transport, the fines can be hefty, ranging from €120 to €350. Be sure to hold on to your ticket to avoid getting fined, whichever type of public transit you're using.

BUS

Porto's transport company **STCP** (tel. 225 071 000, www.stcp.pt) runs wide-ranging bus service, including less extensive late-night bus service in the main Aliados and airport areas

12:30am-5:30am. Late-night service operates hourly. Most single-journey tickets cost €1.95.

TRAM

Porto has gorgeous vintage 1920s wooden **trams** (tel. 225 071 000, www.stcp.pt) that rattle around the city. The three main tram lines are line 1, along the riverfront area between Porto's historic area and the Passeio Alegre garden; line 18, between Massarelos and Carmos; and line 22, a circular route through downtown. Tickets (€3) can be bought on board. A 48-hour tram pass (adults €10, children €5) can also be bought on board as well as from most hotels and tour agencies. Trams come along every 20 minutes 8am-8pm daily.

METRO

Porto's **Metro** (tel. 225 081 000, www.metrodoporto.pt) is a light-rail network that runs above ground in the suburbs and underground in the city center. Trains run every 10-20 minutes 6am-midnight daily. Scenic Line D runs across the Douro River over a bridge to Gaia. Metro also runs to the airport in Maia. Trips are priced by zones and cost just over €1 for a two-zone single trip; cards are rechargeable.

TAXI

Local taxi companies include **Taxis Invicta** (Rua de Cunha Júnior 41B, tel. 225 076 400, www.taxisinvicta.com), **Taxis Porto** (Rua da Constituição 823, tel. 220 997 336, www.taxisporto.pt), and **Taxis do Porto** (Av. da Boavista 1002, tel. 223 206 059, www.taxisporto.pt). Getting a taxi is easy; taxi ranks can be found at the airport and bus and train stations, outside shopping centers and hospitals, near the riverside, and along the main Avenida dos Aliados. Taxis can also be hailed in the street.

CAR

There's no need for a car in Porto, but a car can be useful to explore neighboring cities and the northern region. Hire companies operating at the airport include **Sixt** (Francisco Sá

Vila Nova de Gaia

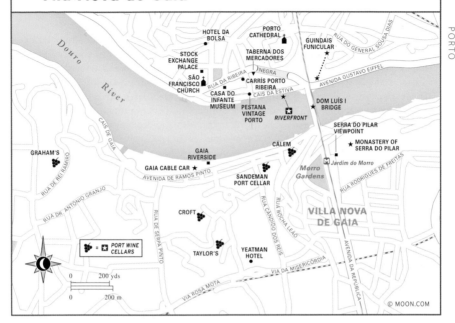

Carneiro Airport, tel. 255 788 199, www.sixt. pt) and **Europcar** (Av. do Aeroporto 322, tel. 229 482 452, www.europcar.pt). Most rental car depots are near the airport. A free shuttle takes passengers from arrivals to the depot, and most are open 7am-midnight daily. There are also a few car-hire offices (9am-1pm and 3pm-6:30pm Mon-Fri, 10am-noon Sat) at Porto's Campanhã train station.

The traffic in Porto can be dense and chaotic, especially on weekdays at rush hours, and parking can be hard to find, particularly in summer and during major festivities such as São João.

VILA NOVA DE GAIA

On the opposite side of the Douro River, Vila Nova de Gaia (VEE-lah NOH-vah d' GUY-yah), known simply as Gaia, is the salt to Porto's pepper. While less colorful than Porto, Gaia has the same ancient feel of old white houses with tangerine roofs clinging to narrow, sloping streets.

Gaia's quaint historic riverside dates to the 17th century, when Portuguese and English merchants started producing and shipping port wine. For hundreds of years, boats ferried large barrels of port from deep in the Douro Valley downriver to Gaia. Wine lodges still line the picturesque riverfront, along with pretty cafés and a splash of touristy shops. Wooden *rabelo* boats still bob on the water, and cable cars glide overhead. Gaia is rife with viewpoints offering stunning vistas of Porto, especially at dusk, when a soft glow falls over the Unvanquished City as its lights begin to twinkle.

Sights
★ PORT WINE CELLARS
(Caves de Vinho do Porto)

Every year, over one million people visit Gaia's port wine cellars to see Portugal's most famous export. Rows of wine casks are stored in these cool, damp caverns. Around one-third of the wine cellars and lodges are open to the public. Each has different brands and history.

Many of Gaia's port lodges were founded in the 17th century by British merchant families, who turned to their Portuguese allies after Britain placed sanctions on French wines. To better suit the British palate, a splash of brandy was added to Portuguese wine, creating the sweet fortified port we know today. Some of the best-known makes include Sandeman, Cálem, Ferreira, Croft, Offley, Graham's, Kopke, Churchill's, and Quinta do Noval, all of which can be tried and tested at Gaia's "caves."

Most of the lodges offer guided tours in multiple languages, including English, taking visitors through the history of port-making, culminating in a tasting session. Basic tours of the cellars (€10-12, including tasting) last about an hour. Lodges are open 10am-6pm daily year-round.

Founded in 1859, **Cálem** (Av. Diogo Leite 344, tel. 916 113 451, https://tour.calem. pt, from €12) is one of Portugal's signature ports, and its cellars, located on the Gaia riverfront, are among the most visited. Tour options include tastings, food, and even fado performances.

Globally renowned since 1790, **Sandeman** (Largo Miguel Bombarda 3, tel. 223 740 534, www.sandeman.com, from €12) has vast cellars in a magnificent 200-year-old building on the Gaia riverfront. Tours include a 1970 vintage tour, with tasting of five select wines, and a 100-Year-Old Tawnies tour.

Founded in 1588, **Croft** (Rua Barão Forrester 412, tel. 220 109 825, www.croftport. com, from €10) is another distinguished name and the oldest port producer that is still active. A visit to Croft's cellars offers a classic in-depth experience into the production of port, with a guided tour and tasting of three ports at the end.

Producing port since 1692, **Taylor's** (Rua do Choupelo 250, tel. 223 742 800, www. taylor.pt, €12) is among Portugal's oldest port houses. Its extensive audio-guided tours provide a wealth of information in 11 languages. Founded in 1820, family-run **Graham's** (Rua do Agro 141, tel. 223 776 484, www.grahams-port.com, €15) has a magnificent 1890 lodge high on a ridge with excellent views. Visits to Graham's lodge—still a working cellar—are by advance reservation only.

Porto Walkers (tel. 918 291 519, www. portowalkers.pt, from €20) takes groups on half-day walking tours that include a trio of different lodges. Knowledgeable guides teach you about the origins of port, and even how to sample the drink properly.

Cálem port cellar

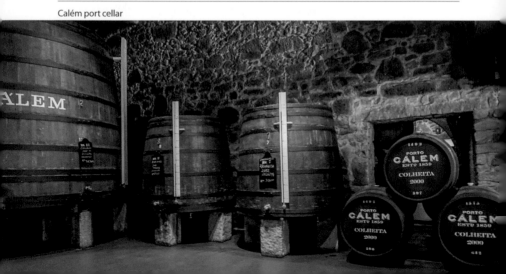

GAIA CABLE CAR
(Teleférico de Gaia)

Have your camera at the ready as you soar in these modern, eco-friendly cable cars over the Douro, the rusty red roofs of the port cellars, and the maze of narrow lanes far below. The **Gaia Cable Car** (Rua Rocha Leão 236, tel. 223 741 440, www.gaiacablecar.com, 10am-8pm daily Apr 26-Sept 24, 10am-6pm daily Oct 25-Mar 23, 10am-7pm daily Mar 24-Apr 25 and Sept 25-Oct 24, adults €6 one-way, €9 round-trip, children 5-12 half price) makes a five-minute journey from the Cais de Gaia Market up to the Morro Gardens, near the top end of the Dom Luís I Bridge.

MORRO GARDENS
(Jardim do Morro)

Carpeting the hilltop at the Gaia end of the Dom Luís I Bridge's upper platform, the **Morro Gardens** (Av. da República, tel. 223 752 862) are an oasis of green in a city of tawny red. The palm tree-shaded park, with its trim lawns, colorful flower beds, and children's play area, is an idyllic spot to enjoy a picnic or watch the sun set.

From Porto, you can reach the gardens by Metro (Jardim do Morro, Yellow Line) or a 3-kilometer (1.9-mi) walk over the Dom Luís I bridge's upper deck. From Gaia riverside, it's a 25-minute (1.8-km/1.1-mi) walk east. You can get there by cable car.

MONASTERY OF SERRA DO PILAR
(Mosteiro da Serra do Pilar)

Looming over the city, the grandiose **Monastery of Serra do Pilar** (Largo de Aviz, Santa Marinha, tel. 220 142 425, www.culturanorte.pt, 10am-5:30pm Tues-Sun Oct-Mar, 10am-6:30pm Tues-Sun Apr-Sept, monastery €2, church and cloisters €4) is an active military barracks but is open to the public. It has interesting architecture, with an unusual circular whitewashed church and domed cupola. Construction on the building started in 1537. It was later occupied by Wellington's troops circa 1809, when Porto was under Napoleonic control. The monastery grounds feature a splendid **viewpoint (*miradouro*)** (24 hours daily, free)—a vast terrace with the best photo ops this side of the Douro.

Accommodations

On 2.8 hectares (6.9 acres), the ★ **Yeatman Hotel** (Rua do Choupelo, tel. 220 133 100, www.the-yeatman-hotel.com, €475) is distinguished by its excellence and refinement. It boasts an acclaimed two-Michelin-star restaurant, a spa, outdoor and indoor infinity swimming pools, and commanding views.

Getting There

Vila Nova de Gaia is a short walk across the Dom Luís I bridge from Porto's riverside. Take the upper platform for the Monastery of Serra do Pilar and Morro Gardens or the lower deck for the riverside and port cellars. Alternatively, Porto's **Metro** (tel. 225 081 000, www.metrodoporto.pt, €1.20 one-way) light-rail system runs regularly between the two cities; take the D Line to Santo Ovidio from the São Bento station, stopping at Jardim do Morro. This line crosses the Dom Luís I bridge's upper deck. Metro trains run every six minutes 6am-1am weekdays, every 15 minutes weekends.

VILA DO CONDE

A short trip north of Porto, Vila do Conde, on the mouth of the River Ave, boasts a rich salt-tinged heritage, from its beginnings as a salt exporter during Roman times to its role in the Age of Discoveries as a shipbuilding port and maritime powerhouse. A medieval town center, interesting museums, beaches, and restaurants make it a popular side trip from Porto.

Sights
SANTA CLARA CONVENT AND AQUEDUCT
(Convento de Santa Clara e Aqueduto)

The town's skyline is dominated by the 14th-century **Santa Clara Convent** (Av. Figueiredo Faria 18, tel. 252 248 445, grounds open 24 hours daily, free), whose stately whitewashed facade reflects in the waters of the river mouth. The building is mostly closed to the public, except a few days in March to celebrate local occasions. Its grounds have a lovely view over the Ave River. Snaking out from the side of convent is the **Santa Clara Aqueduct,** a 17th-century construction with 999 vertical pillars over 4 kilometers (2.5 mi) linking the convent to the Terroso Spring.

NAUTICAL SIGHTS

A trio of attractions within close proximity honor the city's shipbuilding history. For tickets and information, head to the **Vila do Conde Memory Center (Centro de Memória de Vila do Conde)** (Largo de São Sebastião 9, tel. 252 248 468, www. cm-viladoconde.pt). Admission costs €1.10 (€0.50 for ages 6-24) and includes entrance to all three attractions.

On the riverside, once the shipyards, the **Museum of Shipbuilding (Museu da Construção Naval)** (Rua Cais da Alfândega, tel. 252 248 468, 10am-6pm Tues-Sun, last entry 5:15pm) occupies a former Royal Customs house, established in 1487. Throughout the 18th century, the building was successively enlarged to accommodate the booming maritime trade. Permanent exhibitions elaborate on the city's nautical history.

Nearby, bobbing in the river is a replica of a 16th-century **Portuguese carrack** (Rua Cais da Alfândega, tel. 252 248 468, 10am-6pm Tues-Sun, last entry 5:15pm), designed for long-distance journeys to places such as India. On board the rotund vessel, you can explore the decks and crew quarters and see old-fashioned navigational instruments and cartographic material.

In a contemporary building, the **Boat House (Museu Casa do Barco)** (Rua Cais da Alfândega, tel. 252 248 445, 9am-7pm daily June-Sept, 9am-6pm daily Oct-May) focuses on fishing, displaying a replica of a traditional *gasoleiro* fishing boat, alongside several boat models and historical photographs.

BOBBIN LACE MUSEUM
(Museu das Rendas de Bilros)

Traditional lace-making in Vila do Conde can be traced to the 17th century. The **Museum of Bobbin Lace** (Rua de São Bento 70, tel. 252 248 470, www.geira.pt, 10am-noon and 2pm-6pm Tues-Sun, €1.10) contains exquisite examples of lacework, including magnificent wedding dresses, pillow lace, and bobbin lace. You can also watch as bobbin lace is made by hand, nimble fingers follow time-honored traditional techniques.

Beaches

A golden crescent of sand dotted with rocky outcrops at low tide, **Praia da Senhora da Guia** is the main beach, just north of the river mouth. It's very popular, crowded in summer and on weekends. It's served by a busy bar. Just over the southern side of the Ave River, vast **Praia da Azurara** is bordered by extensive dunes and is close to a tranquil lake. Amenities include rentals of sun beds and umbrellas, water-sports rentals, and a series of summer events and parties.

South of Vila do Conde, busy and family-friendly **Praia da Moreiró** is a long bay of isolated sand, fringed by reedy dunes. A bar serves drinks and food, and outfitters rent gear such as umbrellas and chairs. Moreiró beach is 12 kilometers (7.44 mi) south of Vila do Conde, a 30-minute drive on the N13 road.

Getting There

Vila do Conde is located about 30 minutes' drive (25 km/15.5 mi) north of Porto. The easiest route is the A28 motorway, which has tolls.

An express **Metro** (tel. 225 081 000, www. metrodoporto.pt) train leaves every 20 minutes from Porto's Campanhã and Trindade (closest to central Porto) Metro stations on the Red Line (B Line) and takes around 50 minutes to Vila do Conde. A six-zone or Z6 ticket (€2.80 one-way) is needed. Vila do Conde has two metro stops: Vila do Conde and Santa Clara, closest to the monastery and the river.

PENAFIEL

East of Porto, the town of Penafiel is famed for its green wine and a church straight out of a fairy tale.

Sights

SAMEIRO SANCTUARY
(Santuário de Sameiro)

The stunning white dome dwarfs the rest of the 19th-century **Sanctuary of Our Lady of Piety and Holy Steps (Santuário da Nossa Senhora da Piedade e Santos Passos)** (Av. Zeferino de Oliveira 239, tel. 288 212 619, 7:30am-8pm Mon-Fri, 6:30am-8pm Sun, June-Sept, 7:30am-6pm Mon-Fri, 6:30am-6pm Sun Oct-May, free), more commonly known as the **Sameiro Sanctuary**. Climb the stairs to the church tower to enjoy glorious views or picnic in the tranquil gardens. Often compared to Sacré Coeur in Paris, the church is even more spectacular at night, when its dome and peaked turrets are lit up.

QUINTA DA AVELEDA WINE FARM

Approximately 2 kilometers (1.2 mi) west of Penafiel town center, family-run **Quinta da**

Aveleda (Rua da Aveleda 2, tel. 255 718 242, www.aveledaportugal.pt) is the largest producer of Portugal's green wine, exemplified by its Casal Garcia label. Green wine is not aged, making it young, fresh, and sparkling. The color is actually close to that of regular white wine, although there are red and rosé varieties too. The estate dates to the 17th century and has been in the same family for over 300 years. The ivy-clad manor house is surrounded by beautiful English-style gardens, teeming with peacocks, swans, and goats. Guided tours (1 hour, 10am, 11:30am, 3pm, and 4:30pm daily Mar-Nov, advance reservation required, €7.50) end with a tasting.

Getting There

Penafiel is around 40 kilometers (25 mi) east of Porto, 35 minutes by the most direct route, the A4 motorway. By public transport, **CP** (tel. 707 210 220, www.cp.pt, 45 minutes, €2.65-5.70 one-way) trains on the Caíde-Marco de Canaveses line leave Porto's São Bento station about every half hour; Penafiel is about a dozen stops down the line. From the station, it's a 30-minute walk south to the town center, or a three-minute taxi ride.

The Douro Valley

Curvaceous landscapes unfold as the Douro (DOH-roo) River carves through rolling hills and forested mountains, extending over 200 kilometers (124 mi) from coastal Porto to the border with Spain. The breathtaking scenery around every bend changes with the seasons, from luxuriant greens in spring to gold and copper in autumn. Vine-clad terraces zigzag down hillsides in one of the world's oldest demarcated wine regions.

The river's banks are studded with towns and villages where farming is the way of life and historic ruins pepper the landscape. The renowned Alto Douro wine region is steeped in tradition, packed with restored historic villages and home to standout towns like Peso da Régua and Vila Nova de Foz Côa. Farther east still is the dramatic Côa Valley, with its prehistoric rock art.

TOP EXPERIENCE

EXPLORING THE DOURO VALLEY

The best times to visit the Douro Valley are September, for the harvest, or any time in autumn, when the valley is ablaze with color. Main stops include fairy-tale Amarante, the valley's "capital" Peso da Régua, Lamego and its famous hilltop chapel, and Vila Nova de Foz Côa, home of prehistoric rock art.

The Douro Valley

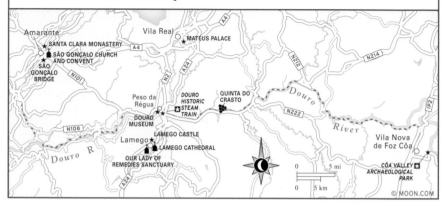

The most scenic ways to explore the Douro Valley are by boat or by train. Both depart regularly from Porto. The valley can be toured by car, but sharp bends and steep inclines mean that the designated driver will miss out on much of the scenery, not to mention wine-tastings.

Cruises

Splashing out on a peaceful cruise upstream is a memorable way to explore the gorgeous scenery of the Douro Valley. Nowadays a series of locks keeps the once-formidable river calm enough to navigate. Cruises departing from Porto, Vila Nova de Gaia, and Peso da Régua range from a day to a week. The day-long cruises from Porto (€60-125) range 10-18 hours and often involve one leg by train, either upriver or downriver. Longer cruises run April-October and frequently include excursions, meals, and entertainment.

Prices range from €200 for a two-day cruise to €2,000 for an eight-day cruise. The number of towns the boat stops at depends on the length of the cruise. Cruise operators include **Cruzeiros Douro** (tel. 226 191 090, www.cruzeiros-douro.pt) and **Douro Azul** (tel. 223 402 500, www.douroazul.com). Douro Azul's fleet of boats includes historic British river barge *Spirit of Chartwell*.

Train

The Douro Valley is one of Europe's best rail journeys. The national rail service, **CP** (tel. 707 210 220, www.cp.pt), operates the **Linha do Douro (Douro Line),** which connects Porto in the west to Pocinho in the east, hugging the river's edge through tunnels and past vineyards and picturesque towns. The full journey takes around 3.5 hours and costs €14 one-way. The Douro Line train runs several times a day, starting from Porto's São Bento or Campanhã stations, and less frequently on weekends and holidays.

The handsome 1925 **Douro Historic Steam Train** (tel. 707 210 220, www.cp.pt) runs from Peso da Régua and Tua on a one-day round-trip (3 hours, varying afternoons late May-Oct, adults €42.50, children 4-12 €19). Tickets can be bought at CP ticket offices or online.

Car

Exploring the Douro Valley by car offers the freedom of impromptu pullovers at scenic viewpoints. Drive any of three port wine routes passing through the Baixa Corgo (below the Corgo River), Cima Corgo (above the Corgo), and Douro Superior (Upper Douro); see www.dourovalley.eu. The N222 road between Régua and Pinhão has been voted one of the best drives in the world and promises incredible scenery at every bend.

Wine Tours

A number of wine-tour operators cover the Douro Valley and offer a range of organized excursions (day tours from €100) to wine- and port-producing farms, with pickups and drop-offs at hotels in Porto and Vila Nova de Gaia. They can even put together tailor-made packages with the estates of your choice, transport, and accommodations. For more on wine farm tours, see **EFun Tours** (tel. 220 945 375, www.efungpstours.com) or **Lab Portugal Tours** (tel. 916 119 101, www.labportugaltours.com).

AMARANTE

Thriving Amarante straddles a gentle bend on the Tâmega River (a tributary of the Douro, on its north bank), the town's storybook buildings reflected in the glassy river. The striking São Gonçalo Bridge unites the town, with the Serra do Marão mountain range rising magnificently in the background. Tall whitewashed buildings with balconies and wrought-iron grills flank the riverbank.

The town is named after a Roman centurion, Amarantus, while the bridge takes its name from the town's patron saint, who made a pilgrimage to Italy and Jerusalem and went on to cure the sick and pair lovers. A grand church and convent named for São Gonçalo, a main highlight of Amarante, are across the river.

Sights

Most of Amarante's sights are along the river and in the town center. The busy local market takes place every Wednesday and Saturday.

SÃO GONÇALO BRIDGE
(Ponte de São Gonçalo)

Over the glassy Tâmega River, the 18th-century São Gonçalo Bridge is simple and sturdy, named after the town's patron saint, a traveling Benedictine monk. Portuguese forces fended off an attack by the French here in 1809. Ornate pylons flank its extremities, its

trio of arches framing the scenery beyond. At one side of the bridge is an image of Our Lady of Pity; at the other is an image of Christ crucified.

SÃO GONÇALO CHURCH AND CONVENT
(Igreja e Convento de São Gonçalo)

Small **São Gonçalo Church** (Praça da República, tel. 255 437 425, 8am-6pm daily, free) has a handsome and complex tiered portico, a 17th-century organ case, and the tomb of São Gonçalo, who died in the mid-1200s. According to local legend, visitors will find love if they touch the saint's statue above the tomb. The church's origins stretch back to the 13th century, although the bulk of its construction took place in the 16th century. A bell tower was added in the 18th century. The interior is notable for its gilded baroque altar, exquisite ceilings, and wood-clad sacristies adorned with sacred art. Behind the church, a lovely, peaceful courtyard boasts fabulous stonework clad with moss.

SANTA CLARA MONASTERY
(Mosteiro de Santa Clara)

Founded in the 13th century, sprawling **Santa Clara Monastery** (Largo de Santa Clara, tel. 255 420 236, 10am-12:30pm and 2pm-6:30pm Mon-Sat, free) was rebuilt and expanded in 1560, accommodating a large community of nuns for the next two centuries. In 1809 it was mostly destroyed in a fire, which tore through the village during the Napoleonic battles with Anglo-Portuguese troops; today just part of the original chapel and a gateway survive. During the late 20th century, archaeological digs uncovered the original outline of the monastery, with four distinct wings, a cloister, and a bell tower. The existing building is currently the municipal library and archive, and the original chapel has been repaired and restored.

Food

Amarante is famous for its **traditional cakes and sweets,** conceived by the nuns at the

Santa Clara convent in honor of São Gonçalo. Pastry recipes emerging from convents were common from the 15th century in Portugal. Conventual sweets *(doçaria conventual)* are based on sugar and egg yolk. Amarante specialties include almond *lérias* and eggy *foguetes*. Most cafés and cake shops in town sell them. Authentic savory dishes include oven-roasted goat *(cabrito serrano assado)* and Maronesa-bred beef.

Just across the bridge from the São Gonçalo Church, **O Moinho Centro Histórico** (Rua 31 de Janeiro 95-165, tel. 255 449 528, 8am-midnight daily, €6) is packed with fresh-baked sweets. This bright, cozy café is a great place for a coffee or a sandwich and a cool drink. There's a lovely garden out back.

Unpretentious **Tasquinha da Ponta** (Rua 31 de Janeiro 193, tel. 255 433 715, 11am-11pm daily, €15) is a rustic tavern serving home-cooked classics such as wild boar and bean stew *(feijoada de javali),* fried squid, and oven-roast lamb. Portions are hearty at very reasonable prices.

Getting There

From Porto, Amarante is a 45-minute drive, 60 kilometers (37 mi) east along the A4 motorway, which has tolls. Trains no longer run to Amarante, but northern bus company **Rodonorte** (tel. 259 340 710, www.rodonorte. pt) runs a direct bus hourly between Porto's Hospital São João stop and Amarante (€7-11). The bus station in Amarante is on the south side of the river, a short 1.5-kilometer (0.9-mi), 20-minute stroll from the town center.

PESO DA RÉGUA

Surrounded by stepped terraces covered in lacy vines, Peso da Régua (PAY-zoo dah RAY-gwah), commonly abbreviated to just Régua, is at the center of wine country, equidistant between Porto and the Spanish border to the east. Régua is the largest town along

the Douro River, so many cruises either stop here midway or finish here. Not as picturesque as nearby towns, hard-working Régua is important in the port wine trade as a crossroads for shipping. The riverfront lacks charm, but wander a few streets back and you'll find a quaint, authentic town.

Sights
★ DOURO HISTORIC STEAM TRAIN

Take a trip back in time on the 1925 vintage **Douro Historic Steam Train** (tel. 707 210 220, www.cp.pt) on a one-day round-trip (3 hours, varying afternoons late May-Oct, adults €42.50, children 4-12 €19) as it crosses rickety bridges, passes through atmospheric countryside and provincial villages, and stops in ornate old stations. Tickets can be bought at CP ticket offices or online. Trips include onboard entertainment courtesy of local folk singers as well as a glass of port wine.

DOURO MUSEUM
(Museu do Douro)

To get a feel for local wine-making culture and history, spend an hour or so at the **Douro Museum** (Rua Marquês de Pombal, tel. 254 310 190, www.museudodouro.pt, 10am-5:30pm daily, €7.50, includes a glass of port), where exhibits take you through the process, from growing and harvesting to fermenting and shipping. Short films, vintage photos, and even a *rabelo* boat add some interest. The building, 18th-century Casa da Companhia Velha, was once the headquarters of the Royal Company of Vine-Growers from the Alto Douro Region, the oldest company in Portugal.

QUINTA DO VALLADO

Established in 1716, **Quinta do Vallado** (Vilarinho dos Freires, tel. 254 323 147, www. quintadovallado.com, 9am-7pm daily) is one of the oldest wine estates in the Douro Valley, producing reds, whites, rosés, and port wines. The historic estate comprises a manor house built in 1733, with a new wing built from locally sourced slate, and handsome grounds.

1: Douro River cruise near Peso da Régua;
2: Santa Clara Monastery and São Gonçalo Bridge in Amarante

Day visitors enjoy tours (1.5 hours, in English 11am and 2:45pm daily, €15), including the working vineyards, state-of-the-art winery, and cellars, that end with a wine-tasting.

The on-site **restaurant** offers lovely views over the Douro River. The refurbished **hotel** (from €210) has 13 rooms, all equipped with modern conveniences like air-conditioning. The estate can organize activities such as walks, bicycle rides, boat trips, fishing, picnics, and wine-tastings. Quinta do Vallado is 3.5 kilometers (2 mi) north of Régua town center. It's about an hour's walk or a five-minute ride in a taxi (€5).

QUINTA DO CRASTO

Quinta do Crasto (Gouvinhas, tel. 254 920 020, www.quintadocrasto.pt, 9am-1pm and 2pm-6pm Mon-Fri, from €20) has roots stretching back to 1615. The vast estate comprises 135 hectares (334 acres), 74 hectares (183 acres) of which are vineyards, and produces 1.4 million bottles of wine and port per year. At its heart is a century-old farmhouse. Visits include guided tours (available in English, must be reserved in advance) with wine-tastings, which can also include lunch or dinner and boat trips on the Douro River. Guests are invited to enjoy a dip in Quinta do Crasto's famous infinity pool, designed by Portuguese architect Eduardo Souto de Moura, or just take in the stunning view over the valley from the poolside. Prebooking a visit is mandatory.

Quinta do Castro is 32 kilometers (20 mi) east of Régua, a 50-minute drive along the N313-2 road. It can also be reached by train from Régua to the Ferrão station (15 minutes, 5 trains daily 9:10am-7:10pm, €2.15). Ferrão train station is a 45-minute walk from Quinta do Castro, but the Quinta can pick up visitors.

Food

Its role as a crossroads makes Peso da Régua's regional gastronomy diverse. Typical dishes include onion soup with red beans, oven-roasted rice with kid and potatoes, and *feijoada á transmontana*, a robust, intense stew.

Hidden at the end of a small dead-end street, unpretentious ★ **Cacho D'Oiro** (Rua Branca Martinho 5050, tel. 254 321 455, www.restaurantecachodoiro.pt, 9:30am-11pm daily, €15) is worth looking for. Its traditional menu is packed with local and regional specialties complemented by a vast selection of Douro wines.

Behind the Douro Museum, gorgeous **Tasca da Quinta** (Rua do Marquês de Pombal 42, ground floor, tel. 918 754 102, 7pm-10pm Tues-Fri, 12:30pm-2:30pm and 7pm-10pm Sat, 12:30pm-2:30pm Sun, €15) serves authentic Portuguese tapas at just six tables. The crepes with homemade jams are a must. Make a reservation; it's hugely popular with both visitors and locals.

Getting There

Peso da Régua is an easy day trip from Porto; take a boat cruise to get there and travel back on the train, which runs along the river. Combined tickets are available via many Douro Valley Cruise organized excursion providers, such as **Cruzeiro Porto** (tel. 925 675 253, www.cruzeiroporto.com, from €60).

From Porto by car, Peso da Régua is 118 kilometers (73 mi) east, a 1.5-hour drive on the A4 motorway, which has tolls. From Amarante, Régua is a 40-minute, 61-kilometer (38-mi) drive southeast on the A24 and A4 motorways, via Vila Real.

CP (tel. 707 210 220, www.cp.pt) runs trains every two hours from Porto's Campanhã station, (2 hours, €7-14). Peso da Régua's train station is a 20-minute walk east of the town center. **Rodonorte** (tel. 259 340 710, www.rodonorte.pt) runs buses hourly from Porto's main terminal to Peso da Régua (2.5 hours, 7am, 8am, noon, and 2:30pm, €9.50), with a transfer in Vila Real. The bus and train stations in Régua are close to each other, on the riverside, about 20 minutes' walk east of the main town center.

LAMEGO

Between two hills, Lamego (lah-MEH-goo) sits primly on the banks of the Balsemão

River, a small tributary of the Douro. It's drenched in baroque and Renaissance influences, seen in the remnants of its 12th-century castle on a hill and in the fabulous Our Lady of Remedies Sanctuary.

Home to Raposeira sparkling wine, Lamego flourished in the 18th century thanks to its production of port, but its origins predate the Roman era. It is also believed that the first Portuguese *cortes*—medieval assemblies of nobles, clergy, and commoners summoned by the king—were held here in 1143.

Lamego has long walks, both in and out of the city. Explore its baroque landmarks, tangle of narrow streets, or the lofty terraces that crisscross the surrounding hills.

Sights

OUR LADY OF REMEDIES SANCTUARY
(Santuário Nossa Senhora dos Remedios)

Perched gracefully on a hill, the **Our Lady of Remedies Sanctuary** (Monte de Santo Estevão, tel. 254 614 392, 7:30am-6pm daily Oct-Apr, 7:30am-8pm daily May-Sept, free) is a triumph of baroque architecture, flanked by a pair of elaborate bell towers and with a grandiose facade. Construction began circa 1750 but was completed two centuries later. Inside, an intricate gilded altar has a statue of Our Lady of Remedies at its heart. But outside is the most impressive part, with a monumental staircase zigzagging down the hillside to the town below. The various levels of the 686-step stone staircase include decorative fountains, tiled friezes, and sculptures as well as benches and picnic spots that take advantage of the views. September 6-8, faithful pilgrims climb the sanctuary's stairs to ask Our Lady for miracles. The three-day festival culminates in a procession on September 8. There is a road to drive up to the sanctuary if you don't want to climb the steps.

LAMEGO CASTLE
(Castelo de Lamego)

Standing high on the hill opposite the Our Lady of Remedies Sanctuary, the 12th-century **Lamego Castle** (Rua do Castelo, tel. 254 612 005, 10am-6pm Tues-Thurs, free) holds a tangle of quaint alleys and narrow streets within its walls. Its square 13th-century tower has thick stone walls. Little of the castle remains, but it's worth the hike for the views from the top.

LAMEGO CATHEDRAL
(Sé de Lamego)

Built in the 12th century by Portugal's first king, Afonso Henriques, **Lamego Cathedral** (Largo da Sé, tel. 254 612 766, 8am-1pm and 3pm-7pm daily, free) is believed to be one of the oldest in Portugal, although little remains of the original building. Its longest-surviving original features are the Romanesque tower's windows with their dexterously carved capitals. The cathedral underwent major renovation in the 16th and 18th centuries, resulting in an unharmonious blend of frilly Gothic, Manueline, and Renaissance styles. A floor-to-ceiling blue-and-white 18th-century tile mural depicting the life of Saint Nicholas adds some interest to the interior, which—thanks to a large skylight—is bright and airy.

SÃO PEDRO DE BALSEMÃO CHAPEL
(Capela de São Pedro de Balsemão)

In the nearby hamlet of Sé, the tiny 7th-century **São Pedro de Balsemão Chapel** (tel. 254 600 230, 10am-1pm and 2pm-6pm Tues-Sun, free) is believed to be the oldest Visigothic chapel in Portugal. Its well-preserved features include Corinthian columns, enigmatic symbols carved into the walls, a painted ceiling, and a statue of the pregnant Virgin Mary. The chapel is 5 kilometers (3 mi) northeast of Lamego, a 14-minute drive along the N226 road, which involves navigating winding rural roads and narrow streets. Walking takes an hour, a scenic downhill stroll from Lamego, but a steep hike coming back. Lamego tourist office (Av. Visconde Guedes Teixeira, tel. 254 099 000, 8am-6pm Mon-Sat) can provide a map.

QUINTA DA PACHECA

Prestigious **Quinta da Pacheca** (Rua do Relógio do Sol 261, tel. 254 331 229, www.quintadapacheca.com, 10am-7pm daily) is one of the Douro's finest wine estates, its origins stretching back to the 1730s. It was also one of the first to bottle wine under its own label. Spread over 140 hectares (346 acres) that step toward the river, it comprises a winery, a posh wine hotel, and quirky cabins in the shape of wine barrels. Eight granite winepresses *(lagares),* constructed in 1916, are still in use today. Guided tours (10:30am-5:30pm daily, €9) include a wine tasting.

Quinta da Pacheca is a 10-kilometer (6.2-mi), 20-minute drive north of Lamego on the N226-1 road. Alternatively, take a **Rodonorte** (tel. 259 340 710, www.rodonorte.pt) bus from Lamego to Peso da Régua (25 minutes, 12:45pm and 6:15pm daily, €5.90), then get a taxi (5 minutes, €6) from Régua to the estate. Quinta da Pacheca is a 50-minute walk south of Régua town center, across the river.

Food

Local specialties include wild rabbit, lamb or goat *chafana* stew, and *bolas de lamego* (buns stuffed with a savory filling like ham or tuna).

Located in the town center, stylish **Restaurante Vindouro** (Rua Macário de Castro, tel. 961 422 784, www.restaurantevindouro.com, noon-10:30pm Mon-Fri, noon-11pm Sat, €20) has a creative menu showcasing contemporary cuisine based on traditional recipes. Reservations are advised.

You'll find down-to-earth regional cooking at family-run **Restaurante Casa Filipe** (Rua Virgílio Correia 58, tel. 254 612 428, 8:30am-11pm daily, €10), behind Lamego Cathedral. Specialties include the local *bola de Lamego,* beans and tripe stew, and a typical Lamego tart for dessert.

The dark, tavern-like appearance of friendly ★ **Trás da Sé** (Rua Virgilio da Correia 12, tel. 254 614 075, 9am-3pm and 7pm-9:30pm Wed-Sun, 9am-3pm Mon, €10) is as traditional as the regional cuisine it dishes

up, which includes oven-roasted kid, *chafana* stew, and *arroz de salpicão,* rice with beans and sausage. Its name is literally its location: "Behind the Cathedral."

To taste genuine local products, head to **Mercado Municipal** (Av. 5 de Outubro, tel. 254 609 651, 7:30am-6:45pm Mon-Sat), where all sorts of food and drink are sold to go.

Entertainment and Events

DOURO GASTRONOMIC TOURISM FESTIVAL

Lamego hosts one of the Douro Valley's biggest annual events, the **Douro Gastronomic Tourism Festival** (tel. 254 609 600, www.cm-lamego.pt, late Oct-early Dec), which showcases the region's fabulous wines along with its rich and varied cuisine. Around 20,000 people attend the 40-day event. Participating restaurants, hotels, and wineries offer special rates.

Accommodations

Four-star ★ **Quinta da Pacheca Wine House Hotel** (Quinta da Pacheca, Cambres, tel. 254 331 229, www.quintadapacheca.com, €315) is a charming, atmospheric retreat in a restored 18th-century house surrounded by vineyards. Enjoy gourmet dining and river views. For a unique experience, stay in one of its wine barrel-shaped luxury cabins.

Also on a wine estate, luxurious four-star **Quinta de Casaldronho Hotel** (Quinta de Casaldronho, tel. 254 318 331, www.quintadecasaldronho.com, €157) has an avant-garde contemporary design, an à la carte restaurant, and an outdoor swimming pool. The scenery around the hotel is amazing.

Surrounded by sweeping vineyards, cozy family-run guest house **Casa Relógio Sol** (Quinta de Tourais, tel. 914 847 709, www.casarelogiodesol.com, €135) offers a genuine slice of Douro living, as well as a seasonal outdoor pool. The two-star **Império Hotel** (Rua José Vasques Osório 8, tel. 254 320 120, www.imperiohotel.com, €55) has 33 bright and basic rooms and serves a decent breakfast.

It's a good no-frills base for exploring the region. Perched on the edge of the Douro River, charming **Vila Galé Collection Douro** (Lugar dos Varais, Cambres, tel. 254 780 700, www.vilagale.com, €185) has 38 rooms and scenic decks, along with a heated indoor pool and an outdoor jetted tub.

Getting There

Lamego is 130 kilometers (81 mi) east of Porto. By car, the most direct route is the A4 motorway, which takes 1.5 hours but incurs tolls. Lamego is 16 kilometers (9.9 mi) south of Régua, a 20-minute drive on the A24 road.

The easiest and most scenic way to get to Lamego without a car is by taking the train from Porto to Peso da Régua, then catching a **Rodonorte** (tel. 259 340 710, www.rodonorte.pt) bus from Régua to Lamego (20 minutes, 10:25am and 4:25pm daily, €5.90), although this is a limited option with only two buses per day. The bus stop is in the city center, on Avenida Visconde Guedes Teixeira, between the castle and the church.

There are around half a dozen daily services between Porto and Lamego operated by **Rodonorte** (tel. 259 340 710, www.rodonorte.pt), **Rede Expressos** (tel. 707 223 344, www.rede-expressos.pt), and **Citi Express** (tel. 707 223 344, www.citiexpress.eu). Journeys take 2.25-3.75 hours; one-way tickets start from €10.90. Most routes require a change in Vila Real or Viseu. There may be fewer buses on weekends.

VILA NOVA DE FOZ CÔA

Nestled in a crook of the Douro River near the Spanish border, far-flung Vila Nova de Foz Côa (VEE-lah NOH-vah d' FOZH KOH-wah) became an archaeological hot spot in the 1990s with the discovery of thousands of mystifying rock engravings, which run along the Côa Valley. A string of small schist villages encircle Vila Nova de Foz Côa, a provincial town where life is much as it has been for centuries. It's known as the "Almond Tree Capital" for the almond trees blanketing the landscape.

Sights

★ **CÔA VALLEY ARCHAEOLOGICAL PARK**
(**Parque Arqueológico do Vale do Côa**)
In the 1990s, researchers inspecting the area for a new dam stumbled across thousands of rock-art engravings from prehistoric times, depicting animals, hunters, weapons, and abstract images. The **Côa Valley Archaeological Park** was created to manage and protect the most important Paleolithic art collection in the world, with more than 60 sites in 17 kilometers (10.5 mi) of the valley. The earliest drawings in the Côa Valley are believed to date back more than 20,000 years.

Guided tours (€15) are offered of the three main sites—Canada do Inferno, Ribeira de Piscos/Fariseu, and Penascosa—via all-terrain vehicles. Each stop includes a guided walk; Penascosa can also be toured in the evening. Reservations are required.

At the gateway to the park, on one of the slopes where the Douro and the Côa Rivers meet, the state-of-the-art **Côa Museum** (**Museu do Côa**) (Rua do Museu, Parque Arqueológico do Vale do Côa, tel. 279 768 260 or 279 768 261, 10am-1:30pm and 2pm-5:30pm Tues-Sun, museum €6) offers more detailed insight into prehistoric artwork. Over four floors, exhibits explore the valley through multimedia, photography, and images of the engravings. Objects unearthed during excavations in the valley are also showcased.

Food

The gastronomy of Vila Nova de Foz Côa is based on fresh fruit and vegetables. Fresh bread is a staple, as are fish from the river and game meats like rabbit and partridge. Almonds, grown widely throughout the region, are another much-used ingredient.

Aldeia Douro (Rua Dr. José Augusto Saraiva de Aguilar 19, tel. 279 094 403, www.aldeiadouro.pt, 11am-midnight Tues-Sun, closed Mon, €15) is a classy modern restaurant and wine bar that brings together the regional cuisine and wines, along with some international dishes. Starters include local smoked sausage and homemade compotes; mains feature the likes of spaghetti carbonara. **Petiscaria Preguiça** (Beco Chão-do-Pombal, tel. 279 789 432, 11:45am-8:30pm Fri-Tues, 11:45am-4pm Wed, €15) is a little jewel serving fresh home-cooked dishes. It's worth finding; the views are stunning too.

Getting There

From Porto, Vila Nova de Foz Côa is a 2.5-hour, 198-kilometer (123-mi) drive east on the A4 motorway, crossing almost all of northern Portugal. Vila Nova de Foz Côa is best explored as part of a Douro Valley trip. From Vila Real, Vila Nova de Foz Côa is a 1.5-hour, 107-kilometer (66-mi) drive east on the IC5 road. There are also three **Rede Expressos** (tel. 707 223 344, www.rede-expressos.pt)

buses daily from Vila Real to Vila Nova de Foz Côa (2-4 hours, morning, noon, and mid-afternoon, €17.60); a change in Viseu is usually required.

CP (tel. 707 210 220, www.cp.pt) runs five trains daily from Porto to Pocinho (3.5 hours, €10.65), the nearest station to the park, at the end of the Douro Line. There are five trains daily from Peso da Régua (€6.85). From Pocinho, take either a taxi to Vila Nova de Foz Côa (€6-8) or a bus (20 minutes, €2-4.40). Bus service from Pocinho train station to Foz Côa is limited, with only a couple per day. From Vila Nova de Foz Côa, take a local bus (every 15 minutes) to Castelo Melhor, on the outskirts of town, or take a taxi straight to the park's main visitors center. It is an easy walk from Castelo Melhor to the visitors center.

Trás-os-Montes

The name Trás-os-Montes (TRAZH-oosh-MON-tesh) translates as "Behind the Mountains," an indication of this region's hidden splendor. Steeped in history, the Trás-os-Montes highlands have natural beauty in sweeping flowered plateaus and majestic mountains as well as historic villages. Age-old traditions thrive in this well-preserved alcove, still relatively off the tourist track, giving visitors a sense of the Portugal of old.

VILA REAL

Where the Corgo and Cabril Rivers converge, Vila Real sits high on a headland, its steep hillsides scattered with churches and whitewashed houses. The city is a sleepy university town with a quaint historic center and a pretty riverside avenue. Vila Real can be used as a base for exploring the Douro Valley.

Sights
MATEUS PALACE
(Casa de Mateus)
The dreamy and romantic baroque design of the 18th-century **Mateus Palace** (tel. 259

323 121, www.casademateus.com, 9am-7pm daily, gardens only €8.50, tours €12.50) is credited to famed architect Nicolau Nasoni. The palace appears on the labels of the popular Mateus rosé wine, even though it was never made here. Guided tours are available in several languages and last 40 minutes. A tour of the wine cellars costs €1 extra; a wine-tasting costs €4 extra.

A mirror-like lake sets the tone for the grandeur of the estate. Inside, the rooms are dressed with regal furniture, fine fabrics, and family artifacts. One wing houses an exhibition on local wine-making, and a fully-set dining room with an intricate carved ceiling is another point of interest. Outside, wander the resplendent gardens with fragrant flowers, ornamental box hedges, small statues, and shady tree-tunnels. There's also an ornate chapel.

Casa de Mateus is 3 kilometers (1.9 mi) east of Vila Real. Take the local **Urbanos Vila Real** (tel. 259 336 806, www.urbanosvilareal.pt) bus to the university (line 1 for Lordelo-UTAD), which leaves from Vila Real's central bus terminal on Rua Dom António Valente da Fonseca every half hour, and ask to be dropped off at Mateus (20 minutes, €1). Taxis cost around €5.

Food and Accommodations

In the city center, informal three-star **Hotel Mira Corgo** (Av. 1º de Maio 76, tel. 259 325 001, www.hotelmiracorgo.com, €79) has great river views, an indoor pool, a restaurant, and its own nightclub. Choose from 122 well-appointed rooms, including 22 suites.

An elegant 18th-century manor converted into a stylish hotel, ★ **Estalagem Quinta do Paço** (Estrada Nacional 322, tel. 259 340 790, www.quintapaco.com, €85) is 1 kilometer (0.6 mi) from the Mateus Palace and 5.6 kilometers (3.5 mi) southeast of Vila Real. It's set in landscaped gardens, with its own chapel, tennis courts, an outdoor pool, and panoramic views of Vila Real.

For a base that's simple, clean, and affordable, **Residencial Encontro** (Av. Carvalho Araújo 72, tel. 259 322 532, www.res-encontro. tripod.com, €38) is a guesthouse and snack bar. Rooms are a little dated but have air-conditioning and private baths.

Information and Services

PSP police station: Largo Conde de Amarante 3, tel. 259 330 240, www.psp.pt
Vila Real Hospital (Hospital São Pedro de Vila Real): Rua dos Lagoeiros 43, tel. 259 300 500, www.chtmad.com
Vila Real Tourist Office: Loja Interativa de Turismo, Av. Carvalho Araújo 94, tel. 259 308 170, www.visitportugal.com
Main post office: Av. Carvalho Araújo 105, tel. 259 330 316, www.ctt.pt, 9am-6pm Mon-Fri

Getting There

Vila Real is 100 kilometers (62 mi) east of Porto, one hour on the A4 motorway. From Peso da Régua, Vila Real is 30 kilometers (19 mi) north, 22 minutes' drive on the A24 motorway.

Northern bus company **Rodonorte** (tel. 259 340 710, www.rodonorte.pt) runs buses hourly from Porto's main terminal to Vila Real (1.5 hours, €9.10). Vila Real's main bus terminal is on Rua Dom António Valente da Fonseca, a five-minute walk from the city center. There are daily buses between Peso da Régua and Vila Real (25 minutes, €5.90), albeit only one in the morning and one in the afternoon. At least a dozen Rodonorte buses run between Amarante and Vila Real every day (30 minutes, €7.10).

CHAVES

On the banks of the Tâmega River, Chaves (SHAH-vezh) is a far-flung fortified settlement whose name translates as "keys," reflecting its strategic position along the border with Spain. Nestled in a fertile, picturesque valley, Chaves has a rich history starting as a Roman military outpost known as Aquae Flaviae. Local landmarks pay testament to centuries of fierce fighting. Today, Chaves is a spa town whose steaming hot spring water is among the hottest in Europe.

Sights
ROMAN BRIDGE
(Ponte Romana)

The excellently preserved **Roman Bridge,** a city landmark also known as Trajan's Bridge, has a succession of 12 arches. Its construction began during the reign of Emperor Vespasian circa AD 78 and was concluded during Trajan's reign in 104. Two facing pillars commemorate the bridge's construction and its colorful history.

MEDIEVAL VILLAGE CENTER
(Centro Medieval)

Wandering the streets, you'll see antiquated buildings with colored doors and wrought-iron balconies draped in fresh flowers. The heart of the medieval center is **Camões Square (Praça de Camões),** with a statue of the Duke of Bragança. This ancient neighborhood contains churches, temples, and monumental old buildings, such as the city hall, which enhance the medieval ambience.

Just off this square are the remains of a sturdy 14th-century **castle keep,** flanked by green gardens. This national monument also houses an interesting **Military Museum (Museu Militar)** (Praça de Camões, tel. 276 340 500, http://museus.chaves.pt, 9am-12:30pm and 2pm-5:30pm Mon-Sat, €1 combined ticket with the Regional Museum), with ancient weapons and armor as well as World War I machine guns and uniforms, and displays of artifacts from the colonial wars. The castle's elevated esplanade offers fantastic views over the city.

Nearby is the petite **Regional Museum (Museu da Região Flaviense)** (Praça de Luís Camões, tel. 276 340 500, http://museus. chaves.pt, 9am-12:30pm and 2pm-5:30pm Mon-Sat, €1 combined ticket with the Military Museum), which houses a wealth of locally unearthed artifacts, such as pre-Roman jewelry, bronze tools, grinding stones, and Roman relics like coins and mosaic tiles. The 17th-century building was once part of the palace of the Dukes of Bragança and has also served as a barracks, a military prison, and a library.

Next door to the castle keep is the 17th-century baroque **Misericórdia Church (Igreja da Misericórdia)** (Praça de Camões, tel. 966 402 040, 4pm-6pm Mon-Sat, 8:40am-10am Sun, free), with a granite facade and twisted columns. Inside are an ornate gilded altar, painted ceilings, and glazed tiled walls depicting biblical scenes.

CHAVES HOT SPRINGS
(Termas de Chaves)
Have a hot soak in restorative **Chaves Hot Springs** (Alameda do Tabolado, tel. 276 332 445, www.termasdechaves.com, 9am-7pm Mon-Sat, 9am-1pm Sun, from €4), which bubble up at a lovely 73°C (163°F) year-round. The hot springs has both medical therapies and indulgent massage and spa services. Prices for treatments are wide-ranging; a simple soak in the pool is €4.

Food
In Chaves you can sample authentic regional Transmontana cuisine. It's famous for delights such as cured ham and minced meat-stuffed pasties, *folar* (sweet dough stuffed with sausage), meaty stews, and stuffed trout.

A local institution managed by a mother and daughter team that has won several awards, **Carvalho** (Alameda de Tabolado, Largo das Caldas 4, tel. 276 321 727, www. restaurante-carvalho.com, noon-3pm and 7pm-11pm Tues-Sat, noon-3pm Sun, €18) gives traditional local recipes a classy modern makeover.

In a traditional guesthouse, ★ **Pensão Flávia** (Travessa Cândido dos Reis 12, tel. 961 693 890, 12:30pm-2:30pm and 7:30pm-10:30pm Wed-Mon, €15) has no menu; ask the waitstaff for recommendations, sit back, and enjoy tasty tapas-size local cuisine.

Behind big bright-red iron doors in a century-old building, smart **Adega Faustino** (Travessa Cândido dos Reis, tel. 276 322 142, noon-midnight Mon-Sat, €12) has checkered red-and-white tablecloths and an old wooden counter. Long wooden tables and a lofty beamed ceiling give the restaurant a laid-back, convivial ambience. The menu is a good selection of regional meat and fish dishes.

Accommodations
Four-star ★ **Hotel Forte de São Francisco** (Alto da Pedisqueira, tel. 276 333 700, www. fortesaofrancisco.com, €110) occupies a 16th-century former convent, later converted into a fort, that today is classified as a National Monument. But there are no traces of medieval hardship; it provides comfortable, upscale lodging with a chic bar and pool. Slightly north of the city center, it is within walking distance of main attractions.

A swanky retreat an 11-minute drive (5.2 km/3.2 mi) out of town, **Hotel Casino Chaves** (Lugar do Extremo, Valdanta Parish, tel. 276 309 600, www.solverde.pt, €175) provides some glitz and glamour, with modern rooms, bars, restaurants, and shows alongside ancient mountain views. Just a few hundred meters from the hot springs, two-star **Hotel Termas** (Rua Tabolado 7, tel. 276 333 280, www.hoteltermas.pt, €40) offers clean and comfortable rooms with frilly decor and an excellent riverside location.

Nearby, in the spa town of Vidago, 25 kilometers (15.5 mi) or 25 minutes' drive south of Chaves, **Vidago Palace Hotel** (Parque de 5-307, tel. 276 990 920, www.vidagopalace. com, €250) is one of the most luxurious hotels in Portugal. The sprawling pink belle epoque palace is set amid a vast century-old park, the source of naturally carbonated Vidago spring water. Embraced by magnificent mountains, this luxurious golf and spa hotel was commissioned by King Carlos I and opened in 1910. Enjoy lavish living areas and furnished terraces, an indoor pool, and an 18-hole golf course. Elegant rooms and suites are equipped with Wi-Fi and flat-screen TVs.

Getting There

Chaves is about 160 kilometers (99 mi) northeast of Porto, 1.75 hours via the A7 motorway. From Vila Real, Chaves is a 50-minute, 66-kilometer (41-mi) drive north on the A24 motorway.

Bus companies **Rodonorte** (tel. 259 340 710, www.rodonorte.pt, 2.5 hours, 7 times 9am-9pm daily, €13.10) and **Rede Expressos** (tel. 707 223 344, www.rede-expressos.pt, 3.25 hours, 2:30pm and 7:30pm daily, €12.60) run regular daily buses between their terminals in Porto (Travessa Passos Manuel and Garagem Atlântico on Rua Alexandre Herculano, respectively) to Chaves, but transferring in Vila Real or Amarante may be necessary. Direct buses are also operated frequently by **Auto Viação do Tâmega** (tel. 276 332 384, www. avtamega.pt, 2.5 hours, €13.80), departing from near Batalha Square in Porto.

There are two Rede Expressos buses from Vila Real to Chaves (1 hour, 4:30pm and 9:45pm daily, €7.60). Rodonorte has six buses (1 hour, about every 2 hours 10:30am-10:40pm daily, €7.60).

Rede Expressos and Auto Viação do Tâmega go to the main bus station on Avenida Miguel Torga (also called Largo da Estação), a 10-minute walk north of the city center, near the old train station. Rodonorte drops off at a bus stop on Avenida Santo Amaro. There is no longer a rail link to Chaves.

BRAGANÇA

Time appears to stand still in remote, historic Bragança (brah-GAN-ssah), on the doorstep of untamed Montesinho Natural Park, with a long fortified medieval wall that embraces the city and its ancient citadel. Beyond the city center, modern museums and new buildings adjoin quaint whitewashed town houses and medieval monuments, surrounded by the plains that stretch as far as the eye can see. Keep an eye out for the granite pig statues, symbols of power or fertility, depending on which folktale you prefer.

Sights and Recreation

Bragança's main sights can easily be covered on foot. Walking from the city's old town center to the castle and citadel is a scenic stroll along the banks of the River Fervença. The town's main **Sé Square** has a distinctive cross in the middle and a church to one side.

BRAGANÇA CASTLE AND CITADEL (Castelo e Citadela)

Bragança's stocky castle is a well-preserved relic of Portugal's turbulent past, its 13th-century citadel protected by a 2-meter-thick (6.6-foot-thick) fortified wall. The city originated from a cluster of fortified structures that were ringed together under the order of King Afonso Henriques. This stronghold was key to maintaining the region's sovereignty from Spain and stands intact today. It gave its name to the noble House of Bragança, the last in the line of Portugal's royal ancestry.

Construction of the Gothic castle was ordered by Sancho I, son of Afonso Henriques, in 1187. The impressive keep rises from the middle of four cylindrical towers. Flanked by quaint whitewashed cottages, the keep today houses Bragança's **Military Museum (Museu Militar)** (Rua da Cidadela, tel. 273 322 378, 9am-noon and 2pm-5pm Tues-Thurs and Sat-Sun, 9am-noon Fri, free), which showcases weaponry from the 12th century to

Bragança

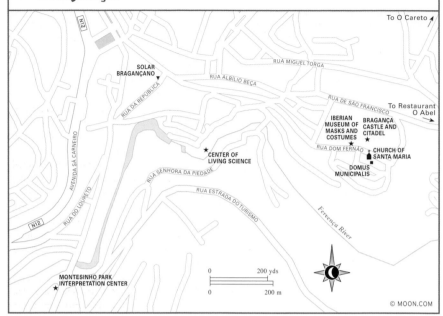

To O Careto

SOLAR
BRAGANÇANO

RUA MIGUEL TORGA

RUA ALBÍLIO BEÇA

RUA DA REPÚBLICA

RUA DE SÃO FRANCISCO

To Restaurant
O Abel

IBERIAN
MUSEUM OF
MASKS AND
COSTUMES

BRAGANÇA
CASTLE AND
CITADEL

★
CENTER OF
LIVING SCIENCE

AVENIDA SÁ CARNEIRO

RUA DOM FERNÃO

CHURCH OF
SANTA MARIA

RUA SENHORA DA PIEDADE

DOMUS
MUNICIPALIS

RUA DO LOUREIRO

RUA ESTRADA DO TURISMO

Fervença River

N12

0   200 yds

0   200 m

MONTESINHO PARK
INTERPRETATION CENTER
★

© MOON.COM

World War I. Also within the castle walls, the 18th-century baroque **Santa Maria Church (Igreja de Santa Maria)** (Rua da Cidadela, tel. 273 329 182, http://diocesebm.pt, 9:30am-5:30pm daily, free) is famous for the stunning illustration of the Assumption on its barrel-shaped ceiling. The **Domus Municipalis** (Rua da Cidadela 112, tel. 273 381 273, www.cm-braganca.pt, 9:30am-6:30pm Tues-Sun, free) is a surviving example of Romanesque civic architecture and the only council chambers in Europe with a pentagonal shape.

IBERIAN MUSEUM OF MASKS AND COSTUMES
(Museu Ibérico da Máscara e do Traje)
The vibrant, three-story **Iberian Museum of Masks** (Rua Dom Fernando O Bravo 24-26, tel. 273 381 008, www.museudamascara.cm-braganca.pt, 9am-1pm and 2pm-5pm Tues-Sun, adults €1, children free) displays a vast selection of colorful couture used in traditional celebrations, ranging from ancient pagan rituals to present-day winter festivals. A selection of arts and crafts by local artisans is also on display.

CENTER OF LIVING SCIENCE
(Centro de Ciência Viva)
The eco-friendly **Center of Living Science** (Rua do Beato Nicolao Dinís 35, tel. 273 313 169, www.braganca.cienciaviva.pt, 10am-6pm Mon-Fri, 11am-7pm Sat-Sun, adults €2.50, children under 7 €1) is like a big greenhouse, a modern glass building that hangs over the river and was converted from a former hydro-electric power plant. Interactive exhibits explore topics on energy and the environment, from electricity to the local ecological footprint. The museum also includes a restored mill, the Silk House (Casa da Seda).

MONTESINHO NATURAL PARK
(Parque Natural de Montesinho)
Venture north into the unkempt beauty of the **Montesinho Natural Park** (Forest Park, tel.

273 329 135, www.montesinho.com), which sprawls over 74,000 hectares (286 square mi) along the border with Spain. Rural villages nestle peacefully among mountains alongside crystalline waters and oak forests. Many of the houses comprising the park's 92 villages are built from natural schist or granite, blending with their surroundings. Villagers have a traditional communal way of farming and sheepherding, protected within the park. Visitors can wander well-mapped hiking trails (www.montesinho.com/en/passeios) and may spot elusive animals like otters and Iberian wolves. Two dozen inns and B&Bs are within the park, some in riverside mills and stone houses. The park's office and website can offer advice about lodging or camping in the park.

Montesinho Natural Park starts about a 10-minute drive north of Bragança on the main N103-7 road. In the park, it passes by the villages of **Rabal** and **França** before reaching the village of **Montesinho,** 23 kilometers (14.3 mi) north of Bragança, a 35-minute drive. Hidden in the depths of the park, a stone's throw from the Spanish border, it's a true time capsule, a serene cluster of granite houses and cobbled streets.

The **Park Interpretation Center (Centro de Interpretação do Parque Natural de Montesinho)** (Casa da Vila em Vinhais, tel. 273 771 416, 9am-5:30pm daily, free), in the village of Vinhais, a 39-kilometer (24-mi), 50-minute drive west of Bragança along the N103 road, offers more information on what to see in the park. From Bragança, rural **STUB buses** (tel. 800 207 609, www.cm-braganca.pt, €2) shuttle visitors from the city hall to villages within the park. However, the best way to really explore it is by car.

HOT-AIR BALLOONING

Ao Sabor do Vento (tel. 939 509 436 or 938 659 144, www.aosabordovento.net) operates scenic hot-air balloon rides (2-3 hours, 7:30am or 4:30pm daily, adults €150, children under 15 €100) over the stunning Transmontano region. It's a relaxing way to appreciate the gorgeous landscape.

Food

Rustic and unfussy, Bragança's gastronomy features locally raised meat and seasonal vegetables, simply cooked in the oven or on open fires. Chestnut honey is a local specialty. Run by a husband and wife team, the **Solar Bragançano** (Praça da Sé 34, tel. 273 323 875, noon-3pm and 7pm-10pm Tues-Sun, €18) is a temple to Transmontano cuisine, using traditional pots and pans to cook up staple ingredients such as partridge, wild boar, and hare. It's all beautifully presented in a wood-clad, chandelier-draped interior.

Bright and friendly **Restaurante O Abel** (Rua do Sabor, Gimonde Parish, tel. 273 382 555, www.oabel.pt, noon-2:30pm and 7pm-10pm Mon-Wed and Fri-Sat, noon-2:30pm Sun, €10), 6.1 kilometers (3.8 mi) east of Bragança on the N218 road, showcases quality local meats, simply grilled on charcoal and accompanied by fresh vegetables.

In Montesinho Natural Park, in the village of Varge, ★ **O Careto** (Carretera, Varge, tel. 273 919 112, noon-2:30pm and 7pm-10pm Tues-Sun, €14) is a warm and welcoming schist-built rural restaurant serving excellent no-fuss farmhouse cuisine. The menu is limited to the day's fresh ingredients and local meat, to be enjoyed in front of a roaring fire. It's worth the 11-kilometer (6.8-mi) drive north from Bragança.

Entertainment and Events

The traditional **Winter Festivities (Festival de Inverno de Bragança Paulista)** begin on the winter solstice (Dec 21) and continue through to Carnival (Feb or Mar). Huge communal bonfires are lit throughout the city and surrounding villages, and locals dress in colorful homemade outfits including historic half-animal, half-human masks. These masquerades, bringing color and cheer to winter, originated in ancient fertility rites. Every two years, at the start of December, the **Mascararte Biennial Mask Festival** showcases these traditions with exhibitions and events.

Other entertainment options include

shows at the **Municipal Theater (Teatro Municipal)** (Praça Professor Cavaleiro Ferreira, Braganza, Norte, tel. 273 302 740, www.teatromunicipal.cm-braganca.pt) and the nightclub and lounge **Mercado** (Largo Forte São João de Deus 204, tel. 936 953 207, www.mercadodisco.com, 2am-6am Thurs and Sun).

Getting There

Bragança is 208 kilometers (129 mi) northeast of Porto, 2.5 hours on the A3 motorway, which has tolls. Bragança is a 1.5-hour, 111-kilometer (69-mi) drive east of Chaves via the N213 road and the A4 motorway. From Vila Real, Bragança is 117 kilometers (73 mi) northeast, a 1.25-hour drive on the A4 motorway.

There is no rail link to Bragança. The bus terminal is in the newer part of town, on Avenida João da Cruz, five minutes' walk north of the city center.

From Porto, **Rede Expressos** (tel. 707 223 344, www.rede-expressos.pt) operates several buses a day between Porto's Campo 24 Agosto station and Bragança (3.25 hours, every 2 hours 9:15am-7:30pm daily, €13.80). The bus makes a number of stops. Regional bus company **Rodonorte** (tel. 259 340 710, www.rodonorte.pt, 3.25 hours, 12 buses 7am-9:15pm daily, €13.90) also operates frequent buses from Porto's Travessa Passos Manuel, near Rua Ateneu Comercial do Porto.

From Chaves, there is one Rede Expressos bus a day (4.5 hours, 2:45pm daily, €12.60), with a transfer in Vila Real. Rodonorte buses (3.25 hours, every 2-3 hours daily, €12) from Chaves also require a transfer in Vila Real. The trip is much longer than by car because of the transfer.

From Vila Real, there are Rede Expressos buses almost hourly (1.75 hours, 10:45am-10:45pm daily, €10.50). Rodonorte also operates services between the two at towns about every two hours (2 hours, 8:20am-10:40pm daily, €10.50). Rede Expressos' buses usually make two stops, while Rodonorte buses stop three times.

Getting Around

Bragança has a local bus system, **STUB** (tel. 800 207 609, www.cm-braganca.pt), which runs a circular route every 30 minutes, stopping at key sights including the cathedral and the main bus station, as well as rural routes. It also provides limited service to villages in Montesinho Natural Park.

MIRANDA DO DOURO

Nestled amid arid mountains on the border with Spain and swaddled by Douro International Park (Parque Natural do Douro Internacional), Miranda do Douro is often called a living open-air museum. This well-preserved hamlet dates to 1286 and even has its own language—Mirandese. It's also home to Portugal's only indigenous breed of donkey and a famous breed of cow—the *vaca mirandesa*, or Mirandese cow.

The tranquil town has a 13th-century castle built during the reign of Dom Dinis, a ruined 16th-century Gothic cathedral, and the crumbling 16th-century Vilarinho Aqueduct, as well as a number of bridges and dams whose stony construction is unique in the region. Located 75 kilometers (47 mi) southeast of Bragança, Miranda do Douro makes a great day trip.

Recreation
RIVER CRUISES

Glass-topped boats sail through the magnificent landscapes of the Douro River gorge. Expert guides discuss the geology, ecology, and ethnography of the valley in Portuguese and Spanish, with limited English translation. Cruises end with a dockside port-tasting.

On the border between Spain's Zamora and Portugal's Miranda do Douro, one-hour **Europarques Cruises** (Parque Natural de Arribes del Duero, Estación Biológica Internacional de Miranda do Douro, tel. 273 432 396, www.europarques.com, 4pm daily

1: Camões Square in Chaves; 2: grapes in the Douro Valley; 3: hot-air balloon near Bragança; 4: the castle walls of Bragança

Sept-July, 11am and 4pm daily Aug, from €18) depart year-round from the Miranda do Douro International Biological Station, 3 kilometers (1.9 mi) south of the town center, on the banks of the Douro River. Longer cruises can be arranged with prior booking.

MIRANDA DONKEY TREKS (Passeios de Burro)

The Miranda donkey (*burro de miranda* or *burro mirandês*) is Portugal's only indigenous breed. Used for centuries for farming, these adorable, docile, shaggy animals are today mostly kept for companionship by the elderly farmers. There are concerns that as their owners disappear, the breed may face extinction; since 2003 it has been listed as an endangered species. Ecotourism has played a role in the Miranda donkey's survival, and donkey-trekking tours have become a popular activity.

Established to protect and preserve the Miranda donkey, the **AEPGA** (Associação para o Estudo e Protecção do Gado Asinino, Largo da Igreja, Atenor, tel. 966 151 131 or 960 050 722, www.aepga.pt) organizes rides from one-hour excursions (from €20 per donkey; rides can be shared by two people) to five-day treks across the plains and along streams, passing through tranquil hamlets. Accommodations and meals are optional.

Food

Superb Mirandesa beef steaks come from a unique local breed of cow, raised 500 meters (1,640 feet) above sea level and typically cooked on a grill and seasoned with sea salt. Other local specialties include *folar de carne* (meat baked in bread), *bola doce mirandesa* (a sticky layered bread laced with sugar and cinnamon), and smoked *alheira* sausage.

Restaurant O Mirandês (tel. 273 432 823 or 273 431 418, www.omirandes.net, 10am-10pm daily, €15) is a gem of local gastronomy. The decor is simple, the wine is served in jugs, and Mirandese beef is the star of the menu. There are two branches: one in the heart of town (Rua Dom Dinis), the other in an inn at the northern entrance to town (Urbanização do Juncal), 10 minutes' walk from the center.

Restaurant and Pizzaria O Moinho (Rua do Mercado 47C, tel. 273 431 116, http://restaurante-pizzaria-o-moinho.business.site, noon-4pm and 7pm-10pm Wed-Mon, €15) serves an interesting mix of home-baked pizzas and regional dishes in generous portions. The views of the surrounding countryside make it stand out; get a table by the window.

Getting There

Miranda do Douro is 75 kilometers (47 mi) southeast of Bragança. By car, the trip on the E-82 road takes one hour, while the N218 road takes 1.25 hours.

By bus, there is one daily **Rede Expressos** (tel. 707 223 344, www.rede-expressos.pt, 1.25 hours, noon daily, €9.50) from Bragança to Miranda do Douro. Local company **Santos Viagens e Turismo** (tel. 279 652 188, www.santosviagensturismo.pt) also operates a couple of daily buses between Porto and Miranda do Douro, passing through Vila Real (€14.10), as well as one or two buses daily, in the afternoon, between Bragança and Miranda do Douro (€10). The bus station is a 400-meter (0.2-mi), five-minute walk north of the town center and is walking distance to the castle and the International Biological Station.

The **CP** (tel. 707 210 220, www.cp.pt) train runs from Porto five times a day, departing every couple of hours to Pocinho (3.25 hours, 7am-5pm daily, €13.35), the nearest station to Miranda do Douro; from there you take a **Santos Viagens e Turismo bus** to Miranda do Douro (2 hours, 2:30pm and 11:45pm daily, €6.70).

Minho

In the picturesque northwestern province of Minho (MEEN-yoo), the soil is rich, the rain abundant, and the vegetation luxuriant. Deep green blankets the valleys. Even Minho's most famous product—*vinho verde* (green wine), a young, fizzy white wine—is green in name if not in color. On the coast, this greenery is flanked by long sand dunes called the Costa Verde and punctuated with captivating villages, an enticing mix of authentic fishing towns and lively seaside resorts.

Considered the birthplace of Portugal, Minho is home to ancient cities steeped in history, evident not only in the architecture and well-preserved landmarks but also in the customs that are part of daily life.

BRAGA

Founded over 2,000 years ago by the Romans, who called it Bracara Augusta, Braga is the country's fourth-largest city and often referred to as the "capital" of Minho. It's also known as the "City of Archbishops," its religious standing reflected in its many churches, chapels, and monasteries and its vibrant celebration of Semana Santa, the Holy Week leading up to Easter.

Braga is lively despite its age. Amid the Roman ruins, churches, and quaint lanes in the town center are trendy bars and restaurants. The student population at Minho University keeps the city fun and oriented toward the future.

Sights
BRAGA CATHEDRAL
(Sé de Braga)

The twin-towered Romanesque **Braga Cathedral** (Rua Dom Paio Mendes, tel. 253 263 317, www.se-braga.pt, 9am-6:30pm daily Oct-Mar, 9am-7pm daily Apr-Sept, cathedral €2, museum €3) is the oldest in Portugal, dating to the 12th century. It was built by the first king of Portugal, Afonso Henriques, and houses the tombs of his parents, Henrique and Teresa. Inside are a beautiful altar, elaborate choir stalls, exquisite gilded woodwork, and tile murals. Spectacular painted ceilings depict Braga's history. The lower floor houses the main Manueline chapel, a cloister lined with Gothic side chapels, and two huge baroque organs still in playing condition. Upstairs, a museum exhibits sacred art, including a statue of the breast-feeding Virgin Mary, and an iron cross used by Frei Henrique of Coimbra to celebrate the first mass in Brazil.

GARDEN OF SANTA BARBARA
(Jardim da Santa Barbara)

The manicured municipal **Garden of Santa Barbara** (Rua Dr. Justino Cruz, tel. 253 262 550, 24 hours daily, free), with its box-hedged borders and bright flower beds, is a lovely place for a peaceful stroll. Sandwiched between modern city buildings on one side and the medieval Archbishop's Palace on the other, it represents the harmonious balance struck by Braga's two halves.

BOM JESUS DO MONTE SANCTUARY
(Monte do Bom Jesus)

Five kilometers (3 mi) northeast of the city center is the stunning **Bom Jesus do Monte Sanctuary** (Estrada do Bom Jesus, tel. 253 676 636, www.bomjesus.pt, 8am-7pm daily June-Sept, 9am-6pm daily Oct-May, free). The first stone of the neoclassical basilica was laid in 1784 atop the magnificent baroque staircase known as the Sacred Way. Flanked by dense forest and lined with little chapels, the chalk-white staircase climbs 116 meters (381 feet) with 600 steps. Made from granite, it is divided into sections devoted to the five senses and the three virtues, represented by fountains and statues, with a different surprise at each landing. At the top,

Minho

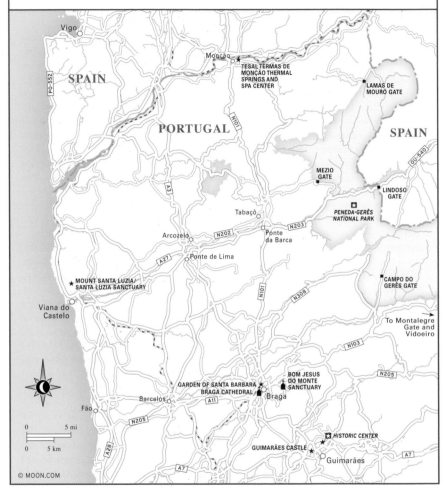

you're rewarded with a lovely garden laced with streams and a magical hidden grotto, as well as vertiginous views. A funicular train (€1.20 one-way, €2 round-trip), inaugurated in 1882, makes a quicker—albeit less eventful—ascent.

A bus marked "Bom Jesus" (€2) leaves every 20 minutes from Braga's train station and the central bus station. Buy tickets from the driver. Bom Jesus is the last stop, and the bus stops at the bottom of the staircase.

Food

Tasca Dom Ferreira (Rua de São Vicente 35, tel. 253 262 870, noon-3pm and 7pm-10pm Mon-Sat, €10) is a charismatic Old World tavern, serving traditional Portuguese dishes on earthenware crockery on red-and-white checkered tablecloths. Specialties include Braga-style codfish, *bacalhau à narcisa*.

A warren of rooms and staircases, **Velhos Tempos Tavern** (Rua do Carmo 7, tel. 253 214 368, noon-2:30pm and 8pm-10:30pm

Mon-Sat, €15) feels like a step back to a by-gone era. The food is old-fashioned home-cooked Portuguese fare like *rojões* (chunks of pork loin), served in heaping portions. Don't miss the *alheira* sausage starter or the *abade de priscos* pudding dessert, made with bacon and port.

In a historic 19th-century building, elegant **Restaurante Centurium** (Av. Central 134, tel. 253 206 260, www.centurium. bracaraaugusta.com, 12:30pm-3pm and 7:30pm-10pm, Mon-Sat, €20) centers its menu on the finest seasonal produce. Octopus carpaccio, creamy codfish, and slices of grilled black pork are on the menu. Charming features include a classy bar and a private garden.

At **Restaurant Anjo Verde** (Largo da Praça Velha 21, tel. 253 264 010, noon-3pm and 7:30pm-10:30pm Mon-Sat, €10), the keywords are innovation and variety. This excellent vegetarian and vegan restaurant is located in a small square next to a pillar of the Porta Nova archway, the gateway to the city. It also hosts art exhibitions and monthly classical concerts.

Don't leave Braga without having a coffee and a cake at ★ **Café A Brasileira** (Largo Barão de São Martinho 17, tel. 253 262 104, 7:30am-1am daily, €5), on a corner of the main Barão de São Martinho square. A striking azulejo tile facade fronts this busy hive of activity, established in 1907.

Entertainment and Events
HOLY WEEK
(Semana Santa)
In March or April, starting the Friday before Palm Sunday and ending Easter Sunday, Braga's **Holy Week** (www.semanasantabraga. com) attracts as many as 100,000 people, who flock to the city to participate in colorful, energetic celebrations whose origins date to the 4th century. The city is bedecked with flowers and lanterns, its streets flooded with processions. A highlight is the Holy Thursday parade of the *farricocos:* barefoot men dressed in hooded purple tunics and carrying torches, reminiscent of the reconciliation of public penitents that took place until the 15th century.

BRAGA ROMANA FESTIVAL
Once a year, over five days in late May-early June, Braga transforms into a living reenactment of the Roman Empire in **Braga Romana** (bragaromana.cm-braga.pt), as the city celebrates its origins. Visitors can sample Roman delicacies and drinks, learn ancient dances and games, and browse handicrafts.

Recreation
Covering 700 square kilometers (270 square mi), the **Peneda-Gerês National Park** is prime adventure territory. Braga-based **Tobogã Canyoning Tours** (Rua dos Prados 21, ground floor, tel. 915 707 938, www.portal. toboga.pt) has experienced guides who specialize in canyoneering and rappelling adventures in the park. No experience is necessary, although height and weight restrictions apply. Tours (from €30) last three hours and cover 1 kilometer (0.6 mi) of terrain. Hotel transfers can be arranged.

Accommodations
Nestled amid romantic gardens, ★ **Hotel do Parque** (Bom Jesus do Monte, tel. 253 603 470, www.hoteisbomjesus.pt, €100) is in a restored 19th-century mansion. Features include a spa and a piano bar, and rooms are equipped with modern amenities. With 53 modern rooms, three-star ★ **Hotel do Lago** (Largo do Santuário do Bom Jesus, tel. 253 603 020, www.hoteisbomjesus.pt, €79) boasts stunning views of the beautiful Serra do Gerês mountains. Clean and comfortable **Ibis Budget Braga Centro** (Av. da Liberdade 96, tel. 253 614 500, www.accorhotels.com, €37) is a good budget option a short distance from Braga's main sights.

Three-star **Hotel Dona Sofia** (Largo São João do Souto 131, tel. 253 263 160, www. hoteldonasofia.com, €65) overlooks a lovely green square near the cathedral and is a 10-minute walk from the train station. It has 34 well-equipped rooms. In the heart of the historic center, **Albergaria da Sé** (Rua Dom Gonçalo Pereira 39-51, tel. 253 214 502, www.albergaria-da-se.com.pt, €50 d, €65 suite) is a cozy four-star guesthouse with 12 spacious rooms, a restaurant, and free parking.

Indulge in a bit of luxury while exploring Braga at the five-star **Melia Braga Hotel & Spa** (Av. General Carrilho da Silva Pinto 8, tel. 253 144 000, www.meliabraga.com, €149 with breakfast, €180 with 2 meals, €214 with 3 meals), a swanky-looking mirrored tower with an outdoor pool and an on-site restaurant.

Information and Services
PSP police station: Rua dos Falcões, tel. 253 200 420, www.psp.pt

Braga Hospital: Rua das Sete Fontes, tel. 253 027 000, www.hospitaldebraga.pt

Tourism office: Av. da Liberdade 1, tel. 253 262 550, www.cm-braga.pt, 9am-6:30pm Mon-Fri, 9:30am-1pm and 2pm-5:30pm Sat-Sun

Post office (nearest to center): Rua do Raio, tel. 253 200 361, www.ctt.pt

Getting There
Braga is 55 kilometers (34 mi) north of Porto, 45 minutes on the A3 motorway.

The **Getbus** (tel. 253 262 371, www.getbus.eu) airport shuttle bus operates a dozen direct buses (50 minutes, 4am-12:45am daily, €8) between Porto Airport and Braga's main bus station (Av. General Norton de Matos), with fewer services on weekends and holidays.

Long-distance bus company **Rede Expressos** (tel. 707 223 344, www.rede-expressos.pt) also operates regular buses between Porto's Campo 24 Agosto bus station and Braga (1 hour, hourly 10am-11pm daily, €6). There are also a couple of late-night buses at 1am and 4am daily.

From Porto's Campanhã station, there are frequent **CP** (tel. 707 210 220, www.cp.pt, 1 hour, hourly 6am-1am daily, €3.20-16.25) trains to Braga, with trains running more frequently at peak times. Faster direct services (the high-speed Alfa Pendular train), with

two stops en route, take just 40 minutes and are more expensive than the regular Urbano trains.

The train station is on the western fringe of the center, and Braga's main bus terminal is closer to the center, on Avenida General Norton de Matos, walking distance to sights such as the cathedral. Taxis and local buses (www.tub.pt) can be found outside the train station and main bus terminal.

Getting Around
Braga's local bus routes (www.tub.pt) are comprehensive and easy to navigate. A 24-hour tourist ticket to ride all buses costs €3.35 and can be purchased on board.

TOP EXPERIENCE

★ PENEDA-GERÊS NATIONAL PARK
(Parque Nacional da Peneda-Gerês)
In the far north of Portugal, hugging a C-shaped swath of the Portuguese-Spanish border, rambling and resplendent **Peneda-Gerês National Park** (www.natural.pt/en) hides stony spa villages, medieval castles, megalithic monuments, and Roman roads amid rugged mountainous terrain. Portugal's only national park, Peneda-Gerês covers over 70,000 hectares (270 square mi), spread across four mountain ranges—Peneda, Soajo, Amarela, and Gerês.

The dramatic, unspoiled landscape ranges from dense forest to bald hilltops, deep ravines, natural pools, streams, and waterfalls, and the park is home to roe deer, Iberian wolves, wild Garrano ponies, Barrosã cattle, and Castro Laboreiro cattle dogs.

There are five **main entrances** to the park:

- **Lamas de Mouro Gate** (Melgaço municipality), on the northern end of the park
- **Mezio Gate** (Arcos de Valdevez municipality), on the western side of the park
- **Lindoso Gate** (Ponte da Barca municipality), on the western side of the park

- **Campo do Gerês Gate** (Terras de Bouro municipality), about 6.6 kilometers (4.1 mi) west of Gerês village, the closest entrance to Braga, the best base for exploring the park
- **Montalegre Gate** (Montalegre municipality), on the eastern end of the park

Each entrance has a visitors office with guidance on the terrain and activities in that area. There is also an **education and activities center** (Lugar do Vidoeiro 99, tel. 253 390 110, 9am-12:30pm and 2pm-5:30pm Mon-Fri, free) in the village of Vidoeiro, 15 kilometers (9.3 mi) southeast of Montalegre.

The park's points of interest include the quirky collection of *espigueiros* (stone granaries on stilts) in the village of Lindoso; the **Geira Roman Road,** which once connected Braga to Astorga in Spain; the **Arado waterfall and bridge,** near Gerês village; and the **Pitões das Júnias** stone village, with the remnants of a 9th-century Benedictine monastery, about 12 kilometers (7.4 mi) northwest of the Montalegre entrance.

Exploring the park is difficult without an organized tour or your own vehicle. A good option is to travel to Braga and sign up for an organized excursion to the park with a company that includes hotel transfers, such as the Braga-based, family-run business **Keen Tours** (tel. 938 690 513, www.keentours. com), which covers everything from hiking and horseback-riding excursions to berrypicking tours. For private lodging, see **Gerês Holidays** (tel. 253 352 803, www.gerescasas. com) for a range of chalets and cottages in Peneda-Gerês.

Recreation

Peneda-Gerês is prime terrain for adventure activities such as canyoneering, kayaking, and hiking. Guided tours and self-guided sign-posted routes are available throughout the park. Contact the **park's head office** (Av. António Macedo, tel. 253 203 480) in Braga.

Discover the park's beautiful spots sliding down waterfalls into translucent pools, zip-lining over gorges, and rappelling down sheer rock faces. Braga-based **Tobogã Canyoning**

Tours (Rua dos Prados 21, ground floor, tel. 915 707 938, www.portal.toboga.pt) has experienced guides for the three-hour tours (from €30), suitable for the moderately fit. No experience in canyoneering or rappelling is necessary, but height and weight restrictions apply. Hotel transfers can be arranged.

Nature exploration company **AktivaNatura** (Largo de São João 13, tel. 916 336 628, www.aktivanatura.com), based in Ponte da Barca, specializes in three-hour kayaking trips (€15), canoeing, and stand-up paddleboarding (from €25). **Soajo Nomadis** (tel. 935 510 931), founded by a local entrepreneur and eco-enthusiast based in Soajo, takes hikers on a web of guided trails and treks (from €12) of varying difficulty spanning the Peneda-Gerês National Park.

Food and Accommodations

For travelers with a car, there is no shortage of quality local hotels, cozy inns, and family-run farmhouses in Peneda-Gerês. **Agúas do Gerês Hotel, Thermal Springs & Spa** (Av. Manuel Francisco da Costa 136, tel. 253 390 190, www.aguasdogeres.pt, €86) is a grand 54-room, three-star hotel in the picturesque village of Gerês, near one of the park's main entrances.

The **Lurdes Capela restaurant** (Av. Manuel Gomes de Almeida 77, tel. 253 391 208, noon-10pm daily, €10), in the heart of Gerês village, is one of the best in the region, serving local fare such as wild boar and slow-cooked kid. A simple, countrified restaurant that might look either dated or charmingly antiquated, it has been handed down in the family for generations.

Getting There and Around

The best way to get to the Peneda-Gerês National Park independently is by car from Braga, a 40-minute drive. The roads inside the park are good. Follow the A3 motorway from Porto to Braga, then the N103 road from Braga to the park's nearest border.

By public transport, take the bus or train to Braga, the best base for exploring the park;

from Braga, local **Empresa Hoteleira do Gerês** (www.ehgeres.com) or **Transdev** (www.transdev.pt) buses run to the closest main entrance, the Campo do Gerês gate in Gerês village, also referred to as Caldas do Gerês. The buses (1.5 hours, €6) run every few hours 7am-7pm weekdays, but on Saturday-Sunday there are only about four buses.

GUIMARÃES

Guimarães (gee-mah-RAYNZH) is often referred to as the "Cradle of Portugal," where the first king, Afonso Henriques, was born in the early 12th century. Guimarães was the first capital of the new kingdom. The city's well-preserved historic features are its main allure. Wander the narrow streets of the quaint UNESCO-listed historic center and head north to Largo Hill (Monte do Largo) to see the castle and the palace.

Sights
★ HISTORIC CENTER
(Centro Histórico)
Wandering Guimarães's excellently preserved buildings, whose styles span several centuries, is a trip back in time. The city's past is showcased in the evolution of techniques, materials, and tastes. The center covers 16 hectares (39.5 acres) with 14th- and 15th-century fortress styles giving way to Renaissance and neoclassical buildings and colorful bourgeois homes. A labyrinth of medieval backstreets frames the main Oliveira Square and its 14th-century freestanding arch. The Old Palace Town Hall is a 16th-century Manueline building with a ribbed-arch gallery. The 16th-century Santa Clara Convent today houses the city council.

GUIMARÃES CASTLE
(Castelo de Guimarães)
Ten minutes' walk north of the center, the town's 10th-century castle is said to be the birthplace of Afonso Henriques, first king of Portugal, in 1112. **Guimarães Castle** (Rua Conde Dom Henrique, tel. 253 412 273, www.cm-guimaraes.pt, 10am-6pm daily, €2) towers

above the city atop a granite hill, Monte Latito, with forested gardens and pedestrian trails around it. It was built in late Romanesque style with Gothic touches, its walls forming a pentagram that contains eight towers, a square, and a central keep, added in the 13th century. Inside, visitors can trek around the castle walls, visit the Chapel of São Miguel, and take in sweeping views of the city.

PALACE OF THE DUKES OF BRAGANÇA
(Paço dos Duques de Bragança)
Amid the forested gardens of Monte Latito, a stone's throw from Guimarães Castle, the sprawling medieval **Palace of the Dukes of Bragança** (Rua Conde Dom Henrique, tel. 253 412 273, http://pduques.culturanorte.pt, 10am-6pm daily, palace €5, with the castle €6) was home to the first Dukes of Bragança. It's a fine example of austere late-medieval construction. The rectangular building is laid out around a central courtyard. Inside, explore multiple rooms featuring ancient furniture, tapestries, and weapons. A stunning chapel has a soaring ceiling, a huge chandelier, and a beautiful stained-glass window. There's also an impressive bronze statue of King Afonso, created in 1874 by renowned Portuguese sculptor Soares dos Reis.

PENHA MOUNTAIN
(Montanha da Penha)
Penha Mountain (Montanha da Penha, tel. 253 414 114, www.penhaguimaraes.com), also known as Monte da Santa Catarina, 6.5 km (4 mi) south of the city center and rising to 586 meters (1,923 feet), is the highest point in Guimarães. It includes enchanting green woodland, a network of caves, and many magnificent viewpoints. A diverse range of activities includes hiking, camping, horseback riding, and miniature golf. There are picnic areas, restaurants, bars, and coffee shops. A scenic **cable car** (Rua Aristides de Sousa Mendes, tel. 253 515 085, www.turipenha.pt, 10am-8pm daily June-Sept, 10am-6:30pm daily Apr-May and Oct, 10am-5:30pm daily

Nov-Mar, €5 round-trip) takes around 10 minutes.

Food

The nuns of the local Santa Clara Convent had a huge influence on local cuisine, as evidenced by the number of traditional *conventual* sweets like *tortas de Guimarães* (a glazed croissant-like pie stuffed with a sweet concoction of squash, egg, and almond) and *touchino do céu* (a cake made with lard). Another staple is the meat cake, pizza-like dough topped with pork, sardines, and other unusual ingredients.

Simple little **Cantinho dos Sabores** (Rua Francisco Agra 33, tel. 253 095 645, 10am-10pm Mon-Sat, set menu €5-8) serves fantastic regional food at low prices. Simple grilled meats, stuffed codfish, codfish with bread, and grilled octopus are all on the limited but well-considered menu.

Charming **Taberna Trovador** (Largo do Trovador 10, tel. 913 205 263, noon-late Wed-Mon, €10) matches tasty tapas made from fresh local products with an extensive wine list. Tongues in spicy sauce, chicken gizzards, and fish salad are some of the intriguing dishes.

Posh *pastelaria* **Manjar dos Doces** (Rua do Salgueiral, Edificio Principe Real Loja A, tel. 253 528 298, 8am-10pm daily, €5) offers a huge range of traditional sweets and cakes, along with a selection of sandwiches on fresh-made bread.

Getting There

Guimarães is 55 kilometers (34 mi) northeast of Porto (45 minutes on the A3 and A7 motorways, with tolls) and 25 kilometers (15.5 mi) southeast of Braga (25 minutes on the A11 motorway).

The **Getbus** (tel. 253 262 371, www.getbus.eu) airport shuttle bus runs a dozen direct buses (50 minutes, 4am-12:45am daily, fewer on weekends and holidays, €8) between Porto's Sá Carneiro Airport and Guimarães's main bus terminal.

Rede Expressos (tel. 707 223 344, www.rede-expressos.pt) operates four buses (25 minutes, 1 bus at 9am, 3 buses in the afternoon, €6) daily between Braga and Guimarães. **Rodonorte** (tel. 259 340 710, www.rodonorte.pt) also runs buses (25 minutes, €5.90) between Braga and Guimarães, five times a day.

Guimarães's **main bus terminal** (Alameda Doutor Mariano Felgueiras) is a 20-minute walk west of the city center.

Direct **CP** (tel. 707 210 220, www.cp.pt, hourly) trains run almost hourly between Porto's main Campanhã station and Guimarães, with slower Urbano service (1.25 hours, €3.20 round-trip) and the direct high-speed Alfa Pendular train (53 minutes, €14.50), which makes just two stops. CP trains also run hourly between Braga and Guimarães (1-3 hours, €3.50-17.15). The train station is south of the city center.

VIANA DO CASTELO

Sprawling across the River Lima, Viana do Castelo (vee-AH-nah doo kash-TEH-loo) is a medieval city with beautiful seaside suburbs. In the historic city center, old buildings line tree-shaded avenues and quaint backstreets. The plethora of architectural styles show the city's history and evolution: Romanesque, Manueline, Renaissance, baroque, and art deco blend with modern structures.

Water is the backbone of the city's history; on the docks of the Lima's mouth, the Gil Eannes ship museum covers maritime heritage from the Age of Discoveries to the modern cod-fishing industry. Local beaches make water the focus of recreation, including surfing and kite-surfing.

Sights

COSTUME MUSEUM
(Museu do Traje)

Located on the main Praça da República square in the city's historic center, the **Costume Museum** (Praça da República, tel. 258 809 306, www.cm-viana-castelo.pt, Tues-Sun 10am-1pm and 3pm-6pm, till 7pm June and Sept, €2) hosts a splendid array of traditional regional and local costumes. Housed in a mid-20th-century bank building and spread over three floors, it displays colorful outfits that range from working clothes to wedding garments, many exquisitely embellished and embroidered, all carefully preserved. Among the outfits on display are traditional costumes worn during local festivals.

HOSPITAL SHIP *GIL EANNES*
(Navio *Gil Eannes*)

Moored on the commercial docks is the **Hospital Ship** *Gil Eannes* (Doca Comercial, tel. 258 809 710, www.fundacaogileannes.pt, 9:30am-8pm daily, €4), a restored mid-20th-century vessel built in local shipyards. The *Gil Eannes* was a state-of-the-art floating medical facility at the time of its launch in 1955. This pride of Portugal's White Fleet assisted cod-fishing vessels in the seas of Newfoundland and Greenland. Now permanently moored, it's a museum and occasional youth hostel. Wander the decks, explore the compartments, and view the original equipment, such as the operating theater and X-ray machine.

SANTIAGO DA BARRA CASTLE
(Forte de Santiago da Barra)

On the edge of the Lima River's mouth, peering over the sea, **Santiago da Barra Castle** (Campo de Castelo, tel. 258 820 270, 9am-5pm Mon-Fri, free) is likely the first castle built along the Lima. Fortification may have existed on this site as long ago as the 13th century; this building was completed under King Manuel I in the 16th century and enlarged a century later to protect the prospering city against pirate attacks. Cross the drawbridge over a moat to wander the castle walls and admire its distinctive Manueline-style Roqueta Tower. A busy Friday market takes place outside its walls.

MOUNT SANTA LUZIA
(Monte de Santa Luzia)

Few churches are as dramatic as the **Santa Luzia Sanctuary (Santuário de Santa Luzia)** (Monte de Santa Luzia, tel. 258 823 173 or 961 660 300, www.templosantaluzia.org,

8am-7pm daily Apr-Sept, 8am-5pm daily Oct-Mar, free), also known as Templo do Sagrado Coração de Jesus (Temple of the Sacred Heart of Jesus). This 20th-century Byzantine Revival building is gracefully poised on top of **Mount Santa Luzia,** 228 meters (748 feet) above the estuary in the suburb of Santa Maria Maior. It can be reached from the city on the country's longest **funicular tram** (€2 one-way, €3 round-trip), which departs every 15 minutes from the local train station. The panoramic views of the coastline are worth the seven-minute journey. Once inside Santa Luzia, visitors can ascend to the domed roof by lift (€0.80), then walk up a narrow stairway to enjoy still more impressive views. The church can also be reached by car or taxi, 3.5 kilometers (2.2 mi) from the center, or a steep 2-kilometer (1.2-mi) hike that is only for the fit. Mass (4pm weekdays, 11am and 4pm Sun) is held here.

The hill behind the sanctuary, with eucalyptus trees, is peppered with stony ruins, thought to be a **fortified Celtiberian settlement** from the 4th century BC.

Food

Viana do Castelo's local cuisine is about fish, particularly *bacalhau* (cod). For dessert, try a Viana Half Moon, a sweet pastry stuffed with cassava paste, ground almonds, egg yolks, and sugar, and dusted with icing sugar.

Located in the city center, poised and polished **O Laranjeira** (Rua Manuel Espregueira 24, tel. 258 822 258, www.olaranjeira.com, 8am-10:30pm daily, €15) is a charismatic restaurant and guesthouse that first opened in the 1940s. The funky flowered wallpaper is just one talking point; authentic local fare served with finesse is another.

Near the Santiago da Barra Castle, **Tasca a Linda** (Rua dos Mariantes A8, tel. 258 847 900, www.tasquinhadalinda.com, noon-11pm daily, €25) is tavern-chic, with an elegantly

---

1: the Palace of the Dukes of Bragança in Guimarães; 2: cows on a road in the Peneda-Gerês National Park; 3: the Santa Luzia Sanctuary in Viana do Castelo; 4: the main square in Braga

simple interior, nice views, and delicious seafood, including stuffed crab and seafood *cataplana*.

Entertainment and Events

Famous for the women's bright multicolored costumes and gold jewelry, the city's biggest event, the four-day **Pilgrimage of Our Lady of Agony** (Romaria da Senhora da Agonia, http://vianafestas.com) has been held each August since 1783. Processions, exhibitions, and concerts are staged in key spots around town.

Recreation
PRAIA DO CABEDELO

Stroll along lovely **Praia do Cabedelo**, a stretch of pristine sand lined by reedy dunes and a few beach shacks. Its rolling waves attract surfers in droves. Expect summer crowds of surfers, kite-surfers, windsurfers, and body-boarders. Local outfitters include **Sports Center Feelviana** (tel. 258 249 841, http://hotelfeelviana.com) and **Vianalocals** (tel. 258 325 168 or 914 193 535, www.vianalocals.com) for surfing lessons, trips, and rentals. **Ondimar** (tel. 912 274 244) rents Jet Skis.

May to October, a ferry (5 minutes, €1.50) crosses the estuary to connect the city to the beach; it leaves every 30 minutes 9am-6pm daily from the quay south of Praça 5 Outubro square. A bus to the beach also departs the local bus station frequently.

Getting There

Viana do Castelo is 80 kilometers (50 mi) north of Porto, an hour by car on the A28 motorway, and 62 kilometers (38 mi) north of Braga, a 45-minute drive on the A11 and A28 motorways.

You can easily get to Viana do Castelo on public transport, both by train and by bus. **CP** (tel. 707 210 220, www.cp.pt) runs Regional trains (1-3 hours, €6.85-16) every couple of hours from Porto's Campanhã station. The slower Urbano train is cheaper but stops often and may require a transfer in the town of Nine; direct Inter-regional trains are faster and more expensive. Trains run every half hour between Braga and Viana do Castelo (1.5 hours, €6-16). The train station is near the city center, at the far end of Avenida dos Combatentes da Grade Guerra, a straight walk down to the riverfront.

Rede Expressos (tel. 707 223 344, www.rede-expressos.pt) buses travel direct between Porto and Viana do Castelo (1 hour, €7.60), departing hourly from Porto's Campo 24 Agosto. Viana do Castelo has a new bus station, just outside the center next to the railway station and a large shopping center called Estação Viana.

MONÇÃO

Separated from Spain by the picturesque River Minho, modest Monção (mon-SSOWN) is untouristed despite the ruins of a 14th-century castle not far from the town center, which is embraced by 16th-century walls. Life revolves around the main square, Praça Deu-la-Deu, with an attractive fountain at one end and a bastion at the other, offering views of Spain, along with old churches and historic monuments.

Visitors come for hot-spring spas and Alvarinho, a fresh and fruity *vinho verde*. Monção claims to be the wine's birthplace, but that is disputed by Spain's Galicia. A three-day Alvarinho festival is held every year over the first weekend in July, involving music, dancing, eating, and, of course, drinking.

Sights and Recreation

Monção's hot springs are sought out for their purported healing properties. Bathing in the steaming water dates back to Roman times. Located on the Minho riverside, the **Tesal Termas de Monção hot springs and spa center** (Av. das Caldas, tel. 251 648 367, www.termasdemoncao.com, 9am-7:45pm Mon-Sat, 9am-5:45pm Sun June-Oct, 10am-2pm and 4pm-8:30pm Mon-Fri, 10am-8:30pm Sat, 10am-6pm Sun Nov-May, hot spring pool €15, day packages from €55) features bubbly jetted tubs, mini waterfalls, and bubble beds. A range of spa treatments (9am-2pm daily), including massages and therapeutic water baths, enhances the experience.

Getting There

Monção is a 135-kilometer (84-mi) drive (1.75 hours) north of Porto on the IC1 road to Viana do Castelo, then the N13 road to Valença and the N101 road to Monção.

The easiest way to get to Monção by bus is from Viana do Castelo, with five daily buses operated by **Rede Expressos** (tel. 707 223 344, www.rede-expressos.pt, 1.25 hours, 12:45pm-11:30pm daily, €7.60). The bus stop in Monção is on Avenida Afonso III, 500 meters (0.3 mi) south of the town center. One Rede Expressos bus runs the 93 kilometers (58 mi) from Braga to Monção (1.25 hours, 6:30pm daily, €9.10).

Madeira and the Azores

Scattered far out in the Atlantic are Portugal's islands, two stunning archipelagoes that are among Europe's most beautiful lesser-known places. An hour's flight south of the mainland, off the coast of Africa, is Madeira, the older and closer of the two archipelagoes. Two hours due west of the mainland, between Europe and the United States, are the Azores, a cluster of nine verdant volcanic islands. Lush, low-key, and laid-back, both archipelagoes ooze unspoiled Portuguese charm while being distinct in character.

Most of the major attractions on both archipelagoes' main islands can be seen in a few days, an option for a short break, although you could spend a week. Majestic Madeira, the sunnier and warmer of the two, has better weather and is rapidly growing in popularity as a winter

Highlights

Look for ★ to find recommended sights, activities, dining, and lodging.

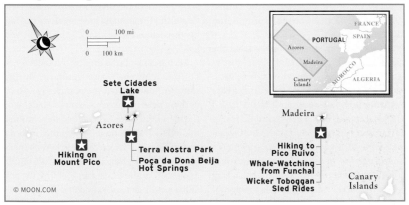

★ **Hiking to Pico Ruivo:** Feel on top of the world as you stand on Madeira's highest peak, with the island—or clouds, depending on the weather—spread out at your feet (page 322).

★ **Whale-Watching from Funchal:** Gaze in awe as these majestic creatures surface from the deep to greet visitors (page 323).

★ **Wicker Toboggan Sled Rides:** Hold your breath as you whiz down Funchal's steep mountainsides on Madeira's novel answer to Venice's gondolas (page 327).

★ **Sete Cidades Lake:** This stunning Azorean landmark is infused with local legend (page 344).

★ **Terra Nostra Park:** Stroll through a paradisiacal Eden packed with beautiful flora before dipping into a relaxing hot-spring pool (page 347).

★ **Poça da Dona Beija Hot Springs:** Soothe aching limbs in the steaming, sparkling waters of the Azores' most famous natural hot springs (page 348).

★ **Hiking on Mount Pico:** Climbing the highest mountain in Portugal is an adventure lover's dream (page 355).

escape for Northern Europeans. The rural Azores, with a moody climate, hot springs, and mist-enshrouded peaks, have a mystical magnetism. Domestic flights by a number of airlines, including national and European low-cost carriers, have competitive and affordable airfares.

PLANNING YOUR TIME

Traveling to either archipelago is quick and easy from mainland Portugal, with daily flights from Lisbon and Porto. There are a few direct flights between Madeira and the Azores. If your primary destination is mainland Portugal, a long weekend provides time to sample either archipelago.

In addition, there are direct flights to Madeira from European destinations outside Portugal, including London, Amsterdam, and Paris. There are also direct flights to the Azores from Europe as well as the United States (Boston) and Canada (Toronto and Montreal).

Madeira's main destination is Funchal, the capital city, on Madeira Island. If you're driving, the island can occupy two or three days, with a day at either end and Funchal as a base in the middle. In a rush, most of the island can be seen in a day. There is public transport, but it can be intermittent and takes a long time to get anywhere. Nearby Porto Santo Island is an unspoiled beach destination a short ferry trip from Funchal; the ferry generally makes one daily round-trip, and the crossing can be hampered by Madeira's infamously temperamental weather.

In the Azores, Ponta Delgada on the island of São Miguel is the main destination and a great base for exploring the island. From Ponta Delgada, regular interisland flights connect the other islands, divided into three groups. Regular intergroup transport is by plane and by ferry. If you intend to see more than one Azorean island, take at least four days, as São Miguel alone has plenty to see.

Madeira is at its best in late spring and early summer, just before the peak tourist season, when the flowers are in bloom. It generally stays dry April-September and is rainiest in winter (Nov-Mar), although much of the rain falls on the northern side of the island, meaning Funchal is often drier. Outside summer holiday season (July-Aug), Funchal gets very busy for two of the island's main events: New Year's and the annual Flower Festival in May. To visit around these times, book flights and lodging well in advance.

Spring is a fantastic time to visit the Azores. Like Madeira, the Azores get busier during summer holidays, but the islands experience nothing near the mass tourism of Madeira or the mainland. The Azores tend to be rainier than Madeira, although the weather on both archipelagoes is unpredictable and changeable, but rarely prone to extremes like on the mainland. While winter can get rainy, the rest of the year is generally mild and pleasant.

Previous: Madeira's capital city, Funchal; a painted door in Funchal; Madeira cow.

Madeira

Off the coast of western Africa, 970 kilometers (600 mi) southwest of mainland Portugal, Madeira (mah-DAY-rah) is one of Portugal's two autonomous archipelagoes. Comprising Madeira Island, smaller Porto Santo, and two clusters of uninhabited islands, the Desertas and the Savage Islands Natural Reserve, the subtropical archipelago is one of the European Union's farthest outposts and a destination that has soared in popularity thanks to its balmy year-round climate and scenery.

Semiautonomous since 1976, the colorful archipelago, in the same time zone as mainland Portugal, is today driven by tourism, with most visitors staying on Madeira Island. The island is also a popular stop for Mediterranean and transatlantic cruises. A daily ferry between Madeira Island and neighboring Porto Santo Island has seen the number of visitors to tiny Porto Santo grow in recent years.

The climate in Madeira is warm and dry most of the year, making it an excellent winter escape for Northern Europeans, and as it is just a short hop from the mainland, it is a short-break destination any time of year.

THE ISLANDS

The Madeira archipelago comprises two inhabited islands, Madeira and Porto Santo, and two clusters of uninhabited islets, the Desertas and the Savage Islands.

Madeira Island

Called the "pearl" or the "floating garden" of the Atlantic, Madeira Island is famous as a botanical bonanza, known for its unusual fruit, including the Madeira banana and banana passion fruit; for Madeira wine and amazing New Year's firework displays; and as the birthplace of soccer megastar Cristiano Ronaldo. The archipelago's main destination, Madeira Island has long been a popular short-break destination for mainlanders. The island's precipitous volcanic landscape rises spectacularly from the deep-blue Atlantic, its jagged peaks clad in tiny whitewashed houses. Inhabited since shortly after being discovered in July 1419 by Portuguese explorers João Gonçalves Zarco and Tristão Vaz, subtropical Madeira Island is latticed by a network of small irrigation channels *(levadas)* that once watered the terraces created for farming in the precipitous terrain, but that nowadays serve mainly as landmarks on popular hiking routes.

Dotted with lakes, waterfalls, and dramatic precipices, Madeira is a haven of tranquility. The weather is generally warm and breezy but can be temperamental; locals warn visitors that they may experience four seasons in one day as they travel around the island. The entire island is skirted by beaches and seawater pools. Most of Madeira's beaches are pebbly and lack soft sand.

Funchal, the main city, with its scenic cable cars and glorious botanical gardens, is toward the east end of the south coast, with the main international airport and seaport.

On the east coast is the town of **Caniçal,** the center of Madeira's whaling industry until 1982. Heading west from Funchal is the town of **Câmara de Lobos,** home to unusual gastronomy, such as the Nikita, a baffling mix of wine, beer, and pineapple ice cream, and the famous hanging kebabs. On the northwestern tip of Madeira is charming **Porto Moniz,** with inviting natural saltwater pools, sandwiched between mountains and the ocean. In the heart of the island is cloudy **Pico Ruivo,** Madeira's highest peak, flanked by incredible vistas and challenging hikes.

Porto Santo Island

A short 15-minute flight or a two-hour ferry ride from Madeira Island, paradisiacal Porto Santo Island is like the Caribbean, with year-round balmy weather, warm turquoise water,

Madeira

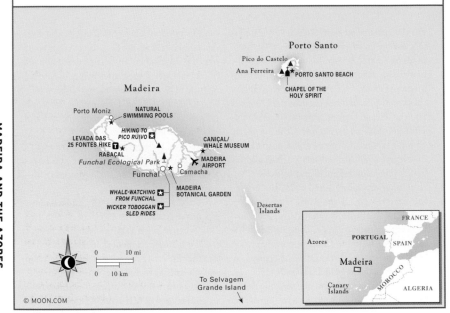

and 9 kilometers (5.6 mi) of soft white-sand beaches. Drier than Madeira Island and just under 15 kilometers (9.3 mi) from one end to the other, Porto Santo is a first-rate beach resort, the ultimate getaway for rest and relaxation. Tourism development has been regulated to be in harmony with the size and spirit of the island. Equipped with an international airport, Porto Santo also offers excellent diving conditions and spectacular mountainside trekking terrain. Dubbed the "Golden Island," it is one of Europe's last undiscovered treasures.

Desertas Islands

The Desertas are a chain of three long thin slivers of desolate terrain just south of Funchal. A few hardy wildlife species inhabit the barren islands, among them feral goats and a tiny colony of monk seals. The only human presence is a handful of wardens, geologists, occasional boaters, and a few research stations.

Savage Islands (Selvagens)

Even more remote and desolate than the Desertas are the Selvagens, or Savage Islands, 230 kilometers (143 mi) south of Funchal and halfway between Madeira Island and Spain's Canary Islands, just off the coast of Morocco. Two small islands and several smaller islets are the designated nature reserve Madeira Natural Park, an important breeding ground for thousands of nesting and migrating birds; it also has extraordinary marine biodiversity. Surrounded by perilous reefs and vast ocean, and with little freshwater and limited access, the Savage Islands have human habitation of only two year-round wardens and, intriguingly, a lone family of British descent. The islands are at the heart of a fierce dispute between Portugal and Spain over the definition of the Selvagens—whether they are islands or merely large rocks—which has major consequences for the borders of Portugal's exclusive economic zone.

GETTING THERE
Air
TO MADEIRA ISLAND

There are many daily flights between mainland Portugal and Funchal on Madeira Island, but only from Porto and Lisbon. There are no direct flights from the Algarve to Madeira.

TAP Air Portugal (tel. 707 205 700, www.flytap.com) operates flights between Lisbon and Madeira Island every few hours year-round, while British low-cost carrier **Easyjet** (tel. 707 500 176, www.easyjet.com) has daily flights between Lisbon, Porto, and Funchal, providing competitive fares, sometimes less than €100 round-trip. Flights take 1.5 hours. It is possible to fly directly to Madeira from London and Manchester in the United Kingdom, Amsterdam, Paris, and Frankfurt, although some routes operate seasonally.

Madeira Airport (Aeroporto da Madeira) (FNC, Santa Cruz, tel. 291 520 700, www.aeroportomadeira.pt) is 20 minutes west of Funchal, connected to the city center by good roads and buses.

TO PORTO SANTO ISLAND

There are direct flights between mainland Portugal and **Porto Santo Airport (Aeroporto do Porto Santo)** (PXO, tel. 291 520 700, www.aeroportoportosanto.pt). **TAP Air Portugal** (tel. 707 205 700, www.flytap.com) and **SATA Azores Airlines** (tel. 707 227 282, www.azoresairlines.pt) operate direct flights between Lisbon and Porto Santo. Porto Santo has a few flights from the United Kingdom and Germany in summer. Getting to Porto Santo is easiest via Funchal or Lisbon. From Funchal (Madeira Island), regional airline **Sevenair** (tel. 214 444 545, www.sevenair.com) is the main carrier to Porto Santo, operating daily flights.

Ferry
FROM MAINLAND PORTUGAL TO MADEIRA ISLAND

At the time of writing there was a summer-only ferry link between Portimão (in the Algarve) and Funchal by Spain's **Naviera** **Armas** (www.madeira-ferry.pt). The ferry continues from Funchal to Spain's Canary Islands.

FROM MADEIRA ISLAND TO PORTO SANTO ISLAND

The *Lobo Marinho* **ferry** (tel. 291 210 300, www.portosantoline.pt) runs daily between Madeira and Porto Santo but generally makes only one round-trip per day, departing from Funchal in the early morning and departing Porto Santo in the late afternoon or evening. The trip takes two hours.

GETTING AROUND
Car
MADEIRA ISLAND

The best way to explore Madeira Island is by car. Main towns are linked by good roads and tunnels that cut through the island's rocky landscape, making travel swift and easy. Outside the major routes, traveling short distances can take time due to the winding roads.

Be warned: Driving in Madeira is not to be taken lightly. Many roads, especially within towns, can be vertiginously steep due to the hilly topography. Rockfalls, wet and foggy conditions, sheer exposed cliffs, long tunnels, and narrow roads are a few of the challenges. Rent a good car with a decent engine and drive at a sensible speed.

There are many rental companies serving the island, and vehicles can be hired through hotels, at the airport, or at offices in Funchal. The best part is that car hire is cheap on Madeira, so it is worth considering even for a one-day adventure.

PORTO SANTO ISLAND

Porto Santo's main attractions are mostly in its biggest town, Vila Baleira, easily seen on foot, although by car the entire island can be covered in a day. The roads are much quieter and flatter than Madeira's, and rented cars can be brought here on the ferry from Funchal. A number of car rental companies operate on Porto Santo, mostly at the airport and in the main town center.

Bus

MADEIRA ISLAND

Generally speaking, public bus services between Madeira's main towns and villages are frequent, cheap, and mostly punctual, but they can be slow and at times bumpy. As a rule of thumb, the nearer to Funchal the destination is, the greater the frequency of bus service.

The distinctive yellow buses of Funchal's main bus company, **Horários do Funchal** (tel. 291 705 555, www.horariosdofunchal.pt), serve the city center and its urban fringes. Information in English is available on the website. **SAM** (tel. 291 201 151, www.sam.pt) operates the main routes between Funchal, the airport, and the neighboring towns of Caniço, Machico, Caniçal, Porto da Cruz, and Santo da Serra. **Rodoeste** (tel. 291 220 148, www.rodoeste.com.pt) covers the north and west of the island, while **EACL** (tel. 291 222 558, www.eacl.pt) serves the east of the island.

PORTO SANTO ISLAND

There will always be a bus waiting for the ferry to take passengers from the terminal to the main town, Vila Baleira. Porto Santo has a public bus service, but due to the island's limited size, the routes are not varied; buses run the same route around the coast and inland. There is also a local tour bus that does a two-hour tour of the island once a day.

Taxi

Taxi travel on Madeira Island is reasonable, and taxis are plentiful. There are also a good number of taxis on Porto Santo Island, and given its size, taxis are an option, as the distances are short.

FUNCHAL

Madeira's capital city is an awesome sight. A sloping mountainside is covered in tiny houses down to the waterfront, where the sheer escarpments end abruptly in the sea. From afar, this slope appears gentle, but up close the vertiginous angles of the steep ridges and narrow roads become apparent. Clumps of tropical foliage sprout between chalky white facades and red roofs around Funchal's main bay.

Funchal (fun-SHALL) is the largest and most populous city in the archipelago, its name said to derive from the fennel (funcho) in the dense forests that once covered Madeira's shores. The first settlers replaced the forests with profitable sugarcane plantations, the main export for many years. Today famous products made from sugarcane include bolo de mel (honey cake, made with sugarcane molasses) and mel de cana (sugarcane honey). Clean and cosmopolitan yet steeped in culture and history, Funchal is the island's main destination year-round. The annual Flower Festival, summer season, and New Year's Eve are peak times. It is also Portugal's leading cruise-ship destination, with huge liners docking at the port on a regular basis, dwarfing the picturesque waterfront.

Funchal's airport is famous for its intriguing runway and dramatic setting. Surrounded by sheer mountains on one side and the Atlantic on the other, often battered by breezy conditions, the runway has a reputation as challenging. Following a series of extensions, the runway today is an innovative feat of engineering, a long platform over the ocean on 180 cement stilts. In 2017 Madeira Airport, also known as Funchal Airport, was officially rebranded Cristiano Ronaldo Madeira International Airport in honor of the island's most famous son, soccer star Cristiano Ronaldo.

Funchal is an enthralling place to explore, with its stunning scenery and unusual attractions, and is particularly enchanting by night, when the slope of houses becomes a blanket of lights twinkling in the inky black of the Atlantic.

Sights

Funchal's historic center, the Old Town, is an idyllic maze of picturesque streets, old houses, colorfully painted doors, and traditional restaurants. The oldest buildings in Old Town date to the 15th century, though few survive.

Funchal

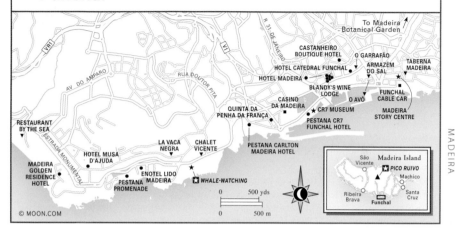

© MOON.COM

Rua de Santa Maria is one of the oldest streets in this area, a narrow cobbled cavalcade of quaint old shops, restaurants, and old-fashioned streetlights.

Easily covered on foot, this area is where you'll find the colorful Lavradores Market and its weird and wonderful fruits and flowers, and the noble main Municipal Square (Praça do Município), with its striking chessboard-like black-and-white cobbling.

Elsewhere, Funchal's port and waterfront area bustles, with one of its main attractions, the Cristiano Ronaldo CR7 Museum and Hotel, pulling in sports fans. A short cable car ride from Funchal's Old Town is Monte, a peaceful suburb with one of Madeira's most famous trademarks, the Wicker Basket Toboggans.

BLANDY'S WINE LODGE

In the heart of Funchal city center, **Blandy's Wine Lodge** (Av. Arriaga 28, tel. 291 228 978, www.blandyswinelodge.com, 10am-6:30pm Mon-Fri, 10am-1pm Sat) provides an opportunity to explore the history of Madeira wine. Acquired by the Blandy family in 1840, it is home to 650 barrels of the famous fortified wine. The comprehensive **Premium Tour** (45 minutes, €5.90) covers two centuries of wine-making history in the cool warehouse with

its thick stone walls; the museum, which contains artifacts such as letters from Sir Winston Churchill; the revered Vintage Room, which houses Blandy's rarest and oldest Madeira wines; and a tasting. The **Vintage Tour** (1 hour, €16.50) adds the opportunity to see the aging process, access to the Blandy family's private collection of vintage Madeiras, and a tasting in the Vintage Room. Both tours are available in various languages, including English.

CR7 MUSEUM
(Museu CR7)

To understand the fuss regarding soccer star Cristiano Ronaldo and his connection to the island, this is the place. If you're not really a soccer fan, you can skip the museum and its artifacts, although the interactive features are interesting. Packed with gleaming trophies won by Ronaldo, photos, fan paraphernalia, and a huge assortment of personal memorabilia, the **CR7 Museum** (Av. Sá Carneiro 27, tel. 291 639 880, www.museucr7.com, 10am-6pm daily, €5)—CR7 are his initials plus his jersey number—maps his ascension from a humble islander who played soccer in the streets to an international superstar, philanthropist, and Madeira's biggest ambassador. Ronaldo's career achievements,

Madeira Wine

You can't leave Madeira without sampling Madeira wine, which is to Madeira what port is to Porto; this robust fortified wine is produced exclusively on the Madeira Islands, with a history back to the Age of Discoveries at the end of the 15th century. Wine producers found the wine had intensified in flavor when unsold shipments were brought back to the islands after long periods at sea in the heat of ships' holds. The heating process distinguishes Madeira wine from others and creates its unique flavor.

During the 18th century, the popularity of Madeira wine grew but was severely compromised in the mid-19th century due to an outbreak of powdery mildew that destroyed crops. In the 20th century, the Russian Revolution and Prohibition in the United States saw two of its biggest markets severed. Madeira wine's reputation as little more than a cooking wine improved toward the end of the 20th century, and it is enjoying fresh popularity in new markets. Ranging from dry to sweet, Madeira wine is consumed as an aperitif or dessert accompaniment, while cheaper versions are used for culinary purposes.

Interestingly, on Porto Santo, grapes are picked from vines that grow flat along the sandy fringes of the beach; these grapes are said to give the wine a distinctive taste. Most of the harvest is shipped to Madeira Island to bolster its wine production, but some locals produce their own homemade varieties, more akin to a rosé in color and strong in flavor.

including his Ballon D'Or, Golden Shoes, and club trophies, are in glass cabinets that fill the ground-floor show area. Outside, a full-body bronze statue of the man welcomes streams of cruise-ship passengers. The museum, run by the icon's family members, is in the same building as a hotel, partly designed by the player. Coincidentally, the founders of Pestana, Portugal's largest hotel group, José Pestana and his brother Manuel, also hail from Madeira.

MADEIRA STORY CENTRE

In an unassuming building in the heart of Old Town, the **Madeira Story Centre** (Rua D. Carlos 27-29, tel. 291 639 081, museum tel. 291 639 082, www.madeirastorycentre.com, 9am-7pm daily, adults €5, children €3) is packed with information on everything Madeira, from its volcanic formation to its culture, gastronomy, and arts and crafts. It explores history from ferocious pirate attacks to outmoded local transport such as hydroplanes to Madeira's trademark flora. A wide selection of typical goods can be purchased from the well-stocked gift shop. The rooftop terrace restaurant has gorgeous views and serves traditional island cuisine.

MADEIRA BOTANICAL GARDEN
(Jardim Botânico da Madeira)

The **Madeira Botanical Garden** (Caminho do Meio, Bom Sucesso, tel. 291 211 200, www.ifcn.madeira.gov.pt, 9am-7pm daily, €5.50) is an exquisite, fragrant oasis of peace and tranquility with rare and exotic flora for an hour or two of strolling. Three thousand plants from all over the world cover 8 hectares (20 acres) on several levels, with views of Funchal. Once a private estate, the garden has been open to the public since 1960, suffering extensive damage in the 2016 wildfires that swept Funchal. Replanted, it is slowly recovering. Good facilities include toilets, a museum, and a café. Steep, unleveled pathways can be inaccessible for people with disabilities.

The gardens, in the rugged hills 3 kilometers (1.9 mi) northeast of Funchal center, are reached most cheaply by bus 31 or 31A from Funchal seafront (€1.95), by taxi (€5-8 one-way), or by cable car from Funchal to Monte (www.madeiracablecar.com, 15 minutes, €11 one-way) and then a shorter cable

1: Madeira Botanical Garden; **2:** Blandy's vintage Madeira wine bottles; **3:** fruit stand at the Lavradores Market; **4:** Funchal's charming historic downtown

car ride from Monte to the gardens (www.telefericojardimbotanico.com, €8.25 one-way). The cable car terminals in Monte are a minute's walk from each other. A combined round-trip ticket for both cable cars costs €31.40 adults. It is possible to walk up to the gardens, but the roads are steep and busy, and it's a long walk. Ride up and walk back down, or jump on one of the thrilling wicker toboggans in Monte.

Food
REGIONAL
Trendy little **Taberna Madeira** (Travessa João Caetano 16, tel. 291 221 789, www.tabernamadeira.com, 11:30am-3pm and 6:30pm-11pm Mon-Thurs, 6:30pm-midnight Fri, 11:30am-3pm and 6:30pm-midnight Sat, noon-3pm Sun, €15) takes typical Madeira produce and makes it cool. Bite-size delicacies include cod fritters, and larger meals feature tuna belly and calf liver, with side servings of cabbage and sweet potato. Tables are limited; reservations are recommended.

On one of Funchal's quirky backstreets, ★ **O Garrafão** (Rua da Queimada de Baixo 25, tel. 291 635 328, 11am-10pm Mon-Sat, €15) serves authentic cuisine at value prices. A limited menu with homemade soups and traditional mains in a cozy setting makes this one of the town's most highly recommended eateries. Don't miss the passion fruit pudding for dessert.

A century-old chalet in the heart of Funchal, **Chalet Vicent** (Estrada Monumental 238, tel. 291 765 818, noon-11pm daily, €20) has classic Madeiran cuisine such as *espetadas* (hanging kebabs) skewered on bay-leaf sticks, oven-roasted goat, old-fashioned tuna dishes, and huge veal cutlets.

FINE DINING
Pricey but unique, swanky **Armazém do Sal** (Rua da Alfândega 135, tel. 291 241 285, www.armazemdosal.com, noon-3pm and 6:30pm-11pm Mon-Fri, 6:30pm-11pm Sat, €30) has a clever and accomplished fusion of traditional Portuguese gastronomy with typical Madeiran influence and strong international nuances. It is in a historic 200-year-old salt warehouse.

SEAFOOD
Overflowing with the freshest seafood, **Restaurant by the Sea** (Estrada da Praia Formosa, tel. 291 763 120, 10am-11pm daily, €15) is off the beaten track, its idyllic waterfront location making this hidden gem a great place to try scabbard-fish eggs, squid, and limpets.

STEAK HOUSE
A taste of South America in Madeira, **La Vaca Negra** (Rua Velha da Ajuda 10-12, tel. 291 764 491, 4pm-11pm Tues-Sun, €22) is highly rated for its steaks. Small and busy, this characterful little joint is a must for meat lovers; reservations are advised.

SNACK BAR
Hundreds of soccer scarves hang from the rafters of quirky little snack bar **O Avô** (Rua da Praia 49A, tel. 291 632 651, www.baroavo.weebly.com, 11am-11pm daily, €10), as interesting as its larger-than-life owner, Ricardo. A great selection of beer and wine accompanies the typical menu, making this a great stop for a light lunch.

Entertainment and Events
NIGHTLIFE
Funchal has varied but contained nightlife, with many trendy places that don't have the rowdy scenes of other holiday islands. Nightlife areas are along the Lido waterfront boardwalk, Rua Santa Maria in the Old Town, and just behind the Pestana Carlton Madeira hotel. The clubs open only on weekends.

At the **Casino da Madeira** (Av. Do Infante, tel. 291 140 424, www.casinodamadeira.com, 3pm-2am Fri-Wed), part of the Pestana Casino Park, have dinner and a show before gambling in the flashy Games Room.

Local Specialties

Madeira has many distinctive, wonderful signature drinks and dishes, from **Madeiran** *poncha* (a potent punch) and the fabled **Nikita** (a mix of wine, beer, and homemade pineapple ice cream, indigenous to Câmara de Lobos) to little **limpets** *(lapas),* the local seafood of choice, and huge **hanging kebabs** *(espetadas da Madeira),* big, juicy chunks of island-reared meat grilled on long skewers that hang over the tables. Fruits unique to Madeira include the Madeira banana and the banana passion fruit. A great place to see and sample these intriguing products is the **Lavradores Market** (Rua Latino Coelho 38, tel. 291 214 080, 7am-7pm Mon-Thurs, 7am-8pm Fri, 7am-2pm Sat), a busy and colorful traditional market in the heart of Funchal.

The island's gastronomy is simple and unfussy. Key dishes are based on the cows that roam the landscape, and *prego no caco* (beef steak on the traditional Madeiran *caco* bread, made with sweet-potato flour) is a popular snack, best accompanied with an ice-cold Coral beer. *Caco* bread is commonly brought to tables in baskets as a starter, hot and smothered in garlicky butter.

It might be an acquired taste, but the Nikita is definitely worth a try.

To enjoy one of Madeira's best-known specialties, hanging kebabs, take a scenic, hilly drive to **Câmara de Lobos,** 10 kilometers (6.2 mi) west of Funchal along the VR1 road. This typical dish is beef marinated in salt, pepper, garlic, and bay leaf, strung on long metal skewers or bay-leaf sticks, and slowly grilled over coals.

Established in 1966, traditional, unpretentious **Restaurante Santo António** (Estrada João Gonçalves Zarco, Estreito de Câmara de Lobos, tel. 291 910 360, www.restaurantesantoantonio. com, noon-midnight daily, €18) has become an institution specializing in *espetadas.* Savor the best local cuisine, including *caco* bread, washed down with a *poncha.*

It's worth seeking out authentic, down-to-earth little ★ **Restaurante Viola** (Estrada João Gonçalves Zarco 594, Estreito de Câmara de Lobos, tel. 291 945 601, noon-midnight Tues-Sun, €18), with cork-clad walls. The huge guitar above the door gives it away. Inside are succulent *espetadas* and the traditional accompaniments: salad, chunks of fried corn bread, *poncha,* sangria, and beer.

While you're in Câmara de Lobos, sample the unique Nikita drink. The original Nikita has been served since 1985 at **Casa do Farol** (Rua da Nossa Senhora da Conceição 11, Câmara de Lobos, tel. 291 945 413, 9am-2am daily, €5), recently reinvented into a swanky tapas bar and restaurant.

MADEIRA

MADEIRA AND THE AZORES

FLOWER FESTIVAL

A tribute to the wonder of nature and arrival of spring, Madeira's weeklong **Flower Festival** (www.visitportugal.com/en/node/155972) is one of Portugal's most famous celebrations, held four weeks after Easter. Funchal bursts into fragrant bloom with flower-decked floats and parades. Folk dancing and singing fuse with flowers and fragrances to stimulate every sense and bring the "floating garden" to life. In the city center, fresh flowers create the famous floral carpets along central Avenida Arriaga. Elsewhere, exhibitions dedicated to the flora of Madeira are put on, and one of the most poignant moments is the Wall of Hope ceremony, staged for over three decades, where hundreds of local schoolchildren, flower in hand, march toward the Municipal Square where they place their flowers into a wall as a call for world peace. Madeira is a bouquet of flowers on a normal day, but when the Flower Festival takes over the island, it is absolutely stunning.

NEW YEAR'S

The island's New Year's celebrations are the legendary highlight of the holiday season, and hotels often sell out months in advance. Madeira's fireworks display is one of the most dazzling in the world. The biggest in Europe, it makes Madeira one of the continent's leading New Year's destinations. Funchal is the epicenter of the fireworks displays, with inky skies and the dark sea.

Recreation

★ HIKING TO PICO RUIVO

Climb above the clouds for the view from Madeira's highest peak, Pico Ruivo, at 1,862 meters (6,109 feet) the third-highest point in Portugal. On a clear day, the summit affords views of the entire island.

There are **two main hiking routes** to the top of Pico Ruivo. The more popular and more challenging route is the **Vereda do Areeiro** (footpath PR1), from the peak of nearby **Pico do Areeiro,** Madeira's third-highest peak, accessible by car and home to a NATO radar unit. This route is not for those with vertigo, as it passes along sheer ridges, narrow ledges, steep slopes, and dark tunnels, stringing together the three highest peaks on Madeira—Pico do Areeiro, Pico das Torres, and Pico Ruivo. The trip is 11 kilometers (6.8 mi) round-trip and takes four hours, so moderate physical fitness and stamina are required.

The second and more moderate route is the **Vereda do Pico Ruivo** (footpath PR1.2), starting from the village of **Achada do Teixeira,** east of Pico Ruivo. This trail snakes along the ridgeline from the village's car park to the summit; the round-trip is 6 kilometers (3.7 mi) and takes three hours. At the end of the hike is a flight of steps to the summit of Pico Ruivo, a 10-minute climb.

Both hikes are challenging and should never be attempted in the dark. The weather is famously temperamental, and up in the heights even more so, as thick blankets of clouds can move in without warning. Be prepared and take warm clothes, a flashlight (particularly for the Pico do Areeiro route), and plenty of drinking water. There are shelters along the walks in the event of a sudden change in weather.

Pico Ruivo is 20 kilometers (12.4 mi) north of Funchal. Public transport to either trailhead, Pico do Areeiro or Achada do Teixeira, from Funchal is intermittent and scarce; the easiest way is by car. To get to Achada do Teixeira, drive around the eastern edge of the island to Santana, along the VR1 and VE1

hiking trail from Pico Areeiro to Pico Ruivo

roads, and then head inland along a winding road to the car park near the village, from where it is a short hike to the summit. The drive from Funchal via Santana takes an hour.

Driving to Pico do Areeiro is a much shorter 20-kilometer (12.4 mi), 40-minute trip along the ER103 road, north from Funchal. The hike to Pico Ruivo summit is longer and more challenging from Pico do Areeiro.

A great option for less experienced hikers is to join an organized tour, which offers shorter hikes and their own transport. Ask about tours at your hotel or the tourist office.

FUNCHAL ECOLOGICAL PARK
(Parque Ecológico do Funchal)

Created in 1994, the vast hilly terrain of the **Funchal Ecological Park** (Reception Center, Estrada Regional 103, No. 259, tel. 291 784 700, 9am-5pm daily, park entry free), 12 kilometers (7.4 mi) north of Funchal, is preserved to promote environmental education and provide recreational opportunities such as picnic areas, hiking, mountain biking, canyoneering, and camping. Covering 1,000 hectares (2,471 acres), it is home to rare native tree species such as the mountain ash, lily of the valley tree, and canary laurel. The park also has a landing strip for paragliders and hang gliders as well as an igloo-like reservoir where snow was stored before being transported to hotels and hospitals in Funchal. More information on hiking, bicycle rentals, and even donkey rides is available at the Reception Center.

★ WHALE-WATCHING

Due to its mid-Atlantic position, Madeira enjoys regular visits from whales, some of whom take up residence June-September. Among the species here are fin, sei, pilot, sperm, beaked, and humpback whales, along with dolphins and rare seabirds. There's a good chance of a whale sighting any time of year. Various companies operate whale- and dolphin-watching trips, mostly from Funchal's marina but also from the fishing town of Calheta on the west side of the island. Trips operate year-round except in poor weather.

The *Bonita da Madeira* (Estrada Monumental 187, tel. 291 762 218 or 919 183 829, www.bonita-da-madeira.com) is an authentic 23-meter (75-foot) wooden schooner that makes three regular themed cruises: Fine Bays, Desert Islands, and Whales and Dolphins (3 hours, 10:30am and 3pm Wed and Sun, adults €33, children 5-12 €16.50). Tours include round-trip transfer from Caniçal, Machico, Santa Cruz, and Caniço to Funchal.

VMT Madeira (Shop 9, Funchal Marina, tel. 291 224 900, www.vmtmadeira.com) operates dolphin- and whale-watching trips (3 hours, 10:30am and 3pm daily, adults €35, children 5-12 €17.50) on a catamaran, more suitable if you're susceptible to motion sickness. VMT also runs catamaran excursions to the Desertas Islands (adults €80, children €40); the all-day excursions run on Saturday only, May-September, departing Funchal Marina at 9am and returning at 5:30pm.

Santa Maria de Colombo (Shop 3, Funchal Marina, tel. 291 220 327, 291 225 695, or 965 010 180, www.santamariadecolombo.com) runs boat trips (3 hours, 10:30am and 3pm daily, adults €35, children 6-11 €17.50) on a splendid replica of Christopher Columbus's flagship *Santa Maria*. Although the trip is more about sailing on this special ship than dolphin-watching, dolphins are still regularly sighted on its voyages.

LEVADA DO FURADO HIKE

The island's unique *levada* irrigation channels offer an invigorating way to absorb Madeira's natural beauty. One of the island's most popular and prettiest walks is the **Levada do Furado (Ribeiro Frio-Portela Irrigation Channel).** Halfway between Funchal and the north coast village of Faial, 15 kilometers (9.3 mi) north of Funchal center, **Ribeiro Frio** is a small inland village where the Levado do Furado hike begins. Also known as the Ribeiro Frio-Portela walk, this moderately challenging full-day trek is about five hours and 12 kilometers (7.4 mi) through forested terrain between Ribeiro Frio and the neighboring village of Portela. The sun-dappled

Madeira's *Levada* Hikes

Madeira is laced with 2,100 kilometers (1,300 mi) of *levadas* (**irrigation channels**), mini-aqueducts that were used to irrigate the island's farmed terraces and supply drinking water. In recent years they have become an extraordinary network of walking paths through breathtaking hidden countryside. You can walk for kilometers on narrow dirt tracks that run alongside the extensive *levadas*, which are specific to Madeira and synonymous with a unique way of exploring the island.

Do your homework when deciding which *levada* to follow. Some provide relaxing, scenic strolls and others can be challenging, with tunnels and vertigo-inducing sheer cliffs. Two popular routes are **Levada do Furado,** starting in the inland village of Ribeiro Frio, and the waterfall-laced **Levada das 25 Fontes,** in Rabaçal. Sturdy, comfortable hiking boots, waterproof clothes, a flashlight, sunscreen, and drinking water are advised for embarking on a *levada* trek, and if the weather is poor, be prepared for wet, muddy conditions.

The *levada* irrigation channels make for unusual and often challenging treks.

LEVADA TOURS AND GUIDES

Lido Tours (Estrada Monumental 284, Monumental Lido shopping center, Shop 18, Funchal, tel. 291 635 505, www.lido-tours.com), among others, specializes in *levada* tours (€27-37) for all ages and levels of physical fitness. In several languages, experienced guides lead treks that last from a few hours to a full day. **Madeira Levada Walks** (Monumental Lido shopping center, Shop 23, 1st Fl., Funchal, tel. 291 763 701, www.madeira-levada-walks.com) guides leisure walks and offers around a dozen treks along the *levadas* (half-day €27, full-day €37). **Madeira Adventure Kingdom** (Estrada da Eira do Serrado 38B, tel. 968 101 870, www.madeira-adventure-kingdom. com) specializes in full-day and half-day *levada* walks (from €25) and other outdoor activities like canyoneering, scuba diving, and jeep safaris.

The **WalkMe mobile guide** (www.walkmeguide.com) was created by local hikers and offers a multitude of information, maps, guides, tips, and a downloadable app to help trekkers in Madeira see the best of the island in a safe and enjoyable way.

path is covered by heather and laurel trees, and trout swim in the *levada* alongside. The route, one of few *levadas* that can be reached by public transport, can become crowded at times. Take **Horários do Funchal** (tel. 291 705 555, www.horariosdofunchal.pt) bus 56 or 103 from Funchal toward Santana, getting off at Ribeiro Frio (40 minutes, €3.35). The route ends in Portela, from where bus 78 can be taken back to Funchal.

Accommodations

★ **Pestana Carlton Madeira Hotel** (Largo António Nobre 1, tel. 291 239 500, www. pestana.com, €152) is the grande dame of the Pestana chain and one of the first five-star hotels on Madeira. Built on the island of the founder's birth, it combines old-school glamour with impeccable service, with views from every room and a gorgeous infinity pool overlooking the Atlantic.

In the heart of historic Old Town, overlooking the main cathedral, three-star **Hotel Catedral Funchal** (Rua do Aljube 13, tel. 291 230 091, www.catedral-funchal.madeirahotels. net, €61) has elegant rooms and an extensive breakfast buffet. Founded in 1972, it's just a short walk from city center attractions.

A splendid old colonial-style manor house plus a newer hotel wing form the ★ **Quinta da Penha da França** (Rua Imperatriz D. Amelia 85, tel. 291 204 650, www.penhafrancahotels.com, €117), with pretty private gardens, two saltwater pools (one heated in winter), and ocean or garden views from all 109 rooms. This family-run hotel is an oasis of tranquility just west of Funchal center. Sleek, modern, low-rise four-star **Madeira Golden Residence Hotel** (Rua do Cabrestante 25, tel. 291 710 100, www.goldenresidencehotel.com.pt, €85), on the cliffs on the western outskirts of Funchal center, is a two-minute walk to Praia Formosa, Madeira's largest beach.

For a tiny taste of how sports stars live, spend a night at ★ **Pestana CR7 Funchal Hotel** (Av. Sá Carneiro, tel. 291 140 480, www.pestanacr7.com, €167), a small industrial-chic hotel on Funchal's marina that is a partnership between Pestana hotels and soccer legend Cristiano Ronaldo, both with close ties to the island. Ronaldo is said to have had a hand in the interior design, which includes banana-print scatter cushions, plush carpets, novel doorknobs, and fake-grass walls. The unusual open-plan kitchen-bar-reception lobby has a sleek industrial feel, while rooms are plush and swank. Guests wake to splendid views of mountains on one side and huge cruise ships on the other. The CR7 Museum is right beneath.

Perched above the Lido open-air pool complex and promenade, the contemporary **Enotel Lido Madeira** (Rua Simplício dos Passos Gouveia 29, tel. 291 702 000, www.enotel-lido-madeira.com, €200) is a gorgeous glass-fronted all-inclusive hotel a short walk from Madeira Casino and Formosa Beach. It has a variety of on-site bars and restaurants as well as many in its immediate surroundings.

Formed from five historic buildings, trendy, singular **Castanheiro Boutique Hotel** (Rua do Castanheiro 31, tel. 291 200 100, www.castanheiroboutiquehotel.com, €180) is a short walk from the heart of downtown, with 81 polished rooms and a lap pool on the roof

deck, with panoramic views of Funchal Bay. Low-key, large-scale four-star **Hotel Musa D'Ajuda** (Rua Nova Vale d'Ajuda, tel. 291 708 000, www.hotelmusadajuda.com, €72) is 3 kilometers (1.9 mi) west of Funchal's city center. Rooms, set around a large pool, are equipped with kitchenettes. The hotel has direct beach access and is just 50 meters (164 feet) from a shopping mall.

Laid-back, affordably priced, city-center three-star **Hotel Madeira** (Rua Ivens 21, tel. 291 230 071, http://hotelmadeira.com, €80) is on the doorstep of Funchal's main attractions and has clean and cozy rooms and a rooftop pool. Fun, family-friendly, affordable hotel **Pestana Promenade** (Rua Simplício dos Passos Gouveia 31, tel. 291 141 400, www.pestana.com, €142) is a 10-minute taxi ride or a 30-minute walk west of Funchal center. It offers simple but spacious rooms on the oceanfront, along with three restaurants, two pools, a spa, and a very popular happy hour.

Information and Services

National emergency number: tel. 112
PSP police: main squadron, Rua Conde Carvalhal, tel. 291 208 400, www.psp.pt
Main tourist office: Av. Arriaga 16, tel. 291 211 902, www.visitmadeira.pt, 9am-8pm Mon-Fri, 9am-3:30pm Sat-Sun
Main hospital: Hospital Dr. Nélio Mendonça, Av. Luís de Camões, tel. 291 705 600, emergency tel. 808 201 414, www.sesaram.pt
Private hospital: Madeira Medical Center, Rua do Hospital Velho 23ª, tel. 291 003 300, www.madeiramedicalcenter.pt
24-hour pharmacy: La Vie shopping center, just back from the marina, Rua Dr. Brito Câmara, tel. 291 231 174
Main post office: Mercado, near the Lavradores Market and Madeira Story Center, Rua Acipreste, 9A, 9am-6pm Mon-Fri

Getting There
AIR
Madeira Airport (Aeroporto da Madeira) (FNC, Santa Cruz, tel. 291 520 700, www.

MADEIRA AND THE AZORES
MADEIRA

Funchal Cable Car

the Funchal Cable Car

To get the most phenomenal views of Funchal and really appreciate its dramatic landscape, take the **Funchal Cable Car (Teleférico do Funchal)** (Caminho das Babosas 8, tel. 291 780 280, www.madeiracablecar.com, 9am-6pm daily, €11 one-way) from Funchal's Old Town (departs from Campo do Almirante Reis) to Monte, soaring high over streets, roads, and dramatic ridges, and through misty clouds on the 15-minute journey. At the top, enjoy the stunning Monte Palace Tropical Garden, within walking distance, as well as the Madeira Botanical Garden, reached by a second cable car from Monte, before whizzing all the way back down to the city center on one of the famous wicker basket toboggans.

aeroportomadeira.pt) is 23 kilometers (14.3 mi) east of the city center, a 20-minute drive on the VR1 road.

SAM (tel. 291 201 151, www.sam.pt) operates the Aerobus airport shuttle between Funchal center and the airport (30 minutes, hourly daily, €5). Buy tickets from the driver. There are other regular buses that connect Funchal center to the airport. A taxi from Funchal airport to the city center will cost €30. A taxi rank with Madeira's distinctive yellow cabs is located right outside the airport.

BUS

Funchal doesn't have a main bus terminal. Most buses depart near the riverfront downtown, and tickets are sold on board or from newsstands. The easily recognizable yellow buses of **Horários do Funchal** (tel. 291 705 555, www.horariosdofunchal.pt) serve the city center and its urban fringes. **SAM** (tel. 291 201 151, www.sam.pt) operates buses on main routes between Funchal, the airport, and the neighboring towns of Caniço, Machico, Caniçal, Porto da Cruz, and Santo da Serra. **Rodoeste** (tel. 291 220 148, www.rodoeste.com.pt) connects Funchal with the north and west of the island, while **EACL** (tel. 291 222 558, www.eacl.pt) connects with the east of the island.

CAR

Rent a car to explore the island. On a short stay, book it in advance to pick up at the airport. On a longer stay, visit one of numerous local car hire companies in Funchal and get a vehicle for a day or two. It's the best way to discover other parts of the island at leisure, as public transport can be intermittent in rural areas. Funchal is linked to the rest of the island with a good modern road network with long tunnels through the mountains.

Getting Around

Funchal's lower city area, along the riverside, is easily explored on foot, but farther inland the hills are steep: In places the grade of the roads can be quite intimidating, even for experienced drivers. With good bus service and the cable cars, it's easy to reach all of Funchal's main sights with minimal effort and without a car.

BUS

Bus company **Horários do Funchal** (tel. 291 705 555) has a useful guide to Funchal's public bus services and networks in English that can be downloaded (www.horariosdofunchal.pt/guia-en/mobile). Fares start from €1.95; tickets can be bought from the driver. Rechargeable cards, which cost €0.50, can be purchased from selling points including newsagents, post offices, and tourist offices, and can be credited with prepaid single journeys. At €1.35 for a single journey, it works out cheaper than buying from the driver. A 24-hour pass for unlimited bus travel is €4.50; three-, five-, and seven-day passes are also available. There is a decent bus network between Funchal and other main points on Madeira Island, but it is limited elsewhere.

CAR

Parking in Funchal center is not a problem, as it has a number of designated car parks, but traffic on the narrow streets can get congested.

TAXI

A distinctive bright yellow color with blue stripes, taxis are widely available in Funchal and a reasonable way to get around town. Flag them down in the street or go to one of the taxi ranks found throughout the city. Fares should be displayed on the meter, but don't hesitate to ask roughly how much a journey will cost before setting off.

MONTE

In the hills over Funchal, 6 kilometers (3.7 mi) north of the city center, Monte (MONT, with a silent *e*) is a small mountainside town where some of the region's main attractions, such as the exhilarating wicker toboggans, can be found. Easily accessed by a scenic cable car from Funchal's waterfront near the old town, this village was formerly a well-being retreat for wealthy Europeans.

Sights
MONTE PALACE TROPICAL GARDEN
(Jardim Tropical Monte Palace)

Covering 70,000 square meters (17 acres), the **Monte Palace Tropical Garden** (Caminho do Monte 174, tel. 291 780 800, www.montepalace.com, 9:30am-6pm daily, €12.50) houses formal gardens, lakes and ponds, and rich flora and fauna, including swans, as well as a museum, Asian gardens, and garden art. On three floors, the funky-looking museum is well organized, with two floors showcasing African sculptures and the third housing a unique mineral collection. The sparkling centerpiece is an exhibition of 300 semiprecious and precious gems, among them rough and cut diamonds. Throughout the lovely gardens are statues and sculptures in stone and metal, creating an intriguing open-air art collection hidden among lush exotic flora.

Recreation
★ WICKER TOBOGGAN SLED RIDES

Whiz down the steep, winding roads of Funchal from Monte to downtown on the famous **Wicker Toboggans** (tel. 291 783 919, www.carreirosdomonte.com, 9am-6pm Mon-Sat, €30 per basket). Madeira's answer to Venice's gondolas, the wicker toboggans are an exhilarating attraction that embodies the region's traditional basket-weaving craft and its creative ways of getting around. Dating to the 1850s, these sleds were originally used to transport people and goods from the hills to downtown. The sled baskets are big enough for two people and travel on runners, pushed and steered by two smartly dressed men called *carreiros*, who have only the soles of their shoes as brakes. These 2-kilometer (1.2-mi), 10-minute runs reach 48 km/h (30 mph) and are an art form as well as one of Madeira's must-do attractions. The toboggans are in Monte, at the bottom of the Our Lady of Monte (Nossa Senhora do Monte) church stairs.

Getting There

The easiest way to get to Monte is the **cable car** (departs from Campo do Almirante Reis, tel. 291 780 280, www.madeiracablecar.com, 15 minutes, 9am-5:45pm daily, €11) from Funchal's Old Town.

Horários do Funchal (tel. 291 705 555, www.horariosdofunchal.pt) runs buses 20 and 21 (20 minutes, €1.60 plus €0.50 bus card) from the main road through Funchal center (Rua 31 Janeiro) to Monte. The buses run about hourly, and sometimes more frequently, on weekdays (about 6am-midnight Mon-Fri) and are also about hourly on weekends (about 6am-8pm Sat-Sun).

A taxi from Funchal to Monte costs around €20.

RABAÇAL

One of Mother Nature's great achievements, Rabaçal (rah-bah-SSAL) is a spectacular amphitheater of natural springs, mountains, waterfalls, and the Laurissilva forest, a botanical rarity that covers around 20 percent of the island and dates back 20 million years. The forest is classified by UNESCO as Natural World Heritage. West of Funchal, Rabaçal is an example of natural heritage best discovered on foot. Pack a waterproof raincoat and comfy boots, maybe a swimsuit, and a camera, and take one of the most popular *levada* hikes.

Recreation

LEVADA DAS 25 FONTES HIKE

Arguably the most popular *levada* walk on the island, the **Levada das 25 Fontes (25 Fountains)** trail is well marked and zigzags through spectacular landscape, starting at the car park on the main ER110 road on the Paúl da Serra plateau in Rabaçal. From here, there's a gentle 2-kilometer (1.2-mi) walk down to the Rabaçal forestry house. A minibus runs at regular intervals between the car park and the shelter (€3 one-way, €5 round-trip). This makes the trek easier on the return. There are toilet facilities at the forestry house but nowhere else on the route.

From the forestry house, the 25 Fontes *levada* leads to the mesmerizing Risco waterfall, passing through the Rabaçal valley and the picturesque cascading waterfalls from which the *levada* takes its name. The trail also passes through astonishing tunnels of tree heather, shaded woodland, fragrant laurel trees, and forest to Risco and its half-moon-shaped lagoon. Construction on the 25 Fontes *levada* started in 1835 and took 20 years. The 4.5-kilometer (2.8-mi) one-way route takes three or four hours through ravines and tunnels and over bridges. The trail climbs to 1,290 meters (4,232 feet) elevation. A number of stone staircases are involved, and the trail can get very crowded with large tour groups, so try to get here before 9:30am to enjoy it at its most peaceful.

Getting There

Rabaçal and the 25 Fontes *levada* are 30 kilometers (19 mi) west of Funchal on the VR1 road and north on the VE4 road to Encumeada; then head west again on the ER110 road toward Gazebo Rabaçal. The route and parking are well signed. From the parking, follow signs on foot to the Rabaçal shelter house and the start of the 25 Fontes *levada*. The drive from Funchal takes an hour.

A round-trip by taxi from Funchal to the 25 Fontes *levada* costs around €90. There is no public transport to Rabaçal. **Rodoeste** (tel. 291 220 148, www.rodoeste.com.pt) runs a bus from Funchal to Encumeada (bus 139 to Santa-Porto Moniz), although it leaves just a couple of times a day and takes over two hours to Encumeada; from there a taxi should cost €16 one-way.

PORTO MONIZ

With dramatic mountains and ocean as a backdrop, Porto Moniz (POR-too moo-NEEZH) is famous for natural saltwater pools, created from lava and filled with seawater by the tide. The journey here is gripping, skirting around the edge of the island through a series of tunnels and along steep hillsides before arriving at the island's northwesternmost point. There is a selection of pleasant sea-view cafés and restaurants as well as hotels.

Sights

PORTO MONIZ NATURAL SWIMMING POOLS

Made from lava that trickled into the ocean to create jagged black formations, the famous, beautiful natural swimming pools of Porto Moniz, on the northwest tip of Madeira Island, fill with seawater. Surrounded by the Atlantic, they make the ultimate infinity pool and are particularly enticing when the weather is hot. Many locals have an invigorating dip as part of their daily routine.

Near the entrance to the town of Porto Moniz are the wild-feeling **Cachelote natural pools** (24 hours daily, free), and a short walk from these are the **managed pools** (Rue do Forte de São João Baptista 7A, tel. 291 850 190, www.portomoniz.pt, 9am-7pm daily, €1.50), which also have a children's swimming pool, a children's play area, sun beds and parasols, lifeguards, changing facilities, a snack bar, and disabled access.

Getting There

Porto Moniz is 50 kilometers (31 mi) and 1.5 hours from Funchal by car on the main VR1 west from Funchal to Ribeira Brava, then through the middle of the island along the VE4 road to the north coast, then west along the VE2 road from São Vicente to Porto Moniz.

By public transport, **Rodoeste** (tel. 291 220 148, www.rodoeste.com.pt) operates bus 139 (3 hours, morning and afternoon daily, €12 round-trip) to Santa-Porto Moniz, via São Vicente village, and bus 80 (3 hours, 9am daily, arriving at noon, €12 round-trip) to Porto Moniz (return bus departing 4pm daily), via Calheta village, both departing from Funchal and passing through lovely villages and around the rugged rim of the island. Bus 139 has fewer stops. Tickets can be purchased at the kiosk on the main Avenida do Mar in Funchal.

CANIÇAL

A 15-minute drive up the coast from Funchal, past the airport to Madeira's easternmost tip, is Caniçal (kah-nee-SSAL), famous for fishing, shipping, and until 1982, whaling, when demand for whale meat plummeted and conservation became the focus. Reminders of Caniçal's whaling history are the modern and interactive whaling museum, with a life-size whale monument suspended inside, and photos and posters on the streets. Today Madeira's whales aren't hunted but act as a tourism draw.

On a relatively secluded and remote tip of the island, the town's port was extensively developed between the mid-1990s and mid-2000s as Madeira's biggest cargo port and is now home to boats of all sizes. On a clear day, the nearby island of Porto Santo can be seen.

Sights

WHALE MUSEUM
(Museu da Baleia)

Caniçal's **Whale Museum** (Rua Garcia Moniz 1, tel. 291 961 858, www.museudabaleia.org, 10:30am-6pm Tues-Sun, adults €10, children 12-17 €8.50, children 6-11 €5) is a large and innovative museum that explores the island's short whaling history from 1941 to 1982, when commercial whaling dried up as the international movement to preserve whales gained force. In an unexpectedly modern building on a hillside overlooking the sea, the museum houses interesting interactive exhibitions, 3-D movies, life-size statues, scale examples of whaling boats and whales killed, and historic whaling paraphernalia, all of which provide insight into how Madeirans hunted the huge mammals and their uses.

The museum is on three floors, divided into the island's whaling history and whale species and conservation. While many exhibits are child-friendly, some are graphic and could be disturbing to the sensitive. Special tours for children are available. The institution that runs the museum conducts scientific research projects and collects and catalogs marinelife from Madeira waters.

Getting There

Caniçal is 32 kilometers (20 mi) and 30 minutes' drive from Funchal along the main VR1 coastal road, east past the airport. Regular public transport is on **SAM** (tel. 291 201 151, www.sam.pt) bus 113 (45 minutes, €3.35), departing from near the park on Funchal's main Avenida do Mar. The bus runs about hourly on weekdays, less frequently on weekends.

PORTO SANTO ISLAND

A two-hour ferry journey or a short flight from Madeira is the much smaller island of Porto Santo, an unspoiled haven of golden sand, tranquil water, and a smaller range of activities, attractions, bars, restaurants, and hotels. Stretching 43 kilometers (27 mi), Porto Santo is the northernmost and easternmost island of the Madeira archipelago, famed for year-round mild weather and a beach—a 9-kilometer (5.6-mi) crescent of pristine sand and warm turquoise water. Dubbed the "Golden Island," it has a Caribbean feel but with the rugged ocher landscape and architecture of Portugal.

Porto Santo's tourism has taken off in recent years, with a few good hotels and elegant four-star all-inclusive resorts. But it is not being overrun or overbuilt, as construction has been regulated to be in harmony with the island's character.

The biggest town is **Vila Baleira,** on the south side, the island's first settlement and

active year-round. Home to most of the island's residents and action, Vila Baleira has low-key, unspoiled charm and an unhurried pace, except on weekends and summer when visitor numbers are higher.

The island's southwest shore is one long, glorious beach, and its northeastern shore is rocky and rugged, spiked with mountain peaks. This makes the southern part popular among sun lovers and the northern coast popular among adventure seekers, although neither becomes crowded. Stretch out on the warm sand, dive, hike, or try stand-up paddleboarding.

Sights and Recreation

CHAPEL OF THE HOLY SPIRIT
(Capela do Espirito Santo)

Small and simple and perfectly formed, the 17th-century **Chapel of the Holy Spirit** (Estrada Regional 120, Campo de Baixo, tel. 291 982 215, open for mass only, 10am Sun, 5:30pm Sat Oct-May, 6:30pm Sat June-Sept, free) in Campo de Baixo was built in the mannerist style and extensively refurbished during the 19th century. A short walk from Vila Baleira, this pretty little chapel has a simple facade with a bell tower. Inside it features 17th-century Flemish paintings of the Last Supper. It is a 2.5-kilometer (1.6-mi), 30-minute walk southwest from Vila Baleira.

CHRISTOPHER COLUMBUS
HOUSE MUSEUM
(Casa de Colombo)

Famed Italian explorer and navigator Christopher Columbus is said to have lived on Porto Santo while planning his global voyages, and the house in which he is believed to have spent several years with his wife has been transformed into the **Christopher Columbus House Museum** (Travessa da Sacristia 2-4, Vila Baleira, tel. 291 983 405, 10am-12:30pm and 2pm-5:30pm Tues-Sat,

1: Madeira's trademark wicker basket toboggans; **2:** Porto Moniz's gorgeous natural swimming pools; **3:** the small fishing village of Caniçal; **4:** Porto Santo Beach

10am-1pm Sun, €2). The small 15th-century stone house is in an alley behind Porto Santo's main church. Spread over several rooms, it houses artifacts relating to Columbus and his expeditions, including a portrait and replicas of 15th- and 16th-century maps, as well as large panels tracing Portuguese maritime history. A separate room showcases artifacts recovered from a Spanish galleon that sank off Porto Santo in 1724. The museum, inaugurated in 1989, also has a lovely little courtyard.

PORTO SANTO BEACH
(Praia Porto Santo)

Porto Santo Beach, one of the island's highlights, is an uncrowded 9-kilometer (5.6-mi) strip of pristine soft sand and warm turquoise water that provide tranquil beach days and the opportunity for long strolls. It is divided into five smaller beaches, each with a name, stretching southwest along the main strip of hotel resorts between Vila Baleira and Calheta Point, the southwestern tip of the island. Widely believed to have therapeutic properties that relieve aches and pains, the fine volcanic sand mixed with particles of ancient coral reefs gives the beach a yellow-and-gray two-tone look. Flanked by snack bars, restaurants, and elegant resorts, Porto Santo is the ultimate beach paradise and one of Europe's best-kept beach secrets.

Stand-up paddleboards can be rented from outfitters and hotels along the beach, including **On Water Academy** (tel. 964 838 535, www.onwateracademy.com, from €25 for 1.5 hours).

CASTELO PEAK
(Pico do Castelo)

Shaped like a volcano, the Castelo Peak has precipitous sides but good conditions for walking. The **hiking trail** to **Castelo Peak Viewpoint** starts in the hamlet of Moledo, just off the Regional Road (Estrada Regional), about a 15-minute, 3.5-kilometer (2.2-mi) drive north from Vila Baleira. The trail passes Facho Peak, the highest point on the island,

and winds through forested hillsides with native flora and fauna before reaching this legendary viewpoint at 437 meters (1,434 feet) elevation. The trailhead is signposted and easy to find. Two trails can be followed: one a shorter and easier 3.2-kilometer (2-mi) loop around the north side of the peak that takes 1.5 hours, and a longer and tougher 4.6-kilometer (2.9-mi) loop on the south side, which takes two hours and is the longest pedestrian trail on the island.

Despite its name, there is no castle; in the 15th century there was a fort on the site where residents took refuge from pirates and invaders. The panoramic viewpoint looks out over the airport, houses, and the ocean, and on a clear day you can see the Desertas Islands and Madeira Island. There are picnic tables.

ANA FERREIRA PEAK
(Pico de Ana Ferreira)

The highest point on the west side of Porto Santo Island, **Ana Ferreira Peak** is unique for its unusual summit, which erupts in an oddly ridged rim of pentagonal basalt rock columns like bizarrely shaped teeth. Nicknamed "the Organ," these peculiar pipes—similar to the famous Giant's Causeway in Northern Ireland, only bigger—were shaped millions of years ago by volcanic activity, when thick lava flows cooled and cracked. Also named the "Piano Quarry," this unusual formation is a fantastic viewpoint, at 283 meters (928 feet) elevation, with views over Porto Santo. The **hike** to Ana Ferreira Peak, whose trailhead starts near the Porto Santo golf course, is easy and short (1 hour, 5 km/3.1 mi) on a road or on dirt tracks, southwest from Vila Baleira.

An exciting way to explore the peak is to take a 4WD Jeep excursion, such as those operated by **Lazermar** (Rua João Gonçalves Zarco 66, Vila Baleira, tel. 963 501 488, www.lazermar.com, 3.5 hours, €25) on a bumpy off-road round-trip, passing through hidden beauty spots and geological places of interest, including Ana Ferreira Peak.

DIVING

Porto Santo is a world-class diving spot thanks to its unspoiled water with a rare high level of visibility. Impressive dive sites include the *Madeirense,* a purposely sunk ship that attracts fish. Providers include **Rhea Dive Center** (tel. 969 333 777, www.rheadive.com), taking divers and snorkelers to Porto Santo's best spots since 2007.

Food

Porto Santo shares typical dishes with big sister Madeira. Signature fare includes *fragateira,* a fish stew for sharing, as well as *gaiado,* sun-dried skipjack tuna. Most of Porto Santo's restaurants and bars are in the main town, Vila Baleira.

Quirky little ★ **Mercado Antigo** (Old Market) (Rua João Gonçalves Zarco, Vila Baleira, tel. 291 984 205, 9am-late daily, €10) is in the island's old fish market. Patrons perch on little stools at cement tables as unfussy traditional fare, including *lapas,* grilled fish, *bolo do caco* sandwiches, and a great *poncho,* is served at cheap prices.

★ **Casinha do Bolo do Caco** (Praça do Barqueiro, Porto Santo quay, Vila Baleira, tel. 291 645 852, 10am-midnight daily, €5) is a little beach shack specializing in sandwiches and snacks made with typical fresh-baked *bolo do caco* bread rolls. These include *bolo do caco* smeared with chocolate spread or stuffed with spicy sausage or bacon and cheese. This is a great place to grab a quick bite during a day at the beach: street food with a smile.

La Siesta (Rua João Gonçalves Zarco da Praia, Vila Baleira, tel. 914 694 474, 7pm-2am Wed-Mon June-Sept, €20) is a quaint wooden beach restaurant with a definite shack-chic vibe. Cozy and in a romantic setting, La Siesta has a menu that showcases inventive gourmet food inspired by fresh island ingredients and prepared with an Asian twist. Dishes include Thai vegetarian curry, scallop carpaccio, and duck *magret.*

Casa d'Avo (Campo de Baixo, tel. 291 982 037, 5pm-2am Mon-Sat, €20), 2.5 kilometers (1.6 mi) southwest of Vila Baleira, off the main ER111 road, is an elegant little restaurant in a lovely setting that serves flavorful traditional Madeiran dishes, nicely presented and based on local products. Madeiran staple seafood *lapas* are on the menu, as are steak with shrimp sauce and other regional favorites such as the *espetada* kebabs and *espada* scabbard fish.

Getting There

AIR

Two kilometers (1.2 mi) north of Vila Baleira, **Porto Santo Airport (Aeroporto do Porto Santo)** (PXO, tel. 291 520 700, www.aeroportoportosanto.pt) is small but has a modern terminal and a 3,000-meter (9.843-foot) runway that accommodates most aircraft. It receives just a couple of daily flights in winter, growing to a handful in summer.

There are a few direct flights between mainland Portugal and Porto Santo. **TAP Air Portugal** (tel. 707 205 700, www.flytap.com) flies from Lisbon to Porto Santo weekly in low season (Oct-May) and more frequently in high season (June-Sept). Regional airline **SATA Azores Airlines** (tel. 707 227 282, www.azoresairlines.pt) operates a direct flight from Lisbon to Porto Santo. Airfares start from €200 round-trip and the flight takes 1.5 hours. Seasonal summer flights come to Porto Santo from Germany and the United Kingdom.

Porto Santo is more easily reached from Madeira Island. Regional airline **Sevenair** (tel. 214 444 545, www.sevenair.com) is the main carrier to Porto Santo, operating daily flights from Funchal. At the time of writing, Spanish airline **Binter Canarias** (tel. +34 902 391 392, www.bintercanarias.com), based in the Canary Islands, was offering cheap direct flights between Funchal and Porto Santo (15 minutes, from €66 one-way) twice daily in summer high season.

Porto Santo Airport is a five-minute drive north of Vila Baleira. The easiest way to and from the airport is in a taxi. There is a taxi rank right outside the airport. A taxi from the airport to the center costs €10-15, depending on the time of day and if you have bags.

FERRY

By sea, Porto Santo Line's *Lobo Marinho* ferry (tel. 291 210 300, www.portosantoline. pt) runs daily between Madeira and Porto Santo (2 hours, €47-72 adults Oct-Mar, €58-81 Apr-Sept), weather permitting; the ferry departs from Funchal in the early morning and departs Porto Santo in the late afternoon or evening. Passengers enjoy a number of bars, restaurants, and even a cinema on board. Cars (€93-121), bicycles, and motorbikes can be transported. First- and second-class tickets can be purchased online, from a ticket office (Av. do Mar e das Comunidades Madeirenses 20, Funchal, tel. 291 210 300, 8:30am-6pm Mon-Fri, 9am-12:30pm and 2pm-5pm Sat; Estrada Monumental 175C, Funchal, tel. 291 210 300, 9am-12:30pm and 2pm-8pm daily), or from the passengers' terminal at the port, up to one hour before departure.

Getting Around

There are plenty of **taxis** on Porto Santo, and a taxi is a reasonable option to go anywhere, as distances on the island are short and fares reasonable. The island's main taxi rank is next to the petrol station on Avenida Dr. Manuel Gregório Pestana Júnior, at the end of Rua João Gonçalves Zarco, in Vila Baleira. You can also call **Vila Baleira taxis** (tel. 291 982 334). A half-day tour of the island by taxi costs around €30.

Besides taxis, the best way to explore Vila Baleira is **on foot,** as most attractions and the main beaches are in and around Vila Baleira. Plenty of local excursions, which can be booked through hotel desks, take you to the island's more remote attractions. Renting a **car** is also an option; if you're staying for a short time, book ahead to get the car at the airport. The island is easy and safe to drive around.

For those arriving by ferry, a **bus** is always waiting to take passengers to Vila Baleira (€1). It's operated by **Moinho Rent-a-Car** (tel. 291 982 141 or 966 066 389, www.moinhorentacar. com), which manages Porto Santo's public bus service; its main hub is next to the petrol station at the beach end of Rua João Gonçalves Zarco, but due to the island's limited size, the routes are not varied. Six daily buses, leaving hourly, do the same route around the coast and inland; costs vary depending on destination.

A local **tour bus,** operated by **Lazermar** (tel. 963 501 488, www.lazermar.com), departs from the city's main taxi rank at 10am and 3pm daily and makes a two-hour tour of the island (adults €20, children 6-12 €10).

Horse-drawn carriages (tel. 964 682 937, up to 6 people, €15 for 15 minutes, €30 for 30 minutes, €50 for 1 hour) are brought out in summer for visitors to enjoy the sights of Vila Baleira and along the coast. They are usually available from the vicinity of the ferry terminal or along the main promenade.

The Azores

It's hard to describe the breathtaking natural mystique of the volcanic Azores. Scattered like emeralds in the middle of the Atlantic, the nine lush islands—some modern and developed, others still largely unspoiled and rural—are among Europe's last best-kept secrets. Tourism has started to take off on the main island, São Miguel, in recent years, and low-cost and charter flights from all over Europe now visit this Edenic oasis. But the islands are still far from being a mainstream destination, and traveling to a relatively uncharted place of idyllic beauty and friendliness makes the Azores alluring. The archipelago's famously changeable weather, which swings from sunny and warm to cool with low-hanging clouds in the blink of an eye, adds to its mystical aura. A short hop from the mainland, luxuriant gardens, soothing hot springs, quaint villages, and dramatic landscapes make the Azores a world away from the everyday.

The Azores were discovered circa 1427 and colonized by the Portuguese from the 1430s. History has it that sheep were the first inhabitants, having been let loose on the islands ahead of human occupation to sustain future settlers. Portuguese settlement was slow, as there was little interest from mainlanders in moving to such a far-flung location, but eventually the first colonizers came mostly from the Algarve, Alentejo, Central Portugal, and Madeira. This intermittent settlement influenced local dialects and gastronomy, which vary remarkably, as do the landscapes and climates of the islands. Interestingly, the Azores also had a large Flemish settlement whose influences are noticeable to this day, most visibly in the many little windmills that pepper the islands.

The climate is mostly wet and mild, influenced by the winds and currents of the Gulf Stream. Small tremors happen regularly on this volcanic archipelago, although few of the islands have had eruptions since human habitation, and the mini rumbles rarely cause damage. This volcanism, which fuels bubbling fumaroles, hissing hot-water geysers, and soothing springs, is a major draw to the archipelago and provides its main attractions.

THE ISLANDS

Located deep in the middle of the Atlantic Ocean, a two-hour flight straight west from mainland Portugal, the Azores archipelago spreads over 600 kilometers (370 mi). Roughly a quarter of the way between Portugal and the United States, this group of nine loosely scattered volcanic islands (actually the tips of some of the biggest underwater mountains on the planet) is divided into three groups: São Miguel and Santa Maria in the eastern cluster; Graciosa, Terceira, São Jorge, Pico, and Faial in the central group; and Flores and Corvo to the west. The time zone in the Azores is one hour earlier than on the mainland.

The largest island, São Miguel, and its capital, Ponta Delgada, tend to be the number-one destination, and it makes a great base. A few days can be spent taking in São Miguel's attractions; just exploring the pretty streets and harborside in Ponta Delgada could take up a day. If you only have time for one island, São Miguel has the archipelago's main landmarks. It also has the airport and port for trips to the other islands. Start with a couple of days in Ponta Delgada and allow another few days to explore one or two of the other islands.

São Miguel Island

Just 42 square kilometers (16 square mi) smaller than Madeira and locally dubbed the "Green Island," São Miguel is in the eastern group and is the biggest and most populous island in the Azores. Its main city, **Ponta Delgada,** is the Azores' capital. The archipelago's outstanding natural beauty is apparent while landing at Ponta Delgada's airport, with the sea to one side and majestic mountains

The Azores

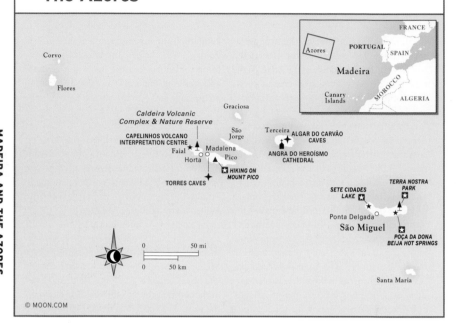

© MOON.COM

flanking the other. Ponta Delgada is densely populated, but just 10 minutes out of town, sprawling green fields dotted with sheep and cattle and a rainbow of colorful flowers justify the island's nickname. Among the highlights of long, whale-shaped São Miguel are incredible **crater lakes,** soothing **hot springs,** and rolling green meadows stretching to the horizon.

Terceira Island

Terceira Island is the second most populous in the archipelago. Almost perfectly round, it forms part of the central cluster of islands along with Faial, São Jorge, Graciosa, and Pico. Its name translates as "third," as it was the third island to be inhabited and is also the third largest in the archipelago. A patchwork of verdant plains and forested mountains, Terceira is nicknamed the "Lilac Island" due to its stunning sunsets as well as an abundance of purple hydrangea. The island's coastline is hemmed by a string of forts built to

protect the main port, **Angra do Heroísmo,** from pirate attacks in the 16th and 17th centuries, after it became a popular stopover point for treasure-laden Spanish galleons en route from the New World. Angra do Heroísmo is the oldest city in the Azores and the historical capital, classified as a World Heritage Site by UNESCO.

Pico Island

Pico's snowcapped summit, **Mount Pico,** is famously the highest point in all of Portugal at 2,351 meters (7,713 feet), dominating the second-largest island in the Azores, often referred to as the "Black Island" due to its dark volcanic terrain. The landmark Mount Pico is one of the major draws for adventure climbing. The island's main town, **Madalena,** spreads along the foot of Mount Pico, fronted by the Faial channel, facing Faial Island, 7 kilometers (4.3 mi) away. Pico has a unique and successful **wine** industry, with vineyards thriving in the volcanic soil. One of the last islands to be inhabited, Pico is today one of the most popular.

Faial Island

Faial is best known for its main town, **Horta,** one of the most colorful and attractive in the archipelago. Horta is a popular **stopping point for sailors** crossing the Atlantic in their yachts, which gives the town an international and cosmopolitan feel. This watering hole for traveling yachties also boasts stunning views of Pico, which it faces. In keeping with other Portuguese islands, Faial has a color-inspired nickname, the "Blue Island," derived from the vast ocean surrounding it and the blue hydrangeas that cover the island. The lush banks of this peaceful haven slope gently upward toward a central **volcano** before dropping into the 400-meter-deep (1,312-foot-deep) caldera. This awesome geological formation provides visitors with fantastic walks and jaw-dropping scenery.

GETTING THERE
Air

The only way to get to the Azores is by air. Following the liberalization of the islands' airspace in 2015, more carriers and flights than ever before serve the archipelago.

All nine islands have an airfield for interisland transportation, but only three (São Miguel, Faial, and Terceira) have international airports. **Ponta Delgada Airport (Aeroporto de Ponta Delgada)** (PDL, tel. 296 205 400, www.aeroportopontadelgada. pt), on São Miguel, is the Azores' main airport and receives the vast majority of international flights. **Lajes Airport (Aeroporto das Lajes),** also known as **Lajes Civil Air Base (Aerogare Civil das Lajes)** (TER, tel. 295 545 454, www.aerogarelajes.azores.gov. pt), on Terceira, is both a civilian airport and a military airbase, managed by the Portuguese armed forces with a U.S. presence. Lajes Airport also has direct international flights, primarily from Europe. **Horta Airport (Aeroporto da Horta)** (HOR, tel. 292 943 511, www.aeroportohorta.pt), on Faial, also receives direct international flights, mainly from Europe.

From mainland Portugal, the Azores are a short and cheap two-hour flight. Round-trip flights can be found for less than €100. The main airlines are national flag-carrier **TAP Air Portugal** (tel. 707 205 700, www.flytap. com), regional carrier **SATA Azores Airlines** (tel. 707 227 282, www.sata.pt), and Irish low-cost airline **Ryanair** (tel. +44 871 246 0002, www.ryanair.com).

- **To Ponta Delgada (São Miguel):** TAP, SATA, and Ryanair have regular direct flights from Lisbon and Porto.

- **To Lajes (Terceira):** TAP and SATA offer regular direct flights from Lisbon and Porto; Ryanair has less frequent direct flights.

- **To Horta (Faial):** TAP and SATA have direct flights from Lisbon; from Porto, flights usually require a stop in Lisbon or Terceira.

SATA provides a free onward service from Porto, Lisbon, Faro via Lisbon, or Funchal via Ponta Delgada, meaning you can request a free onward connecting flight to any other Azorean island. The flight must be taken within 24 hours of landing in Ponta Delgada.

SATA also operates direct flights to the Azores from Boston and Newark in the United States and Toronto in Canada year-round, and from Montreal in summer months. TAP, SATA, and Ryanair operate direct flights from London's airports, including Gatwick and Stansted, to Ponta Delgada. Flights from London to Horta and Lajes entail a stop in Lisbon.

GETTING AROUND
Between the Islands

Traveling among the Azores' islands is pretty straightforward, with regular interisland flights and ferries, although fares fluctuate with the tourism seasons.

All of the Azores' nine islands are connected by **ferry,** operated by **Atlânticoline** (main cruise terminal on Ponta Delgada harbor, Av. Infante Dom Henrique, tel. 707 201

572, www.atlanticoline.pt). Ferries run several times a day between Horta (Faial) and Madalena (Pico), various times a week between the central and western groups of islands, and seasonally (May-Sept) between the eastern group (São Miguel and Santa Maria) and the other islands. Given the Azores' famously unpredictable weather, ferry journeys are always subject to weather conditions.

For islands that are farther apart, for example São Miguel to Pico, it's quicker to take a **flight**. Regional airline **SATA Air Azores** (tel. 707 227 282, www.sata.pt) provides interisland service. The frequency of the short interisland flights varies depending on the season, running more frequently in summer and less frequently in winter.

On the Islands

Hiring a **car** is the way to go if you really want to discover the bigger islands (São Miguel, Terceira, and Pico), particularly if you're going to be spending a few days. Faial, a smaller island, can be explored on a rental **scooter.** Car rentals are cheap and are more flexible than booking often costly excursions. Fuel is cheaper than on the mainland, and the roads are generally quiet and well maintained.

Taxis are a practical way of getting around and are reasonably priced. **Public transport,** however, is designed to be practical for locals, so for visitors it is limited, and even on the bigger islands service is infrequent, particularly on weekends. The bigger islands do have cheap public transport, although buses tend to follow the main coastal roads, and few travel inland.

SÃO MIGUEL ISLAND

The Azores' biggest island, São Miguel (sown mee-GELL), is fun and stimulating. With pools of rusty-red hot spring water and blanketed in wild flora interspersed with pretty towns and fishing villages, the volcanic island is just a little smaller than Madeira Island, but its landscape is vastly diverse. Blanketed by verdant woodland and meadows, São Miguel is home to capital city **Ponta Delgada** and the main international airport, though it shows few signs of pandering to mainstream tourism. Life moves at an unhurried pace that adds to the laid-back feel. São Miguel is also where many of the Azores' most famous sights can be found, such as Sete Cidades Lake and Terra Nostra Park, with evocative landscapes and excellent gastronomy far off the beaten track.

A car is the best way to explore São Miguel. Good highways cover the island. Navigating the quiet winding roads is easy; keep the sea on the left, and eventually you'll come full circle. In a rush the island could be circumnavigated in a day, but it's better to dedicate one day or more to the east and west ends. Include a day in Ponta Delgada, compact enough to cover on foot and the departure point for whale- and dolphin-watching trips.

On São Miguel, make sure you always have a swimsuit and a towel with you, as jumping into steaming hot springs is a tempting treat, whatever the weather—but make sure it's an old swimsuit, as the iron-rich waters can turn clothes orange.

Ponta Delgada

The gateway to the Azores, Ponta Delgada is toward the western end of the island's south coast. Developed from a humble fishing port into a cosmopolitan city, it is quaint and polished and retains its small-town feel. Devoid of high-rises but densely built, the city is easy to navigate on foot, with most of the restaurants, cafés, shops, and bars along several streets in the old part of town that frames the harbor. Here visitors will find aristocratic buildings, pretty cobbled squares, and manicured gardens. Its architecture is distinctively two-toned, with whitewashed walls and black basalt trim. Grand monuments are scattered around, evoking Ponta Delgada's days as a trading port. Most of the vessels that sail into its harbor today are privately owned yachts on transatlantic voyages, the odd transatlantic cruise ship, and ferries to other Azores islands.

A must in Ponta Delgada is whale-watching, with trips departing from the marina at the far eastern end of the harbor promenade. Some of the Azores' most resplendent sights are a short drive from Ponta Delgada.

SIGHTS

Avenida Infante Dom Henrique, a beautiful harborside promenade, is a pleasant stroll from a formidable 16th-century fort on the western tip to a cosmopolitan marina with chic restaurants and trendy bars. The historic Renaissance fortress, the **Fort of São Brás (Forte de São Brás)** (Rua Engenheiro Abel Ferin Coutinho 10, tel. 296 304 920, www. monumentos.gov.pt, 10am-6pm Mon-Fri, €3) is today occupied by the Portuguese Navy and a museum dedicated to Azorean military paraphernalia.

Opposite the fort is one of Ponta Delgada's main squares, the pretty Praça 5 de Outubro, with its charming little central bandstand, flanked by handsome buildings. Farther down are the imposing **Old Gates** to the city, the trio of large freestanding arches with a royal coat of arms on top, built in the 18th century and a symbol of Ponta Delgada. This gateway was formerly next to the old quay but was relocated to the decorative Gonçalo Velho Cabral Square, which stretches before the gateway.

Also of interest in the old quarter, located inside the impressive 16th-century Saint Andrew Monastery (Convento de Santo André), is the **Carlos Machado Museum (Museu Carlos Machado)** (Rua do Dr. Guilherme Poças 65, tel. 296 202 930, www. museucarlosmachado.azores.gov.pt, 10am-5:30pm Tues-Sun, €5), which explores natural history and local farming and fishing. Divided between the monastery and two additional sites within walking distance, the museum collection also includes local sacred art. It's a great option for a rainy day.

The streets throughout Ponta Delgada are an attraction in themselves, boasting fancy black-and-white cobblestone designs in stripes, stars, chains, and other eye-catching patterns.

DOLPHIN- AND WHALE-WATCHING

The Azores' deep waters are home to one of the largest whale populations on the planet, with both resident and migrating species. Seeing whales and dolphins is possible year-round. Spotted dolphins, sperm whales, sei whales, and bearded whales are most frequent in summer, while blue whales are most frequent at the end of winter.

Numerous companies operating on São Miguel specialize in these tours; a sighting is almost guaranteed on every trip. One of the foremost is **Azores Whale Watching Terra Azul** (tel. 296 581 361, www.azoreswhalewatch.com, 2.5 hours, early morning, noon, and mid-afternoon daily, €55-60), whose trips are guided by experienced marine biologists and naturalist guides. Based at the Ponta Delgada Marina and with over 15 years' experience in whale-watching, it provides a thrilling and educational experience. Trips depart from the marina.

FOOD

Big portions of traditional Azorean food are served up at ★ **A Tasca** (Rua do Alijube 16, tel. 296 288 880, 11am-2am Mon-Sat, 5pm-1am Sun, €12), an unassuming backstreet tavern whose rustic wooden tables are usually full due to its reputation as the island's best place to eat. Local fare is given a creative twist without being pretentious, and it's cheap. Due to demand, reservations are necessary.

Another of Ponta Delgada's most popular little taverns, **Saca Rolhas Taberna** (Rua Nova 50, Relva, tel. 296 716 747, www. sacarolhas.pt, noon-3pm and 7pm-11pm Mon-Sat, €18), which translates as "corkscrew," is a cozy eatery where the menu showcases a wide range of typical local fish and meat, along with cold meats, cheeses, homemade soups, and desserts.

The island-inspired interior design of **Restaurante São Pedro** (Largo Almirante Dunn 23A, tel. 296 281 600, www. restaurantesaopedro.com, noon-3pm Mon-Fri, 6pm-11pm daily, €18) reflects its vast traditional menu of Azorean classics. Dishes

São Miguel Island

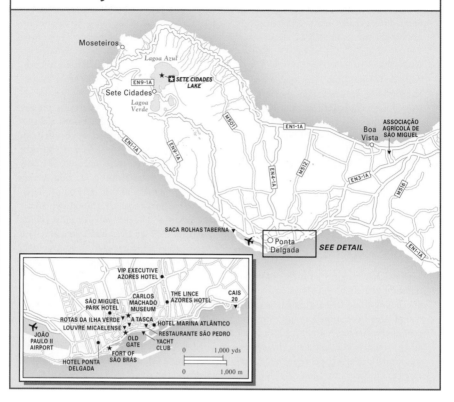

include codfish tenderloin, forkbeard (a deep-sea fish) fillets, and Azorean beefsteaks.

On the main marina at the newer end of the waterfront, the ★ **Yacht Club** (Av. Infante Dom Henrique 111, tel. 296 284 231, www. grupoanjos.pt, 11am-midnight daily, €20) restaurant overlooks the pretty docks. Its waterfront location is the perfect place to enjoy fresh seafood and quality meats in a polished cosmopolitan environment.

For upmarket dining, make the short and easy journey along the freeway to the other side of the island to the **Associação Agricola de São Miguel** (São Miguel Farming Association, Campo do Santana, Recinto da Feira exhibition venue, Rabo de Peixe, tel. 296 490 001 or tel. 926 385 995, www.

restauranteaasm.com, noon-11pm daily, €20), which, despite its countrified name, is actually a refined restaurant in a contemporary exhibition building. The star of the show is local beefsteak, although plenty of other Azorean specialties, like black pudding with pineapple, are on the menu. The restaurant is in the parish of Rabo de Peixe, 15 kilometers (9.3 mi) northeast of Ponta Delgada.

As its name, "Routes of the Green Island," suggests, highly regarded **Rotas da Ilha Verde** (Rua de Pedro Homem 49, tel. 296 628 560, www.rotasilha.blogspot.pt, lunch Mon-Fri, dinner 7pm and 9pm Mon-Sat, €12) takes diners on a vegetarian gastronomic journey through the island's cuisine. This small, charming restaurant has a wide and creative

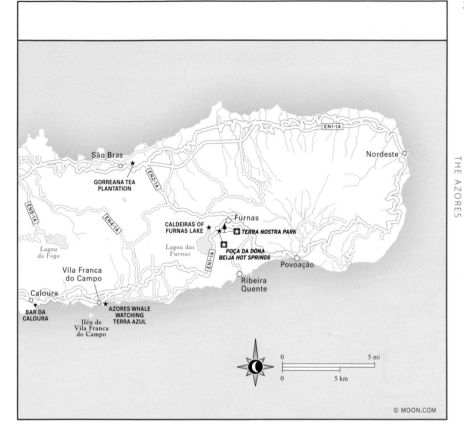

© MOON.COM

range of delicious vegetarian and gluten-free meals made from fresh local produce. Reservations are advised.

An exquisite old hat shop and tearoom in downtown Ponta Delgada, **Louvre Michaelense** (Rua António José D'Almeida 18, tel. 938 346 886, 9am-8pm daily, €8) first opened in 1904. Its century-old display cabinets are reminiscent of an old-fashioned grocery shop, and it is also where locals go to enjoy tea, coffee, and a wide range of delicious island pastries.

Simple, understated **Cais 20** (Rua do Terreiro 41, São Roque, tel. 296 384 811, www.restaurantecais20.pt, noon-5am daily, €12) is a restaurant with amazing sea views and amazing flavors a 30-minute walk or a 4-minute drive east from Ponta Delgada's marina. Among the array of intriguing dishes and tapas, including the freshest island-caught shellfish, are barnacles and limpets, tuna kebabs, and whelk salad. Meat options to try are the local snack *pica-pau* (woodpecker) and small cubes of succulent beef in tasty beer gravy, as well as *pregos* (beef sandwiches). The restaurant is open late in the parish of São Roque, 2 kilometers (1.2 mi) east of Ponta Delgada.

A short drive east of Ponta Delgada in the small parish of Água de Pau is ★ **Bar da Caloura** (Rua da Caloura 20, Água de Pau, Lagoa, tel. 296 913 283, noon-9:30pm daily, €15), a hidden gem in a stunning scenic seaside setting, where excellent fresh seafood and

great cocktails make the journey worthwhile. This is the spot to head to for a great meal in a memorable setting. Água de Pau is 15 kilometers (9.3 mi) east of Ponta Delgada.

NIGHTLIFE

There are a number of trendy bars toward the end of the marina. In addition, many little cafés and taverns that stay open late—some even hosting open-air karaoke—are scattered throughout the waterfront area.

One of the island's most popular haunts, the **Lava Jazz Club and Bar** (Av. Roberto Ivens, tel. 917 350 418, 9pm-midnight Tues and Sat, 5pm-late Wed-Fri) casts the spotlight on a foot-tapping live music scene, as well as providing a popular and cozy place for a drink.

Ponta Delgada's top cultural venue, **Arco 8 Art Gallery & Bar** (Rua Azores Park 191, tel. 296 284 103, www.arco8.blogspot.pt, 9pm-2am Tues-Sat) is on the western fringes of town, a 10-minute walk west of the Fort of São Brás but worth the trip, as the unique warehouse-like building has an alternative art gallery, cocktails, and frequent events.

FESTIVALS AND EVENTS

Held every year on the fifth Sunday after Easter, the time-honored **Cult of the Lord Holy Christ of the Miracles Festival** is the biggest popular festival in the Azores and one of the most ancient in Portugal. The celebration venerates a wooden statue of Christ, tightly guarded in the Sanctuary of the Lord Holy Christ at the **Convent of Our Lady of Hope (Convento da Nossa Senhora da Esperança)** (Campo de São Francisco, tel. 296 284 453, 11am-noon and 5:30pm-6:30pm daily). It is believed that this sacred statue was given in the 18th century by Pope Paul III to a group of nuns who went to Rome to request establishing their convent near Ponta Delgada. Pilgrims from all over the globe pour into the streets of Ponta Delgada to take part in the three days of festivities, whose highlight is a huge procession with hundreds of brightly dressed participants singing and hoisting the revered statue.

SHOPPING

Ponta Delgada has a number of traditional **cheese shops** stocking the finest local products courtesy of the island's famously "happy" cows, and the local market, **Mercado da Graça** (Rua do Mercado, tel. 296 282 663, 7:30am-6:30pm Mon-Wed, 7:30am-7pm Thurs, 7am-2pm Fri-Sat) is an opportunity to get up close with the island's intriguing local produce. Products to take home include cheeses and honeys, hand-rolled cigars, and, of course, the island's famous Gorreana tea.

ACCOMMODATIONS

Excellently located in the heart of Ponta Delgada, three-star **Hotel Ponta Delgada** (Rua João Francisco Cabral 49, tel. 296 209 480, www.hotelpdl.com, €136) offers reasonably priced clean and simple rooms, a heated indoor pool, a sauna, and a Turkish bath.

Back from the western end of the main waterfront promenade, ★ **São Miguel Park Hotel** (Rua Manuel Augusto Amaral s/n, tel. 296 306 000, www.bensaude.pt, €144) is an easy stroll down into a quiet part of town near a large supermarket. Modern, welcoming, and well-presented, it has an outdoor pool, a heated indoor pool, a jetted tub, and very friendly, helpful staff.

The handsome **VIP Executive Azores Hotel** (Rua de São Gonçalo, tel. 296 000 100, www.hotelazoresvipexecutive.com, €99) is a 1-kilometer (0.6-mi) stroll inland from the marina and has sleek yet simple rooms, two restaurants, and an indoor pool.

Contemporary and clean-lined with a modern glass facade, **The Lince Azores Hotel** (Av. Dom João III 29, tel. 296 630 000, www. thelince-azores.com, €120), just a few hundred meters' walk up from the main waterfront, offers casual rooms with full amenities, a posh bar, and an indoor and outdoor pool.

1: Ponta Delgada's waterfront avenue and the Fort of São Brás; **2:** grilled *lapas* (limpets); **3:** a whale- and dolphin-watching trip; **4:** the Gorreana tea fields

Hotel Marina Atlântico Ponta Delgada (Av. João Bosco Mota Amaral 1, 767, tel. 296 307 900, www.bensaude.pt, €120) overlooks the marina and harbor in the heart of Ponta Delgada. An upscale choice, it has classically elegant rooms, a trendy bar, and an indoor lap pool.

INFORMATION AND SERVICES

National emergency number: 112
PSP police: Rua da Alfândega 1, tel. 296 205 500, www.psp.pt
Tourist office: Av. Infante Dom Henrique, tel. 296 308 625, www.visitazores.com, 9am-6pm daily fall-spring, 9am-7pm daily summer
Main hospital: Hospital do Divino Espírito Santo, Matriz, Av. D. Manuel I, tel. 296 203 000, www.hdes.pt
Private hospital: São Lucas Private Hospital, Rua Bento José Morais 23, 1st Norte Direito, tel. 296 650 740, www.hpsl.pt
Main pharmacy: Farmácia Popular, Rua Machado dos Santos 34, tel. 296 205 530
Main post office: Rua Conselheiro Doutor Luís de Bettencourt Câmara, tel. 296 304 071, 8:30am-6:30pm Mon-Fri

GETTING THERE AND AROUND

Ponta Delgada Airport (Aeroporto de Ponta Delgada) (PDL, tel. 296 205 400, www.aeroportopontadelgada.pt) is also called João Paulo II Airport for Pope John Paul II. The small single terminal is on the immediate outskirts of the city, 3 kilometers (1.9 mi) west of Ponta Delgada center, a five-minute drive. There is no shuttle bus or public transport between the airport and Ponta Delgada city, so taxis, rental vehicles, or prearranged transfers are the only options.

There are plenty of taxis outside the airport's arrivals area (€10 into the city); **Associação Taxis Ponta Delgada** (tel. 296 302 530, 296 382 000, or 938 346 759, www.taxispdl.com) offers 24-hour service. Taxis are also found widely throughout the city. Fares vary depending on the time of day and whether you have luggage. Using taxis for short hops in and around Ponta Delgada is

affordable, although as São Miguel's popularity has soared, so have the prices for hiring a taxi for the day to explore the sights.

Excursions and taxis for longer trips can be costly, so **renting a car** generally works out cheaper and provides more flexibility for exploring the island of São Miguel. Fuel is cheaper than in mainland Portugal. Reserve a car well in advance, as they sell out in peak seasons, especially summer.

A half-dozen rental companies operate at Ponta Delgada Airport (see www.aeroportopontadelgada.pt). The desks can get crowded, particularly early in the morning when cars are being returned, so allow more time than usual to drop off the car. Local companies such as **Autatlantis** (tel. 296 205 340, www.autatlantis.com) or **Micauto** (tel. 296 284 382, www.micauto.com) have offices in Ponta Delgada city center and offer competitive rates.

São Miguel has a public **bus** network that mostly covers coastal areas and main sights but not rural inland areas. Buses are cheap but patchy, infrequent on weekends, and can be slow. The three bus companies are **Auto Viação Micalense** (tel. 296 301 358, www.autoviacaomicaelense.pt), **Caetano Raposo & Pereiras (CRP)** (tel. 296 304 260, www.crp.com.pt), and **Varela & Ca.** (tel. 296 301 800). Each operates different routes, but most buses depart from outside the Ponta Delgada tourist office or on the opposite side of the road. For fares and timetables, visit the **Ponta Delgada Tourist Office** (Av. Infante Dom Henrique, tel. 296 308 625, www.visitazores.com, 9am-6pm daily fall-spring, 9am-7pm daily summer).

★ Sete Cidades Lake
(Lagoa das Sete Cidades)

The Azores' most famous vista is postcard-perfect and luxuriant Sete Cidades (Seven Cities) Lake. Five kilometers (3.1 mi) long and 12 kilometers (7.4 mi) around, the largest

1: the Caldeiras in Furnas village; **2:** Sete Cidades Lake

freshwater lake in the Azores is on the western tip of the island. Technically two large twin lakes in the crater of a giant dormant volcano surrounded by vibrant vegetation, the lakes are connected by a narrow, bridged strait and are locally called "Green Lake" and "Blue Lake," differing in how they reflect the sun. Folklore has it that the lakes were formed by the tears of a young princess and a local shepherd who fell in love but were forbidden from seeing each other by the king. The strikingly vivid colors of the lake are said to represent the princess's green eyes and the shepherd boy's blue eyes.

Trails surround the lake, allowing hikers to appreciate the beauty from various angles. A circular walk from the famous **Vista do Rei viewpoint** to the lakeside parish of Sete Cidades and back is around 12 kilometers (7.4 mi) and takes four to five hours. The viewpoint has snack vans as well as parking spaces, and is located at the southern end of the lake.

The mirror-like waters of the lake are also perfect for **kayaking** and **stand-up paddleboarding,** available from rental outfitters on the shore in the parish of Sete Cidades. **Azores Adventures Futurismo** (tel. 296 559 385, www.futurismo.pt) has a lakeside activity center that rents boards and kayaks (from €10 per hour).

This enchanting spot is 25 kilometers (15.5 mi) northwest from Ponta Delgada, a half-hour drive on the EN1-1A and 9-1 roads.

Furnas

The unique valley of Furnas (FOOR-nass) and its eponymous village are under an hour's drive from Ponta Delgada on the eastern flank of the island. This inland hamlet is a spa resort, a busy tourist attraction, and a kooky gastronomic outpost, all fueled by simmering geothermal activity. Geysers and fumaroles hiss and splutter with boiling water; steaming springs form popular, privately managed communal thermal pools, and the island's signature dish, *cozido das Furnas,* is cooked underground on the shores of the Furnas Lake and served in restaurants around the village.

Visitors flock to Terra Nostra Park, an oasis of tranquility in the heart of the busy little hamlet. The nearby Poça da Dona Beija hot springs are another of the island's top attractions.

At the heart of Furnas village are the Caldeiras (calderas—not to be confused with the Caldeiras of Furnas Lake), where visitors can see more steaming geysers and sample various types of hot and cold spring water that flow from public taps. A word of warning: The high iron content in the water gives it a bitter taste that fizzes on the tongue. Don't forget to try another local specialty, *maçarocas de milho* (corn on the cob), cooked in the steaming volcanic water and sold from little stalls in the center of Furnas village. A whole day can be spent in this exhilarating community, although given its popularity, finding parking on its narrow streets can be a challenge.

FURNAS LAKE
(Lagoa das Furnas)

A 10-minute drive southwest of Furnas village, **Furnas Lake,** the second largest on São Miguel, is where huge steel pots are lowered into and removed from the ground to cook the local *cozido* stew before being loaded into waiting vans and zipped off to nearby restaurants. This culinary curiosity takes place in the fumaroles *(fumerolas)* at the northern tip of the lake in an area known as the **Caldeiras of Furnas Lake (Caldeiras da Lagoa das Furnas)** (24 hours daily, €2). Some of the fumaroles have been allocated to local restaurants while others belong to locals, who bring their own pots and pans and ingredients to cook their own *cozido.* To appreciate this unique geothermal gastronomy, visit around noon, when the large metal pots are lifted out after hours of cooking underground. A walkway has been built around the fumaroles so you can safely wander amid the hissing geysers and bubbling mud pools, which regularly spew hot vapor with a distinctive sulfurous stench. The Caldeiras have ample parking on-site.

Furnas Lake itself lacks the breathtaking beauty of Sete Cidades but is compelling with

Rustic, rich, and hearty, Azorean cuisine is bolstered by homegrown cheeses, charcuterie such as regional *chouriço* sausages, and fresh fruit and vegetables; as on Madeira, there are signature varieties. Fresh **pineapples** and local **tea** are to São Miguel what the banana and *poncha* are to Madeira. The dinky little sweet pineapples are grown widely in greenhouses and are unique to the archipelago, often eaten as a snack or as jam or a liqueur.

São Miguel's most famous dish, *cozido das Furnas,* is a one-pot wonder slow-cooked in the volcanic heat of the earth and made exclusively in the village of Furnas. It is São Miguel's take on the traditional *cozido à Portuguesa,* a stew made from several types of meat (often chicken, pork, and beef), *chouriço* and blood sausage, offal, and an array of vegetables, including potatoes, carrots, and cabbage, cooked together and served with rice. The raw ingredients are taken to the Furnas Lake site at dawn in huge sealed pans, placed into deep fumaroles, and then covered with soil and left to cook in the volcanic heat for several hours before being unearthed and hoisted out before lunchtime. Each pan is identified by a nameplate next to its hole, then sped off to the many local restaurants that serve the specialty.

São Miguel's trademark dish, *cozido das Furnas,* is cooked slowly underground in the earth's natural volcanic heat.

In this area, known as the Caldeiras da Lagoa das Furnas, the banks of a vast lake are pitted with boiling fumaroles and bubbling geysers. Walkways have been created around the site so visitors can wander safely. Most local restaurants in the small town serve the specialty and are so in demand that it's a good idea to reserve in the morning. Head off to the Caldeiras and, around midday, watch as the pots are lifted out of the ground before heading back to your restaurant to taste the *cozido.* Some say they can taste sulfur from the volcanic heat in the dish.

Most people make a beeline for ★ **Miroma** (Rua Dr. Frederico Moniz Pereira 15, Furnas, tel. 296 584 422, 9:30am-9:30pm daily, €15), which has a reputation as the best local restaurant for *cozido das Furnas.* This simple, traditional, yet large and lofty restaurant seats 200, meaning you should be able to walk in and enjoy *cozido* most days, even without a reservation; to make sure, book ahead.

its intense heat and sulfurous smell. It's an impressive feeling to experience the trembling power of the earth rumbling underfoot. The **Lagoa das Furnas Loop** (trail PRC6SMI) is an easy, 9.5-kilometer (5.9-mi) circular trail that starts and ends in Furnas village. It is easy to follow, has a good flat surface, and takes around 3 hours to complete.

★ TERRA NOSTRA PARK
(Parque Terra Nostra)

If there were a paradise on earth, it might look like the **Terra Nostra Park** (Rua Padre Jose Jacinto Botelho, tel. 296 549 090, www.parqueterranostra.com, 10am-6pm daily, adults €8, children 3-10 €4), a captivating Eden of sprawling gardens, secret grottoes, shady tree-covered walkways, babbling streams, lily-covered ponds, and a big pool of hot rusty-red spring water that soothes aching muscles and joints. The park is decorated with exotic plantlife from around the world, including more than 2,000 different types of trees.

Over 200 years old, this sublime botanical park was the brainchild of wealthy American consul Thomas Hickling, who had a summer house on the site nicknamed Yankee Hall, and started shaping the gardens in 1775. Yankee Hall today dominates the hill overlooking the gardens' famous Thermal Pool, built in 1780 and extended in later years. The volcanic water that feeds the pool ranges 35-40°C (95-104°F) and is an uninviting, murky dark-orange color due to its iron content, but it is perfect for a dip after walking around the glorious gardens.

TOP EXPERIENCE

★ POÇA DA DONA BEIJA HOT SPRINGS

Indulge in a soothing soak in the invigorating **Poça da Dona Beija hot springs** (Lomba das Barracas, tel. 296 584 256, www. pocadadonabeija.com, 7am-11pm daily, €4), one of São Miguel's most famous attractions. Filled with steaming crystalline water, deep tanks were created to harness the formerly wild spring water and transform it into an open-air spa. The first construction was in 1988 following an influx of visitors to the site after news of its restorative properties spread, but public access was only regulated in 2007 due to the number of visitors. Nowadays the spot is well managed and equipped with a

small car park (although finding parking can still be a challenge), a ticket office, changing rooms, and several large tanks designed to blend in with the surrounding natural landscape of lush greenery, stone walls, and stone-block houses. Nighttime is particularly lovely, when it's all lit up. It's also a novelty to enter the steaming water when it's rainy and cold.

ACCOMMODATIONS

The ★ **Furnas Boutique Hotel** (Av. Dr. Manuel de Arriaga, tel. 296 249 200, www. furnasboutiquehotel.com, €306) embodies the serenity and beauty of Furnas with a hip bar, an outdoor hot-spring pool, and minimalist-modern rooms with distant mountain views. It is just a 10-minute walk to the gorgeous Terra Nostra gardens.

Tranquil, classy **Terra Nostra Garden Hotel** (Rua Padre José Jacinto Botelho 5, tel. 296 549 090, www.bensaude.pt, €288) is nestled in paradisiacal Terra Nostra Park, a 10-minute walk from the Poça da Dona Beija hot springs and a few kilometers from the Furnas Golf Course. It offers contemporary rooms, a refined restaurant, an outdoor hot-spring pool, and a heated indoor pool. A stay includes buffet breakfast, parking, and entry to the park.

Terra Nostra Park

Best Souvenirs: Gorreana Tea

A box of Gorreana tea makes a fantastic gift from the island of São Miguel. Distinctive to the Azores, it is lightweight and compact and can be enjoyed for months. Close your eyes and you'll be back in the Azores with every sip. Boxes of Gorreana tea (€4-8) can be purchased from the plantation or from any supermarket on the island.

GETTING THERE

Furnas is 46 kilometers (29 mi) east from Ponta Delgada, a 40-minute drive on the EN1-1A road. A bus from Ponta Delgada to Furnas village (1.5 hours, €3-5) runs every four hours during the week and once daily on weekends. Ask at the Ponta Delgada Tourist Office for bus timetables and fares.

Gorreana Tea Plantation
(Plantações de Chá Gorreana)

The only tea plantation in Europe is on São Miguel. Since 1883 the family-run **Gorreana Tea Plantation** (just off EN1-1A road, Maia, tel. 296 442 349, www.gorreana.pt, 8am-7pm Mon-Fri, 9am-7pm Sat-Sun, free) has been producing world-class organic green and black teas. In the parish of Maia, 33 kilometers (20 mi) northeast of Ponta Delgada, a half-hour's drive along the EN1-1A road, the 32 hectares (79 acres) of vivid green fields blend perfectly with the rest of the island's emerald tapestry and contrast with the sea. A boutique souvenir store, café, and museum are on the site, along with the factory, to offer insight on how the tea came to the island, how it is produced, and its evolution. Gorreana currently produces 33 metric tons (36 tons) of tea per year, although only a small portion is destined for the Azorean market, with the rest exported to mainland Portugal and other countries. Visitors can stroll at leisure among the fields along the Atlantic, a sight to behold and the perfect place to enjoy a cup of fresh tea. A visit to the plantation and museum, self-guided or guided, is free, as is a tea-tasting offered at the end. A box of Gorreana tea makes a great souvenir.

TERCEIRA ISLAND

As one of the larger islands in the Azores archipelago, Terceira (ter-SAY-rah), the "crossroads of the Atlantic," is a patchwork of distinct landscapes with a heavily forested western coast, a lava field-covered northern side, and a wild central region. The name means "third"; this was the third island in the archipelago to be discovered. Awash with purple hydrangea, it has been nicknamed the "Lilac Island" in part due to stunning sunsets, which give the island a reputation as one of the best sunset-viewing places in the Azores.

Hemmed in almost entirely by dramatic coastal cliffs, Terceira is home to the strategically placed Lajes air base, a military and civilian airfield on the northeast coast. With the sizable seaports of Angra do Heroísmo and Praia da Vitória, and large towns and cities around the coast, Terceira is densely built-up and populous. Nonetheless it is still predominantly agricultural, evident in the sheep and cattle pastures and fields of active farming communities that clad its hilly landscape.

On the island's south coast, the main city, **Angra do Heroísmo,** commonly referred to as Angra, is the historical capital of the Azores. Its heyday during the Age of Discoveries as the main mid-Atlantic stopover and trading point shaped the city's rich, exotic look. It was raised to the status of a city in 1534, becoming the archipelago's first, and was twice designated the capital of Portugal. Centuries later, in 1983, Angra's historic center was among the first places in Portugal to claim a UNESCO World Heritage Site designation.

Sights and Recreation
ANGRA DO HEROÍSMO'S HISTORIC CENTER

Terceira's historic capital, Angra do Heroísmo (ANG-rah doo eh-ro-EESH-moo), is the island's main destination. Quaint streets, buildings in a rainbow of colors, grand monuments, manicured gardens, and stately homes exude the 15th-century style that defines the UNESCO-listed historic center. In 1980 the island was rocked by the second-biggest earthquake ever to hit Portugal—the first was the devastating 1755 Lisbon earthquake—and swaths of Angra were destroyed. But the city was restored within a few years, preserving its exquisite 15th-century allure. The old town is sheltered by magnificent Mount Brasil and slopes down to a picturesque bay fringed by bobbing boats.

The handsome **Angra do Heroísmo Cathedral (Sé de Angra do Heroísmo)** (Rua Carreira dos Cavalos 53, tel. 295 216 670, www.igrejaacores.pt, 10am-6pm Mon-Fri, mass Sat-Sun, donation) is the biggest church on the island and one of its main monuments. Towering over Angra, overshadowed only by Mount Brasil, the cathedral has an imposing Gothic exterior and twin bell towers. The current building was constructed circa 1570 on the site of a former church, São Salvador. Inside, it is smart but plain and understated, with stone arches and a famously large pipe organ.

Terceira boasts one of the finest examples of public gardens in the impressively manicured **Duke of Terceira Garden (Jardim Duque da Terceira)** (Rua Direita 130, Angra do Heroísmo, tel. 295 401 700, 8am-6pm daily, free). Dating from the late 19th century, it forms part of the municipal gardens in Angra's historic center. A pretty central bandstand in the heart of the green oasis is flanked by an intricately designed garden of landscaped lawns, fluidly shaped ponds, and a diversity of towering trees. Four main gardens are delimited by wrought-iron gates, basalt walls, and cobblestones. The highest point is the Alto da Memoria promontory, a gentle climb that provides beautiful views. Just off the main cathedral, these gardens are a little botanical gem.

ALGAR DO CARVÃO CAVES

Vast and dripping with water, the mesmerizing **Algar do Carvão caves** (Porto Judeu, tel. 295 212 992, 2:30pm-5:15pm daily late Mar-May, 2pm-6pm daily June-mid-Oct, 2:30pm-5:15pm Tues-Wed and Fri-Sat mid-Oct-late Mar, €6) take their name (coal pit) from the black volcanic walls. This is a unique opportunity to descend into the depths of an extinct volcano with formidable features that include a huge chimney and spectacular chambers, created from an eruption some 2,000 years ago. The walls change color as you descend through the layers of earth. A mysterious world is revealed on a series of staircases (at least 250 steps, some quite steep) and tunnels to a place once filled with lava. This eerie landscape has an ethereal touch, with dim modern spotlights that enhance the natural light from the chimney.

You'll find a guide or two at the bottom of stairs on a landing; they offer information on the caves, upon request.

The local conservation association **Os Montanheiros** (tel. 295 212 992 or 961 362 215, www.montanheiros.com) manages the caves, which are 11 kilometers (6.8 mi) north of Angra do Heroísmo, a 15-minute drive on the EN3-1A road.

A combined €9 ticket provides access to a smaller lava tube, the **Natal Cave (Gruta do Natal),** 6 kilometers (3.7 km) away.

MOUNT BRASIL
(Monte Brasil)

For the best views of Angra and its sandy bay, climb this attraction-packed mountain, a remnant of a mostly submerged crater. A 15-minute stroll west of Angra's waterfront and marina, covered in shrubbery, Mount Brasil juts out between Angra Bay to the east and the Bay of Fanal to the west. Named after Brazil, a former Portuguese colony, the large rock extends into the Atlantic, giving it

---

1: Angra do Heroísmo's historic center; **2:** fountain in the Duke of Terceira Garden; **3:** entrance to Algar do Carvão caves; **4:** Angra do Heroísmo and Mount Brasil

protective positioning that made it a point of defense for Terceira and the Angra port. Most of Mount Brasil is a government-managed **nature reserve** (Terceira's Forestry Service, tel. 295 206 310, sunrise-sunset daily, free). It is scattered with picnic spots, well-maintained hiking routes, whale lookouts, and viewpoints; and it has asphalt roads to explore on foot or by car. Entry, at the foot of the mountain, is controlled by the military. Most of the mapped hiking trails start at **Relvão Municipal Park (Parque Municipal do Relvão),** at the foot of the mountain, just before the Fortress of São João Baptista and guardhouse.

A number of forts in the island's defensive network were built around Mount Brasil, including the elaborate 16th-century **Fortress of São João Baptista (Fortaleza de São João Baptista do Monte Brasil)** (tel. 295 214 011, free), which looks over Angra. Construction began in 1593 during Spanish occupancy and finished circa 1640. The fortress was used to house troops and protect the trading port from pirate attacks. In the 20th century, it served as a political prison, and is currently used as a military base. Five bastions reinforce the sprawling monument's 4-kilometer-long (2.5-mi-long) fortified wall, within which visitors will find São João Baptista Church, Santa Catarina Chapel, catacombs, and the Governor's Palace. In recent times the imposing fortress's edges have begun to soften and merge into the landscape as its chunky stone blocks are covered in fine moss, but its former sober splendor is still evident. Escorted visits around the fortress are free, but visit times need to be negotiated at the guardhouse.

One of Mount Brasil's best vantage points is the **Pico das Cruzinhas viewpoint,** a short walk from the fortress. Pico das Cruzinhas, one of the mountain's three main peaks, towers above whitewashed Angra and its terracotta roofs, providing panoramic views over the city. The spot is marked with an evocative monument to Portugal's Age of Discoveries, a large stone pillar crowned by the Order of Christ Cross.

Mount Brasil has excellent safe family **hikes** (http://trails.visitazores.com), and a half or a full day can be spent exploring. An easy 7.5-kilometer (4.7-mi) circular hike from Relvão Park takes in the Fortress of São João Baptista, the picnic area, Pico das Cruzinhas viewpoint, and other attractions in 2.5 hours.

Food

Terceira's gastronomy is closely related to that of the Trás-os-Montes region on the mainland, as people from that area were among the first settlers. Typical local dishes are *alcatra* (a melt-in-the-mouth stew made with beef rump, red wine, and black peppercorns) served with *massa sovada* (a slightly sweet puffed-pastry bread), Holy Ghost soups (*sopas de espírito santo,* hearty soups made from dry bread and the stock from boiled meats), and the sweet *cornucópias* (pastry cones stuffed with fruits and flowers).

How much more quintessentially Azorean can you get than excellent beef cooked on a sizzling lava rock? That's what **O Cachalote** (Rua do Rego 14, Angra do Heroísmo, tel. 914 237 459, noon-11pm Mon-Sat, €20) specializes in. Ignore the sterile interior and garish red and green color scheme and enjoy the best steak for miles.

A hub of the finest Terceira cuisine, ★ **Ti Choa** (Grota do Margaride 1, Serreta, tel. 295 906 673, noon-3pm and 6:30pm-10pm Mon-Sat, €12) occupies an old rural farmhouse with rustic decor and ambience. It serves hearty homemade stews including *alcatra* in typical terra-cotta pots, a mixed meat platter with pulled pork and sweet potatoes, and great homespun desserts. The restaurant is on the island's western fringe, a 30-minute drive west from Angra on the EN3-1A and EN5-2A roads.

A rustic farmhouse-style restaurant with local favorites like great beefsteaks, barnacles, *alcatra,* smoked island sausages, and a prawn and squid kebab, **Restaurant A Caneta** (Rua

As Presas 13, Altares, tel. 295 989 162, www. restaurantecaneta.com, noon-3pm and 6pm-10pm Tues-Sun, €20) is 20 kilometers (12.4 mi) north of Angra, on the opposite side of the island, a 30-minute drive on the EN3-1A road. It's worth the trip for the authentic food and ambience.

Accommodations

Budget 12-room inn **Pensão Residencial A Ilha** (Rua Direita 24, Angra do Heroísmo, tel. 295 628 180, €55) is in a great city-center location 100 meters (328 feet) from the marina and the beach. Rooms are clean and simple, breakfast is included, but there's no elevator.

Stately **Terceira Mar Hotel** (Portões de São Pedro 1, Angra do Heroísmo, tel. 295 402 280, www.bensaude.pt, €109) is on the waterfront of Fanal Bay, in an exceptional location at the foot of Mount Brasil. Floor-to-ceiling windows throughout this resort-style hotel make the most of its stunning setting.

Offering good value for money, the tasteful four-star seaside **Hotel Caracol** (Estrada Regional 1, Angra do Heroísmo, tel. 295 402 600, www.hoteldocaracol.com, €100) is across the road from a handy grocery store, a 15-minute walk west from Angra city center. It has bright, pleasant rooms, all with garden or sea views, a beautiful pool overhanging the ocean, and a cement sundeck jetty.

Large and imposing, modern five-star ★ **Angra Marina Hotel** (Estrada Pero de Barcelos, Porto de Pipas, Angra do Heroísmo, tel. 295 204 700, www.angramarinahotel.com, €154) is cut right into the cliff face that hems Angra do Heroísmo. All 157 gleaming rooms have sea views and aquamarine accents. There is a panoramic rooftop restaurant, a spa, and an outdoor pool. It is on the marina side, a 10-minute walk east from the city center.

Information and Services

National emergency number: 112
PSP police: Praça Doutor Sousa Júnior 1, Angra do Heroísmo, tel. 295 212 022, www.psp.pt

Tourist office: Rua Direita 70-74, Angra do Heroísmo, tel. 295 404 810, www.visitazores.com, 9am-7pm Mon-Sat
Main hospital: Hospital de Santo Espírito da Ilha Terceira, Canada do Briado, Angra do Heroísmo, tel. 295 403 200, www.hseit.pt

Getting There

AIR

The main airport is **Lajes Airport (Aeroporto das Lajes)**, also known as **Lajes Civil Air Base (Aerogare Civil das Lajes)** (TER, Vila das Lajes, Praia da Vitória, tel. 295 545 454, www.aerogarelajes.azores.gov.pt), in Praia da Vitória, on the northeastern tip of Terceira, 24 kilometers (15 mi) from Angra do Heroísmo. The drive from Angra to Lajes Airport takes 20 minutes on the VR freeway. There is limited bus service operated by **Empresa de Viação Terceirense** (tel. 295 217 001, www.evt.pt, 1 hour, €3) roughly hourly between the airport and Angra. Taxis (about €20) are available outside the terminal.

The airport has flights from the other islands and a few from the mainland. There are several flights daily between Ponta Delgada on São Miguel and Lajes Airport (40 minutes, high season €90). Interisland flights between São Miguel and Terceira are operated by **SATA Air Azores** (tel. 707 227 282, www.sata.pt).

FERRY

Ferries operated by **Atlânticoline** (www.atlanticoline.pt) connect Angra and Praia da Vitória to other islands, but only from May to September. Ferries run between Ponta Delgada (São Miguel) and Praia da Vitória (Terceira) (6 hours, €50) at least twice per week (generally Mon, Wed, and Fri, but schedules vary) and make the return trip a day or two later.

Getting Around

Given the size of the island, renting a **car** is not necessary. Angra do Heroísmo is easily covered on foot, and parking in the city is extremely limited. If you want to travel away from Angra, hiring a car for a day or two, or bringing one on the ferry, is an option. Getting around the compact, quiet island is straightforward, and there are numerous car-hire companies at the airport and the port in Praia da Vitória, as well as in Angra. The VR freeway connects Angra to Praia da Vitória in around 20 minutes.

Terceira's **bus** service is operated by **Empresa de Viação Terceirense** (tel. 295 217 001, www.evt.pt). With the exception of the bus from Angra to the airport, service is limited and infrequent, especially to inland locations.

Most **taxi** companies on Terceira are small and privately run, but taxis can generally be found waiting around busy areas and main attractions. A recommended company is **Taxi Amigos** (tel. 963 729 390). Exploring the island by taxi is an affordable way of getting around.

PICO ISLAND

Volcanic Pico (PEE-koo), the Azores' "Black Island," is an adventurer's playground, with the highest mountain in Portugal, ancient vineyards, and underground caves to be explored. It takes its nickname from a network of black basalt stone walls that were built to hem in the vineyards.

The second-largest island in the archipelago, Pico is in the central group, 264 kilometers (165 mi) northwest of São Miguel. Most visitors arrive on direct flights from Ponta Delgada (50 minutes) or by ferry from the nearby island of Faial (30 minutes), a short 7-kilometer (4.3-mi) trip across the Faial Channel. The main town on Pico is **Madalena,** a pretty little community spread around the foot of Mount Pico on the western coast of the island.

Pico's rich volcanic soils and distinctive cool-summer microclimate saw the viticulture industry develop from the 15th century onward. Wine production waned in the middle of the 19th century following blights that destroyed the vines. The local economy was buoyed by a brief period of whaling, which stabilized the island financially until whaling ended in the 1970s, by which time new casts had been planted and viticulture once again flourished. The landscape of the Pico Island Vineyard Culture is now a designated UNESCO World Heritage Site.

Among the most traditional and widespread varieties of grapes grown on Pico are the Portuguese *verdelho* and *arinto dos Açores*. *Verdelho* is an autochthonous variety of white wine grape found throughout Portugal but most strongly associated with the islands. *Arinto dos Açores* is a unique grape indigenous to the island, the most important variety in the archipelago and different from the *arinto* found on the mainland; it's believed to be a descendant of *verdelho* and is used to make full-bodied white wines.

Among the more famous wine labels are Lajido, a golden-yellow fortified white wine; Frei Gigante, a fruity white wine; Basalto, a dark red wine; and Terras de Lava, available in red, white, and rosé.

Sights and Recreation

Grand backdrops await newcomers to Pico's shores, among them the island's showpiece Mount Pico and its distinctive snow-frosted summit, which dwarfs the island's landscape. Skirting it are lush green pastures crossed by remote roads whose only users at times seem to be cattle and sheep. Much of the scenery is outlined by black basalt rock, used to build protective walls and houses. Basalt was also used to carve up the vineyards into thousands of small square plots known as *currais*. These primitive stone walls were initially designed to protect vines from ocean winds, although connoisseurs claim the island's unique terroir of salty, Atlantic-blown volcanic soil is clearly noticeable in the flavor of the wines.

Travel and tour websites **Pico—The Azores** (www.picotheazores.com) and **Pico Island Adventures** (www.pico-island-adventures.com) provide information on what to do on the island and how to get around, as well as on guided tours that scale Mount Pico, wine tours, and cave tours.

PICO ISLAND WINE COOPERATIVE
(Cooperativa Vitivinícola da Ilha do Pico)

To get a real taste and understanding of Pico's famously distinctive wines, head to the **Pico Island Wine Cooperative** (Av. Padre Nunes Rosa 29, Madalena, tel. 292 622 262 or 912 533 243, www.picowines.net, 8am-8pm Mon-Fri, 3pm-8pm Sat), producer of some of Pico's best-known brands, including Lajido, Frei Gigante, Basalto, and Terras de Lava. In the main town of Madalena, the cooperative offers guided winery tours (several times daily, €3-6.50) that explain the unique history of local wine-making. Visitors are given the choice of how many wines they would like to sample, and a tasting is included in the tour fee.

★ HIKING ON MOUNT PICO
(Montanha do Pico)

Majestic Mount Pico, Pico's perfectly-shaped 2,351-meter (7,713-foot) volcano, picturesquely snowcapped in winter and the highest mountain in Portugal, dominates the island. To many, it represents the epic Azores hiking challenge. It takes six to eight hours to ascend to the summit and return (about 8 km/5 mi total), which can be a full-day activity if you include a couple of stops for a rest and a bite to eat.

It might not be Everest, but Mount Pico can be deceptively challenging, with steep ascents, harsh terrain, and frequent weather changes. The trail up is marked, and hikers can climb on their own (for a €15-20 fee), but hiring an experienced, informative local guide for the day with a Pico tour operator such as **Épico** (tel. 962 956 196, http://epico.uractive.com) is strongly recommended.

All hikers, with or without a guide, must first check in at the **Casa da Montanha** (Mountain House, Caminho Florestal 9, Candelária, tel. 967 303 519), a civilian safety office, where trekkers are given a GPS locator. The trail to the summit begins here. The actual climb is steady and steep, and requires some degree of physical fitness. There are 47 markers that measure the climb; Pico's crater is marker 44 and upward. Steel yourself for vertiginous vistas and desolate, moon-like landscapes with the odd colorful flower as you near the top, with the clouds beneath you. On a clear day, the view from the top stretches to neighboring São Jorge and Faial Islands. Sunrise and sunset climbs are also organized for an even more memorable experience.

From the Casa da Montanha, at 1,231 meters (4,039 feet) elevation, it's another 1,120 meters (3,674 feet) to the summit. A second, even higher summit, known as Piquinho—essentially a little mountain atop a big mountain—takes another 30 minutes to climb. The **fee** is €15 to climb unguided to the crater, plus an extra €5 to climb all the way to Piquinho. The fee is paid at the Casa da Montanha visitors center.

Mount Pico is 17 kilometers (10.5 mi) inland (southeast) from Madalena, a 20-minute drive on the EN3 road.

TORRES CAVES
(Gruta das Torres)

Dubbed the longest lava tube in Portugal, this fascinating underground formation—a series of caves, grottoes, and tunnels on the slopes of Mount Pico—stretches over 5 kilometers (3.1 mi). Formed 1,500 years ago from cooled molten lava, this incredible natural phenomenon is in the village of Criação Velha, a short drive from Madalena. **Guided tours** (1-1.5 hours, 10:30am, noon, 2pm, 3:30pm, and 4:30pm daily June-Sept, 10:30am, noon, 2pm, and 3:30pm Tues-Sat Oct-May, adults €7, children 7-14 €4, family €13) cover the first accessible stretch of the formation. Packed with stalactites, stalagmites, and lavacicles, the tunnels are deep and dark and not for the claustrophobic. Tours are in groups of 15 at a time, and each visitor is given a helmet with lamps. At the **Torres Caves visitors center** (Caminho da Gruta das Torres, Criação Velha, tel. 924 403 921, year-round), audiovisual presentations in English and Portuguese give in-depth details about the cave. Children under age 12 must be with an adult. The Torres Caves are 6 kilometers (3.7 mi) southeast from Madalena, a 10-minute drive on the ER1 road.

WHALERS' MUSEUM
(Museu dos Baleeiros)

Inside an original whaler's boathouse, this compelling museum comprehensively explores Pico's whaling past. Established in 1988 and very well put together (although not quite to the same level as Madeira's whaling museum), Pico's **Whalers' Museum** (Rua dos Baleeiros 13, Lajes do Pico, tel. 292 679 340, www.museu-pico.azores.gov.pt, 9am-5pm Tues-Sun, €2) includes a film auditorium designed like the inside of a whale, where in-depth videos are shown; an exhibition of whale-hunting paraphernalia; whale-related art; and a library. This small museum in Lajes do Pico, 34 kilometers (21 mi) southeast of Madalena, a 40-minute drive on the ER1 road, houses an entire chapter of the island's history. Some of the exhibits are quite graphic and could be disturbing to the more sensitive or to children.

Food

Pico is often referred to as the orchard of the Azores, as its hard, lava-dried terrain is quite fertile. One of the island's most distinctive fruits is bright ruby-red figs, often turned into a brandy. Great starters on the island are its soft fresh cheeses, cured sausages like *morçela* (blood sausage) and *linguiça* (a type of thin *chouriço* sausage), and the local corn bread. Mains feature rich stews, fish soup, and octopus and squid stewed in wine.

Genuine Azorean food is served at the very busy **Restaurante Marisqueira Ancoradouro** (Rua João Lima Whitton da Terra, Areia Larga, Madalena, tel. 292 623 490, noon-3pm and 7pm-10pm Tues-Sun, €15), where shellfish and fresh fish are the stars. Recommended dishes include fish *cataplanas*, fish or meat kebabs, and fish rice. The restaurant also has great views: Ask for a table on the terrace, weather permitting, to make the most of sunset.

Pico specialties can be found at ★ **Tasca O Petisca** (Av. Padre Nunes da Rosa, Madalena, tel. 292 622 357, 10am-3pm and 7pm-midnight Mon-Fri, 11am-3pm and 7pm-midnight Sat, €10), a little wooden tavern. Try cheese and cold meat platters or chopped chicken gizzards for starters, great tuna steaks, and a dish of the day (€6); expect huge portions at tiny prices.

Upscale Italian-Mediterranean fusion restaurant **Atmosfera** (Rua dos Biscoitos 34, Madalena, tel. 914 232 760, www.almadopico. com, 7:30pm-9pm Wed-Mon, €25) is within the Alma do Pico nature resort, a 10-minute drive northeast from Madalena. It's perfect for a romantic meal, with views of the island's sunsets.

Accommodations

Overlooking Madalena's petite harbor, **Hotel Caravelas** (Rua Conselheiro Terra Pinheiro 3, Madalena, tel. 292 628 550, www. hotelcaravelas.com.pt, €90) is Madalena's only proper hotel, offering basic, clean, and pleasant rooms in a great location a short walk to the ferry terminal. It could use updating, but rooms have private balconies with sea or mountain views, and there is an outdoor pool.

A contemporary nature resort a 10-minute drive northeast from Madalena, ★ **Alma do Pico** (Rua dos Biscoitos 34, Madalena, tel. 914 232 760, www.almadopico.com, 2-person bungalow €95) has modern bungalows nestled in a woodland setting, and exceptional views over the ocean and the volcano.

Getting There
AIR

Pico Airport (Aeroporto do Pico) (PIX, Bandeiras, tel. 292 628 380) is on the northern coast of Pico, 12 kilometers (7.4 mi) northeast of Madalena, a 10-minute drive. The easiest way from the airport to the town center is by taxi (€15-20). Bus 15, operated by **Cristiano Limitada** (tel. 292 622 126, www. cristianolimitada.pt), runs between the airport and Madalena (20 minutes, twice Mon-Sat, once Sun, €2).

Interisland flights from Ponta Delgada on São Miguel Island to Pico (50 minutes, around €80) are operated by **SATA Air Azores** (tel. 707 227 282, www.sata.pt), roughly four times a day Monday-Saturday, fewer on Sunday.

FERRY

One of the easiest ways to get to Pico is to fly to Horta (on nearby Faial Island, with direct flights from mainland Portugal and elsewhere in Europe), and from Horta take one of the regular **Atlânticoline** ferries (www.atlanticoline.pt) to Madalena (30 minutes, several times daily, €3.60).

From Ponta Delgada (São Miguel Island), the seasonal **Atlânticoline** ferry (www.atlanticoline.pt) sails to São Roque on Pico (13-14 hours, €51), leaving Ponta Delgada a couple of times a week and stopping at Terceira, Graciosa, and São Jorge before Pico.

Getting Around

Once on Pico, the easiest way to get around is to hire a car or take a taxi. A **car** hire is the most cost-efficient if you're staying for a while. If you're flying in, arrange to get your car at the airport or try one of the local companies in Madalena, which might offer better rates.

Pico Island's taxi association **Taxis Pico** (www.taxispico.pt) caters to local trips and also offers complete daylong tours of the island (from €120 for four people), smaller tours, and airport transfers.

Buses on Pico are operated by **Cristiano Limitada** (tel. 292 622 126, www.cristianolimitada.pt). The routes are designed for locals to get around, so services and destinations are limited.

FAIAL ISLAND

Pretty Faial (fie-YAL), the westernmost island of the Azores' central group, has become a yachting playground. The island could be considered Europe's westernmost point as the two islands of the western Azores group—Flores and Corvo—are on the American tectonic plate. Many yachties crossing the Atlantic stop at this small island rather than the larger

islands due to its quaint feel. Its marina, in the main city of **Horta,** is the most important marina in the Azores and the fourth most visited in the world.

A dot of green surrounded by endless blue, with a smattering of whitewashed villages, Faial has seen tourism grow in recent years, with most visitors heading for the volcanic black-sand beaches around Horta. The island's nickname, "Blue Island," derives from the ocean encircling it as well as the blue hydrangeas in summer. Faial was also once Europe's main source of blue dye, from the woad plant; from the 17th century, trade routes provided access to indigo from Asia.

At the heart of Faial is the Central Caldera, a deep, 2-kilometer-wide (1.2-mi-wide) crater formed by a large eruption around 1,000 years ago. This caldera and its asymmetrical slopes are main attractions on Faial, which remains the Azores' most seismically active island. The last major event was in 1957-1958, and the island has been quiet since.

Sights and Recreation

HORTA MARINA

In the southeastern corner of the island, the main city of Horta (OR-tah, literally "vegetable garden") with its elegant marina is a legendary stopping point for transatlantic sailors. The nearby **Peter Café Sport bar** (Rua José Azevedo 9, tel. 292 392 027, www.petercafesport.com, 8am-1am daily) is a popular hangout for yachties traveling between the Caribbean and the Mediterranean. A well-known melting pot and an obligatory stop on Faial, the renowned century-old bar (the original in a chain of Peter Café Sport bars) also houses the island's **Scrimshaw Museum (Museu de Scrimshaw)** (Rua Tenente Valadim, tel. 292 292 327, 10am-noon and 2pm-4pm Mon-Sat, €2.50), a collection of artifacts carved from whale teeth and jawbones. As the saying goes, if you sail to Horta and don't visit Peter Café Sport, you haven't really seen Horta.

The city is arranged around a central avenue, called Avenida Marginal or Avenida

Dom Infante Henriques, and its busy marina. Slowly developing urban sprawl has trickled over the hills into the inland valleys. Horta regularly hosts international regattas, and despite being a small community, it has maritime spirit. Don't miss the walls surrounding the marina, covered in colorful paintings by visiting yachties in the hope of clear sailing ahead, an unofficial tradition that pays homage to the island's adventurous character.

BEACHES NEAR HORTA

At the far southern end of Horta, a 15-minute, 1-kilometer (0.6-mi) stroll along the waterfront, past the marina and the town's main shopping area, is the sandy bay of **Porto Pim,** a wonderful family-friendly spot that is sheltered and has safe, shallow water. Porto Pim has a mix of golden sand and volcanic black sand gently lapped by calm sea. This scenic spot is fringed by little pubs and quaint shops. In summer, the beach can get busy, but never too crowded.

To the north of Horta town center, on the island's east coast, are the long black-sand beaches **Conceição** and **Praia do Almoxarife,** littered with smooth round boulders. These adjacent beaches are an hour's walk from Horta and are among the most popular on the island. When the weather is good, majestic Mount Pico can be seen from both beaches, making an extraordinary backdrop. A taxi from Horta center to Conceição or Almoxarife costs around €7 one-way.

CALDEIRA VOLCANIC COMPLEX AND NATURE RESERVE
(Reserva Natural da Caldeira do Faial)

A huge bowl of natural flora, the Caldeira Volcanic Complex and Nature Reserve takes up the center of Faial Island. The monumental crater measures 2 kilometers (1.2 mi) in diameter and is completely lined with myriad shades of greenery peppered with colorful wildflowers and clusters of laurel forest. The popular **Caldeira hike** (Route PRC4FAI, 3.5 hours, 7 km/4.3 mi) is an easy, well-marked official hiking route around the crater rim

through exceptional landscape, with amazing views on either side. The scenery inside the bowl changes as the light shifts, and don't mind the odd cow or horse that might pop up along the way. The trail starts and finishes at the **Caldeira Viewpoint,** a 20-minute drive from Horta, following the winding scenic EN2-2A road. From Horta, head north toward Flamengos parish and follow the signs for "Caldeira." From the viewpoint car park, a tunnel cuts through the volcano to a platform inside the ridge, where you can photograph the interior of the crater if you don't want to do the rim hike. While not a demanding hike, parts of the route are narrow, and a good pair of shoes is a must for the uneven terrain.

The nature park is a dispersed protected reserve that covers 17 percent of the island's terrain, mainly along the Caldeira complex, stretching west to the coastal Capelinhos. The conical Caldeira's highest point is **Cabeço Gordo** peak, at 1,043 meters (3,422 feet) high, on the Caldeira's southern ridge. A web of clearly marked **hiking trails** (http://trails. visitazores.com) stretches across the wider Caldeira complex.

CAPELINHOS VOLCANO INTERPRETATION CENTRE
(Centro de Interpretação do Vulcão dos Capelinhos)

On the extreme western side of Faial Island, 25 kilometers (15.5 mi) from Horta, the Capelinhos Volcano is not so much a volcano as a stretch of eerily barren, inhospitable, dusty land hewn just 60 years ago following the awesome eruption of an underwater volcano that began in September 1957 and rumbled for 13 long months. This extraordinary if terrifying event extended Faial's landmass by 3 square kilometers (1.2 square mi) and caused nearly half of the island's population to flee to the United States. It also provided scientists with a unique opportunity to observe the rare phenomenon of a volcano progressing from eruption to falling dormant.

An abandoned **lighthouse** marks the point where Faial once ended and the new land begins. It is also a marker for the **Capelinhos Volcano Interpretation Centre** (Farol dos Capelinhos Capelo, tel. 292 200 470, http://parquesnaturais.azores.gov.pt, 10am-5pm Tues-Fri, 2pm-5:30pm Sat-Sun, €10), an amazing little underground museum dedicated to the formation of Capelinhos and how the planet was formed. The center was built underground to avoid interfering with the moonlike landscape, and after seeing the exhibits, visitors can climb to the top of the lighthouse to appreciate the otherworldly scenery. Exhibitions and 3-D movies (available in English) are the core of this informative little museum, described by many as one of the best in the Azores.

Food

Faial's typical cuisine is seafood-heavy, and popular local dishes are octopus stewed in wine and fresh fish soup.

As the name claims, **Restaurant Genuíno** (Rua Nova, Horta, tel. 292 701 542, www.genuino.pt, noon-3pm and 6:30pm-10pm Thurs-Tues, €16) has genuine island cuisine, blended with flavors and recipes from around the world. Clean and polished, with wooden tables and white floors and walls, the restaurant serves dishes that include tuna meatballs,

fish-and-chips, steaks with homemade chutneys, and a selection of vegetarian mains. The views over Porto Pim are inspired.

Dockside **Canto da Doca** (Rua Nova, Horta, tel. 292 292 444, noon-2:30pm and 7pm-11pm daily, €17), en route to Porto Pim, offers a more unusual dining experience, as ingredients are brought to the table raw and cooked on lava stones at the table, accompanied by a selection of sauces. It has a great interactive atmosphere, and vegetarian options are available.

Accommodations

Bright and airy, **Azoris Faial Garden** (Rua Consul Dabney, Horta, tel. 292 207 400, www.azorishotels.com, €84) is a sprawling low-rise hotel just across the street from the marina, offering simple rooms with privileged views of the harbor as well as a beautiful infinity pool. Charming, if a bit dated, it also includes breakfast and parking.

Comfortable, modern ★ **Hotel do Canal** (Largo Dr. Manuel de Arriaga, Horta, tel. 292 202 120, www.bensaude.pt, €115) is across from the marina, boasting amazing views of the marina and Pico Island. Tastefully decorated, the rooms are spacious and spotless, and the hotel's top floor has a small spa with

coastline near the Capelinhos lighthouse on Faial

a gym, a hot tub, Turkish bath, and a sauna, free for guests.

Just a short walk from the bay, informal four-star **Hotel Horta** (Rua Marcelino Lima, Horta, tel. 292 208 200, www.hotelhorta.pt, €120) has a restaurant, two bars, and a nice pool. Recently renovated, the 80 casual rooms are equipped with modern amenities.

Information and Services

National emergency number: 112

PSP police: Av. Gago Coutinho e Sacadura Cabral s/n, Horta, tel. 292 208 510, www.psp.pt

Tourist office: Rua Comendador Ernesto Rebelo 14, Horta, tel. 292 200 500, www.visitazores.com, 10am-10pm daily

Main hospital: Hospital da Horta, Estrada Príncipe Alberto do Mónaco, Horta, tel. 292 201 000, www.sns.gov.pt

Getting There

AIR

Nine kilometers (5.6 mi) west of Horta town, a 10-minute drive, **Horta Airport (Aeroporto da Horta)** (HOR, Castelo Branco, Horta, tel. 292 943 511, www.aeroportohorta.pt) has direct flights from mainland Portugal and elsewhere in Europe. A bus operated by **Farias** (tel. 292 292 482, www.farias.pt) runs between the airport and Horta (20 minutes, 3-4 buses weekdays, fewer weekends, €1.40). A taxi from the airport to Horta takes 20 minutes and costs €20.

Other than a direct flight, the easiest way to get to Faial is to fly to Ponta Delgada on São Miguel and then transfer to a free regional interisland flight operated by **SATA** (www.sata.pt) to Horta. To qualify for a free connecting flight with SATA, you'll have to travel within 24 hours of landing on São Miguel. There are usually two daily direct interisland flights between Ponta Delgada and Horta (€80), although there can be up to four flights in season.

FERRY

Atlânticoline (www.atlanticoline.pt) runs ferries in summer from Ponta Delgada to Horta (15 hours, €51) up to twice a week, stopping at other islands en route. There are ferries several times a day between Horta and Madalena on Pico Island (30 minutes, €3.60).

Getting Around

Getting around Faial is cheap and easy, as most attractions are close to Horta and can be reached on foot or with a short, cheap taxi ride. **Taxis** are widely available across the island, including outside the airport. Call **Taxis da Horta** (tel. 292 391 500) or **Associação de Taxistas do Faial** (tel. 292 391 300).

The island is compact, so renting a **car** is an excellent way of seeing a lot in a short time. There are three rental car bureaus at the airport. Given the island's small size and quiet roads, hiring a scooter is also a cheap, reasonable option. Local company **JP Scooter Rent** (tel. 965 516 252, http://jpscooterrent.blogspot.com), in Horta's main Praça do Infante square, at the kiosk in front of the marina, rents scooters (high season from €25 per day).

Buses operated by **Farias** (tel. 292 292 482, www.farias.pt) travel the perimeter of the island.

Background

The Landscape

Portugal is a coastal country whose landscape varies greatly by region, from the rugged mountain valleys of the north to the wooded mounts of Central Portugal and the rolling plains and sunny beaches of the south. Portugal's coastline is characterized by sheer cliffs alternating with golden beaches and coves. Inland, vegetation is predominantly European species in the north and shrubby Mediterranean in the south. The southern region is particularly beautiful in spring, dusted with white almond blossoms and the exotic fragrance of orange blossoms on the air.

Across the middle of Portugal is the Tagus River, and the Douro River crosses the country's width in the north. All of Portugal's main watercourses—the Tagus, Douro, Minho, Mondego, and Guadiana—have their sources in Spain and traverse the country to the Atlantic. Wedged between the Douro and the Tagus is Portugal's Central Region, with the snowcapped Serra da Estrela mountain range and the mainland's highest peak, Torre.

While the landscape inland is predominantly pastoral, dry in summer and vibrant green in winter, the coastline is cosmopolitan and touristy. The two archipelagos—Madeira and the Azores—are subtropical and lush year-round, although their location in the Atlantic means that the mild climates can be unpredictable. The beaches of these volcanic islands are mostly black and pebbly, in stark contrast to the mainland's famous soft golden sands.

GEOGRAPHY

On the southwestern flank of the Iberian Peninsula, Portugal forms a corner that separates the Atlantic Ocean from the Mediterranean Sea. Encased by Spain to the north and east and the Atlantic Ocean to the west and south, Portugal is Europe's westernmost country. Portugal occupies a total landmass of 92,391 square kilometers (35,672 square mi), and the mainland has 943 kilometers (580 mi) of coastline. Situated on the tectonic Eurasian Plate near its southern boundary with the African Plate, mainland Portugal, especially the Algarve, is a hotbed of seismic activity, but most of the tremors are relatively small and generally go unnoticed. The Azores, located on the junction of three tectonic plates—the North American, Eurasian, and African—also sees frequent quakes and tremors, mostly of low and moderate intensity, that go unnoticed.

CLIMATE

Mainland Portugal has one of the mildest year-round climates in Europe, and its more than 3,300 hours of sunshine per year make it a popular winter-sun destination. Notwithstanding, it does have distinct seasons, with mild springs (sunny days but cool nights), hot and dry summers, warm and sunny autumns (a popular time to visit Portugal, along with spring), and bright but chilly and wet winters.

Winter is generally December to February, and summer is June to late September, although some years have seen summer weather reach well into October. Traditionally, the hottest months are July and August, when temperatures can exceed 40°C (104°F) in some places; the wettest month is November, and the coldest January. But it is not unusual in Portugal to have downpours in April and heat waves in June or October. Overall, the consensus is that the best times to visit are June and September-October, with pleasant weather and when the popular resorts are not yet in full-throttle peak summer.

Northern Portugal is generally wetter and cooler than the rest of the country, while the south is warmer and drier. It also snows in winter, but only on the Serra da Estrela mountain range in Central Portugal. Largely influenced by the Atlantic, coastal areas usually benefit from a pleasant sea breeze, even in the scorching throes of summer. There are also distinct microclimates within the country, with the weather in Northern Portugal resembling that of Northern Europe, the south taking on an increasingly North African feel, and inland areas reflecting the climes of Central Europe.

ENVIRONMENTAL ISSUES

In recent years, Portugal has been increasingly afflicted by sporadic weather-related environmental issues such as flash floods,

---

tornadoes, increasingly ferocious and widespread wildfires, and coastal erosion, examples of growing extreme and atypical climatic phenomena. Portugal also battles the palm weevil, a beetle from Asia that kills palm trees. Portugal's natural and architectural heritage is well preserved, and there are no major pollution issues, although large forest fires and growing cities have caused alerts for air quality. Significant investment is being made in Portugal to combat air pollution, especially in Lisbon, where new regulations governing vehicles and new data collection systems were implemented in 2017.

Plants and Animals

Portugal has a diverse palette of flora and fauna whose origins stem from several parts of the globe. Almost identical to the flora and fauna of neighboring Spain, it is a mix of Atlantic, European, Mediterranean, and North African. The distribution of Portugal's vegetation reflects varying regional climates, denser and leafier to the north and sparser and shrubbier to the south. Simply put, the farther south, the more Mediterranean the vegetation becomes. The country has a number of indigenous species of plants and animals, and several native breeds of dogs, cows, donkeys, horses, pigs, and chickens. The countryside is home to an abundance of wild animals, including wolves, foxes, deer, hares, goats, boars, and lynx. The Iberian lynx has been brought back from the brink of extinction thanks to a proactive conservation and reintroduction program.

Portugal also teems with birdlife as it is on a major winter migration route for western and central European species. It has rich fish stocks off the coast as well as a rapidly expanding number of exotic plant species, particularly invasive species. The Azores can claim the peculiarity of having only small wild mammals, such as rabbits, ferrets, rats, mice, and bats, while Madeira's Desertas Islands are home to the endangered Mediterranean monk seal.

VEGETATION ZONES

Vegetation varies from the predominantly European vegetation of the north to the Mediterranean vegetation of the south.

Thick pine and chestnut forests characterize the north, where deciduous trees blanket the landscape. Portugal's central ridge is distinguished by oak and eucalyptus, as is the Alentejo, where, farther south, symbolic cork and holm oaks take over the undulating plains. Farther south still, in the Algarve, the landscape takes on a shrubbier look with predominantly Mediterranean vegetation such as olive, almond, orange, and carob trees as well as vineyards. The lush Azores and Madeira islands abound with mosses and ferns, and throughout the mainland are a number of protected natural parks established to defend regional natural heritage.

TREES

Not so long ago, most of Portugal was clad in forests. Due to deforestation and, more recently, wildfires, just over one-third of the country remains wooded. Vast swaths of the country, particularly Central Portugal, are blanketed by dense holm and cork oak woodlands (the cork oak is Portugal's national tree), which cover approximately 1.2 million hectares (almost 3 million acres) between Central Portugal and the Alentejo region. Portugal is a leading producer of paper and is the world's leading producer of cork, exporting close to 200,000 tonnes (more than 440 million pounds) every year. Corks found in some of the finest bottles of champagne on the planet derive from Portugal. Mountainous and sandy areas are covered in fragrant eucalyptus and pines as well as ancient olive trees and, farther south, almond trees. Palm trees are a common sight, particularly in popular coastal areas. While many of the common palm species are native, many are foreign, introduced by humans.

FLOWERS AND OTHER PLANTLIFE

You would be hard-pressed to travel around Portugal and not notice the national flower, lavender, growing wild and in gardens It is also a popular ingredient in soaps and teas. Thanks to Portugal's year-round mild climate, a stunning range of colorful flora includes orchids, azaleas, proteas, water lilies, the lovely bougainvillea that grows on seemingly every street, jacarandas and gerberas, as well as the birds-of-paradise that are synonymous with the island of Madeira. Among the flowers native to Portugal are daffodil, thyme, and sweet marjoram. Portugal's landscape comes to life in spring.

MAMMALS

Portugal's diverse countryside is home to over 100 mammal species, the most common being wild boars, goats, deer, foxes, rabbits, and the Iberian hare. Wolves still live wild in remote parts of the far north and northeast, and the endangered Iberian lynx is gradually being reintroduced into its natural habitat, the Malcata Mountains and the Algarve-Alentejo border regions, after being brought back from the brink of extinction by a successful breeding program implemented in Portugal and Spain. Driven out of its native territories by dwindling food resources, loss and degradation of habitat, urban development, and illegal hunting, Iberia's largest wild cat is once again roaming the hills of its home. Smaller rodents, such as water voles, dormice, rats, and hedgehogs can also be found throughout the country, while Iberian badgers, otters, common genets, and mongooses are also found in central and northern thickets but are rarely sighted.

SEALIFE

The waters off Portugal's coast teem with life from tiny sardines to huge tuna, and fishing is an important economic activity. Dolphins can be spotted off the south coast, where dolphin-watching trips are popular, while the Sado Estuary, near Lisbon, is home to a resident pod of bottlenose dolphins unique in Europe. Turtles can be found in the tranquil waters of the Algarve's Ria Formosa, as well as in the waters off the Azores. Whale- and dolphin-watching can be enjoyed on the Azores and Madeira, and Portugal has a plethora of interesting dive sites off its shores and islands. The most common fish caught off the coast and staples in the national diet are sardines, mackerel, and tuna, while the craggy coastline is also a source of shellfish such as clams, cockles, crabs, and oysters.

BIRDS

Positioned on a major migration route between Europe and Africa, Portugal hosts common European species that reside here year-round as well as exotic transients. Over 600 species of birds have been logged in Portugal, with at least one new species recorded every year. Due to their unique geographical location, the Azores and Madeira are particularly interesting to bird-watchers, as they host North American species rarely found elsewhere in Europe. Mainland Portugal's many *rias* (lagoons), marshes, estuaries, and salt pans attract beautiful species like flamingos, which can often be seen standing one-legged. Another common sight is the cattle egret, which likes to pick mites off the backs of livestock or eat insects that emerge from soil disturbed by the animals' hooves. The elegant stork is a protected species in Portugal and has become symbolic of the south, even though they can be found throughout the mainland. Their huge nests, which withstand even the most ferocious weather, crown pylons, pillars, and buildings in cities and the countryside, a captivating sight. The soaring Iberian white stork *(Ciconia ciconia)* is revered in Portugal as it eats insects that blight crops. It is also illegal to move a stork's nest in Portugal, so many new buildings, especially those converted from old factories, have to retain the original brick chimneys if they have a nest on top.

REPTILES

When the weather is hot, tiny chameleons, lizards, and geckos come out to bask in the sun and to feast on the insects that come out in warmer months. Small reptiles are common throughout Portugal, particularly in arid southern areas, to the delight of some people and the disgust of others. Portugal is home to several species of snakes, but few are venomous and none are deadly. The most common snakes in Portugal are the ladder snake, the false smooth snake, the grass snake, the Montpellier snake, the viperine snake, the Lataste's viper (the only species thought to be harmful to humans), the southern smooth snake, and the horseshoe snake.

AMPHIBIANS

Portugal's sandy dunes and lagoons are a haven for amphibians and are awash with terrapins, toads, frogs, newts, and salamanders. The natterjack toad *(Bufo calamita)* is commonly found, even though it is very rare in other European countries.

INSECTS AND ARACHNIDS

Unlike its snake population, Portugal has many biting spiders, several of which are poisonous, the most common being the *armadeira* (wandering spider). The *armadeira* is light brown, is slightly furry, and has long legs. Its bite can be painful and cause dizziness, vomiting, and muscle spasms. The *armadeira* generally comes out in cooler weather, growing up to 5 centimeters (2 inches). If bitten, seek immediate medical attention. If left unattended, the bite can cause serious wounds or even loss of a limb. The *armadeira* is not native to Portugal but was brought from South America in banana boxes. Portugal is also home to the notorious black widow spider, distinctively black with a red spot on its back, and tarantulas, which are less common. But both will bite if provoked. Sound advice is to never handle a spider.

Much more common is the dreaded mosquito, prevalent in areas with still water, such as lagoons and canals, and more so during warmer months. There is no risk of malaria in Portugal, although the island of Madeira has had cases of dengue fever. Besides being itchy, a mosquito bite seldom turns into anything more than a nuisance.

Thanks to its wealth of flowers, Portugal also has bees and wasps, which can give a nasty sting, as well as many butterflies and moths, with common species including the swallowtail butterfly *(Papilio machaon)* and the monarch, most often seen in the Algarve.

One of Portugal's more unusual insects is the pine processionary caterpillar, which turns into a moth and lives in pine trees. These toxic caterpillars can often be seen shuffling along in formation, nose-to-tail, in long lines. They have long hairs that make them look cute and fluffy but can cause a painful allergic reaction if touched; they can be fatal to smaller animals like dogs and cats.

History

Portugal is a small country with epic history. As one of the world's oldest nations and ruler of what was one of the world's most powerful empires, yet with one of the youngest settled democracies in Europe, Portugal has remarkable historical achievements. Its name is said to derive from the ancient Portus Cale, the name for the city now known as Porto. From ancient and medieval invasions to the 12th-century reconquests and the founding of the nation, through the Age of Discoveries, when Portugal spearheaded global explorations and established itself as a world power, the 17th-century Restoration of Independence, and the more recent Carnation Revolution and implementation of democracy, Portugal has a storied history. Evidence of these eras can be found throughout the country in relics, architecture, and monuments, which in many cities have been excellently preserved. Portugal's architectural styles are influenced by its wide-ranging history and territorial disputes, and can be loosely divided into five main styles: Romanesque, Gothic, Renaissance, baroque, and neoclassical. Portugal's hand in shaping the world belies its discreet yet determined positioning today, and it deserves its reputation as a nation with an acute sense of adventure and resilience, having successively and successfully rebuilt and repositioned itself in the wake of natural and economic disasters.

ANCIENT TIMES

Portugal is believed to have been inhabited by humans since Paleolithic times, more than 20,000 years ago. The earliest known people to have invaded Portugal were the Celts of Central Europe, who arrived in waves from the first millennium BC, interbreeding with the local native population to form a number of tribes. Like much of Europe, Portugal was invaded by the Romans, who occupied the territory from the 3rd century BC until their demise in the late 4th and 5th centuries AD.

The Roman occupation of Portugal started from the south and took several decades. Rebellion in the north by local Lusitanians hampered the invasion, but after the Romans bribed three rebels to kill their own leader, Viriathus, the country was finally conquered as a whole, and the Roman Empire began to flourish, laying the foundations of the cities and infrastructure of today's Portugal. The cities of Beja and Braga were key administrative sites during the Roman occupation, and many vivid remnants of the Romans' time in Portugal can still be found there. Two of the best-preserved Roman sites in Portugal are in Conímbriga, near Coimbra, and the Milreu Roman Ruins in Estoi, Algarve.

EARLY HISTORY

In the 5th century AD, the Iberian Peninsula was invaded and conquered by a Germanic tribe known as the Visigoths, vestiges of whose presence can be found in Coimbra, Alenquer, and Lisbon. Despite establishing what went on to become known as the Visigoth Kingdom, the invaders' claim didn't last long, and they were overthrown by the Moors, medieval Muslims from present-day Morocco in North Africa, who invaded Portugal circa 711, claiming and settling across the entire Iberian Peninsula. Small pockets of Christian armies lingered and rebelled against the Moors, over the next few centuries driving them back and reclaiming territory during an era known as the *reconquistas* (reconquests). By the 9th century, the north of Portugal was under Christian rule, and by the 12th century the Moors had been completely driven out. One of the main leaders of the Christian armies, Afonso Henriques, famously declared himself the first king of Portugal in 1139, and a fledgling kingdom was founded.

Portugal's early foundations were shaken when territorial disputes with the Spaniards broke out, particularly over the south of

Portugal. However, Portugal's status as an independent kingdom was reinforced in the Middle Ages when Afonso III (third in succession of founding King Afonsos, in what became known as the Afonsine era) conquered the southern city of Faro in the Algarve in 1249, and an alliance was drawn up with the United Kingdom, the Treaty of Windsor, to protect Portugal from further incursions.

AGE OF DISCOVERIES

With the country firmly under Christian rule and the protection of the Treaty of Windsor, Portugal took advantage of the stability to turn its attentions to exploration, an era that was to become known as the Age of Discoveries. Roughly spanning the 15th and 16th centuries, this golden age saw Portuguese seafarers, spearheaded by Portugal's most famous captain, Prince Henry the Navigator, sail off to explore the world. Henry, the third son of John I (João I), at age 21 commanded a military force that captured the Muslim outpost of Ceuta in North Africa in 1415; this was the initial step in Portugal's Age of Discoveries. First, the Portuguese explored the Atlantic archipelagos and the African coast before rounding the Cape of Good Hope in 1488 under the leadership of Bartolomeu Dias, finally reaching India a decade later in 1498, guided by Vasco da Gama. But what really catapulted Portugal to stratospheric wealth and power was the exploration and claiming of Brazil by Pedro Álvares Cabral in 1500. These discoveries elevated Portugal from a tumultuous territory to a leading global power, along with the imperial peers of England, France, and Spain, in terms of economic, political, and cultural clout.

COLONIALISM

Portuguese explorers continued to establish profitable trading routes around the globe and set up a string of trading colonies, forts, and factories throughout the world as they went; the spice, gold, and slave trades were among the most lucrative. By 1571, a series of naval outposts connected Lisbon to places as far-flung as Nagasaki along the coasts of Africa, the Middle East, India, and South Asia. This had a huge positive impact on Portuguese economic growth that lasted for three centuries. While Brazil was undoubtedly the jewel in Portugal's colonial crown, major colonies in the African countries of Angola, Mozambique, and Guinea-Bissau also proved profitable. Other important colonies were established in Cape Verde, São Tomé and Príncipe, Goa (India), East Timor, and Macau. For centuries, the Portuguese pioneered global explorations and excelled in trade, and its colonial empire grew to become one of the largest and longest-lived in world history, spanning six centuries until the handover of Macau to China in 1999.

SPANISH ANNEXATION AND INDEPENDENCE

In 1578 Portugal's king, Dom Sebastião I, was killed in the Battle of Alcácer Quibir in northern Morocco. Because the king died without an heir, the throne was claimed by King Phillip II of neighboring Spain, based on a vague family lineage. Phillip II took advantage of Portugal's vulnerability following the king's death and invaded in 1580, forcing a merger that saw Spain protect Brazil from being claimed by the Dutch but also saw Portugal inherit Spain's enemies, among them England. Even though life was relatively tranquil during the reigns of Phillip II and III, with Portugal retaining its own laws and currency, unrest finally reached boiling point during the reign of Phillip IV, who stripped the country's nobility of all powers and effectively attempted to make Portugal a Spanish province. Seizing Spain's fatigue at the end of the Thirty-Year War, Portugal's John of Braganza led a Portuguese resistance, later known as the Portuguese Restoration War, that lasted 28 years. Finally, on February 13, 1668, Spain officially recognized Portugal's independence. Even though Portugal no longer has a monarch, and hasn't since the revolution of October 5, 1910, the House of Braganza is still seen as akin to the country's royal family, and lays claim to the throne.

EARTHQUAKE OF 1755

Finally thriving in its independence, Portugal was again brought to its knees by the massive 1755 Lisbon earthquake, which razed vast swaths of the country. A succession of three devastating tsunamis and massive fires that raged for days contributed to the apocalyptic chaos that practically wiped out an entire country. In the aftermath, the Marquis of Pombal was nominated by José I to lead the recovery, which, to Pombal's credit, was remarkably swift. Portugal was almost entirely rebuilt in a matter of years, mostly thanks to the wealth coming from Brazil after gold was discovered there. This reconstruction gave way to the distinctly Portuguese Pombaline style of architecture, a mix of late baroque and neoclassical.

BRITISH ULTIMATUM

In 1890 the United Kingdom issued Portugal an ultimatum that all Portuguese troops should withdraw from the belt of African colonies between Mozambique on the east and Angola on the west. The theories about the reasons for this are that the presence of Portuguese troops hampered British plans to build a railroad between Cairo and Cape Town, or that the British government was pressed into taking action by Cecil Rhodes, whose British South Africa Company was founded in 1888. Rhodes's ambition was to create a zone of British commercial and political influence from Cape Town to Cairo, and the Portuguese settlements were in the way.

Portugal complied with the British demands, which were considered a breach of the Treaty of Windsor as well as a national humiliation by republicans in Portugal, who denounced the government and the king, leading to the collapse of the government. It was considered the most outrageous action by the United Kingdom against its oldest ally and was one of the main causes for the Republican Revolution, which ended the monarchy in Portugal 20 years later. On October 5, 1910, a coup d'état organized by the Portuguese Republican Party, in which at least 37 people died, deposed the constitutional monarchy and proclaimed a republican regime, the Estado Novo (first republic). The iconic red, gold, and green national flag was adopted in 1911.

20TH CENTURY

After siding with the Allies in World War I and suffering a postwar spell of turmoil and unrest, on May 7, 1926, Portugal saw another coup d'état that paved the way for the military to seize power and gave birth to the second republic, the Diatdura Nacional (National Dictatorship). This saw the rise of notorious dictator António de Oliveira Salazar, and times of oppression and censorship. Salazar led Portugal through World War II, during which the country remained nominally neutral. Despite supplying troops under the British flag and allowing the Allies to establish air bases in the Azores, Portugal continued to trade successfully with both sides for the duration of World War II. The demise of Salazar came in 1968 when he slipped in a bathtub and suffered a brain hemorrhage; he died in 1970. He handed power to the slightly less radical Marcelo Caetano, who was overthrown in 1974 in what has become known as the Carnation Revolution, the third and last republic.

The Carnation Revolution eradicated dictatorial power without bloodshed or a single shot being fired. This was the start of the democratic republic of Portugal we know today. The revolution also saw the end of the Portuguese colonial empire, with its remaining overseas colonies, including Angola and Mozambique, attaining independence. The Portuguese people who left the colonies to come back to Portugal became known as the *retornados* (returnees). Macau, the nation's last possession, was handed over to China in 1999. But Portugal joining the European Union in 1986 really thrust the country forward, increasing funding for basic infrastructure such as roads, schools, and medical facilities as well as foreign investment, with which Portugal has truly blossomed.

CONTEMPORARY TIMES

Modern-day Portugal is a prospering and socially stable country despite the severe impact of the 2008 global economic crisis. Years of austerity ensued, but Portugal remained true to its resilient roots, and its recovery and payback of its €78 billion bailout have been exemplary. Currently enjoying a period of financial reestablishment, social and economic recovery, record-breaking tourism, and dropping unemployment, the country has yet again managed to get back on its feet following a debilitating blow. A number of reforms are in place to underpin future growth.

In recent years, Portugal has also repeatedly topped the list of most peaceful countries in the world, and it has been voted among the best places to live in Europe, to retire in Europe, and to visit in Europe.

Government and Economy

GOVERNMENT

Organization

The Republic of Portugal is a sovereign democracy. Its current form of government is unitary and semi-presidential (with a president as well as a prime minister), in which the central government has ultimate power. The prime minister is the head of government, while the president is the head of state. The president is head of the armed forces and is responsible for swearing in new prime ministers, based on election results, and convening or dissolving parliament when required. At the time of writing, Portugal's prime minister is António Costa, of the Socialist Party, and its president is Marcelo Rebelo de Sousa of the Social Democratic Party.

The government of Portugal comprises the president of the republic, the Assembly of the Republic (parliament), and the courts, representing the country's executive, legislative, and judicial branches, respectively. The government has political, legislative, and administrative functions and comprises a prime minister, ministers, secretaries of state (junior ministers), and their deputies. Portugal's current government is a Socialist Party (PS) minority government, supported by a leftist alliance of the Left Bloc (BE), Portuguese Communist Party (PCP), and the Ecologist (green) Party (PEV). The autonomous regions (Azores and Madeira) have their own regional political and administrative statutes, governments, and presidents.

Political Parties

Since the dawn of democracy following the 1974 Carnation Revolution, Portugal has had two main parties that dominate the political scene: the center-left PS Socialist Party, and the center-right PSD Social Democratic Party. Following those, the other main parties are the conservative Christian-Democratic CDS-PP People's Party, the BE Left Bloc, the PCP Communist Party, the green party Os Verdes, and, more recently, the progressive center-left PAN—Party for People, Animals, and Nature. The country does have a few right-wing and far-right parties, but they have little political expression.

Elections

Elections take place on the national and local levels. Citizens directly elect a president every five years in the Presidential Election, and a new parliament in the Legislative Election every four years. Portugal's parliament is made up of 230 members elected to four-year terms by proportional district representation. Locally, Portugal has 308 municipal authorities, and every four years local elections choose councils and mayors for four-year terms. Local elections are interspersed with national elections. Portugal also stages European elections for representatives to sit in the European Parliament.

ECONOMY
Agriculture
Agriculture plays a large role in the Portuguese economy, with the farming heart of the country, the Alentejo, known as the breadbasket of Portugal and for grazing. Forestry, farming, and fishing support many families in rural and inland areas, reflected in regional gastronomy. The main products of Portugal, beyond cork and wine, are green vegetables, rice, corn, wheat, barley, olives, oilseeds, nuts, cherries, bilberries, table grapes, and mushrooms. Portugal is also a leading producer of tomato paste, olive oil, and sea salt. Despite vast regions of the country still being agriculture-dependent, investment and funding for the sector is low, and environmental issues such as drought, wildfires, and dwindling fish stocks hamper prosperity.

Industry
Because Portugal is a seafaring nation where trade has historically been a mainstay, it is perhaps unsurprising that it remains an industrious and creative country. The tertiary (services) sector is currently the largest in the country's economy, in which the importance of tourism cannot be overstated. The services sector presently provides jobs for more than two-thirds of the working population and represents over 75 percent of the gross value added (GVA). Industry, construction, energy, and water make up just under a quarter of the GVA and employ one-quarter of the working population, while agriculture, forestry, and fishing are just a tiny slice of the GVA (2.2 percent) and employment (6.9 percent).

Given that in the 1960s fishing and farming were responsible for around a quarter of the country's economy, that sector has suffered a steep and steady downturn over the past half-century.

Although Portugal was a late starter in industrialization—it was one of the last European countries that the Industrial Revolution reached—the economy today is powered by several key drivers, mostly harnessed from the country's natural attributes and ever-developing skills. Chiefly, these are machinery, electrical, and electronics industries; automotive and shipbuilding industries; injection molding; creative clothing, textiles, and footwear; wood pulp, paper, and cork; food processing and fish canning (Portugal's canned fish brands are gastronomic icons); world-class wine and olive oil production; and the all-important tourism.

Industrial production in Portugal soared after World War II, aided by modernization in the 1960s. Portugal's return to democracy in 1974, followed by the nation's joining the European Union in 1986, saw privatized firms liberalized, which allowed the national economy to thrive.

Most of the bigger textile and footwear factories are in the north of the country, while Oeiras, in Lisbon, is home to the country's major multinational companies. Many larger Portuguese companies have also made significant investment in internationalizing, among them retailer Jerónimo Martins, which owns the largest no-frills supermarket chain in Poland and is also investing in Colombia, and national flag-carrier airline TAP Portugal, which is held in high regard for its safety record.

For much of the 1990s the economy grew by more than the EU average, and, despite the crippling economic downturn, it has recently started to regain ground. In 2017, driven by exports and investment, the economy grew at twice the pace of the Eurozone average.

Distribution of Wealth
Despite gradual industrialization in the late 1800s, prior to the 1974 Carnation Revolution, Portugal was socially divided into two main classes: an affluent elite of mainly landowners and impoverished peasants. The revolution eradicated the dictatorship that had kept

the social classes in place, and major changes erupted. The onset of slow modernization in the 20th century saw a new and prosperous middle class begin to emerge, and social indicators began to equalize. Portugal infamously had one of the highest illiteracy rates in Europe, but as education improved, so did development, mainly along the country's coast, which inevitably saw younger people leaving the rural interior for the coast to pursue studies or seek employment. This led to desertification inland, which, while less pronounced today, had an impact on the distribution of investment. With the exception of a handful of major inland cities, the coast is generally a more affluent and desirable place to live, although much of the employment, particularly in the Algarve, is tourism-generated and seasonal.

The economic crisis of 2008 had a debilitating impact on the country's lower-earning families, whose main income came from precarious employment and benefits. Rife unemployment and tough austerity measures saw many families heading for soup kitchens, and young graduates left the country in large numbers to find employment abroad, many in the former Portuguese colonies. That scenario is much improved today, although recent studies have found that Portugal's distribution of wealth is still disparate, one of the most unequal in Europe and with higher-than-average levels of poverty.

Tourism

Tourism is a buoyant key economic driver in Portugal, particularly in coastal areas and especially in the southern Algarve region, where tourism is the main source of employment. Growth has been gradual since 2011, with new hotels opening every year to welcome a record 21 million tourists in 2017, generating €3.39 billion in revenue. This is up significantly from the 15 million visitors registered in 2014, and the 19 million tourists who stayed in Portugal's hotels in 2016. Tourism currently accounts for approximately 12 percent of the gross domestic product, making tourism the second-biggest element of the national economy.

Foreign visitors to Portugal are predominantly European and of British, German, Spanish, and French nationality, or Brazilian. In recent years, growing numbers of American, Russian, Asian, and Scandinavian tourists have arrived.

While Portugal has always been a popular destination among Northern Europeans, particularly the British, who make up the largest tourist group as well as a major expatriate community, it's safe to say never has Portugal's allure been as strong as today. Despite the crippling economic downturn and austere bailout, Portugal managed to maintain its quality over quantity image while identifying new niche markets and investing in creative promotions to become increasingly trendy.

Lisbon, the Algarve, and Madeira see the largest numbers of tourists, accounting for almost one-third of visitors to the country, but the Azores and Northern Portugal are enjoying a newfound demand that has seen visitor figures soar. From 2006 to 2016, foreign tourist numbers in Portugal almost doubled.

The first tourism poster that Portugal launched in 1907 sported the slogan "Portugal: the shortest way between America and Europe," and to this day the country is still one of the main gateways to Europe from the Americas and Africa. There are now numerous direct flights between Portugal, the United States, and Africa as well as connecting flights to major international destinations.

As one of the last Western European countries to develop its tourism, Portugal has more tourists, more revenue, and fuller hotels than ever, and was named the World's Leading Destination at the 24th annual World Travel Awards (WTA) in 2017.

Lisbon and Porto are now revered top European destinations like Barcelona and London, while the Algarve remains one of Europe's leading beach destinations.

People and Culture

DEMOGRAPHY AND DIVERSITY

Portugal has a population of about 10 million. Most densely populated are Lisbon, Porto, Coimbra, Braga, and Funchal (Madeira), while the Algarve and the Silver Coast are popular places to live. As of 2016, the average life expectancy was 81.1 years. However, as life expectancy increases and the birth rate dwindles, Portugal's struggle with an aging population mounts.

Portugal has a literacy rate of 95.7 percent. Education in Portugal is free, as is health care, and is compulsory until the age of 18 or until completing 12th grade.

Portugal's minority groups are primarily legal and illegal immigrants. The largest groups are Brazilians, Eastern Europeans, Asians, and Africans from Portugal's former colonies, such as Cape Verde, Angola, and Guinea-Bissau. Legal immigrants account for about 5 percent of the total population. There are also 40,000-50,000 Roma people in the country. Portugal has strict antiracism and antidiscrimination laws. It is forbidden to collect statistics about race or ethnicity in the country.

RELIGION

Portugal is over 80 percent Roman Catholic, although only around one-third of Portuguese are practicing. Traditional religious festivals and customs are widely observed, as are religious ceremonies like baptisms, last rites, and marriages. Religious observance is strongest in the northern regions and less prevalent in the southern regions and cities.

LANGUAGE

The language spoken in Portugal is European Portuguese, distinct from Brazilian Portuguese, which originates from the European version. A West Romance language, Portuguese is the seventh most widely spoken language in the world and the sole official language of Portugal and former Portuguese colonies Brazil, Cape Verde, Mozambique, Angola, and São Tomé and Príncipe, as well as Guinea-Bissau. Portuguese also has co-official language status in East Timor, Equatorial Guinea, and Macau in China.

While Portuguese is spoken throughout the country, some 5,000 people in the villages in the Miranda do Douro speak their own language, Mirandese, recognized as a co-official language.

English is the most widely spoken second language in Portugal, followed by French and Spanish. Most tours will have a guide who speaks very good English, and signage will usually have an English translation, especially at main monuments and attractions. Generally, the less prominent the attraction, the poorer the level of English.

THE ARTS
Literature

Portugal has a rich literary history, with acclaimed and revered writers of international repute. One of the earliest examples of Portuguese literature is medieval Galician-Portuguese poetry, which shaped early Portuguese literature. A superlative example of this style is the great 16th-century master poet Luís de Camões's epic lyrical text *Os Lusíadas (The Lusiads)*. *Os Lusíadas* is an undisputed classic and one of the most important works of Portuguese literature.

The progression of Portuguese literature can be divided into three main classical phases—Renaissance, baroque, and neoclassical, followed by romanticism and realism. Other Portuguese literary greats include Eça da Queirós; Fernando Pessoa; Antero de Quental; Alexandre O'Neill, a Portuguese poet of Irish descent; and novelist José Saramago, recipient of the 1998 Nobel Prize in Literature.

Visual Arts

Particularly accomplished in ceramics, architecture, sculpting, and painting, Portuguese artists excel in many genres. Famous for glass and crystal ware as well as ceramics, artisans produce striking and colorful objects, many of which have been elevated from time-honed crafts to true art. The country is perhaps best known for its azulejos, hand-painted glazed tiles that historically have been used to create giant plaques depicting everything from battle scenes to drink advertisements. Azulejo murals of myriad sizes and scenes can be found on buildings and monuments throughout the country. Portugal is also famous for terracotta earthenware, a distinctive staple on many of the country's restaurant tables.

Over the centuries, Portugal has produced many fine artists and sculptors, among them Nuno Gonçalves, Joaquim Machado de Castro, Grão Vasco, António Soares dos Reis, and, more recently, Maria Helena Vieira da Silva, Carlos Botelho, and Paula Rego. Portugal is also home to many revered architects, perhaps the most celebrated being Álvaro Siza Vieira, who designed Porto's stunning Serralves Foundation, and Eduardo de Souta Moura, who designed Braga's unique municipal stadium; both have won major international architecture awards.

Music and Dance

Portugal's music and dance originate from its exotic heritage. The country has a huge appetite for traditional festivities, and folk music and dance underpin celebrations nationwide that vary by region. Portuguese folklore is rich and exhilarating, with upbeat music and dizzying dances. Most towns have their own local dance groups, *ranchos,* which perform the traditional dances at local or tourist attractions, such as the themed "Portuguese night" dinners that so many hotels offer.

Portuguese dances include the circle dance, fandango (from the Ribatejo region), two-step waltz, schottische *(chotiça), corridinho* (from the Algarve and Estremadura regions), *vira* (from the Minho region), *bailinho* (Madeira), *vira solto,* and *tau-tau,* among many others. Dances tend to be fast-paced and involve lots of twirling and leg-lifting, which to the uninitiated might look rather jazzy. Folk dancing is generally accompanied by a traditional band or an accordion player as well as folk singing, with everyone dressed in colorful folky outfits. Typical instruments used in folk bands are the guitar, mandolin, bagpipes, accordion, violin, drums, Portuguese guitar, and a plethora of wind and percussion instruments. Portugal is currently enjoying something of a folk revival, with cool bands making it popular among the younger generations.

A very typically Portuguese form of music is *pimba*, a kitsch genre that mixes traditional instruments like the accordion with up-tempo Latin beats and generally involves lyrics that can be tongue-in-cheek and sometimes rude. It might sound cheesy, but *pimba* has generated some of the country's best-loved artists, including Emanuel, Quim Barreiros, and Ágata, who have become national treasures and pretty wealthy.

Two of Portugal's best-known genres of traditional music are the mournful fado, which has two main styles, deriving from Lisbon and Coimbra, and *cante alentejano,* traditional group folk singing from the Alentejo region. Both fado and the *cante alentejano* are classified by UNESCO as Intangible Cultural Heritage.

It's a little-known fact that many former and current mainstream pop stars are of Portuguese descent—including Nelly Furtado, former Journey lead singer Steve Perry, Aerosmith's Joe Perry (both Perrys' original paternal family names were Pereira), Jamiroquai lead singer Jay Kay, Katy Perry (again, from Pereira), and Shawn Mendes, whose father is from Lagos in the Algarve—which only adds to Portugal's newfound cool.

Essentials

Transportation

GETTING THERE

Traveling to Portugal from anywhere in Europe is quick and easy, with regular direct flights from many European cities as well as from Asia, the Middle East, North and South America, and Africa. Even better, flights can be pretty cheap within Europe, thanks to the growing number of low-cost airlines.

The three main airports on the mainland are Lisbon, the country's biggest and busiest; Porto in the north; and Faro in the south. Madeira Airport (also known as Funchal) is on Madeira Island, and on São

Miguel is Ponta Delgada Airport, the main airport for the Azores.

Most flights from outside Europe are to Lisbon, with direct flights from the United States, Canada, Brazil, Morocco, Tunisia, Turkey, Russia, Dubai in the United Arab Emirates, Angola, Mozambique, and China. Porto also has regular direct flights from Newark in the United States, Luanda in Angola, and Rio de Janeiro and São Paulo in Brazil, although far fewer than Lisbon. Faro has almost exclusively European flights, the vast majority from the United Kingdom, Germany, and France.

It is easy to travel to Portugal within Europe, with bus and train services connecting Portugal with Spain, France, Belgium, the Netherlands, and the United Kingdom. Driving to Portugal is also possible thanks to a good international road network and the EU (European Union) open-borders policy.

From North America

Some transatlantic cruises include Lisbon, generally just for a short day trip, but the easiest, quickest, cheapest, and most convenient way to travel between the United States and Portugal is without doubt by air. Flights take seven hours eastbound from the Northeast, and nine hours westbound.

Portugal's national carrier, **TAP Air Portugal** (www.flytap.pt), has regular direct flights between mainland Portugal and New York (JFK and Newark), Boston, Miami, and Philadelphia. U.S. airline **United** (www.united.com) also has direct flights to Portugal.

TAP has invested heavily in the U.S. market, increasing the number of destinations it serves, and has also created the **Portugal Stopover** (www.portugalstopover.flytap.com) program, where U.S. travelers on TAP to other destinations can spend a few days in Portugal before continuing onward. Portugal's national flag carrier also operates onward connecting flights from Lisbon to Porto, Faro, and the islands.

Regional Azores airline **SATA Azores Airlines** (www.azoresairlines.pt) and **Air Canada** (www.aircanada.com) operate direct flights between Portugal and Canada, including a stop in the Azores archipelago.

From Europe
AIR
The vast majority of European flights to Portugal are from the United Kingdom, France, Germany, the Netherlands, and Belgium, all 2.5-3 hours away. Direct flights also operate from Finland as well as Eastern European countries such as Poland, the Czech Republic, and Hungary. Flights from neighboring Spain are only to Lisbon and Porto; oddly, there are no direct flights between Spain and Faro Airport in southern Portugal.

The ever-expanding availability of European flights includes a number of low-cost airlines such as Ryanair (Ireland), easyJet (UK), Vueling (Spain), Eurowings (Germany), and Transavia (France), meaning travel between two European destinations can cost less than €100 return. Prices within Europe are heavily influenced by school holidays at Easter, summer, and Christmas-New Year's as well as peak tourist seasons in Portugal, especially July-August; pricing can vary widely.

TRAIN
Getting to Portugal from other European countries by train isn't as straightforward as by air and can sometimes be more expensive. The train is slightly quicker than traveling by bus.

From the United Kingdom: Getting to Portugal from the United Kingdom takes around 24 hours and involves catching the **Eurostar** (www.eurostar.com) from London to Paris, then a TGV high-speed train from Paris to Hendaye-Irun at the border of southern France and Spain, and from there the overnight Sud Expresso train to Lisbon.

From Spain: There are two overnight sleeper trains: the **Lusitania Hotel Train** (www.cp.pt), linking Madrid's Chamartin Station to Lisbon in about 10 hours, and the **Sud Expresso** (www.cp.pt), which connects Lisbon to San Sebastian in Spain and Hendaye in southern France in about 11 hours. In Northern Portugal, a high-speed train, the **Celta IC** (www.cp.pt), links Porto to Vigo in 3.5 hours.

From elsewhere: Getting to Portugal by train from Belgium, the Netherlands, or Germany requires passing through an international terminal such as Paris or Madrid.

Train passes: The easiest way to get around Portugal—and the rest of Europe—by train is with a **Eurail Pass** (www.eurail.com). This EU-wide rail travel pass for non-EU citizens covers train travel in first or second class. The Eurail pass comes in three options: the Global Pass, covering 5 or more of up to 28 European countries; the Select Pass—covering 2, 3, or 4 bordering countries; or a single-country pass. Prices for Portugal range from €82 for a single-country pass to €307 for a basic Global Pass, although prices vary.

An identical pass is available to EU citizens and official residents: the **Interrail Pass** (www.interrail.eu) ranges from €80 for a single-country pass to €208 for a basic Global Pass, although prices vary.

BUS

The main bus lines offering intercity travel within Europe to Portugal are **Eurolines** (Lisbon tel. 218 957 398, Porto tel. 225 189 303, Bragança tel. 273 327 122, www. eurolines.com) and **National Express** (www. nationalexpress.com). These generally travel to Lisbon, Porto, and Faro in the Algarve from many European countries. The most popular routes are from the United Kingdom, France, Spain, and the Netherlands. Transfers may be required; from London to Lisbon, for example, a change may be required in Paris. There are at least five buses a week between Paris

and Lisbon. Bus prices from Amsterdam to Lisbon start from €110 one-way and take around 36 hours; London to Lisbon is around €115 and 45 hours, and Paris to Lisbon €85 and 29 hours.

The main bus companies operating between Portugal and neighboring Spain are **Avanza** (tel. +34 912 722 832, www. avanzabus.com) and **Alsa** (tel. 902 422 242, www.alsa.com). A one-way trip from Madrid to Lisbon costs around €23, Seville to Lisbon €25, and Corunna to Lisbon €38.

CAR

Europe is connected by a well-maintained motorway network, meaning international travel is straightforward between EU capital cities. Most of Europe exercises an open-borders policy, with no compulsory inspections at borders. Time-wise, for example, driving nonstop from Paris to Lisbon takes around 16 hours; Madrid to Lisbon is 6 hours; and Berlin to Lisbon is 26 hours. Each country has different speed limits, driver alcohol tolerances, and other traffic laws.

Driving from the United Kingdom to Portugal is slightly more complicated, as it requires a ferry between the UK and mainland Europe. There are no direct ferries between the UK and Portugal, so the more common driving routes are from the UK by ferry to France or Spain. Ferries from the UK to France are quicker and cheaper than those to Spain, but also make the journey longer due to added driving time. Ferry trips between the UK and France often take just a few hours, while a ferry to Spain can take over a day. There are many ferry routes between the UK and France, and the website **Direct Ferries** (www.directferries.co.uk) provides a comprehensive map of routes and prices.

Ferry crossings between the United Kingdom and Spain tend to change often, but the main crossings are between Plymouth and Santander, generally once a week, and Portsmouth to Bilbao or Portsmouth to Santander, three times a week. Other good ferry comparison sites are www.aferry.co.uk and www.ferries.co.uk. There are also direct ferries between Ireland and France.

The alternative to the ferry between the United Kingdom and mainland Europe is to take the Channel Tunnel, also known as the **Eurotunnel** (www.eurotunnel.com). Taking just 35 minutes to cross under the channel, the tunnel is cheaper and quicker than a ferry but is not for the claustrophobic. It connects Folkestone in the south of England to Calais in northern France via a 50-kilometer (31-mi) rail tunnel. At its lowest point, it is 75 meters (246 feet) below the seabed and 115 meters (377 feet) below sea level. Costs start from £30 per car (including up to nine passengers), but don't fight over the window seats; the views aren't that amazing.

Most of Europe, with exceptions like the United Kingdom and Ireland, drives on the right-hand side of the road. Manual gear shifts are the norm, although automatic transmissions are available on request when hiring a car.

It is without doubt cheaper and quicker to fly to Portugal from anywhere in Europe than to drive, and tolls and the cost of gasoline can vary noticeably from country to country. But a road trip is always an adventure, as long as you do your research and mapping in advance, and there's no reason why driving to Portugal can't be an enjoyable—if perhaps costly—experience.

From Australia and New Zealand

There are no direct flights between Portugal and Australia or New Zealand. Connecting flights are generally via Dubai in the United Arab Emirates, with a daily direct flight between Lisbon and Dubai on **Emirates** (www.emirates.com), or via Asia. There is also a direct nonstop flight between Australia and London, from where there are many onward flights to Portugal. Most major European air carriers operate code-share flights to major Asian hubs. Singapore, for example, can be reached with just one connection, from Lisbon to Istanbul on Turkish Airlines, or Dubai

on Emirates, or via the United Kingdom or Germany with Singapore Airlines.

From South Africa

There are no direct flights from South Africa to Portugal. TAP flies direct to Maputo in Mozambique and Luanda in Angola, also served by Angolan airline TAAG, and connecting flights can be arranged from there. Major European carriers such as British Airways, Germany's Lufthansa, Swissair, Spain's Iberia, and Air France fly direct to South Africa with connecting flights to Lisbon.

Package Holidays

From European countries, the United Kingdom particularly, package holiday deals that include flights and accommodations can be found at very competitive prices. To spend a week or so in the Algarve, Lisbon, or Madeira, check websites such as www.travelsupermarket.com. Packages usually include flights and one to three weeks' lodging, ranging from self-catering to all-inclusive, and in off-peak seasons can start from as little as £120 ($154) pp for self-catering based on double occupancy for seven nights in a three-star hotel; £250 ($322) including two meals; and £350 ($451) all-inclusive. Prices shoot up in high season, but if you're not fussy about where you stay or when you travel, good deals can be found. If you just want a little taste of Portugal, the ports of Portimão in the Algarve, Lisbon, and Leixões in Northern Portugal are included on some European cruise itineraries by companies such as **Fred Olsen** (www.fredolsencruises.com) and **Princess** (www.princess.com).

GETTING AROUND

Once in Portugal, getting around is easy. The travel network is perhaps not as sophisticated as in France, Spain, or Germany, but domestic flights, good motorways (with tolls), and efficient and inexpensive buses and trains link all the main towns and cities, and cars can be hired from every airport and hotel in the country.

Air

Portugal's main destinations—Faro in the Algarve, Lisbon, and Porto—are connected by regular daily domestic flights. **TAP Express** (www.flytap.pt), a subsidiary of the national carrier, operates hourly flights between Lisbon and Porto, while low-cost **Ryanair** (www.ryanair.com) operates regular daily Lisbon-Porto flights, albeit less frequently than TAP. Ryanair also has regular flights between Faro in southern Portugal and Porto at least five times a week, increasing in frequency in summer. TAP has a few flights daily between Faro and Lisbon, with connections to Porto.

TAP, Ryanair, **SATA Azores Airlines** (www.azoresairlines.pt), and **easyJet** (www. easyjet.com) all operate daily flights between Lisbon, Porto, and the archipelagoes of the Azores and Madeira. All of the archipelagoes' islands are connected by regular interisland flights, which also increase in frequency in busier months.

A multistage **national shuttle service** links the south of Portugal to the north. A small plane leaves Portimão airdrome in the Algarve every morning Monday-Saturday and flies to Bragança in the north, stopping en route at Cascais in Lisbon, Viseu in Central Portugal, and Vila Real in Northern Portugal. This trip takes three hours, depending on the duration of the stops, and costs €95-198 round-trip from Portimão to Bragança. Passengers are allowed to carry 10 kilograms (22 pounds) of luggage. The flight is operated by **AeroVip,** which belongs to the Sevenair group, once a day off-season and twice daily during the busier months from the end of March. **Sevenair** (tel. 214 444 545, www.sevenair.com) also operates interisland flights between Madeira and Porto Santo.

Train

Portugal's train service **Comboios de Portugal (CP)** (www.cp.pt/passageiros/en) is efficient and cheap but complex. It operates on several tiers, from the painfully slow Urbano train service, which stops in every town and village; the modern Intercity service between main cities; and the high-speed Alfa-Pendular, which connects Porto to Lisbon and the Algarve with a few stops between. Taking into account the required time spent at the airport for checking in (passengers are generally advised to arrive two hours before the flight), flying between Faro and Porto can take the same amount of time as the train and often costs the same.

Despite being comprehensive, the national rail network isn't as direct as bus services, and, oddly, some major cities have no train station, while many cities and towns have their train stations on the outskirts, requiring a taxi ride to the center. On the plus side, Portugal's trains tend to be spacious and well-kept on the inside, and offer cheaper second-class tickets and more privacy and comfort in first class, sometimes in private compartments.

Bus

There are many different bus companies in Portugal, including three major intercity long-distance bus companies, Algarve line **Eva Transportes** (www.eva-bus.com), national **Rede Expressos** (www.rede-expressos.pt) and northern **Rodonorte** (www.rodonorte. pt). Local and regional buses link towns, villages, and parishes within municipalities. In Lisbon, the local public transport company is Carris, which operates buses, trams, and funiculars. Bus travel in Portugal is cheap but not always the most comfortable, although long-distance express buses are mostly equipped with air-conditioning, TVs, toilets, and even onboard drinks and snacks. Routes between large cities, such as the Algarve-Lisbon or Lisbon-Porto, depart several times a day, while smaller local services tend to be frequent on weekdays and irregular on weekends and holidays. Pop into a local ticket office to check for updated timetables. The Algarve-Lisbon bus takes 3 hours and costs €18.50 one-way. Lisbon-Porto takes 3.5 hours and costs €19 one-way. Small discounts are given on round-trip tickets.

Car

Driving in Portugal can, in certain places, require nerves of steel and patience. Lisbon and Porto have fast and furious traffic, where delaying at a traffic light will inevitably earn a blast of the horn from behind. There can also be a seeming lack of civility on Portugal's roads, with poor usage of indicators when turning, and overtaking seems to be a national sport. For the most part, navigating Portugal's roads is straightforward, and major road surfaces are of a decent standard.

Portugal has one of the highest accident and road death rates in Europe, but these figures have improved drastically since the 1990s, along with the condition of the country's roads and the policing of them. One road in particular—the N125 road in the Algarve, a major cross-region secondary road that runs parallel to the Algarve's only motorway, the A22 Via do Infante—once was among Europe's deadliest spots. In recent years the N125 road has been significantly overhauled to improve safety and offer a viable alternative to the paid motorway, although congestion, especially in summer, is still a problem. It's widely agreed that while it's much better, the N125 is not yet a good alternative to a motorway.

ROAD SYSTEM

Portugal's road system is decent and major routes are kept in good condition, although the same cannot be said about smaller regional or municipal roads. Some are in urgent need of repair, particularly in rural areas, and on certain stretches signage could use updating.

Motorways are generally in good condition, although major motorways (autoestradas) have tolls, signaled with a large white V on a green background. Secondary and rural roads can be poorer quality, with potholes and sharp bends. In high-elevation areas, such as the Serra da Estrela, snowfall can close roads for hours or even days.

Roads are categorized as follows:

- **Motorways (autoestrada)** start with an **A** (A1, A22) and are major highways between cities or regions. Most A roads have tolls, paid at booths or electronically. Some motorways, such as the A22, are exclusively electronic and have barriers. Electronic toll payment uses the **Via Verde** (www.viaverde.pt) transponder system. More information on tolls and motorways is available at www.portugaltolls.com. Motorways have service areas with cafés, gas stations, and toilet facilities at regular intervals. Emergency telephones are also found at regular intervals.

- **Main highways (itinerário principal)** start with an **IP** (IP1, IP2). These are major roads that are alternatives to the motorways, although the road conditions are inferior, and generally link main cities.

- **Secondary highways (itinerário complementar)** start with an **IC** (IC1, IC2). These roads complement the IPs by connecting them to big towns and cities.

- **National roads (estrada nacional)** start with an **N** or **EN** (N125, also known as EN125) and are the main roads between towns and cities.

- **Local municipal roads (estrada municipal)** start with an **M** or **EM** and are smaller roads within localities.

Portugal is also connected to the rest of Europe by an **international E-road system,** a numbering system for pan-Europe roads. The main European routes crossing Portugal are the E01, E80, E82, E90, E801, E802, E805, and E806.

GENERAL ROAD RULES

In Portugal traffic runs on the right side of the road. Drivers must be over age 18, and seat belts are compulsory for all occupants.

National speed limits are easy to remember, although many drivers seem to struggle to abide by them: 50 km/h (31 mph) in residential areas, 90 km/h (56 mph) on rural roads, and 120 km/h (74 mph) on motorways. Cars towing trailers are restricted to 80 km/h (50 mph).

The rule on roundabouts (rotaries, or traffic circles) is that the outer lane should only be used if turning off immediately. In practice, this rarely happens. Make allowances for it.

You must park facing the same direction as the traffic flow. It's also illegal to use a mobile phone while driving (although at times you might wonder), and that applies to talking and texting.

Punishment for drunk driving is harsh, ranging from hefty fines to driving bans. The legal limit is 0.5 gram (0.02 ounce) of alcohol per liter (34 ounces) of blood, or 0.2 gram (0.007 ounce) per liter for commercial drivers.

DRIVER'S LICENSES

EU citizens require a valid driver's license with a photo on it, issued by the bearer's home country, to drive in Portugal. Drivers from outside the EU require a license and an International Driving Permit, which must be shown both to rental agencies for hiring a car and to the authorities if asked. When you are driving on Portugal's roads, the vehicle's documents must be in the vehicle at all times, and drivers need a valid ID, such as a passport. It is compulsory to have certain items in a vehicle. These are a reflective danger jacket, a reflective warning triangle, spare bulbs, a spare tire, and approved child seats for children under age 12 or 150 centimeters (5 feet). Check that you have these before driving off, as failure to produce them could result in a fine.

CAR RENTAL

The country's airports host many car rental companies, or ask at your hotel. Vehicles can be dropped off at most holiday lodgings. Use price comparison sites like **Auto Europe** (www.autoeurope.pt) or **Portugal Auto Rentals** (www.portugal-auto-rentals.com) to find the best deals. Booking well in advance will mean better prices. Beware of unexpected surprises by double-checking the opening and closing times of the car rental desk at the airport, fuel fees and excess insurance, electronic toll payments (if you want to use motorways with barriers, such as the Algarve's A22, see www.portugaltolls.com), fees to drop the car in a different location from where you picked it up, and cross-border surcharges if you take the car out of Portugal into Spain.

Even though the minimum legal age to drive is 18, most rental companies require drivers to be age 21 or to have held a license for at least five years. Costs can vary greatly, from as little as €10 per day in low season but rising exponentially in high season. If you're just visiting one or two areas, a small car is useful as most town centers, including historic hamlets and large cities, have areas that are a tangle of narrow cobbled streets. To do a lot of touring, a bigger engine is better, which means a more expensive rental.

REFUELING

Diesel *(gasóleo)* is cheaper than unleaded gasoline *(gasolina sem chumbo)* in Portugal, and gas stations can be found in abundance (although this is less the case in rural areas). Most large supermarkets and shopping centers have gas stations that offer low-cost fuel options, and there is almost always a gas station near an airport. The main gas stations in Portugal belong to BP, Galp, and Repsol. Most petrol stations are open 7am-10pm daily, but stations at service areas on motorways or on main roads should be open 24 hours daily. Unleaded gasoline has a 95 or 98 octane rating, although both can be used in gasoline vehicles; the 98 is more expensive. All petrol stations accept debit and credit cards as well as cash.

PARKING

Parking can be hard to find in town centers given the narrow cobbled streets and tourist demand. Big towns and cities have designated car parks and parking areas, which charge fees, especially in popular places like Faro, Lisbon, and Porto. The closer to the city center, the more expensive the parking will be.

AUTOMOBILE ASSOCIATIONS
A contact number for breakdowns should be provided by the vehicle's insurer. When collecting a rental car, always clarify what to do or who to call in the event of a breakdown

or emergency. The **Auto Club Portugal (ACP)** (tel. 808 222 222, www.acp.pt) is the Portuguese equivalent of the American Automobile Association.

Visas and Officialdom

To enter Portugal, all travelers are required to have a valid ID. Most European citizens need only a valid ID or a passport and can circulate freely within the EU by land, air, or sea. People from other countries must have a passport and may require a visa. Always check with the relevant authorities before traveling or with your travel provider. Here are some basic guidelines.

PASSPORTS AND TOURIST VISAS

EU nationals traveling within EU or Schengen states do not require a visa for entering Portugal for any length of stay. They do require a valid passport or official ID card (national citizen's card, driver's license, or residency permit, for example).

European citizens traveling between Schengen countries are not required to present an identity document or passport at border crossings, as an open-borders policy is in effect. However, it is recommended that travelers have ID documents with them at all times, as they may be requested at any time by the authorities. In Portugal the law requires everyone to carry a personal ID at all times.

Citizens of the United Kingdom and Ireland must produce a passport to enter Portugal, valid for the duration of the proposed stay, and can stay for up to three months. After that, they must register with the local authorities. The UK and Ireland are currently EU member states but are not part of the Schengen area, the 26 countries that abolished passport and other border controls at their shared borders. It is not yet known how

the UK's departure from the EU, commonly referred to as Brexit, will affect travel policies.

People from non-EU countries always require a passport, valid for at least six months, and some may require a visa. Australian, Canadian, and U.S. travelers require a valid passport but do not need a visa for stays of up to 90 days in any six-month period. While it is not obligatory to have an onward or return ticket, it is advisable to have one.

South African nationals need to apply for a Portugal-Schengen visa. This should be done three months before travel. Applicants must have a South African passport valid for six months beyond the date of return with at least three blank pages. They also need a recent passport photo (specify to photographer that it has to meet the Schengen visa requirements), a completed original application form, round-trip tickets from South Africa to Portugal, and proof of prepaid lodging or a letter of invitation if staying with friends or family in Portugal, among other requisites.

Traveling with Children

All children under the age of 18 must have a valid ID or passport and be accompanied by an adult. Minors traveling alone or with just one parent or guardian should have a formal document of authorization by the absent parent or guardian. Documentation such as custody court rulings in the event of divorce or a death certificate in the event the child is orphaned should also be presented.

Portugal's borders and immigration authority, SEF, advises that children traveling to Portugal alone or without a parent or legal guardian should be met at the airport or point of entry by the parent or guardian or carry a letter of authorization to travel from their parent or guardian, stating the name of the adult in Portugal who will be responsible for them during their stay and including contact details.

CUSTOMS

Customs is mandatory for all travelers arriving in or leaving Portugal carrying goods or money, although certain limits apply to what can be brought in or taken out. Aeroportos de Portugal (ANA) states that all passengers traveling without baggage or transporting cash or monetary assets under the equivalent of €10,000 or carrying personal items not intended for commercial purposes and not prohibited should pass through the "Nothing to Declare" channel. Passengers carrying over €10,000 or whose baggage contains tradable goods in quantities greater than those permitted by law and that are not exempt from value-added tax (VAT) or excise duty must pass through the "Goods to Declare" channel.

Passengers age 17 or older can bring in the following:

From EU member states: 800 cigarettes, 400 cigarillos, 200 cigars, 1 kilogram (2.2 pounds) of smoking tobacco, 10 liters (11 quarts) of alcoholic spirits, 20 liters (21 quarts) of beverages with alcoholic content under 22 percent, 90 liters (95 quarts) of wine, 110 liters (116 quarts) of beer, medications in quantities corresponding to need and accompanied by a prescription.

For travelers from outside the EU: 200 cigarettes, 100 cigarillos, 50 cigars, 250 grams (0.6 pound) of smoking tobacco, 1 liter (1 quart) of alcoholic spirits, 2 liters (2 quarts) of beverages with alcoholic content under 22 percent, 4 liters (4 quarts) of wine, 16 liters (17 quarts) of beer, medications in quantities corresponding to need and accompanied by a prescription.

Quantities exceeding these must be declared, and passengers under age 17 don't get an exemption for alcohol or tobacco.

EMBASSIES AND CONSULATES

Australian Embassy: Av. da Liberdade 200, Lisbon, http://portugal.embassy.gov.au, tel. 213 101 500, 10am-4pm Mon-Fri

British Embassy: Rua de São Bernardo 33, Lisbon, tel. 213 924 000, emergency tel. 213 924 000, www.gov.uk/world/organisations/british-embassy-lisbon, 9:30am-2pm Mon, Wed, and Fri

British Vice Consulate: Edificio A Fábrica, Av. Guanaré, Portimão (Algarve), tel. 213 924 000, 9:30am-2pm Mon, Wed, and Fri

Canadian Embassy: Av. da Liberdade 196, Lisbon, tel. 213 164 600, www.canadainternational.gc.ca/portugal, 9am-noon Mon-Fri

French Embassy: Rua Santos-O-Velho 5, Lisbon, tel. 213 939 292, https://pt.ambafrance.org, 8:30am-noon Mon-Fri

Irish Embassy: Av. da Liberdade 200, Lisbon, tel. 213 308 200, www.dfa.ie/irish-embassy/portugal, 9:30am-12:30pm Mon-Fri, closed weekends

New Zealand Consulate: Rua da Sociedade Farmacêutica 68, 1st Right, Lisbon, tel. 213 140 780, consulado.nz.pt@gmail.com, www.mfat.govt.nz, office hours by appointment only

South African Embassy: Av. Luís Bívar 10, Lisbon, tel. 213 192 200, lisbon.consular@dirco.gov.za, 8am-12:30pm and 1:15pm-5pm Mon-Thurs, 8am-1pm Fri. The Consular Section (Annex) is open 8:30am-noon Monday-Friday.

Spanish Embassy: Praça de Espanha 1, Lisbon, tel. 213 472 381, www.exteriores.gob.es, 9am-2pm Mon-Fri

U.S. Embassy: Av. das Forças Armadas 133C, Lisbon, tel. 217 273 300, https://pt.usembassy.gov/embassy-consulate/lisbon, 8am-5pm Mon-Fri

U.S. Consulate: Príncipe de Mónaco 6-2F, Ponta Delgada (Azores), tel. 296 308 330, conspontadelgada@state.gov, 8:30am-12:30pm and 1:30pm-5:30pm Mon-Fri

POLICE

Portugal has three police forces: the **PSP** (**Public Safety Police—Polícia de Segurança Pública**) (tel. 218 111 000, www.psp.pt), in cities and larger towns; the road traffic police **GNR (National Republican Guard—Guarda Nacional Republicana)** (tel. 213 217 000, www.gnr.pt), also responsible for policing smaller towns and villages and investigating crimes against animals or nature; and the **PJ (Judiciary Police—Polícia Judiciária)** (tel. 211 967 000, www.pj.pt), the criminal investigation bureau, responsible for investigating serious crimes.

The common European **emergency number** is tel. **112,** which redirects calls to the appropriate services.

Recreation

PARKS

Portugal has one excellent national park, the Peneda-Gerês, and a vast variety of outstanding protected parks and reserves. The **Institute for Conservation of Nature and Forests (Instituto da Conservação da Natureza e das Florestas)** (ICNF, www2.icnf.pt) is largely responsible for managing the country's parks and forests. The associated **Natural.PT** website (www.natural.pt) offers plenty of information in English on Portugal's natural parks and protected areas.

HIKING AND BIKING

With glorious lush mountains, undulating plains, and wild coastline, Portugal offers excellent conditions for active travelers. In addition to trails in parks and reserves, there are regional designated hiking and cycling tracks, such as the **Via Algarviana** (www.viaalgarviana.org) in the Algarve and the **Vicentine Route (Rota Vicentina)** (www.rotavicentina.com) in the Alentejo, with networks of well-mapped and signed routes. Many towns also have *eco-vias* or *ciclovias* (designated cycling tracks) and public bike-sharing schemes.

The website of the national tourism board, **Turismo de Portugal** (www.visitportugal.com), has pages on cycling and walking in Portugal. The website of the tour company **Portugal Bike Tours** (www.portugalbike.com) provides detailed information on cycling routes in Portugal.

BEACHES

Portugal has some of Europe's finest beaches, from the grotto-etched coastline of the Algarve, Portugal's premier beach destination, to the endless, largely undiscovered beaches of the Alentejo, Lisbon's cosmopolitan Estoril coastline, and the rugged beaches of Central and Northern Portugal, popular among surfers. Portugal also boasts one of the highest numbers of Blue Flag-awarded beaches, a European symbol of clean, high-quality beaches.

One of Portugal's less-explored delights is its excellent river beaches (*praias fluviais*), lakes and dams with artificial beaches. Northern and central inland regions are pocked with these little oases of tranquil water and sand, which in warmer months provide a refreshing escape far from the coast. Most have fun water equipment like canoes and pedal boats, sun beds, cafés or restaurants, and toilet facilities. Most are staffed by lifeguards in summer.

SURFING

Portugal is one of Europe's top surfing hot spots. From the Algarve's windswept, rugged west coast to Guincho Beach near Lisbon and Cabedelo Beach in Northern Portugal, the coast has popular surfing hubs that offer consistent conditions for all levels. Portugal's most famous surfing spot is Nazaré, which came onto the global surfing radar in 2011 after U.S. surfer Garrett McNamara set a new world record here for the largest wave ever surfed.

The website of **Turismo de Portugal** (www.visitportugal.com) addresses all kinds of surfing in Portugal (including windsurfing, kite-surfing, and body-boarding), with suggestions on where to go. Surf website **Portuguese Waves** (www.portuguesewaves.com) has detailed information on surf spots and news.

OTHER WATER SPORTS

Bounded by the Atlantic, latticed by rivers, and studded by lakes and dams, Portugal is a boating and water sports playground. Diverse activities for all ages include coastal and champagne sunset cruises and grotto boat trips; parasailing, Jet Skiing, and banana-boating off golden beaches; deep-sea fishing and scuba diving; and stand-up paddleboarding and kayaking along scenic waterways.

The website of **Turismo de Portugal** (www.visitportugal.com) provides information on sailing and mooring. The **Portal do Mar** website (www.portaldomar.pt) offers information on all things nautical.

GOLF

Several dozen first-rate golf courses range in difficulty from amateur to pro. The majority of Portugal's golf courses are in Lisbon and the Algarve, many designed by legendary golfers such as Sir Henry Cotton, Arnold Palmer, Jack Nicklaus, and Sir Nick Faldo.

WILDLIFE-WATCHING

From whale-watching in the Atlantic to bird-watching on reedy lagoons or observing dolphins in the unique setting of the Sado Estuary, Portugal offers an abundance of special and exhilarating wildlife-watching opportunities.

The website of **Turismo de Portugal** (www.visitportugal.com) offers a wealth of information on nature tourism, including bird-, whale-, and dolphin-watching. The **Portuguese Society for the Study of Birds (Sociedade Portuguesa para o Estudo das Aves)** (SPEA, www.spea.pt) provides information on the birds and bird-watching tourism of Portugal.

ADVENTURE SPORTS

Freshening up its image as a traditional beach holiday destination, ingenious Portugal has positioned itself as a magnet for thrill-seekers. It boasts the only bridge-climb in Europe (in Porto), excellent year-round conditions for skydiving and paragliding, and some of the best natural parks in Europe for canyoneering and climbing, such as the Peneda-Gerês National Park and Serra da Estrela Natural Park.

WINTER SPORTS

In the coldest months, mainland Portugal's Serra da Estrela mountain range becomes a snowy wonderland and the only place in the country for skiing and snowboarding.

Food

It's not hard to wax lyrical about Portugal's cuisine: fresh, flavorful, comforting, and generous, it is the soul of an unassuming seafaring nation. Largely Mediterranean, the staples are fresh fish, meat, fruit, and vegetables prepared with olive oil and washed down with excellent national wines. Dishes vary from light and fresh along the coast, with grilled fish and seafood, to hearty meaty stews and roasts in rural inland areas and colorful cosmopolitan fusions in larger towns and cities.

Each region touts its own take on national staples such as the *cozido á Portuguesa* (Portuguese stew) and *caldeirada* (fish stew), as well as typical local sweets—all with a story attached to them. Another staple on most menus and one of Portugal's emblematic gastronomic ingredients is salted codfish, or *bacalhau,* for which the Portuguese are said to have a different recipe for every day of the year. The most famous cod dishes are *bacalhau à Brás* (cod mashed with egg, potato, and onion, topped with crunchy matchstick fries), *bacalhau à Gomes de Sá* (flaked cod layered with sliced potato and egg and baked in the oven), *bacalhau espiritual* (like *bacalhau á Bras* but with grated carrot), and *pastéis de bacalhau* (cod fritters), usually a snack with cold beer.

PORTUGUESE CUISINE
Fish

It is perhaps unsurprising that Portugal, an audacious seafaring nation, is renowned for its bounty of seafood. Coastal areas generally serve shellfish as an appetizer. One-pot dishes such as *caldeiradas* and *arroz de tamboril* (monkfish rice) are not to be missed. Salted codfish is a staple throughout Portugal, and grilled sardines are enjoyed voraciously during summer (sardine fishing is limited in winter to allow stocks to replenish); these, along with *dourada* (golden bream), *robalo* (sea bass), and *cavalas* (mackerel), are among the most common fish on menus. Prawns boiled or fried in olive oil and garlic are enjoyed as a snack or appetizer, while more unusual seafood includes razor clams and sea urchins.

Meats

Most restaurants have grilled meat on the menu, most commonly *febras* (pork steaks), *costeletas de porco* (pork chops), *entrecosto* (pork ribs), *entremeada* (pork belly), and the ubiquitous *frango piripiri* (chicken grilled and served with spicy chili sauce). Note that the word *grelhado* (grilled) usually means on charcoal.

Cured and smoked meats, especially the smoky, spicy *chouriço* sausage, *presunto* (cured ham), and *morcela* (black blood sausage), also represent a huge chunk of Portuguese gastronomy. They are often eaten simply as an appetizer, accompanied by fresh rustic bread, olives, and cheese, or added to stews and soups to enhance the flavor.

Soups

Almost all cafés and restaurants have a homemade vegetable soup on the menu. *Caldo verde,* potato and kale soup with hunks of smoky *chouriço* sausage, is a typical soup served at family tables and traditional festivities.

Bread

Portugal has amazing bread, almost always freshly made. From rustic hobs to seeded baguettes and pumpkin or carob bread, it's hard not to be sucked in by the amazing carbohydrates on offer, especially to soak up those delicious sauces and juices.

Sweets and Pastries

Portugal is renowned for its range of traditional sweets and pastries. Display cabinets in cafés and *pastelarias* (cake shops) throughout the country are piled every morning with freshly baked treats. Portugal is home to the unique *doces conventuais* (convent sweets), generally based on egg yolk and sugar and made to ancient recipes said to originate in the 15th century from the country's convents.

Arroz doce (rice pudding with a sprinkling of cinnamon), *bolo de bolacha* (cookie cake), *pudim flan* (custardy pudding with caramel on top), and *tarte de natas* (creamy chilled pie made from condensed milk with a ground cookie topping) are typical desserts, but the ever-present *pastel de nata* (custard tart) is Portugal's iconic sweet.

DRINKS

Perhaps not as eminent as France, Italy, or Spain, modest Portugal nonetheless boasts a gamut of acclaimed wines, including rosés and unique fresh and fizzy green wines. Even ordinary table wine tends to be palatable, and a small jug of house wine in a low-key restaurant costs as little as €3. Besides wine, Portugal produces beer, the most famous being Sagres, Cristal, and Super Bock. A growing number of craft beers are also on the market.

Traditional Portuguese tipples include *ginja* (a sweet cherry liqueur, also called *ginjinha*), *licor beirão* (a medicinal-tasting liqueur said to aid digestion, made from a long-guarded secret blend of herbs), *aguardente* (brain-blowing firewater), and *amarguinha* (a marzipan-tasting, toothachingly-sweet almond liqueur, often chilled). Besides port and madeira liquor-wines, make sure you try the local *poncha* in Madeira, a mix of alcohol distilled from sugarcane, honey, orange or lemon juice, or other fruit juices.

The legal age to drink and buy alcohol in Portugal is 18. Nondrinkers won't be disappointed with canned iced teas and Sumol sparkling fruit juices, the traditional flavors being pineapple and orange. The Algarve, especially the city of Silves, is renowned for incredibly sweet oranges, and fresh orange juice served here with plenty of ice is a real treat.

The Portuguese are big coffee drinkers, and the standard is a small, strong, black expresso. To get milk in it, ask for *café com leite* or *meia-de-leite* (in a cup and saucer), or *galão* (served in a tall glass), differing only in presentation. "Having a coffee" is synonymous with "catching up," and cafés are the social glue of neighborhoods.

DINING OUT

Restaurants in Portugal are incredibly varied, from down-to-earth, no-frills spots to high-end Michelin-starred eateries. Touristy areas have a wider range of well-known chains and international cuisines. Vegetarian and vegan restaurants are on the rise, while traditional Portuguese eateries can be found in spades.

For real local flavor, try to find a *casa de pasto*, literally a "grazing house," basic, cheap, and cheerful little diners found off the beaten track that cater to local laborers with good home-cooked food. These characterful places tout three-course "dish of the day" menus for as little as €7.50, including a bread basket with butter, pâtés, and olives, a fish or meat entrée, a coffee, dessert, and drinks. If your budget allows, head to a high-end eatery where the menu will be a contemporary take on fresh local products and time-honored recipes. If you have a sweet tooth, find a *pastelaria* (there seems to be one on almost every street) to enjoy a coffee and freshly made traditional cake or a toasted sandwich for just a few euros.

In restaurants in Portugal, it is customary for a basket of fresh bread to be brought out before a meal, along with olives and butter and fishy pâtés. Don't be misled: these items are not complimentary, and if you eat them, they will be charged on the bill. If you don't want them, ask for them to be taken away.

PICNIC SUPPLIES AND GROCERIES

A great way to save money is to buy your own food, and Portugal is a veritable buffet of fresh produce. Larger supermarkets have counters for fresh fish, cold meats, cooked meats, and deli, with the likes of olives and slaws, as well as a fresh bread section, baked in-house or supplied by local bakers.

Most towns have a farmers market at least once or twice a month, generally on Saturday morning, piled high with locally grown fruit and vegetables as well as treats like dried nuts, dried fruits, sweets, and eggs. Municipal markets, usually open mornings Monday-Saturday, are also great for fish, meats, vegetables, and fruit. Some municipal markets have ready-to-go food counters and sell jams, liqueurs, cured meats, and preserves.

MEALS AND MEALTIMES

Portugal has three main meals: a good breakfast in the continental style, with cereals, bread, cold meats and cheese, and jam, generally eaten before work or school; lunch at 1pm-3pm; and dinner starting from 7:30pm-8pm. Main meals tend to be hearty, and lunch and dinner are often preceded by a bowl of soup. The Portuguese also enjoy *lanche*, a light midafternoon snack, as well as a coffee and a pastry midmorning.

Accommodations

Accommodations range from run-of-the-mill hotels and tourist complexes to friendly family-run inns, campsites, budget-friendly hostels, and exclusive luxury retreats. Lisbon and Porto currently exercise a **tourist tax** *(taxa turística);* Lisbon's has a surcharge of €1 per night per guest up to a maximum of seven nights. This is charged directly at reception on check-in. Porto's tourist tax is €2 per guest over age 13 per night, maximum seven nights.

ACCOMMODATIONS RATINGS

Portugal's rating system is governed by national law and implemented by the national tourism board, **Turismo de Portugal** (www.turismodeportugal.pt). Ratings are based on fulfilled minimum requisites stipulated for each category. Star ratings are generally indicative of the level of comfort and facilities an establishment provides and not necessarily subjective factors such as view or atmosphere. Hotels are classified one to five stars; a one-star property is a basic budget lodging, while a five-star hotel offers a luxurious experience. *Estalagens* (inns) rate four to five stars, *pensões* (guesthouses) one to four stars, and apart-hotels rate two to five stars. Campsites are graded one to four stars.

MAKING RESERVATIONS

Most people nowadays make bookings online via price comparison websites or directly with hotels. It's always wise to follow it up with a phone call to ensure everything is confirmed and any special requests are clear. If planning to travel to Portugal in summer, book well ahead, as hotels sell out fast in peak season. Prices can also be much higher in peak season than in low season.

TYPES OF ACCOMMODATIONS
Hotel

All of Portugal's main towns and cities offer hotels spanning three to five stars. The more popular the destination, the greater the choice. Lisbon, Porto, and especially the Algarve are awash with smart hotels, most with their own pools. Prices vary greatly by season and the popularity of the resort. Prices are cheaper in winter. Portugal has several major national hotel chains: **Pestana Hotels and Resorts** (www.pestana.com), **Vila Galé** (www.vilagale.com), **Sana Hotels** (www.sanahotels.com), and **Tivoli Hotels & Resorts** (www.tivolihotels.com), part of the Minor Hotel Group, to name a few. A number of international chains also operate within Portugal, from low-cost to high-end, such as **Ibis** (www.ibis.com), **Best Western** (www.bestwestern.com), **Hilton** (www3.hilton.com), **Marriott** (www.marriott.com), and **Holiday Inn** (www.holidayinn.com), among others.

Among the compulsory criteria, minimum requirements for four- and five-star hotels include air-conditioning, TV, and direct phone lines in all rooms; one- to three-star hotels don't necessarily have to have those features. Three- to five-star hotels must also provide room service, laundry service, and air-conditioning in public areas, whereas one- and two-star hotels don't. All categories except one-star hotels must have an on-site bar, a full bath, 24-hour reception, copy and fax service, and safes in the rooms.

Estalagem (Inn)

Portugal's inns *(estalagens)* are hotel-type lodgings in traditional buildings that, due to their architectural characteristics, style of fixtures and furnishings, and services provided, reflect the region and its natural environs. Inns are classified four or five stars. As a whole, inns must comply with criteria similar to corresponding hotels (24-hour reception, room service, restaurant, bar, air-con in public areas, etc.); the main differences are found in the actual rooms, which tend to be smaller. Generally speaking, inns are more modest than hotels and often rustic and family-run.

Pensão Residencial

Smaller towns and villages will usually have a *pensão residencial,* or just *residencial,* private family-run boardinghouses in shared residential buildings. These provide affordable lodgings in central locations. *Pensões* usually have a restaurant. The word *residencial* is added when the unit provides breakfast only. *Residenciais* are simple bed-and-breakfast lodgings.

Apart-Hotel

Apart-hotels are self-contained apartments with the full facilities of hotels. There is no room service.

Pousada

Pousadas are state-owned monuments such as castles, palaces, monasteries, and convents converted into sumptuous accommodations reflecting the region and era of the monument. **Pousadas de Portugal** (www. pousadas.pt) is a brand that has iconic monument-hotels in exceptional locations, including Pousada Serra da Estrela, a former sanatorium in the snowy Serra da Estrela mountains; Pousada Convento Beja, an ancient convent; and Pousada Castelo Óbidos,

a castle-hotel in the heart of the famous medieval town.

Hostel

Portugal is renowned for excellent hostels, regularly earning European awards. That doesn't mean all of the country's hostels are above par. It pays to do some research and read reviews before booking. For outstanding hostels in Portugal, see www.hostelworld. com.

Aldeamento Turístico (Tourist Resort)

Tourist resorts, also known as tourist villages or complexes, are developments comprising different types of independent lodging, such as bungalows, apartments, or villas, in communal spaces. These resorts must also have an on-site four- or five-star hotel, entertainment facilities, and room service.

Camping

Portugal has over 100 campgrounds. Camping sites are classified by stars, from the most luxurious four stars to the minimum basic one star. Privately owned camping sites are classified in the same way, preceded by the letter *P.* Campsites tend to stay open year-round, as Portugal has a growing number of winter motor-home visitors, but prices can double from low to peak season. High-season prices may apply to holidays such as New Year's. Most campsites have on-site toilets and showers as well as facilities such as swimming pools and markets, bungalows, and chalets, which are reflected in the star rating. Some have sanitary facilities for RVs. Not all accept pets. For more on camping in Portugal, see www. campingportugal.org.

Conduct and Customs

The Portuguese are characteristically warm and welcoming and proud to show off their heritage, although they are also modest and conservative. Striking up a conversation about food or soccer, two of Portugal's best-loved pastimes, is a surefire way of opening communication. Conscious that tourism is a main source of income, the Portuguese are generally friendly and helpful toward visitors, although in rural pockets of the country foreigners are still eyed with curiosity. Staunchly traditional and understated, Portugal is a country where recent acquaintances may be greeted like long-lost friends, but raucous behavior, such as drunken rowdiness, is eschewed. Decorum is much appreciated, which is not to say you can't let your hair down and let loose in the appropriate places. As long as you show courtesy and respect to the locals, you can expect the same back.

GENERAL ETIQUETTE

Typically friendly and humble, the Portuguese love to show off their language skills and impress visitors, and few are the people who don't know at least a few key phrases in English. Likewise, the Portuguese very much appreciate efforts by visitors in learning even just a few words of the national language. Modest and somewhat reserved, the Portuguese tend to be quite formal in greetings among those less well acquainted. Men usually shake hands while women give air kisses on each cheek; women hardly ever shake hands in Portugal. Children are greeted in the same way as adults. Family is the foundation of Portuguese households and takes precedence over most other social and professional affairs.

COMMUNICATION STYLES

The Portuguese appreciate polite directness. Eye contact, a smile, and a firm handshake are the cornerstones of communication. Saying *"Bom dia"* (Good day or Hello), *"Por favor"* (Please), and *"Obrigado/a"* (Thank you) go a long way. Overtly exuberant or loud behavior is not appreciated. The Portuguese tend to socialize on the weekends rather than after work during the week.

BODY LANGUAGE

A big no-no in Portugal is pointing—especially pointing at someone. While conversations can sound heated and loud, the Portuguese are not overly demonstrative with hand gestures or body language. Finger-snapping to get someone's attention is also frowned upon.

TERMS OF ADDRESS

An overtone of formality is required when addressing people, especially strangers. Men should be addressed as *senhor* (abbreviation *Sr.*) and women *senhora (Sra.)* at all times. A young girl would be *menina* (miss), and a boy, *menino.*

TABLE MANNERS

Table manners are relaxed but courteous. Sharing from a bowl while talking animatedly is a mainstay around a family table, although politeness, such as wishing everyone *"Bom apetite"* (Bon appétit) before a meal and saying "Thank you" afterward, is expected. Domestic dining begins at the say-so of the head of the table or the cook, and feel free to raise a glass to toast *(saúde)* everyone. Dining out depends on the type of establishment; laid-back eateries are a family-style affair, while upmarket venues require upmarket manners and dress. Arriving late to a meal with friends is acceptable; arriving late to a dinner reservation is not. If invited to dine at someone's home, take a small gift, such as a bottle of wine or flowers.

PHOTO ETIQUETTE

Places where photos are banned will be signed. Taking photos inside churches during mass is considered disrespectful. If you want to take a picture of a local, Portuguese people are generally happy to collaborate, but always politely seek permission beforehand.

Health and Safety

Overall, travel and health risks in Portugal are relatively low, with food- and water-borne illnesses like traveler's diarrhea, typhoid, and giardia not a concern in Western Europe. Insect-transmitted diseases, such as Lyme disease and tick fever, however, are found in Portugal. A number of precautionary steps can reduce the risk: prevent insect bites with repellents, apply sunscreen, drink plenty of water, avoid overindulging in alcohol, don't approach wild or stray animals, wash your hands regularly, carry hand sanitizer, and avoid sharing bodily fluids.

Basic medications such as ibuprofen and antidiarrheal medication can be bought over-the-counter at any pharmacy in Portugal. For emergency medical assistance, call 112 and ask for an ambulance. If you are taken to a hospital, contact your insurance provider immediately. Portugal also has a 24-hour free health help line (tel. 808 242 424) in Portuguese only. For detailed advice before traveling, consult your country's travel health website: www.fitfortravel.nhs.uk (United Kingdom), https://wwwnc.cdc.gov/travel (United States), www.travel.gc.ca (Canada), or www.smarttraveller.gov.au (Australia).

VACCINATIONS

There are no compulsory immunization requirements to enter Portugal. The World Health Organization (WHO) recommends all travelers, regardless of destination, are covered for diphtheria, tetanus, measles, mumps, rubella, and polio. See your doctor at least six weeks before departure to ensure your routine vaccinations are up-to-date.

Rabies

Rabies has been detected in bats in Portugal, but there is a low risk of infection. The U.S. Centers for Disease Control and Prevention (CDC) recommends the rabies vaccine for travelers involved in activities in remote areas that put them at risk for bat bites, such as adventure travel and caving.

Hepatitis A

Recommended for all travelers over age one and not previously vaccinated against hepatitis A. In 2017 a number of European countries, Portugal included, recorded an outbreak of hepatitis A. It is transmitted through contaminated food and water, as well direct contact with infected individuals via the fecal-oral route.

Hepatitis B

The hepatitis B vaccination is suggested for all nonimmune travelers who may be at risk of acquiring the disease, which is transmitted via infected blood or bodily fluids, such as by sharing needles or unprotected sex.

Yellow Fever

Yellow fever vaccinations are only required for travelers heading to the Azores or Madeira and only if arriving from a yellow-fever-infected country in Africa or the Americas.

HEALTH CONSIDERATIONS
Sunstroke and Dehydration

The sun and heat in Portugal can be fierce, especially June-September and particularly July-August. Apply a strong sunblock and use a hat and sunglasses. Avoid physical exertion when the heat is at its peak (noon-3pm) and keep well hydrated by drinking plenty of water or electrolyte-replenishing fluids. Avoid excessive alcohol during the hottest hours or being out in the sun with a hangover.

Undertow

Some beaches, especially along the western coast, which is fully exposed to the Atlantic, can experience strong undercurrents when the sea is roughest, particularly in winter and spring. During summer, generally May-September, the sea is calmer and beaches are staffed by lifeguards; off-season they are not. Always obey flags.

Tap Water

Tap water is consumable throughout Portugal and is safe to brush teeth, wash fruit, or make ice, although many people drink bottled water, as opposed to tap water, even at home.

Insects

With a balmy Mediterranean climate, Portugal is home to lots of bugs, including mosquitoes, sand flies, and ticks. There is a low risk in Portugal of catching Lyme disease from ticks, which inhabit long grasses and bushes. There is a higher risk of catching tick fever, ehrlichiosis, and anaplasmosis. To minimize the chance of tick bites, avoid areas of long grass and stray animals.

To avoid mosquito bites, use lightweight, light-colored clothing and avoid places with stagnant water. In the hotter months, particularly in early morning or at dusk, apply a repellent.

An outbreak of *Aedes* mosquito-borne dengue fever was reported on Madeira, concentrated in the city of Funchal, in 2012. More than 2,000 cases had been reported by 2013, including 78 cases in travelers. The outbreak is currently under control. There is no vaccine against dengue. To prevent it, apply insect repellent and keep covered when outdoors.

Stray Animals

Portugal still battles errant and abandoned animals. In some places it's not unusual to see stray dogs and cats, even in packs and colonies. A huge amount of work has been done by private and public entities to sterilize and rehome animals, and things have greatly improved since the 1980s, but more work remains. Travelers are advised to not approach, pet, or feed strays. If you are bitten by a stray animal, wash and disinfect the wound, and seek medical advice promptly.

Sexually Transmitted Diseases

Travelers are at high risk of acquiring sexually transmitted diseases (STDs) if they engage in unprotected sex. According to research, Portugal has one of the poorest control rates of sexually transmitted infections; gonorrhea and syphilis are common.

HEALTH CARE
Medical Services

Portugal's state-funded public health service (SNS, Serviço Nacional de Saúde) provides quality care, particularly in emergency situations and those involving tourists. There are also private hospitals operating throughout Portugal, such as the **Hospital Particular do Algarve** (tel. 707 282 828, www.grupohpa.com) group in the Algarve and the **CUF Hospitals and Health Units** (tel. 210 025 200, www.saudecuf.pt) in Lisbon and the north. For minor illnesses and injuries, head to a pharmacy: Most pharmacists speak good English and can suggest treatment. If the problem persists or worsens, seek a doctor. Portugal has two types of pharmacies: traditional pharmacies *(farmácia)*, identified with a big flashing green cross outside, and para-pharmacies *(parafarmácia)*, selling only non-prescription medicines.

Insurance

EU citizens have access to free emergency medical treatment through the European Health Insurance Card (EHIC), which replaces the defunct E111 certificate. Non-EU citizens for whom there is no reciprocal agreement for free medical care between Portugal and the traveler's home country should consider fully comprehensive health insurance for serious illness, accident, or emergency. Opt for a policy that covers the worst-case event, like medical evacuation or repatriation. Find out in advance if your insurance will make payments to providers directly or reimburse you later for overseas health expenditures. Travelers to the Azores and Madeira are advised to acquire wide-ranging travel insurance that provides for medical evacuation in the event of serious illness or injury; serious or complicated problems sometimes require medical evacuation to the mainland.

Prescriptions

A prescription issued by a doctor in one EU country is valid in all EU countries. However, a medicine prescribed in one country may not be authorized for sale or available in another country, or it might be sold under a different name. EU doctors can issue cross-border prescriptions valid in all EU countries. Opt for paper copies of prescriptions as opposed to electronic copies.

If you're traveling from outside the EU, have enough of your prescription medication to cover the trip. Talk to your doctor beforehand and travel with a doctor's note, a copy of any prescriptions, or a printout for the medication. Medications should be carried in labeled original bottles or packaging, although this is not compulsory. Some prescription medicines may require a medical certificate; always check with your doctor. Ask for an extra written prescription with the generic name of the drug in the event of loss or if your stay is extended. Portuguese pharmacies will accept prescriptions from countries outside the EU, but drugs have to be paid for in full. Even without the state subsidies, drugs are generally cheaper in Portugal than many other EU countries and the United States. Alternatively, visit a Portuguese doctor and obtain a prescription in Portugal.

Many types of medication—including heart medication, antibiotics, asthma and diabetes medicines, codeine, injectable medicines, and cortisone creams—can only be acquired in Portugal with a prescription.

It is illegal to ship medication to Portugal. When traveling, always transport medicines in carry-on luggage.

Birth Control

Birth control is widely available throughout Portugal. Female contraceptive pills, patches, and rings can be bought over the counter in pharmacies, as can the morning-after pill, without a prescription. Condoms are also widely available in pharmacies, supermarkets, petrol stations, and some nightlife venues.

SAFETY
Crime

Portugal has a relatively low serious crime rate, but opportunistic crime is recurrent, particularly in busy places popular among tourists, such as Lisbon and the Algarve. Popular beaches are hot spots for car theft, so keep valuables on your person or at least hidden from view. Don't leave anything of value, such as passports or computers, in vehicles. Pickpocketing is also common, particularly on the busy trams in Lisbon and Porto. Use a concealed cross-body pouch to carry cash and your ID, and keep money and documents separate. Take the same precautions you would at home—keep valuables safe and avoid walking alone at night or on backstreets.

Harassment

Harassment is not something visitors to Portugal will usually have to deal with. Opportunistic petty drug pushers in busy nightspots and overenthusiastic restaurant or bar staff trying to attract clientele are about the extent of the pestering. Saying a polite but firm "No, thanks" and walking away are generally enough to deter unwanted attention.

Drugs

Since 2001, Portugal has a decriminalized drug system, and being caught with a small amount of some recreational drugs, such as marijuana, is no longer a crime but a medical health issue, addressed with rehabilitative action like therapy as opposed to jail. This health-focused legal shift saw drug-related deaths drop dramatically, but that's not to say it's okay to do drugs in Portugal; drug use is prohibited. The law does not differentiate between citizens and visitors, and tourists caught with drugs will be subject to the same process, which could include fines or being brought before a dissuasive committee or a doctor. Producing or dealing drugs in Portugal is a serious criminal offense punishable with lengthy jail terms. The use of recreational drugs is common in the nightlife areas of places such as Lisbon and Albufeira. Beware being approached by people selling drugs.

Walking Madeira's *Levadas*

Walking the *levadas* (ancient irrigation channels) in Madeira can be challenging. Walkers need to do their research in advance and choose only the *levadas* that are suited to their physical ability. The trails can be narrow, uneven, vertiginous, and slippery. There are sporadic reports of tourists going missing on Madeira after becoming lost or falling down a *levada*. Suitable clothing and footwear are essential, as is taking supplies like water, energy bars, and a lightweight raincoat. It is recommended that less experienced walkers join a group or a guided tour. Leave details of where you intend to walk with your hotel reception, and if you have a mobile phone, take it with you.

Travel Tips

WHAT TO PACK

Key items to pack include mosquito repellent and sunblock (sunblock is expensive in Portugal) plus a hat for May-October, a windbreaker for all seasons (Portugal can be breezy year-round), and warm sweaters, a jacket, and a light raincoat for winter. Comfortable shoes for walking are advised if your trip is more than a beach holiday, especially if you're traveling to the Azores or Madeira, and don't forget an electrical adapter for chargers. Pack a concealable pouch to carry documents and cash while out and about exploring, and never carry cash and documents together.

BUDGETING

As one of Europe's most affordable countries, Portugal still offers value for money. Far cheaper than London, Paris, or Barcelona, Portugal doesn't have to be expensive. As with all the sunshine destinations in Southern Europe and the Mediterranean, hotel rates peak in summer and drop in winter, meaning spring and autumn can offer the best value in terms of lodging and weather. Car hire rates fluctuate with the tourist seasons, and airfares are influenced by EU school holidays. Portugal has a range of inns, vacation rentals, and some of the best hostels in Europe, so how much you spend depends on you.

A British study found Portugal's Algarve was Europe's third-cheapest holiday destination for sun-loving Britons in 2018, mainly driven by a strengthening pound. Including everyday items such as coffee, beer, meals, wine, public transport, and sunblock, it is still much cheaper than other European destinations.

Examples of average costs include:

- small expresso coffee: €0.70
- 1.5-liter bottle of water: €0.50
- sandwich: €2
- local bus ticket: €2
- theme park or water park admission: €15-25

- museums: €2-5
- small glass of wine or beer: €1.50-2
- hotel room: €60-90

MONEY

Currency

Since 1999 Portugal's currency has been the euro; before that it was the escudo. There are 100 cents in 1 euro (€1).

Changing Money

The ability to exchange currency varies greatly by location. In tourist-dense Lisbon, Porto, and the Algarve, foreign currency can be exchanged at almost every hotel, currency exchanges, and even some shops. Airports have exchange bureaus, although their commission rates, along with those in hotels, are more expensive. Keep an eye on exchange rates in the months before you travel to see how they fluctuate, and change some cash beforehand when the rates are favorable. In Portugal, hunt around, do some groundwork, and compare rates to choose the best option. It is almost always more favorable for UK travelers with British pounds to change their cash for euros in the United Kingdom; in Portugal the Scottish pound can sometimes be refused. For up-to-date exchange rates, see www.xe.com.

Banks

Banks in Portugal are generally open 8:30am-4pm Monday-Friday. In larger towns and cities, they will stay open during lunch, but in smaller locales, banks close 1pm-2pm. Portugal's banks close Saturday-Sunday and national holidays. Banks rarely offer foreign exchange services.

ATMs

ATM cash withdrawal machines *(multibanco)* can be found widely in most towns and cities. Smaller villages may have just one or two, normally at bank branches, in supermarkets, on main streets and squares, and at major bus and train stations and airports. Charges apply to foreign transactions. There is an option for instructions in English. Maximum withdrawals are €200 a time, but this can be withdrawn several times a day.

Credit Cards

Credit cards are widely accepted in bigger towns and cities, but not so much in smaller locales. Visa, Mastercard, and American Express cards are widely accepted in hotels, shops, and restaurants. Gas stations usually only take debit cards and cash.

Sales Tax

The standard sales tax rate in Portugal is 23 percent. On wine it is 13 percent, and on medications, books, and optical lenses 6 percent. In Madeira the tax is 22 percent, and in the Azores 18 percent. Many stores throughout Portugal have adopted the Europe Tax Free (ETS) system, which allows non-EU shoppers to recover VAT or sales tax as a refund. Stores adhering to the ETS system have an ETS sign at the entrance. For more information, see www.globalblue.com/tax-free-shopping/portugal.

Bargaining

Haggling is increasingly a thing of the past in Portugal, as standardized retail prices are enforced in municipal markets and farmers markets. However, haggling at a flea market is still part of the experience.

Special Discounts

Students, seniors (65 and over), and children generally benefit from discounts on state-run services such as monuments, museums, municipal swimming pools, and public transport.

Tipping

Restaurants tend to be the only places in Portugal where tipping is exercised, and a tip reflects how much patrons have enjoyed the food and service. As a general rule, 10-15 percent of the overall bill is the standard, but in less formal eateries it's okay just to leave any loose change you have, but at least €1. Gratuities are not included on bills. Waitstaff in Portugal appreciate tips, but they are not compulsory.

OPENING HOURS

In the past most shops and services in Portugal would close 1pm-3pm for lunch. This is still in practice in many establishments, although a growing number of state and private entities such as banks, post offices, and pharmacies now remain open during lunch.

Major national monuments like castles, churches, and palaces are open every day of the week, and those that aren't tend to close on Monday. Almost all close on bank holidays, such as Christmas Day, New Year's Eve, and New Year's Day. Smaller museums and monuments also close for lunch.

Attractions stay open longer in summer, opening an hour or so earlier than in winter and closing an hour or so later. Theme parks, especially water parks, and even some hotels and restaurants close for a month or two in winter.

COMMUNICATIONS

Phones and Cell Phones

MAKING CALLS

Portugal's country code is +351 (00351). To call a phone number in Portugal from abroad, first dial the country code. Within Portugal, there are regional prefixes (area codes), and all start with 2. Lisbon, for example, is 21, Faro is 289, and Porto is 22. These are incorporated into phone numbers, which are always nine digits. There is no need to dial 0 or 1 before the area code. Mobile phone numbers start with 9. Toll-free numbers start with 8. Portugal's main landline provider is **Portugal Telecom** (www.telecom.pt).

MOBILE PHONES

The main mobile providers are **Nós** (www.nos.pt), **Meo** (www.meo.pt), and **Vodafone** (www.vodafone.pt). Mobile phone coverage is decent throughout the country, particularly in major cities and populous areas along the coast, although it can be patchy in rural or high-elevation areas. Foreign handsets that are GSM compatible can be used in Portugal. Using a prepaid SIM card in Portugal is recommended, particularly for non-EU visitors. They are widely available from the stores of the main mobile phone providers, which can be found on retail streets and shopping centers. You will need a copy of your passport or ID to buy one.

In 2017 the EU abolished roaming surcharges for travelers, meaning that people traveling within the EU can call, text, and use data on mobile devices at the same rates they pay at home, but this applies only to EU countries. Surcharges may apply if your consumption exceeds your home usage limits.

Internet Access

Portugal has an up-to-date communications network, with good phone lines and high-speed internet. Wi-Fi is widely available, and most hotels will either have free Wi-Fi throughout or in designated Wi-Fi areas. Elsewhere, major cities offer Wi-Fi hotspots, as do some public buildings, restaurants, and cafés. Internet cafés can be found throughout Portugal.

Shipping and Postal Service

Portugal's national postal service is **Correios de Portugal** (tel. 707 262 626, www.ctt.pt), with post offices in all population centers. Postal services range from regular *correio normal* to express *correio azul*. Shipping costs for a 2-kilogram (4.4-pound) package range from €4.50 sent domestically to €15 sent abroad. Postcards and letters up to 20 grams (0.7 ounce) cost €0.86 within Europe, €0.91 to other countries. Express mail letters cost €2.90.

Other shipping services operate in Portugal, including **FedEx** (tel. 229 436 030, www.fedex.com) and **DHL** (tel. 707 505 606, www.dhl.pt).

WEIGHTS AND MEASURES

Customary Units

Portugal was the second country after France to adopt the metric system, in 1814. Length is in centimeters, meters, and kilometers, and weight is in grams and kilograms. Temperatures are in degrees Celsius.

In addition, shoes and clothing sizes differ from the British and U.S. systems. For example:

• shoe sizes: U.S. men's 7.5, women's 9 = U.K. men's 7, women's 6.5 = Portugal 40

• women's dresses and suits: U.S. 6, 8, 10 = U.K. 8, 10, 12 = Portugal 36, 38, 40

• men's suits and overcoats: U.S. and U.K. 36, 38, 40 = Portugal 46, 48, 50

Time Zone

Mainland Portugal is in the Western European time zone (WET), the same as the United Kingdom and Ireland. Complying with European daylight saving time (DST), clocks advance one hour on the last Sunday in March and lose one hour on the last Sunday in October. The Azores archipelago is always one hour earlier than mainland Portugal. Madeira is in the same time zone as the mainland. In relation to the United States, Portugal is seven or eight hours later than Los Angeles, four or five hours ahead of Miami and New York, five or six hours ahead of Chicago, and ten or eleven hours ahead of Hawaii.

Electricity

Portugal has 230-volt, 50-hertz electricity and type C or F sockets. Type C plugs have two round pins; type F have two round pins with two earthing clips on the side. Travelers from the United Kingdom, the rest of Europe, Australia, and most of Asia and Africa will only require an adapter to make the plugs fit. Visitors from the United States, Canada, and most South American countries require an adapter and for some devices a voltage converter. These are available in airports, luggage shops, and most electrical shops. Universal adapters are a great investment as they can be used anywhere.

VISITOR INFORMATION

Portugal is a tourism-oriented destination with widely available visitor information. Each region—Porto and the North, Central Portugal, Lisbon, the Alentejo, the Algarve, Azores and Madeira—has its own tourism board to promote the area, while the national **Turismo de Portugal** (www.turismodeportugal.pt) promotes the country as a whole. Each main town has at least one tourist office, as do popular villages. Most hotels provide good information on what to do and see locally. Portugal's official tourism website, www.visitportugal.com, provides a wealth of information on history, culture, and heritage as well as useful contacts.

Tourist Offices

Tourist offices can be found in every city, town, and village that has a tourist attraction or monument. Major cities and destinations like Lisbon, Porto, and the Algarve have numerous tourist offices where visitors can drop in with questions and get maps, public transport timetables, and excursion information. Tourist office staffers speak good English.

Maps

Download maps of Portugal and its various regions free from www.visitportugal.com. Most hotel reception desks have maps of the vicinity, or ask at tourist offices.

Traveler Advice

OPPORTUNITIES FOR STUDY AND EMPLOYMENT

With a recovering economy firmly on the way up, job opportunities in Portugal are improving. The Algarve has casual summer employment in bar and restaurant work, and the southern half of the country has agricultural jobs picking oranges and farming vegetables. Elsewhere there are opportunities teaching English and IT and sciences, fields that are expanding and have positions for English speakers on occasion. Websites such as **Jobs in Lisbon** (www.jobsinlisbon. com) list jobs for English-speaking professionals. There are also work-lodging exchange schemes in Portugal, home to a growing number of permaculture communes and organic farm-stays. Websites like **Helpx** (www.helpx.net) and **World Wide Opportunities on Organic Farms** (WWOOF; www.wwoof.pt) promote opportunities for holidaymakers to work in exchange for free lodging.

Portugal has many international students and is popular for studying abroad; it's one of the top countries for the EU Erasmus student-exchange program (European Community Action Scheme for the Mobility of University Students). Universities are geared toward welcoming foreign students, and most have their own residences, albeit usually off-campus. Flat-sharing is common, although rents can be high, especially in Lisbon. Many of Portugal's universities and campuses offer undergraduate programs, and Portugal has a solid reputation for outstanding postgraduate studies. For more information in English on studying in Portugal, see www. studyinportugal.edu.pt.

ACCESS FOR TRAVELERS WITH DISABILITIES

Portugal prides itself on being an accessible destination for travelers with disabilities, and massive efforts have been made to become inclusive for all. The main airports have services and facilities for wheelchair users, and infrastructure is gradually being modernized to facilitate mobility. There are a number of wheelchair-friendly accessible beaches along the coast, with equipment and facilities for all to enjoy the beach safely and comfortably. Some monuments, however, are not wheelchair friendly, and people with mobility issues might struggle with everyday infrastructures (such as cobbled streets and high sidewalks).

In 2018 the national tourism board launched an interactive app, **TUR4all Portugal,** that contains a wealth of information about facilities and services for those with special needs visiting Portugal. It can be downloaded for free from www. accessibleportugal.com.

TRAVELING WITH CHILDREN

Youngsters in family-friendly Portugal are fawned over and welcomed practically everywhere. It's not unusual to see children dozing on their parents' laps in a café late on a summer night. Restaurants are very accommodating of younger diners, although kids' menus can be limited to the staple chicken nuggets or fish fingers.

Activities for children range from Lisbon's Oceanarium to Coimbra's Little Portugal and the many water parks in the Algarve; zoos in most major towns; fantastic beaches; and play parks in almost every public garden.

Kids also benefit from discounts on public transport, at museums, and at most main attractions.

When the weather is warm, tourist trains and ice cream are found throughout towns and villages, while most resorts and hotels have kids' clubs or at least activities and facilities for children. For some grown-up-time, ask your hotel to arrange a babysitter.

To enter and leave Portugal, all minors must have their own passport and be with both parents. If children are not traveling with both parents, legal documentation with formalized permission from the other parent is required. Portugal's border and immigration officials will ask for such papers.

Breastfeeding is applauded in Portugal, although it's rarely done in public, and if it is, it's done discreetly.

WOMEN TRAVELING ALONE

Portugal is a great destination for women traveling alone, given that it is one of Europe's safest and most peaceful countries, and people as a whole are respectful and obliging. If you want to share lodging or to meet new people, Portugal has clean and cheap, well-regulated and well-run hostels, a great way to mingle with fellow travelers. Most people speak decent English and are happy to assist. Besides petty crime in major towns and cities, the serious crime rate is low, and lone women travelers should have no problems. As with any place, common sense should prevail, and taking dark backstreets or walking along deserted streets at night should be avoided.

SENIOR TRAVELERS

With a year-round pleasant climate and placid, laid-back lifestyle, Portugal is a magnet for senior travelers and a top destination for Northern European retirees who make it their second home. Compact, peaceful, and well equipped, with medical facilities (providing you have the right insurance coverage), it meets the needs of travelers of all ages. Geographically, Lisbon and Porto are hilly and a challenge on foot; sticking to the flatter downtown and riverside areas and using the plethora of public transport can help travelers avoid issues with aches and pains.

Portugal has discounts for senior travelers (65 and over) with ID on public transport and in museums, and plenty of attractions, like wine-tasting and spa visits, to appeal to the mature tourist.

LGBTQ TRAVELERS

LGBTQ travelers will find Portugal mostly welcoming; it legalized same-sex marriage in 2010, the eighth country in Europe to do so. Portugal is currently a popular destination for same-sex weddings. Most Portuguese have a laid-back attitude toward LGBTQ visitors, although attitudes toward same-sex couples can vary by region. Despite being progressive, Portugal is traditionally a Roman Catholic society, and inhabitants of remote and small towns might raise an eyebrow or scowl at same-sex displays of affection, but rarely will verbal or physical hostility be directed at you.

While the LGBTQ scene is still underground in much of Portugal, Lisbon and Porto, and to a lesser extent the Algarve, have a vibrant and inclusive LGBTQ scene. Lisbon and Porto host colorful pride marches and have numerous gay bars, nightclubs, and LGBTQ-friendly accommodations, although tourists being denied a room or a table based on their sexual orientation or gender identity is not unheard of. The **International Gay & Lesbian Travel Association** (IGLTA, www.iglta.org) provides a wealth of information on LGBTQ travel in Portugal, including organized trips, tours, tips, and travel advice.

TRAVELERS OF COLOR

Portugal is widely regarded as one of Europe's safest, most peaceful, and most tolerant countries, and allegations of color-motivated discrimination and attacks are rare. However, in recent times there have been sporadic reports of incidents involving racial bias, specifically at the doors of popular nightspots in Lisbon. Management of these venues strongly deny that bouncers discriminate against clubgoers' entry based on their race, but allegations to that effect have made the rounds on social media. That said, Portugal is home to large communities of Africans from the former colonies, and while racially motivated incidents do happen, they are extremely rare. For the most part, travelers and immigrants of all colors are welcomed and accepted in Portugal, which has one of the most integrated immigrant communities in Europe.

Resources

Glossary

adega: wine cellar
arco: arch
autoestrada: motorway (abbreviated A)
avenida: avenue
azulejo: hand-painted ceramic tile, usually blue and white
bacalhau: salted codfish
bairro: neighborhood or district
capela: chapel
castelo: castle
cataplana: seafood stew cooked in a copper pan
cidade: city or town
espetada: skewered meat
estação: station
estalagem: inn
estrada municipal: local municipal road (abbreviated M or EM)
estrada nacional: national road (abbreviated N or EN)
fadista: fado singer
fado: a genre of traditional Portuguese music that is soulful and often mournful
farmácia: pharmacy
feira: fair or open-air market
ferroviária: railway
festa: festival
fortaleza: fortress
forte: fort
foz: river mouth
ginja: cherry liqueur; also known as *ginjinha*
gruta: cave
igreja: church
ilha: island
itinerário complementar: secondary highway (abbreviated IC)

itinerário principal: main highway (abbreviated IP)
jardim: garden
lago: lake
lagoa: lagoon or pond
largo: small square or plaza
levada: irrigation channel
litoral: coastal
livraria: bookshop
loja: shop
lote: lot or unit
Manueline: lavishly ornate Portuguese architectural style, widely employed in the early 16th century; owes its name to the reign of King Manuel I
mercado: market
miradouro: viewpoint
monte: hill or mountain
multibanco: ATM
museu: museum
paço: palace
palácio: palace
parafarmácia: pharmacy with only nonprescription medications
parque: park
pastel: pastry
pensão residencial: boardinghouse or bed-and-breakfast
Pombaline: distinctly Portuguese architectural style of the 18th century that is a mix of late baroque and neoclassical; named after the first Marquis of Pombal, who led the rebuilding of Lisbon after the 1755 earthquake
poncha: alcoholic punch associated with Madeira
ponte: bridge

pousada: monument (such as a castle, palace, monastery, or convent) converted into luxurious accommodations
praça: square or plaza
praia: beach
quinta: wine farm or estate
rabelo: traditional flat-bottomed boat
reconquista: Christian reconquest of Portugal
retornado: Portuguese citizen returned from former colonies
ria: lagoon or estuary
rio: river
rua: street
santuário: sanctuary or shrine
sé: cathedral
serra: mountain range
tasca: simple, small eatery
vila: village or town
vinho: wine

Portuguese Phrasebook

PRONUNCIATION
Vowels
The pronunciation of **nonnasal vowels** is fairly straightforward:

a   pronounced "a" as in "apple," "ah" as in "father," or "uh" as in "addition."

e   pronounced "eh" as in "pet." At the end of a word, it is often silent or barely pronounced.

i   pronounced "ee" as in "tree."

o   pronounced "aw" as in "got." At the end of a word or when it stands alone, it is generally pronounced "oo" as in "zoo."

u   pronounced "oo" as in "zoo."

The **nasal vowels** are much more complicated. Nasal vowels are signaled by a tilde accent (~) as in *não* (no), or by the presence of the letters **m** or **n** following the vowel, such as *sim* (yes) or *fonte* (fountain). When pronouncing them, it helps to exaggerate the sound, focus on your nose and not your mouth, and pretend there is a hidden "n" (or even "ng") on the end. Note that the **ão** combination is pronounced like "own" as in "town."

Consonants
Portuguese consonant sounds are easy compared with the nasal vowels. There are, however, a few exceptions to be aware of.

c   pronounced "k" as in "kayak." However, when followed by the vowels **e** or **i**, it is pronounced "s" as in "set." When sporting a cedilla accent (ç), it is pronounced with a longer "ss" sound as in "passing."

ch   pronounced "sh" as in "ship."

g   pronounced "g" as in "go." However, when followed by the vowels **e** or **i**, it is pronounced "zh" like the "s" in "measure."

h   always silent.

j   pronounced "zh" like the "s" in "measure."

l   usually pronounced as in English. The exception is when it is followed by **h,** when it acquires a "li" sound similar to "billion."

n   usually pronounced as in English. The exception is when it is followed by **h,** when it acquires a "ni" sound similar to "minion."

r   pronounced with a trill. When doubled (**rr**), it should be pronounced with a longer roll.

s   pronounced "s" as in "set" when found at the beginning of a word. Between vowels, it's pronounced like "z" as in "zap." At the end of a word, it's pronounced like "sh" as in "ship."

x   pronounced "sh" as in "ship" when found at the beginning of a word. Between vowels, the pronunciation varies between "sh" as in "ship," "s" as in "set," "z" as in "zap," and "ks" as in "taxi."

z   pronounced "z" in "zap" when found at the beginning of a word. In the middle or at the end of a word, it is pronounced "zh" like the "s" in "measure."

Stress

Most Portuguese words carry stress on the second-to-last syllable. There are, however, some exceptions. The stress falls on the last syllable with words that end in **r** as well as words ending in nasal vowels. Vowels with accents over them (**~, ´, `, ^**) generally indicate that the stress falls on the syllable containing the vowel.

PLURAL NOUNS AND ADJECTIVES

In Portuguese, the general rule for making a noun or adjective plural is to simply add an **s**. But there are various exceptions. For instance, words that end in nasal consonants such as **m** or **l** change to **ns** and **is**, respectively. The plural of *estalagem* (inn) is *estalagens*, while the plural of *pastel* (pastry) is *pastéis*. Words that end in nasal vowels also undergo changes: **ão** becomes **ãos, ães,** or **ões,** as in the case of *irmão* (brother), which becomes *irmãos*, and *pão* (bread), which becomes *pães*.

GENDER

Like French and Spanish, all Portuguese words have masculine and feminine forms of nouns and adjectives. In general, nouns ending in **o** or consonants are masculine, while those ending in **a** are feminine. Many words have both masculine and feminine versions determined by their **o** or **a** ending, such as *menino* (boy) and *menina* (girl). Nouns are always preceded by articles—*o* and *a* (definite) and *um* and *uma* (indefinite)—that announce their gender. For example, *o menino* means "the boy" while *a menina* means "the girl." *Um menino* is "a boy" while *uma menina* is "a girl."

BASIC EXPRESSIONS

Hello *Olá*
Good morning *Bom dia*
Good afternoon *Boa tarde*
Good evening/night *Boa noite*
Goodbye *Tchau, Adeus*
How are you? *Como está?*
Fine, and you? *Tudo bem, e você?*
Nice to meet you. *Um prazer.*
Yes *Sim*

No *Não*
I don't know. *Não sei.*
and *e*
or *ou*
Please *Por favor*
Thank you *Obrigado* (if you're male),
    Obrigada (if you're female)
You're welcome. *De nada.*
Excuse me (to pass) *Com licença*
**Sorry/Excuse me (to get
    attention)** *Desculpe* (if you're male),
    Desculpa (if you're female)
Can you help me? *Pode me ajudar?*
What's your name? *Como se chama?*
My name is . . . *Meu nome é . . .*
Where are you from? *De onde é que vem?*
I'm from . . . *Sou de . . .*
Do you speak English? *Fala inglês?*
I don't speak Portuguese. *Não falo
    português.*
I only speak a little Portuguese. *Só falo
    um pouquinho português.*
I don't understand. *Não entendo.*
Can you please repeat that? *Pode repetir,
    por favor?*

TERMS OF ADDRESS

I *eu*
you *você* (formal), *tu* (informal)
he *ele*
she *ela*
we *nós*
you (plural) *vocês*
they *eles* (male or mixed gender), *elas*
    (female)
Mr./Sir *Senhor*
Mrs./Madam *Senhora*
boy/girl *menino/menina*
child *criança*
brother/sister *irmão/irmã*
father/mother *pai/mãe*
son/daughter *filho/filha*
husband/wife *marido/mulher*
uncle/aunt *tio/tia*
friend *amigo* (male), *amiga* (female)
boyfriend/girlfriend *namorado/namorada*
single *solteiro* (male), *solteira* (female)
divorced *divorciado* (male), *divorciada* (female)

TRANSPORTATION

north *norte*
south *sul*
east *este*
west *oeste*
left/right *esquerda/direita*
Where is . . . ? *Onde é . . . ?*
How far away is . . . ? *Qual é a distância até . . . ?*
far/close *longe/perto*
car *carro*
bus *autocarro, camioneta*
bus terminal *terminal das camionetas*
subway *metro*
subway station *estação do metro*
train *comboio*
train station *estação de comboio*
plane *avião*
airport *aeroporto*
boat *barco*
ship *navio*
ferryboat *ferry, balsa*
port *porto*
first *primeiro*
last *último*
next *próximo*
arrival *chegada*
departure *partida*
How much does a ticket cost? *Quanto custa uma passagem?*
one-way *uma ida*
round-trip *ida e volta*
I'd like a round-trip ticket. *Quero uma passagem ida e volta.*
gas station *bomba de gasolina*
parking lot *estacionamento*
toll *portagem*
at the corner *na esquina*
one-way street *sentido único*
Where can I get a taxi? *Onde posso apanhar um táxi?*
Can you take me to this address? *Pode me levar para este endereço?*
Can you stop here, please? *Pode parar aqui, por favor?*

ACCOMMODATIONS

Are there any rooms available? *Tem quartos disponivéis?*
I want to make a reservation. *Quero fazer uma reserva.*
single room *quarto de solteiro*
double room *quarto duplo*
Is there a view? *Tem vista?*
How much does it cost? *Quanto custa?*
Can you give me a discount? *É possivel ter um desconto?*
It's too expensive. *É muito caro.*
Is there something cheaper? *Tem algo mais barato?*
for just one night *para uma noite só*
for three days *para três dias*
Can I see it first? *Posso ver primeiro?*
comfortable *confortável*
change the sheets/towels *trocar os lençóis/as toalhas*
private bathroom *banheiro privado*
shower *chuveiro*
soap *sabão*
toilet paper *papel higiênico*
key *chave*

FOOD

to eat *comer*
to drink *beber*
breakfast *pequeno almoço*
lunch *almoço*
dinner *jantar*
snack *petisco*
dessert *sobremesa*
menu *ementa*
plate *prato*
glass *copo*
cup *chávena*
utensils *talheres*
fork *garfo*
knife *faca*
spoon *colher*
napkin *guardanapo*
hot *quente*
cold *frio*
sweet *doce*
salty *salgado*
sour *azedo, amargo*

spicy *picante*

I'm a vegetarian. *Sou vegetariano* (if you're male), *Sou vegetariana* (if you're female).

I'm ready to order. *Estou pronto para pedir* (if you're male), *Estou pronta para pedir* (if you're female).

Can you bring the bill please? *Pode trazer a conta, por favor?*

Meat

meat *carne*

beef *carne, bife*

chicken *frango, galinha*

pork *porco, leitão*

ham *fiambre*

cured ham *presunto*

sausage *salsicha*

Fish and Seafood

fish *peixe*

seafood *frutas do mar, mariscos*

shellfish *marisco*

codfish *bacalhau*

sardines *sardinhas*

tuna *atum*

shrimp *camarão*

crab *caranguejo*

squid *lula*

octopus *polvo*

lobster *lagosta*

Eggs and Dairy

eggs *ovos*

hard-boiled egg *ovo cozido*

scrambled eggs *ovos mexidos*

whole milk *leite gordo*

skim milk *leite desnatado*

cream *creme de leite*

butter *manteiga*

cheese *queijo*

yogurt *iogurte*

ice cream *gelado*

sorbet *sorvete*

Vegetables and Legumes

vegetables *verduras, legumes*

salad *salada*

lettuce *alface*

spinach *espinafre*

carrot *cenoura*

tomato *tomate*

potato *batata*

cucumber *pepino*

zucchini *courgette*

eggplant *berinjela*

mushrooms *cogumelos*

olives *azeitonas*

onions *cebolas*

beans *feijões*

Fruits

fruit *fruta*

apple *maçã*

pear *pêra*

grape *uva*

fig *figo*

orange *laranja*

lemon *limão*

pineapple *ananás*

banana *banana*

apricot *damasco, abricó*

cherry *cereja*

peach *pêssego*

raspberry *framboesa*

strawberry *morango*

melon *melão*

Seasoning and Condiments

salt *sal*

black pepper *pimenta*

hot pepper *pimenta picante*

garlic *alho*

oil *óleo*

olive oil *azeite*

mustard *mostarda*

mayonnaise *maionese*

vinegar *vinagre*

Baked Goods and Grains

bread *pão*

pastry *pastel*

cookies *biscoitos*

cake *bolo, torta*

rice *arroz*

Cooking
roasted, baked *assado*
boiled *cozido*
steamed *cozido no vapor*
grilled *grelhado*
fried *frito*
well done *bem passado*
medium *médio*
rare *mal passado*

Drinks
beverage *bebida*
water *água*
sparkling water *água com gás*
still water *água sem gás*
soda *refrigerante*
juice *sumo*
milk *leite*
coffee *café*
tea *chá*
with/without sugar *com/sem açúcar*
ice *gelo*
beer *cerveja*
wine *vinho*
Do you have wine? *Tem vinho?*
Red or white? *Tinto ou branco?*
Another, please. *Mais uma, por favor.*

MONEY AND SHOPPING
money *dinheiro*
ATM *multibanco*
credit card *cartão de crédito*
Do you accept credit cards? *Aceita cartões de crédito?*
Can I exchange money? *Posso trocar dinheiro?*
money exchange *câmbio, troca de dinheiro*
It's too expensive. *É muito caro.*
Is there something cheaper? *Tem algo mais barato?*
more *mais*
less *menos*
a good price *Um preço bom.*

HEALTH AND SAFETY
I'm sick. *Estou doente.*
I have nausea. *Tenho nausea.*

I have a headache. *Tenho uma dor de cabeça.*
I have a stomachache. *Tenho uma dor de estômago.*
Call a doctor! *Chame um doutor!, Chame um médico!*
Call the police! *Chame a polícia!*
Help! *Socorro!*
pain *dor*
fever *febre*
infection *infecção*
cut *corte*
burn *queimadura*
vomit *vômito*
pill *comprimido*
medicine *remédio, medicamento*
antibiotic *antibiótico*
cotton *algodão*
condom *preservativo*
contraceptive pill *pílula*
toothpaste *pasta de dentes*
toothbrush *escova de dentes*

NUMBERS
0 *zero*
1 *um (male), uma (female)*
2 *dois (male), duas (female)*
3 *três*
4 *quatro*
5 *cinco*
6 *seis*
7 *sete*
8 *oito*
9 *nove*
10 *dez*
11 *onze*
12 *doze*
13 *treze*
14 *catorze, quatorze*
15 *quinze*
16 *dezesseis*
17 *dezessete*
18 *dezoito*
19 *dezenove*
20 *vinte*
21 *vinte e um*
30 *trinta*

40 *quarenta*
50 *cinquenta*
60 *sessenta*
70 *setenta*
80 *oitenta*
90 *noventa*
100 *cem*
101 *cento e um*
200 *duzentos*
500 *quinhentos*
1,000 *mil*
2,000 *dois mil*
first *primeiro*
second *segundo*
third *terceiro*
once *uma vez*
twice *duas vezes*
half *metade*

TIME

What time is it? *Que horas são?*
It's 3 o'clock in the afternoon. *São três horas da tarde.*
It's 3:15. *São três e quinze.*
It's 3:30. *São três e meia.*
It's 3:45. *São três e quarenta-cinco.*
In half an hour. *Daqui a meia hora.*
In an hour. *Daqui a uma hora.*
In two hours. *Daqui a duas horas.*
noon *meio-dia*
midnight *meia-noite*
early *cedo*
late *tarde*
before *antes*
after *depois*

DAYS AND MONTHS

day *dia*
morning *manhã*
afternoon *tarde*
night *noite*

today *hoje*
yesterday *ontem*
tomorrow *amanhã*
tomorrow morning *amanhã de manhã*
week *semana*
month *mês*
year *ano*
Monday *segunda-feira*
Tuesday *terça-feira*
Wednesday *quarta-feira*
Thursday *quinta-feira*
Friday *sexta-feira*
Saturday *sábado*
Sunday *domingo*
January *janeiro*
February *fevereiro*
March *março*
April *abril*
May *maio*
June *junho*
July *julho*
August *agosto*
September *setembro*
October *outubro*
November *novembro*
December *dezembro*

SEASONS AND WEATHER

season *estação*
spring *primavera*
summer *verão*
autumn *outuno*
winter *inverno*
weather *o tempo*
sun *sol*
rain *chuva*
cloudy *nublado*
windy *vento*
hot *quente*
cold *frio*

Index

INDEX

N

List of Maps

Photo Credits

All interior photos © Carrie-Marie Bratley except: title page photo © biathlonua | dreamstime.com; page 2 © filipeb | dreamstime.com; page 3 © radub85 | dreamstime.com; page 6 © (top left) nikolais | dreamstime.com; (top right) mosessin | dreamstime.com; (bottom) sepavo | dreamstime.com; page 7 © (top) joyfull | dreamstime.com; (bottom left) dwnld777 | dreamstime.com; (bottom right) emicristea | dreamstime.com; page 8 © (top) golasza | dreamstime.com; page 9 © (top) dziewul | dreamstime.com; (bottom left) hlphoto | dreamstime.com; (bottom right) mango2friendly | dreamstime.com; page 10 © elxeneize | dreamstime.com; page 12 © (top) xantana | dreamstime.com; (bottom) jackmalipan | dreamstime.com; page 13 © sohadiszno | dreamstime.com; page 14 © (top) tenetsi | dreamstime.com; (bottom) afagundes | dreamstime.com; page 15 © studiof22byricardorocha | dreamstime.com; page 16 © (top) zhykharievavlada | dreamstime.com; (bottom) vector99 | dreamstime.com; page 17 © cro magnon / alamy stock photo; page 22 © (bottom) nito100 | dreamstime.com; page 23 © (top) sepavo | dreamstime.com; page 24 © (bottom) sohadiszno | dreamstime.com; page 27 © (bottom) rosshelen | dreamstime.com; page 29 © (top) vonderrusch | dreamstime.com; page 32 © feightstudio | dreamstime.com; barbaracerovsek | dreamstime.com; page 33 © (top) tiagofernandezphotography | dreamstime.com; page 47 © (left middle)zhykharievavlada | dreamstime.com; (right middle)4kclips | dreamstime.com; page 51 © (top) tomas1111 | dreamstime.com; (right middle)photoweges | dreamstime.com; page 57 © (bottom) dennisvdwater | dreamstime.com; page 103 © (left middle)azurechina | dreamstime.com; (right middle)fazon1 | dreamstime.com; page 136 © (top) stefanovalerigm | dreamstime.com; (left middle)presse750 | dreamstime.com; (right middle)typhoonski | dreamstime.com; page 159 © (left middle)stuartan | dreamstime.com; (right middle)vincenthanna | dreamstime.com; (bottom) akersholt | dreamstime.com; page 171 © (bottom) zts | dreamstime.com; page 175 © 2circles | dreamstime.com; page 179 © (top) fosterss | dreamstime.com; (left middle)xavierallard | dreamstime.com; (right middle) sohadiszno | dreamstime.com; (bottom) christophecappelli | dreamstime.com; page 182 © milosk50 | dreamstime.com; page 196 © (left middle) zts | dreamstime.com; (right middle)jimmigokins | dreamstime.com; (bottom) taolmor | dreamstime.com; page 234 © (top) digitalsignal | dreamstime.com; (bottom) bennymarty | dreamstime.com; page 240 © jma468 | dreamstime.com; page 247 © (top) wqsomeone | dreamstime.com; (left middle)aurore426 | dreamstime.com; (right middle)anafidalgo | dreamstime.com; (bottom) mrallen | dreamstime.com; page 253 © (top) swissmargrit | dreamstime.com; (left middle)2circles | dreamstime.com; (right middle) homydesign | dreamstime.com; (bottom) eranyardeni | dreamstime.com; page 263 © (left middle) jackmalipan | dreamstime.com; page 272 © (top) dimaberkut | dreamstime.com; (left middle)nmessana | dreamstime.com; (right middle)sohadiszno | dreamstime.com; page 284 © (top) sergio85simoes | dreamstime.com; (bottom) venemama | dreamstime.com; page 297 © (top) venemama | dreamstime.com; (left middle) 2circles | dreamstime.com; (right middle) g0r3cki | dreamstime.com; (bottom) afearonwood | dreamstime.com; page 307 © (top) peizais | dreamstime.com; (left middle) mpzsapopt | dreamstime.com; (right middle) peizais | dreamstime.com; (bottom) saiko3p | dreamstime.com; page 319 © (left middle) villarionov | dreamstime.com; page 322 © ivusakzkrabice | dreamstime.com; page 331 © (bottom) presse750 | dreamstime.com; page 345 © (bottom) perszing1982 | dreamstime.com; page 351 © (top) saaaaa | dreamstime.com; (left middle) vidalgophoto | dreamstime.com; (right middle) saaaaa | dreamstime.com; (bottom) eyewave | dreamstime.com; page 359 © hdamke | dreamstime.com.

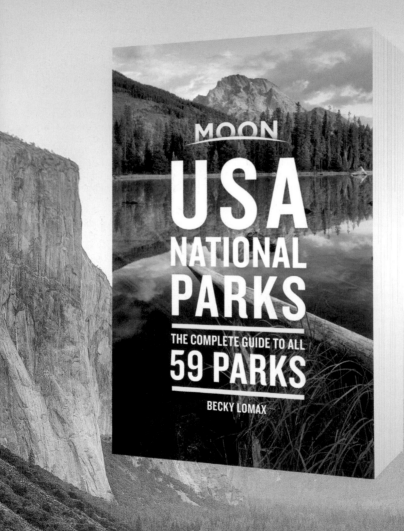

ACADIA
NATIONAL PARK
HILARY NANGLE

ARCHES &
CANYONLANDS
NATIONAL PARKS
W. C. McRAE & JUDY JEWELL

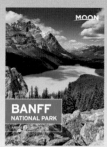

BANFF
NATIONAL PARK
ANDREW HEMPSTEAD

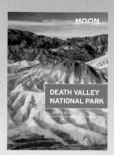

DEATH VALLEY
NATIONAL PARK
JENNA BLOUGH

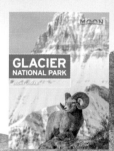

GLACIER
NATIONAL PARK
BECKY LOMAX

GRAND
CANYON
KATHLEEN BRYANT

GREAT SMOKY
MOUNTAINS
NATIONAL PARK
JASON FRYE

MOUNT RUSHMORE
& THE BLACK HILLS
Including the Badlands
LAURAL A. BIDWELL

ROCKY MOUNTAIN
NATIONAL PARK
ERIN ENGLISH

YELLOWSTONE
& GRAND TETON
Including Jackson Hole
BECKY LOMAX

YOSEMITE,
SEQUOIA &
KINGS CANYON
ANN MARIE BROWN

ZION &
BRYCE
Including Arches, Canyonlands,
Capitol Reef, Grand Staircase-
Escalante & Moab
W. C. McRAE & JUDY JEWELL

In these books:

- Full coverage of gateway cities and towns
- Itineraries from one day to multiple weeks
- Advice on where to stay (or camp) in and around the parks

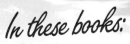

MOON ROAD TRIP GUIDES

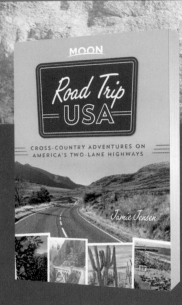

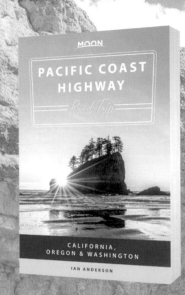

Road Trip USA

Criss-cross the country on America's classic two-lane highways with the newest edition of *Road Trip USA!*

Packed with over 125 detailed driving maps (covering more than 35,000 miles), colorful photos and illustrations of America both then and now, and mile-by-mile highlights

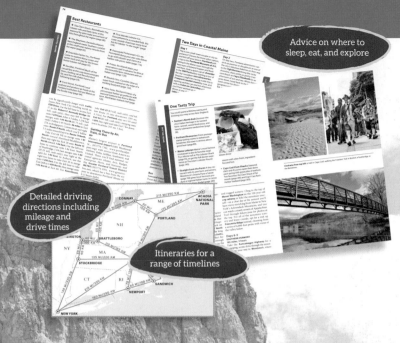

Advice on where to sleep, eat, and explore

Detailed driving directions including mileage and drive times

Itineraries for a range of timelines

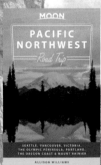

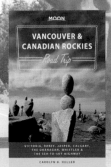

Trips to Remember

ANGKOR WAT

TRIP OF A LIFETIME
GALÁPAGOS ISLANDS

ICELAND

JENNA GOTTLIEB

TRIP OF A LIFETIME
MACHU PICCHU

MOROCCO

NORWAY

DAVID NIKEL

TRIP OF A LIFETIME
PATAGONIA

WAYNE BERNHARDSON

ROME, FLORENCE & VENICE

ALEXEI J COHEN

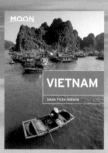

VIETNAM

DANA FILEK-GIBSON

Epic Adventure

Drive & Hike
APPALACHIAN TRAIL

THE BEST TRAIL TOWNS, DAY HIKES, AND ROAD TRIPS IN BETWEEN

TIMOTHY MALCOLM

CAMINO DE SANTIAGO

SACRED SITES, HISTORIC VILLAGES, LOCAL FOOD & WINE

BEEBE BAHRAMI

USA NATIONAL PARKS

THE COMPLETE GUIDE TO ALL
59 PARKS

BECKY LOMAX

Savvy City Combinations

BARCELONA & MADRID
JESSICA JONES

PRAGUE, VIENNA & BUDAPEST
JENNIFER D. WALKER | AUBURN SCALLON

SANTA FE, TAOS & ALBUQUERQUE
STEVEN HORAK

ROME, FLORENCE & VENICE
ALEXEI J. COHEN

More Guides for Urban Adventure

ASHEVILLE & THE GREAT SMOKY MOUNTAINS

BOSTON
CAMERON SPERANCE

BUENOS AIRES
NICHOLAS MILLER

CHICAGO
REBECCA HOLLAND

HANOI
DANA FILEK-GIBSON

MEXICO CITY
JULIE MEADE

MONTRÉAL
ANDREA BENNETT

NASHVILLE
MARGARET LITTMAN

NEW YORK CITY
CHRISTOPHER KOMPANEK

PORTLAND

VANCOUVER
CAROLYN B. HELLER

WASHINGTON DC

MAP SYMBOLS

═══════ Expressway	○ City/Town	✈ Airport
─────── Primary Road	◉ State Capital	✗ Airfield
─────── Secondary Road	⊛ National Capital	▲ Mountain
∙∙∙∙∙∙∙ Unpaved Road	★ Point of Interest	✦ Unique Natural Feature
─────── Feature Trail	• Accommodation	Waterfall
- - - - - Other Trail	▾ Restaurant/Bar	⛟ Park
∙∙∙∙∙∙∙∙ Ferry	■ Other Location	⬛ Trailhead
═══════ Pedestrian Walkway	⋀ Campground	⛷ Skiing Area
▭▭▭▭▭ Stairs		

⚲ Golf Course	
🅿 Parking Area	
▱ Archaeological Site	
⬤ Church	
⬛ Gas Station	
Glacier	
Mangrove	
Reef	
Swamp	

CONVERSION TABLES

$°C = (°F - 32) / 1.8$
$°F = (°C \times 1.8) + 32$
1 inch = 2.54 centimeters (cm)
1 foot = 0.304 meters (m)
1 yard = 0.914 meters
1 mile = 1.6093 kilometers (km)
1 km = 0.6214 miles
1 fathom = 1.8288 m
1 chain = 20.1168 m
1 furlong = 201.168 m
1 acre = 0.4047 hectares
1 sq km = 100 hectares
1 sq mile = 2.59 square km
1 ounce = 28.35 grams
1 pound = 0.4536 kilograms
1 short ton = 0.90718 metric ton
1 short ton = 2,000 pounds
1 long ton = 1.016 metric tons
1 long ton = 2,240 pounds
1 metric ton = 1,000 kilograms
1 quart = 0.94635 liters
1 US gallon = 3.7854 liters
1 Imperial gallon = 4.5459 liters
1 nautical mile = 1.852 km

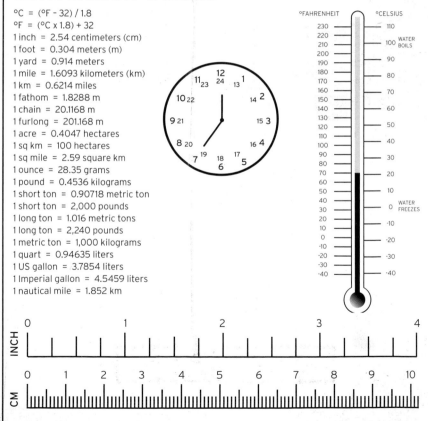

MOON PORTUGAL

Avalon Travel
Hachette Book Group
1700 Fourth Street
Berkeley, CA 94710, USA
www.moon.com

Editor and Series Manager: Kathryn Ettinger
Copy Editors: Christopher Church, Linda Cabasin
Graphics Coordinator: Rue Flaherty
Production Coordinator: Rue Flaherty
Cover Design: Faceout Studios, Charles Brock
Interior Design: Domini Dragoone
Moon Logo: Tim McGrath
Map Editor: Kat Bennett
Cartographers: Kat Bennett, Allison Ollivierra
Indexer: Greg Jewett

ISBN-13: 978-1-64049-180-9

Printing History
1st Edition — April 2019
5 4 3 2 1

Front cover photo: Belém Tower in Lisbon © Claudio Cassaro / SIME / eStock Photo
Back cover photo: Lisbon skyline at night © Sean Pavone | Dreamstime.com

Printed in China by RR Donnelley

31901064787577